Great Britain

Report Together with the Appendix

Presented to Both Houses of Parliament by Command of Her Majesty

Great Britain

Report Together with the Appendix
Presented to Both Houses of Parliament by Command of Her Majesty

ISBN/EAN: 9783337161101

Printed in Europe, USA, Canada, Australia, Japan

Cover: Foto ©ninafisch / pixelio.de

More available books at **www.hansebooks.com**

REPORT

OF

THE COMMISSIONERS

APPOINTED TO INQUIRE INTO

THE CONDITION OF THE VOLUNTEER FORCE IN GREAT BRITAIN;

TOGETHER WITH

THE APPENDIX.

Presented to both Houses of Parliament by Command of Her Majesty.

LONDON:
PRINTED BY GEORGE EDWARD EYRE AND WILLIAM SPOTTISWOODE,
PRINTERS TO THE QUEEN'S MOST EXCELLENT MAJESTY.
FOR HER MAJESTY'S STATIONERY OFFICE.

1862.

CONTENTS.

	Page.
COMMISSION	iii
REPORT	v
APPENDIX	1

COMMISSION.

VICTORIA R.

Victoria, by the Grace of God, of the United Kingdom of Great Britain and Ireland, Queen, Defender of the Faith.

To Our right trusty and well-beloved Cousin and Councillor Charles Viscount Eversley, Lieutenant-Colonel in the Hampshire Regiment of Yeomanry Cavalry, and one of Our Aides-de-Camp, with the rank of Colonel in the Yeomanry ; Our right trusty and right well-beloved Cousin and Councillor Henry John Earl of Ducie, Captain of Our Body-Guard of Yeomen of the Guard ; Our right trusty and well-beloved Cousin Charles Stewart Viscount Hardinge, Lieutenant-Colonel in the Second Administrative Battalion of Kent Rifle Volunteers ; Our trusty and well-beloved Francis Wemyss Charteris Douglas, commonly called Lord Elcho, Lieutenant-Colonel in the Fifteenth Middlesex Rifle Volunteers ; Our right trusty and well-beloved Samuel Baron Overstone ; Our right trusty and well-beloved Councillor Edward Pleydell Bouverie ; Our trusty and well-beloved Walter Barttelot Barttelot, Esquire, Lieutenant-Colonel in the Second Administrative Battalion of Sussex Rifle Volunteers ; Our trusty and well-beloved Sir Archibald Islay Campbell, Baronet, Lieutenant-Colonel in the First Lanarkshire Rifle Volunteers ; Our trusty and well-beloved Sir George Augustus Wetherall, Lieutenant-General of Our Forces, Knight Commander of the Most Honourable Order of the Bath ; Our trusty and well-beloved Henry Eyre, Esquire, Major-General of Our Forces ; Our trusty and well-beloved William Montague Scott McMurdo, Companion of the Most Honourable Order of the Bath, Colonel in Our Army, Inspector-General of Volunteers, and one of Our Aides-de-Camp ; Our trusty and well-beloved Adam Steuart Gladstone, Esquire, Lieutenant-Colonel in the Fifth Lancashire Rifle Volunteers ; Our trusty and well-beloved Edward William Venables Vernon Harcourt, Esquire, Major in the Fourth Cinque Ports Artillery Volunteers, greeting :

Whereas it hath been humbly represented to Us that it is expedient that a Commission should forthwith issue to inquire into the present condition of Our Volunteer Force in Great Britain, and into the probability of its continuance at its existing strength, and to report whether any Measures should be adopted for the purpose of increasing its efficiency as an auxiliary Means of National Defence.

Now Know ye that We, having taken into Our consideration the premisses, do hereby nominate and appoint you, the said Charles Viscount Eversley, Henry John Earl of Ducie, Charles Stewart Viscount Hardinge, Francis Wemys Charteris Douglas, commonly called Lord Elcho, Samuel Baron Overstone, Edward Pleydell Bouverie, Walter Barttelot Barttelot, Sir Archibald Islay Campbell, Sir George Augustus Wetherall, Henry Eyre, William Montague Scott McMurdo, Adam Steuart Gladstone, and Edward William Venables Vernon Harcourt, to inquire into these Matters.

And it is Our further will and pleasure that you, or any Seven or more of you, do obtain information touching the Matters aforesaid, by the examination of all Persons most competent, by reason of their knowledge and experience, to afford it, and also by calling for all Documents, Papers, or Records which may appear to you, or any Seven or more of you, calculated to assist your researches and to promote the formation of a sound judgment on the subject, and that you, or any Seven or more of you, do report to Us, under your Hands and Seals, your several proceedings by virtue of this Our Commission, together with your opinions touching the several Matters hereby referred for your consideration.

And We will and command, and by these presents ordain, that this Our Commission shall continue in full force and virtue, and that you, Our said Commissioners, or any Seven or more of you, may from time to time proceed in the execution thereof, and of every Matter and thing therein contained, although the same be not continued from time to time by adjournment.

And for your assistance in the due execution of these presents, We have made choice of Our trusty and well-beloved Thomas Frederick Wetherell, Esquire, to be Secretary to this Our Commission, and to attend you, of whose services and assistance We require you to avail yourselves from time to time, as occasion may require.

> Given at Our Court at Balmoral, this Sixteenth Day of May, in the year of Our Lord One thousand eight hundred and sixty-two, and in the Twenty-fifth Year of Our Reign.

By Her Majesty's Command.

G. C. LEWIS.

REPORT.

TO THE QUEEN'S MOST EXCELLENT MAJESTY.

WE Your Majesty's Commissioners appointed to inquire into the present condition of the Volunteer Force in Great Britain, and into the probability of its continuance at its present strength, and to report whether any measures should be adopted for the purpose of increasing its efficiency as an auxiliary means of national defence, do most humbly report to Your Majesty as follows:

In entering upon the task confided to us under Your Majesty's commands, we deemed it right in the first place to take steps for ascertaining the actual condition of the Volunteer Force at the present time; and for that purpose, as well as to obtain other requisite information, we addressed a series of questions to every commanding officer of Volunteers in Great Britain, and we also examined such witnesses as we believed to be well acquainted with the subject.

The information thus sought has been readily afforded to us. The actual number of enrolled members of the force on the 1st of April 1862 was 162,681, of whom 662 were light horse, 24,363 artillery, 2,904 engineer, 656 mounted rifle, and 134,096 rifle volunteers; of the rifle volunteers 48,796 were organized in 86 consolidated battalions, and 75,535 in 134 administrative battalions; and we are much gratified in being enabled to state that the present condition of the Volunteer Force is, generally speaking, satisfactory, and we believe that by steady perseverance in the course hitherto pursued, and by due discipline, it will be a valuable auxiliary to the British Army as a means of national defence.

On its first formation this force received considerable assistance from honorary members of corps, officers, and others, and the funds so raised have been for the most part expended in the establishment of head-quarters, drill grounds, rifle ranges, &c., and in the purchase of clothing and equipments. The current annual expenses of corps have generally been met by subscriptions from their own members.

The time, however, is approaching when the uniforms will require to be renewed, and as there is reason to apprehend that the honorary subscriptions and donations may not be maintained at their present amount, the cost of new uniforms, and the subscriptions necessary to defray the annual expenses of corps are together felt to be a burden, the pressure of which will seriously affect the force by causing a large diminution of its numbers.

Under these circumstances, we have had great difficulty in arriving at a conclusion, both with regard to the amount of the aid required and the mode in which it ought to be administered, owing to the great discrepancy of opinion on this point which the evidence has brought under our notice.

Several witnesses, whose opinions are deserving of attention, deprecate any grant in money, and recommend that whatever assistance is afforded should be in kind. Others recommend a grant varying from 12s. to 50s., and even more for every effective.

After a careful consideration of the whole subject we have come to the conclusion that it is expedient that some further assistance in aid of the volunteer movement should be rendered by the Government, but it is essential in our judgment that whatever aid may be so granted should be strictly regulated with reference to the real efficiency of the force.

As the most expedient way of carrying out this principle, under existing circumstances, we recommend:—

> That there should be a grant from the Government of 20s. per man for every light horse, engineer, mounted rifle, and rifle volunteer, who can produce a certificate, according to a form to be prescribed by the Secretary of State, signed by the commanding officer and adjutant of his corps, or by the commanding officer and adjutant of the administrative battalion to which his corps belongs, that he has attended nine drills, six of which in the case of a consolidated battalion, and three of which in the case of an administrative battalion, should be battalion or troop

drills, in the course of the preceding twelve months; that he is efficient in drill, has been fully instructed in the manual and platoon exercise, and, in addition to the above drills, has gone through a course of musketry instruction to be laid down by the Secretary of State; and also that he was present on parade (unless absent by leave of his commanding officer with the approval of the Secretary of State) on the day of inspection; and an additional grant of 10s. per man for every volunteer who can produce a similar certificate that he has fired a certain amount of ball cartridge, according to regulations to be laid down by the Secretary of State.

That in the case of a recruit 30 drills, including a short course of musketry instruction, should be substituted for the drills already enumerated, in order to qualify him for receiving such certificate.

That a power should be reserved to the inspecting officer to disallow the certificate of any man or body of men whose inefficiency may be manifest on parade.

That the existing definition of an effective should be repealed.

That divisional or brigade field days and official inspections should not be reckoned in the number of drills above specified.

That every rifle should be seen and examined once a year by a person appointed by the Government, and that no corps should be entitled to receive any portion of the Government grant for any member whose rifle is reported in an unserviceable state through neglect.

That officers commanding volunteer corps, or administrative battalions, in the event of such corps or battalions obtaining further aid from Government, should be permitted to expend the grant under the following heads:—

    Head quarters.
    Drill grounds.
    Care and repair of arms.
    Ranges.
    Clothing and accoutrements.
    Cost of conveyance to and from battalion and brigade drill, and rifle practice.
    Forage for serjeant instructor's horse in the case of mounted corps.

That in the case of artillery volunteers a further grant, beyond that already made by the Government, of 30s. per man should be made for every man who can produce a certificate signed by the commanding officer and adjutant of his corps, or by the commanding officer and adjutant of the administrative brigade to which his corps belongs, that he has attended twelve gun drills in the course of the preceding twelve months; has been present at the gun practice of his battery, and is an efficient gunner; also that he was present on parade (unless absent by leave of his commanding officer with the approval of the Secretary of State) on the day of inspection. During the first year of service attendance at 30 drills, of which 24 should be gun drills, should be substituted for the conditions above enumerated.

In the event of such further aid being obtained, commanding officers should be permitted to expend the grant under the following heads:—

    Head quarters.
    Drill grounds.
    Care and repair of arms.
    Construction of expense magazines.
    Store rooms.
    Gun and drill sheds.
    Expenses incidental to target practice.
    Articles for repository exercises.
    Cost of conveyance of men and guns, on duty.
    Accoutrements and clothing.

That in the event of any corps being desirous of expending the whole or any portion of the Government grant in clothing, sealed patterns of colour applicable to the four branches of the service should be issued, to which such corps should be required to conform.

That all corps in the receipt of the Government grant should be required to adopt accoutrements approved by the Secretary of State, and all corps belonging to administrative battalions to adopt such colour as the Lord Lieutenant shall direct.

That in addition to all other allowances, a sum not exceeding 4s. per head per annum for each member who has been certified as efficient, in any corps where the head-quarters are distant beyond five miles from the place of meeting of the administrative battalion to which it belongs, should be granted to the commanding officer of the battalion in aid of the expenses of conveying the members of such corps to battalion drills.

That the adjutant should be responsible to the War Office, in the event of his being employed to act as paymaster, for all sums received on account of such corps, and for their having been expended strictly according to regulation, and that he should be put on the same footing as an adjutant of disembodied militia.

A witness of long and distinguished service in the Army, who is now the adjutant of an administrative battalion in the midland counties, has spoken in strong terms of the inefficiency of many of the drill instructors attached to volunteer corps; and he has suggested that a school of drill instructors should be formed, somewhat on the same principle as the School of Musketry at Hythe. We consider this suggestion deserving the attention of Your Majesty's Secretary of State; but in the meantime we recommend that special provision should be made for training non-commissioned officers as drill instructors, and that all drill instructors should be attested to serve for a period of three years.

We also recommend that the drill instructors at present attached to corps in an administrative battalion should as soon as possible be placed under the orders of the officer commanding the battalion, who should have the same power and authority when visiting any corps of his battalion for the purpose of inspection as he now exercises at a battalion parade.

The system now in operation, under which officers appointed by the Secretary of State to inspect volunteer corps examine and report upon the competency, or otherwise, of officers and non-commissioned officers of the corps so inspected, such examination being conducted in the field, and all cases of marked incompetency being brought confidentially to the notice of the Secretary of State, is of essential importance, and ought to be strictly maintained.

We recommend that in order to afford to volunteers every possible assistance in acquiring a more perfect knowledge of drill and of our military system, and with the view of promoting that cordiality and feeling of confidence in each other, which would be of vital importance to the regular troops and volunteers in co-operating against an enemy, volunteer corps should, wherever practicable, be united with troops of the line for exercise and instruction, as already sanctioned by the Secretary of State with the concurrence of the General Commanding-in-Chief.

We have much satisfaction in reporting that arrangements have been made in some parts of the kingdom between officers commanding corps of artillery volunteers and the farmers, gentry, and others, for obtaining a supply of horses and oxen, when requisite, for the purpose of moving guns of position, free of expense to the Government; and we are of opinion that such arrangements should be encouraged and extended wherever possible.

We have also been informed that there are a number of men on the sea coast and in various parts of the country, who are desirous of learning their drill at ship's guns, but who are ineligible for the Royal Naval Reserve; and we think such men should be encouraged to avail themselves of any opportunities offered them by the Admiralty of acquiring a knowledge of ship gun drill, and should be embodied in the existing batteries of artillery volunteers on the coast.

It appears in evidence that numerous cadet corps have been established in connexion with volunteer corps, and public and other schools, and we suggest that, having regard to the future strength and permanence of the Volunteer Force, encouragement should be given to the formation of such cadet corps.

We also think it desirable, that those corps which are fit for it should take part occasionally in brigade and divisional field days; but evidence having been given to the effect that the subsequent attendance at regimental parades is apt to fall off, we are of opinion that brigade and divisional field days should, as much as possible, be postponed until the close of the battalion drill season.

We are also of opinion that in order to ensure a good average muster, and to obviate the breaking up of companies in battalion drills, it is desirable to raise the strength of companies in consolidated battalions.

In measuring the amount of further pecuniary assistance to the Volunteer Force which this Commission humbly recommends to Your Majesty, reference has been had solely to the maintenance of the present efficiency of the force as regards its strength and discipline. If it be desirable that any positive limit should be placed upon the total number of the force, the duty and responsibility of deciding that question must rest exclusively with the responsible advisers of the Crown.

The permanence and efficiency of a Volunteer Force must essentially depend upon the sympathies of the public, and upon the general support, whether pecuniary or other, to which those sympathies give rise. The Volunteer movement, in its progressive advance to its present condition, has been materially aided by the efforts and contributions of those who, from age or other circumstances, have found themselves precluded from giving their personal service, and the further aid now recommended by this Commission would fail to accomplish its intended purpose if it weakened that general support on the part of the community at large.

We also beg leave to refer, as affording further explanation of the reasons upon which our Report is founded, to the evidence, documentary and oral, collected by this Commission, and which constitutes the appendix to this our Report.

         EVERSLEY.
         DUCIE.
         HARDINGE.
         ELCHO.
         OVERSTONE.
         EDWARD PLEYDELL BOUVERIE.
         WALTER B. BARTTELOT.
         A. I. CAMPBELL.
         G. A. WETHERALL, Lieut. General.
         H. EYRE, Major General.
         W. M. S. MACMURDO.
         E. W. HARCOURT.

Although I agree to the Report generally, I cannot sign it without stating that I consider a capitation grant open to objection on principle, and of doubtful efficacy for the object it is desired to attain.

I also think that the proposed amount (bearing in mind the aid already given) is in excess of the actual requirements of the force.

With this qualification I have signed the Report.

                    H. EYRE, Major General.

I have been unable, in consequence of illness, to attend the meetings of the Commission; but, on a consideration of the printed evidence, I agree in the recommendations of the Report.

                  ADAM S. GLADSTONE,
                      Lieut. Colonel.

APPENDIX.

CONTENTS.

	Page
ANALYSIS OF EVIDENCE	2
ALPHABETICAL LIST OF WITNESSES	16
MINUTES OF EVIDENCE	17
LETTERS AND MEMORANDA	205

ANALYSIS OF EVIDENCE.

ACLAND, LIEUT.-COL. THOMAS DYKE:
Commands a mounted rifle volunteer corps, and an administrative battalion, in Devonshire, 3967. The corps consists of one company, with a certain number of dismounted men; it is well provided for, and requires no assistance beyond that already given, 3968–3974. The administrative battalion consists of eight corps, with two mounted corps attached, 3976. Volunteer corps should, if possible, be self-supporting, 3980; and any assistance given by Government should be subject to strict conditions as to efficiency, 3981, 4026, 4056. A man should have passed through a course of musketry instruction, and perhaps all the preliminary drills, in order to be an effective, 3982–3984. There has been great difficulty in some parts of Devonshire in getting ranges, 3986. The commanding officer of an administrative battalion should have more responsibility than he has at present; but if money were given to the different corps, it should not pass through his hands, 3988–3990. He should have the power of ascertaining what progress is being made in the drill of the different corps under him; the adjutant should keep him informed on this point, and should have an orderly-clerk or serjeant-major for the purpose, 3985, 3991–3993. The plan of compounding for the adjutant's travelling expenses is a bad one, 3995. The present mode of appointing and paying drill-instructors in small corps, should be altered; the best arrangement would be to place them under the commanding officer and adjutant of the administrative battalion, and, failing this, the most convenient course would be to give a money payment to the officers of each corps to be spent on the payment either of an occasional drill instructor, or of a resident orderly, or of both. This would cost less than the present system, and would go further to ensure a supply of proper men, 3996–4013, 4041–4042. The expenses incurred in travelling to battalion drill fall, as a rule, on the officers; and this imposes a limit on attendance and also on the appointment of officers, 1014, 1015. The Devon County Volunteer Association gives money for brigade but not for battalion drills, 4019. It is now endeavouring to encourage a high figure of merit in shooting, by giving battalion prizes, 4020, 4021. There is no insuperable difficulty in keeping the several companies at their proper strength, 4022. It is not necessary to enforce universally all the details of the Hythe system, 4023–4025. In the administration of Government aid each corps should state its own wants; the field officers and the assistant inspector should give their opinions on the application, and the War Office should then exercise a final judgment, 4027–4033, 4056. It is desirable that the volunteers should, as far as possible, clothe themselves, 3938–4040. If the present arrangement with regard to drill instructors remains unaltered, the case of subdivisions should be specially considered, 4043. Every rifle in the possession of a corps ought to be produced when the corps is inspected, 4043–4049. The inspection should carry practical consequences to the funds of the corps, 4053. A man should be judged to be effective by the results of his work, and not by the time he has spent on it, 4054.

BELL, MR. SHERIFF GLASSFORD;
STIRLING-CRAWFORD, LIEUTENANT-COLONEL;
STIRLING, LIEUTENANT-COLONEL WILLIAM;
MCGRIGOR, CAPTAIN ALEXANDER B.;
LOCKHART, MR. JAMES:
Concur generally in the evidence given by Colonel Dreghorn. The Committee, originally appointed at Glasgow to consider the appropriation of the fund to be collected for the purpose of the volunteer movement, reported that its first object should be to facilitate the formation of volunteer corps, especially among the artizan and working classes; and its second object, to promote the efficiency of the corps after they were formed. Understand the word artizan to cover all persons who have limited incomes, varying perhaps from 50l. to 100l.

BELL, MR. SHERIFF GLASSFORD, &c.—continued.
a year, 4288–4292, 4304–4305. If the Government made a grant it is probable that all corps would accept it. The Glasgow officers are of opinion that the grant should not be under 2l. a head, but as a compromise they decided to ask for only 1l. a head. Besides the general fund, there were special funds and sources of assistance to particular corps at Glasgow; none of them are any longer available, 4289, 4293. The present number of volunteers, at Glasgow, is from 6,000 to 7,000, but the continuance of that number cannot be relied on unless further assistance is given, 4298. Assistance should be given in money, 4298–4303. If the artizans were eliminated from the Glasgow Volunteer force there would not be more than eight or ten companies left, 4303, 4304. The social tone of the artizans has been greatly improved by their enrolment in volunteer corps, 4305. In an artizan corps, even if the Government issued cloth, the whole of the other expenses would fall on the officers, 4305. A uniform granted by the Government might be taken away from a man who did not attend a certain number of drills, and he might be made to pay a certain sum of money, 4321. About 4,000 of the Glasgow Volunteers are artizans, 4330. They would contemplate a discontinuance of the volunteer movement with considerable disgust, 4331–4334. The withdrawal of 4,000 artizan volunteers from Glasgow for actual service would not, under the circumstances which would in that case exist, disorganize the industry of the city, 4335–4340. If the power of resignation with 14 days' notice were abolished, the commanding officers would have more power over their men, 4344–4355. If the Government renewed the offer to purchase rifles with which the corps have supplied themselves, it might be accepted in Glasgow, 4355–4358.

BERESFORD, MAJOR MARCUS:
Commands the 7th Surrey Rifle Volunteers, 608. The corps has 475 members, of whom from 120 to 160 ordinarily muster at each battalion drill, 611, 612. The corps is rather decreasing in numbers, 617–619; and will probably decrease more when new uniforms are required, 641. The expenses of the corps exceed its receipts, and will continue to do so, 620–640. The efficiency of the corps cannot be maintained without assistance from Government, 643. This assistance should be in the form of a capitation grant, 648. If the subscriptions were retained, 10s. a head would be a sufficient Government grant to cover all ordinary expences except clothing, 650–654, 674–678, 706–709. The corps pays nothing extra to its adjutant, 656. The expenses which fall upon officers of the corps do not deter persons from undertaking the duty of officers, 657, 658. The Government grant should be paid to the commanding officer, subject to specific appropriations, and an accurate account of it should be rendered, 662–667. This arrangement would not invalidate the voluntary principle of the force, 660, 661; nor lead to any inconvenient control of the commanding officer by the members of his corps, 668–670. It is desirable to increase the number of companies in a corps, and not to increase the maximum strength of each company, 618, 619, 679–701. It is essential that Government should give some assistance towards clothing, 710; and, including this, the Government grant should be 20s. a head on the nominal strength of the corps, 711–721. The law which allows a volunteer to resign with 14 days notice should not be altered, 723.

BINGHAM, COLONEL CHARLES:
Is Deputy Adjutant General of Artillery, 3930. The volunteer organization for moving guns of position on the coast is one of the best arrangements that could be made, and should be extended as much as possible, 3933, 3934. The Government assistance given to the Artillery Volunteers might fairly include the gratuitous carriage of ammunition, the construction of expense magazines, the construction, in certain cases, of store-rooms for

BINGHAM, COLONEL CHARLES—*continued*.
Government stores, the residence for the gunner in charge, the erection of gun-sheds, the expense of sending out their targets for practice, skidding luff-tackle, ground and other rollers, scotches, selvages, straps, and dragropes; but the expense under some of these heads would be great, 3935–3955. The Horse Guards authorities have no control over the volunteer officers; but the Artillery Volunteers are organized under the commanding officers of Royal Artillery in the districts, as far as their matériel and practice are concerned, 3957–3961. The Artillery Volunteer Force is of the greatest importance as an auxiliary to the Royal Artillery, and ought to receive, as it does, every possible assistance from the Government, 3964.

BLACKBURN, CAPTAIN JOHN GEORGE:
Commands the 31st Lancashire Rifle Volunteer Corps, 2623. The corps musters 221 men, who are mostly artizans, 2625–2663. Two-thirds attend parades regularly, 2626. Members attend drill once a month, or pay a fine, 2628. The volunteer force is not at present on a solid foundation, nor ever can be, so long as subscriptions are obtained from the men, 2634, 2636. Means by a solid foundation greater certainty as to their pecuniary resources, 2654. None of the corps in Lancashire, with one or two exceptions, can be maintained unless they are assisted, 2644, 2645, 2708, 2709. The power of resigning after 14 days' notice should be abolished, and the members enrolled for three years, 2653, 2740, 2741, 2745. To make the volunteer force a permanent one, all expenses of instruction and maintenance should be borne, and armouries, rifle ranges, and uniforms provided by the Government; the officers paying for bands and for everything not really necessary for the efficiency of the corps, 2655, 2687, 2691. The men of his corps are in a state of efficiency, and able to join in general movements if called out for service, 2657. Officers should be bound to obtain certificates of fitness after one year, 2662. Could have a strong and efficient force in Oldham, if members were exempt from money payments, 2663. Popular feeling in favour of the volunteer force would be increased by acts of recognition and acknowledgment of its services on the part of the Government, 2669, 2670. Its association with the regular force would be acceptable to the volunteers, 2672, 2673. Objects to the arms being left in possession of the men, 2676. Recruits readily take the uniforms of men who have resigned, 2684. Finds no falling off in the subscriptions and donations of honorary members, but they are very precarious, 2686. Officers are willing to contribute themselves, but are annoyed when obliged to call upon the men for their subscriptions, 2688, 2702. Every corps should have an establishment entitling it to an adjutant, 2692. The volunteer force should not be greatly augmented but kept near its present strength as a nucleus round which in case of emergency large numbers of all classes might be collected and speedily brought to a state of efficiency, 2711–2716. All members, when effective, should be exempted from civil duties, such as those of jurors, special constables, &c., 2718, 2719, 2720, 2722, 2723, 2724. The volunteer force does not at all interfere with the recruiting for the militia, 2725. Thinks it undesirable for serjeant-instructors to engage in trade or any other occupation, 2728, 2729, 2730, 2732, 2733. Present system of discipline is amply sufficient, 2736.

BOURNE, LIEUTENANT-COLONEL JAMES:
Commands the 4th Lancashire Artillery Volunteer Corps of eight batteries, 3167–3169. A fund of 3,500*l.* was raised for brigade purposes by subscriptions from the officers and men, and a donation of 1,200*l.* from the town. The clothing was paid for out of this fund, 3171, 3172, 3237. The men are principally clerks in merchants' houses; 50 or 60 are mechanics of the higher class, 3173, 3174. Has great doubt of a fund being raised to renew the clothing, 3176–3251. The men are supplied with short carbines and sword bayonets, and eight garrison guns, small 24-pounders, for drill purposes. Platforms of wood for those guns were provided by the corps, 3177–3178, 3199. Has battalion drill once a week during the summer months; attaches importance to it as giving occupation to the men when they are all assembled, having only facilities for drilling a certain number at one time at gun drill, 3184, 3186. Divisional field days are of no use to artillery volunteers, unless they were supplied with guns and ammunition, and placed under the command of an artillery officer, 3185, 3195. Has a gun range at which practice with shot and shell is carried on, 3187, 3188. Does not see how opportunities for drill can be increased. The fort at which

BOURNE, LIEUTENANT-COLONEL JAMES—*continued*.
they practise is four or five miles from head quarters. The men are marched down by batteries in succession, and boarded there for certain periods, during which they have two gun drills per day, or practise in the morning and evening, the men returning to their duties in the town and sleeping at the fort at night, 3189. 24-pounders are mounted in the parade ground, close to the storehouse, where more guns could be placed, but this would be of no great advantage, as the course is gone through by separate detachments of batteries, and drill is carried on every evening, 3190 3194. There is no organized association in his district for range firing with great guns; it would not be of much advantage to artillery corps, 3196–3198. 30 drills per annum, including company, carbine, and gun drill, should constitute an effective artillery volunteer; the present number is not sufficient, 3200–3203. The attendance is much better at gun practice, especially with shot and shell, than at gun drill, 3204, 3205. The men go through a superficial course of theoretical instruction in gunnery, and in boring and fixing fuses. Such instruction is most necessary for artillerymen, and especially for non-commissioned officers, 3206–3208. Very few of his men have been through repository drill; such a mode of varying the drill would be most advantageous, 3215–3218. Considers the corps under his command to be in a very healthy condition, 3221. Government aid is necessary to secure its permanence and efficiency, 3222, 3250–3254. It should be given in the form of a money grant to the extent of 1*l.* 5*s.* or 1*l.* 10*s.* a head. It should be under the control of the commanding officers, and applied to the payment of all expenses for drill purposes and instructors, the rent of storehouses, the custody and repair of small arms, headquarters, carriage of ammunition, drill grounds, and the expense of attending parades, 3223, 3229–3233. At the commencement of the movement the corps paid 130*l.* for instructors belonging to the coast brigade of Royal Artillery, 3226–3228. He would be satisfied to be supplied with the items he has named on the terms upon which they are supplied with floating targets, the Government specification being adhered to with a maximum price. to be reduced by the commanding officer as much as possible, and the money so expended to be refunded by Government, 3234–3236. The income of his corps is about 800*l.* a year, 650*l.* of which is expended annually under the heads he has enumerated, leaving a balance of 150*l.*, which may or not be applied to the renewal of clothing, 3238, 3239. He does not include clothing in the 25*s.* or 30*s.* to be given to the commanding officer, 3240, 3241, 3242. Sees no way for the provision of clothing unless the Government relieve the men and officers from the expenses to which they are now liable. From the class of men forming his brigade, has no doubt they would clothe themselves were they relieved by Government of the other expenses. They now subscribe 18*s.* a year, 3243, 3245. Considers that if Liverpool were menaced by an invading force his corps would render most valuable service, 3246, 3247. Its efficiency is not now exposed to very serious danger arising from pecuniary difficulties, 3248. The artizans in his brigade are very orderly, well-disposed, and amenable to discipline, 3255. The band costs the officers from 160*l.* to 180*l.* a year, and is not included in these expenses. The volunteer movement has had a very beneficial effect, morally and socially, in Liverpool and its neighbourhood, 3258.

BOUSFIELD, MAJOR NATHANIEL:
Is major of the 1st Lancashire Rifle Volunteer Corps, 2272. It is a consolidated battalion of 10 companies, and 698 men, 2273, 2274, 2276. The corps was at first composed entirely of gentlemen. Tradesmen, their sons and assistants, are now enrolled. Three companies of artizans have also been formed, 2277. Has a regimental fund raised from an annual subscription of one guinea, paid by each member in the corps, 2278–2280, and expended in storehouse accommodation, band, and storekeeper, 2281. There is one large range for the force in Liverpool, supported by subscriptions, and used by about 4,000 volunteers; its annual cost, including markers and others, is near 1,000*l.*, 2282–2284, 2331–2333, 2339, 2340. No extra allowance is given to the adjutant or drill serjeants, except when the latter are used as storekeepers, 2285–2287. All the arms are kept in storehouses situate in different parts of the town, near the head-quarters of the companies. The men are taught to clean the arms, but to prevent their being taken home, men are paid to do it at the store, 2288–2293. The artizans were principally clothed by the officers, none

B 2

BOUSFIELD, MAJOR NATHANIEL—continued.
from the funds, 2294. Anticipates no difficulty in the renewal of clothing, except by the artizans, 2295. Government assistance should be applied in the payment of arm cleaners, instruction of buglers, bugle-major, and rent of storehouses. Practice ranges should be provided, and travelling allowances made for attending drills, &c. Adjutants should have lodging allowance. The allowance of ammunition should be increased, 2296. Is averse to a capitation grant, 2297. Government should pay the actual cost, and leave the men to provide their own uniforms and bands, 2298. To his corps of 700 men, 500l. a year should be given by Government, which would not include clothing, 2300–2302. This would be wholly inadequate for corps composed of artizans, or who required clothing; three artizan companies only in his corps require clothing, 2303–2306. Anticipates a falling off from pecuniary considerations only, 2308, 2309. Including clothing and everything, fully 30s. a man is required from Government to place the force in a satisfactory condition, 2310–2314. In his corps 20s. for 500 and 30s. for 198 men would be sufficient, 2315–2318. A capitation grant would be objectionable to the members of his corps, 2319–2321. Assistance should be given to certain branches of the service only, 2322. Separate regulations would be required for different corps; would leave it to each commanding officer to say whether he would receive aid in the form of a capitation grant or by any other mode; estimates ought to be required, 2323–2326. Non-effectives should be included in the calculation of a capitation grant; they are tolerably efficient, and fall in at reviews, &c., 2327–2330, 2420. The Government, serjeants require extra pay for cleaning arms, 2333–2336. It is not possible for all volunteers to clean their own arms, 2338, 2339. The volunteers in his corps could not be under stricter control than they are at present, 2341, 2342. In 1860 had 220, and in 1861 150 of his men in camp under canvas for seven weeks. It answered very well, and many of the men want another camp this year, 2343–68. If uniform were issued by the Government, it should be in cloth and an allowance should be given for making up, 2369. Everything personal to each man should be provided by himself, 2370–2372. Finds no good in working men as volunteers, except when they are in the employ of their commanding officer, 2374, 2375. There would be a difficulty in getting the men to wear second-hand clothing, 2376, 2405. Where artizan corps are officered by their employers anticipates no inconvenience in Liverpool from strikes, 2378. Has some officers totally incompetent who obtained commissions by obtaining 50 or 60 men. 2380–2382, 2385, 2411. Has now no difficulty in transferring men from one company to another, 2384. Thinks every officer should be subjected to an examination, and that lord lieutenants have the necessary power for that purpose, 2387–2391. Suggests, for securing the permanent efficiency of the volunteer movement, an examination of all officers as to efficiency, a monetary grant for a storehouse, drill instructors, arm cleaners, adjutants with lodging allowance, instruction of buglers, and an increased allowance of ammunition, 2394, 2395, 2400, 2405. In his corps three companies (artizans) would require more than others, 2396, 2397. If one-half or two-thirds of the force were proved to be in the same position as those three companies, it would modify the views he has expressed, 2398. No man should be a volunteer who is not self-supporting; the place of those who require clothing and maintaining is in the militia, 2399. The uniform in his corps costs 5l. for tunic, shako, forage cap, belts, pouch, and trousers; great coat is extra, and provided by all, 2401, 2402. An early decision on the question of Government aid is of pressing importance, 2406–2409. None of the officers in his corps, except himself, have been attached to a regiment of the line for instruction, 2410. Less than 24 drills every year should not be allowed to constitute an effective; many men attend more, 2416–2418. His drill instructors have nothing to do during the day, which is injurious, leading to drinking and idleness; reducing their number or allowing them to engage in other occupations would not be advisable; if they could get light work it would be useful, or they might be ordered by Government to clean the arms; light work would not interfere with their duties except on Saturdays; their conduct is generally good, 2423–2434. Finds it impossible to carry out the theoretical instruction laid down by General Hay; has musketry classes, but the men do not care for them, 2435. Every man, in his corps has had ball practice, but not fired his 90 rounds, 2436, 2437. Thinks there should be a larger gratuitous supply of ammunition for prize shooting, 2440–2449.

BOWER, LIEUTENANT-COLONEL JOHN:
Commands the 1st Hants Light Horse Volunteer Corps, of 44 men, 4213, 4214. There will be no difficulty in renewing the clothing, and the corps is not in absolute want of anything, 4216–4227. The Government should give forage for the serjeant instructor's horse, 4217. It would be an advantage to the corps if the Government would issue a lighter weapon to them than the short Enfield, 4222. The corps is a peculiar one, and requires a proper designation, 4224–4226. The present allowance of ammunition is not enough, 4227–4230.

BOYS, CAPTAIN HENRY, R.N.
Is 1st Lieutenant of the 2nd Cinque Ports Artillery Volunteer Corps, of one battery and 64 men, 3260–3263. The men are drilled at guns belonging to the corps mounted at Sandwich at an old battery, used only as a magazine by the corps, 3264–3267. The members are got together for drill eight or ten times a month during summer, and three or four times a month during winter, 3268. They are pretty perfect in their garrison gun drill, 3269. They are armed with carbines, 3270. Attaches no value to the possession of carbines by artillery volunteers for service, but they would not be satisfied without them, 3271. They have small arms drill three or four times a month, 3272. A drill instructor is attached to the corps, whose travelling expenses from Sandown to Sandwich they have to pay, 3273–3277. The artillery volunteers would not object to being placed even more than at present under the control of the district officers of Royal Artillery, 3282, 3283. There are several rifle volunteer corps in the neighbourhood, 3284. Recruiting for one arm interferes with recruiting for the other, 3285–3287. On the coast, artillery is the more important arm, 3286. The men generally prefer the artillery, 3288. The corps has battalion drill eight or ten times a year, 3289, 3290. All field days are good for the men, 3292. There is an organized association in the district for prize firing with great guns, 3294. Such associations would be of great advantage to artillery corps generally, 3295–3297. The corps is supplied with two 24-pounder garrison guns for drill purposes, and two 18-pounder field guns of position on the coast for shot practice, 3298. Platforms for these were provided by the corps; application was made for the expenses, but refused. They were not erected according to a specification, 3299–3303. Considers for each description of gun drill 10 drills a year necessary to constitute an effective, 3304. The attendance is better at gun practice than at gun drill, 3305. All the men have been instructed in boring and fixing fuses, and partially in the general principles of gunnery, 3306. It is essential for a gunner to be acquainted with these subjects before being appointed a non-commissioned officer, 3307. Varying the drills secures better attendance, and doing so by repository exercises, which are necessary for artillerymen, would be appreciated by the men, 3322–3324. It would be advantageous to artillery volunteers to know how to shift everything belonging to a gun or carriage, 3325. Thinks a system could be organized in his neighbourhood like that which exists in Sussex for moving guns or travelling carriages, 3327, 3328. Gun-boats or floating batteries in charge of the coast-guard, and manned by seamen from the naval reserve, should be stationed at various ports on the coast, and the artillery volunteers should provide marines, still attached to their batteries on shore, for those vessels when they should be called out, 3330. Does not think that this plan would interfere in any way with the naval reserve, 3331. It would be a great advantage if the artillery volunteers were provided with light 6-pounder guns or 12-pounder howitzers, 3332, 3333. Thinks his corps generally is in a healthy condition with reference to its finance, 3335. Government aid will be necessary to ensure the permanence and efficiency of his corps, 3336. If aid were afforded, would prefer a money allowance of so much a head to be made to the commanding officer for the purpose of paying the travelling expenses of volunteers in going to reviews and meetings, and to establish gun sheds, 3337. The men generally march about three miles to gun practice, 3338–3343. Various classes of men are enrolled in his corps, 3344. One half is clothed entirely, and one third partly, from the funds of the corps, one third clothing themselves, 3349–3351. There are a good many honorary members belonging to the corps, who pay a guinea a year to the fund, 3352–3354. Does not think the subscription from honorary members will fall off, but there will be no more donations, 3355. The officers subscribe largely, but are not called upon to

BOYS, CAPTAIN HENRY, R.N.—*continued*.

pay other expenses, 3356. Considers his corps to be at this moment in a state efficient for actual service, and that in case of a sudden emergency it would render real and valuable assistance, 3358, 3359. The poorest men in the corps feel the expenses of moving about to the different meetings to be the heaviest, 3360.

BRIGGS, LIEUTENANT-COLONEL GEORGE:

Commands the 1st Administrative Battalion of the West Riding of Yorkshire Rifle Volunteers, of eight and a half companies, averaging 75 men each, 1804-1807. All the companies attend battalion drill twice a year; four companies once a week, 1808, 1809. The volunteers travel by railway at the same rate as the regular troops, 1814. Has a battalion fund of 150*l.* a year, raised from subscriptions of staff officers and contributions of 12*l.* per company, and applied to battalion drill and head quarters expenses, 1815-1818. Each company has a separate fund of its own, 1819. The men have been assisted in providing clothing; apprehends difficulty in renewing it, and a falling off in the subscriptions, 1820-1822. One corps in York has four companies and one range, 1823-1825. All the expenses are borne by the four companies together, 1826. The adjutant receives no extra allowance; has the use of a room at head quarters, 1827-1829. His pay is not sufficient; he has harder work, and receives less than a militia adjutant; he keeps a horse, 1830, 1837-1842, 1860-1869; he visits and attends to the drill of the outlying companies, 1831. The position of commanding officer of an administrative battalion should be more defined and regimental than at present, 1834, 1907. The adjutant visits the corps for drill at least once a quarter, oftener in the summer months; the musketry instruction is carried on under his supervision; the greater part of the effectives have gone through the course, 1843-1850. The Government serjeants are engaged by the commandants of the separate companies, and receive an additional allowance out of the funds of each, 1851-1853. Registers of attendance are strictly kept, 1855-1859. Captains of companies are responsible for the correctness of returns of effectives; they are not always correctly kept, 1870, 1871. 24 drills a year should be required to constitute an effective, 1872, 1873. Recruits usually join in spring and summer, 1876. The arms are always inspected by the adjutant, 1877, 1878. Further Government aid will be required to keep up the battalion; a capitation grant of 5*s.* a year would be sufficient, and supply the place of the present battalion fund, 1879-1885, 1908-1910. To keep up the companies a capitation grant of 1*l.* 1*s.* for each effective should also be given, through the colonel of the battalion to commanding officers, to be applied at their discretion to certain objects only, 1886-1908, 1911, 1912. An early decision on the question is important, 1899. The battalion is increasing in numbers, 1901. Some assistance is necessary for the continuance of the force, especially in the rural districts, 1902. The band funds have been kept distinct from the corps funds, 1903. If the private subscriptions ceased, a considerable number of the members would provide their own uniform, 1904. Has no control over the finance of the corps composing his battalion, 1905. Thinks there would be a difficulty in getting members to wear second-hand uniforms, 1906. A member who attends drill and musketry instruction 24 times a year is considered an effective, 1914, 1915. An administrative battalion should have one colour of uniform only, 1916. If further aid is given, stringent rules should be laid down as to returning men effective or non-effective, 1917-1919. Members muster about two-thirds when he visits them, 1920-1922. Has no power to enforce attendance; the adjutant sees to the drill, 1923-1925. Has no control except on parade; volunteers would be better pleased with a stricter system of discipline; the officer commanding an administrative battalion should be placed in the same position as the commanding officer of a yeomanry regiment; at present he cannot interfere to correct irregularities himself, and can only represent them to the authorities, 1926-1937. The drill instruction should be under his direction, with power to enforce any system he may lay down, 1938-1941. The Government serjeants are under the authority of the adjutant, but the commanding officers order their own parades, and are apt to disregard the system of drill recommended by the adjutant, 1942, 1943. There is great difficulty in obtaining serjeant instructors, 1945. A new Act of Parliament is absolutely necessary to remedy the defects he has pointed out, 1949. The adjutant exercises a general superintendence over the musketry instruction, but each corps has its own instructor, 1950.

BROOKS, MAJOR THOMAS:

Is major of the 3rd Manchester Rifle Volunteer Corps, of 10 companies and 731 men, 3439-3441. The corps is composed principally of artizans and tradesmen, 3444. The fund is spent principally in the expenses of the orderly-room, drill grounds, storage of arms, and clothing, 3446. In one year nearly 300*l.* of the fund was expended on a band, which will for the future be supported by a special subscription, 3448, 3449. There are two battalion drills out of uniform twice a week, and once a fortnight in uniform, 3451. The corps has decreased this year, owing partly to the great distress in Lancashire, 3453, 3454, 3511-3513. In good times there would be difficulty in maintaining the force at its present strength, the subscriptions being too high, 3455. The rifle range of the corps is eight miles from Manchester. The men are taken there and back by the railway for 6*d.* each, which is paid by themselves, 3456, 3457, 3544. All the men have passed through a course of musketry instruction, 3458, 3466, 3468. The average muster at each battalion drill out of uniform is 250 to 300, and in uniform 550 to 600, 3464. Every man must make himself effective or leave the corps, 3465. Eight companies could be maintained of the corps irrespective of clothing without Government aid, 3471. Aid should be given in money at so much a head, to be expended in defraying the regimental expenses, at the discretion of the commanding officer, 3475-3481; or the commanding officer might send in an estimate under certain heads, according to which the money might be granted, or assistance might be given in kind instead of money, 3482-3484. The issue of cloth would not be so satisfactory as that of ready-made clothing, on account of the expense in making it up. Many members would object to receiving complete suits of clothing from Government, 3485-3487. Volunteer corps in which the men are not able to clothe themselves would be willing to accept clothing, while others who can afford to clothe themselves would not consent to receive such uniforms, 3493. Has a general knowledge of the condition of the movement in South Lancashire, 3594. It is not subject to any serious danger as to its present condition; a better class of recruit is now obtained, 3595. The present condition of the volunteer force is satisfactory, but not financially so, 3596, 3597. The pecuniary pressure upon the artizan class in his corps threatens considerable danger to its maintenance and efficiency, 3598, 3599. Considers the corps to be in a highly satisfactory state with regard to discipline and organization, and also as to the condition of its arms and accoutrements, 3600, 3601. In the event of South Lancashire being suddenly menaced by a foreign force, his corps would render effectual assistance to the regular army; there would be an increased disposition to enter the force, and the men so brought in would be rapidly rendered efficient, 3602-3605. The volunteer force, as it now exists, is a valuable nucleus for augmentation in time of emergency, and the certainty of that opinion would be increased by limited pecuniary aid from Government, 3506, 3507, 3509. The movement is in a satisfactory condition both as to its present efficiency and its probable permanence, reserving only the question of pecuniary aid, 3510. The number of drills required to constitute an effective should be 35 a year, 3514-3521. Above two-thirds of his corps have gone through a course of 35 drills, 3522. None have been obliged to leave the corps through not passing the 24 drills, 3523. Many other corps are in as efficient a state, 3524. Is well acquainted with the state and feelings of the artizan class in South Lancashire, and sees no objection to their being drawn largely into the volunteer force, 3525, 3527. In case of emergency a large volunteer force, including a considerable part of the artizan population, might be safely relied on for the discharge of their military duties, 3528, 3533. Is convinced that it would be quite prudent to arm and train a large portion of the artizan class in military discipline, 3534-3536. The social habits and general conduct of the volunteers are invariably improved by the volunteer organization, 3537, 3538. The artizans in his corps are its most efficient members, 3539. Has sufficient power to enforce discipline under the volunteer regulations, 3540, 3545, 3546. In South Lancashire there are great difficulties in getting rifle ranges, 3541, 3542. The enrolment of artizans does not interfere with recruiting for the line or militia, 3547. There are about 3,000 volunteers in Manchester, two-thirds of whom are artizans, 3549, 3550. Experienced a difficulty in finding officers, but not entirely in consequence of the large subscription; 3551. Thinks the captains are competent to command their companies, 3552. The volunteers would rather have more military supervision than less, 3553; and desire to

B 3

BROOKS, MAJOR THOMAS—*continued.*

be oftener assembled in large bodies for inspection, 3551, 3568-3570. In the event of the volunteers being called out for actual service, the millowners and other employers would have no objection to volunteers being enrolled in any number, and the arrangements need not occasion any inconvenience to trade or industry, 3528-3532, 3555-3560. Great anxiety is felt in his neighbourhood with reference to the question of Government aid; and the effect of nothing being done would be a loss of a great many volunteers, 3561-3567.

BUCKLEY, LIEUT.-GENERAL EDWARD PERY, M.P.:

Commands the South Wiltshire Administrative Battalion of Rifle Volunteers, consisting of nine companies, and numbering 700 men, 2754-2757. Had three battalion drills last year and one this year, 2758. Owing to the battalion being much scattered, has never mustered 400 at one time; attendance at battalion drill is more important than at reviews, 2759. The travelling expenses of each battalion drill are about 46l., and are sometimes defrayed by the men, and occasionally made up by the captains, and from local funds, 2761-2765. Has no battalion fund, 2766. The members in the first instance clothed themselves; there will be great difficulty in the renewal of the clothing, and members consider it a grievance to have to provide new clothing and are holding back in the hope of assistance, 2767-2768. Volunteers know their value a little and expect something to be done for them, 2810, 2811. All the companies are provided with ranges, 2769-2772. The battalion would be very efficient in case of a demand for its service to resist invasion, and could be brought expeditiously to one point to assist the regular army, 2776-2778. The force generally would be useful and valuable for the purposes of internal and national defence, 2779-2780, 2784. Officers commanding administrative battalions have very little power, 2786, 2789. Thinks that the returns of effectives and non-effectives are correctly rendered, 2790. A capitation grant for each effective should be given by Government to commanding officers for the purposes of providing clothing and defraying the expenses incurred by attendance at battalion drills, 2796, 2797. Members who had attended a certain number of drills, learned the manual and platoon exercise, and gone through the third class of musketry instruction, might be considered effectives, 2799-2805. The men would not object to receive assistance in clothing, if it were judiciously given, 2809. An adjutant's allowance is not sufficient, 2812. The Lord-Lieutenant should decide what the uniform colour of the company or battalion should be.

CAMPION, CAPTAIN W. F.:

Commands the 13th Sussex Rifle Volunteer Corps, of one company and 73 men: it forms part of an administrative battalion, 2450-2453. The numbers keep up very fairly, 2454. Some belong to St. John's College, a few are artizans, and more than a third farmers, 2455-2457. Has a fund supported by honorary members, 2458, 2459. Uniforms are provided by the men themselves or out of a special fund raised in the neighbourhood, 2460, 2461, 2498. Attendance at drill is getting slack, 2462, 2463. The average attendance of his corps at battalion drill is about 70, including the band, 2464-2466. The Government serjeant has 2l. a quarter extra for cleaning the arms, 2474, 2522, 2523. Sees no difficulty in maintaining the corps in its present state of efficiency, 2475. Does not require any further assistance from Government, 2476, 2496. Has no doubt but that the men will renew their uniforms themselves; is averse to giving them clothing. The travelling expenses on account of battalion drills are paid out of the funds of the corps, 2479-2481. All the corps in a battalion should wear the same uniform, 2480-2483. Has a balance in hand of 100l. invested in stock, 2496. The incidental expenses of his corps can be permanently met by subscriptions raised in the neighbourhood, 2504, 2505. Entertains no apprehension as to the maintenance of the volunteer force in its present state of efficiency, 2506, 2507. Does not think that any special measures are now requisite for maintaining it, 2508. The adjutant is very useful, visits his corps once a month or every two months; he does not superintend the musketry instruction of his corps, 2509-2512. The serjeant-instructor has a great deal of spare time, but he is always ready to work; he keeps the arms clean, attends all parades and at the orderly room, and keeps the muster roll and books of the corps, which are accurately kept; the arms are kept in the armoury, but some of them are necessarily out, 2515-2520.

DARBY, CAPTAIN GEORGE:

Commands the 3rd Sussex Artillery Volunteer Corps, of two batteries and 108 men, 2922-2924. Formed his corps with a view to organising a mode, which might be generally extended, of conveying artillery to the coast. Has now for that purpose above 600 draught beasts, volunteered by farmers in the district, most of whom are enrolled as honorary members in his corps, 2925, 2928-2997. To move the guns of his battery at the late Brighton review, they supplied horses, teamsters, and forage, free of charge, 2926-2928. Could command these horses when necessary. Has contrived a plan by which agricultural may be changed at once into artillery harness, 2929, 2930. Ammunition, side-arms, and small stores are supplied by Government, 2931, 2932. On renewal of the uniform, 30 men will have to be wholly, and 19 men partially, clothed out of the funds of the corps, 2935. Furnishes the officer commanding the royal artillery in the district, under whose superintendence practice is carried on, with quarterly returns of practice and returns of stores, 2936-2938. The organization of Artillery Volunteers is of a more military character than that of Rifle Volunteers. Thinks the men like it better, and would not dislike being placed even more than they are at present under the superintendence of the officer commanding the royal artillery in the district, 2940-2943. All the members go through a regular course of artillery drill, 2947-2949. Attaches no importance to the use of carbines by artillery volunteers, 2950-2954, 2959-2964. The corps should be relieved from expense for the storage and care of the arms, 2955. Rifle matches and county timecegs are of little use in keeping up the artillery volunteer force. The less the volunteers are taken away from their occupations, the better it will be for the permanence of the movement, 2964-2968. Uses 68 prs., 32 prs., and 18 prs. for drill and practice, 2969. Thinks that after the first year, 12 drills per annum should constitute an effective, 2971, 2972, 2974-2978. The attendance is better at gun practice than at gun drill, 2973. The members go through a course of theoretical instruction in boring and fixing fuses, trajectory, and the science of artillery generally, 2979. A better attendance is secured by varying the drills, 2992. The members of his corps give assistance to the coast brigade of Royal Artillery when required, 2995, 2996. It is desirable that Government should provide sheds for drill, and for the care and storage of the arms, and also pay for getting the targets out to sea; the whole would cost about 5s. a head per annum, 2999-3000, 3009, 3030, 3031, 3041. Aid should be given in kind, 3002. Artillery volunteer corps should be principally formed on the coast, and rifle volunteer corps inland. Volunteer corps should never attempt to use light field guns, 3007, 3010. In case of invasion, artillery volunteer corps would be required to man existing batteries, and to move guns of position and heavy stores, 3008. The artillery volunteer service is generally popular in his district, 3011. The members of his corps are principally drawn from master blacksmiths, carpenters, farmers, and tradesmen, superior labourers, and skilled artizans, 3019-3021. In case of emergency, his corps would be ready and prepared for active service, 3022-3025. The quantity of ammunition allowed is always fired off, 3027-3029. The corps practises with the same kind of shells as are used by the Royal Artillery, and in doing so, the men regularly change rounds, 3036, 3039, 3040. Thinks it objectionable for Government to supply clothing to volunteers, 3041.

CRAWFORD, LIEUT.-COL. *See* BELL, MR., &c.

DE GREY AND RIPON, THE EARL:

The 1st Devon and 1st Middlesex Rifle Volunteer Corps were formed some years before 1859. In the spring of 1859 the then Government determined to accept the service of other volunteer corps. They were to occasion no cost whatever to the public, and the general intention was, that they should be formed as separate and independent companies. When the present Government came into office 11 of these new corps had been formed, and applications increasing almost daily in number continued to be received. Lord Herbert first determined to supply 25 per cent. of the rifles required by the corps. Shortly after, he sanctioned the organization in consolidated battalions, and ultimately decided on giving 100 per cent. of rifles. The next step taken was to supply adjutants, and to unite the small rural corps in administrative battalions. At the end of last session the Government took a supplementary estimate for the purpose of supplying drill serjeants. The position in which the matter stands at present with regard to Government assistance is, that a volunteer gives his

DE GREY AND RIPON, THE EARL—*continued.*

service, and provides himself with everything except arms, ammunition, and the persons required for his drill and inspection, 4594, 4624, 4625. It is practically impossible to put the force under a more extended military discipline without entirely altering its character, and completely changing the basis upon which it now rests, 4595, 4596. The organization of the administrative battalion grew up from the circumstances connected with the development of the movement in the country. It is desirable that the commanding officer of an administrative battalion should have a somewhat more extended power of command than he now possesses, but this power cannot be given him without an alteration in the Act of Parliament, 4597. It is desirable that the drill instructors of administrative battalions should be placed under the orders of the commanding officers of the battalions. 4597–4599, 4621, 4622. It would not have been possible or wise to enforce strict uniformity in the rules of the corps, 4600, 4601. In case of invasion it is not probable that the volunteers would be moved from their own homes until they were actually wanted in the field, 4603, 4604. If any further assistance is given to the volunteers, there should be some test of efficiency beyond the present test of effectiveness, 4605, 4628–4631. If any considerable sum of public money were disbursed to each corps, the adjutants could, without difficulty, be employed as paymasters, in accordance with the precedent of the militia adjutants, 4607–4609, 4619, 4620. The spending of a large sum of public money on the force would necessarily involve a limitation of its total strength in time of peace, 4610–4614, 4636–4640. A capitation grant to the force would not involve any important trouble or expense at the War Office, 4615–4618. No further Government aid should be given to any corps, which either was not a consolidated battalion, or did not form part of an administrative battalion, 4621, 4622. It is desirable that the decision to which the Government may come on receiving the report of this commission should be considered as defining the permanent basis of the corps, 4625. The main responsibility, both as to the corps to be raised, and as to the officers to be nominated, must remain with the lords lieutenant, 4627. In time of peace, it would be inconsistent with the character and constitutional nature of the force that it should be placed under the command of the general officers commanding districts, and the present position of the artillery volunteers affords no precedent for such an arrangement, 4641–4645. In case of the volunteers being called out for actual service, they would not act as an independent force, and it is desirable that they should now, as much as possible, be associated with the regular troops, 4646–4651.

DENYS, MAJOR SIR GEORGE, BART. :

Is major of the 1st Administrative Battalion of the North Riding of Yorkshire Rifle Volunteers, consisting of 12 companies, and about 750 men, 4376. Not more than half the men pay for their own clothing. 4379. There is no provision for the renewal of the clothing. 4387. Further material assistance from the Government is necessary to prevent half the corps in the battalion coming to an end, 4388. The men are tolerably welldrilled, 4391. The adjutant receives no extra pay, 4396. The drill instructors are generally over-paid, 4397, 4398. The great defect of the corps is the inefficiency of the officers and non-commissioned officers, 4399. If the Government relieves the officers of the expenses which now fall on them it may institute some test of their efficiency, 4400–4402. The volunteers in his district are perfectly fit for garrison duty, and in three months' time, if embodied, could be made equal to the disembodied militia, 4403–4405, 4410–4414. The more nearly the force assumes the character of the regular army the more efficient it will be, 4406, 4407. If the Government give further assistance, every corps should be made to keep accounts, as they are kept in the regular army; and the commanding officers of the corps should be responsible to the commanding officer of the administrative battalion, who should himself be responsible to the War Office, 4415. The commanding officer of an administrative battalion should enforce a uniform drill throughout the battalion, 4416. The more immediately the drill instructors can be placed under the authority of the general commanding the district, the better; drill instructors generally conduct themselves well, but they have too much time on their hands, and they have been spoiled by over-pay, 4420.

DILLWYN, MAJOR LEWIS LLEWELLYN, M.P.:

Commands the 3rd Glamorganshire Rifle Volunteers, consisting of four companies, 4232, 4233. Some further assistance to the force is necessary, in respect to both clothing for the privates, and assistance towards the regimental expenses, 4237. Cloth should be given for the uniforms, and officers should be relieved from the regimental expenses which now fall on them, and which sometimes prevent the best men becoming officers, and oblige the officers to economize in other ways in their relations with their corps, 4238–1244. The numbers of the force should be limited, if further aid is given to it, 4240, 4254–4259, 4263. Aid should only be given on account of efficient men, 4245–1247. To limit the numbers of the force by withholding further aid would be a prohibition of the volunteers in certain districts, and would destroy some of the best corps, 1248–4253, 4260–4262. The volunteers throughout Glamorganshire are in an efficient state, and will become more efficient if the suggestions already enumerated are adopted, 4261–4273. The volunteer movement has had good effect on the moral and industrial character of the people of the county, 4274–4276. The corps does not contain the class of men who would be likely to enter the militia or the regular army, 4277, 4278. In case of invasion, there would be no difficulty in getting the men together, because most of the works would stop or be at half work, 4281, 4282.

DREGHORN, LIEUTENANT-COLONEL :

Commands the 3rd Lanarkshire Rifle Volunteer Corps of nine companies and about 600 men, 1468–1472. The number of effectives is kept up, 1473. Is provided with rifle ranges and drill sheds paid for by the corps, 1474, 1475. The annual subscription of 2s. 6d. each has not been very well paid by the men, 1476, 1477. Nearly 2,000l. were raised for the first two companies, 1478. Doubts very much being able to maintain the efficiency of his corps, as the members will not renew their clothing without assistance, and the public will not again subscribe any large amount, 1479–1482. At the commencement of the volunteer movement in Glasgow a fund of 3,000l. was raised and spent in aiding the men to meet the expense of their uniforms, 1485–1491. A proposal was made to apply that amount to providing head quarters and ranges, but rejected, 1492–1494. Those companies who did not provide their own clothing will be less likely to be able to renew it, 1495–1497. Very little has been done with honorary members; subscriptions from the public and the men are the only sources of income, 1498, 1499. The organization in Glasgow has been entirely by companies, and the subscriptions differ in almost every two companies, 1500–1503. There are from 6,000 to 7,000 volunteers in Glasgow, of whom three-fourths will disappear unless aid is given, 1504, 1505, 1512. A money grant for each effective should be given to the commanding officers to provide clothing and aid towards boots, rifle ranges, &c, 1506, 1507. The battalion is 100l. in debt irrespective of the company expenses, 1508. The uniform and accoutrements cost 3l. 6s., 1509–1511. Only a money grant would keep up the members, the financial difficulty being the only one, 1513, 1514. A grant of 30s. for each effective would be sufficient, and would not be objected to by the volunteers if administered through commanding officers, 1515, 1516, 1535–1551. It should be applied to the assistance of those members who required it, and to the formation of a battalion fund, 1517. If the 30s. were given, subscriptions from the privates could be almost entirely done away with, 1518. None of it should be applied to the band expenses, 1519. There are companies of self-supporting volunteers in his corps; their attendance and efficiency does not differ much from that of the others, 1523–1525. The artizan companies, who are clothed by their employers, attend very well, 1526–1527. More than one-third of the volunteers in Glasgow equipped themselves at their own expense, 1528–1531. None of the working men in his corps belong to a class who would join the militia, 1534. Any one of respectable character, whatever his earnings may be, is admitted into his corps, except mere labourers, 1536, 1537. Almost all his men are liable to the ballot for the militia, but thinks none have joined to escape it, 1538, 1539, 1583. Volunteers who have received assistance are as zealous and as regular in attending their drills as those who have paid everything for themselves, 1540, 1541, 1559. The issue of so many yards of cloth to each company would be less objectionable than that of ready-made clothing, 1542. The price of the uniform could not be reduced enough to enable volunteers in his corps to provide it themselves, 1544, 1545.

B 4

DREGHORN, LIEUTENANT-COLONEL—continued.

None of the volunteers are men who might go into the militia or the line. Finds the introduction of artizans into his corps to be very useful, 1546, 1576–1578. A grant of 2l. a head would cover the whole expenditure, 1549, 1550. It is not right that volunteers who give their time should be called upon to give money also, 1552. The enrolment of volunteers improves their social habits, and has the best effect upon artizans, 1554–1556, 1573–1575. The members give their time regularly to their drills, and many have passed through a musketry instruction course; has company drills every week, 1563–1565. The volunteer force is supported by extraneous aid given by certain individuals, the mass of the public who derive the benefit do not pay anything towards it, 1568–1571. The volunteer force would be increased by the enforcement of the ballot for the militia, 1582. Exemption from civil duties would have no effect in inducing men to volunteer, 1584, 1585. Volunteers prefer serving under military command when gathered in large numbers, 1586, 1587. Would hold the men responsible for the clothing issued to them from Government funds, and would not let a man resign until the uniform was worn out, unless he paid for it, 1588, 1592. Thinks volunteers would not accept uniforms which had already been in use, 1593, 1594. An early decision on the question of Government aid is of importance with regard to the permanence of the force, as the uniform generally is now worn out, 1595, 1596, 1603, 1605. Meetings were held at Glasgow at which the view taken was that a capitation grant should be made by Government to be expended at the discretion of the commanding officer solely upon things essential for the maintenance of the force, 1597–1600. Anything like payment for their services would be repudiated by the volunteers, 1601. The Government money would be perfectly safe and well administered in the hands of commanding officers, 1602. While in London met many volunteer officers who had made up their minds on the subject of Government aid in the same sense in which he has spoken, 1606, 1607.

EDWARDS, LIEUTENANT EDWARD:

Is adjutant of the 1st Administrative Battalion of Warwickshire Rifle Volunteers, consisting of 10 corps, 3666–3668. Between 400 and 500 men muster at battalion drills, 3670. Has opportunities of seeing every man in the battalion, 3671, 3672. Two thirds of the members on an average have passed through a course of musketry instruction, and all are thoroughly drilled, 3678–3683. The rifle instruction is carried on by the serjeant instructors, 3684–3686. Beyond the superintendence of drill and musketry instruction, an adjutant of an administrative battalion has very little to do, 3687–3690. The commanding officer of an administrative battalion has hardly enough control over the management of the different corps in it, but it would not be advantageous to the service to make any alteration in the matter, 3691–3694. Receives no extra allowance from the volunteers, 3700–3701. Sustains a considerable loss in travelling expenses, 3704–3710. In a few weeks the Warwickshire Volunteers might be made an efficient force, 3711–3715, 3762, 3784–3789. But their clothing will soon need renewal, and they are not prepared to pay for renewing it, 3716, 3717. Their arms and accoutrements are in a satisfactory state, 3719–3726, 3779 There are three ways in which the Government may assist the volunteers, 3732; first, by establishing a central school for drill instructors, from which they should be temporarily detached from service with volunteer corps, and by giving them better pay than the present drill instructors, who are worth very little, 3733–3758; secondly, by defraying under certain regulations the railway expenses incurred in attending battalion drill, 3759, 3760; and thirdly, by assistance in the provision of clothing, 3760. The Government should not issue cloth to the volunteers, but allow to each corps a sum of money equal to the amount of subscriptions from its effective members, 3761. With this money the commanding officer should pay all expenses and start a clothing fund, 3772. A single colour should be prescribed for the uniform of the whole force, 3764–3770; and the commanding officer should obtain suits of clothing from the Government factory at Pimlico, 3790–3801. The number of volunteers in the county is increasing, but there are considerable arrears of subscriptions, 3776, 3777. The facility with which men can leave the force has no bad effect, 3783. The enrolment of volunteers does not interfere with recruiting for the militia, 3802.

ENFIELD, THE VISCOUNT:

Is Honorary Colonel of the 29th Middlesex Rifle Volunteer Corps, 745. Unless some means are adopted to remedy the financial difficulty there will be a great falling off in the numbers of the force, 747, 748. It is not probable that the members of the corps will be able to bear the expense of renewing their uniform, 756, 780, 781. If it had not been for the expense of the band the corps would have been able to pay its way, 761. The corps gives extra pay to its drill instructors, but not to its adjutants, 763, 764. If any Government grant is given it should be vested in the commanding officer, and he should be held responsible by the Government for it, 774. The grant should be 20s. for every efficient man present at the official inspection of the corps, 775, 816. A corps ought to keep up one band at a moderate expense, 783, 785. The application of the Government grant should be limited to certain items, 789; and the commanding officer should send in annually a proper account of its expenditure, to be regularly audited, 790, 796. All the companies of the corps, except two, consist almost entirely of artizans, 799. About 50 per cent. of the members is the maximum muster, 800, 801. It would be advisable to double up small corps, and, if possible, to divide London into districts, permitting men to volunteer only within their own districts, 806–808.

EWENS, CAPTAIN ALEXANDER:

Is Adjutant of the City of London Rifle Volunteer Brigade, consisting of 1,217 men, 1364, 1365. A paid quartermaster should be appointed to the London corps generally, who would have charge over transit, commissariat, ammunition, armoury, and camp duties, 1366, 1367–1397. The balance in hand at present is over 2,000l., 1370, 1371. Apprehends a falling off in the subscriptions and donations, 1372–1379. The expense of the band is 600l. a year, the total annual expenditure for the last 3 years averages 3,000l., derived from subscriptions and donations, 1380–1385, 1389–1393. The want of officers in his corps is not caused by the expenses to which they are liable, 1402. Receives 200l. a year from the corps. 1412. Extra pay is given to four drill instructors, 1417. Their Government pay is not sufficient. 1427. The corps has fallen off nearly one-fourth, partly on account of the expenses and late hours, 1439–1441, 1462–1467. There is a secretary to the corps with a salary of 120l. per annum, 1445–1448. Musters 400 to 600 men on field days, 1459.

GROSVENOR, THE EARL:

Commands the Queen's Westminster Rifle Volunteer Corps of two battalions, the largest corps in London, 2106, 2107. The pay of adjutants should be increased so as to put them on the same footing as those in the militia, 2108–2111. His adjutant receives 50l. out of the funds. 2112, 2113. When he had a vacancy, received innumerable applications for it, 2115. The Government pay allowed to serjeants is sufficient, 2117. They get fees for looking after the arms, &c., 2118. The minimum number of a company in towns should be 110, 2119–2125. Government assistance is necessary to maintain the volunteer force in its present condition, 2126–2151. A minimum grant of 1l. a head should be given through the commanding officer on the guarantee of a certain number of attendances at drill, and applied entirely at his discretion, 2127–2131, 2151. Would spend such a sum in obtaining a larger range and knapsacks and defraying travelling expenses to drills, &c., 2132–2135. Thinks efficient adjutants cannot be obtained for the present pay, 2138, 2139. The annual subscription is 1l.; there is great and increasing difficulty in getting it paid, 2140–2142. The attendance is not so good as last year, as the men think they know their drill, 2145, 2146. Early field-days lead to that belief, 2147. Field-days should be held at the close of the season, 2149, 2150. Regulations for volunteers should be few and simple, 2151.

HARCOURT, MAJOR EDWARD W. V. VERNON:

Has been in communication with the Admiralty in reference to certain questions put by him to Capt. H. Boys, and with the object of explaining why he put these questions, hands in a letter, dated War Office, 7th Nov. 1861, informing him that the Commissioners of the Admiralty have intimated their willingness to appropriate a ship occasionally to the drilling of the corps under his command, but have stated also that no vessel is likely to be available for the purpose for some time to come, 3365, 3366.

HARMAN, LIEUTENANT-COLONEL:

Is Assistant-Inspector of Volunteers in the Northern Division, which contains 107 corps, and 15,000 or 16,000 men, 4057–4059. Their condition is generally satisfactory, except in point of finance, 4060, 4095–4099. The majority of corps in the North are composed of artizans who consider it enough to give their time and attention; and there is no provision for renewing the clothing, which is beginning to be worn out, 4061, 4062. At inspections the town corps muster about half their enrolled strength, the country ones about two-thirds, 4063. The commanding officer of an administrative battalion has not sufficient authority, 4066–4068.* The arms are generally in good condition, 4069–4071. In administrative battalions the officers are generally very deficient, especially the field officers, 4072, 4073, 4129–4149. In consolidated battalions the officers are in a higher state of efficiency, 4132–4149. A man should be reckoned an effective if he comes up to a certain standard, not if he attends a certain number of drills; and no Government grant should be given for any man who does not come up to that standard, 4087–4087, 4391–4094. The adjutants would have more authority if they had some other title, such as "deputy assistant inspector," 4088. A test of efficiency should be applied to officers as well as to men, 4101. Adjutants might perhaps in some cases have the authority of deputy assistant inspectors, under the orders of the field officers commanding the battalions, 4102–4107. The volunteers should be all clothed nearly alike, 4110, 4111. The present equipment of the volunteers is sufficient for peace time, but would require completion before they could take the field effectively, 4112–4124. Drill serjeants should be placed more immediately under the control of the adjutant, and should be sent from the head-quarters of the administrative battalion to such of the corps as might require instruction, 4134, 4136. The travelling allowance for adjutants is insufficient, 4135. The pay of an assistant inspector is insufficient, 4136–4144. Has no defined powers as assistant inspector, but has experienced no difficulty from the want of them, 4145–4161.

HUDSON, LIEUTENANT-COLONEL JOSEPH:

Is Superintendent of the Royal Army Clothing Factory at Pimlico, 3900; believes that it is intended to confine the issue of Government cloth to four colours, 3903, 3907–3909; thinks the volunteers would get their clothing better, and perhaps rather cheaper, by availing themselves of the issue of cloth by Government, 3904–3906, 3917–3924. The Government clothing establishment could not at present undertake to issue the clothing made up; but perhaps the Government could contract for it as they do in the case of the army, 3928, 3929.

HUGHES, MAJOR THOMAS:

Commanded the 19th Middlesex Rifle Volunteer, 1045. There are 702 men on the muster roll of the corps, and within the last year there have been 30 or 40 more withdrawals than entrances, 1048. The financial position of the corps is satisfactory, and there will be no difficulty in getting the uniforms renewed, 1049–1060, 1088, 1123–1128. The Government serjeants have lodging, coals, and candles given them by the corps, but no extra allowance, 1065–1067, 1151. The force has been demoralized by excessive expenditure, and if the Government give any further assistance, it should only do so on conditions which would put an end to this extravagance, 1070–1075, 1097, 1098, 1100–1115. It is necessary to give further assistance if the present numbers are to be kept up, 1074, 1082, 1083, 1097, 1100–1103, 1129–1131. Twelve shillings for each effective who has passed into the first class, and appears at the inspection, would be a sufficient grant from Government to keep the corps in a satisfactory state, 1076–1078. The grant should be expended in accordance with a specification sent in by the commanding officer, 1079–1081, 1165–1169. It should only be given for first class men, because the force, whatever its numbers, should be in the highest possible state of efficiency, 1084–1086. The tendency to diminished numbers is owing to the failure of those who entered the force from frivolous motives, and constitute its least valuable portion, 1090–1096, 1116–1120. The adjutant receives no extra allowance, 1152–1155, and is sufficiently employed, 1158, 1159. Further Government aid would not alter the character of the force, 1162–1164. The corps is the poorest in London; three companies of it are composed of men from the Working Men's College, and the rest consist of artizans, clerks, warehousemen, shopmen, &c., 1087, 1171–1175.

HUMBERSTON, CAPTAIN PHILIP STAPLETON, M.P.:

Is Captain Commandant of the 6th Cheshire Rifle Volunteer Corps, 4162. The subscriptions have the effect of keeping men away from drill; an allowance of 1l. for every effective would pay the current expenses of his corps exclusive of clothing, and 2l. would enable it to keep up its numbers and clothe the same number of men that it now has who are clothed by means of the subscriptions, 4163. An equivalent should be given to the volunteers for their services, and they should also have facilities for shooting and for obtaining ranges, 4167–4170. There should also be a power of stopping roads on their behalf; 4167–4168. Adjutants should have higher pay, 4171.

INNES, CAPTAIN ALEXANDER.

Commands the 1st Kincardineshire Artillery Volunteer Corps, of two batteries and 120 men, 100 of whom are effective, 3045–3046. The corps is not attached to a brigade, 3047. Has company and battery drills regularly, 3048. Has a private battery close to head-quarters, mounting three 32-pounder guns of position. Takes detachments to Aberdeen, 14 miles distant, where there are two batteries of royal artillery, for the purpose of drill with 68-pounders, 3049–3051, 3063. A drill-instructor in receipt of regular pay is permanently attached to the corps, 3052–3054. The members are armed with carbines, 3056. A small proportion of the members provide their own uniforms, but a considerable number are clothed by private contributions: one battery composed of fishermen living on his estate was supplied entirely by himself with a dress such as is worn by the Royal Artillery when employed on the Mediterranean stations, 3058–3061. Has had between 80 and 90 drills in the course of the year, and considers that the statutory number of drills necessary for an effective should be increased, 3061, 3062. His battery is very complete in its formation; the platforms were supplied by Government, but the rest of it principally by himself, 3064–3067. Has a magazine for about 60 cases, 3068. Has a Government instructor, a corporal in the Const Brigade, who takes charge of the guns and stores, 3070–3072. Has a range in front of the battery where the men practise about 20 times a year with shot and shell, 3075–3077. Government aid would tend very much to the efficiency of the volunteer force. One half should be given to those volunteers who had served as such for five years and the other half for the purpose of improving the administration of the force, 3078–3080, 3135. The volunteers would have no objection to be placed even more than at present under the district officers of the Royal Artillery, 3090–3093. The use of the carbine by artillery volunteers is of great importance and an inducement to volunteers to enrol and maintain themselves, 3094. The seafaring men of his corps are not armed with carbines, 3095. There is an association for prize firing with great guns and carbines, 3097, 3098. Has not been able to have battalion drill, 3099. Twenty-four drills in marching, gun drill, and parades in the course of the year would be enough to keep up the efficiency of an effective volunteer, 3100–3104. Is supplied with 32-pounders. Has provided at his own expense tackle, skids, and guns for repository work, 3104. Generally has gun practice and gun drill together, 3105. There are two rifle corps in the same district, but recruiting for one arm does not interfere with that for the other, 3109. All the men go through a course of theoretical instruction in boring and fixing fuzes, trajectory, and the science of artillery generally, 3110, 3111. Varying the drills is beneficial to the men and secures a better attendance; repository exercises are also very salutary; facilities for obtaining a knowledge of gun drill at ships' guns should be afforded seafaring men near their own homes, 3125–3132. His corps generally is in a healthy condition, 3133. Government aid, although it is not absolutely necessary, would very materially assist it, 3134. The battery which is composed of seafaring men is at present in a state capable of rendering efficient service, and his men generally are in a state fit for actual service with field guns, 3136–3138. A non-commissioned officer of the Royal Artillery is in charge of the guns generally and the side arms, to keep them in order, for which he is responsible, 3158, 3159. The constitution of the volunteer force as a useful and military body must depend on its organization and superintendence by competent and qualified officers; great advantage is derived from the instruction and assistance afforded by the supervision of officers appointed by Government to inspect and superintend the force; it should be felt that the force is under the more active encouragement and superinten-

c

INNES, CAPTAIN ALEXANDER—*continued.*

dence of the deputy lieutenants; the duties, authority, and standing of the officers should be better defined and vindicated; great advantage would be derived by affording the gunners more extended instruction in mounting and dismounting heavy ordnance, by practice with guns of different calibre, by mutual interchange of ammunition, and by opportunities for assembling of several corps together, 3166.

JONES, LIEUTENANT-COLONEL DOUGLAS :

Is Assistant Inspector of the North-eastern Division of Scotland, containing about 153 corps, 1953-1955. They are not all in an efficient state, 1956. Some are deficient in drill from want of proper instruction, and in equipment, 1957-1961. Government instructors cannot be provided for all at present, 1958. Consolidated are better drilled than administrative battalions, 1959. The best instructors are those obtained by commanding officers through their own friends in the army, 1962. Good instructors are essential to volunteer corps, 1963-1964. Does not always obtain satisfactory musters at his inspections; a little more than half the members turn out on an average, 1965-1967. Many keep away in consequence of not being sufficiently drilled, 1968. The pouches are defective, 1969-1970. Good waterproof haversacks would be better at present for volunteers than knapsacks, 1971, 1972. Very few are equipped with haversacks, 1973. The clothing of the men is not complete, 1975. None have great coats, 1976, 1977. Light cloaks are preferable to great coats for volunteers, 1980. Something in addition to the tunic is desirable, 1981. Has heard no complaints about insufficiency of the pay for adjutants, 1982. The present pay of drill instructors is not sufficient; they ought to be men of tact, and good drills, and superior to militia serjeants, who receive more pay. 1983-1989. The serjeants receive gratuities chiefly for cleaning arms, 1990-1991. One serjeant is sufficient for two companies when together, 1992-1995. A militia adjutant would be perfectly fit for the appointment in a volunteer corps, 1996. Volunteer adjutants are sufficiently paid except as regards travelling allowance to adjutants of administrative battalions, but the circumstances are different in different battalions. With two or three exceptions the adjutant in his division are very good; nine have been raised from the ranks, and 20 are from Her Majesty's European and East Indian army. In the artillery they have chiefly risen from the ranks, 1997-2007. There will be great difficulty in maintaining the corps at their present strength unless assistance is given, 2008. To each effective who thoroughly knows his duty, and has passed through the musketry instruction course, clothing should be given; and an allowance for each should be made to the commanding officer, who should account to the Government how it was expended, 2009-2011. All the adjutants have not qualified themselves by going to Hythe, 2013. At inspections, examines the musketry drill and practice returns, but the corps are not bound to produce them, 2014-2017. Great attention is paid to the registers of musters, drill, and musketry instruction; they are kept by the serjeant instructors, 2018, 2019. These registers should be subject to the supervision of the inspector, 2020. Drill is more important than shooting, 2021, 2022. The volunteers are thoroughly trained in the manual, platoon, and aiming drill, which they can practise in the winter under cover, 2023. Men who are considered effectives by the commanding officer judging with the assistance of the adjutant, should be returned as such, irrespective of the number of drills they may have attended; 2024-2029. The inspecting officer when he went round could see whether the men individually had been properly drilled or not, 2030 2031, 2035-2036. The manual and platoon drill is not a good test, 2032; nor is the 24 drills, 2037-2038. About one-third, or one-fourth of the corps in his division are self-supporting, one half contribute a portion, and one-fourth give nothing whatever, 2043-2045. Unless further aid is given, the numbers will decrease, especially in the case of artizans, who are the best drilled men, 2046-2056, 2081. An early decision on the question is of importance, 2057. In some corps new clothing is immediately required, 2058, 2059. Volunteers on joining should provide their own clothing, and be supplied with uniform and accoutrements by Government after being two years effective, 2060-2062. Second-hand clothes would be worn by those who would wish to be provided for, 2064-2066. Clothing would be the most acceptable aid that could be given; some corps, who can

JONES, LIEUTENANT-COLONEL DOUGLAS—*continued.*

afford to provide clothing their own, would not accept from Government, 2067-2069. The subscriptions in the corps in his district vary from 5s. to 2l. a year, and a portion of the men pay nothing, 2070. Marching money should be given to administrative battalions to defray expenses of battalion drill, 2072. Would like to see all the incidental expenses of volunteer corps defrayed by Government, 2077. Artizans who have volunteered have improved very much in a social point of view, 2078, 2079. They form nearly one-half of the volunteer force in his district, 2080. There is unnecessary extravagance with regard to bands; by a little effort they might be formed at little expense, 2084, 2085. If Government insisted upon annual returns of shooting being made, it would be an advantage, and would be liked by the corps, 2087-2091, 2095-2098. Volunteers would be more satisfied if a stricter system of discipline were gradually enforced, 2092-2094. Rifle ranges are easily obtained in Scotland, except in the large towns, 2103.

KNIGHT, LIEUTENANT-COLONEL FREDERICK WINN, M.P. :

Commands the 1st Administrative Battalion of Worcestershire Rifle Volunteers, consisting of 11 companies and 936 men, 3571-3573. Has 11l. per company from the county fund applied to travelling expenses for field days, 3574, 3609. The battalion is composed of men of every class, 3575. The men will not generally re-clothe themselves, 3577. They will not be able to get subscriptions again; in the three years at least 1,000l. have been spent from each district for each company, 3578. Has an adjutant, who receives 130l. a year in addition to his pay; the adjutant ought to have a serjeant-major allowed to him, 3582. The adjutant is constantly at work and sees the corps very frequently; the men have gone through a course of musketry, 3583, 3584. The battalion drills are generally wing-drills of from two to four companies; they are well attended, 3590, 3591. Officers should be those whom the rest of the men will follow and like to serve under; many of the subalterns are very competent and take great pains with their duties, 3593, 3594. Cannot go on much longer without Government aid, 3595. There are three heads under which assistance ought to be given:—1st, the increase of the efficiency of the permanent staff; 2nd, uniform; and 3rd, incidental expenses, including head-quarters, armouries, drill grounds, repair of arms, company's stationery, &c. grants, pontoon kettles, canteens, and expense attending field days, and petty cash disbursements, 3596-3602. In addition to what is at present paid for the staff, 2l. should be allowed by Government for each volunteer to cover all expenses, except for bands, 3603-3606. Has not the least doubt of the returns of effectives and non-effectives being correctly kept, 3610. Not less than 24 drills a year are required for recruits; after the first year two drills a month in summer and one drill a month in winter would be required, exclusive of target practice, 3611-3613. It is absolutely necessary for the adjutant to have an office, and at his own house; there is no battalion orderly-room; the adjutant should have an allowance for house rent, 3617-3620. The battalion will not continue to exist at all unless something is done for it; the allowance for clothing would be taken by almost every man, by nine-tenths certainly, 3621-3627, 3629, 3630. An immediate decision upon the question is important, 3628. In Worcestershire there are two battalions, 21 companies, and 1,636 men, 3631. The force in that county is at present in a satisfactory condition as to the arms and accoutrements, and its discipline and organization, and in case of emergency it would be prepared to render efficient service, 3632-3637. The existing force may be maintained, and rather increased in numbers and efficiency, if assistance of the kind he has mentioned is given, 3638, 3639. Has found no difficulty in obtaining proper officers, and those of the Worcester volunteers are fully competent to command their companies on a battalion field day, 3641, 3642. If no assistance should be given, the corps would fall away when the time comes for renewing the clothing, 3643-3645. Volunteers should be exempt from service on juries; many of his men belong to the class who are eligible to serve, 3646-3649. Has never found any difficulty in enforcing his orders; his position as commanding officer of an administrative battalion is satisfactory, 3653-3660. At field days the senior lieutenant-colonel should command, if he is competent, 3661, 3662.

LAIRD, MR. JOHN, M.P.:

Many volunteers on the coast would learn gun drill if the Admiralty placed gunboats at their disposal at certain hours, 2528–2530, 2532, 2537. This would not interfere with the Royal Naval Reserve, 2531. At present the artillery volunteer practise at Rock Fort, four miles down the river, and a steamer is generally hired to take them there for drill. They are not allowed to fire shot there, 2533–2535. A gunboat for drill would be more convenient, 2536. In Birkenhead and the neighbourhood four companies of rifle volunteers were first formed, composed of the better class, who paid all their own expenses. Then five additional companies were formed, composed of working men, who are assisted greatly by their officers and others. The artillery volunteers were raised on different principles, and composed of men in large works, and generally wholly or partly clothed by their employers. Payment for clothing by the men is an important element in the movement, 2540, 2542. Employs 2,500 men, of whom about a twelfth are volunteers, 2541, 2542. Exclusive of clothing, the expenses of corps are from 25s. to 30s. a head per annum. Men who give their time and provide their clothing cannot be expected to bear the other expenses, 2543. Unless aid is given the corps cannot go on, 2544. To ensure the permanency of the movement would require 25s. or 30s. per effective, exclusive of the uniform, for travelling expenses to drill, storehouses, extra pay to serjeants, and many other expenses, 2545, 2546, 2548, 2549, 2571, 2588, 2592. There is difficulty in obtaining efficient officers on account of the expense, as they are considered responsible for any deficiency, 2546–2548, 2563. In the rifle volunteer corps extra pay is given to Government serjeants, 2550. Working men and artizans should find their own clothing, but be relieved from all other expense, 2551, 2552, 2584, 2593, 2595. Regarding the different classes of which the force is composed, Government aid may reasonably be expected, 2553; which may be higher for artizans and working men than for other classes, 2554, 2589, 2558–61, 2593. A capitation grant paid to the commanding officers, to be properly accounted for, would be the simplest way of giving assistance, 2555–2557. Rifle prizes have done good, but they should have been of much less value, 2565–2567. There is only one review in Cheshire in the year, on account of the expense, 2568. The patriotic feeling in which the movement originated remains undiminished, and members would enrol themselves if it were not for the expense, 2569, 2570. The Government would be amply justified in advancing 30s. a head to assist the volunteer movement; it would be the best expenditure possible, 2572, 2576. The volunteer movement exercises a valuable moral and social influence on the volunteers, and has been of great value beyond originating a means of protection, 2573–2575. Government assistance and efficiency should depend one upon the other, but too much interference would do harm, 2577–2580. If assistance were given, any number of respectable mechanics could be obtained, 2581. The intelligent classes in his neighbourhood concur in the opinion he has expressed before the Commission, 2582, 2583. Enrolment of the working class does not interfere with recruiting for the line or militia. Some of the men get 30s., 40s., and 50s. a week; the lowest would be perhaps 20s., 2597–2599. At first the men obtained arms for themselves, 2601, 2602. Any issue of clothing should be made on one principle, not with one class of men paying and the others not, 2603.

LAYE, CAPTAIN HENRY THOMAS:

Commands the 3rd North Riding of Yorkshire Artillery Volunteer Corps of one battery, and 80 men, 3367–3371. The corps has its own guns, two garrison 32-pounders, 3372, 3373, 3400. The men are armed with carbines, 3375. The battery is supported by a fund raised in the district, 3377. The men subscribe 10s. each annually. The officers subscribe more, 3378, 3379. The fund is not applied to the provision of clothing, but to pay the carriage of ammunition &c., 3380, 3381. The men clothe themselves, except 10 or 12, 3382–3384. The members are artificers, builders, and architects, 3383. Anticipates no difficulty in renewing the clothing, 3385. Government aid would be of great assistance, 3386. The corps is supported by honorary members and liable to fluctuation, 3387. There are rifle volunteers in his district. Recruiting for the one arm does not interfere with recruiting for the other, 3388, 3389. Finds no difficulty in getting the men to drill, 3390. Has two drills a week regularly, besides recruit drills. Some members have attended 170 drills in the course of the year, 3391. Has carbine and big gun drill, 3392. The men attach great importance to the carbine;

they could not do without it, and it makes the corps popular, 3393, 3394. Has battalion drill. It is of the greatest importance, but the corps wants money to move, 3395, 3396. A gunner should attend a few more than 24 drills a year to be considered an effective, 3401. The officers of the corps are competent and zealous in attending drill, 3406. The corps was drilled by a master gunner, and it has also the services of an adjutant, 3407. Had a moving magazine built at a cost of about 1l. 10s., in which he brings the cartridges, 3409, 3410. Has been put to expense for conveyance of stores, 3411–3414. And also for storing the Government stores, 3415–3417. The men have all gone through the fuse drill, 3418. Has no organized method of moving guns on travelling carriages by horses, 3421. Some of the men would learn gun drill on board ship if facilities were afforded them, 3423. His corps is financially in a healthy condition, 3424. If 1l. a man were allowed by Government it would set the corps up well; would prefer the aid in that form, the commanding officer to use it to the best of his judgment, 3426–3429. The poorest men in his corps receive about 4s. a day as wages, 3431. They are valuable men, and he would not like to lose them, 3432, 3433. The clothing costs each man 5l., 3434.

LINTOTT, MR. WILLIAM:

Is a private in the 7th Sussex Rifle Volunteer Corps, and is well acquainted with the feelings of the members, 2158–2160. The spirit which gave rise to the volunteer movement is sufficiently strong to inspire confidence in the permanence of the force; 2161, 2236, 2237. The numbers do not diminish, 2162. When the corps was first formed 50 out of 80 men were supplied with uniforms and accoutrements out of the fund, the others provided their own, 2163–2167, 2185, 2270, 2271. Corps consists of between 90 and 100 members, and forms part of an administrative battalion, 2164, 2165. An account of the expenditure is rendered every year, 2168. The balance in hand is very small at present, 2169. The money is expended in rent of armoury, ranges, and incidental expenses. Until this year 60l. were paid annually for serjeant instructors, 2170, 2171. There is no annual subscription; the fund, which hitherto has been 100l. a year, is supported by honorary members, 2172–2174. There will be very great difficulty in renewing the clothing, 2175. The attendance at drill is as good as ever, 2176. There are battalion drills four times a year; the attendance is very good, 2177–2179, 2189. There is nothing likely to interfere with the efficiency of the corps but want of money, and especially funds to provide clothing; if money is given the corps will increase, 2181, 2183. The corps is recruited from mechanics principally, gentlemen, tradesmen, and farmers, 2184. Attendance is not so good for some time after battalion drills and field days, 2188. Artizans and mechanics attend best; this arises from the others members having to come from a distance, 2193, 2194. Travelling expenses to battalion drill are defrayed out of fund, 2198. The drill serjeant receives no extra allowance, 2199–2201. The expenditure for clothing presses very heavily on the funds; if relieved of that the corps would ask for nothing more, 2215–2217, 2238, 2239. Relief from expense of attending battalion drills would tend very much to the permanence of the corps, 2218. The chief difficulty artizans have to contend with is the money they are out of pocket, 2219. If clothing were given it would require 100l. a year to cover the other incidental expenses, 2220, 2221. There would be no difficulty in getting the men to wear second-hand uniforms, 222*. There are company drills once a week; they are pretty well attended, 2232, 2233. 30s. a head is necessary to maintain the efficiency of the corps, 2242. It should be given to the commanding officer, to be expended according to an annual estimate, under Government supervision, 2244–2248. The muster roll is accurately kept, 2249, 2250. Many members attend more than the 24 drills a year, 2251. The majority of the men would have sold their rifles to Government, if the offer of the Government to purchase them had not been withdrawn, 2252–2254. Prizes given by the officers and honorary members are shot for once a year, 2256, 2257. The band expenses are very small, and defrayed by a special fund obtained from the public, 2259–2262. Some of the bandsmen, not all, are effective members, 2263. Some give up their instruments and go into the ranks, 2264. The men are very ready to give their time, but feel that nothing else should be required of them, 2265–2268. Very few of the individual members have been put to any expense, 2269.

LOCKHART, MR. JAMES. See BELL, MR., &c.

LUARD, LIEUTENANT-COLONEL RICHARD:

Is Assistant Inspector of Volunteers in the southeastern district, 3804. The corps in the district are rather more slack in attendance at drill than they used to be, 3805, 3806. About two-thirds assemble at inspection, but some few subdivisions fail entirely, 3807-3809. There are about 9,000 volunteers in the district, 3813. The expense is greater than was expected, but it does not interfere with the supply of officers, 3814, 3815. Assistance should be given in kind, not in money, 3817, 3896-3899. The Government should give drill instructors to subdivisions, and pay, under certain regulations, the travelling expenses of men who attend battalion drill, 3818-3828. The Government might also fairly pay all the expenses of ranges and targets, 3828-3831. The clothing should be issued by the Government at so much a suit, 3832-3835. Has heard no complaint of the drill instructors being badly paid, 3836, 3837. They are efficient. as a rule, 3844. The officers are the weak point of the movement; the field officers are more zealous than the captains and subalterns; it is doubtful whether any system of examination of officers would work well, 3838-3842. After a volunteer knows his drill he might be reckoned as an effective with fewer drills annually than are now required, 3843-3848. The power of the officer commanding an administrative battalion is defective, but there appears to be no remedy, 3849-3871. The volunteers under his inspection are fairly efficient, and with the assistance already specified their efficiency may be maintained, without giving clothing, 3872-3888. It is desirable to put the drill instructors of an administrative battalion directly under the adjutant, and to let him drill them at his head-quarters and send them to the different corps at the discretion of the commanding officer of the battalion and himself, 3889. There is not much difficulty in obtaining drill instructors, 3890. The allowance for travelling expenses to assistant inspectors is insufficient, 3892.

LYTTELTON, THE LORD:

Is Lord Lieutenant of the county of Worcester, 1721. There are 21 volunteer corps in the county, 1722. There has been no falling off, 1723. The maintenance of the force without assistance is very doubtful, 1724. The corps have hitherto been supported by subscriptions and donations, expended at the discretion of commanding officers in providing rifle ranges, clothing, &c.; the battalions, by a county fund recently established administered by himself through the colonels of the two battalions in defraying the expenses of battalion drills, 1725-1730, 1737, 1738, 1740-1745. Battalion drills, which are well attended, are encouraged by the commanding officers at considerable trouble and expense, 1731, 1732. Some assistance, principally towards provision of clothing, is requisite to promote the efficiency of the corps, although great efforts would be made to go on if it was not given, 1733, 1734-1747. The volunteers have been wholly or in part clothed by the subscriptions, and it is doubtful whether they will be repeated, 1735, 1736. County meetings and shooting matches are most popular and the expenses easily met, 1739. Expense of attending battalion drills is a great burden, 1746. Prefers the estimate plan to a capitation grant, 1748, 1749. 250l. in donations, and 70l, or 80l, a year has been raised by the county fund, and all spent in battalion drill expenses, 1751, 1752. Could not raise a county fund to meet all expenses, 1753; and greatly doubts being able to do so from local subscriptions for each corps, 1754. The members contribute by subscriptions, 1755. The artizans form the smaller proportion, but a good many are enrolled, 1756-1758. Volunteers ought not to be expected to give a money contribution as well as their time and services; it would be just as much a volunteer force if they were not required to do so, 1759-1762, 1763. The permanent maintenance of the volunteer force is of the greatest importance, 1761. On a corps being enrolled, obtained first from the commanding officer his personal assurance that the corps should be maintained in a state of efficiency for a certain number of years, 1765. Has never had any unsatisfactory proposal to form a company, 1768. The corps were organized solely through the captains, 1769. Some volunteers have provided their own clothing, 1770. The rest were supplied with clothing by the finance committee of each corps, 1771. Sees no objection to men being enrolled who cannot provide their own uniforms, but would object to any system which interfered with recruiting for the line or militia, 1772-1775. All his corps are dressed in the same uniform, 1776. The cost is between 3l. and 5l., 1777. Those who cannot afford to give their time cannot afford to clothe themselves, 1778. Has heard frequent complaints of irregularity in drill attendance, 1779. Approves Government aid being regulated by some test of merit, 1780. Does not see how the present expenditure can be decreased, 1781, 1782. If the subscriptions of the privates ceased, and accoutrements were provided, there is little doubt of the men clothing themselves, 1783. Expects no difficulty in getting the men to wear secondhand uniforms if good, although they might have some feeling against it, 1785. Each corps has a band supported from the funds; it is very popular, and they would not like to be without one, 1786-1790. Delay in the decision of the question of Government aid would not affect the volunteers in his county, 1791, 1792. It is sometimes difficult to obtain efficient officers; few changes take place among those appointed, 1793-1795. They mention the difficulty of expense, but do not personally complain, 1796. The adjutants do not receive any extra pay, 1797. Has great difficulty in getting the rifle ranges, 1798. There are no heavy expenses connected with the head-quarters, 1800. The adjutants are beyond all value in the volunteer force, 1801, 1802. Volunteers in his county are not men who would join the army or militia, 1803.

MABERLY, LIEUT.-COL. EVAN:

Is an officer in the Royal Artillery, and has inspected many artillery volunteer corps on the south coast, 4173, 4174. They are in every stage of efficiency; generally they are in a satisfactory state, but in some instances that is not the case; there are many corps of which too much cannot be said in praise, 4175-4181, 4205, 4206, 4209. All the corps in the district have facilities for gun drill and practice, 4182-4192. The difference in the efficiency of different corps is owing to the great difficulties the members have in some cases to contend with, 4195. The proper remedy for defects would vary according to circumstances; but generally the best security for progress and efficiency is in the appointment of active and good officers as adjutants of brigades, 4196-4199. The inspections of last year showed that from a third to over half the artillery volunteers of the district would be of considerable value as a supplement to the regular troops, 4200-4203, 4208-4212.

MACGREGOR, CAPTAIN JOHN:

Commands a company in the London Scottish Rifle Volunteers, and is musketry-instructor of that corps, 2604. The Volunteer movement has had a good moral, social, and hygienic effect on those who have taken part in it, 2605-2608. The volunteer force is more efficient than could have been expected; nothing would cause it to decline more than an unnecessary expression of the fear of its doing so, the truth, however, should be ascertained and met, 2609-2611. The movement was impelled by two different sets of forces, one is a desire to be connected with military efficiency, the other regards an amusing social and healthful recreation; the first is permanent, the other intermittent and subject to competition with other amusements or engagements, 2612-2614. The really efficient members only in a corps ought to be estimated in giving Government assistance, 2616. Men who give their time should be supplied by Government with means of instruction, such as butts, targets, rifle ranges, and instructors, 2617, 2618. Government should supply clothing to those corps only who wish for it; men who are effective for two years should have 2l. or 2l. 10s. for a new uniform; they should bear the first expense themselves, 2619-2621. Would divide the force into three classes, men who are continually effective, men who have once been effective, and men who are not yet effective; these three classes should be considered separately; encouragement should be given to file and volley firing, 2622.

McGRIGOR, CAPT. ALEXANDER B. See BELL, MR., &c.

MACLEOD OF MACLEOD, LIEUTENANT-COLONEL:

Commands the 1st Middlesex Engineer Volunteer Corps, which consists of 724 members, about three-fourths of whom are mechanics and artizans, 427-431. The corps is efficient in drill, 432; and receives special instruction in engineering, 433-436. The financial position of the corps is satisfactory, although its requirements are greater than those of ordinary corps, 437-463. It is desirable, though not essential, to release members from their subscriptions, and to give a Government grant of 20s. for every man who attends a certain number of drills, 464-466, 468. A more military character should not be impressed on the force, 467. It is undesirable to increase the number of corps except in very special cases, 470. About 250 members of the corps ordinarily attend a battalion parade, 489. About 150 have received musketry instruction, 491. The majority of the members would

MACLEOD OF MACLEOD, LIEUT.-COLONEL—*continued*.
renew their uniforms when necessary, 525–528. If further Government assistance were given to the force, it should be in the form of a capitation grant, paid in each case to the commanding officer, and spent under certain predetermined heads, at his discretion, 529–538, 548–550. This would have no prejudicial effect on the corps or its members, 541–547. The Government should see that the money was properly expended, 553, 554. It is not necessary to lessen the number of drills prescribed by the present Volunteer Act to constitute an effective, 555–557. It is not desirable that Government should enforce a uniform set of rules, 568–570. A uniform system of drill is very desirable, 571. The present mode of appointing officers in the corps works well, 561, 662, 572–575. It is not advisable that the public money should be spent on uniform in any shape, 588. There is a difficulty in obtaining drill instructors, 592–595. The corps gives no extra allowance either to its serjeant instructors or its adjutant, 596, 597. A stricter system of discipline than exists at present is not desirable, 598–600. The Government grant should not be given to a man in proportion to the amount of expense he incurs by attending drill, &c. 601–603.

MACMURDO, COLONEL W. M. S.:
In London it is impossible that the recruiting should assume the form of local corps, 4421. In administrative battalions it might be a good arrangement to put the drill instructors of the different corps directly under the authority of the commanding officer of the battalion; but a special provision would be necessary for the purpose, 4422, 4423, 4572, 4573. An administrative battalion is a provisional arrangement, and in case of war, the several corps composing it would probably become so many battalions. The command of each of them would thus become a more important function than it is at present, and the commanding officer of the administrative battalion would probably be the first person appointed to one of these commands. Meanwhile, he has the power of an inspecting officer; the Secretary of State could not give him more; and what he has is sufficient for its present purpose, 4426–4465, 4479–4481. There would be no difficulty in employing adjutants of volunteers as paymasters, and their travelling allowances should, in any case, be increased, 4466–4468. Many of the small corps are fit to form the nuclei of larger ones, and the larger corps might in these cases be made fit for service in 20 days, 4563, 4473–4476. The establishment of a central school for drill instructors might be advantageous; and if it were adopted, it would not be necessary to increase the pay of the instructors, though their allowances might be increased, 4482–4490. The relations between the artillery volunteers and the district commanding officers of Royal Artillery spring out of the fact that the stores and guns furnished to the volunteer batteries remain in the charge of the Royal Artillery, 4491–4500. The work of the assistant inspectors is lessened by the union of corps in administrative battalions, but there is no reason against employing officers of the line on the duty of inspecting volunteers, 4501–4506. It is the duty of the assistant inspectors of rifle volunteers, if they have time, to inspect also the artillery volunteers with regard to their general state, 4511. The volunteers generally have so improved since last year, that a report made of a last year's inspection would not show the present state of the force inspected, 4513–4515. It is not advisable to map out London into brigade districts for command, 4516. An effective is a man who attends 18 drills according to the regulation, and the inspection of his corps, 4517–4521. There should be an understanding that every volunteer should go through certain setting up drills, and pass a certain examination, after which he should be entitled at once to step into a battalion, and then pass through a smaller number of drills, 4522–4528. An obvious test of efficiency, irrespective of the statutory number of drills, is advisable, and there would be no difficulty in finding and applying one, 4529–4552. A marked improvement has taken place in the efficiency of the officers, 4553, 4554. It is not desirable at present to establish any arbitrary test of the efficiency of officers, 4555–4568. About two-thirds of the rifle arm have gone through a course of rifle instruction, and the proportion is increasing, 4569–4571. The annual pecuniary charge now incurred by Government on account of the volunteers is about 1 *l.* a head, exclusive of the arms, 4574–4580. The object of the volunteer service is to be prepared at a time of danger, and there would be time before a war actually broke out to render the volunteers efficient for the field, 4581–4585. It is neither advisable nor possible to clothe all the volunteers in one coloured uniform,

MACMURDO, COLONEL W. M. S.—*continued*.
4586–4589. There should be a staff uniform for adjutants, drill instructors, &c., 1592. The force is in a satisfactory state of efficiency with reference to the objects for which it is raised, and estimating its efficiency by what it is capable of becoming at very short notice. Of the rifle volunteers, about a third require little more to fit them to take their place in a line of battle, and the proficiency of the rest is, speaking generally, and all things considered, satisfactory. The efficiency of the artillery volunteers is in most cases highly satisfactory, and their importance cannot be over-rated. The engineer arm is of extreme importance, and its progress quite satisfactory, 4593.

PAGE, CAPTAIN S. FLOOD:
Is Adjutant of the London Scottish Rifle Volunteers, 865. The establishment of a company of rifle volunteers should be increased in large corps from 100 to 150 men, and sections of 20 men should be allowed, 868, 875–878, 894, 895, 953, 954, 1010–1012. The average attendance of the corps is 199 out of 673 members, 871–874. A uniform system of drill should be adopted for the whole force, 883, 884. This year, 216 members of the corps passed through the course of musketry instruction, and last year rather more than 200 did so, 885–893. The inability of members to pay the subscription is one of the difficulties of the corps, 896–904. There should be a Government grant of 20*s.* for every effective member, to be applied to military expenses, and the commanding officer should be held responsible for its administration, 905–908, 983–986. The Government serjeants receive from the corps, 5*l.* in money, and the value of 15*l.* in quarters. Their position is not so good as that of militia serjeants, 909–920; although they need to be superior men and are difficult to obtain, 934–941. The allowances given to an adjutant of volunteers are insufficient, and his position is not so good as that of an adjutant of militia, 921–933, 942–944. The adjutants in towns have not enough work, and a considerable number of them might be dispensed with if weak corps were amalgamated, or if one adjutant were appointed to several corps, 946–952, 955–964. It is important that an adjutant should have passed through a course at Hythe, though he need not conduct the musketry instruction of his corps, 965–968. There should be a staff uniform for the adjutants and Government serjeants, 969–972. If the subscriptions are retained it will be necessary that the Government should pay some one to carry on the financial business of the corps, 974–981. As an inducement to volunteers to attend at drill, those who do so should be exempted from serving on juries, and from the payment of some tax of about the same amount as the hair powder tax, 988–1013. The legal definition of an effective should be altered, so as to diminish the number of required drills in the case of men who had attained to a certain standard, 1014–1016. There should be no examination of officers before they receive their commissions, but their efficiency should be tested at the inspections, and inefficient officers should be attached to regiments of the line, 1017, 1018. The discipline of the force is improving, but the numbers are diminishing, and will diminish unless aid be granted by Government, 987, 2020–1023. The officers are almost necessarily put to inconvenient expenses, 1024–1031, 1035, 1036. The Government should establish a central school of arms, 1037. One set of regulations should be strictly enforced throughout the force, 1043, 1044.

PERKINS, LIEUTENANT-COLONEL EDWARD MOSELEY:
Commands an administrative battalion of rifle volunteers in Durham, consisting of 11 companies, and numbering 620 effectives, 2820–2823. On one occasion mustered 620 men at a battalion drill, but the average attendance is 200, 2824. Has sufficient authority as commandant of the battalion, 2826. Has no battalion fund; expenses of battalion drills are defrayed by the officers of the different corps, 2827, 2828. Two of the corps have public funds; in two others all the expenses fall upon the officers and their friends; another has a public subscription; and the rest, composed of working men, are supported by the proprietor of the works and the officers, 2829. Some of the members provide their own uniforms, but the artizans generally are clothed by public subscription, 2830. Each corps has an armoury and rifle range paid for out of the general funds of the corps, 2831–2833. Anticipates very great difficulty in the renewal of uniforms, 2834. The question of expense affects the men more than the officers, 2836. The drill serjeants receive a small pay in addition to what they receive from Government, 2839. Government assistance is of vital consequence to the maintenance and efficiency of the volunteer force, 2840. Uniform and equipment should be provided, an allowance made to meet the expense attending battalion drills, and 150 rounds each

C 3

PERKINS, LIEUT.-COL. EDWARD MOSELEY—*continued.*
of blank and ball cartridge allowed to every enrolled member, 2841, 2842, 2867. The expense of transport for each battalion drill is 2s. a head, 2843, 2844. The whole expense would be about 3*l.* 12s. a man per annum, 2856, 8857. Assistance should be given in materials, 2861. Would have no difficulty in getting the men to wear second-hand clothing, 2865. The feeling in the neighbourhood is in favour of scarlet as the colour of the uniform, 2867. Thinks if assistance is not given some battalions will soon become extinct, 2868–2870. A prompt decision of this question would do a great deal of good, 2871. The service has now become very popular, and there is no doubt of every member becoming efficient. If liberal assistance is afforded, and a uniform colour adopted, great satisfaction will be felt, 2876. If the coast of Durham were menaced by an invading force, he thinks he could bring up the 770 effectives of his battalion in an efficient state to support the regular force in resisting invasion, especially if they were supplied with equipment, and could oftener meet together for battalion drill, 2877–2881, 2884. Many of the battalions would, in a very short time, be able to take their places with the regular troops and militia, 2882. Others would require more military discipline and training, 2883. Training will not be kept up unless new clothing is found for the volunteers, 2886. In the present state of the force, its efficiency is limited and imperfect, with certain aid from Government it might be rendered much more efficient, but for distant operations still further training and the habit of using camp equipment would be requisite. 2889–2896. If the different corps were properly handled together for a fortnight they would become thoroughly efficient in their drill, 2900, 2901. His corps is composed principally of artizans, and he finds that volunteering has produced in them a marked improvement physically and socially, 2903–2905. A feeling exists among volunteers who give their time and services that they should not be called upon to contribute in other ways, 2906, 2907. Field officers should be exempt from service on juries, 2907, 2908. The course of instruction in musketry is inapplicable to rural corps from the nature of the different members' employment, 2911–2915. The officers in his battalion give a higher subscription than the men, and make up almost all deficiencies, 2916.

PETTIE, MR. JOHN :
Is a serjeant in the London Scottish Rifle Volunteer Corps, 822, 823. The volunteer service has a good effect on the artizan volunteers, physically, morally, socially, and politically, 828, 829, 851–853, 857, 858, 863, 864. It would be more attractive to them if the facilities for shooting were improved, 839–843. Unless some assistance is given, a large number of the artizans now in the corps will leave it, 849, 850. If the artizan element in the force should fail, it will be entirely for financial reasons, 854, 855. Artizan volunteers prefer military men for their officers, 859, 860.

RADSTOCK, THE LORD :
Commands the West Middlesex Rifle Volunteer Corps, 1. Corps consists of 579 members, of whom 150 muster at battalion drill, 3–5, 263. There is no falling off in the actual strength, though there may be in the numbers on paper, 8–27. The continued efficiency of the corps depends on the action of Government in the next twelve months, 34, 35. The sources of danger are the direct and indirect expense to which the men are subjected, the deficiency in equipment, and the defects in organization and discipline, 36–42. Small corps should be amalgamated, 44–52, 115–120, 127–131. There should be one uniform for the whole force, 53–63, 121, 136, 137, different from that of the army, 138–144. The uniform of the corps costs 3*l.*, and the accoutrements, 15s., 65–68. The corps is mainly supported by the subscriptions of its members, which is a cause of weakness; but the subscriptions do not cover all expenses, 69–94. The pressure of expense repels good officers, and keeps down the numbers of the force, 95–99. Every corps should have a defined recruiting area, 103–107. There should be one system of rules, 125, 171–179, and of drill, 125, and of organization, 126. Every corps should have a defined recruiting district, 103–107, and every district a certain quota of volunteers, 132. The field equipment of the force is totally inefficient, 145–164. The organization of the force is defective from the absence of a thoroughly military character, and a uniform system of discipline, 165–170. Discussions in the corps, whether on its military or its civil affairs, are objectionable; and there should be no election of officers, but before any officer, commissioned or non-commissioned, is appointed, the commanding officer should ascertain privately the feeling of the members on the subject, 180–211. The efficiency

RADSTOCK, THE LORD—*continued.*
of the officers of a corps depends practically on the commanding officer, 212–224. In consequence of the want of a uniform system of discipline, some corps become lax in order to be popular, and these drag the rest of the force down to their own level, 228–236. The legal definition of an effective might be altered, 237 ; by reducing the required number of annual drills in the case of a man who had come up to a certain standard, 280–288, 301–303, 309–312. Brigade and divisional field days increase the strength at the parades which precede, and diminish it at the parades which follow them, 266–268. It is more important to have in the force a nucleus of well trained soldiers, than to accustom a large number of men to the use of arms without making them absolutely efficient, 289, 300, 304–308. A fair amount of musketry instruction is necessary in order to make a man really effective, 313–318. There should be a Government grant of 20s. for every man present on parade on the day of inspection, 328–333 ; and an additional Government grant of 10s., for every such man who has his equipment, knapsack, and great coat, 335. There should be a national holiday on which the inspections should take place, 334, 335, 348, 349. Brigade districts should be formed, and united under an officer of division, and the number of men present at the last inspection should be the test referred to in arranging the formation of new corps in the districts, and the increase of existing ones, 335–345. A company should not lose its Government serjeant in consequence of its sinking to a sub-division, 346, 347. The best way of giving Government aid to the force is by a capitation grant, to be spent in each case at the discretion of the commanding officer under certain regulations, and subject to proper account, 352–360, 409–412. A Government grant would enable corps to dispense with public subscriptions, which are a source of weakness, and are generally falling off, 361–364, 426. A capitation grant need not alter the character of the force, 365–372. The revival of the militia ballot would have a good effect on the volunteer force, 373, 374. The pay of the Government serjeants is not sufficient, 376–381. The pay of adjutants is sufficient, 382–386. In each brigade district there should be a brigade armourer, and an efficient brigade staff of unpaid officers, 387–399. The proposed divisional brigade system should supersede the present system of inspection, 400. It would not be prudent to entrust the management of the financial affairs of a corps to the Government serjeants, 406–408. If indirect assistance were given by Government, it should be, in the case of his corps, for drill grounds, head-quarters, rifle ranges, and care of arms, 414–419.

RANELAGH, THE VISCOUNT :
Commands the South Middlesex Rifle Volunteer Corps of 16 companies, and about 1,300 effectives, 1252, 1255. Is provided with rifle grounds, sheds, and everything necessary, the cost of which was defrayed out of the donations and annual subscriptions, 1256, 1257. The annual subscription is 1*l.* 1s. each member, which would cover the expenses of the corps if it was out of debt, 1258, 1259. The members provide their own uniforms ; has no reason for saying they will not renew them, 1261–1263. Could not get a really efficient instructor for the Government allowance, 1264. Has battalion drill every Saturday and in winter every Thursday also, but company drills are better attended, 1266. Brigade and divisional meetings are essential to the maintenance and efficiency of the corps, 1267. Every man passes through company drills before taking part in battalion drills, 1268. Men who are not able to supply themselves with uniforms should not be admitted in the volunteer force ; their place is in the line or militia, 1269–1273. A large volunteer force of men of a respectable class could be secured and their numbers and efficiency increased by organizing a system of militia under which 500,000 men could be called out, and exempting those who were effective volunteers, 1274–1276. A reduction of the number of corps formed in London would be advantageous, 1277, 1278. The volunteer force should be treated as part of a general system of organizing the whole country for defensive purposes ; the militia being composed of those who cannot afford to pay for their arms, accoutrements, &c., and the volunteer force receiving only those who can ; the latter should have a distinct organization and be commanded and officered on a system of its own, 1280, 1281. The force can be permanently maintained in its present position, 1282. In each county or district there should be an unpaid volunteer staff under the lord lieutenant composed of retired military men, 1283–1297, 1304, 1313, 1325. Competent men in all counties would be found willing to serve on the staff without remuneration ; rank and position could be given them,

RANELAGH, THE VISCOUNT—*continued.*
1299–1301. The staff duty would not be very onerous except on occasions of county reviews and field days, 1302, 1303. Each county should have an état-major, a regular organized system, and its own means of transport and commissariat, 1305, 1306. The senior volunteer officers could take command in a county where there were only 3,000 men; in counties where there were from 10,000 to 18,000 men there could be a divisional or brigade staff, 1307–1310. The volunteers should have every facility to learn their work, the senior volunteer colonel having the command at field-days, &c., 1311, 1312. The volunteer force should be always kept separate from the regular army, and commanded only by volunteer officers. An inefficient colonel would be expelled by the force of public opinion, and by mutual criticism the volunteers would perfect themselves, 1313–1335. The volunteer force generally requires further aid from Government, 1336. Head-quarters, armouries, and drill-grounds, should be provided by Government, 1337. The gratuitous issue of clothing by Government would destroy the independence of the movement, 1344. Corps which spend large sums on bands have no right to ask for further aid, 1345, 1346. The Government pay to drill instructors is not sufficient, 1347–1352. The work of his adjutant is hard for the pay, 1353, 1354. The men are allowed to take their arms home, 1355. Last year 500 of the men passed though the first period of musketry instruction, 1356, 1357. No expenses are paid by the officers; in consequence, military men are obtained who would not otherwise join, 1358–1360. Assistance towards providing railway expenses at battalion drills and field-days would be a great boon. An officer should retain his rank after 10 years service. Exemption from serving on juries would be a boon to the privates. The posts of adjutants, and drill and musketry instructors should be thrown open to the volunteer force, 1361, 1362.

RUSSELL, CAPTAIN CHARLES WHITWORTH :
Is adjutant of the 2nd Administrative Brigade of Devonshire Artillery Volunteers, 4359, 4360. Volunteers should have a knowledge of every gun and carriage they are likely to be called upon, in case of actual service, to work, 4361. They should be furnished with the appliances for repository drill, 4372, 4375. Thinks the volunteers would be perfectly fit to man the fortifications, in the event of a war, 4374.

STIRLING, LIEUT.-COL. WILLIAM. *See* BELL, MR., &c.

TEMPLER, CAPTAIN JOHN CHARLES :
Commands the 18th Middlesex Rifle Volunteer Corps, 1176. The corps is increasing, and its funds are in a satisfactory position, 1177–1188, 1205. There are only three artizans among its members, 1189, 1238. Town corps can be kept up without assistance, but country corps cannot, 1192. A volunteer is entitled to a complete indemnity for all expenses, and to give him this there should be a Government grant of 42s. a head, 1193–1196, 1215–1219. The essential distinction between the volunteer force and other forces is that the one is not paid and the others are, 1220–1223. When a volunteer has attained a certain efficiency, the number of drills now required to keep him on the list of effectives should be diminished, 1224–1236. The corps has at present no desire for assistance, 1237. If Government clothed the men, they would be entitled to require them to appear at the annual inspections, 1239–1241. A man should not be considered an effective unless he has some knowledge of rifle shooting, 1242–1249. It is desirable that further facilities should be given to volunteers for the acquisition of rifle ranges 1250, 1251.

WARRENDER, MAJOR GEORGE :
Served formerly in the Line and in the Guards. Commands an administrative battalion of Haddington Rifle Volunteers of five companies and one subdivision, 1608–1610. Each company manages its own finances, and has its own organization and rules, 1612, 1616. Has no battalion fund, meets the casual battalion expenses himself, 1614. The Government allowance for postage, stationery, &c., is adequate, 1615. There is an inspection of arms every month in each company, 1617. Each company has an armoury which costs from 2*l*. to 3*l*. a year, 1618–1623. In No. 1 company the arms are taken home by the members, in the other companies they are kept in the armouries and are kept in better order, 1619. When members do not produce their rifles for inspection for two months, permission to take them home is withdrawn, 1621. The captain is held responsible for the arms being kept in proper order, 1622. The serjeant

WARRENDER, MAJOR GEORGE—*continued.*
instructor generally cleans the arms kept in the armoury, for which he receives 10*l*. a year and materials, 1624–1626. Government serjeants are generally well satisfied, 1627. The adjutant receives no extra allowance, 1615–1628. The best class of non-commissioned officers are the best men for adjutants of administrative battalions, 1629, 1632. The adjutant has no authority over the captains and his visits are not considered as inspections, 1630, 1631. There is great difficulty in getting the different corps together for battalion drill, 1633, 1634. The travelling expenses are met by the captains and by small subscriptions from the men, 1635–1638. There are 408 rifle volunteers in the county of Haddington, 1639. At the commencement a county fund was raised of about 800*l*., and a further sum of 200*l*., which has been expended in providing targets, drill instruction, and equipment, exclusive of clothing. Funds for providing clothing to those who did not provide their own, were procured from friends in the neighbourhood, 1640–1645. The result of an inquiry held in the county showed that out of 550 Volunteers, only 100 were self-supporting, and that 500*l*. a year would be necessary to meet the incidental expenses for the force, exclusive of clothing, 1646–1649, 1666–1672. Commands a company in Berwickshire ; the condition of the force in that county is the same as that in Haddington, 1650. No. 1 company is self-supporting, and composed of merchants and clerks, but there is some difficulty in getting the subscriptions, 1651–1653. His battalion has no means of self-support in itself, and will fall away unless assistance of some kind is given, 1654, 1655. The different companies in Berwickshire are nearly in the same condition, 1656. A voluntary assessment of two-twelfths of a penny on the rental was made in that county for one year, and 10s. 6d. was allowed for each effective volunteer, 1657–1661. In Haddington it was proposed, but objected to, 1662, 1663. The assistance given to his company will not be continued, 1665. Last year the battalion met together three times ; the five companies are within a radius of 5¼ miles from head-quarters, 1673–1677. Each company has a drill serjeant, 1679. One instructor with a higher rate of pay should be appointed to two or more companies, 1680, 1681, 1689, 1693, 1694. The outlying companies are almost entirely agricultural, or else clerks and mechanics, 1682. The others are of all classes, but principally of mechanics and artizans, who are often apprentices, with only a bare subsistence, 1683. The battalion he commands is composed of very good material, and the men would not enter the army nor generally the militia, 1684, 1685. In his company 18 or 20 half clothed themselves, 18 wholly, and the remainder were clothed entirely by their employers, and from the funds raised for the purpose, 1686. The latter attend drill better, 1687. Drill serjeants for subdivisions would be a great boon, but a great tax upon Government, 1689, 1690. A soldier on leave of absence drills the subdivision, which is in as good order as the companies, 1691, 1692. The general impression in his district is, that the Volunteers should not be required to give more than their service, and that the pecuniary burden should be borne by Government, 1695–1699. Aid should be given by a money grant, 1700–1702, 23*s*. a head, according to the annual return which should be furnished in December, would be barely sufficient to maintain the efficiency of the volunteer force ; about one-fourth more would be required to cover all expenses, except for attending battalion drills, 1703–1709, 1714–1716, 2152. Clothing provided gratis to members might belong to the corps until they had served a certain time, and in cases of retirement might be issued to others, 1711–1713. The corps would be more efficient with Government accoutrements, 1717. Recruiting for the rifle volunteer corps does not interfere with recruiting for the volunteer artillery in the neighbourhood, 1718. An early decision is most desirable on the question of Government aid, 1719, 1720. In Haddington six or eight volunteers in one corps have joined the militia. If Government wished to increase the militia at any time, volunteer officers could render great assistance, 2151. Great regret would be felt if the corps had to be dissolved for want of money, as volunteering has been very beneficial to the health and habits of the men. Volunteers who are assisted are more easily dealt with, and attend drill better than those who provide everything themselves. Two volunteer corps in one place should be placed under one commanding officer ; adjutants should receive better pay, 2152. The musketry instruction in his battalion is under the superintendence of the adjutant, 2154, 2155. Companies receiving assistance should first consent to be battalionized. 30 or 40 only out of 500 or 600 men are likely to re-clothe themselves, 2156.

ALPHABETICAL LIST OF WITNESSES.

Acland, Lieut.-Col. - - - 164	Hughes, Major - - - - 55
Bell, Mr. Sheriff - - - 183	Humberston, Captain, M.P. - - 175
Beresford, Major - - - 37	Innes, Captain - - - - 131
Bingham, Colonel - - - 163	Jones, Lieut.-Col. - - - 90
Blackburne, Captain - - - 113	Knight, Lieut.-Col., M.P. - - 146
Bourne, Lieut.-Col. - - - 135	Laird, John, Esq., M.P. - - 107
Bousfield, Major - - - 99	Laye, Captain - - - - 141
Bower, Lieut.-Col. - - - 178	Lintott, Mr. - - - - 97
Boys, Captain, R.N. - - - 138	Lockhart, Mr. - - - - 183
Briggs, Lieut.-Col. - - - 86	Luard, Lieut.-Col. - - - 158
Brooks, Major - - - 142	Lyttelton, the Lord - - - 82
Buckley, Lieut.-Gen. - - - 119	Maberley, Lieut.-Col. - - 176
Campion, Captain - - - 105	MacGregor, Captain - - - 111
Crawford, Lieut.-Col. - - - 183	McGrigor, Captain - - - 183
Darby, Captain - - - 126	Macleod of Macleod, Lieut.-Col. - 30
De Grey and Ripon, the Earl - 199	MacMurdo, Colonel - - - 190
Denys, Major Sir George, Bart. - 188	Page, Captain - - - - 47
Dillwyn, Major, M.P. - - 180	Perkins, Lieut.-Col. - - - 121
Dreghorn, Lieut.-Col. - - 72	Pettie, Mr. - - - - 45
Edwards, Lieut. - - - 152	Radstock, the Lord - - - 17
Enfield, the Viscount - - 42	Ranelagh, the Viscount - - 64
Ewens, Captain - - - 70	Russell, Captain - - - 187
Grosvenor, the Earl - - 95	Stirling, Lieut.-Col. - - - 183
Harcourt. Major - - - 140	Templer, Captain - - - 60
Harman, Lieut.-Col. - - 170	Warrender, Major - - - 76, 96
Hudson, Lieut.-Col. - - - 161	

MINUTES OF EVIDENCE

TAKEN BEFORE

THE COMMISSIONERS

APPOINTED TO INQUIRE INTO

THE CONDITION OF THE VOLUNTEER FORCE IN GREAT BRITAIN.

Tuesday, 27th May 1862.

PRESENT:

Viscount EVERSLEY.
Viscount HARDINGE.
Lord ELCHO.
Lord OVERSTONE.
Lieutenant-Colonel BARTTELOT.
Lieutenant-Colonel Sir A. CAMPBELL.
Major-General EYRE.
Colonel MacMURDO.
Major HARCOURT.

VISCOUNT EVERSLEY IN THE CHAIR.

Lord RADSTOCK examined.

1. (*Chairman.*) You are the colonel of the West Middlesex Rifle Volunteer Corps?—Yes.
2. The corps consists of eight companies, does it not?—Yes.
3. And according to the paper before us of 609 members?—The last return gives 579.
4. Do you muster at battalion drill as many as 609 usually?—Not half that number, and taking into account wet days not much more than a quarter.
5. (*Lieut.-Col. Barttelot.*) About 150?—I think that is about the average.
6. What is the establishment of your corps?—800.
7. That is the maximum?—Yes.
8. Do you find any decline in the number of your corps?—I think on paper there is, but not in the actual strength, and that arises from its being difficult to find out what men have left. You imagine that a man has left you who has never resigned, and after a time you trace him out; you find that he has gone to another part of the country, without sending in his resignation: I think that there will be a very great falling off. There is not an actual falling off; but very likely on paper I should come down to 500, if I could get in all the resignations.
9. (*Col. MacMurdo.*) I suppose you can tell by finding that the subscriptions fall off?—Yes.
10. (*Major-Gen. Eyre.*) They are not struck off after being absent for a certain time; they are still retained on paper?—Sometimes; we should not strike a man off for six months; he may go into the country and then come back again. Some of them go to China and some to India.
11. (*Chairman.*) Have you any rules that require notice to be given to the captain of the company when a member leaves the corps?—Yes; but when they are gone you cannot carry the rule into effect.
12. (*Sir A. Campbell.*) When a man has been absent for five or six months do you inquire into the cause of his absence, and ascertain the reason?—It is very difficult to do that; a captain may send to a man's address, and does do so, and he is told that the man has left his lodgings, but said he was coming back.
13. (*Col. MacMurdo.*) His arms in that case would be returned?—Yes.

14. The whole of your arms are in the possession of the individual members?—Yes.
15. (*Major-Gen. Eyre.*) A man may have gone to the Cape, taking his rifle with him?—I do not think that would take place.
16. (*Lord Elcho.*) Have you any men on your books this year who have neither appeared nor paid the subscriptions of last year?—That is a difficult matter, as there are some men who appear and pay no subscription, and some who pay their subscription but do not appear. If a man appears we do not strike him off, or if he pays his subscription.
17. Do you keep your men on if they appear, although they do not pay their subscriptions to the end of the year when you are making up the accounts, or is there any rule about the payments of the subscriptions that a man is struck off at a certain period after the subscription becomes due?—It varies very much in different cases; for instance, with regard to some men, you may know that they are perfectly well able to pay their subscriptions, but they are away.
18. (*Chairman.*) How are these subscriptions paid? Do the officers and men subscribe in the same proportion, or is there a different rate for each?—They all subscribe the same.
19. What is the annual subscription?—A guinea.
20. (*Lieut.-Col. Barttelot.*) Is that in the rules of the corps, that they must pay a guinea?—Yes.
21. A man is not considered an effective member unless he does pay it?—" Effective" relates more to the number of drills; there is no reason why he should not be an effective, but it is rather too difficult to tell about the subscriptions, as they are paid in advance. A man pays a guinea when he joins, and that naturally would become due at the end of twelve months afterwards; but in reality you must give him twelve months' law; it is not legally due until the end of the second year.
22. That depends upon your rules?—Yes; but there is no rule that the guinea should be paid in advance.
23. (*Major Harcourt.*) What do the arrears of subscriptions amount to; is the sum large?—No, I should not think so; I think there are about 500

D

Lord Radstock.
27 May 1862.

men whose subscriptions you can calculate may come in within three or four months.

24. (*Col. MacMurdo.*) Have you any reason to apprehend a very serious falling off in your corps?— That enters into quite a different question.

25. Your return shows on the 1st of April 592 men, and if you think that 500 will pay their subscriptions within three months, that would show a falling off of only 92?—Yes; I do not think that the falling off is to be looked at quite in a money point of view only. My corps is raised principally from a class who can afford to pay the subscriptions; and when these men get tired of it, which, of course, is quite possible, then you want to recruit; and it is a question as to what is the extent of the class from which you recruit, whether it can furnish you so many men willing to pay the guinea.

26. I believe you had 29 recruits in the last quarter as against 27 resignations?—That may be so; there is no doubt that the practical available strength of the corps is where it was.

27. Have you any reason to apprehend that they will fall away?—Then comes a different question; it remains unaltered at present.

28. (*Chairman.*) Why do you think they will fall away?—I think that there are three or four main questions which relate to the force in general, which, I think, would apply to all corps, and which I conceive are of the greatest importance in viewing this question aright.

29. (*Lord Overstone.*) You have stated that you are colonel of the West Middlesex Rifle Volunteer Corps?—Yes.

30. Have you held that position from the first formation of the corps?—No.

31. When did you commence?—I think about two years ago.

32. Were you before that connected with the corps?—Yes, I was captain of a company.

33. You have been connected with the corps, and you have had the means of observing its progress from its commencement?—Quite so; I was the first man that went out to drill.

34. Bearing in mind all your past observation of the progress of the corps, and considering its present condition, do you entertain any serious apprehensions that the efficiency of that corps is now in danger?— It depends very much upon the action of the Government the next twelve months.

35. Are the Commissioners to understand from that answer that if the Government continue the course which they at present have pursued, you do apprehend immediate danger to the efficiency of the corps? —Undoubtedly.

36. Will you have the kindness to state what are the circumstances which have led you to that conclusion?—I have jotted down one or two points as to the general condition of the force, and as illustrative of my own experience.

37. Will you be good enough to take those points seriatim, stating first what is the ground and nature of the apprehension that you entertain, and then illustrate it by any experience that you have of your own corps?—I will begin by stating what I conceive to be the weak points of the force; of course one of the main difficulties of the force is the cost to individual members, that is, not only the subscription, but the cost of the uniform; I apprehend that that cannot be put at less than from 2*l.* to 3*l.*; a man for effective men; the total cost to a man belonging to the volunteer corps is from 2*l.* to 3*l.* per annum.

38. (*Lieut.-Col. Bartlelot.*) Merely referring to London?—Yes.

39. (*Major Harcourt.*) Does that include accoutrements?—Yes. Then of course the loss of time is a very serious thing. The men are all drawn from the money-making classes, and every hour that is taken from them is so much out of their pockets.

40. (*Lord Overstone.*) Are the Commissioners to understand that you think that the sources of danger to the efficiency of the corps arise from the expense to which the men are necessarily subjected, and also the indirect charge upon them by the loss of valuable time?—Yes; that is one of the dangers.

41. Is there any other general cause that you would first allude to before you examine the causes in detail? —Yes; there are other defects.

42. If there are other main causes dangerous to the efficiency of the force, will you enumerate them before you begin to examine each in detail?—Yes. There is a deficiency in the equipment, both in the uniform and in the field equipment. The uniform and much of the field equipment are defective. The organization is defective and the discipline is defective. Those are the four heads under which I propose to review the defects of the force.

43. Having stated the various considerations which led you to apprehend the diminished efficiency in the corps, unless some palliative is applied, are you prepared to state to the Committee any palliatives which have suggested themselves to you as likely to prove efficient?—I am.

44. Be kind enough to state them?—I would allude to the great disproportion of the staff. There are too many battalions formed. Each battalion or each corps has a little organization of its own to collect subscriptions. It has its band and its headquarters, so that five corps of 200 men may have five organizations, each one of which would do for a corps of 1,000 men if they were all consolidated.

45. In what way does that apply to your particular corps?—The principle is this. In my neighbourhood there are perhaps three or four corps having separate organizations, the whole of which, if they were consolidated, could all work together at the same expense and machinery at which one is working.

46. (*Chairman.*) You say that one of the great objections is that there are so many battalions, all of which ought to be included in one, so that you should have only the expense of one staff and headquarters for one corps, and I suppose a band for one corps?— Quite so. In general, I think, the battalions are too weak, and therefore the expenses of organization are unnecessarily increased.

47. Will you be kind enough to proceed with the question of cost, as that was the first point you mentioned?—Owing to there not being one uniform it is much more expensive for one regiment to get it than if there were only one for the whole force, which could be contracted for at a much smaller price than when each corps has its own uniform made by a separate manufacturer, supplied by a separate contractor, and with separate facings.

48. Is there any other expense that you can mention?—There are the expenses at headquarters coming under the general expenses of the corps, headquarters, shooting grounds, and some man to look after your financial business, a secretary, or whatever he may be called. These are general expenses, which of course are well known to the Commission, but that is one main element of expense.

49. (*Lord Overstone.*) That is one which you think is capable of being better arranged?—Yes; and by a diminution of the battalions I think the expense would be diminished.

50. (*Chairman.*) The answers you have now given could only have reference to populous districts where many battalions are found within reach of each other?—Still I apprehend that in the less populous districts there is an amount of local machinery which might be reduced, and transferred to some central machinery, which could be carried on at less cost.

51. There is one item of expense which you have alluded to, as to the cost of the band; do you think that the battalions would be as well satisfied to march to the ground without their band. Has not that a good deal to do with keeping up the spirit of the men?—Undoubtedly: it is a very important thing.

52. (*Col. MacMurdo.*) You would have one band instead of five?—Yes; I think so; and if the administrative battalions were more consolidated that expense would be reduced; there might be portions

of the band distributed, they would not each want a whole band.

53. (*Lord Elcho.*) You have stated that the cost of the uniform was 2*l.* or 3*l.* per annum. I believe that your corps chiefly wear tweed, and not cloth?—I meant to say the total expense, not the expense of the uniform, but including the subscriptions and other incidental expenses.

54. What do you think the uniform costs?—The uniform and accoutrements cost 3*l.* 15*s.*

55. How long, in your opinion, should they last?—Of course some men who attend very frequently would want a supply every year almost; some men use them almost every day in the year, and some men shoot in their uniform every day in the year, but I should think on the average two years.

56. (*Col. MacMurdo.*) Do you supply any uniform out of the funds of the corps?—No; except to the paid marker.

57. (*Major Harcourt.*) Have your men any undress for shooting?—No.

58. (*Sir A. Campbell.*) Do you oblige them to shoot in uniform?—Not for private practice.

59. (*Lord Hardinge.*) You have stated that you think it desirable that there should be one uniform colour for all corps?—Yes.

60. What colour would you propose?—Grey.

61. The Government grey?—No; it is too light.

62. Do you think that the advantage which the corps now possess of obtaining Government cloth at a certain per centage cheaper than that which is supposed to be procured by contract is a material advantage with regard to diminishing the expense to the corps?—Not unless the corps are compelled to adopt it; the corps would not change their colour unless there was a general understanding that they were all to take to the same; then there would be a saving.

63. Taking a corps clothed in rifle green or Government grey, do you think that that is any material assistance to the volunteer corps?—I cannot answer, as that depends upon the wear of the cloth. I consider that my tweed is a better wearing one than the Government tweed; it costs more, but I believe it is cheaper in the end, as it will last longer.

64. (*Sir A. Campbell.*) Have you seen the patterns that were sent out lately?—Yes.

65. (*Lord Hardinge.*) What is the cost of your uniform, deducting the equipments from it?—As nearly as possible 3*l.*

66. (*Major-Gen. Eyre.*) You would deduct 15*s.* for the accoutrements?—Yes.

67. (*Lord Hardinge.*) That is deducting the expense of the equipments?—Yes; the accoutrements are 15*s.*

68. (*Lieut.-Col. Bartelot.*) In the 3*l.* for the uniform do you include leggings?—I am really not prepared to state.

69. (*Col. MacMurdo.*) How did your balance stand in your last annual statement; was there a deficiency or a surplus?—A surplus in the fund, but the surplus is not altogether to be relied upon, because suppose there is a little sinking in the foundations of a butt there will be the expense of 300*l.* or 400*l.*, which perhaps eats up all the balance.

70. Are there not many arrears in your subscriptions, or do they come in regularly?—I believe that I have 500 men who pay.

71. (*Lord Elcho.*) Who have paid this year?—Yes; in the current year.

72. (*Col. MacMurdo.*) Do you depend upon yourselves, or rely upon the outside subscriptions of honorary members and others?—I think we depend upon both.

73. What do the honorary members pay?—Two guineas.

74. (*Lord Elcho.*) Have you 50 honorary members who pay two guineas each?—I cannot answer that question with certainty. I should think I have; but I could not say that I should have them next year.

75. (*Col. MacMurdo.*) Your main source of main-tenance is your own subscriptions?—Yes; the only thing I can rely upon.

76. (*Lord Elcho.*) Have you had recourse to any prosecutions for subscriptions?—No.

77. (*Chairman.*) If those subscriptions do not fall off, are they quite sufficient to maintain the corps in its present state of efficiency?—I cannot help thinking that the subscriptions are one main cause of the weakness. There are a great number of my men who pay a guinea, but it is a stretch for them to pay it; they are clerks with very limited incomes, and they have got families; and it is a great pinch for them to pay a guinea. The guinea just turns the point. They may be willing volunteers, but having the guinea to pay, the whole of the domestic influence is brought to bear to induce them to leave.

78. (*Sir A. Campbell.*) Do you find that the resignations take place mostly at the time when the annual subscriptions become due?—The subscriptions are paid at the time the men enter, not on a particular day in the year; it is as they enter.

79. (*Lord Hardinge.*) Is the subscription of one guinea paid according to one of your rules?—Yes.

80. Those rules have been approved by the War Office and by the Lord Lieutenant?—Yes.

81. You could not alter the amount of the subscription without first submitting the matter to the Lord Lieutenant and to the War Office?—Supposing that I did not choose to obey the law, it would be very difficult to say what tribunal would call me to account.

82. (*Lieut-Col. Bartelot.*) If you altered the subscription to 10*s.* you could not recover a farthing of it without the sanction of the War Office? For instance, if you reduced it to half a guinea without authority, you could not recover a halfpenny from any man?—That is a legal question which I cannot answer.

83. (*Lord Elcho.*) Does the subscription of a guinea cover all the expenses that fall upon the men; for example, does it cover the expense of their conveyance to their butts, or do you allow them anything for that; or does it pay for attending the brigade drills?—No.

84. Will you give a general idea of what the expenses are that are covered by the subscription?—The subscription is a guinea, and, taking the uniform to last two years, I should put it at 30*s.*, but then there is a saving in the man's ordinary clothing, which I estimate at 10*s.*, but the cost of his uniform is 1*l.* a year; there are incidental expenses, such as attending brigade field days, and going down to fire at the shooting ground, which I put at 10*s.* a year putting them altogether.

85. (*Lieut. Col. Bartelot.*) That would be 2*l.* 11*s.*?—It is impossible to estimate it to a nicety; it might be 5*l.* or 6*l.* for some men, and with others not so many shillings.

86. (*Lord Hardinge.*) When your regiment goes to Brighton for a divisional field day, do the men pay for their own tickets generally?—Yes.

87. With regard to the other expenses to which you have alluded, does any expense fall upon the officers for conveyance and so on?—My principle is not to impose any additional expense upon the officers. My object is to get the best officers I can get; those who have the most military capacity, and many of them are men of not superabundant means, and therefore I take every precaution that the officers should not incur any extra expense beyond what is absolutely necessary.

88. (*Chairman.*) Suppose your corps were ordered for a brigade field day to Brighton, you say that you as much as possible prevent expense falling upon the officers?—Yes.

89. How are the expenses defrayed beyond what are actually paid by the men?—They are all paid by the men.

90. All out of the fund?—For instance, the conveyance of the band, that of course would come out of the funds.

91. (*Lord Hardinge.*) The men, generally speaking, I believe, provide their own refreshments?—Yes.

Lord Radstock.
27 May 1862.

Lord Radstock.
27 May 1862.

92. (*Lord Elcho.*) Is the subscription to the band compulsory?—No; I try to do away with that altogether; as far as possible I try to save any extra expense beyond the guinea.

93. How then do you support the band?—Partly from external means and partly from subscriptions, mostly amongst a few.

94. Not from the funds of the corps?—Sometimes they may get a grant of money to it; there has been, I think, one of 50*l.* to it.

95. (*Lord Overstone.*) You have stated that you are very jealous of allowing any avoidable expenses to be thrown upon the officers; does that feeling arise from any observation of yours of the tendency of officers either to refuse to take the duty, or to resign it after they have taken it, in consequence of the pressure of pecuniary expenses?—I have no doubt that that does occur.

96. It is within your experience and belief that pecuniary expenses pressing upon officers tend to diminish the efficiency of the corps as regards the obtaining of officers and the danger of losing them afterwards?—Undoubtedly.

97. From your statement it appears that the expense of a volunteer corps is the main ground for apprehending the danger to its efficiency, and you have suggested several arrangements for the purpose of effecting a more economical management of the funds. Do you think if those arrangements were effectually carried out that they would completely remove the difficulty and danger that arise from the expense, or do you think that further measures would still be desirable?—Further measures are undoubtedly desirable.

98. A volunteer entering the service incurs two sacrifices; one, the pecuniary sacrifice involved in the subscription, and the other the sacrifice involved in the loss of his time and his labour. Which do you conceive presses most severely upon their feelings?—It depends very much upon the different circumstances. In some cases the arrangements of the drill may be faulty, and they may feel that they are losing their time for nothing, if the drill is badly arranged, and the battalions badly arranged, so that a man has to go four or five miles, when by a different distribution he would have only to go one, and a man will say that that is unnecessary, and that weighs upon him much more than if he saw that it was absolutely indispensable.

99. Taking it generally, the circumstance of the loss of time would, of course, be augmented by the feeling that it was unreasonably lost, but do you think that the loss of time which is necessarily involved in joining a volunteer movement predominates in the estimation of the general volunteer body over the pressure arising from expense?—I apprehend that that affects the volunteer force, and that there are vast numbers of men who would join us if those two sources of expense could be diminished.

100. I presume that you are not at present going into the question of the remedies; the loss of time, I presume, is an unavoidable sacrifice?—To a certain extent it is.

101. (*Sir A. Campbell.*) Is it not possible to arrange the drills so that the times should fall in the leisure hours, and not in the business hours of the volunteers?—To a great extent it is, but there again the faulty arrangement of the battalions operates very severely, and I can illustrate that in this way: instead of the battalions being raised exclusively from their own neighbourhoods (I am speaking, of course, of London now), they are completely mixed up; for instance, I may have some of my men, perhaps 100, living three miles off, whereas the men living close round my head quarters may go four miles off. They have been induced by some difference in uniform, and thus, of course, they get tired of volunteering.

102. (*Col. MacMurdo.*) They do not join other corps nearer to their neighbourhood?—I think that when once they have joined and have got tired of it, it is very difficult indeed to get them again.

103. (*Lord Hardinge.*) You have no defined area of recruiting?—No.

104. Would it be possible to have a defined area for recruiting?—I think it is indispensable; the force cannot exist without it.

105. (*Lord Elcho.*) Do you mean compulsorily?—Not compulsory enlistment, but compulsory districts.

106. (*Lord Hardinge.*) That would not apply to national corps, such as the Irish and the Scottish?—I do not know how far a general principle is to be modified for individual cases.

107. Have you not known instances of new corps being raised almost within a stone's throw of the head quarters of an existing corps?—Yes, quite so; and that is a point which I will enter into under the head of organization.

108. (*Lord Elcho.*) Have you any entrance fee as well as a subscription?—I have by the rules, but I have dispensed with it.

109. What was the amount of it?—Half a guinea.

110. Do you believe that it checked recruiting?—Yes; and I was obliged to do it, as all the other regiments in my neighbourhood did away with it.

111. Do the officers pay anything on receiving their commissions?—No, beyond the fees to the lord lieutenant's office.

112. (*Lord Overstone.*) I understand your view upon the subject of expense to be that the cost of a volunteer corps is at present a serious impediment to its efficiency?—Undoubtedly; the cost to the men.

113. And you are also of opinion that a considerable proportion of that burden may be removed by better and more efficient arrangements?—Yes.

114. But you are still of opinion that there will remain a pressure of a pecuniary character which requires a further remedy?—Quite so.

115. (*Sir A. Campbell.*) With regard to the size of the battalions, you stated that if there were fewer battalions there would be less headquarters expense. I understood, from what you stated afterwards, that that meant if the battalions were concentrated in different parts of London, so that you would have perhaps 1,000 men in each district, and that would involve less expense?—Yes.

116. Do you suppose that there would not be any difficulty in inducing volunteer corps to consent to such an arrangement, and that it would not cause a falling away of the numbers?—I think that unless a re-arrangement of the system is made the force will fall to pieces. I think it is a question of two evils.

117. (*Major Harcourt.*) Must not that be done by an agreement between two commanding officers?—I think it can be done.

118. Do not you think that an agreement between the commanding officers, that they should not take men from neighbouring corps, might overcome the difficulty?—I do not think that there is any practical way of carrying it out in that way.

119. (*Sir A. Campbell.*) Do you not think that if such amalgamations were carried out by orders from head quarters they would be the cause of many men resigning on account of being transferred from one corps to another?—I do not think so. It is merely a matter of administration; you need not remove them from the command of their own officers. All the effect of it would be to make those officers part of the system. I will take an instance. There are three small battalions, whose real and positive strength is not more than 300 or 400, and if those three battalions were put together, and they had one uniform given to them, they would become one battalion, and still be to a certain extent, as far as the companies go, completely under their own officers. The amalgamation would be, I think, complete. They would be part of a system, instead of being in units.

120. (*Lord Hardinge.*) There would be greater *esprit de corps* in larger battalions?—Undoubtedly.

121. (*Lieut.-Col. Barttelot.*) You think it absolutely necessary that the volunteer force should be clothed

in one colour?—I think that would much increase the efficiency of the force.

122. (*Lord Elcho.*) Are you aware whether the results which you anticipate would follow, do actually take place where what you suggest exists; take, for example, the Queen's at Westminster?—I am not able to form an opinion about that particular corps, but I do not think that you can judge of the efficiency of any system from any particular instance, unless you are sure that you eliminate from that instance all the other causes that may affect the system. The system may be good in itself, but there may be other causes, from badness of administration and so on, which may vitiate the results of the system.

123. You assume that if that which you propose is found to fail it is because of defective administration, and not owing to any defect in the system itself?—It is part of the defect of the present system of the force generally; a thing which may be possible with one battalion, if the whole force were constituted on the same principle, would be impossible if each battalion were organized on different principles.

124. That is to say if the rules of each corps are different, as in their method of drill and carrying out the various details of the regiment?—Yes.

125. You would recommend one uniform system of rules, and one uniform system of drill?—Undoubtedly.

126. And one uniform system of organization?—Yes; I have a proposal to that effect.

127. (*Col. MacMurdo.*) Applying that principle to your own case; you have eight companies, would you propose that a small battalion, consisting of four companies, should be joined to yours compulsorily, supposing that the corps consisted of men entirely of a different class from the men of your own battalion?—I believe that if one definite system were struck out, and carried out with efficiency, the men would come in better; if it were put upon one recognized military system the force would be not only far more efficient, but the numbers would be greater, and it would come out far better than it does now.

128. (*Lord Hardinge.*) Is it not the fact that many of the metropolitan corps which have been sanctioned by authority have not any specified range attached to the corps?—I believe so.

129. Your plan of amalgamating the small battalions, and making them larger battalions, would in a great measure facilitate that question of range, would it not?—Undoubtedly.

130. Where is your range?—At Wormwood Scrubbs.

131. Then assuming that the smaller corps in your neighbourhood were amalgamated with your battalion, the whole of the amalgamated battalions would be in a position to shoot at your present range at Wormwood Scrubbs?—But other arrangements would have to be made as a matter of course, for if 500 men have paid for a thing they would not like to see 500 other men come and use it.

132. (*Chairman.*) I understand your view to be this, that in every district there should be a certain quota of volunteers within it?—Yes.

133. Could your plan be made to come into operation by prospective arrangements, so that it should commence in 12 months, or in two or three years?—I think that any remodelling of the force that might take place must have time.

134. (*Lord Overstone.*) With regard to the second head, namely, the pressure upon the volunteer force from a sense of their loss of time, do you think that by better arrangements with regard to the periods of drill and other considerations, that pressure might be in some degree relieved?—Yes.

135. A large proportion must necessarily adhere to the system?—Yes.

136. (*Chairman.*) Have you anything now to state on the head of defective equipment?—I think that the want of one uniform is destructive, to a great extent, of discipline. It destroys the soldier-like feeling when one regiment is in one uniform and another regiment in another. They imagine that it is merely playing at soldiers, and they do not look upon themselves as part of a national force which has a recognized existence.

137. (*Sir A. Campbell.*) Do you think that the *esprit de corps* is not to a certain extent kept up by the difference in the uniform?—Different facings would be enough, I think, for that.

138. (*Lord Overstone.*) I presume that your view of the difference in equipment would be to conform as nearly as possible to the practice of the regular army?—Yes.

139. (*Lord Hardinge.*) What is your opinion as to adopting scarlet for the volunteer force?—I think that would destroy to a great extent the idea of the distinctive character of the volunteers. I can hardly say whether it would be popular, but I think the expense would undoubtedly be greater, and it would also tend to remove the idea that they were to act as light troops. Directly they were dressed as the regular army they would be compared with them with regard to steadiness at drill, and they never could compare with the regular army but as light troops, who would act to a great extent in concealment or as skirmishers. They have a distinct character of their own.

140. (*Chairman.*) You would not adopt scarlet, but you would adopt one uniform colour for all regiments?—Yes.

141. (*Lord Overstone.*) Is it not essential, on a variety of considerations, to retain really both an ostensible and an effectual distinction between the volunteer force and the regular army of the kingdom?—Undoubtedly.

142. (*Lord Elcho.*) The volunteers have to go out in all weathers?—Yes.

143. The army does not do so?—No.

144. Would it not be the case that scarlet would very soon become purple?—I have no doubt of it.

145. (*Chairman.*) Have you any observations to make as to any other article of equipment?—The total inefficiency of the field equipment is a most serious consideration.

146. (*Lieut.-Col. Bartteloi.*) Will you begin with the accoutrements, the pouches, and state whether, as far as you know, your pouches and belts are of an efficient character, or whether they are not deficient in the quantity of ammunition they are required to carry?—My own men carry 60 rounds, but I was rather referring to the cooking utensils, the camp equipment.

147. (*Col. MacMurdo.*) Will you state where the deficiency is?—It is simply this. If the force were ordered out at 24 hours' notice, and were marched 10 miles into the country, the men would have no means of cooking their food; and they would have no mode of providing themselves with any sort of comfort.

148. Independently of the camp equipment, are your men provided with capes or cloaks?—I think about 25 per cent.

149. Not more?—No.

150. (*Lord Elcho.*) That is not a compulsory part of the uniform is it?—No.

151. Is there a regimental pattern?—Yes.

152. Is it a cape or a cloak?—It is a sort of Inverness.

153. Do you know the cost of it?—30*s*.

154. (*Lord Hardinge.*) Is it your opinion that in the event of the volunteers being called out at 24 hours' notice they should be provided with their own great coats and haversacks, and that they should not rely upon what may be issued out to them from the Government stores?—I should much rather have them ourselves than have them in stores.

155. (*Lord Overstone.*) We have spoken of the possibility of diminished efficiency in the volunteer movement which may occur either from the diminished number of men enlisted, or from the inefficiency of a greater number of the men for their purposes. I apprehend that your observations under the head of diminished efficiency are addressed entirely to the latter consideration?—Quite so.

ord Radstock.
7 May 1862.

156. (*Col. MacMurdo.*) You confine the defective equipment to knapsacks and great coats?—Yes.

157. If they had great coats of their own, would not that greatly increase the expense to the volunteers themselves?—Or to the Government.

158. Supposing that knapsacks were given to your men, and that certain fluctuations took place in your corps from many resignations, how would you dispose of the knapsacks of the men who resigned: would you consider them as Government equipments?—I think they might be treated just like the rifles.

159. Would you teach the men to carry the knapsack with a certain kit?—Undoubtedly.

160. Would not that fall upon the number of men who came to drill?—That would depend upon whether it was done with discretion or not, whether you had it very often, or whether you worked the men very hard; it would depend entirely upon the way in which it was done.

161. Is there any other part of the equipment which you consider defective besides the knapsacks and the great coats?—No; I think not.

162. (*Major-Gen. Eyre.*) You do not allude to the rifles?—No.

163. (*Lord Elcho.*) Do your men wear leggings?—Yes.

164. Do you consider those leggings an essential part of the equipment?—Speaking generally, I do.

165. (*Chairman.*) Will you be kind enough to state your views upon the subject of defective organization?—The main defect is, that there is not a thorough military character impressed upon the force. The corps were originally raised under the idea that they were to be a sort of rifle clubs, where the men would have at least as great a right to make arrangements as their commanding officers. The rules of most corps were framed on that principle, recognizing meetings, and, in fact, all the different incidents of a club. I conceive that this has been very prejudicial to the efficiency and to the vitality of the movement, the men being allowed to discuss certain points among themselves, and to decide by vote, merely perpetuates a source of discussion. If a man has an order given him, and he knows he must obey it, the discussion at once ceases, but if he thinks that by agitation or discussion he can get that order reversed, or by getting up a meeting he can get a certain course of proceeding reversed, he may go on making agitations for months and years; whereas by an organization of a distinctly military kind, where it is an understood thing that an order is an order to be carried out, the men would at once submit, and would like it infinitely better.

166. Do not the rules of the corps embrace that, so that no order is ever disputed that is given by an officer?—I am particularly well situated in my arrangements, as those who have enlisted are a very good class of men, and they have never given me the slightest trouble; but there is no doubt that, looking to the force generally, it is a very serious weakness, and one that will entirely destroy it in a very short time unless it is manfully faced and dealt with.

167. (*Major Harcourt.*) Is it not within the power of any commanding officer to overcome that, and is it not his own fault if such a thing exists in his corps?—It depends on circumstances.

168. (*Lord Hardinge.*) Do you think it possible or desirable that the Government should frame regulations, such as would lay down one uniform system of discipline for the corps generally?—Yes, quite so; I think it indispensable.

169. (*Lord Overstone.*) Do you give that answer after fully considering what must be the effect of such peremptory orders upon the volunteer force?—Yes; it depends upon what the regulations are.

170. Judicious regulations issued by the Government, although imperative, would not, you think, seriously militate against the volunteer feeling?—No.

171. (*Lord Elcho.*) Is it not the case that a committee was appointed of volunteer officers at the commencement of the movement to draw up a set of rules?—Yes.

172. Is it not the fact that those rules have not been accepted as the rules of the force; that is to say, that each corps has taken them perhaps as the basis, but has engrafted upon them whatever it fancied?—Yes.

173. Subject always to revision at the War Office?—Quite so.

174. At the present time, practically, every corps in the kingdom is organized and established under a different set of rules?—Yes; quite so.

175. The rules are drawn up by the commanding officer; they then go to the Lord Lieutenant, who signifies his approval, and then they are submitted to the War Office, for the sanction of the Secretary of State?—Yes.

176. (*Lord Overstone.*) You are of opinion that the code of rules which now exist in every different regiment ought to be rendered one and the same for the whole of the volunteer force?—Yes, and enforced by authority; for if not enforced by authority some commanding officers who carry out a proper system are injured by others who carry out the system in an inefficient manner, and thus create discontent among the men in those regiments where the system is observed strictly.

177. You think that the code of rules ought to be one for the whole of the volunteer force, and that it should be enforced by sufficient authority?—Quite so.

178. Do you think that that may be accomplished with due regard to the vitality of the volunteer feeling?—Yes.

179. (*Lord Hardinge.*) Do you think that if one uniform system of discipline were established, and one uniform system of regulations, such as have been hinted at, the volunteers generally would readily comply with them?—Undoubtedly.

180. (*Sir A. Campbell.*) You mentioned just now that discussions take place sometimes?—Yes.

181. On what points do you allow discussions to take place and where?—By the rules of the corps they are allowed to take place for the civil business of the corps.

182. Not for the military business of the corps?—No; but it is always difficult to define the exact line. I am not speaking as to my own experience, for I have never had one difficulty of any serious moment; anything that has arisen has been immediately settled.

183. (*Col. MacMurdo.*) In what respects are these discussions objectionable?—The very name of volunteer makes a man imagine to a certain extent that he can do as he likes, and it takes some months to din into him that he is to do as he is told.

184. But those discussions are not about military matters, are they?—I suspect that they do arise.

185. Are they not rather as to the disposal of the funds to which the men contribute themselves?—Quite so; but if they can find fault with the commanding officer upon one point, and can say, "This commanding officer has administered these funds badly, we think he ought to have done so and so," his authority is greatly destroyed.

186. According to the rules of your corps you are assisted by a large council of 12 members?—Yes.

187. Do they dispose of the funds only with your sanction?—Quite so.

188. (*Lord Hardinge.*) Are you aware whether it is the practice in any corps, or in corps generally, when certain vacancies occur in a regiment, to hold meetings and discuss the claims of the different officers or non-commissioned officers for promotion?—Undoubtedly.

189. Is that in your opinion objectionable?—Yes, most destructive.

190. (*Col. MacMurdo.*) And yet, according to your rules, you allow the council to recommend to you gentlemen for promotion?—Quite so. As I have stated before, the rules of all the corps were based in early days upon the idea that it was a modified rifle club.

191. Is Rule No. 5, that the officer in command will, on the recommendation of the council, propose to the Lord Lieutenant gentlemen for commissions, carried out?—Practically, I appoint all the officers.
192. Without the assistance of the council?—As a matter of form and as a matter of courtesy, I pass it through; still, if it comes to a push, I should stand upon my right, and say that nobody can appoint an officer but me.
193. (*Lord Overstone.*) You issue a *congé d'elire*?—It is practically that.
194. (*Lord Elcho.*) Is it not desirable, without giving any actual power to the corps, and reserving the full power and responsibility which ought to rest with the commanding officer, that he should ascertain to a certain extent how far the appointments would be acceptable in the corps?—I think that if a commanding officer cannot find that out himself he is not fit for his post.
195. But you think that it ought in no way to be done by any meetings or discussions in the corps?—Undoubtedly it ought not.
196. (*Chairman.*) No discussion does take place, I presume, in your corps as to the appointment of officers?—When they were first formed, there was a requisition sent to me to appoint a man as an officer. I was convinced that he was unfit for it, and I refused to give him the appointment. There was a little grumbling, but nothing further.
197. From the beginning of your career, have you had no difficulty whatever as to the appointment of officers?—It is always a difficult question.
198. The discretion has been left entirely to you as commanding officer, has it not?—Practically, it has.
199. Have you taken pains to ascertain what the feelings of the men were before you made an appointment?—Yes; but the very fact of my having, as a matter of form, to pass it through, to a certain extent ties my hands.
200. (*Lord Elcho.*) How was your own appointment made. You said that you had been a captain; was it by the council of the corps?—No; my appointment was in this way. There was a committee formed for the purpose of raising the corps, which I joined, and I became the chairman of that committee. Then it was put that I should be proposed for the captain of the first company.
201. Did the council appoint you?—Yes, I was appointed by my council.
202. (*Major Harcourt.*) Do you take the same view of the appointment of non-commissioned officers as of officers?—My own plan in the appointment of non-commissioned officers is this. The captain of the company knows the different situations of the men; those who have got time; and he also knows their different feelings and tempers, and I leave to him the appointment of the non-commissioned officers, subject to my approval; and then, in order to secure their efficiency, I inspect them twice a year, and if they prove inefficient on two inspections, I reduce them.
203. Do your captains consult the feelings of the men in the appointment of non-commissioned officers?—Indirectly they do, but not by anything like a meeting.
204. Do you not think that the efficiency of non-commissioned officers, as well as their efficiency in drill, depends a great deal upon their standing with the men?—Undoubtedly.
205. Do you think that that can be found out entirely by the captain?—He is not fit for his post if he cannot find that out.
206. As to the social position of a man, he is not competent to form an opinion upon that?—Yes, he finds it out.
207. It is not recognized that the men should be consulted in the appointment of the non-commissioned officers?—It is not recognized; but you have within your rules that which is always *in terrorem* over your head.
208. (*Lord Overstone.*) Your view is that, as a matter of military discipline, full authority ought to be invested in the colonel commanding?—Yes.
209. But, as a matter of practical wisdom, considering the peculiar character of the volunteer force, the commanding officer will necessarily consult and ascertain the feeling of the corps more than in a regiment of the line?—Yes; he will ascertain by private inquiries what is the feeling of the men.
210. (*Major Harcourt.*) Should you strongly object to the election of a non-commissioned officer by the men, subject to your approval as to his efficiency?—It would not work with us; the difficulty is to get a good man to take it. We work the non-commissioned officers so hard, that the difficulty is to get a man to take it.
211. (*Lieut.-Col. Barttelot.*) Is not that quite contrary to the principle that you wish to lay down, that the men should have no power of electing?—I think it would be a very unsafe principle to introduce.
212. (*Sir A. Campbell.*) If a company is vacant, is it your usual practice to promote the lieutenant of the company, or to promote the lieutenant in the regiment whom you consider to be the most fit?—It varies; some companies are purely local companies, and then you have to look at that circumstance; for instance, I have one company from the London University, and of course it is very desirable that all their officers should be living amongst them, knowing them all as friends.
213. If you brought an officer from another company, although notoriously a better soldier, you do not think it would work?—It would depend as to how much he was a better soldier. I wish to remark that the one great fault in the organization is that there is no central authority to secure the efficiency of the officers.
214. (*Lord Hardinge.*) Further than, I presume, the authority of the inspecting officer?—He has the power of judging of the efficiency of officers in the mass, but not individually. Upon the inspection of battalions, where there are 20 or 30 officers, he cannot tell what their efficiency is.
215. But can he not have each company out if he pleases, and ascertain whether the captains and subalterns are up to their work or not?—It would be very difficult, I think, from an inspection of that sort, to ascertain really the fact; you might hit upon one man and not upon another. You might hit upon one good man out of 20 bad ones, or *vice versâ*.
216. Your remark would equally apply to the militia; they have no central authority?—I am not aware what their system is.
217. (*Chairman.*) In the militia the officers appointed have to undergo a certain amount of examination?—Quite so.
218. Is any such examination insisted upon in the volunteers?—I do myself.
219. Do you insist upon any subaltern officer that you appoint undergoing a certain amount of discipline with regular troops?—Yes, unless a man is thoroughly up to his work; then I excuse him from being attached to a regiment.
220. After all it depends, does it not, very much upon the colonel of the regiment whether his officers are efficient?—The whole of the volunteer movement depends upon the officers commanding the regiments.
221. It is quite within the power of the colonel, if he chooses to insist upon all those officers going through a certain amount of discipline with regular troops, to qualify them for command?—Quite so.
222. Have you anything further to add on the subject of organization?—Nothing further.
223. Will you now go to the defects in discipline?—The great difficulty as to discipline is that which I have already hinted at; there is no recognized code of discipline, not only one code of rules for corps but a code of discipline are wanted; there ought to be a distinct principle laid down as to what is allowable and what is not allowable. From the want of a central authority the discipline becomes very much

D 4

Lord Radstock.
27 May 1862.

impaired in this way, that the commanding officers to a certain extent bid one against another; I do not mean to say that they do so designedly, but practically it is so, and one corps is at first more popular than another, very often for laxity in discipline.

224. In your opinion there should be some general rule of the service, to prevent a man who has been turned out of one corps being taken into another?—Yes.

225. (*Major Harcourt.*) What power has a commanding officer of enforcing any of his orders upon his captains or his subalterns?—He has no adequate power.

226. No power to enforce any command?—No; I should say that the power is very undefined.

227. (*Lieut.-Col. Barttelot.*) Do you feel that you have every power on parade?—Your power depends in the main on the public opinion of your men; the only ultimate power which a commanding officer has, is in the public opinion of his men, and if he draws the bit in the least degree tighter than the public opinion of the men will warrant, he loses his men.

228. (*Col. MacMurdo.*) By Rule 13 of your own corps, it is laid down that "the senior officer in "command shall have power, subject to the approval "of the commanding officer, to inflict fines for dis-"obedience not exceeding 10s., or less than 2s. 6d.?"—Yes.

229. That may not be adequate, but there is a power given over the men by fining them?—The answer to that is, that a man will pay his fine and go.

230. Moreover there is an Act of Parliament to enable you to dismiss a man for disobedience of orders?—That is no punishment to him; he does not care.

231. (*Sir A. Campbell.*) Is it within your knowledge that there have been any difficulties in carrying out any order on parade?—Not in my own regiment.

232. (*Col. MacMurdo.*) You have stated that a code of discipline was wanted; is the Act of Parliament insufficient in that respect, and the rules of your corps, and if so in what particulars?—I think that neither the Act of Parliament nor the rules are at all applicable, they do not help you; whenever a practical difficulty occurs the Act does not give you a distinct category of offence; nor does it give you a distinct power to deal with the difficulties that arise.

233. Suppose a man discharge his rifle in the ranks, you would have the means of dealing with that offence as laid down by your own rule?—Yes.

234. Supposing a man disobeyed you on parade, you would have the means of dealing with that; you could arrest and take him before a magistrate and have him fined, and you might afterwards dismiss him from the corps?—Yes; but still you could never carry that out further than the public opinion of your corps would warrant you, and that public opinion rests to a great extent upon the practice of the corps surrounding them; I am dependent not only upon my own discipline, but I have to measure the average discipline of all the corps around me.

235. (*Chairman.*) Therefore if the discipline was made uniform in all the volunteer corps, that defect would be cured?—Yes

236. (*Lieut.-Col. Barttelot.*) Does it not also rest upon the character that a man bears in the corps?—Yes, to a certain extent.

237. (*Lord Hardinge.*) Do you think that any alteration might be made in the Act of Parliament with regard to what constitutes an effective member?—Undoubtedly.

238. (*Lord Elcho.*) Have you any system of drill in your regiment, meaning by system regular periods for certain descriptions of drill, in the course of twelvemonths?—I will describe to the Commission what a man goes through: On joining the corps he goes through the ordinary stages of drill under the serjeant instructor, and when he is thoroughly instructed, he is passed by the adjutant into the ranks, and takes his place in his company. At the beginning of every year we have a setting-up drill.

239. Is that at the beginning of your regimental year?—No, it is at the beginning of the year; in January or towards the end of the winter we begin then the setting-up drill.

240. When do you have your battalion drill, do they commence at a certain time?—I have a battalion out all the year round.

241. You have no fixed period when you have battalion drills?—No. After the setting-up drill has been going on for some time, I say that no man shall fall into a battalion who has not passed through the setting up drill.

242. When do you exclude those who have not passed the setting-up drill from battalion drills?—Generally about two months after the setting-up drill has commenced.

243. Before the month of March?—About that time; but the battalion drill has been going on all the time; for instance, I begin the setting-up drill on the 1st of January, and on the 1st of March I say that no man who has not passed the setting-up drill shall fall in with the battalion.

244. Between the 1st of January and the 1st of March is the regiment going out to be exercised in battalion drill?—Yes.

245. Then you have battalion drill all the year round?—Yes.

246. Once a week?—Yes, with the exception, perhaps, of eight or ten weeks in the year.

247. Then you do discontinue it during a part of the year?—Yes, in August and September.

248. Do you have those battalion drills in the winter time, in the dark?—Yes.

249. Do you march in the dark in winter?—Yes.

250. Where do you have your battalion drills in the dark?—In the barrack yard at St. John's Wood.

251. Is the attendance of the men good at those battalion drills in the dark?—Yes.

252. As good as they are later in the year?—Almost better, and I can explain why. In the winter the men have very little opportunity for recreation, and they are glad to have exercise. In the summer they have cricket, boating, and a variety of things which call them away.

253. (*Lieut.-Col. Barttelot.*) Would it not be better if those battalion drills were confined to certain periods of the year instead of extending over the whole year?—I think it is a very difficult question; for some it would and for some it would not. A great many of the men in my regiment come to drill for the sake of exercise; they like it and they come once a week regularly, and if the drills were to be discontinued, they would acquire other habits of exercise, and would not come at all. Then there are other men who never come near us in the winter time, but they do come in the summer.

254. (*Major-Gen. Eyre.*) Unless there is a grand field day?—Yes.

255. (*Major Harcourt.*) Do you mean that you would rather have your regiment inspected at the end of March than at the end of July?—Yes.

256. (*Chairman.*) Would they be as efficient at the end of March as in July?—More so.

257. (*Major Harcourt.*) At what time of the year has your regiment generally been inspected?—Generally in June.

258. Always at the same time?—No, once in the winter.

259. Would it not be more convenient to the men that it should take place at one time in the year?—I do not think it matters very much.

260. (*Col. MacMurdo.*) At the last inspection it appears that there were 234 members absent without leave?—Yes.

261. What was the reason assigned generally for that absence?—Those figures relate to the strength on paper, those are part of the men who were on paper and who were not at parade. I should say that about 100 of those probably were away or had left. We cannot tell exactly what has become of them. A certain other proportion of those were men

whose business engagements would not permit them to attend; sickness, and other causes.

262. (*Lord Elcho.*) You have stated that the strength of your regiment on paper is 609?—Yes.

263. What do you think has been the average attendance at the battalion drills, whether in summer or winter?—I gave an answer to that in the early part of my examination, and I gave roughly 150 as the approximate attendance.

264. In your regiment you cannot ever reckon as the average attendance upon more than one-third of the strength on paper?—No.

265. Do you find that the average attendance on divisional and brigade field days is considerably in excess of the average attendance at the ordinary battalion parades?—Undoubtedly.

266. Do you find that the brigade and divisional field days have any effect upon the subsequent attendance at battalion drills in increasing or diminishing the attendance?—Yes. They increase them at the parades before, and diminish them afterwards; they act as a stimulus, in fact.

267. Latterly, since those great field days have taken place, your regimental parades have not been so well attended as before?—No.

268. Can you speak generally as to whether that has been the effect upon the force at large?—Undoubtedly.

269. Do you think that on that account it might be desirable that the brigade field days should be confined to the close of the season, rather than at the commencement, when the men have gone through a regular course of training and drill, and that those only should take part in those brigade field days who had attended at the regimental drills?—The men who take part in the divisional field days are those who have gone through those regimental drills. No man can take part in a battalion drill, and of course, therefore, not in a brigade field day, until he has passed through his annual setting-up drill.

270. Have you any rule as to the number of those battalion parades which he must attend before you let him take part in a battalion or divisional parade day?—Every year he must pass through the setting-up drill.

271. After he has passed into the battalion drill, do you require a certain number of attendances at those battalion drills, before you let him attend a brigade or divisional field day?—No.

272. (*Major-Gen. Eyre.*) That is your own arrangement?—Yes.

273. (*Chairman.*) A man who had attended one battalion drill would be allowed to go to a divisional drill, if he was willing to do so?—Yes.

274. (*Lord Elcho.*) You would assume him to be fit from having passed through the setting-up drill?—Yes.

275. Have you any special method in your regiment of distinguishing the attendances at drill?—The rolls are called.

276. I ask you the question under the impression that there does exist in your regiment some means of marking or distinguishing the men who have attended a certain number of drills, in order to distinguish them from others?—Yes.

277. What is it?—Those who pass the setting-up drill are called the first-class drills, and then they are allowed to take part in the others.

278. Do they bear any distinguishing mark?—No; the bulk of the regiment go through.

279. (*Major Harcourt.*) Do those who are put in the other class have any exemptions?—No, because there is no compulsion.

280. (*Lord Elcho.*) Do you think that the present number of drills which are required by the Act to constitute an effective is the *minimum* which should be required, or do you think that the number might be reduced?—I should say that 24 drills ought to be enforced in the first year, and eight in the subsequent year.

281. Are you aware that the number prescribed by the Act of Parliament is 18 and not 24?—My impression was that it was 24.

282. Let us assume that 18 is the present number of the drills required by the Act of Parliament, should you consider that number in excess of what is absolutely required to ensure sufficient efficiency?—Yes, it is in excess.

283. How would you propose to diminish the number?—I should propose that each man for his first year should be considered a recruit, and that he should have 24 drills, and that in any subsequent year, he should have eight drills only. I think that that would be quite enough to keep it in his mind.

284. Those eight drills being battalion drills?—I should leave that to the discretion of the commanding officer.

285. Would it be advisable to fix those eight drills as battalion drills, but that a man should be exempt from the others, and if he passed an examining drill like your setting-up drill, he should be at once passed into a battalion?—I should prefer to leave it to the discretion of the commanding officer.

286. (*Lord Hardinge.*) You are aware, probably, that the militia have 21 days' drill in the course of a year?—Yes.

287. On what grounds do you advocate a reduction in the number of the drills specified by the Act of Parliament?—It is simply a question of numbers. You may get perhaps 10,000 men in the country to go through 50 drills in a year, and you may get 40,000 men in the country who could go through 20 drills in a year, but if you want to get the number into the force which I think ought to exist, you must in my opinion reduce the requirement to the lowest possible amount.

288. (*Col. MacMurdo.*) Might not some reason be found for that in the superior intelligence of the men?—Undoubtedly.

289. (*Lord Overstone.*) Do not you consider that one of the most important considerations connected with the volunteer movement is its tendency to accustom a very large part of the population of the country to the use of arms, and to a certain elementary knowledge of military discipline?—That is undoubtedly so.

290. Do not you think that a population so accustomed to the use of arms would be more available in a case of sudden emergency for the defence of the country than a population not so accustomed?—It all depends upon the time which there is to organize them.

291. Do you not think that the main consideration in the volunteer movement is rather to accustom a very large number of the population of the country to the most elementary habits connected with military operations than to form a small *nucleus*, much more limited in number, although more advanced in military discipline?—I think that there must be a mean taken between the two extremes. I think that while it is possible to reduce the force too low, by over-strictness, on the other hand, a large number insufficiently instructed would be merely like a flock of sheep for want of proper organization.

292. Do you think that the two considerations,—a strict and efficient military organization, and the opposite consideration of mere elementary habits of a military character must be duly regarded and happily combined to produce an efficient volunteer force?—Yes, only I would lay greater stress upon the efficiency and military character of the force than upon the other considerations.

293. Do you think, considering the principle and the purposes of the volunteer force, that those would be more satisfactorily accomplished, say by a force of 50,000 men who had undergone pretty steady and continuous military discipline, rather than by 500,000 men much less closely and efficiently disciplined or accustomed to the use of arms, and to most of the elementary operations of regiments?—It would depend upon the organization that existed.

294. What do you mean by organization?—For

Lord Radstock.

27 May 1862.

E

Lord Radstock.
27 May 1862.

instance, in my own battalion, I reckon that I have 500 available men, and in the course of a few years I should have 500 other men who will have passed through that battalion, and who will still be available to me, but who from having other pursuits had not remained volunteers; but the organization remaining complete, and the efficiency of the men undiminished, I could at once take in those at a day's notice or a week's notice, and take those 500 men into the field with the 500 that I had already.

295. Supposing a regiment of 1,000 men, which underwent a change of 500 men every year, at the end of ten years 5,000 men would be thrown into the country, accustomed to a certain extent to military operations; in the case of an invasion of the country, and a sudden call upon the population to arm, do not you think that that regiment of only 1,000 strong when the emergency came would render more service in preparing the country for its defence than would be rendered by a regiment which had kept itself at 1,000 strong unchanged through the whole period?—That would depend upon the time there was to organize them; if I had six months to organize those 5,000 men, and to officer them, and to put them into shape, that would undoubtedly be the best, but if the time was limited, and there was only a week to prepare, undoubtedly the smaller number would be more useful.

296. (*Major-Gen. Eyre.*) You would be better without the 5,000, would you not?—Yes.

297. (*Chairman.*) The smaller number would form a nucleus around which a larger body could be formed in a smaller space of time, provided that smaller number were thoroughly well-drilled and disciplined?—Yes.

298. (*Lord Overstone.*) But the formation of the nucleus would be greatly promoted, would it not, by the fact of those by whom it was to be formed having previously undergone some elementary, although incomplete, military discipline?—Unless the organization of a regiment is complete, they cannot work into shape the materials which they have given to them.

299. But assume a given number of the regiments to be thoroughly organized, would not those regiments be able to draw around them a very much larger and more efficient force in proportion as the people who were to be called in to their aid had been previously accustomed, although imperfectly, to a military organization?—Yes.

300. Do you not think that it is one important consideration in the organization of the volunteer movement, that it should be based upon the principle of passing many men through the discipline of the volunteer corps, and so filling the country with men more or less, although incompletely accustomed to the use of arms and to the practice of military operations?—It would be a question of degree. Supposing that I have a regiment which has dwindled down to 300 men who are efficient, both officers and non-commissioned officers, I could absorb 700 men who were imperfectly drilled, and I would undertake to keep them together; but if I had 3,000 or 4,000 men thrown upon me I should be helpless, unless I had time.

301. (*Lord Hardinge.*) Assuming that the volunteer force in a time of peace was nothing more than a nucleus, is it not very desirable that that nucleus should be made as efficient as you can make it?—Yes.

302. If you reduce the number of the drills from 18 to eight, will not the efficiency of your battalions be impaired?—I think not to such an extent as to make it hurtful as a nucleus. If you keep up the number of drills, I believe that the attendance will flag so seriously that the numbers will go off so much that you will not have enough material to keep your organization together. You require a certain number of men to practice your officers and non-commissioned officers, and if you reduce that material too much you will not get enough material upon which to practice your organization.

303. In reducing the drills you say that you will

get more men to join you, but will you gain in numbers what you lose in efficiency?—Undoubtedly; the number of drills, I think, is that which makes a man know his place in the ranks; he may not be so smart, but he will be able to maintain his place.

304. (*Lord Overstone.*) In following the volunteer movement, have you not found that the existence of a large number of officers who have passed through the army and have then retired from it, has materially facilitated and aided the organization of the volunteer movement?—I have not found it in my own case.

305. But speaking generally, has it not been found that the existence throughout the country of a considerable number of officers who have passed through the regular discipline of the army and have retired, has been very useful in aiding the progress of the movement?—Speaking generally, it has.

306. Do you not think that that is an illustration of the principle that the volunteer movement itself, by dispersing throughout the country, a large body of persons who have gone through its discipline more or less completely, will fill the country with a body of persons who can be called to its aid in a case of emergency?—The difference is this, that in the case you have supposed the army officers are those who are to a certain extent efficient organizers.

307. And the volunteers are those who are imperfectly trained?—Yes.

308. (*Major-Gen. Eyre.*) And, perhaps, to a certain degree not trained all; for example, as to musketry instruction?—Quite so.

309. (*Lord Hardinge.*) Do you think, taking into account the time which every volunteer must lose, in your own corps for instance, and considering that the drill must take place in an evening, when the men's daily employment is over, that 18 drills in a year are too much to expect a man to go through?—I think they are too much to expect any large number of men to take a pleasure in going through.

310. (*Lord Elcho.*) Is it not the case that at the annual inspections of corps there are, in nine cases out of ten, very many men who have not attended eight battalion drills in the course of the year, but who appear at the inspection?—Surely; but then I should doubt whether there were any men who had not attended drills of some sort.

311. Do you believe that you would have complete efficiency in the corps if you had eight compulsory battalion drills, and the men were obliged to go through some sort of examination to show that they were fit to be passed into the battalion drills?—I think it might work.

312. Do you think that efficiency might thereby be insured, taking into account the intelligence of the volunteers, and what you know of them?—Speaking generally, I should say yes.

313. (*Major-Gen. Eyre.*) We have talked a good deal of numbers compared with the efficiency of small bodies; do you think that any part or any proportion of any such large bodies would be of any use on an emergency unless they had gone through a fair amount of musketry instruction?—I should say no; unless a man can fire off his rifle he will have no confidence in himself.

314. Is not that what we may consider in the volunteer force as their peculiar tendency, and what we ought to look to?—Yes; I think their main qualification is to act as light troops.

315. (*Lord Overstone.*) Is it not the fact that any young man who has gone through a moderate number of the ordinary drills of the volunteer force obtains through that discipline a certain habit of using his rifle?—That will depend very much upon the practice of the corps. In my own corps no man is allowed to fall in with a battalion until he has fired blank cartridge.

316. What I want to ascertain is this, whether on forming a volunteer regiment, although the attendance at the drills may be irregular and incomplete, still if there be a certain amount of attendance, it does not necessarily involve, on the part of the indi-

vidual so attending, the acquisition of certain habits as to military movements and the handling of military instruments?—It depends very much upon the practice of the different regiments.

317. Is it not very desirable that attention should be specially directed to that consideration?—Quite so.

318. (*Sir A. Campbell.*) Would you make it necessary, in addition to the eight battalion drills, that they should pass through a course of musketry instruction?—I have rather overlooked that point, but in my own regiment no man can fall into a battalion until he can fire blank.

319. (*Col. MacMurdo.*) That instruction would be included in his 24 drills in the first year?—Yes. I ought to add to the 24 drills, that he should be passed into a battalion, and competent to use his rifle.

320. (*Major-Gen. Eyre.*) Is the musketry instruction necessary to passing into a battalion?—No; firing blank is.

321. (*Sir A. Campbell.*) By firing blank, do you mean platoon exercise, or musketry instruction?—That is not compulsory.

322. Do you include position drills and such like in your drills to constitute a man an effective?—They do, of course, in class firing and in regimental firing under a competent man, if sent out by order.

323. (*Lord Elcho.*) What proportion of men has gone through class firing?—About two-thirds.

324. Do you find that the men who go through class firing are regular attendants at drill?—Not always.

325. By whom is the musketry instruction given?—By the musketry instructor of the corps.

326. Is he an officer who does nothing else?—Yes, he is the captain of the company.

327. (*Major-Gen. Eyre.*) Is he any expense to your corps?—No.

328. (*Chairman.*) Will you favour the Commission with your views as to the remedies for the defects which you have pointed out?—Under the head of cost I have already suggested that there should be one uniform as a means of reducing the cost, also that the number of the battalions should be reduced, and for the remaining cost I would propose that the Government should pay 1*l.* per head for every man present on parade.

329. What do you precisely mean by that?—I mean a man that is actually there for inspection.

330. Only on that day?—I mean that he should have been seen; that there is a *bonâ fide* man there, armed and equipped, who is to a certain extent able to go through his drill; he is worth, in my opinion, 1*l.*

331. (*Col. MacMurdo.*) If he comes only one day in the year?—If a man can go through an ordinary field-day in a regiment without upsetting the regiment, then he is *pro tanto* efficient, and he is worth a certain sum of money.

332. According to your view, the 1*l.* per head should be restricted to those men who were present on the day of inspection?—Quite so.

333. (*Lieut.-Col. Barttelot.*) You mean a man fully armed and accoutred, with every thing in good order?—Yes.

334. (*Lord Elcho.*) Is it not the case that on parade you might have from many causes a great many men such as clerks in offices absent whose business occupations would prevent them from attending the inspections, and would you suggest any means of meeting that?—I consider it a point of importance that there should be one day in the year on which every volunteer should be able to attend in his place, that there should be in fact a volunteer's day upon which the whole force should be turned out; that there should be a national holiday, on which every man should take his place in the ranks. I believe that to be a point of the utmost importance. The general weakness of the present volunteer movement is that they feel they are never wanted, and I think that there ought to be in each year a call from the country, and it ought to be recognized that they are wanted once a year, and that would be a day to which they would all look forward; it would give them a soldier-like feeling and an *esprit de corps* which I believe would carry them through the rest of the year. One of the most discouraging circumstances connected with the present force to those who are interested in it is that they never can get a regiment together.

335. (*Chairman.*) According to your proposition if all the volunteers should be called together on one particular day in the year, it would be impossible that they should be inspected?—I think it might be done by arrangement; I think you might increase the number of Inspectors by a plan which I would propose. I think there should be one day in the year in which it should be imperative that every volunteer should take a part, and I would propose that if a man has his equipment, his knapsack and greatcoat, an additional 10*s.* should be given to the commanding officer. I think that he would be worth 10*s.* more. Then with regard to the organization, I think that brigade districts should be formed, and that men should only be allowed to enlist in their brigade district; and that in brigade districts already existing, no new companies or battalions should be formed where less than 80 men per company were present on parade, or less than 800 men per battalion. I believe that the main fault of the force is that there are too many battalions and too many companies, and that you must apply stringent remedies in order to get the force into proper condition.

336. (*Lord Elcho.*) You mean a minimum of 80 obtained by companies and battalions already existing?—Yes, or in the case of a battalion applying for two more companies, then the question would be, were there 80 men per company at the last inspection.

337. (*Chairman.*) In the battalions already existing?—Yes; and that no company should be formed with less than 60 men present, and no battalion should be formed with less than 480 men present.

338. (*Major-Gen. Eyre.*) For drill?—Yes.

339. (*Sir A. Campbell.*) Are they to be inspected before they are formed?—Yes, of course, until fresh companies were formed they would be borne as supernumeraries on the strength of the other battalions until they were sanctioned as a fresh battalion.

340. (*Major-Gen. Eyre.*) You mean over the 80?—Yes; supposing, for example, in this parish there are 10 companies of 80 men each present, there might be perhaps 200 other men who are volunteers, and if they wish to be enrolled in another battalion they should be borne as supernumeraries on this battalion here until they got 480, then they would be formed into a separate battalion; you must provide for the men somewhere.

341. (*Sir A. Campbell.*) But they must be inspected before they can be enrolled?—Yes; then I should recommend that the brigade districts should be united under an officer of division.

342. You mean a military officer?—An officer appointed by the War Office; I do not say necessarily a military officer.

343. You mean that the divisions should consist of an aggregate number of brigades?—Yes.

344. (*Lord Hardinge.*) The officer would be a divisional general?—Yes, he would be a sort of referee; when called out they would be under his orders, he would not have very much to do with them, but he would have the general superintendence of them.

345. (*Lord Elcho.*) He would have the command in the field?—Yes. I do not know that there is anything further which I have to suggest.

346. (*Lord Hardinge.*) You were going to say something about the serjeant instructor to be paid by the Government when the companies became reduced?—I should recommend that the Government, where they have given a serjeant instructor, should not take him away until the company has fallen off

Lord Radstock.

27 May 1862.

E 2

Lord Radstock.
27 May 1862.

to one half the strength compared with what it was formerly.

347. As long as the subdivision remained a subdivision they should keep their Government serjeant?—Yes.

348. (*Lord Elcho.*) Do you see any way of getting that one day in a year, because, although the Government might order the volunteers to turn out on such and such a day, how are they to get the time and liberty to go?—I suppose it would be very easy; there are other holidays which exist by Act of Parliament.

349. (*Lord Hardinge.*) When you say that they should be assembled on one day specially appointed, I presume you mean that there should be a review in Hyde Park, and another review at Warwick or in the Midland counties, and another review in the south-eastern district?—Quite so.

350. (*Lord Elcho.*) Do you think that it would be desirable that the expenses of the volunteers attending such reviews, and likewise the expenses of the administrative companies in the rural districts attending battalion drill should be borne by the Government?—It would be to a certain extent covered by the 1*l.*

351. Do you look upon that as covering all those items?—Yes.

352. (*Lord Overstone.*) Do you not think, considering the importance of retaining the essential character of the volunteer force, that any pecuniary advantage to be derived from the Government, if necessary, would be more wisely and safely administered in the way of paying certain incidental expenses, or part of them, rather than by a direct capitation grant?—I think that the circumstances would be so very various in different corps that no Government could lay down any scheme. My principal expenses, as a town corps, are for headquarters and practice grounds; those are the two main expenses; but in country corps those very often do not exist, for there are ranges in gentlemen's parks, and they get some houses lent to them for headquarters, and therefore they would have no expenses of that sort.

353. Do not you think that the main head of expense would be either the expense of obtaining good drill serjeants, or the expense of obtaining good shooting grounds with butts, and the appurtenances, or the expense of conveyance to the place of general assembly for battalion drill, and that in one or other of those forms the subvention from the Government might be applicable both to a town regiment and to a country regiment?—I think that the multiplicity of the details would be so great that you could not administer a fund better than in the way of a capitation grant.

354. (*Lord Hardinge.*) In the case of a capitation grant you would propose to leave that sum of money to a regiment to be expended entirely at the discretion of the commanding officer?—Yes, accounting as to how he spent it.

355. He would have to furnish to the War Office a very accurate account of how the money had been expended?—He would pass his accounts and have his regimental books to show.

356. You must recollect that it would be Government money, and that he would have to account to this office for every item of the money so spent?—Yes.

357. What security would the Government have that this capitation grant was properly expended?—They would have security of two sorts; first they would have the direct vouchers for the expenditure which would in my case, and in the great majority of instances, be in lump sums, for instance, for the butt or for headquarters; and they would have that indirect security which would be a far greater check, the whole neighbourhood, who would know how the whole amount was expended by the commanding officer, and he might be compelled to publish his accounts.

358. Take the first year in which this capitation grant was made, what security would the Government have that a considerable part of the grant was not expended in an expensive band?—The answer to that is that I am not at all sure, that that might not be a good way of supplying the money, as the money which went to pay the band would save payment by the members, and their money would be applicable to other purposes.

359. Do you think that the Government would sanction any considerable expenditure in the different regiments for band purposes?—I think that if they can get volunteers they would pay very cheaply for them at 1*l.* or 30*s.* a head.

360. (*Lord Elcho.*) Supposing such a system as you have pointed out were resorted to, the Government paying so much per head, would it not be for the Government to draw up certain heads, under which that money must be expended, and under no other, such as the custody of the arms, the drill places, the conveyance to the drills, clothing and anything of that kind, but restricting within certain limits the way in which the money ought to be expended?—I think that that course might be adopted.

361. (*Major Harcourt.*) Do not you think that if a money grant were made it would rather stop one of our present sources of income, namely, the public contributions?—I do not think that the force can really be efficient until it is almost entirely paid by the Government; one of the greatest taxes on the volunteer force is having to raise money; and I think that it is far more weakening to the force to have to attend to civil matters of that sort than the real discipline of the regiment.

362. (*Lord Elcho.*) Do you believe from your knowledge of the state of the force that we can reckon upon a permanent 10 per cent. upon our expenditure from the public for the support of the volunteer corps?—No.

363. (*Chairman.*) Do you say that if this proposition were sanctioned of 1*l.* or 30*s.* per head that you would not obtain any subscriptions whatever from the members of the corps?—I think that in certain places you might get them from those who were most desirous to make their corps more comfortable, to give them a library, or other extra encouragement; but if a corps were to depend at all upon raising money outside from the public in general, it would be I think a very great source of weakness and tend to disgust the men more quickly than anything else.

364. (*Major-Gen. Eyre.*) Have the contributions of the public fallen off from year to year?—I believe in a general sense they have. I happen to have a special means of counteracting that by the kindness of one or two individuals who take an interest in it; but, apart from that, there is no doubt that it is more difficult to get in regular contributions.

365. (*Lord Hardinge.*) Do you apprehend that your proposed capitation grant would alter the character of the force?—No.

366. Do you think that if the Government made a capitation grant they would insist upon having the force more under military control?—I think that it would be more desirable to have a more distinct control, but it depends upon what you mean by military.

367. I mean this: Suppose that brigade districts were formed, and that the volunteers should be commanded by officers of the line, would that be acceptable to the force?—I believe myself that the policy of the Government would be to get the best volunteer officers they could, or at any rate those who had been in the volunteers. I do not mean that volunteer officers alone should be appointed to brigades.

368. What should you say as to divisional commands?—I think that, of course, at first you must select officers for those commands in general, but after a time I think it would be very desirable that officers

for divisional command should be as much as possible selected from those who have been brigadiers.

369. (*Lord Overstone.*) I presume you would feel the force of the principle that has been alluded to, namely, that in proportion as the Government is called upon to assist directly by a pecuniary grant, the Government to a certain degree would feel a corresponding obligation to exercise a more direct control over the whole volunteer movement?—Yes.

370. Looking at that fact, and not with regard to your own feelings as a commanding officer, anxious principally for the effective discipline and efficiency of your corps, but looking to the influence of such interference by the Government upon the minds and feelings of the men separately, do you think it would be a safe procedure?—I think it would be perfectly safe for this reason, that the interference of the Government would merely extend to the system, it would fall upon the commanding officers and not affect the position of the men, it would be merely matter of organization, and it would rest upon those who were in charge of the force, the commanding officers and officers commanding brigades, and they would be willing to submit to the control, having a more recognized status given them.

371. (*Lord Elcho.*) You say that it would not fall upon the men; you know that at present the only hold which the country has upon a volunteer is that he has to give 14 days' notice, at the end of which he may cease to be a volunteer?—Yes.

372. Have you considered whether, in the event of a further subvention from the state, it would be advisable that the state should require some greater security than it now has for the continued services of those men, and that they should enlist, so to speak, for a longer period than 14 days?—I do not think there would be any advantage in that unless you were prepared at once to adopt a system of compulsion; you may have a man on your books and compel him to be on them for six months, but there is no advantage unless he attends; you cannot compel him to attend, you must either retain the volunteer system as a thing which a man can enter into for amusement, or love of his country, or you must make it compulsory like the disembodied militia, and do it by ballot.

373. (*Chairman.*) Suppose the ballot for the militia were resorted to, you would then have some hold upon the volunteer?—I think that that would have a very beneficial effect.

374. You would not allow of any exemption for a volunteer who was not an effective man?—No.

375. (*Lord Elcho.*) Have you ever considered any of the legal exemptions that might be extended to volunteers as an inducement to them to volunteer?—I am not aware of any.

376. At the present moment, serjeants are furnished by Government,—do you find that, for the allowance which they receive from the Government, you can get first-rate men?—No.

377. Have you been obliged to add to the government allowance for that purpose?—Yes.

378. Have you got good men now?—Yes.

379. What extra pay do you give them?—I give them nearly about ten shillings a week extra.

380. To each serjeant?—Yes.

381. At present you find practically that the pay is insufficient?—Yes.

382. Do you find that the adjutants are sufficiently paid?—Practically I think so, the supply is so very abundant.

383. Do you consider the present system as to the adjutants essential to the efficiency of the corps?—Yes.

384. (*Chairman.*) Have you to give any assistance to the adjutant of your corps?—No.

385. (*Sir A. Campbell.*) Do you think the supply of well qualified officers for adjutants is sufficient?—I can hardly judge of that beyond general rumour.

386. You have not been aware that officers who would otherwise have been ready to accept such positions have declined them on account of the smallness of the pay?—No.

387. (*Major-Gen. Eyre.*) You have spoken of a want of control over the rifles, can you suggest any better means of controlling them?—Yes; one of the reasons of that is not having brigade districts; if there were brigade districts there might be a brigade armourer; there is no check upon the commanding officers now.

388. (*Lord Elcho.*) Your officers, I believe, go through a general course of instruction, and are attached, every one of them, to regiments of the line?—Nearly every one of them.

389. (*Lord Hardinge.*) Would you have a brigade staff?—Yes; but I should insist upon efficiency; the brigadier should be responsible for the efficiency of those under him.

390. Are you aware that the staff officers of the regulars are now appointed after going through a course of study at the staff college?—Yes.

391. How could you ever expect to obtain such competence in volunteer officers?—I do not think you would get it either from volunteer officers or from regular officers. I think that regular officers who were competent to pass through the staff college would obtain employment on the staff of the army.

392. When you say that you would have volunteer officers, that is based upon the assumption, is it not, that the Government could not furnish you with military men to fill those appointments, if such appointments were necessary?—I think that it would be indispensable that all staff appointments should be of those who had been volunteers, making the officer commanding either the brigade or the division responsible for their efficiency.

393. (*Col. MacMurdo.*) Should they be paid?—No.

394. How could they perform their duties?—In the same way as any other volunteer officers.

395. But these would be staff appointments?—A man would be in the same position; he would not have so much to do as a field officer; he would only be called out perhaps one or two days in the year.

396. He would not have to accompany the divisional commander in his inspections?—He might do that; it would not entail upon him much trouble.

397. But it would entail upon him very great expense?—So does the command of a regiment.

398. (*Lord Hardinge.*) Do you think that any volunteer officer would qualify himself to go through a severe examination such as would make him competent to fulfil the duties of deputy quartermaster-general to a division of the force?—I think that a modified course might be proposed, and I believe that many would qualify for that and go through it.

399. (*Col. MacMurdo.*) Unpaid?—Yes.

400. (*Sir A. Campbell.*) Is this divisional brigade system to supersede or to go along with the present system of inspection?—I should say to supersede it; I think that the assistant inspector of volunteers might be the assistant adjutant-general of a division: but let me be understood, I have been speaking of the brigade staff.

401. (*Lord Elcho.*) Have you any paid clerk, or orderly clerk, for the transaction of the non-military business of the corps?—I have a secretary.

402. Is he paid?—Yes.

403. By whom is the financial part of the business done; who receives the subscriptions?—He does.

404. What do you pay him?—50*l.* a year.

405. For those purposes your serjeants are at present unavailable?—Yes.

406. If they were permitted to do that part of the business, would their duties as instructors permit of their performing both duties?—I think, speaking generally, it would be unwise to put them in such a position.

407. Unwise; upon what ground?—I think it would be a very great temptation to men in that class if they had to handle money; or it would necessitate such a close supervision as would lead to more trouble than the thing was worth.

Lord Radstock.

27 May 1862.

E 3

Lord Radstock.
27 May 1862.

408. The pay-serjeant of every regiment of the line handles money, does he not?—The daily pay.

409. (*Major Harcourt.*) Is there any other reason why you prefer a capitation grant for the volunteers to any other mode of assistance further than this, that you think it would complicate the accounts less in this office?—I think it would be impossible for this office to frame any schedule of payments to include all the various points.

410. That is your only reason for preferring that mode of payment?—Yes.

411. (*Sir A. Campbell.*) You are of opinion that one corps would require one thing, and another corps another?—Yes.

412. (*Lord Overstone.*) Are there not some three or four or five heads of subvention on the part of the Government, under one or other of which the requirements of the volunteer corps might be put?—To a certain extent; but the main head would be uniform in many cases, the uniform being the thing generally that would be most expensive. Suppose the Government give me 100 suits of clothing, I fit them on to the men, and at the end of the year 50 men go, and you would not get the next set of volunteers to take the clothes of those 50 men; that would be one of the main items of expense. Besides, if clothing were given, men would never take proper care of their clothes.

413. (*Chairman.*) Have you any further remarks to make?—I can sum up the impressions that I have on my own mind in this way, that the vitality of the force is its military character, and if it is attempted to make the force popular and to increase its numbers it will deter all those who are most useful and most energetic from taking any further part in it; and although it may appear to be a dangerous experiment to impress a decidedly military character upon it, yet that it will strengthen the hands of those who are the life and soul of the thing, namely, those who have real military tastes and instincts; and in order to carry out any organized military system it is perfectly indispensable to have a brigade staff which should have the power of enforcing a uniform discipline, and uniform modes of proceeding. At the present time, the weakness of the force arises entirely from there being no power to give direction and concentration to the efforts of those who are engaged in it; and unless some distinct authority is created, which is positive and easily applicable, a power by which to enforce a uniform system, the force will be in its present state, each commanding officer doing what is right in his own eyes and all the best of the men becoming disgusted and withdrawing from the force.

414. (*Lord Overstone.*) Assuming that a direct capitation grant was considered objectionable and was not sanctioned, can you state to the Commission in what other more indirect form a subvention from the Government would be rendered most effective in your corps?—I suppose under two or three heads.

415. Will you state what those two or three heads would be in your judgment?—Quarters and shooting grounds would be two of them.

416. Would you desire any aid in the form of a facility for obtaining drill serjeants?—I do not know that there is anything more necessary on that point.

417. Or aid to defray a portion of the expenses incurred at reviews or at the divisional drill?—I think that would be a very proper subject of expenditure.

418. Do you think that if in two or three points that sort of present partial expense was relieved it would go to any material extent to overcome the difficulties you have alluded to under the head of expense?—I do not think that it would be felt; for instance, take the case of paying a man's expenses to go to reviews, they do not grudge that a bit; they are willing to pay that.

419. That is not one of the forms in which, in the case of your regiment, a subvention would be desirable. What are the points as to which, according to your experience of your own regiment, a subvention in an indirect form would be effective?—Drill grounds, head-quarters, rifle ranges, care of arms.

420. (*Lord Elcho.*) Have you any armourer that you pay?—Yes.

421. How much a year?—10s. a week, besides Government pay.

422. (*Chairman.*) Do you mean an armourer who takes care of the arms, or who repairs them?—He does all the small repairs.

423. (*Lord Elcho.*) You have mentioned repairs of arms, ranges, and head-quarters?—Yes.

424. Suppose the Government took upon itself the payment of those three heads, to what extent could you then reduce your subscription?—I cannot say off hand.

425. Would you be able to reduce it one-half?—Barely.

426. In the event of your own suggestion being adopted, which is a capitation grant of 1l. a head, would that enable you to do away wholly with your subscriptions?—I think it would.

The witness withdrew.

Adjourned to Friday next at half-past twelve o'clock.

Friday, 30th May 1862.

PRESENT:

Viscount EVERSLEY.
Earl of DUCIE.
Viscount HARDINGE.
Lord ELCHO.
Lord OVERSTONE.
Lieutenant-Colonel BARTTELOT.

Lieutenant-Colonel Sir A. CAMPBELL.
Lieutenant-General Sir G. A. WETHERALL.
Major-General EYRE.
Colonel MACMURDO.
Major HARCOURT.

VISCOUNT EVERSLEY IN THE CHAIR.

Lieut.-Col. Macleod of Macleod.
30 May 1862.

Lieut.-Colonel MACLEOD OF MACLEOD examined.

427. (*Chairman.*) I believe you command the First Middlesex Engineer Volunteer Corps?—Yes.

428. It consists of eight companies, with 100 men to a company?—Yes.

429. When was that corps formed?—One company was formed in January 1860; there were three more added in the year 1860; two more were added early in 1861, and two more in November 1861; eight companies in all.

430. How many members have you at present on the muster roll?—Including the band and all ranks, 724.

431. Of what classes is your corps composed?—About three-fourths are mechanics and artizans; the remainder are draughtsmen, clerks, architects, and engineers.

432. What is the present state of your corps with regard to its efficiency in company and battalion drill?

—I think, upon the whole, it is satisfactory. Each company has one day in each week set apart for company drill, and the corps devotes another to battalion drill. Upon the whole, I consider the state of the corps satisfactory, and I hope that the Inspector will think it is so when he comes to inspect the corps. Being engineers, however, our attention is not wholly directed to company and battalion drill.

433. Your corps, I apprehend, receives special instruction in engineering, in addition to the ordinary battalion drill?—Yes.

434. I suppose that instruction is principally given to companies?—It is given to the whole corps. We have classes in field works. A class meets every Wednesday for instruction in throwing up batteries and breastworks of different kinds; other classes for pontooning, for barrel piering, for loopholing walls and laying platforms, and a variety of other exercises of that description are in course of formation. I wish to afford to each man in the corps the opportunity of attending three days in the week, one for company drill, one for battalion drill, and a third for engineering works.

435. Do you find that there is a great desire on the part of the men for this sort of instruction?—Yes; I find that the attendance on company and battalion drill slackens when the men think they know all that we can teach them, and the same remark will probably apply hereafter to engineering works. But whenever there is anything new to teach I have plenty of applicants for admission to the class. There is no difficulty in getting a good attendance when there is anything new in the way of instruction to be given. I should mention, perhaps, that many of the mechanics and artizans attend drill very zealously. I think they seem to consider drill more as an amusement for the evening, and a relaxation after the work of the day, than as a duty.

436. Then the drill is really their relaxation?—Many appear to me to consider it so.

437. Will you state to the Commissioners what the financial position of your corps is?—The financial position of my corps is satisfactory. In order to furnish the best information to the Commissioners, I have brought with me the balance sheet for 1860, which was submitted to the first annual general meeting; it is in manuscript. For the year 1861 a printed balance sheet was prepared, and submitted to a meeting in February last. I have brought with me several copies of that for the information of the Commissioners (*handing in the same*).

438. Can you give the Commissioners, in round numbers, a statement of the receipts and expenses in each year?—In 1860 the receipts from the subscriptions of members amounted to 432*l.* 15*s.* 7*d.* We have had no assistance in any other shape, with the exception of a theatrical entertainment last year, by which we cleared upwards of 70*l.* That theatrical entertainment was given at Camden House, Mr. Woolley, the owner of it, being an honorary member of our corps; we meant to have repeated it this year, but the theatre was burnt down.

439. Do you include the honorary members?—Yes, but there are very few of them. As I have stated, the receipts for 1860 were 452*l.* 15*s.* 7*d.*, and the expenditure in that year was 204*l.* 14*s.* 9*d.* This statement does not include either the band fund or the uniform account. Early in the year 1860 the late Lord Herbert told me that he thought Volunteer Engineers should be as much as possible of the same class as the Royal Engineers. We had then 25 per cent. of artizans and mechanics, and he wished me to recruit in that direction up to 75 per cent. I thought it would be necessary in order to get such members to allow them to pay for their uniforms by instalments. I therefore started by doing so with three companies, and the result was that we advanced a sum of 1,200*l.* for uniforms, and received payment from the members by instalments. That I have kept separate from this account, and therefore the receipts for 1860, of 452*l.* 15*s.* 7*d.*, in subscriptions of members, and the expenditure of 204*l.* 14*s.* 9*d.*, are exclusive of the band and uniform.

440. And what you lent for uniforms?—Yes. In 1861 the receipts from members were 454*l.* 8*s.*, and the expenditure 205*l.* 0*s.* 6*d.*

441. What were the principal items of expenditure included in that amount?—In 1861 it included charges of 49*l.* 1*s.* for drill, and 21*l.* 3*s.* 6*d.* for instruction in fortification. We had to purchase a quantity of wood to make fascines and gabions.

442. Was nothing of that sort furnished from Woolwich?—No; we did not ask for wood. It was not in any list furnished from the War Office, and I did not think it would have been granted.

443. Did you receive any tools from Woolwich?—Yes; we have had spades, pickaxes, a platform, and various other things supplied to us. The War Office has dealt liberally with us, and will, I hope, continue to do so. Of course we shall want many things to carry on the special instruction of the corps. Other items of expense were the cleaning of arms and attending armoury, also advertisements and printing. The whole amount was 205*l.* 0*s.* 6*d.*

444. How much of that was expended in the hire of a field for earthworks and that sort of drill?—For the years 1860 and 1861 we had no rent to pay, having the advantage of a piece of ground near us. Prince Albert also gave the corps the temporary use of a piece of ground behind the conservatory in the Horticultural Gardens, for the purpose of throwing up earthworks, and this, for the first two years, prevented the necessity of our hiring any place. But our expenses will be considerably increased this year. We shall have to pay 40*l.* for a field that we have engaged, to throw up earthworks in, and we shall have to pay 100*l.* for a house and garden which we have taken as headquarters in our neighbourhood, that garden being used also for engineering purposes. We are now making a half sunken battery in it, on a reduced scale. We also pay 40*l.* a year for the use, two days a week, of a rifle range at Ealing. On Tuesdays and Fridays we have the use of that range.

445. Then your future expenses will amount to about 200*l.* a year more than your past expenses?—Yes; I estimate that the receipts from members for this year will be 500*l.*, and I reckon that the expenditure will be 450*l.*, chiefly arising from those additional expenses to which I have referred,—a field to work in, a rifle range, and headquarters.

446. How are these funds procured; do your officers pay a higher amount of subscription than the men?—The officers pay one guinea per year.

447. Only one guinea?—That is all.

448. Is that independent of their subscription to the band?—Yes; they pay one guinea a year to the band, and one guinea a year subscription. The members who are not mechanics and artizans pay one guinea. Mechanics and artizans pay 3*d.* a week, or 13*s.* a year.

449. The privates in the corps pay 13*s.* a year?—Not all; clerks and others who are privates pay one guinea.

450. Upon the whole you anticipate 500*l.* next year?—Yes.

451. And your expenses you expect will be rather more than 400*l.*?—£450; we shall have a balance of about 50*l.*, I hope, when all is paid.

452. The ground for practising earthworks is as essential to a corps of engineers as rifle practice ground to a corps of infantry?—Quite so; but we are obliged to have both.

453. Your expenses have been greater in proportion than the expenses of an ordinary corps?—We have greater requirements. A serious difficulty has been to find a suitable place near enough to break ground in, for the builders in our neighbourhood would not let us go below 2 feet, and that for a sunken battery would be insufficient.

454. With regard to the clothing and accoutrements of your corps, three of the companies have been clothed as you have described,—you have advanced a

Lieut.-Col. Macleod of Macleod.

30 May 1862.

E 4

Lieut.-Col. Macleod of Macleod.
30 May 1862.

sum of money as a loan to a member to provide his own uniform; I presume that all the other members have provided their uniforms without any assistance?—Yes.

455. Of what does the uniform consist?—We have a cloth scarlet tunic, a busby, a blouse or serge coat, one of which I have brought here as a specimen (*producing the same*); it is a capital dress to work in, and throws off the rain, and you can put any amount of clothing underneath it in cold weather. That is the ordinary undress blouse.

456. I understand that your uniform consists of a dress jacket and trowsers, an undress blouse, an undress cap, and leggings?—Yes; and accoutrements.

457. What do the accoutrements cost?—They cost 13*s*.; the scarlet cloth tunic costs 1*l*. 6*s*. 3*d*.; the busby costs 12*s*. 6*d*.; the scarlet serge blouse costs 12*s*. 6*d*.; the accoutrements cost 13*s*.; the trowsers, with red stripe, cost 14*s*.; the leggings cost 7*s*.; and the cap costs 5*s*., making 4*l*. 10*s*. 3*d*. That is the sum that we now give; when we paid for those companies to which I have referred it was at a larger figure; we paid at the rate of 5*l*. 3*s*. for a member's full dress outfit when those three companies were first formed.

458. Have the men any great coat?—No.

459. Or knapsack?—No.

460. Has any part of the money which you advanced to the men for the purchase of their uniforms been paid back?—In 1860 and 1861 we received back about 1,000*l*. out of 1,200*l*.; we advanced, say in round numbers, 1,200*l*., and received back 1,000*l*. There is, therefore, still 200*l*. outstanding; I expect to receive back at least 100*l*. of that, but we shall probably lose, as several of the men have died, and there are some defaulters, 100*l*. upon our advance.

461. You calculate upon losing 100*l*. upon the whole amount?—Yes; I think that that is probable.

462. Do you find that there are many arrears in the annual subscriptions?—I believe that for the two years ending the 31st December 1861 the arrears were between 50*l*. and 60*l*. from the whole corps. I cannot say what they are now.

463. You have stated that the members subscribe 3*d*. a week; how is that collected?—The captains of companies collect the money through the serjeants, each of whom has a squad under his special charge, and at the end of each quarter they hand the amount over to the treasurer.

464. In the prosperous state of the finances in your corps, do you think it requires any aid from the public?—I think that although the present financial state of the corps is on the whole satisfactory, and I have no reason to complain of the manner in which the subscriptions are paid, or to suppose that the members will discontinue their payments, I do think that the subscription falls heavily upon many of the men, and my own opinion is, if the Commission could see its way to recommending that a payment should be made from the public purse, that the members ought to be released from their subscriptions altogether.

465. Do you mean not to receive any subscriptions from the members of the corps?—I think that the members of the corps should be released from their subscriptions of a guinea and 13*s*. I think that if they were released from those subscriptions upon their having attended a certain number of drills in the year, it would have a favourable effect upon the attendance and upon the corps generally. At present members give both time and money. I think they would freely give their time, if the expenses were defrayed by the public. Supposing that 1*l*. was the sum proposed to be given per head, I am sure that the men would, for the sake of keeping up the corps, gladly attend any number of drills that might be required.

466. Your suggestion is that 1*l*. per head should be given for those men who had attended a certain number of drills. I presume you mean battalion drills as well as company drills?—Yes, I mentioned the sum of 1*l*., because I think it would enable me to carry on the corps in a satisfactory and efficient way, without trenching too heavily upon the men's resources.

467. Supposing that this aid was given by the Government, do you think that a greater amount of discipline could be insisted upon, or that it would be desirable to give the force a more military character?—I should be inclined to leave that as it is at present. I think that volunteers value freedom, and in my opinion it would be injurious to the volunteer force to give it a more military character than it has now. I find men sometimes who belong to the mechanic and artizan class objecting to take the oath of allegiance, not because they are not most loyal men, but because they fancy that it binds them more than they like to be bound; and I am quite sure that the power of resigning after a fortnight's notice is very important indeed to the volunteer force. I do not think that it would be desirable to give the force a more military character than it has. I would not increase the number of the drills.

468. Supposing that things remain as they are, and no aid is given by the Government, do you anticipate any diminution in your numbers or any falling off in the efficiency of your corps?—No, I do not. I think that we might hope to carry on as we have done hitherto; a number would resign, but we should have others coming in. I think that the corps could be kept up as it is at present. We are not diminishing in numbers.

469. I presume that your corps is not recruited in any particular district?—It is recruited from all parts of the metropolis, but chiefly in my own neighbourhood; there are, however, some from other parts of London, who have probably some special reason for connecting themselves with an engineer corps.

470. Do you think that any advantage would be gained by limiting the number of corps in London?—I think it would be very undesirable to increase the number of corps, except under very special circumstances. I can mention one case in support of this opinion. Not very long ago a gentleman had undertaken to establish a corps of odd-fellows, and he came to one of my captains and told him what he was about to do. My captain said, "But this is not working for " the advantage of the volunteer force generally, for " you will take men from other corps." He said, "Yes, " but my object is to get up a corps; however, you " need not be alarmed, for I shall only take three of " your men; there are only three odd-fellows in your " company." The captain said, "But you will get men " from other corps." He said, "Yes, and I shall get " up a large corps very shortly." I am happy to say that corps has not yet been established, and I hope it never will. I mention it just to point out that there are persons desirous of increasing the number of corps for their own objects, and to increase the number of the corps unduly will, I believe, have a very prejudicial effect; and therefore I think there ought to be great care on the part of the authorities not to sanction the establishment of any new corps. It occurs to me, that if the Government would decide what should be the maximum of the force, a check would at once be given to the present objectionable facilities of entering it. At present there is almost a system of bidding for men to enter corps. I believe there are persons who get together a considerable number of volunteers, and then go and offer them to different corps. There is a desire on the part of those corps to get those volunteers. I think that that is an objectionable system, and I think that to lessen the facility of becoming a volunteer would create a wholesome desire to belong to a corps into which only meritorious persons were admitted.

471. Have you taken your corps to any divisional or brigade field days?—Yes, I find that the corps like to avail themselves of every opportunity that offers for joining with other corps, and I think that although they like to go for amusement and relaxation, yet I

think that they like to go for instruction also. My opinion is that field days, say of 2,000 or 3,000 men, are most useful and instructive; and although my own men would be very sorry to be left out of such a day as Brighton or Wimbledon, and that, in short, they would all wish if possible to go, still, I think, they would like better, as affording more instruction, a field day when there were perhaps 2,000 or 3,000 men only.

472. Have you found that after attending these field days, early in the year especially, the attendance at the ordinary battalion drills has been rather more slack?—Since Brighton, I think it has been. The last three battalion drills that I have had were attended, the first by 120 men, the second by 140, and the third by 160. Now that is rather under the usual number. I think there has been a smaller attendance since Brighton.

473. You are of opinion that it would be an advantage to retain those brigade and divisional field days, and especially that they would be of still greater advantage if they could be held in the latter part of the year?—I think it would be so; but there are some difficulties in the way. Easter Monday and Whit Monday fall early in the year, and those are the two great holidays for working men.

474. (*Col. MacMurdo.*) Have you got a drill shed? —Yes.

475. Will you state the dimensions and the cost of that drill shed?—The drill shed was erected from a design by Captain Fowke. It is 90 feet long by 40 feet wide, and it cost 69*l*. 19*s*. 5*d*.

476. Did you buy all the materials?—Yes.

477. Is it the same in construction as the annexe at the Exhibition?—Yes, it is.

478. Is it well adapted for volunteer corps generally?—Admirably, I think. Captain Fowke was obliging enough to give the design to our corps, and we have had several applications from other corps for the plan and specification, so that, selling it as we have done at a guinea a piece, we have realized a little sum for the band fund, I believe 8 or 10 guineas.

479. (*Lord Elcho.*) Have you any regular system of drill commencing with setting-up drill and going on to battalion drill?—Yes.

480. Will you be good enough to describe your system?—We have setting-up drills in the spring; a setting-up drill for the officers is going on now. On several Tuesdays and Fridays lately there has been an officers' drill under the major; I have been in the ranks myself, and on those occasions the attendance has been very satisfactory.

481. The officers' setting-up drills?—Yes.

482. How many drills do you require your men to attend; is there any fixed number?—No.

483. Have they to pass through those setting-up drills before they are passed into the battalion drills? —We have not been very particular as to that; some men take a longer time to learn their duties than others. I have passed them into the battalion when they were considered by the captains of their companies fit for it.

484. Supposing they were so passed into the battalion, how many drills in the battalion should you think sufficient from your knowledge of the volunteers to make them as efficient as you could expect or desire them to be?—If they attend well on company drills, I should think that six or eight battalion drills would be quite ample.

485. You have stated that the attendance of your men at battalion drills has fallen off since the Brighton field day, and that it was on different days, 120, 140, and 160?—Yes.

486. That was below the average?—Yes.

487. You have stated the strength of your regiment to be 724?—Yes.

488. From which you must deduct 60 for the band?—Yes.

489. What is the ordinary attendance at an ordinary battalion parade?—About 250.

490. Can you reckon permanently on more than one-third of your regiment ever appearing at an ordinary battalion parade?—No, taking 600 as our strength in round numbers, I should not expect that at an ordinary battalion parade we should have more than 200 or 250.

491. How many of your men have received musketry instruction?—About 150.

492. Have they gone through class firing?—No; I should not think that above 10 have passed through class firing. We have only had our range about two months.

493. Out of those 724 men, including the band, not above 10 have actually gone through their class firing?—No.

494. In three years?—We have had no range, and we have been unable to direct our attention to shooting.

495. Was that in consequence of not having funds to procure a range, or from the impossibility of finding a range?—It was the impossibility of finding a range. For some time I directed the whole of my attention to getting a rifle range on Wandsworth Common. Lord Spencer was kind enough to give me a lease of the ground, but I met with so much opposition on the part of the inhabitants there that I was obliged at last, although very reluctantly, to give it up. We still have that ground leased to us by Lord Spencer, and we propose during the summer to use it for engineering purposes; but as to ever having a range upon it, I am afraid that that must be given up as impossible.

496. Supposing that you could have had that ground, and had erected a range upon it, how would you have erected it? Would the funds of the corps have enabled you to do it?—No; we proposed that the butt should have been erected by the officers of the corps, who were each to subscribe a certain sum, according to their rank. It would have cost us 800*l*.

497. That would have been a special extra subscription?—Yes.

498. And which could have been in no way met by the ordinary annual subscriptions?—No.

499. At present you hire a range at Ealing; is there not another range that you hire for one day in the week?—Yes; there is another range that we hire for one day in the week, and that range belongs to the London Scottish. I omitted to mention it, because that range is only used by one company of my corps, namely, the Wandsworth company, the members of which find Wimbledon more convenient than Ealing.

500. There is a certain rent paid for that range; I believe 25*l*. a year?—Yes.

501. Does that come out of the funds of the corps, or is that found by the company that uses it?—That is paid for by the company that uses it.

502. How is it paid?—It is done in this way,— that company, and another company also, make their own financial arrangements; they pay the corps one-fourth of the whole subscriptions, and retain three-fourths for local expenses.

503. So that it does come out of the funds of the corps?—Yes.

504. You receive less from those companies than from any of the others?—Yes; but that does not affect my calculation with regard to the 500*l*.; that 500*l*. will include one-fourth of the subscriptions of the two outlying companies.

505. (*Sir A. Campbell.*) And one-fourth only?— Yes.

506. In fact your total subscriptions, including the full subscriptions of those companies, would be more than that?—Yes, it would be 500*l*., plus three-fourths of the subscriptions from the two outlying companies.

507. (*Viscount Hardinge.*) Do you not consider with regard to your corps, that your speciality is engineering, and would you not lay greater stress on their proficiency in throwing up earthworks than you would upon rifle shooting?—Certainly; but I find that the men are disposed to like shooting. In fact,

F

Lieut.-Col. Macleod of Macleod.
30 May 1862.

the difficulty under which this corps labours is, that their attention has to be directed to so many things. Our honorary colonel, Sir John Burgoyne, said, "First be soldiers," and we have done the best we could to effect that object. Then said he, "Go in for engineering." Then we have shooting, and in short I am obliged to ask the members to give three days a week, and even that is not enough.

508. (*Lord Elcho.*) Do you send any men to Wimbledon?—We shall send eight men, one for each company.

509. Who have gone through the musketry course? —Yes.

510. Do you believe that if you had an available range open it would be a source of attraction to the men of your corps, and enough to keep it up?— Yes; our present difficulty is, that we have only been able to get the use of a range on Tuesdays and Fridays; Saturday, however, would be a better day for the men, and I fear a very large proportion of them will never be able to shoot.

511. What is the distance from headquarters?— We go by railway, and reckoning by time, it takes an hour to go from headquarters to the range.

512. What is the fare?—Sixpence there and back.

513. Every time that one of your men goes out to shoot it costs him sixpence?—Yes.

514. How are the expenses incident to attending brigade field days borne?—Every man pays his own railway fare.

515. Nothing is found for him?—No.

516. Nothing from the funds of the corps goes to the band?—No, the band fund is separate.

517. Is that a compulsory payment?—It is compulsory, inasmuch as the members, at a general meeting, passed a resolution that every member should contribute half-a-crown to the band fund, and that the officers should contribute a guinea.

518. So that, practically, the subscription of each member is 15s. 6d.?—Yes.

519. Do the guinea and the 2s. 6d. form a sufficient fund?—Yes. One hundred and thirty pounds is about the annual cost of our band, and the half-crown and the guinea pretty nearly pay it.

520. Have you had any difficulty in obtaining the 13s. from the men?—As I have said before, I think there will not be a deficiency of above 50l. upon the whole of the subscriptions up to the end of last year.

521. Have you had any recourse to the power given you under the Act of Parliament to prosecute, in order to recover the subscriptions?—Yes. On two occasions we applied to a magistrate to assist us in recovering subscriptions, but the chief object of the application was to get repayment for the uniforms supplied; the magistrate at Hammersmith said that he had no jurisdiction as to uniforms, and sent us to the county court, to which, however, we did not go. In the cases respecting which we applied to a magistrate, the sums that were due for subscriptions were very trifling indeed.

522. Did that have a salutary effect upon the others, and did the subscriptions come in afterwards?—I think it had a good effect.

523. Have you struck off many men for non-payment?—None.

524. (*Viscount Hardinge.*) You have stated that three-fourths of your men are mechanics and artizans. Can you tell the Commissioners what they earn per week on the average?—I cannot. I have one company composed of men who are in the employment of an extensive building firm, and another company consists of workmen belonging to an engineer establishment; and those men, I take it, are in the receipt of from 20s. to 50s. a week.

525. (*Lord Elcho.*) What probability is there that those men in your corps who have had their uniforms furnished to them, for which they have paid by instalments, will renew their uniforms when required?—I think they would renew their uniforms. Some of them may not; but I think that the majority of them would renew their uniforms when required to do so.

526. Would you have to enter into some arrangement for the purpose?—Yes, I think we should.

527. Would you do so after the experience you have had of the past?—Yes, I would do so with a large majority of the men. Most of them have paid well. Certainly there were some exceptions; but although we have been losers, on the whole the advances have been very creditably repaid.

528. But do you think that under such an arrangement you may reckon the loss at 10 per cent.?— I think that we shall lose 100l. out of 1,200l.

529. (*Viscount Hardinge.*) Have you taken advantage in any way of the Government offer and obtained cloth at a cheaper rate?—No; I have not been disposed to do so. I have found upon inquiry from the tailors that the gain would not be great, as they would have to charge more for the making.

530. You must bear in mind that this Government cloth will be carefully inspected by Government officers, and that you will be sure of obtaining a good article?—That would be an advantage, no doubt, but the tailors whom we employ have supplied us well, and as the foreman is a member of my corps, I am sure that if he furnished bad cloth the members would complain.

531. Your cloth is made up by a contractor?— Yes.

532. Entirely?—When I say that, I do not mean that I require members to go to a particular contractor, but in the case of members of the band, whom we clothe, and in the case of those who pay for their uniforms by instalments, we employ a contractor.

533. Would the issue of cloth by the Government, supposing it were issued in a piece, be a great assistance to your men, I mean to give the cloth gratis?— Yes, it certainly would be, but not so great as might be supposed; my own opinion is, and I have thought a good deal about it lately, that the best course is to let every volunteer find his own clothing, and that any assistance the Government can give should be in another direction. I find that some of those to whom clothing is given take very little care of it.

534. And very often does it happen that that is a man who attends less frequently at the drill?—I cannot so well speak as to that, because we have given no uniforms to effective members; the men I referred to belong to the band.

535. (*Lord Elcho.*) The result of your consideration of this question of Government aid is that it is your opinion that perhaps practically the best form in which it could be given would be a capitation allowance of so much for each volunteer?—Yes.

536. To be given not in any way to the individual volunteer, but to the commanding officer to expend for the good of the regiment in the way which he thinks best?—I think so; but if it were thought desirable not to leave it so much to the discretion of commanding officers, I should not have any objection to limit it to certain things, such as drill grounds, headquarters, rifle ranges, and appliances for special instruction.

537. You would confine it within certain limits? —Yes, to prevent the money being applied to any improper use.

538. Do you think it would be possible to give any assistance that might be required in kind?—No; I think not decidedly. I think it had better be given to be spent on certain things, at the discretion of the commanding officer.

539. (*Lord Overstone.*) I gather from your evidence that you feel considerable confidence as to your own corps, and you think you could maintain its efficiency without extraneous aid?—I think so.

540. Notwithstanding that, you are still of opinion that it would be a matter of expediency and prudence that aid should be obtained by a direct pecuniary grant from the Government, thereby enabling you to relieve your members from their annual subscriptions? —Yes; that is my opinion.

541. Have you carefully weighed the probable moral effect of such a course upon the character of

the members of the volunteer force?—Yes ; if a volunteer provides his own uniform and gives his time, which, as I have stated, may amount in my corps to at least three evenings in the week, I think that it would not have any demoralizing effect upon him to receive assistance in the nature of that which has already in some degree been extended to him. Instructors are already provided, and I would extend to him, as I have stated, assistance for the purpose of obtaining a rifle range, drill grounds, and other accommodations of that description. I think that the commanding officer would be the best judge as to how the money ought to be laid out, subject of course to his rendering accounts, and showing that what he receives had been properly expended.

542. The object of my question is to draw your attention to the distinction between the effect of a direct pecuniary grant avowed as a pecuniary payment by the Government to a corps, and the effect of an advance perhaps to the same amount ultimately but in a more indirect form, to assist the corps in bearing its various engagements, or, rather, relieving the corps from some charges which it is now subject to. I wish particularly to ascertain your opinion as to the different effect upon the feelings of the persons who constitute the corps in case of their receiving a direct pecuniary payment, contrasted with their being aided by Government pay, in the way of finding tools and providing a rifle range, and defraying the expenses of conveyance, and aiding in the expense of throwing up field works, or any other of the indirect forms through which aid might be extended to the corps, without its assuming what is ordinarily considered rather the humiliation of a direct payment?—I do not think that the fact of the payment being made in money to the commanding officer for special purposes would have any demoralizing effect upon the men.

543. You think that the sense of a direct payment would not militate against the principle upon which you have laid great stress, that it is extremely desirable that the men should feel that it is an honour and a privilege to belong to their corps?—I think that the men would consider that they were entitled, as they have hitherto been considered entitled, to some aid in the form of instruction and so forth, and that merely to extend it, as I propose, to what has been found absolutely necessary for the well-being of the corps, such as rifle ranges, &c., could have no prejudicial effect upon them.

544. What sort of influence or interference is now exercised by the members of your corps over the conduct and proceedings and management of the officers of the corps?—Under the regulations there is a committee to aid me in all financial matters, that committee meets frequently, and I avail myself very much of their aid ; it is formed of one officer of each company, and one member of each company not being an officer, and I take every opportunity of letting them know the position of everything connected with the corps ; I endeavour as much as possible to advise with them and to associate all of them in one common interest, so that each shall aid individually as well as collectively.

545. In the volunteer force I presume, of course, that every member of the force feels more entitled to exercise an independent judgment, and some interference or control in the general management of the corps, than would be the case in the regular military force?—I believe so, certainly.

546. That being so, do you not think that considerable danger and inconvenience might arise precisely in proportion as you entrust a commanding officer with a discretion in the management of funds received directly from the Government?—I have mentioned before, that I thought it desirable to confine within certain limits the expenditure of the money intrusted by the Government to commanding officers. If this were done, I do not think that there would be any prejudicial influence exercised by the members of the corps upon the commanding officer in the expenditure of the money.

547. If the money is to be paid to the commanding officer, with the express understanding that it shall be applied only to certain purposes, do not you think that considerable danger will arise, although the apparent inconvenience of making the corps the recipient directly of Government money would be avoided, from subjecting the commanding officer to the inconvenience and responsibility, apparently at least, of administering that fund?—I do not see what danger could possibly arise. I think that it would be very difficult for the Government to carry out the administration of such money satisfactorily ; in my own case I question whether it would be possible for the Government to go into all the minute arrangements which it would be necessary to make in order to deal with the expenditure of the money ; at all events the different corps could get what they want much better themselves.

548. I believe you have already stated that you have received from the Government the tools that are used in your earthwork operations?—Yes ; some of them.

549. Could you not, upon the same principle, receive from the Government a rifle range or a field in which to work, or the expenses of conveyance when you have to incur expenses in conveying your men to certain places for battalion drill and other purposes? —Certainly ; if the Government were to provide a rifle range or a field, then of course it would not be necessary for us to lay out any money for such objects ; that would be sufficient. But then arises the question whether the Government would be able to provide such accommodation in rifle ranges, drill grounds, and headquarters as each corps would require, and whether they could do so as cheaply and well as the different corps could for themselves.

550. After having had your attention pointedly drawn to the different considerations which affect direct pecuniary aid from the Government, or pecuniary aid in an indirect form, you are still deliberately of opinion that the direct form of aid would be the most practicable and desirable?—Certainly, I do think so. Looking at it in every point of view, I do think that a direct payment of so much per head would be the best mode of dealing with the question.

551. (*Lord Elcho.*) Do you know of any precedent for the Government so dealing, as you have suggested, with the volunteer force ; I mean in money?—No, I am not aware of any.

552. Are you aware of how the commanding officers of the Yeomanry corps receive what is called contingent allowance to be spent upon the corps?—I am not aware of the arrangement to which you refer.

553. (*Viscount Hardinge.*) You have stated that it would be impossible for the Government, were they to administer the funds proposed, to go into minute details respecting rifle ranges or any other part of the expenditure. Would not the Government, if they gave further aid in the shape of a capitation grant, have to examine very narrowly the details of the expenditure, and demand accounts from each corps?— Certainly ; I think that they should demand accounts at the end of the year, and that they should have such accounts submitted to them. When I spoke of the difficulty of the details, I meant that private persons can often make advantageous arrangements, which official correspondence would complicate, or perhaps altogether prevent.

554. Still, at the same time you admit, that in the case of a capitation grant the Government would necessarily have to go into considerable details of expenditure?—Yes ; I think that the Government ought to see that the money has been properly expended.

555. You have stated that you think the members of your corps ought to be released from their annual subscriptions after attending so many day's drill, what is the minimum amount of drill that you would think on those grounds sufficient?—I think I should not

Lieut.-Col. Macleod of Macleod.

30 May 1862.

F 2

Lieut.-Col.
Macleod
of Macleod.

30 May 1862.

he disposed to alter the number of days provided by the Act of Parliament. I believe that they would willingly attend that number of drills.

556. Are you aware what the number of drills specified by the Act of Parliament is?—I think it is 24 drills.

557. You are not aware that it is 18?—I was not aware of that.

558. Are you aware that by the regulations of the War Office no member should be returned as effective who has not been present at the annual inspection, of course excepting those who bring satisfactory excuses?—Yes, I am aware of that.

559. Have you strictly complied with that regulation?—This year our inspection does not take place, until the end of next month. With regard to last year, we had two days' inspection, the first day was for battalion drill, the second day was for engineering, and I believe that all my men were present with the exception of those who had leave of absence.

560. Have those men who have been present at the inspection all been passed into the battalion?—Yes, I think all have.

561. You have stated that you would leave the discipline pretty much as it is now in the volunteer corps. Have you ever experienced any inconvenience as to the appointment of officers or non-commissioned officers?—No; I appoint the non-commissioned officers after examination, and on the recommendation of captains of companies. With respect to officers, I have always recommended them for appointment on my own responsibility, but I have invariably consulted the members of a company whether the person I proposed to appoint would be acceptable to them; generally when there has been a vacancy I have requested the members to select two names, and I have made the appointment from those two.

562. Is that according to your rules?—No, there is no rule; I consider that the appointment of the officers should rest with me, but that I should endeavour to feel my way and ascertain that the appointments would be well received; I think that in the volunteer service it is of great importance that the officers should be popular with the men.

563. Do you think it is desirable for the Government to frame one set of rules for the whole force; you are aware, I presume, that at present each corps has its own separate set of rules?—Yes.

564. Would it be desirable, in your opinion, to alter that system?—The rules are nearly all founded upon the original rules adopted at the War Office at the commencement of the volunteer movement.

565. I presume you can only speak from hearsay as to other metropolitan corps?—I think it would be better to leave each corps to make its own rules.

566. For what reasons?—I have not considered the question much, but there must be many points of difference between the corps, and on that ground I think it desirable they should have an opportunity of making their own rules.

567. Having regard to the metropolitan corps, what differences do you allude to that would make it necessary to have a different set of rules for each?—In my own corps, for instance, with respect to the annual subscription, some pay one guinea, while others pay 13s.

568. But this is purely a financial question that does not affect the discipline of the corps. My question related to the rules affecting matters of discipline?—I may, perhaps, quote the following rule from our regulations as an example of a difference, for I doubt if it is to be met with in the rules of other corps: "All candidates to become officers must possess the special acquirements prescribed by the War Department, and will compete by a general practical and scientific examination, to be conducted as may seem best to the Secretary of State for War." Those rules were submitted by me to the Secretary of State for War, and he put in— "if he should think fit to give any directions on the subject." He has not seen fit to give any directions upon the subject, and therefore that portion of the rule has been inoperative.

569. What objection would there be to the Government laying down a special regulation for the examination of officers, if it were judiciously done?—I think it would probably prevent a good many men who would otherwise be very eligible indeed from entering a service in which they would have to undergo an examination.

570. Putting aside the question of examination, I ask you whether, generally speaking, rules judiciously framed by the Government might not be drawn up in a way that would be acceptable to the whole volunteer force?—I think it is desirable to observe general principles, undoubtedly, in the formation of rules; but I think there are, probably, shades of difference connected with every corps, which would make it desirable that each corps should have its own rules.

571. As to the system of drill, do you see any objection to the volunteer force having one uniform system of discipline, going from the setting-up drill upwards?—I think a uniform system would be very desirable.

572. (*Sir A. Campbell.*) You have stated that you have certain companies which are composed entirely of men in the employment of one firm; are those companies officered by their employers or by the overseers of their employers?—The captain and first lieutenant of the company of engineers are both in the firm. The company which is formed of men in the employment of the builder, is commanded by his brother-in-law.

573. Do you consider that a desirable mode of appointment?—I do, always with the reservation that they are eligible as officers.

574. (*Earl of Ducie.*) Have you ever had any difference of opinion with your men as to the selection of officers?—Never but once; one of the members had formerly been in the Turkish service, and was a capital drill; this man made himself so acceptable to a company of mechanics and artizans that they were extremely desirous of having him appointed as an officer; but as I could not recommend him for such an appointment, I told them so very frankly, and they acquiesced at once in my decision.

575. Do you generally find that the men are anxious to recommend persons having a good social position as officers?—Yes; and I think that the officers should have a good social position to have any weight with the men.

576. You have stated that the earnings of the men varied from 20s. to 50s. a week?—That was rather a guess.

577. Do you know that you have any men in the receipt of wages so low as 20s. a week?—Yes, I am sure there must be some.

578. Are they numerous?—No, I should think not very numerous. I have frequently asked applicants about whom I entertained any doubt whether they could afford to pay for their uniform, and have generally been informed that they were in the employment of a father or uncle, and would be assisted by them.

579. The persons who are in receipt of the lowest wages as you have mentioned are probably rising young artizans?—Yes, young men entering business, apprentices, perhaps, or those who have just served their apprenticeship.

580. (*Lord Overstone.*) What is your opinion of an effort being made to obtain further subscriptions from the honorary members, both as to the probable success of such effort and its expediency?—I have very few honorary members, and I think that there is no probability of increasing the number. My experience rather is, that honorary members, after having given one or two subscriptions, seem little inclined to continue them.

581. (*Sir A. Campbell.*) With regard to those artizans who receive small wages, do they lose any part of their wages by attendance at drill?—No.

Occasionally men may have left their work, and lost perhaps a quarter or half a day. We were invited to send a guard of honour to the Horticultural Gardens on the occasion of the opening of the great Exhibition, and 100 men were selected to form that guard of honour, they were the men who had attended the greatest number of drills in the course of the year, so many from each company, and I believe that some of those men sacrificed half a day's wages in order to go.

582. But that does not occur at the ordinary drills? —No; we do not drill until 7 o'clock in the evening.

583. (*Lord Elcho.*) You have stated that your subscription is a guinea for clerks, and 13s. for artizans? —Yes.

584. Is it not the case that there are many clerks in the receipt of 70l. and 80l. a year who can less easily afford their subscriptions than artizans who are in the receipt of 50s. a week?—Yes; I believe that may be so, and that artizans are often better able to pay than clerks; but then my object is to get artizans and mechanics, and not clerks.

585. You have said that you expect that when the time comes for renewing the uniform, you will have recourse to the same practice that you adopted when you first began, namely, to establish a sort of guarantee fund, and to allow the men to pay by instalments?—Yes.

586. Your guarantee in that case will be your present subscriptions?—Yes.

587. Suppose the plan which you have suggested to be adopted, and that the Government should make a capitation grant founded upon certain rules, you think that there would be no necessity for the subscriptions, but in that case you would have no fund to enable you to make an arrangement with regard to the clothing?—Unless the officers would guarantee the payment of the amount.

588. Do you think that in cases where there are corps which in a great measure have been clothed by extraneous aid, and which have not in themselves the means of renewing their uniforms, it might not be desirable to have a discretionary power, supposing a capitation grant to be given, to spend part of the money in the purchase of a second uniform, supposing that the men were ready to accept it?—My opinion is formed only from my experience of a London corps, but I do think it is not advisable that the public money should be spent upon the uniform in any shape.

589. (*Major Harcourt.*) You stated that the captains of companies are employed to collect the monies due by the men for their uniforms?—Yes.

590. Have you reason to suppose that they have suffered any loss, and that they have paid any money out of their own pockets?—No, none of them; all that I require them to do is to account for what they have received.

591. (*Viscount Hardinge.*) With regard to the tools furnished to you, are there any articles or materials that you think the Government could gratuitously supply, and which are not mentioned in this list?—Yes, there is a gabion invented, by Serjeant-major Jones, which I should like to have, there is a specimen of it in the Exhibition. I should also like to get some wood for gabions and facines; it would be very useful to us.

592. Have you got your full number of drill instructors?—I have two drill instructors, but that is not my full number.

593. What is your full number?—I am entitled to three drill instructors.

594. Cannot you procure them?—No; I have laboured under the greatest difficulty for the want of them; I have often applied, but cannot get them; the Royal Engineers have not got enough for themselves.

595. Have you had the two temporarily attached to you?—Colonel Clapman, of the Royal Engineers, informed me that they had no good instructors to give us, and that I must look about and try to find men for myself. I succeeded at last in finding a serjeant of the Royal Engineers, who had left the service for a considerable time. I procured his appointment, and he now receives the usual rate of allowance which is given to instructors. Another man, who belongs to the Royal Engineer force at South Kensington, and who used to drill us, has been under instruction for the last two months at Chatham, and I expect him up every day.

596. Do you give those two instructors any extra allowance?—None.

597. Do you give your adjutant any extra allowance?—None.

598. (*Major-Gen. Eyre.*) Do you consider that you have perfect power to enforce your orders?—Undoubtedly; my orders are always obeyed.

599. Do you think that there should be one uniform and clearly-defined system of discipline for all the volunteer corps?—I think there would be difficulties in carrying out any very strict system of military discipline. I think that volunteers would be very apt to feel and to resent any undue interference with them.

600. You think it would be unpopular?—Yes.

601. If I understand you rightly, every man who attends the drills, supposing them to amount to 18, is more or less out of pocket; that is to say, if he goes to the rifle range it will cost him 6d., or if he sacrifices a day's work he will be out of pocket?—I do not consider him out of pocket in attending the ordinary drills.

602. Not from loss of his time?—No. The day's work is over at seven o'clock. He is not out of pocket in attending from seven till nine.

603. Not necessarily out of pocket?—No.

604. Supposing him to have in some way to incur expense, and that Government aid were given to the extent of 1l. a man, would you allow that to be given to a man in proportion to the number of days that he had attended and been so put to expense?—I do not think that that would be at all desirable, and very open to abuse. I think that would never do.

605. (*Sir A. Campbell.*) And not even for travelling expenses?—No; I think that it would be impossible to carry out such a system as that. The only way in which I think aid could be given by the Government would be by supplying rifle ranges and drill grounds.

606. (*Earl of Ducie.*) Are not the visits to the rifle range and attendance at drills a substitute for other amusements and relaxations which the men had before?—I think to a certain extent they are. Mechanics and artizans have their own amusements; some perhaps go to public houses and smoke, but I think the better class do not; I think that many consider it a relaxation and amusement to come to drill.

607. But that class which can least afford it would be, if they were not attending drill, spending their money in some other amusement equally expensive, and perhaps less advantageous to them?—Probably so, but I cannot say.

Lieut.-Col. Macleod of Macleod.

30 May 1862

The witness withdrew.

Major MARCUS BERESFORD examined.

608. (*Chairman.*) You command the 7th Surrey Rifle Volunteers?—I do.

609. It consists of six companies?—Yes.

610. And the establishment per company is 100 men?—Yes.

611. How many men have you on the roll?—475.

612. At your ordinary battalion drills, how many of those men do you muster?—We generally have from 120 to 160. Sometimes considerably more, sometimes less, about once a month 220 to 260

Maj. M. Beresford.

F 3

Maj. M. Beresford.

30 May 1862.

613. How often do you have your battalion drills?—Every Saturday.

614. Are there company drills besides?—Yes; every Wednesday, and recruit drill every Monday.

615. Have you a rifle range?—I have, with the permission of Lord Elcho, the use of his range at Wimbledon twice a week; the two ranges 2nd and 3rd class.

616. Have many of your men gone through a course of musketry instruction at Hythe?—None with the exception of the adjutant; he has just gone through a course of instruction there and obtained a first-class certificate.

617. Do you find that your numbers diminish or increase?—I have received a considerable accession of men lately in the shape of a company of 80 men from the London Armoury company, less 25 who were before in the employment of that establishment and who were transferred to their own company; otherwise I think we are on the decrease rather than not.

618. Can you account for that in any way?—Yes, I can; the Lord Lieutenant of the county has limited me to six companies of the maximum of 100, and the consequence has been that within the last three months I have been compelled to refuse two or three offers of bodies of men numbering over 40 and over 60 because I had no vacant commissions to recommend the gentlemen for who made the offers. I have been obliged to forego admitting men to my regiment for the reason above stated, and it has acted most prejudicially to the increase of the strength of the regiment generally, the number of officers per 100 men being also limited to three.

619. You think that that has acted disadvantageously?—Decidedly.

620. Have you a regimental fund?—I have.

621. How is it formed?—It consists of the annual subscriptions of the rank and file, of one guinea a head per annum, paid in two half-yearly sums of 10s. 6d., and a subscription by honorary members of two guineas each per annum.

622. What do the officers pay?—The payment by the officers is three guineas, that is, that they each give a subscription as an honorary member, and each of them also a guinea as an effective member.

623. Have you a band fund which is perfectly distinct?—Yes; that is paid for by the officers, the privates pay nothing towards it; there is no compulsory payment by the privates but the guinea a year.

624. Do your privates supply themselves with their own uniforms?—Yes.

625. Have you assisted them from the regimental fund?—No, upon no occasion; but I should state that in the early stage of this regiment, before I had anything to do with it, excepting being an honorary member, there seemed no prospect of its being carried out, and I was solicited to have my name sent in for the command. It was supposed then that there were at least 70 or 80 men ready to join, but in anticipation that the corps would not be established, they joined other corps, and I found 8 men left, and in order to give a stimulus to the thing I was obliged to enter into an arrangement, and I advertised that I would equip 120 men, giving them credit for the equipment. I became responsible. I equipped 120 men, and I lost about 400l. by it. There are some 80 of those men who do not now come to drill, because they owe money for their equipments, and I have sent them circulars, telling them that if they will come to drill I shall not press them for the money, but they do not like to come because they owe me money; the amount I became responsible for was all paid off by me before the expiration of last year, and I have lost about 400l.

626. What was the total amount?—Originally it was quite 800l.

627. What is the financial position of your corps; have you a balance sheet?—Yes.

628. Just hand it in, and describe generally the state of your finances?—This is not a printed balance sheet, it was not prepared for this occasion. I prepared it last year when we were in debt, but I will send in a *bonâ fide* copy of the balance sheet at any time if the Commissioners wish for it. Briefly our expenses last year were over 1,127l.

629. What were your subscriptions?—I have the receipts for twelve months from the 1st July to the 30th of June, and the subscriptions were 837l.

630. What were the principal items of the expenditure?—Rent 206l. altogether, wages 296l.

631. The rent, I presume, was for headquarters?—Yes, and the drill shed.

632. What were the wages for?—They consisted of payments to an orderly-room clerk, to the serjeant-major, drill serjeant, and a man who cleans the arms; the drill serjeant assists in that work also; all the arms are kept on the premises in our armoury.

633. They are not given to the individual members to take care of?—No; they are in the armoury. I give the serjeant-major 30s. a week.

634. (*Col. MacMurdo.*) Independently of his Government pay?—Not now; this is for the last year; he has the same pay now, but of course what the Government pay him is deducted from the 30s.; these items are chiefly for 1861; the printing came to 59l.; the stationery to 23l. 10s.; travelling 7l. 10s.—(that was for the officials, the serjeant-major going to Wimbledon and Plumstead, and other men); clothing 44l. 15s., that is the clothing of the serjeant-major, and there are two or three officials whom we find in clothing; the expense of clothing this year will not exceed 20l. Then ammunition cost 33l. 18s. 7d.; law costs last year 130l. In March last year we moved into different headquarters; we were in Southwark and now we are in Lambeth. The agent of the landlord gave me authority to take possession, which we did; but the tenant who lived next door became alarmed and he went to the landlord and said that he should leave his house and that all the other tenants would do so likewise, and in consequence of this, and of the agreement not having been signed, an action was commenced in Chancery to eject me, but it did not succeed. The next item is, band instruments 23l. 13s., but that is not for our band, it is for bugles and big drum. We had also a dinner at Freemason's Tavern, and there is an item of 33l. which was paid out of the funds of the corps. The dinner cost 130l., but a large part of it was paid by the officers. A portion of the expense connected with the presentation of a bugle we considered ought to be paid out of the funds of the regiment, and it amounted to 33l. The miscellaneous expenses were 65l., for postage and odds and ends of all sorts. There was also a sum of 35l. premium paid to Messrs. Churchill and Sim to give up the lease which had been deposited with them by our predecessor, who was a bankrupt. Those items amounted to 820l. paid in cash, and with the unpaid bills Dec. 31 to 1,120l. I reckon our expenses during the current year at about 500l.; our rent will be reduced to 170l., including hire of rifle range, and wages, in consideration of what the Government allow, to 120l., as I have dispensed with the secretary and clerk also, and some other items will disappear. There will be no ammunition now, no law costs, except for the lease of the field and parade ground, no bugles, no "presentation" expenses, but the miscellaneous items will be as much as before.

635. Do you anticipate that your future income will be more than will cover your expenses?—No, I do not; the expenditure for the current year will be about 500l.

636. (*Earl of Ducie.*) The receipts being estimated at 320l.?—Yes. If we continue to have subscriptions from the rank and file.

637. (*Chairman.*) You anticipate that those subscriptions will amount to 320l.?—Yes, fully that.

638. And your expenses to 500l.?—Yes.

639. (*Lord Overstone.*) The funds that you anticipate you put down at about 300l.?—Yes; I think

TO INQUIRE INTO THE CONDITION OF THE VOLUNTEER FORCE IN GREAT BRITAIN.   39

they will quite equal that. I am rather depending upon letting the large drill shed which we have built lately. That has been built by a loan from one of my brother officers; he advanced the money and we have to pay off so much a year, and I look upon getting 100*l.* a year for the use of that and our drill ground. We have quarters, mess room, armoury, magazine, parade ground, a drill shed, and a drill field of three acres, all close together; we have been at very great expense, and we have just spent between 600*l.* and 700*l.*; it is a large shed 150 feet long by 60 feet in the clear.

640. That is an expense that will not occur again?—No, it will not, and I hope to get the cost of the shed back in the course of five years, by letting it to other corps.

641. Do you anticipate any diminution in the numbers of your corps?—I do. I do not see any hope of getting any additional men, for the reason I have already assigned; there are very few resignations, but I think when it comes to the question of new uniforms the numbers will decrease. The class of members that I have in my regiment consists chiefly of clerks in different establishments, and of artizans. I can state exactly what I received last year in guineas and half guinea subscriptions, and the number of defaulters. The number of the members who attended 24 drills or more during that year was 238. A very large number of them attended a great many drills. I exhibited the returns to Colonel MacMurdo some time ago, showing the number of men who had attended from 60 to 90 drills, and several of them over 30 and 40.

642. (*Viscount Hardinge.*) In one year?—Yes. I have one company of 80 men who all attended more than 24 times, not less than 30 drills in a year. The number who paid a guinea, for 1861, was 270; the number who paid half a guinea, for 1861, was 54; and those who neither paid the guinea nor the half guinea were 88, making in all 412, the strength of the regiment; but I should mention that the bulk of those 88 are men who owe money on the equipment account, and who, therefore, will not come.

643. Do you think that the efficiency of your corps can be maintained without assistance from the Government?—No; I am sure it cannot.

644. In what way do you think that assistance could be most beneficially afforded?—Perhaps I may first state that the nominal strength of the regiment being 475, the present effective strength of those who have attended drill during the last quarter is 338, showing a considerable increase. The number of men who have paid one guinea for this year is 78, and the number who have paid 10*s.* 6*d.* for this year is 112. It is quite optional whether they pay a guinea in the first quarter of the year or not; it is due thus: 10*s.* 6*d.* in January and 10*s.* 6*d.* in July. As to the mode of assistance, I do not think that the regiment ought to be put to any expense for cleaning arms, for instance.

645. How many of them have paid nothing at all this year?—They are represented by the difference between 190 and 395, as 80 members pay no guinea subscription, these three numbers making the total of 475.

646. (*Chairman.*) I understood you to say that nothing, in your opinion, should be paid to the men for the care of the arms?—No, certainly not. It takes two men the whole week to clean our arms. There is a recruit drill on Monday, company drill on Wednesday, and batallion drill on Saturdays.

647. Do you think there is any other expense that ought to be defrayed by the Government?—Yes, there is the question of rent. It costs me now 170*l.* a year, but that includes our quarters, parade ground, field, and rifle range; they come altogether to 170*l.*

648. In what way should the grant be made; by way of a capitation grant or should it be a special payment for those items of your expenditure?—I should consider a capitation grant better than anything else.

649. (*Col. MacMurdo.*) In what way would you apply it?—I should give an account of its application if necessary; and I should apply it in the payment of those items which I have enumerated. The circumstances and expenses of volunteer regiments vary much.

650. (*Chairman.*) What in your opinion should be the amount of such a grant?—I think in my own case, if I did not dispense entirely with the subscriptions of the privates, that 10*s.* annually per head would cover the expense, and leave us really free from the annoyance of having to beg for money. In December last, in order to provide funds for the amount that we were in arrear, in consequence of our law expenses and other matters, I and my brother officers subscribed 140*l.*, and that still left us owing 150*l.* for the last year. One of my brother officers this year lent the regiment 500*l.* for five years, in order to build the drill shed and to discharge the 150*l.* owing for 1861.

651. (*Col. MacMurdo.*) Have you made an estimate for your drill shed?—It is completed and paid for. It cost 368*l.*

652. (*Chairman.*) Do you think that a grant of 10*s.* a head, in addition to the subscriptions from the corps, would completely carry you through?—I think it would, if the rank and file are still to be called upon to subscribe.

653. What would your subscriptions then be reduced to?—They would be reduced to 10*s.*

654. What subscriptions would the officers pay?—An officer would pay three guineas a year as he does now. It must be remembered that the whole expense of the band falls upon the officers. I pay so much a year towards it, and the other officers pay according to their rank; the captains contribute six guineas a year, the lieutenants five guineas, and the ensigns four guineas, then we always have a collection at the end of the year to cover any deficiency.

655. What is the total cost of your band?—Not less than 100*l.* a year; then we found uniforms for the band, which were paid for by the officers. Nothing tends so much to bring the men together as a band; and when it plays on the parade ground, the members come there and bring their friends with them, and they can walk about there just as well as they could in a park.

656. Do you pay anything to your adjutant in addition to what he receives from the Government?—No.

657. (*Lord Overstone.*) You have spoken of the expenses which fall upon the officers, do you think that the pressure of that expense tends to check or discourage persons from undertaking the duty of officers, or to induce those who have undertaken it to resign?—No, I cannot say so.

658. Do you think that the expense which now falls not necessarily, but which morally presses upon the officers is at all a serious consideration with them?—I do not find it so in my own case in the 7th Surrey. The officers feel that as they hold commissions they ought to subscribe handsomely.

659. Do you think that a direct money grant from the Government is expedient for the purpose of supporting the volunteer movement?—I do most decidedly; I believe that the circumstances of every corps differ. I know that the circumstances of mine differ from others.

660. Do you consider that the sense of receiving direct pecuniary assistance from the Government would invalidate the voluntary principle upon which the whole force is founded?—Not in the least, as there would be no money payment to the volunteers.

661. Do you think that persons would not feel that either the honour of belonging to a volunteer corps or their free discretion as a volunteer body was invalidated by the sense that they received direct pecuniary assistance?—Not the least in the world. The assistance would be *indirect*.

662. If direct pecuniary assistance were given by

Maj. M. Beresford.

30 May 1862.

F 4

MINUTES OF EVIDENCE TAKEN BEFORE THE COMMISSIONERS APPOINTED

Maj. M. Beresford.
30 May 1862.

the Government, do you contemplate that it should be given to the commanding officer?—Yes.

663. Should it be placed in his hands under certain restrictions or perfectly free?—Under restrictions, that they should give a proper account of it. In my own case it would be quite immaterial; I want money to meet the expense of cleaning the arms. I think that that should be defrayed by the Government.

664. Do you think it is necessary that the money should be given direct to the commanding officer, subject to specific appropriations, or not, or would you be satisfied that the Government should intervene in a more direct form, such as bearing the expenses necessary for cleaning arms, for rent of quarters, parade ground, and so forth?—I should certainly advise that the Government should accompany any grant of that kind with restrictions.

665. If it be accompanied by restriction, that is to say by specific appropriations, would not that necessarily involve the rendering of a very accurate account by every commanding officer, and a very strict supervision of that account?—Decidedly; but every commanding officer ought to be prepared to give such an account.

666. Have you considered the extent of the ministerial trouble and the cost which this would involve?—I should think it would be very small indeed; the accuracy of the books should be certified by one individual; an auditor or accountant who should examine the accounts, and they are very simple.

667. (*Col. MacMurdo.*) Would it be very easy to do that for 1,500 corps?—I suppose that one accountant could do it easily for all the metropolitan corps.

668. (*Lord Overstone.*) Do you think that the placing of the money directly in the hands of the commanding officer would generate any feeling in the members of the corps generally that they were entitled to exercise some sort of control through the medium of public opinion upon the conduct of the commanding officer in the distribution of that money?—I think not.

669. You do not find that the desire through the medium of public opinion on the part of the corps generally to control the action of the commanding officer is inconvenient?—Not in the least.

670. You have not experienced that evil in any degree?—No; I am quite unfettered by committees or courts of any sort.

671. (*Lord Elcho.*) Have you a financial committee?—I have a regimental committee, which is called together once in three months, or oftener, as may be necessary, but it assists rather than controls me. I have our accounts audited every year by two auditors selected from the officers. The money, which is all paid into the bank, is in the custody of the treasurer of the regiment, Mr. Johnson, the chairman of the quarter sessions for Surrey. When I want money he sends me a cheque. The Government might avoid all expense of accountants if on giving pecuniary assistance to corps it were stipulated that every corps should appoint a treasurer, who should be a gentleman of known respectability, and that two officers should act as auditors to check the cash book, as in the 7th Surrey.

672. What sum of money do you contemplate receiving from the Government?—I think it would be from 250*l.* to 300*l.* a year.

673. Upon the supposition that you received 300*l.* a year from the Government, what number of men in really an efficient state do you conceive you could maintain?—Before I answer that question I should wish to be informed whether the Government proposes to do anything with respect to new uniforms.

674. My question was framed upon the assumption, according to your own principle, that you were to receive a direct pecuniary subvention from the Government, not exceeding 300*l.*, to be paid to you as commanding officer, and then in consideration of that I ask you what number of men you think you could maintain in a perfectly efficient state?—I should say decidedly at least 400 men, and if the restriction which I at present labour under were removed, a very considerably larger number, 600 men.

675. What restriction do you refer to?—I mean the limitation of the companies.

676. That having been imposed by the Lord Lieutenant?—Yes.

677. (*Earl of Ducie.*) If the number of your companies was increased the subvention from the Government would require to be proportionally increased, or do you mean that the 300*l.* would enable you to bring out 600 men?—I spoke of 10*s.* a head; I think that that would just cover it, if the rank and file are still expected to subscribe.

678. (*Lord Overstone.*) Having made the statement that the sum of 300*l.* from the Government would be amply sufficient to assist you, upon the assumption that you receive that amount of aid from the Government what number of men could you hold out an assurance would be maintained in a perfect state of efficiency?—I should say at least 400.

679. (*Lord Elcho.*) You said if the restrictions were withdrawn; that I suppose means if you were enabled to form more companies?—Yes.

680. What is the present strength of your companies?—I have two of 80, and the rest, which are supposed to be 60, were formed before we were limited to 100; they are approaching 60 or below that.

681. Your present maximum strength is 100 is it not?—Yes.

682. You say that you have companies of 80, and of various strengths, what number do you average per company on parade in an ordinary battalion drill. Do you see half of your company on the average?—Not on the average.

683. Suppose a company is composed of 80 men, do you see 40 of that company?—Not every Saturday.

684. Supposing a company to consist of 80 men, do you see on the average 25?—Yes; I should say so, quite that.

685. At your battalion parade do you generally drill with six or with four companies?—With six on Saturdays, if the muster be strong enough.

686. What is your average strength?—I cannot say at this moment.

687. Would it be better if they were stronger?—Decidedly.

688. Is there a prospect of a great increase in your corps?—Yes, decidedly.

689. Do you mean if you could add to the number of the companies borne upon your books?—Yes.

690. (*Viscount Hardinge.*) Do you mean an increase of the number of the companies, or an accession of strength to the existing companies?—I mean to the number of the companies; I wish to increase the number of the companies.

691. (*Lord Elcho.*) Do you think that if you had eight companies you would have enough, and do you believe that you would have eight full companies on parade?—Not as a regular thing; I should never have less than six.

692. What is the largest muster that you have ever had?—I had at Brighton 320 men.

693. Including the band?—Yes; and I think that the largest muster that I have ever had was about last May twelve months, when we were inspected by Colonel MacMurdo; then there were nearly 400 men present of all ranks.

694. Is it desirable in your opinion to increase the maximum number in the companies to 150?—It would not be of the least use in the world.

695. Would it not have the effect of taking more men on to the parade?—No.

696. If you had 150 men on your books, you would be more likely, would you not, to have a good muster than if you have only 100 men per company?—If you have more companies there is a competition on

the part of the men of the several companies, a spirit of emulation.

697. That would equally exist, would it not, if you increased the number in the companies?—No; if you raised the maximum to 150, I do not see how you could have so many companies.

698. Would it not be better to have six companies of 150 men, thereby insuring a good muster on parade, than to have eight companies of 100 each, which would result in having a much smaller number on parade per company?—I think not.

699. (*Col. MacMurdo.*) I understood you to say that you could not bring in those 40 men to whom you referred unless they came in as a distinct body?—No, unless I could admit the officer with them. Such bodies of men generally come accompanied by some gentleman who wants a commission.

700. Could they not come in by way of filling up the other companies?—Yes, I could do that. I have one or two weak companies, and I could amalgamate them and call them companies No. 3, or No. 5, or No. 6. I was offered over 40 men on Saturday last.

701. How did you propose to bring in the leader as an officer, was there a vacancy in the establishment?—No; it was because there was no vacancy that I could not accept the men, the men would not come without him.

702. (*Lord Elcho.*) What probability is there that the uniform will be renewed in your regiment?—I think it will last another year.

703. But when worn out what probability of a renewal will there be?—I do not believe that 12½ per-centage of the men will renew their uniforms, that is, I do not believe that they will be able to renew them.

704. (*Lord Overstone.*) Why do you fix upon that remarkable per centage of 12½ per cent.?—In this way; I look at the men who have paid a guinea for the year, the number is 78, and that is a good deal more than 12½ per cent., but there is a considerable number, in fact I do not know of more than about that per-centage of the men who are able to find their own uniforms.

705. (*Lord Elcho.*) Have you any scheme in your own mind for the renewal of the uniforms?—None whatever, except by Government assistance.

706. Did you include in the 10s. a head which you mentioned the renewal of the uniform?—Certainly not.

707. Then you look upon the 10s. a head, I presume, merely to meet certain incidental expenses which are common to all volunteer corps?—Yes.

708. Not including clothing?—No.

709. That is a separate branch of the subject?—Quite so.

710. Do you anticipate that without receiving assistance in the shape of clothing from the Government, your corps will cease to exist?—I do, or the greater part of it.

711. In what way, if you could obtain what you wish, would you desire the Government's assistance to be given; in cloth, or in the uniform made up, or in the shape of a sum of money towards it?—I should much prefer it in money, my experience of Government cloth is, that I do not think it is of much value.

712. (*Col. MacMurdo.*) What has been your experience of the quality of Government cloth?—In some regiments, such as I inspected the clothing of at Dover, I never saw more scandalous stuff in my life. When I was at Dover I went into that question particularly, and the cloth was full of shoddy.

713. What are your views as to the way in which assistance should be given by the Government?—It should be given in money, with restrictions as to accounting for it; there should be some checks. I am perfectly satisfied that you could get the uniforms made up of better materials and quite as cheaply as the Government could supply the cloth and people to make them.

714. What amount would you consider requisite to provide for such an outlay—how much per head?—The first uniform that we had in the 7th Surrey cost 7l. 10s., including belts and everything; I reduced that down to four guineas.

715. What is the present cost of your uniform?—Four guineas.

716. (*Sir A. Campbell.*) How long will the uniform last?—Four years.

717. (*Lieut.-Col. Barttelot.*) Of what does the uniform consist?—A tunic, trowsers, cap, and belts.

718. Do you wear a helmet?—No.

719. (*Viscount Hardinge.*) You have referred to 80 men who you said did not attend in consequence of being in debt to you, are they effective members now?—Not many of them.

720. And they are not returned as such?—No, they are not. The returns which I made are *bonâ fide* returns.

721. (*Lord Elcho.*) Would you undertake to keep up your regiment and clothe it and find all that is requisite, including incidental expenses, for 1l. a man?—The question of clothing is imminent now, but I think I could if the 1l. per man were paid on the nominal strength of the regiment.

722. (*Sir A. Campbell.*) If either the cloth for the uniforms or the uniforms themselves were supplied at the public expense, what security would the Government have that the men would remain in the regiment until the uniforms were worn out?—None at all while the present regulations last, under which a man can resign in 14 days.

723. Would you propose to alter that regulation?—I think not, if you altered it I think it would be fatal to the movement.

724. (*Major-Gen. Eyre.*) Is your recruiting confined to any particular area?—No, it consists of men chiefly in that particular neighbourhood, Camberwell, Newington, and Southwark.

725. Does the fact of its not being so confined at all interfere with others, or are you interfered with by others?—No, not that I am aware of.

726. (*Lieut.-Col. Barttelot.*) How do you appoint your non-commissioned officers?—According to merit. I make all the appointments myself.

727. (*Chairman.*) Do you appoint all the officers as well as non-commissioned officers?—Yes, I recommend the whole of them to the lord lieutenant.

728. Have you anything further to state?—I wish just to mention with reference to taxes that the year before last I applied to the Inland Revenue Department to remit the house tax; they had the matter for a considerable time under consideration, and they very considerately waived that tax, except a small sum for the serjeant-major's quarters. I then also made an appeal for the purpose of being excused poor rates, and I was told by the vestry in Kennington that if they had the authority of the Government they would be very glad to do it, that they wished to let us off all those taxes if possible, but that authority has not been obtained.

729. Those apply to the headquarters of the regiment?—Yes, I do not think that the serjeant-major's quarters should be taxed, he is there as having the custody of the armoury and of the books.

730. (*Col. MacMurdo.*) They are on the premises, the headquarters?—Yes.

731. (*Chairman.*) Have you any further observation to make?—I may mention that I have no rifle range, and that each year I am obliged to go as a beggar to Lord Elcho, who has very kindly acceded to my request. It is the only thing that we want besides money, and if he had refused we should have had to go down to Plumstead. The rifle range is our only great want.

732. (*Major-Gen. Eyre.*) You collect your arms in the armoury?—Yes.

733. It seems to be more frequently the practice to leave them in the possession of the men, do you find any difficulty with the men as to that?—No, they chiefly live in the neighbourhood, and when we march home to headquarters, they deposit their arms.

Maj. M. Beresford.
30 May 1862.

G

42   MINUTES OF EVIDENCE TAKEN BEFORE THE COMMISSIONERS APPOINTED

Maj. M. Beresford.

30 May 1862.

734. After the drills does every man come and leave his arms there?—Yes.
735. And somebody else cleans them?—Yes, I have two men constantly cleaning arms.
736. (*Sir A. Campbell.*) You do not let the men clean them?—No.
737. (*Chairman.*) Do you consider it is desirable that there should be a certain number of drill days fixed for every year?—Most certainly; and that the several corps of a county should drill together. I have been out twice with Lord Elcho's regiment, and once with the 12th Surrey.
738. (*Col. MacMurdo.*) Do you think that the War Office should regulate these things?—Yes.
739. But how would it be if certain corps declined to come?—I do not think that they would if the commanding officers were not allowed to indulge their own views about these things so much. If you put it honestly to the men, and say "Would you like to go out," the men would always wish to go.
740. (*Lord Elcho.*) Have you found that attendance at brigade field days affects the subsequent battalion drills?—Yes, for a month at least.

741. You then find a falling off?—Yes, but after a month it comes round.
742. (*Sir A. Campbell.*) But beforehand does it improve the attendance?—It does decidedly; I say to the men, "Unless you attend so many drills or come pretty regularly you will not be allowed to fall in," and that has always had a good effect; they then have something in store.
743. (*Chairman.*) Have you any other further suggestion to make?—Only this, that I think commanding officers should not have the power of refusing to let their men go if they do not choose to go themselves to Brighton, Wimbledon, or other places on the occasion of grand field days, where they might fall in with other regiments, or go individually in uniform to those places; I say that if they exercise that sort of authority it is enough to damp the ardour of those men.
744. Do you propose that the men should be allowed, when their own regiment is not going, to go themselves and join other regiments if the commanding officers of those other regiments approved of their falling in?—Yes.

The witness withdrew.

Viscount Enfield.

Viscount ENFIELD examined.

745. (*Chairman.*) I believe you are no longer a volunteer officer?—No; I am honorary colonel.
746. The Commissioners understand that you wish to make some suggestions to them?—Hardly suggestions. I thought perhaps I should be able to answer any questions which the Commissioners might think fit to put to me, having had some 16 or 17 months' experience in the command of a regiment.
747. Has your experience in command of a regiment led you to suppose that the volunteers can be maintained in their present state of efficiency?—I should say certainly not.
748. In what respect do you think there is any failure?—Simply in financial matters; that is the great difficulty. I do not think there is any falling off in the enthusiasm of the men or the good feeling which exists among the officers and the men, but I believe, speaking only from my experience of my own regiment, that the financial difficulty is so great that, unless some means are adopted to remedy that, there will be a great falling off in the numbers.
749. Had you any regimental fund?—Yes.
750. Did the officers contribute to that fund to a certain extent?—The annual subscription was a guinea for all ranks, but the officers have now a graduated scale of expenses as to their band fund, which was a great disturbing element in my corps as to the finances. We pay in proportion to our rank.
751. Did you keep the expenses of the band separate and distinct?—Yes.
752. Did your annual subscriptions cover the expenses of the corps?—Our annual meeting was held at the end of January, and this year we had a slight balance in hand; all the expenses of last year were covered.
753. (*Viscount Hardinge.*) At what date was that?—I think it was on the 14th of January, but I am not quite certain.
754. (*Chairman.*) Did the members of your corps clothe themselves entirely?—I believe so, from the time I had the command entirely. I am not sure whether before it was a consolidated battalion some of the uniforms were not given, but every man since I had the command paid for his own uniform.
755. Without any assistance from the regimental fund?—Yes; except the uniform of the band.
756. When the clothing requires renewal, do you think that the men will be able to bear the expense of it?—I have great doubts on that point. If I were asked to say yes or no, I should say no. The uniform is very inexpensive; the whole cost, including the shako, was under 5*l.*
757. Did that cover the accoutrements, as well as

the cost of the clothing?—It would cover the cost of the old accoutrements, but not of the new pouch and belt that we were to have.
758. The uniform consists of a tunic, trowsers, and shako?—Yes; and a forage cap.
759. No knapsack?—No.
760. Any cloak or great-coat?—There is a greatcoat, but the men in the regiment do not assume it generally. Any member who chose to wear it was allowed to appear in it. I have not included the cost of the great-coat.
761. What was the principal expense?—The band. If it had not been for that, I believe that my corps would have been able to pay its way; but instead of being content with one band it had two bands; and I believe that to be the disturbing element in the finances of a portion of the volunteer force.
762. What did the bands cost?—I am afraid I cannot state the exact sum, but I think it cost very nearly 300*l.* a year. The main portion of our expenses was something like 380*l.*, which included a share of a rifle range, headquarters, pay to the serjeant major and to drill instructors.
763. Did you give any additional pay to the drill instructors?—Yes, in two cases. I think we gave quarters and 7*s.* a week to a musketry instructor and armourer serjeant, who came with very good recommendations. They would not come for the Government allowance, and we gave them 7*s.* a week extra and quarters.
764. Did you pay anything extra to the adjutant?—Not to my knowledge. I believe not, except quarters. He lived rent free in our head quarters, where the serjeant-major and the armourer serjeant lived.
765. The bands were the great expense?—Yes.
766. Would not one band have been sufficient?—Quite so; and I always tried to induce them to be content with one band; but I was over-ruled, both by the officers and by the volunteers who assisted in the council which we had to conduct the affairs of the regiment, and I gave it up as hopeless.
767. (*Lord Overstone.*) Did I rightly understand you to say that in your opinion it is essential that the Government should intervene in a pecuniary way for the purpose of supporting an expenditure which you have stated to be, in your judgment, an improper one?—Certainly not. I stated, I believe, that I was afraid, unless some change was adopted as to the volunteer force, it might go down in numbers, but I did not venture to suggest that the Government should bear any additional pecuniary expenses. I consider that to be a very delicate question, and a very difficult one to deal with. I have not made up

my mind upon it. I said that unless some change was adopted as to the way in which the expenses of the volunteer corps were met, that there would be, I feared, a very great falling off in the numbers.

768. You stated that the expenditure in your corps was 300*l*. a year for bands, and 380*l*. for other expenditure?—Yes; speaking from memory.

769. You consider that the cost for the bands was very extravagant?—Yes.

770. Under those circumstances, do you not think that a reasonable and proper regard to economy and good management on the part of your corps would be the proper remedy for its difficulties?—Yes; but there is this: I have always found, both at the meetings of the council of the regiment, that were held once a month, and also at the annual meetings, that the volunteers would get up and say that unless they had the advantage of two bands to accompany them when they marched out the regiment would probably not attend; and last year, on Whit Monday, an incident occurred. We were to march out into the country for battalion drill. The drum and fife band attended, but the full band did not attend, and several of the men fell out and said that they would not go out unless they had the two bands to accompany them. I remonstrated with them, but it was of no avail, and the men left me.

771. (*Sir A. Campbell.*) Did the men fall out after they had once fallen in?—Yes.

772. (*Col. MacMurdo.*) What course did you pursue?—I stated that I considered it to be a very unsoldierlike proceeding, but there are no means of enforcing discipline; unless a man chooses to obey he may give me notice and go away; I thought it best not to take any further notice of it.

773. You are aware, I presume, that you could have placed those men under a guard during the drill and have suspended them afterwards?—Yes, but that would have been rather a harsh measure, and I thought it not wise to adopt it.

774. (*Viscount Hardinge.*) You are perhaps not prepared to offer any suggestions to the Commission as to the shape in which any further aid should be given to the volunteer force?—Only this, that supposing it was determined that additional Government aid should be granted in money, I should be very sorry to see it vested in anybody but the commanding officer; supposing that he had a certain sum placed in his hands, and he was held responsible by the Government for it, I think there would not be such difficulties arise; for instance, with regard to maintaining two bands, the commanding officer might say to his counsel I am responsible for this sum of money, and I will have it laid out in the most economical and best manner for the interests of the corps; but if the commanding officer was to be controlled in any way by the members of the regiment as a council I think there would be great difficulties, which I should be very sorry to see a man placed in. Suppose a commanding officers with four or five other officers to assist him, some disputes and jealousies would most probably arise, but I do not think that if the money were placed in the hands of the commanding officer it would be wasted.

775. You have probably heard the question canvassed as to the shape in which Government aid should be afforded; would you prefer a capitation grant to a gratuitous issue of clothing by the Government?—Individually I should like 1*l*. a head for each efficient man present at the official inspection of the corps.

776. (*Lord Overstone.*) In your judgment could a Government justify itself to the public in giving any direct pecuniary aid to maintain the efficiency of a regiment which declares that it will not perform its duties or keep up its organization unless it has two bands at its command?—I should say certainly not; but permit me to say that it is a very different question where it is money voted by the members of a corps, and where it is money which is contributed by the Government; I think that when the volunteers contribute it themselves they look upon their corps as self sustaining, and they think that they have a fair right to take exception to the arrangements made by their commanding officers or the council. I think, as I stated before, that the commanding officer ought to be held alone responsible, and he might then be able more easily to check any attempt at insubordination or interference as to the disposal of money than in the case of my own regiment, where there is the difficulty which I have mentioned as to the two bands.

777. I ask you whether in the case of a corps which exhausts its own available funds in the maintenance of an extravagant band, the Government could justify itself to the public for granting any pecuniary assistance direct from the Government funds for the purpose of meeting the other more necessary expenditure of the regiment?—When your Lordship uses the words "exhausting its own available funds," I must remind you that I have already stated that we had a balance in hand, even after the expenses of the two bands were paid.

778. I mean so far exhausting their own funds as to require Government aid?—That has always struck me as one of the most difficult points with regard to the volunteer force, as to whether the Government would be justified in granting a rate in aid for what I must call very extravagant expenditure as to bands. Everybody has their own hobby upon that subject, but my aim always has been, if possible, to put down extravagant bands.

779. Do you not think that the volunteer principle in organization is this, that so long as they provide for their own expenditure they are entitled to exercise the most free discretion as to that. But before they can come with reason, or with propriety, to ask for a subvention from the Government, they must come as it were with clean hands, that is, they must show that they are not incurring an expenditure beyond that which is reasonable and necessary for the avowed purposes of their organization?—Most certainly.

780. (*Lord Elcho.*) Suppose we leave the band out of the question entirely, whether it be one or two, do you consider that there will be subscriptions enough raised in your corps, so that when the uniforms come to be worn out there will be a sufficient number of men in your corps able to supply themselves with a second suit, so as to ensure the permanence of that corps?—I have very great doubts upon that subject.

781. Wholly irrespective of the bands?—Yes; I have not taken the question of the uniform into consideration; at present the uniform is in very good order, and I hope it will last this year and another year; but I have never considered the question of the expense of the uniform.

782. Are there many men in arrear with their subscriptions in your corps?—This year I cannot say; but last year we were obliged to take legal proceedings against some of them who were in arrear; and when the summonses were issued the men came forward and paid. And we had a surplus in hand after we had paid all our expenses.

783. Putting all extravagance out of the question, for bands or otherwise, whether they are met by extra subscriptions or the subscriptions of the corps, I presume that you consider a band on a moderate scale an essential component part of a regiment?—Yes; one band at a moderate expense ought certainly to be kept up.

784. Without a band, I suppose there would be very great difficulty in getting the men to march?—I think it would be almost impossible.

785. And the extent to which the band is carried is entirely a question of prudence?—Yes.

786. (*Chairman.*) Your Lordship's opinion as to a capitation grant has no reference whatever to the clothing?—No. I have not considered that question; but I cannot help thinking that in some corps there would be a great feeling, amounting, I was going to

G 2

Viscount Enfield.
30 May 1862.

say, to degradation; and certainly that is the nearest to what I desire to express. I think that the men would dislike to be clothed at the Government expense; but that they would not dislike knowing that a sum of money was placed in the commanding officer's hands to keep up their status.

787. (*Viscount Hardinge.*) Would the men mind having cloth issued to them?—I do not think they would mind that. I think that if a proposal were made to my own regiment, and they were asked whether they would prefer Government assistance in the shape of 1*l.* or 15*s.*, or whether they would prefer having cloth issued at the contract price, they would say that they would prefer the money at so much per head instead.

788. (*Lord Elcho.*) You would not contemplate, whether it was 15*s.* or 1*l.*, that the money should be given to the man himself under any circumstances?—Most decidedly not. I think that that would lead to extravagance, and all the evils of the present system would be tenfold increased.

789. (*Chairman.*) The money being given to the commanding officer, the application of it would be limited to certain items?—Yes; and he could resist any application of the money to what he considered unfair purposes.

790. (*Viscount Hardinge.*) What security would the Government have that the money was properly expended?—The security would perhaps be difficult to get; but every commanding officer, I should say, ought to send in every year a statement of the exact expenses to the proper authorities, with a balance sheet, supposing that the aid came in the shape of money.

791. Such an account would have to be examined and audited by the Government, would it not?—I think so, in order to ensure that the money had been fairly expended.

792. (*Lord Overstone.*) Do you mean an account giving a general statement of how the money had been expended, or an account accompanied with vouchers to be regularly audited?—The more closely it was examined the better, but that perhaps would entail a great deal of further expense at the War Office; probably they would require to have more clerks and more persons to look into those vouchers; but a plain statement on the one hand of so much for headquarters, so much for armourer serjeant, so much for band, so much for rifle range, so much for expenses for drill instructors, and so much for other expenses, specifying them, would, I think, fully answer the purpose.

793. (*Sir A. Campbell.*) Certified of course by the commanding officers?—Yes, something like what takes place in the militia. "I have examined these "accounts, and, to the best of my belief, they are "correct."

794. (*Viscount Hardinge.*) Are you aware how many corps there are in the force generally?—No.

795. Are you aware that there are about 1,500?—No, I have no notion how many there are.

796. If the vouchers were produced according to your proposal the War Office would have to look into the accounts of 1,500 corps?—Yes, and I suppose that that would entail very great additional expense in clerks. I think that something might be allowed for the discretion of the commanding officer, and that a simple statement with a balance sheet of the expenses and receipts on the one hand with his certificate at the bottom, stating that he had examined the accounts, and that to the best of his belief or upon his honour he believed them to be correct, would be as fair and simple a way of meeting the difficulty as any other.

797. (*Chairman.*) The establishment of your corps is 10 companies of 100 men each?—Yes.

798. How many men were enrolled?—I think 815.

799. Were they all of the artizan class?—They varied; two companies were not of the artizan class; they were composed of men rather in a better position of life,—clerks in offices; but the other companies consisted almost entirely of the artizan class.

800. (*Sir A. Campbell.*) What have been your musters?—About 50 per cent. on great occasions. I think last year that I had exactly 50 per cent. present; I never had more.

801. At the ordinary battalion drills what has been the muster?—They vary very much; sometimes very bad indeed. I never had more than 50 per cent. I took down 50 per cent. to Wimbledon, and 50 per cent. to Brighton.

802. (*Lieut. Col. Barttelot.*) What is your strength at the present time?—I think it is 610.

803. (*Col. Mac Murdo.*)—Have the numbers fallen off?—Yes; very much indeed; men are not able to pay their subscriptions, and they have come and said "I am insolvent, and must beg to have my name struck off."

804. (*Viscount Hardinge.*) Do you give any extra allowance to the adjutant?—I believe not; if anything is given, it is done without my sanction and knowledge; they do give him quarters.

805. (*Lieut. Col. Barttelot.*) Do you recruit in any particular part of London, or all over London?—I believe it is understood that we do not recruit out of our own district; there is a certain district which is assigned to a certain number of regiments.

806. (*Lord Elcho.*) Would it be advisable, do you think, to double up small regiments?—Certainly.

807. And to divide London into districts, permitting men to volunteer only within their own districts?—Yes, if possible; I think that would prevent a little poaching on the part of commanding officers, and it would be a great advantage.

808. Would the men like it, do you think?—I think that it would work practically well. I find in my own case that the men who have to come a shorter distance to drill attend more punctually than those who have come a longer distance.

809. (*Maj.-Gen. Eyre.*) Are your arms deposited in the armoury?—Yes; I used to call them in four times in the year. I allowed the men to take them home, making the captains of the companies responsible for their production if necessary, for the purpose of being kept in proper order. I called them in two or three times in the year, and I generally found them in a very good order. My armoury was not large enough to hold them all; but it would hold a great many. They are not kept in the armoury, except when called in as I have stated.

810. (*Sir G. A. Wetherall.*) Do you limit your recruiting to artizans and labourers, and to men who earn a certain amount of wages?—No; but I require that a man's respectability should be guaranteed by some member of the corps.

811. (*Col. MacMurdo.*) When I inspected your corps last year you had no rifle range. Have you obtained one since?—Yes; we have joined with Colonel Bigg's regiment, the 20th, and with Colonel Jenkes's, the 37th.

812. In one range?—Yes; the 37th, the 29th, and the 20th have one range between them.

813. Where is the range?—At Willesden.

814. What does it cost each man to go down there?—He is taken there and back for about 1*s.* 6*d.*

815. (*Lord Overstone.*) If you were personally responsible for maintaining the efficiency of the present volunteer movement, what steps would you take?—With great respect, I must decline answering that question.

816. What step do you think this Commission ought to recommend for that purpose?—That is a very wide question, but I think I may sum it up under two heads. First, with regard to expense, I should say so much per man for a regiment which presents a certain number of men at their official inspection. I would not pay attention to any returns. I should say that on a given day when a certain number of men are officially inspected, I would give that regiment so much per head. I will not specify the sum, but I think 1*l.* would be ample. I think it might be done

for less. Then I would discourage to the greatest degree the expenditure in bands, which I look upon as wholly useless, and consider that they have been productive of the greatest mischief with regard to the finances of corps.

817. (*Viscount Hardinge.*) You would probably qualify your answer when you say the bands are wholly useless, because you stated before that a corps would probably not be got to march out without a band?—I mean a good drum and fife band, which could be maintained at a very small expense. I consider that necessary, but I think the expense of the brass band is a matter which in a rich corps might be afforded, but in a poor corps ought not to be tolerated.

818. (*Chairman.*) Have all your men had rifle practice?—We have a range where they might all have gone.

819. Where actual shooting takes place?—Yes, but I cannot say that they have all gone.

820. Have a large proportion gone?—Yes, but not all.

821. (*Lord Elcho.*) Is the expense of attending brigade field days borne by the men themselves?—Yes, but that has been very trifling.

Viscount Enfield.

30 May 1862.

The witness withdrew.

Mr. JOHN PETTIE examined.

822. (*Chairman.*) You belong to the London Scottish Volunteers?—Yes.

823. What rank do you hold?—I am colour serjeant.

824. Can you speak to the influence of volunteering on the artizans?—Yes, I am an artizan.

825. In what trade are you occupied?—In building.

826. Do you belong to a company composed of artizans?—No.

827. Have you observed in the conduct of the artizans of that class who belong to your corps the influence that it has upon their conduct in private life?—Yes.

828. Will you just state to the Commissioners what the results of your observations have been?—They have evidently got an object that detaches them from irregular courses, they have fixed times when they know their services will be required, and they prepare for those times, and that causes them to be more regular in their habits in other respects.

829. You consider that they have improved in their habits and that they have become more orderly than they were before?—Yes, I do.

830. Do the men in your company find their own uniforms?—I am not attached to a company which is composed exclusively of artizans; there are in the London Scottish, or there were originally, 340 who entered as artizans, being admitted without paying any entrance fee; about 50 of those availed themselves of the privilege of gaining admission without paying the entrance fee, and provided their own uniforms. The others had their uniforms provided for them, with leave to pay by instalments, through a committee of artizans; at present 170 have paid entirely, and about 110 owe sums ranging from 3*s.* to 3*l.* That is the financial position in which they are; but if I may volunteer a suggestion, the circumstances under which we were formed were exceptional, and any loss that may occur now would be a higher per centage than if we began again with our present experience.

831. You think that most of the arrears will be paid in the end?—Not the arrears incurred in this first organization; there will be an average default of about 10 per cent. My knowledge of the artizan volunteers is not confined to those that I am speaking of in our own corps, but I consider that the average loss will be about 10 per cent., taking in all the corps in the metropolis.

832. Do you consider that that class of artizans if assisted in that way would be able to find their own uniform, that is, if allowed to pay for it by instalments?—A great number will, but there are other expenses which may cause some to leave in consequence of not being able to provide their uniforms, and pay the other expenses also.

833. Is there not this advantage in a man paying for his own uniform, that he is more likely to take care of it?—I think not. I think that in all cases where a volunteer is effective he will be careful of his uniform.

834. Even if it were provided by the Government?—Yes.

835. (*Lord Overstone.*) Do you think that a man would be as careful of clothing provided at another person's expense as of clothing provided at the expense of which was met by himself?—Yes, I believe so. My opinion is, although I have no facts to sustain it, that he would be more careful, knowing that it would be subject to inspection.

836. (*Chairman.*) A volunteer can now quit a regiment on giving 14 days' notice?—Yes.

837. Then what security would the Government have, in case they provided the clothing, that the volunteer would not leave the regiment?—It would depend upon the manner in which the aid was administered. If it was administered through the commanding officer, then it would be his property, and would be left when the resignation was accepted.

838. Do you think that it would be more acceptable to a volunteer to be clothed in that way, and that commanding officers should receive a sum of money to enable them to provide the clothing?—I believe so; and there are many things that would make me believe that you would not get any recruits on holding out to them that the uniform would be given to them, if it were publicly known that it was to be provided at the expense of the Government; but if the aid was given through the commanding officers, subject to their discretion in the way of affording it to such volunteers as might require it and be deemed worthy, then no one could say who had got their uniforms for nothing and who had not.

839. Can you suggest any means by which to render the volunteer service more acceptable to the artizan class?—The facilities for shooting might be improved, for ball practice developes a competitive spirit that makes volunteering more attractive; it is very attractive now amongst them; many of those who cannot join are very fond of it; and there is no jealousy even amongst the very lowest class of workmen against those who are in the ranks. It is very attractive to many who cannot enter on account of the expense and time necessary, for the number of parades that are always taking place would call upon their time more than they could afford; and also when they do join they are able to do nothing but march out and parade. But they like the shooting; and if there were covered drill grounds in the large towns, or in the parks, and each drill ground had a diminished target, if it was only 50 yards range, but so as to get them to fire off and hit the target. They get a liking to it, which attaches them to the service. I have noticed, that those who can shoot ball, will sacrifice a good deal rather than leave the corps.

840. Would it not be almost impossible, in populous districts, to provide these rifle grounds?—It might be so; it is a question for the authorities. There are many artizans who have been ardent volunteers, but have become disheartened because they cannot get away to ball practice; but I see that the others are much more strict in their attendance if they can hit the target.

841. (*Sir A. Campbell.*) Are they more strict in attendance at drill after that?—Yes.

842. (*Major-Gen. Eyre.*) Which do they like;

Mr. J. Pettie.

G 3

Mr. J. Pettie,
30 May 1862.

battalion drill, or company drill, or ball practice?—I could hardly place them in competition, for they are fond of parading, but so soon as they once find that they can shoot they seem to be taken up with that entirely. It engrosses their conversation and attention, and they would be less likely to lose battalion or other drills after that.

843. That attaches them to the force more than the drills?—Yes.

844. And makes them more useful, does it not?—Yes. As to the usefulness of the force I have a very strong opinion in favour of it, and believe it would largely develop the force.

845. (*Sir G. A. Wetherall.*) You have stated that all the men, even those who are in debt now, would be able to pay their instalments for their clothing were it not for other causes of expense. What are those causes of expense?—There is the yearly subscriptions in every corps, and it is too high for artizans. They have also to incur many minor expenses, and to many of them time is money.

846. (*Earl of Ducie.*) What are the average wages of those artizans of whom you speak?—They vary from 25s. to 2l. a week.

847. There are none who receive wages as low as 20s. a week?—There are several on my list who came in as artizans with the permission of Lord Elcho, but who are junior clerks, and who receive much smaller wages than artizans, some of them as low as 15s. a week. They are smart young men, but they cannot pay up so well as the others.

848. (*Lord Elcho.*) In point of fact, from your knowledge of the wages received by artizans and the salaries received by clerks, there are many of the latter who are much less able to pay their subscriptions than many artizans are?—That is the case.

849. In the London Scottish corps in which you are, do you believe that the artizans who now form a portion of that corps will be able to continue to pay their 1l. subscription and to provide themselves with a new uniform?—I do not think that they will.

850. Do you consider that unless something is done for them, either in diminishing their subscription or in helping them to a new uniform, a very large proportion of the artizan element in the London Scottish will disappear and will not be replaced?—That will be the case: I know from the remarks that I hear made every day amongst them that they will have to resign.

851. From your experience of the results of volunteering as evidenced in the class to which you belong, has it had the effect of improving the men physically and morally, and generally of making them better members of society?—That is my experience. I consider, as a jobbing workman, that in the trades with which I am particularly connected their increased money value to an employer is about 3s. a week, that is to say, I believe that a man who is a volunteer is worth 3s. a week more to a jobbing master than a man who is not a volunteer.

852. Have you found that from your own personal experience as an artizan in jobbing labour?—Yes. I frequently take contracts and employ men to help me; therefore I speak from experience as well as from observation.

853. Do you think that experience will be borne out generally?—Yes; whenever a man is wanted for work. In all firms it may not be so, but when a man is really wanted for a workman, I consider him worth 3s. a week more than if he is not a volunteer.

854. Do you believe that there is an anxious desire on the part of the artizan class to remain in the volunteer force, and on the part of others to join them?—Yes; there is.

855. If they do not join in greater numbers than they hitherto have done, do you believe that that results from any distaste on their part for the service, or that the expenses incidental to it are greater than they can bear?—It is entirely the expense. You would otherwise be able to have as many men as you liked when you wanted them, as they have taken a liking to it.

856. Supposing it were thought desirable to aid the volunteers in providing a uniform, should you think it desirable to give the uniform to those who first came forward as volunteers, or would you make them provide their own first uniform and only provide them with a second uniform after they had proved that they were efficient, zealous, and well conducted?—I think it might be necessary to make them pay for their first clothing, it would test their sincerity, and they would feel more independent. But the Government might give the belts and pouches; there must be some test of their sincerity and motives in joining.

857. Is this statement which I have heard made true, that there are many artizans who were rather wild in their political views, and who have sobered down and become much more rational in those matters since they have been volunteers?—I know that their political conduct is different; as to their opinions I do not know that they have changed, but they are more attached to the Government in every way, and less likely ever to promote political agitation. I may state as a fact that the headquarters of political agitation in the metropolis were in John Street, Fitzroy Square, and they have given a complete company from that institution, which is now in Cleveland Street; and I think I may refer to Major Hughes for the character of that company.

858. That company belongs to Major Hughes's regiment?—Yes. This place was formerly the headquarters of chartism; and knowing the mechanics and those who have influence with them, I may say that nearly all the men who really have weight are now loyal adherents to the volunteer service.

859. In forming these artizan corps or companies, what do you consider to be the best plan to adopt, to attempt to amalgamate them with other classes, or to keep them distinct as corps or as companies?—If one was commencing to organize a regiment, I think it might be best to keep them distinct; but it would depend upon what class they would be officered by, for they want military men for officers. I think that there is a document in the War Office which came from the first body of artizans that was raised independently of public support, and they solicited or memorialized the War Office, stating that they desired to be officered by military men entirely, and that they did not aspire to any rank above that of serjeants.

860. Do you not think from your own experience that perhaps the most comfortable way of organizing them, instead of attempting to mix them with other classes would be to keep them apart in companies in the same regiment?—That would depend upon whom they are officered from; they would do the best in that way to be kept apart if they had military gentlemen to officer them; but they would not like it so well if the persons who were merely richer than themselves were made their officers; if they were attempted to be formed as artizan corps exclusively they would be better pleased to be officered by military men.

861. Does not the attendance of the men at their parades depend very much upon the opinion which they have of the captain who commands their company and his efficiency?—Yes, entirely.

862. Where you have an efficient captain you generally have an efficient company and good attendance?—Yes, decidedly.

863. (*Viscount Hardinge.*) You have stated that you thought a volunteer artizan was worth 3s. more to his employer than another man not a volunteer; I suppose you mean both morally and physically?—I think not only morally and physically, but the man who seems to have a motive keeps to his work; a volunteer has a motive, and you know what it is; there is nothing in volunteering that can injure the interest of the employer; if he is a volunteer you know when you can have him; you know the evenings that he wants to get away, and that he has in

some way got a purpose; the greatest evil amongst working men is when they are purposeless. They are then almost valueless, and have no self-respect.

864. (*Sir G. A. Wetherall.*) Discipline gradually induces more careful habits in the men?—Yes; it also gives them personal dignity.

Mr. J. Pettie.
30 May 1862.

The witness withdrew.

Adjourned to Tuesday next at half-past 12 o'clock.

Tuesday, 3rd June 1862.

PRESENT:

Viscount EVERSLEY.
Earl of DUCIE.
Viscount HARDINGE.
Lord ELCHO.
Lord OVERSTONE.
Lieutenant-Colonel BARTTELOT.

Lieutenant-Colonel Sir A. CAMPBELL.
Lieutenant-General Sir G. A. WETHERALL.
Major General EYRE.
Colonel MACMURDO.
Major HARCOURT.

VISCOUNT EVERSLEY IN THE CHAIR.

Captain S. FLOOD PAGE examined.

*Capt.
S. F. Page.*
3 June 1862.

865. (*Chairman.*) You are adjutant of the London Scottish Rifle Volunteers?—Yes.

866. Had you previously been adjutant in any other corps?—Yes; I was adjutant of the City of Edinburgh Rifle Corps for nearly a year.

867. In your opinion, can the rifle volunteer corps be maintained without difficulty in their present state of efficiency?—No; I think there are many difficulties.

868. Will you be kind enough to state to the Commissioners what those difficulties are, and how they can be remedied?—I think that one of the greatest difficulties that we labour under now is the size of our companies. I have made out the averages for the present year of the men of my own regiment on parade, and also of the officers and of the serjeants, and I find that the number of those we have had on parade is, on the average, one officer to eight men, and one serjeant to seven men, and the consequence has been that we are compelled on parade to break our companies up, so that although we have eight companies in our regiment, we never parade with more than six; and that in every way has a very bad effect upon our men. The joining of the volunteers is principally owing to friends, they join a particular corps, and they join a particular company owing to having friends in that corps or that company; and when they come on to parade they are often separated from those friends, and when they find that this has happened once or twice, they stay away and do not come to parade at all. If our companies were increased from 100 to 150 there would be no necessity to break up the companies, and my impression is that the attendances on parade then would be very largely increased. In a military point of view it has a bad effect to parade with very small companies, because when on divisional and brigade field days we parade with larger companies, the movements are done badly; the movements having been practised with small companies, they are then carried out with large companies.

869. What is the establishment per company in your corps?—One hundred men of all ranks.

870. Is that the maximum?—Yes; the minimum is 60.

871. What do you think is the average attendance?—Our average attendance for the whole regiment for the present year, including officers, non-commissioned officers, and men, is only 199.

872. Speaking of the whole corps?—Yes.

873. What has been the average attendance per company?—25, including officers and men; our officers nearly all attend, and a majority of our serjeants always attend; but I have seen our parades with one officer to five men, and one serjeant to six men.

874. (*Viscount Hardinge.*) What is your number on paper?—673.

875. (*Col. MacMurdo.*) Would you make the minimum number in a company 100?—Yes; and the maximum 150.

876. Are you aware of the difficulty of obtaining in some corps even a minimum of 60?—In administrative battalions I think the minimum might be still 60, if you could raise only a single company; but I would not permit a second company to be raised until the first company amounted to 150.

877. (*Major-Gen. Eyre.*) Do you speak of the metropolis only?—In the provinces I would still keep the minimum at 60; but I would not let a second company be raised before the first company amounted to 150. In the metropolis and other large towns, such as Edinburgh, Liverpool, &c., I would make the minimum 100, and the maximum 150. A very short time ago there were two companies forming a separate corps by themselves, paraded with our own; and there were 48 men present, five officers, and eight serjeants; they had one company, considerably below the minimum in men, with nearly the full allowance of officers, and quite the full allowance of serjeants for two companies.

878. (*Viscount Hardinge.*) You would have 50 men as the minimum of a subdivision?—I can conceive that in some places where they cannot raise 50 men they may have a sufficient number of men for a subdivision; in that case I would sanction a subdivision of less than 50 men, or even a section of 20 men.

879. (*Major-Gen. Eyre.*) Are the men who stay away the least proficient, or the most proficient?—I am afraid that as a rule they are the least proficient.

880. You do not think they stay away because they are proficient, up to a certain mark?—There are some few instances of that, perhaps, but many stay away because they have not paid their subscriptions, and a great many men in London cannot attend every Saturday; some of the men are employed in offices, and one office may supply five of their clerks, three of whom can get away on one Saturday, and another three can get away on the following Saturday, and so on.

881. (*Viscount Hardinge.*) How many did you muster at Brighton?—I think 340.

882. Had all those men who were present on parade at Brighton been regularly passed into the battalion by you?—In theory they had, but not in practice. Our system is this; we have the six setting-up drills, and after that a certain number of company drills; and the supposition is, that each man gets a drill card after he has passed through the six setting-up drills. The majority of those present had their drill cards, but some of them had not.

883. Would it, in your opinion, be desirable that there should be one uniform set of rules with regard to attendance at drills, specifying that no man should be passed into a battalion until he had gone through

G 4

Capt.
S. F. Page.
3 June 1862.

a certain number of setting-up drills or company drills?—I think that if a man passes the adjutant in manual, platoon, and position drill, and afterwards in the setting-up drill, he might be exempt from any further setting-up drills or attendances at company drill for that year, and be at once passed into a battalion; but there should be setting-up drills and company drills to qualify a man to pass into the battalion.

884. Would you recommend that system to be applied generally to the whole volunteer force?—I think it of the utmost importance that there should, if possible, be one uniform system for the whole force. I think it is possible that it might be necessary to have one system for administrative battalions, and another system for consolidated battalions.

885. (*Major-Gen. Eyre.*) Supposing that the meeting on the coast had been for positive and active operations against the enemy, what proportion of your corps do you think would have been able to use their rifles effectively?—We have this year 216 men only who have passed in musketry; but there are a great many others who, from having constantly fired with blank cartridge, I imagine would be able to use their rifles effectively.

886. Do you think that that would have been of the least use to them?—I think it would.

887. (*Sir A. Campbell.*) When you speak of a man having passed in musketry, do you mean that he has a knowledge of platoon exercise, or that he has passed through the school of musketry course?—I do not mean the platoon exercise; no man is passed into the ranks or eligible to come to the musketry class until he is proficient in the platoon exercise; by passing, I mean going through a short course of musketry instruction, including position drill, and a short course, hardly of lectures but of explanations, as to what the rifle can do, and how it is to be taken care of, &c.

888. Not the whole minimum course specified in the volunteer regulations?—It is quite impossible to carry that out in London; we did carry it out in Edinburgh.

889. (*Earl of Ducie.*) What number of your men have passed through their classes?—Last year we had 240 men who fired.

890. And who passed through all the three classes?—No; just over 200 only passed through the three classes.

891. Have they not completed the course this year?—They have only just commenced.

892. (*Sir A. Campbell.*) Are they allowed to commence musketry practice before they have been through the minimum course specified in the Volunteer Regulations?—We have a course which is neither the minimum nor the maximum, but a course for each man, which is less than the minimum course specified in the Volunteer Regulations.

893. A special regimental course?—Yes; and I must say that I think there is no necessity for men of intelligence, as a majority of volunteers are, passing through that minimum course annually.

894. You say that in consequence of the smallness of the numbers in your companies equalisation is always necessary, and that produces a difficulty among the men. If the companies mustered more numerously would you be able to do away with equalisation?—It is not for the sake of equalization that we break up the companies. We often move with unequal companies, as ordered in the Field Exercise; it is because our attendances are so small that we have not a sufficient number of men to enable us to move with eight companies.

895. (*Sir G. A. Wetherall.*) Suppose you came with 100 men per company, and other battalions had only 60 men per company, would your men decline, for the sake of equalization, to be sent to the other battalions?—Certainly not; we have had no instance of the men declining; they are sufficiently disciplined to go wherever they are told: but the effect of the state of things I have described is bad, because, although they obey without hesitation, they will not come to parade if they are constantly liable to be separated from their friends and from their own officers.

896. (*Chairman.*) Will you be good enough to describe to the Commissioners the next difficulty which you have to contend with?—I think that one of our great difficulties is the matter of the subscription. We have several men in our corps to whom the 1*l.* a year is a matter of great moment; they cannot afford to pay it; and one of the reasons why, the attendances have fallen off, has been the fact, that several men owe money to the corps, and they do not like to attend parade for that reason. I have received several letters from members owing money to the corps, begging that proceedings might not be taken against them, and expressing a hope that nothing might be done, as they could not afford to pay the subscriptions.

897. I believe that they are only expected to pay a guinea a year?—Until February in this year there was an entrance fee of 1*l.*, payable in addition to the 1*l.* a year, but at a general meeting of the corps that was held in February, the entrance fee was done away with, and the only money which the men are now asked to subscribe is the 1*l.* a year. That does not include the band; that is purely a voluntary matter. A man gives what he likes, or he need not give anything.

898. What proportion of the men in your regiment are able to afford a subscription of 1*l.* a year?—I should imagine that there were about 250, or nearly 300, to whom 1*l.* a year, in addition to uniform and other necessary expenses, is a matter of serious moment.

899. (*Viscount Hardinge.*) Do the men in the company which is composed of working men pay 1*l.* annually?—We have no company entirely and solely composed of working men. Upon a man joining and declaring himself to be an artizan, he paid 5*s.* for his first year and no entrance fee at all; but now they are all placed on one footing and they are all liable to pay 1*l.*

900. You have one company composed of working men?—We have two companies principally, but not entirely composed of artizans.

901. (*Chairman.*) Are those men supplied with clothing at the expense of the corps?—No, at their own expense. One of our rules was, that every enrolled man should provide himself with uniform and accoutrements in accordance with the sealed pattern, but the artizans were permitted to pay for their uniforms by instalments.

902. (*Viscount Hardinge.*) Have they done so?—There is a large outstanding debt still.

903. (*Earl of Ducie.*) What is the amount of it?—I do not know.

904. (*Chairman.*) Then the clothing for those men was paid for out of the funds of the corps?—No, the corps does not hold itself responsible for that money.

905. What remedy would you suggest for this state of things?—I think that if the force is to be kept up at all, there must be a grant of so much per head for every effective man, which will almost entirely, if not quite, do away with the necessity for any subscriptions.

906. (*Lord Overstone.*) Do you mean that there should be a Government grant of 1*l.* per head?—I think that perhaps 1*l.* would do for London; I cannot say for the country.

907. (*Chairman.*) A capitation grant of 1*l.* per head?—Yes.

908. To what expenses should that 1*l.* be applied?—I think it should be applied to military expenses; that it should be applied towards the range expenses; towards the expense of headquarters, and if our serjeants are still to receive the pay which they do, and we are compelled in each instance to add to their pay, I should say that it should be applied also to that purpose.

909. Will you state to the Commission what addition you are obliged to make to the pay of the ser-

jeants?—Our present serjeant-major was serjeant-major of the 61st regiment, and when he came to us he was receiving what he considers equivalent to 5s. 10d. a day; 3s. 3d. pay, 1s. 3d. for quarters, 4d. for clothing, and 1s. for rations; the Government allowance to him as serjeant-major of the volunteer corps is 3s. 1d. a day; we allow him 29l. a year, and in addition to that we provide him with quarters, which cost us 45l. a year.

910. (*Major-Gen. Eyre.*) Do you mean to say that he was receiving in the 61st regiment as serjeant-major the different sums which you have mentioned?—Yes; the 3s. 3d. pay and quarters and clothing and rations.

911. (*Sir G. A. Wetherall.*) Then he put his annual clothing at 4d. a day?—Yes, and he adds this, that whilst serving he paid 10d. a day in the serjeants' mess, which consisted of three wholesome and substantial meals. In London he cannot get three meals daily for that amount, and besides, he loses the comfort of the mess.

912. (*Col. MacMurdo.*) He has his pension, has he not?—No, he is not a pensioned man. We may have serjeants from the line after they have served 18 years.

913. (*Chairman.*) How many serjeants have you?—Three. Then there is another matter; the education of his children is now thrown upon him, which costs a large sum of money, whereas he was able before to send them to a regimental school.

914. (*Col. MacMurdo.*) Are you aware that the Government did not contemplate that the serjeant-majors of regular regiments should become serjeant-majors in volunteer corps, but that the regulations point to obtaining serjeants?—I think that it is very important that we should, if possible, have as serjeant-majors of volunteer corps men who have had experience as serjeant-majors in regiments of the line. The difference between serjeant-majors and ordinary serjeants in the orderly room work, and the management of the drills, and many other things, is of the very greatest importance. Our other two serjeants are pensioned serjeants, to one of whom we pay 20l. a year without quarters, and to the other of whom we pay 10l. a year without quarters.

915. Why is that difference made in the pay of the two serjeants?—Because we are compelled to find quarters for one serjeant; in London it is quite impossible, or almost so, to have any distinct orderly room hours. We are compelled to have a man invariably during daylight at headquarters, that if a member has any business to transact he may transact it as he passes to or from his business. We have tried shutting up the orderly room at certain hours, but during those hours a great number of the volunteers come, and would be able to transact any business that they might have at that time, and they are naturally very much disappointed, if having got away from their business, they find no one there to attend to them.

916. But why is there such a difference between, as between paying one serjeant 20l. and the other serjeant 10l. only?—One of the two is our serjeant-major, and we give him more pay; he has more to do than the other.

917. (*Lord Elcho.*) There is also a difference, I believe, in the pay given by the regiment to the other two serjeants?—Yes; one is our armourer, and we pay him less.

918. (*Viscount Hardinge.*) What do the extra allowances paid to those serjeants amount to in the aggregate?—£59 in money, and 45l. in quarters.

919. You mean the quarters for the serjeant-major?—Yes.

920. Who finds the quarters?—The corps.

921. (*Col. MacMurdo.*) Can you, from your experience as adjutant, state whether the allowances made to the adjutant are sufficient?—I certainly think that the adjutants' allowances in London are not nearly sufficient. For example, if you take the allowance for a horse, it is 2s. a day; that is 14s. a week for a horse, not including any groom or servant. Livery for a horse costs about 23s. a week; in addition to that we get 8s. a day pay, and the house rent that we pay, if married, as I am, is more than that. We get 2s. a day less than the adjutants in the country. The adjutant of an administrative battalion gets 2s. a day for travelling expenses, but our house rent in London exceeds their travelling expenses very materially.

922. Is there much difference between London and Edinburgh?—Not a very great deal. It is very nearly the same thing. There is a very slight difference in the house rent.

923. Do you keep a horse?—I do not.

924. Do you find that the allowance for a horse covers your occasional hire of one?—The Marquis of Abercorn lends me a horse always.

925. Then the allowance for a horse goes to your general pay?—Yes.

926. (*Sir A. Campbell.*) But that is only an exceptional instance, that an officer in your regiment provides you with a horse?—Yes.

927. (*Viscount Hardinge.*) What is the amount of your pay and allowances?—My pay and allowances are 8s. a day pay, and 2s. a day for forage, and 1l. a quarter for each company, that is, 32l. a year. In addition to that, during the last year, in accordance with the warrant, the corps has given me 25l. a year in lieu of my railway and other necessary expenses; they give me the one sum instead of my keeping an account of what I spend and charging it to the corps.

928. (*Col. MacMurdo.*) Is the allowance for stationery, in your opinion, sufficient?—The allowance for stationery is to cover contingent expenses in connexion with correspondence, &c. with the War Office, and some time ago we referred to you, sir (Col. MacMurdo), from Edinburgh, to know whether this was to be applied to the general stationery expenses of the corps, to which you said "No;" and of course our expenses in London in connexion with correspondence with the War Office amount only to a few shillings annually.

929. In Edinburgh do you consider it sufficient?—Quite sufficient.

930. (*Lieut.-Col. Barttelot.*) Do most of the adjutants in London keep their own horses?—I believe not. There is one instance of one corps in London who bought their adjutant's horse and gave it to him. They have very few mounted parades, and his horse costs him about 80l. a year.

931. (*Viscount Hardinge.*) Do you know whether the adjutants in the metropolitan corps have extra allowances made up for them?—I think that very many of them have. Some have large sums.

932. (*Lord Elcho.*) Do you know what the Queen's give to Major Mayno?—I am not quite sure, but it was, I think, a large sum.

933. (*Sir A. Campbell.*) Have you ever made any comparison between the position of an adjutant of volunteers and that of an adjutant in the militia, as regards the pay and as regards the duty?—I think it is just this, that we work for nine months in the year, and the adjutant in the militia works for about one month, and he gets, I believe, half as much more pay than we do.

934. (*Lord Elcho.*) Have you ever made the same comparison between the duties of a serjeant of militia and a serjeant of volunteers?—Yes, and for a serjeant-major in London I can imagine no more tiring work than having to sit nearly all day long at a particular place with very little indeed to do, being as it were, tied to the office, at all hours of the day, and having to work at inconvenient hours at night; our serjeants, too, get very much less pay than the serjeants of militia; I believe that a serjeant of a militia regiment gets 1d. a day more pay than our serjeant-major gets, and in addition he gets quarters and clothing.

935. Is it necessary that the serjeant-major of a volunteer regiment should be a very superior man?—I think it is of the utmost importance that he should be as superior a non-commissioned officer,

Capt. S. F. Page.

3 June 1862.

H

Capt.
S. F. Page.
3 June 1862.

both in his knowledge of the work, intelligence, manner, and bearing, as possible.

936. It requires a man of considerable tact to be in that position, does it not?—Very much so indeed.

937. Before you got your last serjeant-major you made very extensive inquiries, did you not, in all directions in search of one?—Yes.

938. Had you any difficulty in finding one?—I happened to hit upon this one by chance, but we could not hear for some months of a man who we felt could be trusted, without my own presence, so that he should be able to drill our volunteers in such a manner as that he should make them do what he required them to do, and yet at the same time not speak to them in any but the most courteous and proper manner.

939. Do you believe it is possible to obtain the class of men who are required in that position for the allowances or for the salary given by the Government?—I believe it is perfectly impossible in London, at any rate, to get any serjeant of the description that is required as serjeant-major for volunteer corps for the Government allowance.

940. Is it more easy to get a sufficient number of good serjeants for militia regiments than for volunteer regiments?—Yes; my impression of the militia is, that the men in the militia are spoken to more roughly by the serjeants than in a line regiment.

941. Are you aware that the pay of a militia serjeant is higher than that of the volunteer serjeant?—Yes, they get quarters and clothing in addition to their pay.

942. (*Viscount Hardinge.*) Are you quite correct in saying that the militia adjutant receives half as much again as you do?—I think so; but I am not quite sure.

943. Are you aware that the militia adjutant receives about 300*l.* a year?—Yes.

944. And that the volunteer adjutant, taking your own case as an example, receives about 230*l.* a year, if you take into account all your allowances?—Yes; I was wrong in what I said.

945. (*Lord Overstone.*) Could you give in a tabular statement, setting forth the relative pay of the militia serjeant and of the volunteer serjeant, and another, setting forth the relative duties imposed upon the two?—Yes: I could draw such statements up.

946. (*Lord Elcho.*) What is your opinion as to the necessity of adjutants for the volunteer corps?—I think, in the first instance, that they were absolutely necessary; but I am not quite sure that it is necessary to have them now. I am sure of this, that we have not enough to do; and that the enormous sum which is now paid to the adjutants of volunteers might be saved by not having so many; of course the difficulty would be in providing for those officers who would not be continued as adjutants; but we are not permitted to do any non-military duty; an adjutant is not permitted to take any part in the non-military or financial affairs of the corps; and the consequence is that we pass the entire day with very little indeed to do. The whole of the adjutants' military work in the office may be performed in two or three days in a week, with the exception of one week in the year, which is the last week in July, when we have to prepare the muster rolls of the corps; on the other hand, every night, or nearly every night, during the winter, there is some work going on, but I feel quite confident that one adjutant would be able to do the work of two regiments in London, where there is no great distance between them.

947. (*Sir A. Campbell.*) Would that include the superintendence of musketry instruction and target practice?—It would not; there are very few adjutants in London that have much to do with the musketry instruction. I have nothing to do with musketry instruction; there is a volunteer musketry instructor; each company has a company instructor, and an assistant instructor, and those gentlemen are only too willing and too glad to be permitted to work in the corps.

948. (*Lord Elcho.*) The musketry instruction is an entirely voluntary and gratuitous service, is it not?—With the exception that we apply one of our paid serjeants to the musketry instruction.

949. (*Major Harcourt.*) With regard to the adjutants, do you not think that it would be easy for an adjutant to find almost as much to do as he could get through?—I think it is quite impossible, if he confines himself strictly to his military duty, as we are ordered. I do not mean to say that we have not work to do in the evenings, but we have nothing to do in the day.

950. (*Viscount Hardinge.*) Should you be in favour in London of amalgamating two weak battalions?—I think it is a matter of great importance that the metropolitan force should be divided into brigades by districts, forming those national or professional corps already organized into a separate brigade, but whether in merging them into brigades you would sacrifice the individuality of corps, I think is a matter for great consideration.

951. Of course, if you were to amalgamate a certain number of corps, you would be able to knock off a certain number of adjutants?—Yes; but it would be very hard indeed to amalgamate two corps and bring them under new field officers, men whom they might not work with, and of whom they know nothing, perhaps; and I think it is very essential that the volunteers should have confidence in, and should be able to work with, their officers.

952. You have probably heard instances mentioned of new corps having been raised almost within a stone's throw of the headquarters of an existing corps?—Yes; and of course it is a matter for the War Office to consider whether they have done wisely in authorizing and not preventing the raising of such corps. I cannot but think that there are too many corps in London.

953. It would appear that you see insuperable difficulties in the way of amalgamating them?—Yes; I think that every corps which does not at the present time number on its muster rolls 600 should be reduced to four companies, and that every corps that does not muster 900 should be reduced to six companies, and the staff now allowed for six companies be allowed for four, and so on, retaining the officers as supernumeraries until absorbed.

954. (*Chairman.*) Do you mean six companies of a maximum strength of 150 per company?—Yes.

955. (*Viscount Hardinge.*) Your plan of making the adjutant do duty in two or three battalions could not be made to apply to the administrative battalions, could it?—I do not know sufficiently about the duties of the adjutants in administrative battalions to be able to speak to that.

956. But you would have one system for the metropolis and another system for the rural districts?—I should think that one adjutant might, for example, do the work in Liverpool or in Manchester, or in Edinburgh, and in large towns generally, one adjutant being appointed brigade-major to each brigade. Officers connected with administrative battalions will speak as to the working of this system in the rural districts.

957. (*Lord Elcho.*) The Inns of Court corps is only six companies strong?—Only six.

958. How does that work? Are their companies generally full, or have they to be broken up?—I believe I am correct in saying that they have never been broken up. Colonel Brewster told me that they had never been broken up.

959. (*Sir A. Campbell.*) Can you go through battalion drill properly without equalizing the companies?—Yes, except when marching past; and in brigade drill, under Colonel MacMurdo, I have seen one of our companies 19 file, and one or two of the others 13 or 14. We should equalize before we were inspected.

960. In Edinburgh the regiment, I believe, consists of two battalions?—Yes.

961. How many companies are there?—Twenty-two companies.

962. How many adjutants are there?—Two.
963. In your judgment, would one adjutant be sufficient?—The work in the Edinburgh regiment is constituted very differently from that in any other consolidated battalion that I know of. It is, in point of fact, an administrative battalion, because each company is separate from the other. There is no battalion finance. Each company is responsible for its own finance. I was for a long time the only adjutant to the two battalions; but as soon as the War Office circular was sent out that a second adjutant might be appointed, it was determined that one adjutant should have the entire charge of the drill, and the other should have the entire charge of the musketry. My successor as adjutant is an officer who has never been to Hythe, therefore he has the entire charge of the drill, while the other adjutant, who was serjeant-major at the school of musketry at Hythe, has the entire charge of the musketry.
964. Is that system found to work well?—Very well indeed.
965. Do you think that in general it would not be desirable to have the musketry instruction conducted under the charge of an adjutant?—I do not see any necessity for it whatever.
966. Do you think that you can sufficiently depend on volunteer officers?—Yes. It is by no means a difficult thing now, owing to the facilities which have been given by the War Office, to go through a course of instruction at Hythe. We have had, I think, six officers and one serjeant who have gone through a course of instruction at Hythe, and we find that they are perfectly well able to carry out the musketry instruction.
967. (*Col. MacMurdo.*) Is it your opinion that the adjutant of a volunteer corps should not be perfectly well up in his musketry instruction?—No; I consider it a matter of the greatest importance that he should have passed through the school of musketry, and be able to settle all points of detail.
968. An adjutant who had not been at Hythe would labour under a disadvantage?—Yes, and in a very short time his authority with his men would be lessened.
969. (*Lord Elcho.*) Have you formed any opinion as to there being a special staff uniform for staff serjeants and adjutants of volunteer corps?—Taking the serjeants first, I cannot but think that it would be a good thing in many ways if the Government were to provide them with a uniform, that is a staff uniform, by which you should at once be able to distinguish them.
970. At the present time the uniform is found by the corps, is it not?—Yes.
971. That expense has to be added to the other expenses which are borne by the corps?—Yes; the present uniform is found by the corps; I am perfectly confident that our own serjeants have not quite the same authority in drilling our men as the serjeants from the Guards had. Both in Edinburgh and when I first came up to London I wore my own uniform on parade, and I am confident that that gave me, when first I came to the two corps, greater authority; I do not mean to say that I have to complain of any less power or authority with them now, but there was a certain feeling, that of looking up to the adjutant as a military man, and I believe that it would be a very good thing indeed if both the adjutants, at their own expense, and the serjeants at the expense of the Government, were provided with staff uniforms.
972. (*Col. MacMurdo.*) Are you aware that in the pay of the serjeant instructors an allowance of 2*d.* is reckoned for clothing?—I was not aware of that; but that only makes the pay up to 3*s.* 3*d.* I suppose.
973. (*Viscount Hardinge.*) Have you any estimate of the annual expense to which your corps is put for keeping up a range, the rent of headquarters, and so on?—No; I have nothing to do with the financial arrangements of the corps.
974. (*Lord Elcho.*) At present the adjutant is debarred from having anything to do with finance matters, and the serjeants are equally so debarred?—Yes.
975. Is it possible, in your opinion, that the concerns of a volunteer corps can be managed without somebody being held especially responsible for the finance?—It is quite impossible that they can be well managed without somebody being responsible for the financial affairs of the corps. The adjutant is positively prohibited from having anything to do with them. We have received a circular from the Secretary of State for War saying that it was not expedient (but not prohibiting it) that the serjeants should have anything to do with those matters; but we have been compelled to allow our serjeant-major to manage and pay the small cash accounts which come in and require payment on the spot; we can have no volunteer who is constantly in attendance to transact the small financial business of the corps.
976. If the serjeant did not do that the corps must employ an orderly room clerk, whose services could probably not be obtained for less than 40*l.* a year?—Yes, 40*l.* or 50*l.* a year.
977. (*Major Harcourt.*) Is it not the case that the supernumerary lieutenant is obliged to act as paymaster?—Yes, he does act as paymaster by taking charge generally of the financial affairs of the corps; but it is only generally. I think it is too much to suppose that any gentleman in London, for they are nearly all in employment, could give up his entire time to take the entire charge of the finance.
978. Is it not possible to find a person who would be willing to have a commission in the volunteer corps, and who had plenty of time on his hands, and who would for the sake of a commission perform the duties of paymaster thoroughly?—I think not in London; we have not found it so.
979. (*Lord Elcho.*) It would require, would it not, in your corps a person to be constantly, or at all events for certain hours in the day, at the office to receive subscriptions, and to settle the small cash accounts?—Yes, to receive subscriptions, give receipts, &c.
980. (*Viscount Hardinge.*) Who performs that duty now?—The serjeant-major.
981. Are you aware that in many corps a considerable salary is given, such as 50*l.* a year, to the secretary to the finance committee?—Yes; but we cannot afford to give 50*l.* a year to any orderly room clerk or paymaster's clerk, but we have felt the want of it; if the present subscriptions are to be retained I think it will be absolutely necessary that there should be either an orderly room clerk or a paymaster's clerk, to be paid by the Government, in order to carry on the business of the corps.
982. (*Lord Overstone.*) I understand it to be your opinion that the efficiency of the present volunteer movement is in danger from two causes,—one, defects in administration, and the other pecuniary pressure?—Yes.
983. Confining your attention to the latter cause, namely, pecuniary pressure, is it your opinion that some regulation under which the Government should aid to the extent of 1*l.* per man, would be a desirable remedy?—Yes.
984. Do you think that would be an effectual and complete remedy?—I think it would.
985. Do you think it important that that 1*l.* per head should be a specific sum advanced as such; or would it meet your views if that assistance were rendered indirectly by the Government, to be applied to the various purposes which have been enumerated by you; for example, towards the expense of a range, headquarters, serjeants, &c., on the principle that the total advance would be applicable to things of that nature?—I cannot think that that would make much difference. Each corps should be able, I think, to tell the Government in what manner they wish the money to be expended.
986. Do you think that the better course would be to pay a specific sum to the colonel commanding each regiment, he being responsible for the administration

Capt.
S. F. Page.

3 June 1862.

Capt.
S. F. Page.

3 June 1862.

of that sum; or would it be equally efficient for the purpose in view, if advances in an indirect form, were made by the Government, the amount being, generally speaking, equivalent to 1l. per head?—I still think it would make no difference, for the commanding officer of each corps might say upon what individual things he would like the money expended; it would of course lead to very great complication, for I think it would be found that no two corps would apply for the money to be spent for exactly the same purposes, or if they did, certainly not in the same proportions. I think it would simplify matters if the money were given to the commanding officer, he being held responsible to the Government for its administration.

987. Can you express any opinion as to what would be the relative condition either of your own corps, or of the volunteer movement generally, upon the supposition, first, that it is left in its present condition, and on the supposition, secondly, that your suggested plan of Government aid were applied to it?—Our attendance last year was, upon the average, 285; our attendance, on the average, this year is 199; and I believe it will be found to decrease in very much the same proportion if the force is continued as it now is.

988. Do you attribute that decrease entirely to the pecuniary difficulties you have alluded to?—Partly to pecuniary difficulties, and partly to the fact of the breaking up of the companies, partly to the number of parades a volunteer must attend to become an effective, also to the fact that there is very little inducement to the volunteers to sacrifice their holiday, Saturday after Saturday, and come out to drill. I cannot but think that there might be an inducement held out that would attain the object we have in view, that of bringing the men out to parade, in order to make them efficient.

989. What inducement do you allude to?—At the present time an effective volunteer is exempt from the militia ballot, and he is also exempt from the hair powder tax, but he has no other exemption of any kind or sort, and I cannot but think that if an effective were permitted to wear a badge (we find that the marksmen's badges are very much sought after), to carry with it some exemption, such, for instance, as exemption from serving on a jury, or as the hair powder tax is now no boon to the present force as it was formerly, there might be an exemption from taxation; each volunteer choosing what it should be, and he might be exempt from a tax of about the same amount as the hair powder tax, which is, I believe, 1l. 3s. 6d., the tax for a male servant is 1l. 1s., the tax for a horse I think is 1l. 1s., for a dog 12s., and armorial bearings 13s. 6d., and if the volunteers were permitted to choose which of those they would be exempted from, I think they would feel that they had gained something by becoming volunteers.

990. Do not you think that the volunteer movement originated in a feeling which was spread throughout the country of serious danger from foreign invasion?—I do.

991. Do you not think that that feeling must necessarily vary in its strength and in its activity, precisely in proportion as the apprehension out of which it sprung varies?—Yes, I do.

992. Do you think that the remedies which you have now suggested would be anything like an efficient substitute for the diminished feeling of apprehension as to national security?—I think that if we do not introduce something of this kind the force will dwindle away and at last disappear.

993. Do you think that the remedies which you have suggested in the latter part of your evidence can possibly be looked upon as a sufficient substitute for that feeling of serious apprehension as to the national security in which the volunteer movement originated, and with the decay of which the volunteer movement is apparently failing?—I think that it would be an inducement added to the feeling, I cannot think that the feeling has entirely passed away; I believe that the volunteers themselves are conscious that as individuals they have, in coming forward and enrolling themselves, done their duty, and considerably strengthened our position on the continent; but at the same time, inasmuch as the same necessity does not exist for their presence, I think it is our duty to devise means to keep the force permanently together, and in some way to let them feel that they obtain advantages by being volunteers, so that although the feeling has not entirely disappeared, yet, having partly disappeared, there should be an inducement added to what remains of that feeling.

994. Do you think that it would be a safe principle of procedure to mingle to a certain degree or to substitute the feelings to which you have recently alluded in the place of that one which was the more predominant feeling?—The force is now formed under the Act of George 3d, which does exempt them from a tax; it is in no way altering the principle: it is merely substituting something that would be a present advantage to them, instead of leaving it to be said the principle is in existence without conferring any benefit; on principle we give you some advantage, but in practice we really do not give you any.

995. (Chairman.) I understood you to say, that the Act of George 3d exempted the volunteers from a tax on an article which is now no longer in use, and you propose to substitute some other exemption that would really be a relief to them?—Yes.

996. The effect of that, I presume, would be to add 1l. a year to the other 1l. which you propose as a capitation grant from the Government, that is to say, that the exemption from the tax would be equivalent to giving up 1l.?—They are exempt now from the tax on hair powder, but it is no boon to them. I think it is a matter of very great importance that some incentive or inducement should be held out to them, for without it I think we shall hardly be able to keep the force in anything like its present state, and we shall find year by year it will become less, an evil that must, if possible, be avoided.

997. (Lord Elcho.) The ballot is not in force now?—I believe not.

998. Practically there is no exemption?—No.

999. Hair powder is never used, so that the exemption from the tax upon that is no exemption?—No.

1000. What you mean is this, that the present volunteer force as embodied exists under an Act of Parliament in which there were certain exemptions?—Yes.

1001. As an inducement to volunteers?—Yes.

1002. Those exemptions, partly from the law not being enforced in one instance, and in the other from a change of fashion, have ceased to be exemptions?—Yes.

1003. And you would suggest others upon the same principle?—Yes, exactly upon the same principle.

1004. (Lord Overstone.) You think that these exemptions would be valued by the volunteers as marks of distinction and privilege. Do you think that they would be principally valued on account of their pecuniary value, or because they exempted the volunteers from services of a disagreeable kind?—I think that with reference to exemption from serving on juries it would have a most beneficial effect upon all who would benefit by it, for a man would feel that in qualifying himself for a volunteer he obtained an exemption from the disagreeable duty of serving on a jury. On the other hand, I think that the exemption from a tax would be perhaps viewed more almost as an honorary distinction than as a material pecuniary benefit.

1005. Your opinion is that in order to retain the present volunteers it is requisite that some inducement should be given beyond that of the public principle of volunteering for the defence of the country?—There is already provided an inducement in the exemption from the militia ballot, and also the hair powder tax; it is not that we wish to provide an additional inducement so much as we want to change that which is now really no inducement into something that is.

1006. As I understand you opinion it is this, that in the former volunteer movement there were certain exemptions given as an inducement to men to enter the force, those exemptions have now become of little value, and you think that exemptions of equal value to them at the present time ought to be substituted in their place?—Yes.

1007. Your opinion is that unless public feeling is supported or strengthened by some such means as these it will not of itself be sufficient to sustain the present movement?—I believe so.

1008. (*Viscount Hardinge.*) What proportion of the members in the metropolitan regiments do you think keep male servants?—I do not know.

1009. If you were to exempt those members from paying 1*l.* a year for a male servant they would be *pro tanto* able to pay their subscription of one guinea?—Yes, it would be a boon; but I think it is a matter of importance that there should be a boon.

1010. (*Sir A. Campbell.*) Do you propose that the boon in addition to the 1*l.* should be given to the commanding officer?—Yes, certainly. I wish to carry out the Act of 50 years ago, and make it really beneficial now.

1011. (*Chairman.*) You propose to do this either in the way of relief from taxation or by conferring on them the privilege of not serving on juries?—I think that the exemption from serving on juries would be a new boon and a new inducement added to the old principle of a remission of a certain amount of taxation. I wish to give them the benefit both of exemption from being on juries and from some one tax.

1012. (*Earl of Ducie.*) An exemption from a certain portion of the assessed taxes would only relieve those volunteers who were already in tolerably easy circumstances?—Yes; but the object is to induce them, by extending to them some privilege, to attend regularly at their drills and qualify as effectives; and I think that these little inducements would have that desired effect.

1013. (*Sir A. Campbell.*) Do not you think that the knowledge that, by becoming efficient, they would be the means of obtaining for their corps a certain proportion of Government aid, to be paid to the commanding officer, would be sufficient to induce them to come in?—No; I think not.

1014. (*Sir G. A. Wetherall.*) You have stated that in your opinion 1*l.* should be given by the Government to every effective volunteer; what do you consider an effective volunteer?—The present regulations compel a volunteer to attend 24 parades in the year in order to make him "effective." I think that that regulation might be well altered, and that if a volunteer passes the adjutant in the manual, platoon, position, and company drill, after that he need only attend eight battalion parades, exclusive of brigade or divisional parades. Having passed the adjutant, I think that eight battalion parades would be sufficient, he would then be efficient, and should therefore, I think, be looked upon as "effective."

1015. (*Viscount Hardinge.*) Do you think that the Government, if they gave further assistance to the volunteers, would be disposed to dispense with the present number of days' attendance at drill, which, according to the Act, constitutes an effective?—I am afraid that, if the number is not altered, we shall not obtain anything like a fair proportion of our men as effectives. I judge from the fact of the very small attendances, and I know it is not only so in our corps but in others.

1016. Are you aware that in point of fact the number of days specified by the Act of Parliament is 18?—I know that in the Act it is 18, but in the regulations it is 24.

1017. (*Chairman.*) I think you stated some time ago that the officers were very punctual in their attendance?—Yes, they are most regular and punctual, and I cannot but think that it would materially assist us in our endeavours to make our officers efficient if part of every inspection, when inspected by Colonel MacMurdo, say the first hour of the inspection, was devoted entirely to company drill under company officers, so that the inspecting officer might really see not only the battalion parade, but how an officer could work a company by himself. At the present time, many of them, partly from few opportunities, and also knowing that there is no test, are not as competent to command and to manoeuvre a company by itself as they are to command a company in battalion drill.

1018. There is no examination of the officers before they receive their commissions?—No. I do not think it would be well that there should be before they receive their commission, and if there was any examination afterwards, I would limit it entirely to manœuvring a company by itself and also as part of a battalion. I think, on the other hand, that now having been so long in existence, if an officer were found not to be efficient, he should be compelled to be attached to some regiment of the line for a month, and obtain from the officer commanding that regiment a certificate that he was efficient, or be called upon to resign.

1019. (*Sir G. A. Wetherall.*) What proportion of effectives have you in your corps?—According to the legal qualification, it is difficult to say, for the present year, the qualification does not end till the 31st of July; but taking the date that the Commissioners have assigned for this year, which is the 1st of April, we have 382 who have attended 12 parades.

1020. (*Lord Overstone.*) Is it your opinion that the volunteer force is now generally dwindling in efficiency?—I should rather say that it is decreasing in numbers, but that those who remain are increasing very materially in efficiency.

1021. Do you think that the efficiency, as far as discipline is concerned, is rather advancing than retrograding?—Not only rather, but I should say that the force is most materially advancing in discipline and efficiency, and the knowledge of the work in those who do attend is very much greater than it was.

1022. Is not that a very natural and legitimate state of a volunteer force during a period in which the apprehension as to the safety of the country is not seriously shaken?—Yes, perhaps so, if we were likely to retain the present numbers; but what I fear is that, having fallen down from an average of 285 to 199 in one year, the decrease will continue, and I greatly fear to contemplate the small numbers we shall fall down to next year, and we cannot expect the officers to continue to attend regularly, if their companies are constantly taken from them and broken up.

1023. Your apprehension is that inconveniences and difficulties will attend you in keeping up the present numbers in the force, whilst the spirit out of which the movement originated is rather diminishing?—I think so.

1024. (*Viscount Hardinge.*) Are your officers now put to any inconvenient expense?—We do not recognize the fact that they are, but they are; for example, it is very hard indeed for an officer commanding a company in a battalion such as ours to offer to his company prizes to be shot for, and for the officer of another company not to do the same thing. We find that it is absolutely necessary in the appointment of officers that their means should be considered, owing to that fact; and I know of more cases than one in which most efficient gentlemen have declined commissions or promotion because they felt that they could not bear the necessary expense.

1025. Does not each company rather expect its captain to give a rifle prize?—Yes, I think they look for it.

1026. Upon whom does the expense of the band fall?—The expense of the band is met by an entirely voluntary subscription; and there again, if a captain gives 3*l.* 3*s.*, a lieutenant will give 2*l.* 2*s.*, the ensign will give 1*l.* 1*s.*, and the serjeants 10*s.*, and the men 5*s.*; but it is purely optional. Many men do not subscribe anything.

1027. (*Sir A. Campbell.*) Do all of your officers subscribe to the band?—Yes; in every instance.

Capt. S. F. Page, 3 June 1862.

Capt.
S. F. Page.

3 June 1862.

1028. (*Viscount Hardinge.*) Have you any idea what your band costs per annum?—Our band has just been newly organized, and, in point of fact, we have no band of our own; it is a professional band. We give uniforms, and we have a bandmaster, to whom we pay 50*l.* a year. He scores off all the music, and he looks after the instruments, and he is bound to bring us on parade a certain number of musicians who can play. Our band consists of from 12 to 14 men, and we pay them 7*s.* a head each time they come to play. We estimate our annual expenditure for band at about 200*l.* or rather less.

1029. Could you get on without a band?—Certainly not.

1030. Do you think you could get on with fifes and drums?—Certainly not. We have in addition to the band six pipers, the pipes were presented to us by Scotch ladies living in London; but the pipers, with the exception of the pipe major, to whom we pay 25*l.* a year, are voluntary. But having six pipers we never muster more than four on parade, and very often two, and sometimes we go out without one. I think it would be impossible to keep the corps together without a band.

1031. (*Major-Gen. Eyre.*) In one case it is stated that the band cost 600*l.* a year. Do you think that a corps that can furnish that amount for a band can be in much difficulty?—I imagine that that refers to the London rifle brigade, a corps which has been largely assisted by gentlemen living in the city.

1032. (*Sir A. Campbell.*) I suppose that the evidence you have given to-day would generally apply as well to Edinburgh as to London?—I have had London much more in my mind; and without looking through the evidence I have given, I should be sorry to say that it equally applied to both.

1033. Is it probable that what you have stated with regard to the falling off in numbers, in case no aid should be given, will equally apply to Edinburgh?—Hardly so much. There is but one regiment in Edinburgh, and the volunteer spirit in Edinburgh is most strong; and I think throughout all Scotland it is very strong. I fancy from what I know, having seen several officers of the Edinburgh volunteer corps, that the attendances are not much falling off there. The distances in Edinburgh to the parade ground and butts are very small, and it does not cost a man anything to attend.

1034. In fact you think that Edinburgh has not been over enrolled?—I think that it has been very much over enrolled in the number of its companies; and that it would have been better had there been half the number of companies, because although the men turn out, the attendances in companies are small, and they have to be broken up.

1035. (*Sir G. A. Wetherall.*) Are you aware that in the army the officers have been forbidden to give prizes for good shooting?—Yes.

1036. Do you think it would affect the zeal of the volunteers if it were ordered that amongst them the giving of prizes should be discontinued?—I think without exception that it would be the most fatal thing that could happen to the force; without an inducement being held out of shooting for rifle prizes it would be almost impossible to render the force permanent.

1037. (*Chairman.*) Have you any further suggestions to offer to the Commission?—There is one, and it is with reference to a school of arms. I cannot but think that it would be a most material advantage for us in all large towns, if, now that gymnastics and schools of arms have been taken up by the authorities, our serjeant-instructors were sent there to go through a course of instruction, so that they might be able to instruct our volunteers. I think that some central place should be supplied by the Government at no very great expense, the serjeants taking it in turns to go and give instruction; and every effective member might go through a course of gymnastic exercise with the singlestick, and boxing, and so forth. This would, I am convinced, tend to render the service popular and the force permanent.

1038. (*Lord Elcho.*) If the Government allowed you to send individuals, selected from the corps, to be instructed as drill-serjeants, at no expense, would it be acceptable to the corps?—I do not think you could entirely depend upon volunteers as your drill-serjeants, unless you had a large number of them, so that it might make the work easy; in London the men are too much engaged in business.

1039. You think that you could not find the men for it?—We might find them, but it would be necessary to have a large number to carry it out; it would be infinitely inferior to depending upon our present Government drill-serjeants. We find that our drill serjeants have so much more weight with our men than volunteer instructors have.

1040. You have laid much stress upon the strength of the companies and the difficulties arising out of the want of numbers, and you stated that you had been unable to equalize?—It is not so much for the purpose of equalization that we break up our companies, but because the numbers that we have on parade, if divided by eight, which is our strength of companies, makes our companies too small for parade movements. The men do not object to being equalized, but they dislike being broken up and being put with other companies. We are so few on parade that we cannot move with eight companies.

1041. Still you wish to amalgamate them in order to instruct them?—Yes.

1042. Do they object to that?—They never object; they go; but they so much dislike it that when this has happened two or three times they stay away from drill. There has never been one instance of objection, but with the most perfect good feeling, and without the slightest hesitation, they go wherever they are told; but they stay away afterwards.

1043. (*Chairman.*) Is there any other suggestion you have to make?—There is one point with reference to one set of regulations being strictly enforced throughout the entire force, although the present rules as to the different corps may be necessary in some instances; and there may be some necessity to keep them still up as standing orders, because some corps have, like ourselves, different arrangements about their bands, but in this kind of way it works hardly; for example, if one corps tries to carry out strictly the regulations as to the inspection of arms, or that kind of thing, and another corps close by does not, the men in the corps where the orders are strictly carried out consider that they are hardly treated, because they are more strictly looked after than the men in the other corps.

1044. You would have one set of rules applied to the whole force, to be issued from the War Office?—Yes, one set of regulations; and with reference to the regulation by which the arms must be inspected once a month, we find in practice that it is perfectly impossible to inspect our arms once a month; the system that we have adopted is this, our captains on parade, and our musketry instructors, are held responsible that the arms of those men who do come to parade are in good order. We give a card of permission (signed by the commanding officer) to the men to keep their arms in their own possession; but we find, as to those men who do not come to parade, that we have no possible means of inspecting their arms monthly. The commanding officer inspects our arms himself personally once a year, and last year we had 13 only out of the whole corps who did not send in their arms for inspection, but each one of those 13 have since that time been seen by the officers commanding companies; and I would respectfully submit to the Commission that if the arms are in good condition, and the commanding officer is held responsible that they are so, there is no necessity that they should be seen so frequently, as we find that it does not work.

The witness withdrew.

Major THOMAS HUGHES examined.

Maj.
T. Hughes.

3 June 1862.

1045. You commanded the 19th Middlesex Rifle Volunteers?—I did, but Colonel Bathurst now commands the corps.

1046. Of how many companies does that corps consist?—It consists now of ten companies.

1047. The establishment is 100 men per company?—Yes.

1048. How many men were there originally raised?—Originally 240. There are at present 702 on the roll. I think that within the last year we have lost 30 or 40; that is to say, there have been 30 or 40 more withdrawals than entrances. I think the reason of this is, that we have thrown upon our captains of companies the responsibility as to the men's subscriptions, that is to say, they have to return every month so many effective members, and to pay the subscriptions for those they return. Therefore they have been particular lately in striking out all doubtful members.

1049. What is the amount of the subscription?—12s. a year, or 1s. a month.

1050. If a captain has a company consisting of 100 men he is responsible for 5l.?—Yes, per month.

1051. Is there any arrear of subscriptions?—Yes. The captains owe last month's subscription, and some small balance besides. When I say they owe, I do not speak as a lawyer. Although we make them responsible in the corps, we could not by law enforce that responsibility against them, but in the corps they are considered responsible and we look to them to produce the amount.

1052. I presume that there are no arrears?—Our present position is this; we give the captains for the last month's subscriptions a margin of about three weeks, and therefore when I say that there are no arrears at the present moment the position of things is this, that there is about the subscription for the last month not paid, but which will be paid in this month. There are some pounds owing, but we are so within the mark that that which is owing from the companies would more than cover the liabilities of the corps.

1053. Are the officers expected to pay higher subscriptions?—No, their subscription is the same as the men's. Of course there are many voluntary things which the officers do, but the subscription is the same.

1054. What are the principal expenses which are defrayed out of the funds of the corps?—The principal expenses are the expense of headquarters, and, till lately, drill instructors and extra ammunition.

1055. Do you include a drill shed?—We drill in the open air always; there is a small covered place, but that we are very seldom in. Until very lately our expenses included a drill serjeant, but now we are at no expense for a drill serjeant, all the extra work beyond what the Government serjeants do is done by volunteers. Another expense is the band, our band expenses are very small, because we have always felt that that was an expense to be kept down as much as possible, therefore we took none but volunteers. We pay the bandmaster a very small salary, and we have no band except what the volunteers furnish; we pay them nothing, but we give the boys their clothes, and these and the bandmaster's salary amounts to between 50l. and 60l. a year.

1056. (*Col. MacMurdo.*) Is that paid out of the funds of the corps?—Yes, and that is the total amount of the cost of the band, under 60l. a year. Our other expenses are simply for extra ammunition. We have the common expenses of a house and of arranging for going to field days, and small sums for advertising and so on. But we stand literally at very small expense, I should mention that we have a certain fee to pay at Plumstead every week; we have the use of the Government range not having one of our own, and we have every day that we go Plumstead to pay a certain fee to the Government people there who are in charge of the range.

1057. (*Chairman.*) Are the expenses of the journey to and from Plumstead paid by the men?—Yes.

1058. Are the expenses of attending all the brigade and divisional field days also paid by the men?—Yes, always.

1059. Have you ever contributed anything towards the uniform of the men?—When the corps was first started we got a certain sum of money subscribed by strangers outside the corps. We had then something under 200l. subscribed by persons outside the corps, and when this money came in a sum of 50l. was voted to assist those members of the corps who could not purchase their own uniforms. I was then in command of the corps, and the giving out of this money was left in my hands. It was not to be known who had it, but the money would just come to me, and if they wanted assistance I was to consider how much should be allowed to them out of the 50l. The applications in that way did not exhaust the 50l., for a certain balance was returned by me. Since then we have never allowed anything; the men have found their own clothes entirely.

1060. When the clothing of the men requires renewal, do you think there will be any difficulty in getting it renewed?—I believe that there will be none whatever, so far as I have seen. My experience is that there is no difficulty as to the clothing. Our corps is, I suppose, the poorest in London, there not being more than seven or eight gentlemen in it; but as to the clothing I see no difficulty. We have never found any. The only difficulty has been to keep the clothing as simple as possible; in fact, that the men should get cheap clothing instead of dear clothing. We have a certain number of men in the corps, almost the first men who joined it, and who influence the corps a good deal, and they are strongly against any expense in the shape of ornaments. Altogether the men pay down pretty well, and there is no difficulty about the uniform. The men you want will pay, and ought to pay, for their uniforms, and they will be just the men who will keep the uniforms simple and cheap.

1061. What is the expense of your uniform?—Within a few shillings of 3l.

1062. What is the expense of the accoutrements?—I mean for the whole thing, 3l. pays for belt and everything. I should say that lately the men have carried a cross belt. That we resisted, but they wear it now, and I think that the cross belt would bring the whole cost to 1s. or 2s. over 3l. Within the last few months we have allowed the members to vote upon the matter, and they carried the cross belt.

1063. Have you not any knapsack?—No.

1064. Nor a great coat?—There is a great coat, but we do not enforce it. We have a haversack, and that is included in the estimate.

1065. You stated just now that you did not contribute any additional sum to the drill serjeants?—Yes.

1066. They merely receive the pay received from the Government?—Yes, but we give them lodging. We have a house at headquarters, and there are a certain number of rooms which we give them; that and coals. They have their pay. We give them nothing more.

1067. That is paid for out of the regimental fund?—Yes.

1068. How often do you have battalion drills?—Once a week. We have battalion drill on Saturdays and adjutant's drill on Wednesdays.

1069. You do not, I presume, allow a man to attend a battalion drill who has not attended a certain number of setting-up drills?—We have three classes. The adjutant begins at the beginning of the year in January, and he passes the men through those classes. There is a certain efficiency required in each class; when a man joins he goes into the third class, and having acquired a certain degree of efficiency he is put into the second class. That will enable him to attend the adjutant's drill. The adjutant examines him again when he has passed through his second

H 4

Maj.
T. Hughes.

3 June 1862.

class, and if he is declared fit he is put into the first class, and then, and not before, he attends battalion drills and field days. We have found that to be a very useful rule. Unfortunately in the turn which things have taken in the volunteers, it is very difficult now to give the men the idea that it is a favour to let them join your corps, but having classes in that way operates as a stimulus, which is very useful.

1070. What is the turn which things have taken to which you just alluded?—I think all the excessive expense to which most corps have gone in the shape of prizes and bands, and so on, has demoralized the corps. Now the men are constantly in the habit of leaving, or of threatening to leave, corps which are not managed as they like.

1071. You are of opinion that these expenses are unnecessary?—Yes, I do consider them unnecessary; and I was going to say that they have ruined us, but that is not so, because there is a very sound part in the metropolitan force, a very sound nucleus in every corps, of men who come from right motives, considering that it is their duty to take part in the defence of the country if necessary. But a very large proportion of them come from the vanity of the thing, and because there are those immense prizes held out to them. There is extraordinary expense gone to in entertainments of all sorts, and follies which have in my opinion done more harm to the volunteer movement in the metropolis than any other single thing.

1072. (*Viscount Hardinge.*) Can you see any reason why the system of economy which you have introduced into your corps, and which, from your own evidence, appears to have been highly successful, should not be applied to the other metropolitan corps?—I think that unless this Commission should, or Parliament should enforce some economy of that sort, no good will be done whatever by this inquiry. I think that that is the first thing that is wanted to be done. If any help is given to the volunteers at all, it should be given upon some such plan as this,—that no Government relief should be given to any corps which expends above a certain per-centage of its funds upon bands and entertainments, silver prizes, and so on, and all those extravagances.

1073. What does your band cost?— £60 a year, or a little under. We made a strong resistance to any band, but we were obliged to have one.

1074. (*Chairman.*) Do you think that the efficiency of the corps, if your plan of economy were adopted, could be preserved without any assistance from the Government?—No; I think there must be some assistance given. But I think that the great object in giving it will be, to give it only on condition of the corps keeping down the extravagances which have grown up to so large an extent, and that corps whose returns and accounts show that they have expended such large sums as are spent every day on follies should not be assisted to the same extent as those corps which show by their accounts that they have simply expended all their funds on necessaries.

1075. (*Viscount Hardinge.*) I dare say you are aware that some corps expend from 300l. to 600l. per annum on their bands?—Yes; one at least spends more than that.

1076. (*Chairman.*) To what extent do you think it would be necessary to grant assistance to the volunteer corps?—No man can speak confidently of any but his own corps. From what I have seen of the country corps I believe they are very poorly off, and I am sure that they must, if they are to go on, have very considerable assistance. But, speaking entirely for my own corps now, I think that what would be quite sufficient to keep us effective in every respect would be to take off the shoulders of the men their present subscription. I mean to say, that if they got 12s. a year, which is the amount of our subscription—not per head, but per effective man, who has passed into the first class and appears at the inspection; if we got that sum we could keep our corps perfectly effective and going on satisfactorily.

1077. You would not anticipate any diminution in the numbers if that plan were adopted?—I think not.

1078. (*Earl of Ducie.*) Could you by an increased expenditure increase the efficiency of your corps?—No; but we could increase our numbers.

1079. (*Viscount Hardinge.*) Would you recommend that the 12s. should be spent entirely at the discretion of the commanding officer?—I have scarcely considered that point.

1080. Would you prefer that the aid from the Government should be given in a more indirect way, and that an estimate should be sent in from a corps showing the expenses for headquarters, a range, serjeants, and so on, and that the assistance should be given indirectly under those heads, rather than by a direct grant to be expended at the discretion of the commanding officer?—Speaking off-hand, I should prefer that each corps should send in a specification, so much for a range, so much for headquarters, and so on. My reason is that I think there would be a better hold upon the expenditure. My object is to have an efficient force at as cheap a rate as possible to the country; and I think that whatever will have the effect of minimising the relief that must be granted, taking care that that relief is applied entirely to the necessary wants of the corps, and not to extravagance, would be the best plan.

1081. If a capitation grant were made by the Government, to be spent entirely at the discretion of the commanding officer, the Government would have no security that it was not spent upon bands?—None whatever.

1082. (*Lord Overstone.*) In addition to the consideration which you have very properly mentioned, that of its being important to have the most efficient force at the smallest possible cost, and therefore, on that account, that the Government advance should be as small as possible, do you not think that the sense of receiving Government aid is in some degree antagonistic to the great principle of the volunteer movement?—Yes, I think so. It is unfortunate that there should be a necessity, and it is with great reluctance that I would receive a penny.

1083. Notwithstanding that, you still think that Government aid, to some limited extent, and in some qualified form, is still desirable, if not absolutely necessary?—I think it is absolutely necessary, if you desire to keep up the force at anything like its present numbers.

1084. Have you formed anything like a deliberate judgment upon the question whether, during a period in which the apprehension of serious danger to the safety of the country is not strong, it is desirable to make great efforts to keep up the force in its present state of efficiency, or when the danger was the greatest?—I think that whatever force you have it is absolutely necessary to keep it in the highest possible state of efficiency. It is quite another question whether it is desirable to keep up the force at any particular number, say, 150,000 or 100,000; but whatever force you have, it would be useless, unless you keep it in certainly as efficient a state as it is in now.

1085. I understand you to mean that whatever the number of the force may be, the most essential principal is that that number should be kept in a high state of discipline and organization?—Quite so; and that is the reason why I stated that whatever aid is given should be only given to first-class men. You should entirely keep out of sight all those who are not reported by the adjutant to the commanding officer as first-class men.

1086. Do you think that during a period of comparative confidence and absence of alarm a more limited number of men, still kept up in a state of high efficiency, would be sufficient for every essential purpose of any volunteer movement?—Guarding myself as merely expressing my own private opinion, I answer Yes.

1087. I think you have stated that your corps is one of the poorest in the metropolis?—I believe it to be the poorest.

1088. Notwithstanding that, you feel perfectly satisfied that the clothing of that corps ought to be and may be properly left to the resources of the corps itself?—Yes; and I say so for this reason, which I have given before, that there was a certain sum of money set apart for the purpose of assisting members who so desired it, and who chose to come to me and say that they were too poor to clothe themselves; and out of the subscriptions that came from the public for that purpose they were assisted. But the fund so set apart was not exhausted, and I returned a part of it, after keeping it for a sufficient time, into the funds of the corps, and ever since then we have never assisted any member by a single penny, except the boys in the band. We were obliged to dress them, but that is included in the 60l. a year.

1089. Is it the result of your observations that there is at the present time a decided tendency to diminished efficiency in the volunteer corps, either as to their numbers or their discipline and numbers?—I think there is a decided tendency to a falling off in their numbers; but so far as my own experience goes, those who stick to it, stick to it from a good motive; and they become more and more efficient, and more and more reliable. In my own corps there is a large per-centage who will do that, and upon whom we can thoroughly rely. There is also in the corps a certain surplus upon whom we feel that we have a very insecure hold, and who may go any day.

1090. Do you attribute that tendency to diminished numbers to any one specific cause?—I attribute it, not to any one specific cause, but to several specific causes.

1091. Will you be good enough to state what you consider to be the principal causes?—In the first place, there has been an entire re-action in a certain portion of the force, arising from such causes as want of purpose, disappointed vanity, and so on. Then, unfortunately, we have had, in the public press and in other quarters, a very false stimulus applied to the volunteers. They have been petted and spoiled, and the consequence has been that we have got in a lot of men who did not come in seriously from a patriotic desire to do their best for the defence of the country; and these men are now tired of the work, and falling away fast. Then there are prize meetings, and balls, and all such things as those; great entertainments at which large sums are spent upon the frivolous part of volunteering. There are very great inducements of that kind held out, and those inducements have been brought to bear upon a lot of men who have not come in seriously, and boys who have not come in seriously. But these, I think, are beginning to slack off, and I have no doubt that if matters go on as they are we shall lose a very considerable number in that way. I think that there is a small proportion whom we shall not really lose, but whom we shall nominally lose; men who have made themselves competent and thoroughly efficient in drill, but who find now that the attendance is burdensome, and therefore they drop out of the ranks, but they are men upon whom we can rely. The Act of Parliament requires so many attendances, and those attendances it is not convenient for them to give; but I believe that in the event of any serious demand being made for their services, as in the case of an invasion, we should get them again directly. We cannot return them as effectives, but we should have them again. I look upon them as not being lost, and I should very much like to see a law passed by which we could retain those men on the strength of the corps instead of losing them.

1092. I understand your view to be that the volunteer movement was originally constituted under two classes of motives: one, the light and frivolous, and therefore the non-permanent motive, and the other a deep sense of public feeling and principle?—Not exactly. I think that the volunteer movement started under a real sense of public duty; and that the men who first came in, came in on the right principle.

They came in to do the thing as reasonably and effectually as possible, and it was not until all this fuss was made, and they were told, by some of their leaders and the press, that they were better than soldiers, and they began to get 50l. prizes to shoot for, it was not until then that we got the element which has been to us, from the beginning, an element of trouble and anxiety, and in fact an element which I, for one, do not value highly. However, I must say that many of those who came in afterwards, and to whom I refer as coming in from finding that it was a thing for which they were praised up.—I think that many of those who came in afterwards have since taken a very right part; and I think they look upon the work now as a duty, and many of them are as sound members as the others. But I have found in my own corps that there is a nucleus of those first men who did come in, upon whom we have to rely; it is around them that the rest gather; they leaven the rest, and so far as they leaven the rest the corps is the better for it.

1093. Can you form any judgment as to the extent to which the present volunteer force could be maintained upon the supposition that those habits which you designate as frivolous and injudicious were abandoned?—I can judge only from my own corps; and I think that we should lose, perhaps, about 15 per cent.

1094. (*Lord Elcho.*) Would they be of a class which would be a great loss to you?—Not in my opinion.

1095. (*Lord Overstone.*) Do you think that that portion of the volunteer force which has been either drawn into it, or which is now retained in it under the motives which you have alluded to, is by any means equal in value, for the real purposes of the force, to that portion of the force which is retained in it by the higher principle which you have alluded to?—Certainly not, speaking of my own corps.

1096. Do you think that you can with any degree of accuracy distinguish between those two classes?—In my own corps I can, and therefore perhaps I should state the reasons why I can. My corps is a peculiar corps. The three first companies were formed in the working men's college in the north of London, in which I have been for years one of the council, and therefore I know the men intimately. I had been connected with them both as teacher and as a member of the council for a long time, and therefore I knew the men much more intimately than I should suppose any commanding officer ordinarily could know the men who came to him. Therefore I stand in a peculiar position; my experience would scarcely be of any great value, because it is a special experience, and therefore I wish to guard myself by saying that I can speak only of my own corps.

1097. I understand you to be of opinion, founded of course upon your experience, that the most prudent mode of dealing with the volunteer force would be to extend a limited amount of Government pecuniary aid upon conditions which should exclude those corps in which the expenditure had been carried on in an extravagant manner?—I think if that could be done it would be very desirable.

1098. Do you think it would be difficult to do that?—I have been considering the matter a good deal since the appointment of this commission, and I have found that it is very difficult to see how it could be very well done; still I think it may be done.

1099. Can you throw out any suggestion as to the mode of approaching that result?—My own impression is that in any corps in which more than a certain proportion of the funds or annual income was spent in a certain manner, say on bands, prizes, balls, &c., that there is no reason why assistance should be given to those corps.

1100. You are of opinion that the advisable course for this Commission to take would be to devise, if possible, some terms or conditions on which Government assistance should be rendered; those terms and conditions being framed with a view, if possible, to

Maj.
T. Hughes.

3 June 1862.

I

Maj.
T. Hughes.

2 June 1862.

limiting the Government assistance to cases in which there had previously been no foolish expenditure ?—Decidedly.

1101. But you think that Government assistance to a certain extent is essential towards maintaining the efficiency of the volunteer corps ?—Yes.

1102. You would recommend as the result of your experience and judgment that Government assistance should be given to that extent and upon the conditions suggested ?—Yes ; if I could do without a penny I would not have it. I think it is the business of a volunteer force to do without a penny if they can avoid taking it from the country. But my belief is, that in order to keep the volunteer force in a state of proper efficiency certain aid must be given to certain corps.

1103. I understand your feeling to be that the receipt of Government aid is in itself to a greater or lesser degree antagonistic to the principle of the volunteer movement, but notwithstanding that, some interference on the part of the Government is necessary, but that it should be guarded by many very cautious restrictions, in order to prevent the growth of extravagant and foolish habits of expenditure ?—Yes, and I think that you would be doing the greatest possible benefit if you could work out any plan by which the extravagance, the stupid and demoralizing expenditure which has taken place, could be cut down.

1104. (*Lord Elcho.*) You have mentioned as one example of that demoralizing and foolish expenditure, balls ?—Yes.

1105. Without giving any opinion as to whether it is wise or unwise to have bazaars, balls, and concerts, is it not the case that those bazaars, balls, and concerts have not been so much expenditure on the part of the corps for amusement, but the object has been to raise funds to carry on the corps ?—I do not know.

1106. You have spoken generally of balls and concerts having taken place in other corps, and I ask you whether it is not the case, that instead of money being expended for those balls and concerts for the amusement of the corps, they have not been given with the object of raising funds to meet the expenses of the corps ?—I believe that that has been so in general ; but I also know that in several cases those entertainments have resulted in throwing a considerable amount of extra expense upon the corps.

1107. That is to say the speculation has failed ?—Yes.

1108. But it was not with the view of spending the money of the corps that they had recourse to those balls and concerts, but to obtain funds for the corps ?—Yes, in many cases it has been so ; but in some corps the expense has been deliberately incurred ; in some corps it has not been simply a method of obtaining funds, but it has been deliberate extravagance.

1109. Do you know of any corps in which balls have been given for the sake of the balls themselves, and not for the sake of getting money for the use of the corps ?—Yes, I do.

1110. Supposing that the line that you have suggested should be drawn, namely that those corps only should receive Government assistance which had not been frivolous in their expenditure, how many corps in London do you think would so receive assistance ?—Three or four, perhaps.

1111. Out of about 40 ?—Yes ; but bear in mind that I do not mean to say that those corps which have done many of these things should be absolutely excluded, but what I mean is, that a scale should be laid down, if possible, so that those corps which had spent 50 per cent. of their incomes upon such matters should not receive the same amount of assistance as those corps which had spent, say, only 5 per cent. ; it is clear that they do not want aid who apply these large sums to improper purposes.

1112. You have mentioned prizes as being a frivolous part of the movement ; do you consider that rifle shooting is an inducement to men to volunteer and to remain in their corps, and an amusement which is likely to be permanently attractive ?—I think it not only an amusement which the men like, and not only likely to be permanently attractive, but I think it is of immense importance to keep up the practice of rifle shooting, and to encourage the men to give their best energies to it. I consider that of the highest possible importance, but I think that that can be done without giving high prizes.

1113. You do not object to prizes, but you think that the prizes given are too high ?—I object to all prizes in principle. We must have some, but the lower they are kept the better. I think that rifle shooting would be quite as well kept up, like cricket or boating, by a small medal, or a little silver or bronze rifle, or some similar thing ; but you do not want a tea pot that costs 50 guineas—only something for a man to show to his friends and enable him to say that he has been out on such and such a day and helped his corps or his county to win.

1114. It is not to the principle, but to the abuse of the principle of shooting for prizes that you are opposed ?—Entirely so.

1115. With regard to bands, would you object to a corps spending its money on a band provided that the money came from special subscriptions on the part of members of the corps, and was not taken out of the annual subscriptions or the ordinary funds of the corps ?—I am sorry to say that the bands are a necessity ; I quite admit that it is necessary for each corps to have a band, and it is the duty of the commanding officer of each corps to get that band as cheaply as possible, and to get it by volunteers if possible, and if he cannot so get it to get one as cheaply as he can.

1116. I understood you to say that you had two classes of men in your corps, one class that joined you from a sense of public duty, and another from rather more frivolous motives, is that so ?—It is. There are two distinct classes.

1117. Those who were actuated by public principle joined you at first, but latterly you have been joined by men from other motives ?—Yes, generally speaking those who came in afterwards came in from lower motives.

1118. (*Colonel MacMurdo.*) Have those who first joined you fallen away much ?—Not at all ; the nucleus of the corps is as sound as it can be. The few of the good men who have gone are men upon whom we can put our hands any day. The subscription of 1s. a month is something, although it is not much ; but the necessary attendance is a pull upon them. The time is so much out of their pocket, because they are men who live by their daily wages ; but if there were any real demand for their services we could get them. But of the other class of men who have left us many have gone into other corps, where perhaps they get a finer dress, or where their friends are ; altogether we have lost more than we have gained in the last year.

1119. (*Lord Elcho.*) Have you lost many of the men who first joined you ?—We have lost a few of those, but, as I have stated before, we know generally where they are, and can get them.

1120. In your corps what were the inducements which led the other class of men to come to you, because I presume that you have avoided high prizes and balls, and those frivolous inducements to which you have referred ?—Simply this, there was great excitement about the matter, and every youngster in London was wanting to get into some volunteer corps. They looked about to see which corps they could get into in the cheapest way, and they found that in ours the subscription was perhaps the smallest in London, and they came accordingly. That I think was the principal reason, that our subscription was very small, and so we got those other men. The reasons why they have gone are many ; some of them got tired of it, and some of them liked to get a finer uniform.

1121. The expense of your corps being less, and the cost of the uniform being less than in other corps, you think have been the inducements of many men to come to you who would otherwise have gone into other corps?—Yes, I think so.

1122. You have stated that you do not anticipate any difficulty with regard to clothing your corps, and you have also stated that a fund was raised out of which those who chose to come forward and apply for it were assisted. Have you had any defaults in the repayments?—I kept the books and accounts for the first nine or ten months, and during that time the instalments were almost universally paid. But with respect to that matter the clothing fund was placed in the hands of one of our captains, whom I should advise the commissioners to examine. He consulted me while I was in command, but since that time I have no special knowledge. We have never had to sue any member.* I have been surprised at the punctuality with which, on the whole, the instalments have been paid. When I became commanding officer, and undertook the responsibility, I fully expected to have to make up a considerable deficiency on account of defalcations, and that the men would often not repay the instalments which they undertook to pay; we let them pay, some of them, as low as 1s. 6d. a week, and, as I have stated, I fully expected, as the then commanding officer of the corps, to have to make up a considerable sum. But I have never paid a penny, and I do not believe that Colonel Bathurst has ever paid a penny.

1123. Are you of opinion that your artizans will be able to renew their uniform?—Yes.

1124. Many of them?—All the good ones.

1125. What proportion of them do you think will be able to renew them?—I believe that all the good men will be able.

1126. Do you reckon that 50 per cent. of them will be able to renew their uniforms?—About half, I think, will certainly do it.

1127. About half of them would renew their uniforms?—About half of the artizans. Our corps is composed of about half artizans and half clerks and others. I think that about half the artizans are thorough good men, and will renew their uniforms; as to the clerks, it is not so important to them. I think that probably every one of them will renew his uniform, at any rate that this expense will not deter one of them from going on.

1128. Do you believe that the other half of the artizans would continue in the corps if their clothing was provided for them, and they had no expense to meet but the subscription?—I do not say that the other half will not remain in any case, but I feel confident as to the half, that the half will go on, that they have put their hand to it and that they will not go back, and that they will do whatever is necessary, even at great sacrifice to keep to it. I will not say that the other half of the artizans will go unless they get their clothing, but I think it is possible that they may.

1129. Without assistance do you think that your artizan corps can be kept up to its present strength?—No.

1130. In expressing the feeling that you would not receive a penny if you could avoid it, do you believe that that is the general feeling of the volunteer corps?—No, I do not believe it is the general feeling, but I believe that all the best men in the volunteers would feel so.

1131. Do you not think that the volunteers would, if they could afford it, continue to pay their subscriptions, and if they fall off it is their poverty and not their will which leads to it?—Yes, in most cases.

1132. Is it the case in your opinion that they benefit from volunteering universally?—I believe it is so.

1133. Have not the expenses fallen very heavily upon individuals?—Speaking from general knowledge and from rumour I believe it is so, but speaking from my own individual knowledge I should say no. I believe that the expenses have fallen very seriously on individuals in many corps, but it has not been so in ours.

1134. What is the cost of your uniform?—Three pounds.

1135. How long do you reckon it will last?—Three years.

1136. Do you think that an outlay of 3l., or 1l. a year for uniform, and 12s. for subscription is a very heavy tax which an artizan pays for the privilege of serving his country as a volunteer?—Yes; I think it is very heavy, but I think it is a tax which all those men who are worth anything have willingly undertaken. No doubt they would be very glad to be relieved from a portion of it, and I believe that the country ought to be very grateful to the men who pay it.

1137. Have you any rifle range?—No. We shoot at Plumstead.

1138. How many of your men have fired at all with ball?—My impression is that more than half of the corps have done so this year.

1139. Have you found your musters fall off very much since the Brighton field day?—Yes.

1140. What has been the smallest number which you have had at battalion parade since that time?—At one battalion parade we were I think under 130.

1141. Is it the fact that since the Brighton field day you have mustered at battalion parade only 25?—Never at battalion parade.

1142. (*Viscount Hardinge.*) You have stated that you deprecate field days?—No; I think them very useful indeed, but I deprecate all excitement about them, all the fuss that is made about them.

1143. (*Col. MacMurdo.*) Is it a review that you deprecate?—I do not deprecate it, but I deprecate the perpetual excitement that there is about it, and the men being led to think that volunteering cannot go on unless there is this excitement and a perpetual effort to keep the excitement up. The men who are worth anything will stay, and therefore when we have these field days the more quiet they are the better, and the less excited the volunteers are about them the better.

1144. (*Viscount Hardinge.*) Did the working men in your corps pay for their fares to Brighton and back?—Yes, every man of them.

1145. When they go to practice at Plumstead do they pay?—Yes, they pay every Saturday, and a very great tax it is upon them.

1146. (*Lord Elcho.*) Does it cost them 1s. each?—No, 6d.

1147. (*Viscount Hardinge.*) What do you pay for your headquarters?—We pay 40l. for the whole of the house; the adjutant lives there and he takes a certain portion of the rent off our shoulders.

1148. Where do you drill?—In the playground of the London University; we have our battalion drills and adjutant drills there in the winter; we have our company drills in a space behind the college, we have laid it down in gravel and we drill the college companies there; there is company drill also at the quarters of the out companies, and the battalion and adjutant drills are in the University ground, unless we go to the Regent's park.

1149. Do you think that the expense of headquarters could be reduced in the metropolitan corps? It is a very serious expense.

1150. Do you see your way to any reduction in that item?—I do not know what it costs in any corps but my own, but I know that many of them must be very expensive. I do not think we can reduce our head-quarters' expenses.

1151. Do you give any extra allowance to the Government serjeants?—Lodging, coals, and I believe candles.

1152. Do you give any additional allowance to the adjutant?—We give none, but he pays us for his lodging.

1153. (*Col. MacMurdo.*) Does the adjutant subsist

Maj. T. Hughes.

3 June 1862.

---

* The witness wishes to correct this statement. He finds on inquiry that since he gave up the command seven summonses have been issued for arrears, all in one company.

Maj.
T. Hughes.

3 June 1862.

upon his pay?—I am sure he does, at least I do not know what else he has to subsist upon.

1154. Has he ever complained of his pay and allowances?—Never.

1155. (*Viscount Hardinge.*) Are you aware that the adjutants receive a considerable sum in addition to their pay?—I have heard so, but our adjutant does not. He was a non-commissioned officer.

1156. (*Col. MacMurdo.*) In the early part of your evidence you stated, I think, that among the expenses which fall heavily upon the corps extra ammunition was one?—Not now, we pay nothing now; we have not paid anything for a long time.

1157. You find that the Government allowance is quite sufficient?—Yes, quite sufficient.

1158. (*Major Harcourt.*) Does your adjutant find sufficient work to employ him the whole day?—I should think he did.

1159. Is he employed in the day time as well as in the evening?—I think so; our corps is scattered; we have out-lying companies, we have one at Price's patent candle manufactory, then there is another company at Paddington, and there is another close to Regent street, so that the adjutant has a great deal of work to do in consequence of the scattered nature of the corps.

1160. (*Lieut.-Col. Barttelot.*) Do you keep your rifles in the armoury?—Each member of the first class has his own rifle.

1161. (*Lord Overstone.*) Do you think that we ought to consider this volunteer movement as a sort of *levée en masse* of nearly every person physically capable of bearing arms, defraying the expenses of the movement from whatever source the money can be obtained from, or do you think it ought to be looked upon in principle as a self-supporting institution, the persons joining it finding the means of defraying the expenses connected with it for the purpose of keeping them down to the lowest possible amount?—I feel very strongly that it is the duty of every man now who can do so to learn the use of arms in order that he may be able to take part in the defence of the country, and the more reasonably that can be done the better. If you can excite sufficient patriotism amongst the men of England, or get sufficient funds subscribed to enable them to do so without coming to the Government, I think it would be better, but I feel, nevertheless that at present there must be aid given. But the right principle is, decidedly, that men should come forward to defend their country, if possible, at their own expense.

1162. (*Viscount Hardinge.*) Do you think that further aid in whatever shape given will to some extent alter the character of the force?—No, we have aid already; we have rifles, adjutants, and drill serjeants.

1163. Do you mean that further aid would not alter the character of the force?—I think that indiscriminate aid would demoralize it still further ; but further aid, if properly applied, will not alter the character of the force.

1164. (*Lord Overstone.*) Is it your opinion that it is important to maintain the general character of this force as a self-supporting force, and that whatever aid is obtained consistently with that principle should be in such limited amounts and upon such terms as should not invalidate the great principle of its being a self-supporting movement?—Yes.

1165. (*Lord Elcho.*) You have stated that supposing 1*l.*, or any definite sum, was given to be expended by the commanding officer in the way that he thought best for the good of his regiment, the Government would have no security that it was properly spent?—I did not mean to say that; it depends upon the character of the commanding officer.

1166. Might not the application of the money be restricted to certain things?—That is just what I wish to see.

1167. You have suggested that commanding officers should send in certain specifications; in that case you must trust to their honour quite as much as you would in any other case, must you not?—It is one thing to make a man sit down and go through the returns sent in by his adjutant, saying we want so much for headquarters, and so much for other purposes, for then a man begins to think seriously what he will sign, but if you say to him, "it is to be 1*l.* a man," "yes," he would say, "I shall spend that all right."

1168. Supposing that the alternative is a specification in the spending of a certain sum in certain cases would it not come practically to the same thing?—I think not.

1169. You have proposed that a commanding officer should send in with the assistance of his adjutant a specification saying that he requires a certain sum for certain things; the alternative that I suggest is that a certain sum should be allowed to a commanding officer which he at his discretion should expend upon certain fixed things for the benefit of his regiment, not excluding bands and those things which are considered legitimate expenses?—I do not see any real difference except that the trouble would come beforehand in the one case, and afterwards in the other.

1170. (*Lieut.-Col. Barttelot.*) You have stated that you have lost several of your best men from your corps who are unable to attend the number of drills prescribed by the Government. If that number were reduced to eight drills a year, do you think that you could have retained those men?—Yes, I think so.

1171. (*Earl of Ducie.*) You have stated that your corps is a very poor one, partly composed of artizans and the remainder consisting of clerks?—Yes, and warehousemen, shopmen, and others.

1172. What are the average wages of the artizans?—We have among them some skilled engravers, pianoforte makers, and other highly paid mechanics, others are mere common labourers ; the wages of labourers in London are 18*s.* a week, which is the minimum in our corps, except that we have a few boys who are still to a certain extent supported by their parents ; shoemakers may average less, but 18*s.* a week is the lowest recognized wages.

1173. Are there many men receiving wages so small as that?—No, not many ; very few.

1174. Are they mostly single or married men?—Mostly single men, certainly.

1175. Are two-thirds of them single men?—Of those I know, most of them are; there are three companies composed of men from the working men's college, and certainly rather above two-thirds of them are unmarried.

The witness withdrew.

Capt.
J. C. Templer.

Captain JOHN CHARLES TEMPLER examined.

1176. (*Chairman.*) You command the 18th Middlesex Rifle Volunteer Corps at Harrow?—Yes.

1177. Of how many companies does that corps consist?—Of two companies at present ; I have only just received the acceptance of the services of a second company, and perhaps merely for the purposes of this examination it might be as well to consider the 18th as consisting of a single company.

1178. How many men are there in the company?—On the 1st of April there were 100 effectives and five officers ; we were 105 in all.

1179. Is that your strength at the present time?—That has been increased, for within the last month we have enrolled some 26 men more.

1180. How are the funds of your corps raised?—They are raised partly by the subscriptions of the members, that is each enrolled member pays half a guinea a year, each honorary member pays two guiness. We have besides private donations and other sums by letting off our range to other corps.

1181. Have you had any difficulty in obtaining your subscriptions?—None whatever.

1182. Do you see no chance of their falling off?—No.

1183. Do the officers pay more than the men?—No.

1184. They all pay alike?—Yes.

1185. Have you a drill serjeant attached to your corps?—Yes.

1186. More than one?—Only one.

1187. Do you pay him out of your funds more than the Government allowance?—Yes, we do; we pay him 90*l.* a year and his uniform, and that is considerably more, nearly as much again as the Government allowance, but we farm him with the school, that is to say he undertakes also the drill instruction of the public school. We are bound during three terms of the school time to supply him with an assistant. The 18th Middlesex, therefore, is exceptional on that ground, as we have a little assistance which is not common in other corps.

1188. As your corps is increasing and the funds are in a satisfactory position, you do not apprehend anything which is likely to diminish the efficiency of the corps?—Nothing.

1189. (*Col. MacMurdo.*) Of what classes is your corps composed?—Before I came here I took occasion to look through the list, and I found that it was composed of about 40 tradesmen, and I think we have 30 other members with no artizans or labourers among those 30. There was one sculptor, one artist, one general in the army, one member of Parliament, also a captain in the navy, one clergyman, one master in the Exchequer, two justices of the peace, six or seven fellows of the universities of Oxford and Cambridge, and the rest were professional men; there were besides only 1 think three artizans and about five farmers; the whole were men all actively engaged with the exception of two; we have only two disengaged men, I mean persons who follow no profession, and gentlemen in that sense of the word.

1190. Your corps is upon the whole in good circumstances?—Yes.

1191. Have you had opportunities of observing the state of the volunteer force generally, and of forming an opinion upon it?—Yes.

1192. Will you state to the Commissioners whether you apprehend any falling off in the force, and the causes of it?—That is a large question, and I should be glad to divide it, as the reasons that apply are different as to whether the corps is metropolitan or rural. By metropolitan I mean not only London, but Manchester, Liverpool, Glasgow, and, perhaps, one or more other great centres. With regard to the metropolitan force, from circumstances known, perhaps, to some of the members of the Commission, I have had a great opportunity of knowing them. I think that there is no fear whatever as to them, while as to the country corps there is very great fear that they cannot be kept up, unless some money assistance is rendered by the country. I speak as to this from direct communications from commanding officers and friends from Dorset, Devon, and Somersetshire, and from the returns published from time to time in the Volunteer Service Gazette from many other parts of England, which I believe will be found correct. These communications all go to show that unless some decisive assistance be rendered by the country to what may be called the rural corps, they will soon cease to exist as an effective part of the volunteer force.

1193. Have you any particular views as to the form in which that assistance should be given?—Yes. I may say that having looked at the subject with very great scrutiny and care, and that during the whole time that we have been formed, more than two years and a half, indeed, from December 1859, I have come to the conclusion, slowly perhaps, but with entire conviction, that the volunteer is entitled to a complete indemnity from all expenses;

Capt.
J. C. Templer.

3 June 1862.

if you are about to lay down any rule to be co-extensive with England, without excepting the great centres, such as London, Manchester, Liverpool, and Glasgow, where there is opportunity and means for a good deal of aid independent of the Government, that is, if you find that you can only legislate by adopting one general rule, I think that general rule should be based on the principle of complete indemnity, not only from battalion expenses and ranges, but with reference to the uniform also. In short, I would give the volunteer everything, and merely call upon him for his time.

1194. (*Viscount Hardinge.*) Have you ever calculated what that would amount to per man?—I should say it would amount at least to two guineas per man.

1195. Would two guineas per man completely indemnify him for all expenses?—I think it would, exclusive of the rifle and ammunition, of course. I would not pay it to the man, but to the commanding officer, to go into the funds of the corps; he would consult his committee, at least I presume he would like to have the moral support of and lean upon his committee, although he being chairman would have the greater weight in determining how the money should be best expended for the good of the corps. In many cases a great deal of the establishment expenses have been incurred, and consequently you have not in keeping up a corps now so large an expenditure as you would have had at first; for example, in my first year the expenses were about 600*l.*, in the last year they fell to 400*l.*, and this year I hope to do it for still less, probably for 200*l.*

1196. Would two guineas per man cover the expenses for clothing, accoutrements, travelling expenses on field days, and going to rifle ranges?—I think it would; I think you would give a complete indemnity by that, though it would no doubt require considerable economy.

1197. What do you pay for your uniform?—Five guineas over all; that includes an undress tunic, but we can do it cheaper now. Upon any renewal of the uniform it would cost not more than 3*l.* to 4*l.*, or say under 4*l.*

1198. (*Col. MacMurdo.*) You can do it cheaper in consequence of the Government supplying you with cloth under cost price?—There is some doubt about that, whether it is a saving or not; as far as it has gone it appears that there would be a saving.

1199. (*Viscount Hardinge.*) You would put down 3*l.* 10*s.* for the clothing without accoutrements?—No; with accoutrements.

1200. At what amount do you put them?—The cross belt and waist belt only cost 16*s.*, and the ornaments would make it a little more; they would be about 5*s.* more.

1201. Do you see any reason why the cost of the uniform in any corps should exceed 3*l.* 10*s.*?—Certainly not; we paid five guineas, but undoubtedly the expenses now as compared with the expenses when we formed may be considerably reduced.

1202. Do you see any reason why the uniform, generally speaking, should cost more than that amount, taking into consideration the assistance which the Government give you now in clothing?—No, I do not.

1203. (*Lieut.-Col. Barttelot.*) Do you belong to an administrative battalion?—No.

1204. (*Lord Elcho.*) Have you had considerable correspondence with the volunteers throughout the country?—Yes, very considerable.

1205. The result of that, as I gathered it from what you have stated, is an impression on your part and on the part of your friends that further assistance is required in some shape to maintain the force in its present strength?—Decidedly.

1206. Has that correspondence with the volunteers throughout the country at all touched upon the question of uniform?—With many of them, certainly.

1207. From your knowledge of the force generally do you believe that any very large portion of the

I 3

force has been supplied with uniforms from other than their own individual funds?—You mean of course excepting the honorary members?

1208. Yes?—Certainly; almost all.

1209. A great part of the corps is at present clothed not at the expense of the individuals themselves, but from extraneous sources?—Quite so, that is by subscriptions and extraneous aids.

1210. What proportion of the whole force should you think have been so supplied with uniforms, assuming it to be 150,000?—I cannot say; I should think in round numbers two-thirds of the whole force.

1211. Your calculation is that two-thirds of the whole force have been supplied with uniforms from extraneous sources, and that they have not been provided at their own expense?—I should think so, except the metropolis; I think the fair way would be to except the great centres.

1212. (*Viscount Hardinge.*) On what data do you found that answer, that two-thirds of the whole force have been so clothed, merely from hearsay?—No; it is from correspondence; but it is probably a very rough guess, I could not test it numerically.

1213. In the county of Dorset the corps are probably, financially speaking, worse off than in many other counties?—I think that they are not worse off than in Somersetshire, or indeed than in any other purely rural districts.

1214. Are they well supported by honorary members and gentlemen in the neighbourhood?—Not very well.

1215. (*Lord Overstone.*) You have stated that in your opinion the volunteer is entitled to a complete indemnity, in what sense do you use the word "entitled?"—I imply that I think he gives a very large amount in giving his time, particularly the lower class of volunteers, the working men and tradesmen, who have to maintain themselves and families by their daily labour.

1216. You mean by entitled, I presume, that it would be reasonable and prudent to base any arrangement for work upon that principle?—Quite so.

1217. Of course you are aware that there are three principles on which a military force can be maintained; one, that of the regular army in which the whole expense is defrayed by the Government, the other the opposite extreme, that in which the parties volunteering take upon themselves to find the means of defraying the whole expense, and the third and intermediate course is where the volunteers contribute their personal service, their time and labour, to be supported entirely in all other expenditure; upon which of these principles do you think that the defensive force of this country ought to be based?—I should say on the third. The defensive force need not, and perhaps ought not, to be exclusively based upon the volunteer principle. The regular army should bear its share; but I have no hesitation in saying that the third is the proper principle, as applied to the volunteers, upon which the defensive force of the country should be based.

1218. Would you carry the volunteer principle to the extent of limiting the contributions of the parties to their personal services, and obtaining the pecuniary means from other sources, such as public subscriptions or Government aid?—I would, as applied to the whole force; it is a question undoubtedly of principle; but the principle of aid once admitted, the amount is but a question of degree. When once you say that you will give some support, there is no difference in the principle whether that support is partial or entire; supposing that two guineas a man would be sufficient, it is by no means an unreasonable sum to pay per year for an effective soldier, and I am supported in that view by the present statute law. By the 36th section of the Volunteer Act the Commissioners will find that our fathers took this very view of the subject. I believe that even now by the law we can go and claim, *even for the purposes of military instruction*, and not only in the event of a threatened invasion, from the paymaster wherever he exists something like 1*l*. a man, and two guineas for the commanding officer.

1219. What do you refer to when you say that our fathers took this view?—It was under this Act that the volunteer force was raised in 1803; and in the 36th section will be found these words. "Be it " further enacted, that when any corps of volunteers " shall have assembled to do military duty upon any " appearance of invasion, *or for the purpose of im-* " *proving themselves in military exercise,* it shall be " lawful for the Commissioners of His Majesty's " Treasury to direct that any sum not exceeding one " guinea for every volunteer who shall so assemble, " shall be paid to the captain or other commanding " officer of the said corps, and the sum shall be " laid out in providing necessaries for each such " volunteer," and then, as if they were almost afraid of its detracting from the proper character of the volunteers, it goes on to say, "Provided always, that " nothing herein contained shall extend to authorize " the captain to draw for any such sum for the use of " persons serving in the said corps who shall not " desire to be entitled thereto," so also you might limit it to such of the corps as might wish to receive it; there might be many volunteers, the Inns of Courts for instance would be an excellent example in which they would not ask for it; but supposing it were asked for, would you let the defence of the country be prejudiced by the loss of a valuable body of men, simply because they were not as wealthy as some of the others might be?

1220. Is it your opinion that in organizing the present volunteer movement it would be expedient to draw into the movement every person willing to contribute his physical services, finding the necessary money from other sources than his own means?—No; the great limit, I think, would be laid down from the different positions of men themselves; you could not draw them all in. There would be no need to seek the lowest stratum of society which could supply the militia or the regular army with men.

1221. If you abandoned that limitation which arises from throwing upon parties the necessary expenditure, what is the next line upon which you would rest for putting a limitation to the extent of the movement?—I think that the principle would be fairly met by keeping the broad line of demarcation between the men who received payment, and those who did not; in this case the man receives nothing; it does not go to him, it is spent for him, he never touches it; he gives himself, that is all he brings; and his time is a very solid subscription. It is in itself a broad line of demarcation; the soldier is paid, and the militia man is paid, he gets actually money.

1222. I understood you to say that you would not carry the movement so far as to include every person who was willing to give his personal services and his time, but you would restrict it in some way or other?—I think it is restricted by the different positions of men; there is a stratum of society in London, for example, that never could give their time to it.

1223. Do you think that the sacrifice of time is sufficient without a pecuniary sacrifice?—Yes, decidedly.

1224. If all the expense was defrayed out of the public purse would you then make any greater demand on a man's time than is at present made?—No; on the contrary, it has occurred very strongly to me that it should be reduced. I think that directly a volunteer has shown himself to be a thoroughly efficient member of his corps by either passing through an examination or undergoing such test, or obtaining such certificate as might be deemed necessary to establish the fact of his being thoroughly efficient, the statutable number of drills might be very fairly relaxed; and I should strongly recommend, although things may not be quite ripe for it yet, but next year, that as soon as a man has been three years in the force, and is clearly a good effective man, that ten compulsory drills should be sufficient to keep him on the effective list. I think that the present rule should be relaxed, because I think it would be hard to lose men whom we know to be thoroughly effective, but who are unable to go through the statutory number of 24 drills. I think it is beginning to be felt very generally, and possibly it will be more so. An example may be gathered from the Swiss. I believe the Swiss plan of defence is to have a third reserve, and that third reserve consists wholly of men who are masters of their drill but past the highest activity of youth; they are very valuable men for the defence of the country and they are only required to be out for two days in the year.

1225. (*Viscount Hardinge.*) Do not you think that thoroughly efficient men take great pride in punctual attendance, and actually attend more than the 24 drills?—Yes; you never have to press them if they can come at all, but why have a self-imposed disability that can only work to the detriment of the force? The good man is sure to come if he can; why strike him off if he cannot? He is equally good if he keeps 10 or 20 drills.

1226. The only question would be whether the Government would consent to dispense with what might in their opinion tend to diminish the efficiency of the corps?—They ought to do what is best for the country and for the whole force. It ought not to be a question of bargain at all.

1227. (*Lord Overstone.*) Do you not think that in proportion as the Government is called upon to bear the expense of the movement the Government would be entitled and would be bound to exercise a corresponding degree of interference in regulating that movement for the purpose of securing its efficiency?—Not more than at present, and I think that the principles of Government interference, although it is a very delicate question, were admirably laid down by Lord de Grey nearly twelve months ago, at a meeting at which Lord Elcho was present, upon which occasion an address was presented to Lord do Grey upon his retiring from office; and he laid down in a very few sentences, but as clearly as possible, the principle upon which the War Office authority was to be exercised. His words were:—" The great " principle which has directed all the dealings of the " Government with the volunteers has been, that, while " it was our duty to maintain and enforce adherence " to certain broad rules of order and discipline, without " which no body partaking of a military character " could exist for any useful purpose; it was essential " to the success of a movement of this kind, popular " in its nature, as springing from the spontaneous " patriotism of the nation, that it should be permitted, " within the limits of those necessary rules, to develop " itself in the freest and most unfettered manner. " Heartily concurring in these principles, I endeavoured to apply them in the daily conduct of the " business of my office, and while I always maintained " the just and proper authority of the Secretary of " State, I trust that I never forgot that I had to deal " with a body of volunteers who were freely sacrificing " their time, their money, and their personal convenience in the service of their sovereign and their " country, and who were on every ground entitled to " receive the utmost consideration at the hands of " the Government."

1228. Were those principles so laid down by Lord de Grey bearing in mind that the Government would be called upon to bear a large share of the expense of the movement?—I conclude that his Lordship had the whole subject before him, for even then the expense was a large question; I mean that the question was well afloat as to what aid should be given.

1229. (*Viscount Hardinge.*) Was that touched upon in his reply?—Not expressly, but we were assisted with the rifle and with ammunition; I am not sure but that we had some other assistance also at that time.

1230. The adjutants?—Yes, and the adjutants. I think that his Lordship must have considered the expenses defrayed by the Government, for what he said recommends itself at once to the common sense, unless a light hand is kept on the force it will be dissolved; like a snow wreath we shall melt away.

1231. (*Lord Overstone.*) That is a consideration that may press in either direction. It may be true that unless a very light hand is kept on the force the pressure of Government authority might squeeze up the whole movement, but is not that rather an argument against extensive pecuniary interference by the Government on the principle that with pecuniary interference there must go hand in hand administrative interference?—In my view of the question, I should say that the volunteer movement rests entirely upon the patriotism of the country, and in the case of men who bring their willing and zealous services for the defence of the country, men many of them engaged in providing the means of subsistence for themselves and families, I think it is very hard to call upon them to be out of pocket plus their services, remembering the very moderate limit at which that amount of expense is fixed.

1232. (*Viscount Hardinge.*) If the Government gave to the volunteer force further aid, might they not say we must have a *quid pro quo*, and have at all events the same efficiency that we have now?—If you look at it as a mere question of bargain, it would be so, but the efficiency is a matter of fact to be marked by certain tests; the man certainly ought to be effective before his corps receives the benefit of the aid, and the corps should lose it on his ceasing to be effective.

1233. I suppose you will admit that there is a certain standard of efficiency at which, generally speaking, the volunteer corps have arrived?—Yes.

1234. And it is desirable that that should not be diminished?—Certainly; you see that they have to learn it first, and assuming that they have reached a certain state of efficiency the question is whether they may not be maintained in that with less compulsory attendance than now.

1235. (*Lord Elcho.*) You would admit, I suppose, that the Government, whether they gave much or little, but especially if they gave much, would have a right to expect that the volunteer force was well disciplined and thoroughly efficient?—Clearly so.

1236. And that whatever was necessary to secure that efficiency should be fixed, whether the drills were more or fewer than the statutory number?—Yes, and it would be a great thing if you fixed it, not perhaps as absolutely final, but final with regard to the present generation; it would be a great thing if we could get such an amount of aid on the one hand and such an amount of drill on the other as would satisfy our generation. I am certain that the continued agitation is a bad thing for the force. It is better to have it settled at once, then we shall know what we are about; we ought not to be perpetually, like Oliver Twists, asking for more.

1237. (*Chairman.*) With regard to your own corps there is no desire for any fresh assistance?—Certainly not, while our present extraneous assistance lasts; but we stand very exceptionally, we get a great deal of assistance; our subscription is only half a guinea from our effectives, that is 50 guineas a year about, and our expenditure in the last two years has been 1,000*l*.

1238. (*Lord Elcho.*) Is your corps composed much of the artizan class?—No; it is composed of the tradesmen class; we have only three artizans.

1239. (*Col. MacMurdo.*) You are probably aware that at inspections generally not more than one half of the members are present?—Yes.

1240. Do you think that if the Government clothed as well as armed the force they would be entitled to insist upon the clothed men being seen at least once a year by the inspector?—Yes, clearly so; it would be a very fair and proper arrangement that the men should be there; there is no statutable power at present to enforce the attendance at inspection, and we had some little difficulty last year upon that very point,—it occurred in many instances that a man came

Capt. J. C. Templer.

3 June 1862.

Capt.
J. C. Templer.

3 June 1862.

and said, "I have attended 24 drills, and you cannot strike me off." In strictness I believe he was right; he said, "I am good and efficient for this year;" but, however that may be, it would be quite a fair thing to make it compulsory in future. I am sure the men would think so themselves, and they would look forward to the inspection with pleasure.

1241. You think it is quite necessary that the Government should be entitled to see the whole of the men in the corps, except those who were absent with the leave of their commanding officers on the day of inspection?—Yes, it would be a capital guard against shams.

1242. (*Sir A. Campbell.*) Do you consider that efficiency in the use of the rifle is an essential part of the efficiency of a corps?—Certainly, I do.

1243. You have suggested that the men might attend 10 drills; would you add to that any rifle practice, or would you include in those some rifle practice?—I would add the rifle practice to the 10 drills—the 10 should not include the practice with the rifle—he should shoot in his classes; possibly the third class would be sufficient, but he ought to shoot the shoulder ranges at the least.

1244. Still you would require something?—Yes.

1245. (*Lord Overstone.*) Might Government aid be extended on any principle having reference, for instance, to the number of attendances at drill, or to efficiency in drill, or in the use of the musket?—I think the best principle would be that a man was really effective, and that in the opinion of his commanding officer he was fairly in the actually effective list.

1246. (*Lord Elcho.*) Have you ever considered whether it would be an inducement to men to attend drills and to remain in the corps if they were allowed to wear badges distinguishing the effectives from the non-effectives, like the good conduct stripes in the army?—I do not think that would work well.

1247. The marksman's badge is much sought after?—Yes, it is very much, but a badge for drill would introduce a very uncertain element; it is such a question of degree, smart men or not smart men.

1248. Would you insist upon the men acquiring a knowledge of rifle shooting?—I would not require too high a proficiency; if a man fired his third class, I think that that should be enough; we have very good drills who are not very good shots, and *vice versâ*, both being attentive men.

1249. But you would require a man to go through that class?—Yes, you ought not to have any man in the regiment who cannot shoot.

1250. (*Chairman.*) Have you any further suggestion to make?—There is one point with regard to the metropolitan corps; we have very great difficulty in getting ranges, the present statutes do not meet the difficulty; perhaps they may be regarded as merely the first steps, but undoubtedly there ought to be some power of dealing compulsorily with landowners for ranges, somewhat similar to the powers which are granted in railway Acts.

1251. Was not it made a subject of inquiry previous to the organization of any rifle corps whether they had a range within a certain distance?—Not a range, but the promise of a range, and the promise fell through in many instances. I know of an instance in my own neighbourhood now where the men have about six or eight miles to go to shoot, and it is very hard upon them. It is at Stanmore, where through the groundless opposition of a single landowner, not the proprietor, an excellent range of 1,000 yards and upwards has been lost to the Stanmore corps. A compulsory power would prevent all that kind of opposition; itneed very rarely be resorted to, as the mere power would facilitate mutual arrangements. It is very desirable that the Commission should give expression to this view, as there is not a dearth only, but, I may say, a famine of ranges. It really is a very important point, and I think it would be well accepted; it might be guarded in every way, so that no land should be taken except under the sanction of some Secretary of State's warrant; if we had some power of that kind we might go and deal with the landowners, and it would give a great impulse to the movement. I had a difficult and protracted negotiation at Harrow on the subject, which eventually was successful, and we have now an excellent range of 1,000 yards, which the public school has also the advantage of. Without it I doubt if the corps would long be held together.

The witness withdrew.

Adjourned to Friday next at half-past 12 o'clock.

Friday, 6th June 1862.

PRESENT:

Viscount EVERSLEY.
Earl of DUCIE.
Viscount HARDINGE.
Lord OVERSTONE.
Lord ELCHO.
Lieutenant-Colonel BARTTELOT.

Lieutenant-Colonel Sir A. CAMPBELL.
Lieutenant-General Sir G. A. WETHERALL.
Major-General EYRE.
Colonel MACMURDO.
Major HARCOURT.

VISCOUNT EVERSLEY IN THE CHAIR.

Viscount RANELAGH examined.

Viscount Ranelagh.

6 June 1862.

1252. (*Chairman.*) I believe you command the South Middlesex Rifle Volunteers?—I do.

1253. Consisting of 16 companies?—Nominally of 16 companies.

1254. How many men have you on the muster roll?—Between 1,200 and 1,300.

1255. (*Viscount Hardinge.*) Do you mean 1,200 effectives?—Yes; attested men. Non-effectives are not sworn in.

1256. (*Chairman.*) I believe you are provided with rifle grounds and sheds, and everything necessary?—Yes; I would not undertake the command of the regiment until I had got all that; that is my idea of making the volunteer movement permanent.

1257. Out of what funds were those expenses defrayed; the cost of the rifle sheds, and so forth?—Out of donations and annual subscriptions.

1258. Do your officers and men contribute the same amount per annum?—They contribute equally one guinea.

1259. Do you find that a subscription of one guinea a year covers all the ordinary expenses of the corps?—If we were out of debt it would. I think that I do not press the neighbourhood so much as I might; the donations are unusually small for so large and rich a neighbourhood.

1260. Is the interest of the money which you have borrowed for the erection of those buildings paid out of the subscriptions?—We pay no interest, but have gone into debt on my own and Captain Appleyard's responsibility.

1261. Do your men clothe themselves, or are they assisted in providing their uniforms?—They clothe themselves.

1262. When that clothing requires renewal, do you think they will be able to meet the expense?—They could; but the question is, whether some of the men may not be tired of it. I have no reason for saying that they will not do it.

1263. They all clothed themselves in the first instance, and they have shown no lack of zeal since; they are as earnest as they ever were?—Yes.

1264. Do you pay the adjutant and the drill instructor anything beyond the Government allowance?—To our serjeant-major we make up, I think, 10s. a week more, as we found that we could not get a really efficient man for the Government allowance.

1265. Is your band paid for separately?—Our band is the subject of great annoyance; it is a volunteer band, but it is paid for out of the funds of the corps and some subscriptions. I cannot state what I pay for that band, but it is not so expensive as most of the volunteer bands.

1266. How often do you have your battalion drills; once a month?—Every Saturday, and in the winter every Thursday also. We got a great many men, good men, who come regularly, but many come only on great occasions; to counteract this, many have been very good attendants at the company drills during the winter; the fact is, my particular regiment owes its discipline to the good attendance at company drills during the winter. My battalion drill is the worst attended.

1267. Do you think that the brigade and divisional meetings are essential to the maintenance of the spirit and efficiency of your corps?—Yes; if it had not been for such reviews as Chiselhurst, Brighton, &c., &c., according to my opinion, the volunteers would hardly now exist in London; by this time, I think, they would have been heartily tired of it.

1268. Do you insist upon every man passing through a certain number of company drills before he takes part in brigade or divisional operations?—You mean before taking part in battalion drill; brigade and divisional movements are easy in comparison. At our inspection last year I did not forbid any men to come into the ranks, and yet I think that we went through the book, minus four manoeuvres, and how we did it I leave Colonel MacMurdo to say.

1269. Is it your opinion that the volunteer force can be maintained in its present efficient state without aid from the Government or from the public?—That is a great question. In the first place I may not agree with you as to what constitutes a volunteer force. I have my views about that; I think that there are many men in the volunteers who have no business to be there, that their proper place is either in the line, or in the militia. I think that there are many men who have got their uniforms as volunteers, who have no business with them, they have got them by means of the donations of the inhabitants of different districts; those donations have been, according to my idea, wrongly applied in furnishing uniforms; when they are worn out that district or the gentry may not like to supply them again, and I say that those are not the men that ought to be in the volunteer force.

1270. Your opinion is that the men who ought to constitute the volunteer force are men above the class to which you have referred, and able to supply themselves with uniforms?—Unquestionably.

1271. I presume that you have endeavoured to recruit in that direction?—Yes.

1272. (*Viscount Hardinge.*) You allude specially to working men, do you not?—You may put any interpretation you like upon what I have said. I allude to men who cannot pay for their own uniforms.

1273. (*Chairman.*) You think that men who cannot pay for their own uniforms ought not to be admitted into the force?—Yes.

1274. Do you think that you could secure a sufficient number of men of an independent class without the addition of the others?—Yes. If you are in earnest in this country in telling every man that he must provide for the defence of the country, and subscribe his quota, I think that I can show you how you can increase the volunteer force very considerably.

1275. Will you favour the Commission with your views upon that point?—In the first place, looking at the military position of this country, compared with what it was 10 years ago, and admitting the fact, as we ought, that we might be invaded, I think the first duty is to enforce the ballot. I think that you ought to have an organized system of militia by which, at any moment, you could call out, if necessary, and be able to put your hand upon 400,000 or 500,000 men; that does not make it necessary that you should call them out at the present time or have out more than the 50,000 or 80,000 which you have under the present system; but it should be held over the heads of the 500,000 that they are liable to be called upon at any time, and I think that by that means you would draw gentlemen into the volunteers who would not like the militia, and so keep up a respectable class of volunteers.

1276. You think that you would then be able to secure the efficiency of the volunteers, because you would not allow any man to claim exemption from the ballot, unless he was thoroughly efficient?—I think it would draw all the respectable class into the volunteers instead of going into the militia, while a man who could not afford to pay for his uniform would be obliged to go into the militia, and that would be his proper place.

1277. Do you think it would be advantageous to reduce the number of battalions that are formed in the neighbourhood of London?—I should say so decidedly; a great many evils spring from the present system; there is a Foresters' corps, and an Odd Fellows' corps, and other old and absurd corps; but the principle of their constitution in point of fact is to induce a good many men to leave other regiments to go into something that is new; you do not add to the strength of the volunteer force by them. There is another great evil in these small corps; when the men come to drill and they find only 14 or 15 present, they get sick of it, and give it up; they get no exercise and no drill, and so they leave; but when you are in large numbers, it is just the other way, the men meet their comrades and they get a good drill, and it works well.

1278. You are of opinion that if these small corps could be discontinued, the larger corps would become fuller?—Yes.

1279. Are the men in your Lordship's corps recruited in any particular district, or all over London?—Others have broken this arrangement with the apparent sanction of the lord lieutenant; for instance, I have got a company out of this office, and I have a company of lawyers; this may arise from the circumstance that I have such first rate head quarters, or they would not have joined me.

1280. (*Lord Overstone.*) Do I correctly understand your Lordship's opinion to be, that you think the present volunteer force is based upon an erroneous principle, and that it ought really to be treated as part of a general system of organizing the whole country for defensive purposes; the militia force being a body into which those who cannot afford to pay for their own arms and accoutrements should be enlisted, and the volunteer force to act as a complement to the militia, and receiving those only who can afford to pay their expenses?—Yes; that is my firm conviction, with this addition, that the volunteers should be an entirely distinct force from the army and from the militia.

1281. Distinct in what sense of the word?—I think that it should have a separate organization to be commanded, officered, and organized entirely on a system of its own.

1282. Do you think that the volunteer force in its

Viscount Ranelagh

6 June 1862.

K

Viscount Ranelagh.
6 June 1862.

present condition can be permanently maintained?—I do.

1283. Do you think that any measures of importance are requisite for the purpose of giving greater certainty to its permanent maintenance?—Yes, I do.

1284. What do you think those measures should be?—I suppose that part of that question means, how can you popularize it, or make it more able to support itself?

1285. Looking at the present state of the volunteer force, first, as to its organization and discipline, do you think that any essential changes in its organization and discipline are necessary for the purpose of maintaining its efficiency?—If you will be kind enough to separate the questions, and ask me first upon discipline, I will give an answer.

1286. Then do you think that any essential change in the discipline is necessary for the purpose of securing the permanent efficiency of the volunteer force?—I think that at the present time the volunteers, as a body, are efficient; in every county, however, there ought to be a staff. I think in this metropolis, if the force were divided into district brigades and divisions, we should be more efficient; we ought to be able to march into Hyde Park under our own staff with 15,000 or 20,000 men at a few hours notice, and manoeuvre with credit to ourselves; but as things are, I think that in a case of war there would be the utmost confusion—the most ridiculous confusion with no organization of any kind that I can see. I can see no organization and no staff formed, and I therefore think that we ought to be in such a state that 150,000 men might be transported to any spot under an efficient staff.

1287. Is your Lordship prepared to state to this Commission specifically any important changes in the present discipline of the force which you think essential to maintain its efficiency?—Speaking for my own regiment, I should say, if you want to make us more efficient, and to keep up our numbers, you would pay for our head quarters.

1288. But my question referred to the discipline?—I really do not quite catch the question.

1289. I understood you to state that you thought there were important changes which might be effected, first in the discipline, and secondly in the organization of the volunteer force?—Organization, not discipline. I really cannot suggest anything as to discipline; as far as the discipline of the force has gone, I think it is one of the most marvellous things that I have ever witnessed; it is the most remarkable feature in the annals of this country, and I cannot offer any suggestion upon that point.

1290. Your Lordship does not suggest any important change as to discipline?—I do not, with the exception of the want of a good volunteer staff.

1291. (*Viscount Hardinge.*) Do you think it desirable as regards the discipline of the force that any general set of rules should be framed such as would meet the requirements of each corps. You are aware that there was a committee of which you were president, which committee framed a set of rules that were supposed to be model rules, and a previous witness has stated that those rules were framed when it was thought that these corps partook more of the character of rifle clubs than military corps. Do you think that the Government could frame any general set of rules that would be applicable to all the volunteer corps?—I must take the liberty of contradicting the gentleman who said that those rules were drawn up more as rules for rifle clubs. I know that my intention, and that of the majority of the committee concerned in drawing up those rules, was not to have anything to do with clubs; everything was meant to be in the hands of the commanding officer.

1292. Then in fact you would not recommend any alteration in the present system with regard to those rules?—No, I think not.

1293. (*Major-Gen. Eyre.*) You would have no fancy rules?—No.

1294. (*Lord Overstone.*) Passing to the subject of organization, are you prepared to suggest to this Commission any important changes in the organization of the volunteer force with a view to maintain its permanent efficiency?—Yes, I am quite prepared. I should recommend that in every county there should be a volunteer staff. I should not wish to break through any of our national ideas as to the power of lord-lieutenants arising from a system of national habits and institutions; I would still leave the lord-lieutenant to be the nominal head of that staff, as the Queen is the head of the army. I would have this staff composed of retired military men, the senior colonels of regiments. I would have a thoroughly well digested and organized staff, and that staff should be prepared to enter into everything connected with the volunteer movement, and be one that would work in time of peace as well as in war time. I should carry out the same principle in towns. I can give you all this in detail if you please, but the principle is to have in every county a staff. I would not have a staff such as you have got in the militia, consisting of fine gentlemen in cocked hats, but I would make it a really *bonâ fide* military staff, and I dare say you would find men glad enough to serve on such a staff, and be glad to give their services to the force. I would also have "intendants" or civil staff, whose duty resembles that of deputy-lieutenant; I would make it a really *bonâ fide* staff, and let the senior colonel, if he were a man of ability, have the command, but that would depend upon circumstances. But I repeat, let every county have its volunteer staff.

1295. (*Colonel MacMurdo.*) Do you mean a paid staff?—Certainly not. Nothing connected with the volunteers ought to be paid for, unless it is the head-quarters, and ranges for metropolitan corps. We are looking now for economy, and I believe firmly that if this volunteer movement is carried out, and the ballot enforced, you will have a very large body of men who will come forward, and constitute a nucleus in case of emergency. The great volunteer principle is that nobody should be paid.

1296. (*Major-Gen. Eyre.*) Do you object to the paid serjeants that you have now?—No; but that is a thing that already exists. I do not think that you can get men to do that work unless they are paid.

1297. But still you say that a great many must be paid for, who are they?—The adjutant must be paid for, the musketry instructor must be paid for, and the drill serjeant must be paid in most instances.

1298. (*Lieut.-Col. Barttelot.*) With the exception of what you receive now from the Government in the shape of an adjutant and drill serjeant, you do not recommend that the Government should do anything further?—I have not said that.

1299. (*Earl of Ducie.*) Are you of opinion that competent gentlemen could be found in all the counties to fill these staff appointments to which you have referred?—Yes; there are men who have served years in the army, and would like the work, and become the best staff in the world.

1300. But do you think that they are to be found in sufficient numbers in every county in England?—Undoubtedly they are, and not only so, but if you give the volunteers five years, in five years they will make a much better staff of officers than you have in the army, because the one would do it *con amore*, and the other would do it as a duty. I cannot speak in too strong terms of volunteer intelligence.

1301. (*Sir A. Campbell.*) Do you think that these gentlemen would be willing to serve without remuneration?—I think so; you would give them rank and position. You find the deputy lieutenant serving without remuneration; you find me serving without remuneration, and very hard work it is.

1302. (*Earl of Ducie.*) Deputy-lieutenants have not, I think, very onerous duties to perform?—They are supposed to be so; the staff duty would not be a very onerous duty to perform.

1303. But these staff officers would be full of employment on all occasions of county reviews and field-days?—Yes.

1304. (*Major-Gen. Eyre.*) How would the staff that you propose be constituted?—Take the case of Colonel Barttelot, who is a retired officer. Suppose him not to have a volunteer regiment, and he was in a county, and I was lord-lieutenant, I should ask him to come, and other men who had been in the army.

1305. But what would the staff appointments be?—You know as well as I do what the état-major is in the French army; you may call these appointments what you please—quartermaster-general, adjutant-general, deputy quartermaster-general, and deputy adjutant-general; but the staff would be the same in every county. I would have an état-major, which you never have had in this country yet, an efficient and zealous état-major.

1306. Do you mean for each county?—Yes; it should be in communication with the Government; each county should have a regularly organized system, its own means of transport and commissariat; thus, instead of having one commissary-general in London buying bullocks, each county would supply its own.

1307. (*Col. MacMurdo.*) A staff implies also a general to whom that staff would belong. Would you have a general officer in each county?—Pardon me, in a county you would not appoint a general to 2,000 or 3,000 men.

1308. What staff would you have in a county where there were only 3,000 men?—Why should not the senior colonel take the command on a field day.

1309. As a brigadier-general?—Yes; or as senior colonel.

1310. Then, again, in those counties where there were 10,000, 12,000, or 18,000 men, what staff would you have?—A divisional or brigade staff.

1311. Should the general be a volunteer officer?—That would depend upon circumstances. Her Majesty could choose whom she thought right, but in peace time I would give the volunteers every facility to learn their work; in peace time I would give every volunteer every chance he could have of learning his work, in preparation for the evil day. If that is not done, when the evil day does come according to the present system there will be immense confusion, for there are not so many general officers now who can command 4,000 or 5,000 men, and if this country was invaded, you must remember that the army would require to be very much increased. You would have the pensioners out, and an enormous force of militia, and the question is, have we got officers in this country who have had experience enough to be able to step into their places when the emergency came? I think that you would run very short of men; in addition to the regulars, militia, and pensioners, you would very likely have 500,000 volunteers, and who are the officers who are going to command these men, unless you give a certain number a chance of learning their business as to organizing, transporting, and going through the whole system beforehand. You will have frightful confusion, men not knowing their work, and not knowing what to do, and you should give them the opportunity of comprehending what they will have to do. In Middlesex you have 18,000 or 20,000 men, and I should say let the senior colonel command; do not call him a general, if the term is offensive, call him by any other name; but let him learn how to command, in the same way as we proposed in the year 1860, and which was agreed to by all the colonels in London, but who chose afterwards to alter their minds; I have all their names here approving of the principle.

1312. Do you mean approving of the principle of the senior colonel commanding in a county?—Yes; even up to 20,000 men.

1313. Do you mean that the senior colonel commanding in a county should be the officer to command the volunteer force in the county, to whom the divisional staff and the assistant quartermaster-general and the assistant adjutant-general should report?—

No; I have stated before that we must respect preconceived prejudices, and therefore I would still leave it in the hands of the lord-lieutenant; he should be the nominal head of the board, and the staff should be under him; therefore he would be the representative of the Government, and he would guide the rest. If he did not approve of more than two or three field days, he would stop them, and therefore the senior colonel, or the next colonel, would only be carrying out the orders of the executive; he would only for the time being command. For example, I am going down on Whit-Monday to Lord Cowper's at Pansanger; I command, I am senior colonel, and afterwards they march past; they do not march past me, but they march past the lord-lieutenant. I say, carry out that same system. The lord-lieutenant is still the governor of the county, and they would be under his supervision and care; but the mere command in the field should be entrusted to those men whom you wish to teach in a time of peace how to learn their work for a time of need. I want to see the intelligence of the country well developed, and those men who are clever taught. The volunteers should be able to criticise one another, and you cannot criticise the regular soldiers. I should like to know, take Brighton for instance, who would like to sit down and criticise Lord Clyde? I may, because I am an independent man; but other men will not do it. In the army you cannot do it; you would be tried by a court-martial, if you began to attack your superior; but if you leave us alone, we shall criticise one another until we arrive at perfection, and shall never do any harm. This is a movement of public opinion, and it would be dangerous to mix it up with the army; and I think the great difficulty is being in any way connected with the army; I think it would be dangerous from the privates up to the seniors, and more particularly in the seniors.

1314. Suppose that a colonel commanding the force in a county was criticised to such an extent by those under his command that several refused to obey his orders to attend the meetings on general brigade days, would not that cause great embarrassment in the county?—This is by no means likely; a very inefficient old twaddler would probably be expelled by the force of public opinion, whom you could not get rid of by any other means.

1315. He being the senior colonel?—Yes.

1316. How could that state of affairs be remedied—that is to say, the senior colonel being criticised to such an extent that other battalions would not join him on his field days; by what means would you remedy that state of things?—Public opinion would be the remedy, and this is a force entirely in which public opinion will out. Suppose a regular officer was commanding instead of a volunteer officer, you would have the same criticism, and there would be the danger of mixing the regulars up with the volunteers.

1317. (*Major-Gen. Eyre.*) Might not the critics to whom you have referred be the twaddlers, and might not they be very bad judges?—The volunteer force is one of public opinion.

1318. I thought you stated that they would so criticise each other that the old twaddlers would be driven out; but does it follow that the critics in the case supposed would be good judges?—You may apply that style of reasoning to every subject under the sun.

1319. (*Lord Overstone.*) What would you say to a system under which boys in a public school were able to criticise the headmaster out of his office, in consequence of alleged incompetent scholarship?—I think they ought to be well flogged.

1320. Would you apply the same rule to the volunteer force, and flog the men who criticised a good officer out of his position?—You cannot argue against that which is done and which will continue to be done. I am endeavouring to show the Commission the danger of mixing the two elements up, and pointing out the result. How could you correct a volunteer? You cannot flog a volunteer nor put

K 2

Viscount Ranelagh,
6 June 1862.

him in the black hole ; these are our difficulties, we must bear the brunt of criticism. I hope the regular soldiers will not put themselves in the false position of being criticised, it is one of great danger to them.

1321. Does not your lordship adopt the principle that criticism upon the acts of Government is valuable or dangerous precisely in proportion to the competency of the critics?—Yes.

1322. Do you think that volunteer soldiers would be competent critics of the conduct of the officers who had the command of them?—I do not say that ; I only say what they will do, and it cannot be prevented.

1323. (*Col. MacMurdo.*) What would be the result of criticising a colonel commanding the volunteer force in a county ; would he be compelled to resign ; he must, if he continues in the service, continue to be senior colonel, and what course would you take to get rid of him?—How would you do if you had got an inefficient colonel in London ; what means have you got of getting rid of him ?

1324. Am I to be the critic?—Yes ; how would you get rid of him ?

1325. I must leave that to the Secretary of State to answer. You are proposing a scheme to this Commission, and I am desirous to understand it ?—I am proposing a scheme, but I must be a very clever fellow if I can provide for every contingency. I say that for the organization of the force in this country it ought to be divided into counties or districts ; and there should be an efficient staff in each county. I would put the lord-lieutenant at the head of it, and I would put the commanding officers as a kind of committee ; we should then get together the best elements for making a good staff or état-major. Then the question is, who is to command, and I suggest that the senior officer in that county should command. I think that that is very natural ; it is what has generally been done hitherto, and I do not think that I am proposing anything new ; I should say let the military men leave us alone. I have mentioned the dangers arising from criticism ; to criticise an officer in Her Majesty's service is a very serious thing, and one which I think the officers themselves would not like.

1326. (*Viscount Hardinge.*) If the senior colonel should prove unfit for his post, how would you provide for that?—I really have not thought of that seriously, but common sense tells me that he would very soon feel it, and because of that very criticism arising from public opinion.

1327. Do you mean that he would feel it to this extent, that he would say to the lord-lieutenant, or to the board which you have mentioned, that he would rather not undertake the duty ?—If he were unfit to command, and the volunteers would not go to parade with him, he would be a colonel without men to command.

1328. (*Sir G. A. Wetherall.*) Is it not within your knowledge that there are many officers commanding volunteer corps who are not fit to command, but whose regiments do go to parade regularly ?—Yes, but how long will that last ?

1329. It has lasted since the establishment of the force ?—True, the reason being that many of those colonels are moneyed men, and men of influence.

1330. (*Major-Gen. Eyre.*) Do not you think that if you lay down that very marked line of separation which you have expressed a desire to lay down between the volunteer corps and the regular troops, you will interfere with that very cordial feeling which now subsists between the two ?—On the contrary, I take quite a different view. I wish to avoid that which I think will inevitably take place. Let us, for example, go down to Brighton, and suppose an enemy to be near us. You have strict discipline on one side of a street, where you have a force of disciplined men who are ordered to their beds by tattoo at eight or nine o'clock. On the other side of the street you have a large number of volunteer regiments, composed of lords, dukes, and tradesmen ; but they will not go to bed at eight o'clock, and you cannot force them. They will be sitting up and smoking.

1331. (*Sir G. A. Wetherall.*) Suppose an enemy was at Brighton, the first principle of discipline is obedience ; do all your men obey you ?—No doubt of it ; but it is different discipline. I have thought this matter over as much as any man, and every day and every hour I am the more convinced of the truth of what I have said ; and if I do not fully explain myself now, I can do so afterwards. You must give me credit for what I have stated upon the subject of discipline, and I do not say one word against the discipline of the volunteers ; on the contrary, they will go to a certain extent, but they will not go to the extreme of tapcism or the old galvanized ideas of the time of Dundas. They will do very much as I have seen other corps on service do ; but when you call upon them to come out, they must do it according to their own fashion, and in their own way. You will not get the volunteers into bed at eight o'clock at night, at tattoo, of that I am sure ; and, again, if on one side of the street, as I have stated before, you have strict discipline, and on the other side of the street you have not, and one set of men allowed to do what the other set may not, what will be the effect on the army ?

1332. (*Col. MacMurdo.*) Your lordship has been in camp before the enemy. Supposing you were in command of troops once more, and those troops were composed of regulars on one side of a street and of irregulars or volunteers on the other, and that at eight o'clock your orders for the night in front of the enemy were that no lights were to be allowed after sunset ; would you then allow either the regulars or the volunteers to have any lights ?—Certainly not.

1333. Then would they not all be brought under one rule of discipline ?—Yes. You put it very tritely and very well ; they would be so ; but that would only happen occasionally in camps, and in immediate contact with an enemy. This is a large force of 50,000 or 60,000 men, which may be sent into towns; the volunteers would there expect to be allowed a considerable amount of latitude, to disperse for a certain number of hours, and the people would receive them well, a feeling which they would not extend to the regulars. The force is different altogether.

1334. You are aware that, in front of the enemy, they would all be under the same Mutiny Act ?—Yes, but you would not enforce it as if you were dealing with regulars.

1335. (*Chairman.*) Supposing that this force were disciplined entirely and governed by their own staff, would not this difficulty arise in case of an invasion, and their services being required, that they would be brigaded with regular troops and must be under the command of a military officer ; and if the discipline were not the same as that of the military force with which they were brigaded, how do you think that would work ?—That, viz., the being brigaded with regulars, is the very thing I do not advise. I would work the volunteers separately. Let me suppose that we hear to-night that an enemy is landing at Brighton, and 15,000 or 20,000 volunteers are hurried off. General So-and-so is to take the command. I know that he will not risk his reputation by going pell mell into a town and occupying the houses with volunteers ; but he will, as I believe has been done before, occupy a certain position, cover certain roads, and secure his communications. If volunteers were driven back, it would be no disgrace to them ; but to the regular officer commanding it would be a disgrace ; the mere fact of being beaten back would be a disgrace. The volunteers must be used as an irregular force, and not as a regular force.

1336. (*Viscount Hardinge.*) Did you not state that you thought the volunteer force generally required further aid from the Government ?—Yes, I think they do.

1337. Will you state in what shape you think that further aid should be given?—My experience has reference only to the metropolis. I think that the Government might give us headquarters, armouries, and places suitable for recruit and company drills.

1338. Do you think that each officer should send in an estimate of what he required?—No; if the Government give headquarters there would be no necessity for any estimate. I lay great stress upon headquarters; and I would refer, as an example, to the volunteer London Artillery, Victorias, and the Devonshire corps; they have kept together because their headquarters were very good, and that is what you must do here in London.

1339. The rent of headquarters would vary in different localities?—Yes.

1340. Would you propose that each officer should state to the Government what amount of rent he would require?—That may be very difficult. The Government may choose to say that they will give so much per head effectives; that is one way of doing it.

1341. You mean, I presume, that the expenses of headquarters, armoury, &c., should be paid by the Government, but that it should not exceed the rate of 1l. a head?—I will not say that, for in different localities land varies in price; round London, it is 1,000l. an acre, and near Penshurst, for example, 100l. an acre.

1342. In fact there would be an estimate sent in from each corps?—That must be left very much to the discretion of the Government; the largest benefit that you can give us is to give us headquarters.

1343. Referring to the metropolitan corps, and assuming that there are difficulties in the way of a capitation grant, do you think that clothing should be given gratuitously, either in the piece, or made up, and that it would be acceptable?—To give them clothing I think would be perfectly ridiculous; if you do so, you destroy the independence of the movement.

1344. It has been proposed by previous witnesses that the Government should make a capitation grant, so much per head, to be expended entirely at the discretion of the commanding officers; do you approve of that suggestion?—There is a way of doing everything; you may call it a capitation grant, or the Government might say, we will give you the money for your armouries or your grounds. I should not call it so much a head.

1345. You are aware that in some corps they have spent large sums of money on their bands, in some corps as much as 300l. and as much as 600l. a year. Do you think that they would have a fair right to come to the Government and ask for further aid?— Certainly not; when you see a regiment marching out with 40 or 50 men, they are only touting for numbers. I think it is very unfair upon well organized battalions.

1346. Is not one of the evils which has attended the movement in the metropolis this, that many corps have been very extravagant in their bands?—I dare say that it is an item that would tell against them.

1347. I think you have stated that you do not give any extra allowances to the drill serjeants or the adjutant?—Yes, excepting the serjeant-major.

1348. Are you aware that it is the practice in many corps to do so?—I have heard so.

1349. Do you think it is necessary to give any extra allowance to the drill serjeants and adjutant?— The country adjutants are very well paid. I have several armourers, and I only pay them 11s. a week.

1350. Are your serjeants well satisfied with the Government pay?—The serjeant-major, certainly not, as he could get better wages elsewhere.

1351. How comes it that you have only one serjeant?—I cannot get them; I have only one drill serjeant who is a good one.

1352. And could you get them if the Government gave them higher pay?—I think that a little higher pay would be an inducement.

1353. (*Lieut.-Col. Barttelot.*) Do you find that the adjutant's pay is sufficient?—I am very fortunate in my adjutant; he is a man of independent means, otherwise I think the work is hard for the pay. Some adjutants have nothing to do, and others are very hard-worked; my adjutant, Captain Turner, is a very conscientious man, and I think that he has much more work to do than any adjutant in a regiment of the line.

1354. Do you employ him every day in the week? —Yes; he goes to headquarters twice a day, and he writes an amazing number of letters.

1355. Do you keep your arms at headquarters, or do you allow the men to take them home?—I allow the men to take them out, but every man signs a paper and becomes responsible for his rifle.

1356. (*Major-Gen. Eyre.*) What proportion of your corps can use the rifle at the target?—This year we have not got in our returns; last year out of 1,200 men we had over 500 who had passed through their classes, and I think that this year we shall have 600.

1357. (*Earl of Ducie.*) Who have passed through the three classes?—Through the first period.

1358. (*Viscount Hardinge.*) Are the captains of companies in your corps put to any considerable expense?—Not sixpence. As regards the men I have laid it down as a rule, as our subscription is a guinea, that I would not ask them for one sixpence more, with the exception of one shilling for a havresack. I have not altered the uniform, and the band is not compulsory, but is maintained by contributions; and the only thing that I have asked them to do has been lately to have knapsacks, but that is not compulsory.

1359. By that means you have obtained probably, and which I presume you consider an advantage, a considerable infusion of military men into your corps? —If I had not had military men, I could not have come into the park as I did, three months after the regiment was formed, in the face of 20,000 people.

1360. In corps where certain expenses fall upon the captains, a good many who have served in the line would be deterred from joining them, would they not?—Yes.

1361. What I mean is this, that in those corps where the captains of companies are obliged to give expensive prizes to be shot for, many officers who had served in the line would not be able to take command of companies in some corps if they were expected to do the same thing?—Common sense would show that; but to go back to your question as to Government aid, I may mention that I have been written to by many members of other corps, who have asked me to mention that it would be a great boon if a certain sum were given them for field days, to provide for railway expenses. I have received many letters to this effect.

1362. (*Chairman.*) They want some assistance for the battalion drills?—Yes. There are other means by which I would propose to popularize the volunteer movement. I think that the commanding officers and field officers after a certain period of time, say eight or ten years, might very well have their rank confirmed, that is, that an officer should retain his rank after 10 years. With regard to the privates, I have also considered what we should give them, and I know of nothing unless you exempt them from serving on juries and inquests; I think that would be a boon. Then comes the question of the adjutants, the drill serjeants, and the musketry instructors, who are now paid by the Government. I think I would throw those posts open to the force. I would allow as adjutant a man who had served as a volunteer for three or five years; and as to the musketry instructor and drill serjeant, I would also let their places be competed for. I know one volunteer, a very good man, who is quite fit to be an adjutant, and I know in my own regiment two or three serjeants who are quite equal to any serjeants of the line. I would throw all paid volunteer appointments open to the

Viscount Ranelagh.

6 June 1862.

Viscount Ranelagh.
6 June 1862.

usual competition. I throw out these suggestions with the view of popularizing the volunteer movement, and I would even carry it so far, referring now to a scheme of Lord Elcho's, for charging something like a farthing in the pound as a kind of rating, that if this scheme be carried out, all volunteer effectives should be exempt.

1363. Is there any other suggestion that you wish to offer?—None. I have not been able fully to explain my ideas, but I am quite ready to write down a detailed plan if the Commissioners at all care for it. I have a very strong feeling upon the matter, and I have endeavoured to answer the questions, though of rather a discursive nature, which you have put to me.

The witness withdrew.

Capt. A. Ewens.

Captain ALEXANDER EWENS examined.

1364. (*Chairman.*) You are adjutant of the City of London Rifle Volunteer Brigade?—Yes.
1365. Of how many men does that brigade consist?—I think the number is 1,217.
1366. I believe you wish to make some suggestions to the Commissioners upon some points?—The only thing that I wish to mention is this; I think it would be very essential to have a paid quartermaster for the London corps generally.
1367. (*Col. MacMurdo.*) What would be his duties?—To look after transit, commissariat, ammunition, armoury, and, when required, camp duties.
1368. On whom do those duties fall now?—On me.
1369. (*Viscount Hardinge.*) Do you think, considering the great expense that the corps is put to for its band, which has lately come to the knowledge of the public through the newspapers, that it could not afford out of its income to pay for a quartermaster?—It might perhaps for this year; but what may happen next year we do not know.
1370. Do you know what the balance in hand is at the present moment?—Yes.
1371. It is very large, is it not?—The money balance is about 1,500*l.*, but with assets and liabilities we are over 2,000*l.*
1372. Have you any reason to apprehend any falling off in the subscriptions?—Yes.
1373. Upon what grounds?—I cannot tell certainly, but should ascribe to expense and want of time.
1374. Do you receive any annual subscriptions from your honorary members?—Yes; a very small amount.
1375. Those annual subscriptions, I presume, will continue?—They have decreased to a nominal sum.
1376. (*Earl of Ducie.*) Does this 2,000*l.* consist of part of a capital sum not expended?—No; it is taking into consideration liabilities and assets.
1377. Have you any reason to anticipate a falling off of your donations?—Yes.
1378. What are the grounds upon which you anticipate that?—Some months ago we employed a collector to obtain donations, and he has generally failed.
1379. Does he report to you as to his failures?—No.
1380. What is the expense of your band?—About 600*l.* a year.
1381. What is the total annual expenditure of the corps?—About 2,500*l.*
1382. Can you tell what proportion the expense of the band bears to the whole annual expenditure of the corps?—About one-fifth.
1383. Can you state what is the total annual revenue of the corps?—It varies in different years.
1384. Can you state the revenue for this year, or for the last year?—I cannot; I have three balance sheets for the last three years.
1385. What has been the total annual expenditure for each year during the last three years?—It averages over 3,000*l.*, which includes the heavy expenditure at the Crystal Palace.
1386. Can you state what are the principal items of that expenditure?—No; but they will be correctly shown in answers to the Commission papers.
1387. Are there not some large items in so large an expenditure?—Yes, Crystal Palace, bands, &c., &c.
1388. Have you given the expense of the band, or are there further expenses in addition to the band?—Yes.

1389. What is the total cost of the band?—About 600*l.* per annum.
1390. From what sources mainly is that sum of 3,000*l.* and odd derived?—From the subscriptions of the men.
1391. What is the subscription per man?—One guinea.
1392. That would be 1,200*l.*; whence does the rest come?—We started, I believe, with a revenue of 8,000*l.*
1393. Was that obtained by donations?—Yes, by life subscriptions, donations, and subscriptions to the band.
1394. I wish to ascertain what is your annual revenue; the subscriptions, I presume, fall in annually, or do you mean donations for life?—Donations for life; honorary members subscribe two guineas a year.
1395. How many members are there subscribing two guineas a year?—I cannot tell you.
1396. Can you state the total amount of the honorary subscriptions per annum?—I can give you our receipts and expenditure for the last three years; 1859–60, receipts 8,879*l.* 0*s.* 6*d.*, payments 3,749*l.* 7*s.* 7*d.*; 1860–61, receipts 7,221*l.* 7*s.* 7*d.*, payments 4,825*l.* 4*s.* 3*d.*; 1861–62, receipts 4,490*l.* 0*s.* 3*d.*, payments 2,190*l.* 13*s.*; leaving us a balance, of assets in excess of liabilities, of 2,368*l.* 7*s.* 3*d.*
1397. (*Chairman.*) You think that the public ought to pay for the quartermaster of the regiment?—The regiment will not do it, and no man will work without it.
1398. (*Col. MacMurdo.*) You are aware that a supernumerary officer is allowed to perform the duties of quartermaster, and another to perform the duties of paymaster?—Yes.
1399. I see that your estimate does not comprise the officers?—No.
1400. What are the subscriptions of the officers?—The annual subscription for all grades is one guinea a year, and one guinea entrance; but the band subscriptions are in these proportions: lieutenant-colonel, 12 guineas; major, 10 guineas; captains, 7 guineas; lieutenants, 5 guineas; ensign, 3 guineas; surgeon, 7 guineas; and assistant surgeons, 5 guineas.
1401. Are there any other expenses to which the officers are liable?—Nothing, except active expenses. I have a list here of an officer's expenditure for the first year.
1402. Have you any reason to suppose that the want of officers in your corps, as it appears you are not filled up to the establishment, for there are six subalterns wanting, is attributable to the expenses which deter officers from joining the corps?—No; we have more than 12 applicants now.
1403. Why are they not appointed?—Because there was a misunderstanding between Colonel Hicks and the Court of Lieutenancy.
1404. How long is it since Colonel Hicks left?—Some months.
1405. What steps have you taken to make up the establishment of the corps in officers?—The recommendation which was laid before the Court of Lieutenancy stayed there for several months, but they were appointed as soon as Colonel Ward joined; he has proposed more.
1406. (*Viscount Hardinge.*) Why do you think that the honorary subscriptions from honorary members of two guineas per year will fall off, or be withdrawn?—I cannot tell; I only know from being

told that they vary. I have nothing whatever to do with the subscriptions, or with the money.

1407. Then you state that merely from hearsay?—Yes; from the Secretary.

1408. (*Lord Overstone.*) You cannot give the Commission any estimate as to what is the annual income that can be fairly calculated upon?—No.

1409. (*Lieut.-Col. Barttelot.*) Have you not two adjutants?—Yes.

1410. You are one of them?—Yes.

1411. Do you receive anything besides your pay from the corps?—Yes.

1412. How much do you receive?—200*l.* a year.

1413. Does the other adjutant receive anything besides his pay?—He has received a gratuity; no income.

1414. (*Lord Overstone.*) The number of men in your corps is 1,200?—Over 1,200.

1415. Can you form any estimate of what is the necessary annual expenditure for keeping in a fair degree of efficiency, and with a proper regard to economy, 1,200 men?—I cannot. I do not attend any of the civil meetings.

1416. (*Lieut.-Col. Barttelot.*) Do you pay a clerk?—Yes; one clerk.

1417. (*Col. MacMurdo.*) Is anything paid to your drill instructor besides what he receives from the Government?—Yes, there is to four; to two serjeant-majors, and to the musketry instructor, and to the orderly room clerk.

1418. Are there any Government serjeants who do not receive anything?—Yes.

1419. Why should there be a difference between them?—They are a different class of men.

1420. The Government serjeants are instructors, are they not?—Yes.

1421. Why should one serjeant-instructor receive an extra allowance, and the others not?—Because the services of some are more valuable to the corps than others.

1422. They receive an extra allowance?—Yes; and the musketry instructor, who is a first-class man from Hythe, receives pay.

1423. An extra allowance?—Yes; and the man who does the orderly room clerk's work receives 12*l.* a year from the corps and 12*l.* from me.

1424. (*Lord Elcho.*) Is it one of the serjeants who is allowed by Government who does the orderly room work?—Yes, and he does the drill as well.

1425. (*Col. MacMurdo.*) How many of your serjeants do not receive any extra allowance?—One.

1426. What duty does he perform?—He drills a recruit squad, and he attends to the marking of the shooting, and he writes in the orderly room.

1427. Is he satisfied with the Government pay; is it sufficient for him to carry on with?—No; I think not.

1428. (*Lord Elcho.*) Do you mean from individual members, or does he receive the gifts by companies?—Individual members.

1429. Merely individual presents?—Yes.

1430. For drilling them?—No; for general work.

1431. Did you look out for those serjeants yourself?—No; the two serjeant-majors were appointed before I joined.

1432. The two serjeant-majors had been in the regiment before you joined, and before the warrant came out, I suppose, sanctioning an establishment of serjeants for the volunteers?—Yes; two only were employed and paid by the regiment before I joined.

1433. Since the Government supplied those serjeants, have you had to look out for any?—Yes; two more.

1434. And to only one of those have you found it necessary to give an extra allowance?—Yes.

1435. Do you find him with quarters?—No.

1436. (*Col. MacMurdo.*) One of your serjeant-majors belongs to the Tower, does he not?—Yes, he is a yeoman warder.

1437. How much extra allowance do you give him?

—I cannot say positively; but I think it is 3*l.* or 4*l.* a month.

1438. Do you provide him with lodgings?—No; he has a house in the Tower; but I hope you will understand that when speaking of money matters I really do not know, for I do not attend to them.

1439. (*Lord Elcho.*) Has there been any falling off in the number of your corps?—Yes.

1440. What is the greatest strength that the corps has ever borne on its muster rolls?—I cannot state positively, but over 1,600 on the muster roll.

1441. It is now 1,200; was it ever 1,600 in your time?—Yes.

1442. Were there ever 1,600 men who paid their guinea subscription in one year?—I think not.

1443. Do you know what is the greatest number who have ever paid their subscriptions in one year?—I do not.

1444. Do you know whether there is any difficulty now in getting in the subscriptions?—We are in arrear, at least so I am told.

1445. Who has charge of the finance?—The secretary and the colonel; he has charge, with a committee to assist him, and the secretary who keeps the books.

1446. Have you a secretary besides the orderly room clerk?—Yes.

1447. Do you know what that secretary's pay is?—£120 a year.

1448. You have had a secretary from the beginning, have you not?—Yes.

1449. Were there not some defalcations in the corps?—Yes.

1450. To a large amount?—Something like 900*l.*

1451. Of the 8,000*l.* which had been collected, you were cheated out of 900*l.*?—Yes; it just amounted to that, as far as I can tell you.

1452. (*Col. MacMurdo.*) What is the purport of the paper you have handed in?—It is only to show the expense of one officer.

1453. The expenses of one officer appear to have been 93*l.* 15*s.* 10*d.*?—Yes, for the first year.

1454. (*Chairman.*) Is there an expense of a similar kind every year?—No.

1455. (*Major-Gen. Eyre.*) In fact that is the price of his commission?—He was a private up to the time of his commission.

1456. I do not see the uniform for the officers in this paper?—You will see it under the word "tailor."

1457. (*Chairman.*) Have you any other suggestion to offer besides as to the payment to the quarter-master?—No.

1458. (*Lord Elcho.*) Has the attendance at drill fallen off much?—No; it falls off during the hot months, but during the winter it continues on the average about the same.

1459. What does it average at the battalion parades; have you seen a third of the whole corps, or 400 men, present at the battalion parades?—Not in Guildhall, we cannot do it there, but on Saturdays and on a field day out then we do see from 400 to 600 men.

1460. How many did you muster at Richmond the other day?—I think there were 688.

1461. (*Lord Overstone.*) Are you prepared to give any decided opinion as to the cause of the falling off in your numbers?—Not a decided opinion, only my own idea.

1462. What is your idea of the cause of the falling off?—The expenses, the late hours, and other attractions.

1463. You think that the causes are partly causes which are removable by an alteration of the regulations, and partly causes which arise entirely from expenditure?—Yes.

1464. (*Lord Elcho.*) What do you mean by late hours?—Returning home so late from the Saturday field days; we have a great number of married men who live in the suburbs, and when they arrive in London there are no trains or busses to take them to

Capt. A. Ewns.

6 June 1862.

*Capt.
A. Ewens.*

6 June 1862.

their homes, they are, consequently, put to the expense of a cab or obliged to remain in town.

1465. (*Major-Gen. Eyre.*) On other days an earlier hour would not suit them ?—They could not come on other days at an earlier hour.

1466. (*Lord Elcho.*) Where do your ordinary battalion parades take place on the Saturdays ?—We always parade at Guildhall, and march out ; we go to Hyde Park, Regent's Park, Hampstead Heath, Blackheath, and Bushy Park.

1467. At what hour do you usually get back ?—At 11, 12, 1, and 2 o'clock in the morning.

The witness withdrew.

*Lieut.-Col.
Dreghorn.*

Lieut.-Col. DREGHORN examined.

1468. (*Chairman.*) You command the 3rd Lanarkshire Rifle Volunteers ?—Yes.
1469. Is that an administrative battalion ?—No, it is a consolidated battalion.
1470. Of how many companies does it consist ?—Of nine companies.
1471. How many men are there in each company, 100 men ?—That is the maximum.
1472. How many men have you on your master rolls ?—I think there is somewhere under 600.
1473. Do you find that the numbers diminish ?—Not much ; we are not much diminished in effective members.
1474. Are you well provided with rifle ranges and drill sheds ?—We are pretty well provided in that respect.
1475. Have those been paid for by the subscribers ?—They have been paid for by the corps.
1476. Is there an annual subscription raised in the corps ?—Yes, there is ; an annual subscription should be raised in it.
1477. Of how much per man ?—I think it is a small sum of 2s. 6d. for each man, and so much for each officer, but that has not been very well paid by the men.
1478. What has been the total amount raised by the subscriptions ?—I am not quite prepared to say, but for the two first companies of the battalion in the first two years when we provided our own rifles, we raised nearly 2,000l. for the two first companies ; they were the two first nearly, except Sir Archibald Campbell's, which was the first company that was raised in Lanarkshire, and the one that I was connected with was the second. At that time the Government did not provide rifles at all, and the men were obliged to provide their own rifles and other things, and we raised as nearly as possible for the first two years about 2,000l.
1479. Have you any doubt as to being able to maintain the efficiency of your corps ?—Yes, I have very considerable doubts, and I expressed those doubts at a public meeting in Glasgow two years ago.
1480. Will you have the goodness to state to the Commission the grounds upon which you entertain those doubts ?—I find that there are a number of young men, even in what are called the self-supporting companies, who find a difficulty in renewing their uniforms ; for example, there is in my regiment the son of a friend of mine, a most respectable man in a manufacturing business, and who is considered a man in a good position ; I was asking him what had become of his son at the drills lately, and he said to me, " To tell you the truth his uniform is done, " and he did not like to say that he was not able to " renew it." He had supplied his own uniform in the first instance, but he found it difficult to renew it.
1481. Do you think that that is generally the case throughout the corps ?—That is just an instance in the self-supporting companies, but in the artizan companies it is almost universal ; I am quite persuaded that the artizan portion will not again renew their uniforms, unless they be paid for in some other way than by their subscriptions.
1482. In what way should you propose to supply the deficiency ?—We have no mode of supplying it unless we go among the public generally and represent to them the loss it would be to allow the battalion to go down, and get subscriptions in that way, or unless the Government give them assistance. People have got tired, I think, of subscribing ; we have had very great difficulty in getting people to come forward and subscribe again to any large amount.
1483. Are you speaking now of the honorary members of the corps ?—We do not get much from the honorary members, we have not very many of them ; probably we have got altogether some 50l. or 60l. from them.
1484. You are speaking of the subscriptions received from the ordinary members of the corps ?—Yes.
1485. (*Sir A. Campbell.*) At the time when the volunteer movement first commenced in Glasgow there was a public subscription raised ?—Yes.
1486. That subscription amounted, did it not, to somewhere about 3,000l.—Yes.
1487. How was that subscription administered and by whom ?—By a committee appointed by the subscribers at a public meeting.
1488. Of whom did the committee consist ?—I think it consisted of the commanding officers generally of the volunteer corps.
1489. Did it not consist of captains of companies already enrolled ?—I think it did.
1490. And a few other names ?—Yes, outside.
1491. The money raised by that subscription was spent entirely, so far as it has been spent, in aiding the men to meet the expense of their uniform ?—Precisely so.
1492. Do you recollect whether there was any proposal made within the committee to administer that subscription, that instead of being applied to the uniforms it should be applied to the purposes of head-quarters, practice ranges, and other permanent expenses of the volunteer force ?—Yes.
1493. The proposal was made but was rejected by a majority of the committee ?—Yes.
1494. That committee being composed of captains of companies who themselves had become in some instances responsible for the uniforms ?—Yes, precisely so.
1495. Were any of the companies in your regiment assisted out of that subscription ?—Two of them, I think.
1496. Do you apprehend that those companies are more or less likely to maintain their numbers than the companies who did not receive such aid ?—I think that they are less likely to maintain their numbers unless they get aid from some other source.
1497. That is to say, as far as your experience goes, that those companies of volunteers who originally did not provide their own uniforms will be less likely to be able to do again ?—I have no doubt of it.
1498. That public subscription is the only source, with the exception of the subscriptions of the members, which has been to any extent available in Glasgow for the expenses of the volunteer corps ?—Yes.
1499. There has been very little done with honorary members ?—Very little.
1500. The organization in Glasgow has been an entirely company organization ?—Yes.
1501. Practically speaking it remains so, does it not ?—Yes.
1502. And with respect to financial matters ?—Yes.
1503. Consequently in a financial sense the sub-

scriptions differ in almost every two companies in the town?—Yes.

1504. Can you express any opinion as to the probable defection in numbers in the total force in Glasgow, or is your experience confined entirely to your own regiment?—From what I have heard I should suppose that a very large proportion of the volunteer force in Glasgow will disappear unless there is some aid given to them. On the other hand I think that if there is substantial aid given to the volunteers the numbers will be kept up.

1505. (*Lord Elcho.*) What are the present numbers in Glasgow?—I should suppose some 6,000 or 7,000.

1506. (*Chairman.*) Will you explain to the Commission what you mean by a substantial aid?—A money grant to each effective man to enable him to provide a uniform.

1507. (*Sir A. Campbell.*) Would you propose that it should be given to the individual or to the commanding officer of the corps?—I should say to the commanding officer of the corps; besides that, I would contemplate giving them some aid towards the erection of butts and rifle ranges, and such things as those.

1508. (*Chairman.*) I understood you to say that you were provided with rifle ranges?—Yes, but we have the annual expense of them to keep up, the annual rent of the ground upon which they are erected at this moment, although with the exception probably of Sir Archibald Campbell's regiment, the one that I command is just about as free of debt as any of the others, but still I find that notwithstanding all our exertions, and the subscriptions that we can get from the men,—and I have subscribed within the last six months 50*l*. towards the battalion fund,—we are now nearly 100*l*. in debt for battalion expenses, irrespective of the company expenses. The expenses connected with the uniforms we have never interfered with as a battalion.

1509. What is the cost of your uniform?—The cost of the uniform was originally 2*l*. 18*s*.

1510. And the accoutrements?—I think they came to somewhere about 8*s*.

1511. Making together about 3*l*. 6*s*.?—Yes, that was for the original companies that I am talking of. I really do not know very much about the others, because they came into the battalion after those companies were formed, and I never made much inquiry.

1512. (*Sir A. Campbell.*) Can you form any opinion as to the number out of the present 6,000 or 7,000 volunteers who will probably fall off if things remain as they are?—I should say that there will not be a fourth in existence unless some aid is given.

1513. Do you think that there are any other means in the place of a money aid which would effect the object of keeping up the numbers?—I do not think that there are.

1514. You think that the financial difficulty is the only one?—Yes; and there is a reason for it, it is this, the men who would take a money grant if given by the Government would not take clothing, they would consider it a species of degradation to be handed a pair of trowsers or a coat, or anything of that description. I am persuaded that it would not do in any other way than in the form of a money grant.

1515. You think that there would not be any such sense of degradation in the case of a money grant being given to be administered through the commanding officers to aid them in their expenses?—No, I think there would be no such objection.

1516. Have you considered what amount of grant would be necessary, or in what form that grant should be given?—My own impression is that if a grant of 30*s*. for each effective man were given that would answer the purpose. I have heard others who have had fully as much experience as I have had strike at a higher sum.

1517. To what purposes would you restrict the application of a grant amounting to 30*s*. per man?—I would restrict it in the first instance to assisting such of the men as required it. Some of them would not take it, I know that some men in my battalion would not take it at all, they would provide their own uniforms; in the first instance I would assist those men who were not able to provide their own uniforms with a part of the money, and then I would apply any surplus of it to the battalion fund; for example, I find that among the artizans of the corps it is a difficult thing to get them to pay half a crown or 3*s*. subscription towards the battalion fund, and in short the captains of companies have a feeling of delicacy in asking them for it.

1518. I suppose that 30*s*. a head would enable you to do away almost entirely with the subscriptions from the privates?—I think so.

1519. Would you consider it a proper application of the money that a portion of the fund should be applied to the expenses of the band?—No, I should not.

1520. You would leave that to extraneous aid?—Yes, I would; we have two bands connected with my regiment, but they are kept up by the two companies to which they are attached.

1521. Can you form any opinion of the amount of expense which is incurred in the regiment exclusive of the band, and exclusive of uniforms, for incidental expenses?—No, I am not prepared to say what the amount is.

1522. Can you state to the Commission the total expense of maintaining a regiment of your strength, or a regiment 1,000 strong?—No, I cannot.

1523. (*Earl of Ducie.*) You have stated that in your regiment there are distinct companies of self-supporting volunteers?—Yes.

1524. Is there any difference between them and the other companies with respect to their efficiency?—No, I do not think there is much.

1525. Is there any difference with regard to their attendance at drill?—No; there are some companies that we are associated with connected with public works; the companies having been got up by the proprietors of those works, and they can command the attendance of the men at any time; they attend very well.

1526. Are they companies composed of artizans?—Yes.

1527. Have those artizan companies been assisted in obtaining their uniforms?—I understand that the proprietors of the works did originally clothe them either partially or wholly.

1528. (*Lord Elcho.*) Of the 6,000 men, how many do you suppose have found their own uniforms and accoutrements?—I should think that they have all more or less contributed towards their own uniforms.

1529. Do you think that one-third of them have equipped themselves entirely at their own expense?—I should say so.

1530. You think about one-third have?—Yes, or more than that.

1531. (*Sir A. Campbell.*) They have done it entirely at their own expense?—I should say so.

1532. (*Viscount Hardinge.*) What is the average rate of wages that those working men receive?—It differs very much, according to the particular branch of trade in which they are engaged.

1533. What should you say was the lowest rate of wages that they receive?—I should say that very few of them get less than probably 18*s*. a week.

1534. You do not think that any of them belong to a class of men who would enrol themselves in the militia?—Not so far as my regiment is concerned.

1535. You have stated that you think the men would not like to have clothing issued to them directly from the Government; would it not ooze out who had been assisted by the grant if administered by the commanding officer, and who had not?—Yes, but I do not think they would have any objection to the thing if it were given in money. I do think that

L

Lieut.-Col. Dreghorn.
6 June 1862.

they would have an objection to receive clothing in kind.

1536. (*Sir G. A. Wetherall.*) You do not limit your enrolments to men who earn a certain amount of wages, but you take any one of good character?—Yes, any man of respectable character.

1537. You do not mind whether his wages are great or small?—No; but we should not take in mere labourers.

1538. Do you think that any men enrol themselves for the purpose of escaping from the ballot for the militia?—I do not think that there is one.

1539. Have you many men in your corps who are liable to the ballot?—Yes, almost every one of them is.

1540. (*Lord Elcho.*) You have stated that some of your men required and received assistance towards their uniform or towards something?—Yes.

1541. Have you found that those men to whom the assistance has been given, either towards their uniform or something else, have been as earnest and as regular in attending the drills and in supporting the cause as volunteers who have paid everything for themselves?—Yes, I think so.

1542. (*Viscount Hardinge.*) Suppose the Government issued so many yards of cloth to each company or to each battalion, do you think that such a principle as that would be acceptable to the men?—I think that it would be less objectionable than furnishing them with made-up clothing.

1543. (*Sir A. Campbell.*) You have stated, I think, that the uniform costs 3*l*. 6*s*. without accoutrements?—No, with accoutrements; but I think they are cheaper now.

1544. Do you think it would be possible by reducing the quality of the uniform and supplying one that only costs 15*s*. to bring it within the power of the men to clothe themselves?—If you could give them a uniform at 15*s*. I think you might also bring it within their power to clothe themselves, but I understand that that is perfectly impracticable. I have seen the uniform to which you allude; in the Exhibition they have samples of it, and there are some of the officers connected with my regiment who happened to have seen some samples of this cloth, and they said that it was perfectly absurd to think that it would stand any wear.

1545. You do not think that it is possible to reduce the price of the uniform to so low a point as to bring it within the power of the men under your command to provide it for themselves?—I do not think so.

1546. (*Lieut.-Col. Barttelot.*) It has been reported that a great number of men have enrolled themselves who ought not to have enrolled themselves; is it within your knowledge that there are many men who have enrolled themselves as volunteers who should not have been volunteers; I mean, are they men who might go into the militia or line?—No, I do not think that that is so. Originally, when the movement was started, I was very hostile to introducing the artizan element into the volunteer movement at all, and we excluded them in the two first companies that I was connected with, but latterly, when we found that the practice of introducing artizans was prevailing elsewhere I began to change my mind about it and to think that they would be a very useful adjunct to the corps, and we have so found it.

1547. (*Lord Overstone.*) Have you well considered and formed a definite opinion upon the question, whether or not it is expedient that a number of persons should be drawn into the volunteer force who are not in circumstances to enable them to pay their own expenses as connected with that force?—I have formed an opinion upon the subject, but I think you are decidedly better able to judge of the expediency than I can be.

1548. Our judgment is necessarily founded on the opinions of well informed officers, like yourself; will you be kind enough to state your opinion and the grounds upon which it is formed?—I am not quite prepared to state an opinion.

1549. You have already said that you think assistance from the Government, represented by 30*s*. a head, would be efficient for its purpose; can you form any opinion what proportion to the whole expenditure in a corps that aid from the Government would bear?—I have always thought that between 35*s*. and 2*l*. a man should meet the whole expenditure in a volunteer corps.

1550. Do you think that 2*l*. a head would probably cover the whole expenditure in a volunteer regiment?—Yes.

1551. Would it be expedient that Government, out of that 2*l*., should contribute 30*s*., leaving the other 25 per cent. to be a part of the expenditure to be borne by the corps itself?—Yes. It is matter of opinion whether it is proper to keep up the numbers or not; I merely give that opinion upon the supposition that it is right to keep up the numbers; if it is thought that the numbers should be diminished then of course the aid should not be given.

1552. Do you think it is consistent with the principle of the volunteer force that 75 per cent. of the whole pecuniary expenditure should be borne by the Government and 25 per cent. be borne by the volunteers themselves?—I do not think it is right and fair that men who give their time gratuitously, and who are willing to do so, should be called upon to give money towards it also, to the exclusion of the general public who are deriving the benefit from the movement.

1553. Do you not think that in the constitution of the movement, which is essentially a volunteer one, if one set of persons contribute their time and their services, the expenditure necessary for it ought to be sought principally from other persons who cannot give their time, but who are capable of contributing their pecuniary aid?—Yes; but I think that it can only be given in a fair and legitimate way, by being made universal; I may mention that I was for sometime one of the magistrates of Glasgow, and am now a county magistrate, and I have been so for many years, and in that way I have had occasion to go when subscriptions have been required, and endeavour to raise subscriptions for particular funds, such as the Crimean fund, or in the case of people being thrown out of employment,—and there are a few benevolent men in Glasgow, to whom you can go with the certainty of obtaining money, but I think that it would be perfectly unfair that such men as those should be called upon to support such a movement as this, while others are entirely escaping from it.

1554. (*Sir G. A. Wetherall.*) Do you think that the enrolment of volunteers improves their social habits?—Decidedly so.

1555. Are the artizans more trusted by their employers?—Yes, I think that it has had the best possible effect. I recollect about 12 years ago in Glasgow, when I was one of the magistrates, a riot taking place among the work people who were out of employment, but I do not think that now this volunteer movement has taken place there is any risk of any such thing taking place, although the people are out of employment just now. I think that this volunteer movement has mightily improved them; they have taken the oath of allegiance to Her Majesty, and come in contact with other classes of the community, and that has had the best effect, that is my experience.

1556. (*Sir A. Campbell.*) This year has afforded you a very good opportunity of testing that?—Yes; even some of the volunteers themselves are partially out of employment. I know a number of them in my own regiment who are upon half time.

1557. (*Lord Elcho.*) In forming companies do you find it better to separate the classes or to mix them together?—We do not wish to make any distinction at all if possible.

1558. (*Viscount Hardinge.*) Which companies attend drill the best, the artizan companies or the self-supporting companies?—That depends very much upon particular circumstances.

1559. Do you think that at the present time the man whose uniform is paid for by the finance committee is generally speaking as good an attendant as the man who provides his own uniform?—I do, decidedly.

1560. Do you think that if further aid were given to the volunteers by the Government they would object to a longer period of service and a longer notice of resignation?—I do not know, but I think it would be important if it were possible to have the period lengthened.

1561. Do you think that if further aid were given they would submit to having a greater amount of control exercised over them than is now exercised over them?—I am not prepared to say that.

1562. (*Lord Elcho.*) That would depend, would it not, upon what control it was and how exercised?— Yes.

1563. (*Chairman.*) Do you find that they give their time regularly to the drills?—Yes.

1564. How often have you battalion drills?—We have not a battalion drill very frequently, the companies being spread throughout the city, and Glasgow is an immense city; the head-quarters of one company is at Busby, some miles away, but they have company drills almost every week.

1565. Have many of your men passed through a course of rifle instruction?—Yes, in the corps, but not at Hythe.

1566. (*Viscount Hardinge.*) If further aid were given do you think that Government would have a right to insist upon the same amount of efficiency that exists at the present time, or should they require a still greater amount of efficiency?—I am not prepared to say that the Government should insist upon the force doing more than they are doing now.

1567. Are you prepared to admit that if further aid were given from the Government it would in some way indirectly alter the character of the movement as being a self-supporting one?—So far as the money that was given to them is concerned it would alter the character of the movement to that extent, because I would understand that a volunteer regiment should be entirely supported by themselves if they were able to do it.

1568. (*Lord Elcho.*) Do you think that you can now call the volunteer force, or even a large portion of it a self-supporting force, that is to say, that the funds to meet the regimental expenses and other incidental expenses come from the regiment itself, and that in the different corps you could find money to enable those corps to exist?—No.

1569. At the present moment, taking that view of the meaning of self-supporting, a very large portion of the volunteer force is not self-supporting?—Unquestionably not.

1570. It is supported by extraneous aid, is it not, received from benevolent persons?—Yes.

1571. Your experience as a magistrate leads you to think that that extraneous support comes only from a few individuals, and that the mass of the public who derive the benefit do not pay anything towards it?—Yes.

1572. Your opinion with regard to a benefit which is universally spread over the whole of the community is that the support which is given to it should come from the whole of the community, and that the only way of doing it is by obtaining Government assistance?—Yes.

1573. You have stated from your experience of the artizans that they have improved in their general condition and character, and you believe if we had the employers from your district before us they would say that they found them better workmen?—I do not know that they would say it made them better workmen, but so far as my experience has gone, I think that towards the Government and towards their fellow men generally they are much better members of society than they were before.

1574. More loyal subjects and better members of society?—Yes.

1575. (*Sir G. A. Wetherall.*) Do you think that the habits of order which they have partially acquired make them more regular in the attention they pay to their own civil employments?—Yes, I think so.

1576. (*Lord Elcho.*) Of those 6,000 men to whom you have referred, who are mostly artizans, as I understand from you, composing the Glasgow volunteer force, what proportion, or is there any proportion, that would naturally enter into the army or into the militia?—I think there are very few of them.

1577. Your impression is that the services of those 6,000 men, either as militiamen or men enlisting into the regular army would be lost to the State were it not that they were volunteers?—I do decidedly think so. I do not think that they are of that class which generally enlist either into the regular army or into the militia.

1578. And you think that they in no way interfere with enlistments into the regular army?—I do think so. I do not believe that a single man in my regiment would have enlisted either into the militia or into the regular army; they are of the class of mechanics, and not of that class that generally enlist.

1579. (*Sir G. A. Wetherall.*) But it would affect the militia, would it not, because although the ballot is not in force, it is the law?—Yes, just so; but I do not think that there are many of them who would be available; they would find substitutes rather.

1580. (*Lord Elcho.*) Is it not the case that if the ballot were enforced, we are all of us liable to be drawn for the militia between certain ages?—Yes.

1581. (*Viscount Hardinge.*) Do you know whether the militia regiment in your county is tolerably well up in its numbers?—I am not aware of that.

1582. (*Lord Elcho.*) Perhaps the most practicable way of filling up the ranks of the volunteers would be the enforcement of the ballot for the militia?— Yes, I think that it would bring in a class of men that we have not got in it just now.

1583. Have you considered the question of exemptions as an inducement to men to become volunteers? —I do not think that has had the slightest effect with us.

1584. Do you think that any exemptions could be given that would induce men to volunteer, and when they had once volunteered, to remain in the force, such as making them exempt from any civil duties such as serving on juries, and serving as special constables?—No, that would have no effect.

1585. (*Lord Overstone.*) Do you not think that it would be a good principle to substitute an exemption from one civil duty as an inducement to them to undertake another civil duty?—I do not think so.

1586. (*Sir A. Campbell.*) Do you think that in the Glasgow corps generally, there is any indisposition to serve under military command when gathered together in large numbers?—No, I do not think there is.

1587. Your men, for example, would be quite ready, if gathered together in a brigade to serve under a military officer as well as under a volunteer officer? —I think more so.

1588. (*Viscount Hardinge.*) With regard to the clothing, supposing that you, as commanding officer, issued clothing out to a certain number of men, provided by funds contributed by the Government, what would you do in the case of a man who left the town and took his uniform with him?—We should hold him responsible to the commanding officer for his uniform if it was provided by the Government, and the funds were derived from Government; I would put it in the same way as the arrears due by him, and that he should be liable to pay them up when he leaves the regiment.

1589. How would you proceed against a man in such a case as that?—There is a very summary mode of procedure prescribed by the Act of Parliament.

1590. Take the case of a man resigning who had received his clothing from you as commanding officer,

Lieut.-Col. Dreghorn.

6 June 1862.

Lieut.-Col. Deyghorn.
6 June 1862.

that clothing in all probability would be returned into store for the moment, would it not?—I do not know that.

1591. Take the case of a man who resigns and who is in debt to the corps?—I would not accept his resignation as long as he was indebted to the corps. I would hold that he was either indebted to the corps or to the Government if part of his uniform was paid for either by the one or by the other, and therefore he would not be entitled to resign.

1592. You would not let a man resign who had received his uniform from you, and which had been paid for out of Government money?—Not until he had paid back the money or until his uniform was done.

1593. Assuming that he had paid back the money, the suit would then be returned into store, would it not?—If he paid back the money he would be entitled to do what he thought fit with the uniform.

1594. But take the case of a uniform that would be under certain circumstances returned into store, would you re-issue that uniform to a new member?—I do not know that, I do not think they would take it.

1595. (Sir A. Campbell.) Do you think that it is of importance, with regard to the permanency of the force in Glasgow and its neighbourhood, that some decision should be come to immediately as to what the Government intends to do?—Decidedly.

1596. Do you think that further delay would be prejudicial to the movement?—Yes.

1597. (Lord Elcho.) There have been several meetings lately, have there not, in Glasgow?—Yes.

1598. The view taken at the meetings at Glasgow I believe was that a certain capitation grant should be made by the Government?—Yes.

1599. Am I right in assuming that it never entered into the head of any one connected with these meetings that any portion of the money was under any circumstances to find its way into the pockets of the volunteers themselves as a payment for service or anything of that kind?—It never did.

1600. It was solely intended to be expended at the discretion of the commanding officer upon things which he considered essential for the maintenance of his regiment?—Precisely.

1601. They would repudiate anything like payment for their services?—Yes.

1602. (Viscount Hardinge.) What security would the Government have that the money was properly expended by the commanding officers?—I think that they would have the best guarantee possible. Suppose, for example, that I take Glasgow, and I presume that that would afford a proper criterion of the character of the officers generally throughout the country. I hold that it would be perfectly safe in the hands of the officers of the battalion, and that it would be perfectly well administered.

1603. (Sir A. Campbell.) What are your reasons for thinking that promptitude of decision on the part of the Government is essential?—Because the uniform of a number of the men is done, and they cannot appear on parade; they are found fault with for not doing so, and I have been told privately that they have a good deal of pride about them; a number of these men do not wish their poverty to be made known, and they would rather send in their resignation than say "My uniform is done, and I cannot afford to provide a new one."

1604. (Lord Overstone.) Your opinion is that to afford pecuniary aid to support the volunteer movement, derived from the general taxation of the country would be a sound and desirable step to take?—Yes.

1605. And you think that a decision upon the subject is urgently required?—Yes, I do.

1606. (Lord Elcho.) You are not connected with any other part of Scotland I believe?—No; I happened to be in London at the time when a great meeting was to be held here, but not with the purpose of attending it, I was here upon public business at the time; and I met with a great many volunteer officers from various parts of England, and I found that they had made up their minds very decidedly upon the subject.

1607. In the same sense in which you have spoken?—Precisely, and rather stronger.

The witness withdrew.

Maj. G. Warrender.

Major GEORGE WARRENDER examined.

1608. (Chairman.) I believe you command an administrative battalion of Haddington Rifle Volunteers?—Yes.

1609. You were formerly in the Guards, I believe?—Yes, and in the line; I held a captain's commission in the line, and I exchanged afterwards into the Guards.

1610. Of how many corps does the battalion consist of which you have the command?—Five companies and one subdivision.

1611. Are those corps at a considerable distance from each other, or are they near together?—Of the five companies there are two at headquarters, and the greatest distance that they are apart is five miles and a quarter, except the subdivision.

1612. Are there separate funds for those corps?—It is entirely an administrative battalion, and each company manages its own finances.

1613. I suppose that each corps has its own rifle range?—The two companies at head quarters have one between them; I believe it is in contemplation that they should have two separate rifle ranges, but not having been made into one command under a captain-commandant, and the two corps being composed of different classes of men, they both clash in spirit and the discipline is rather different. It has been contemplated to divide them altogether, unless they were brought entirely together, which they do not seem to wish at present, but which is must desirable.

1614. Have you any battalion fund?—We have no battalion fund; this is under the heads of C., D., E., and F. in the printed questions addressed to officers commanding battalions, and I think the first head is with reference to the rent paid for headquarters. My principle on starting was to make the whole machinery of the battalion as simple and as economical and as uncumbersome as possible. With regard to the adjutant, we require no headquarters, for the real use of them would be to summon prisoners, to conduct the routes, and all that sort of business, and therefore we require no headquarters beyond a place to write letters in; the adjutant had a house to live in, and therefore I concluded that the best thing was for him to write the letters in his own house, so that he kept all the battalion papers and books in his own house. Each corps had enough to do to meet its own expenses, and a few casual battalion expenses are met by me, or as they best may.

1615. Is he paid a higher sum than what he receives from Government?—Nothing more; then with regard to the furniture at headquarters, the room that he wrote his letters in was simply a small closet, and he only wanted a table and some drawers to hold the papers. As to printing, stationery and postage, there was an allowance of 4l. for every company, which was received, and which in the army is devoted to that purpose; I concluded that that was the simple way instead of calling upon him or the other officers to pay for it; it more than amply covered the whole of the printing, stationery, and postage. The printing will not be required again for a long time, the postage was marked down as it took place; it was only the adjutant's, and it has not amounted to the sum allowed by the Government, so that the adjutant sustained no loss; I considered that it was not to be made a gain of but to be spent for the service.

1616. (Viscount Hardinge.) Was the 4l. per company totally independent of the Government allowance for stationery?—No, the Government allowed that, and that more than covered it. I concluded that the adjutant was not supposed to make a profit out of it, but he was to spend it in the correspondence of the battalion,—I defray my own postage with headquarters, and each corps defrays its own expenses of correspondence with headquarters,—but all that went through him. I concluded that paper and everything were to be found by him. Then with regard to battalion drill, I found that the five companies existed under a different condition as to standing orders, and everything of that sort; my idea was a standing order to bring them under one system, and I got the officers together and explained to them my wishes, but I found that they all existed under such different conditions that if I was to establish one system and issue one kind of standing order the result would be that it would not be obeyed, therefore I thought that the wisest thing to do was to make everything as simple as possible. I found that it was probably the best plan to make each captain interested in his own company, as each company drew its funds from different sources. In two cases there were two noblemen, one Lord Elcho's father, who almost entirely supported one corps, and Lord Tweeddale, who was very much in the same position. Another corps consisted of men who supported themselves; the two remaining companies were supported, not by any one individual, but by many individuals in their locality, very much by their officers, in both cases the officers were not persons of great social position, but very respectable persons. One was a farmer paying a large rent, but who lived by his farm, another was in a large seed business, which, in an agricultural district, is a good business, but he was a merchant. Those people had spent large sums upon their corps, and I concluded that the best thing was to lay down very broad rules for them, and to suggest to them what was the right discipline to carry on, but to leave it in a certain degree to the discretion of each officer as to how he managed his company, taking care to assure myself that the War Office orders were carried out strictly; the general system was one that could be assimilated with the army system. There is a certain amount of orderly duty carried on in each company, in one company by officers, in another company by non-commissioned officers when the subaltern officers live far from headquarters.

1617. With regard to the inspection of the arms, and seeing that they are kept in a dry place, and properly cleaned, do you hold the captain of a company solely responsible for that?—He has a distinct order upon that subject, a standing order, but it is unequally carried out, but in each company there is an inspection every month; the officer whose charge it is to look after that sends in a report, or rather it is written down in a book, and at the end of the month he hands over everything with an inventory to the other subaltern, who, in his turn, does the same duty, and inspects the arms of those men who have leave to carry them away from headquarters, which is a thing, however, that I do not encourage, for I do not think that it conduces to discipline. In other companies, where the officers live far from headquarters, I find that they cannot do that; I say to the captains "You must carry out the same "system," but they put it into the hands of the non-commissioned officers.

1618. Each company, I presume, has an armoury?—Yes.

1619. What proportion of the arms in each company are kept in the armoury, and what proportion of them are kept in the private residences of the men?—In No. 1 company, which is composed of men of independent means, they are almost all, with hardly any exception, kept in their own houses; in No. 2 company, which is a company composed entirely of agricultural labourers, principally foresters of Lord Tweeddale, they are kept in the armoury, and no arms can be in better order. In No. 3 company also, at headquarters, which is composed principally of mechanics and artizans, and where the discipline is more strict than in No. 1 in the same locality, there the same care is taken as the captain insists upon their being kept in store; the result is that their arms are in better order than in No. 1 company, which is composed of a higher class of men.

1620. How often are the arms of No. 1 company inspected?—I cannot tell you now, but the first thing I shall do when I get back will be to examine the books to which I have referred; they are inspected two or three times a month, but it is only lately that I have established this order; the War Office order was enough to start with, but it was not acted upon sufficiently by each commanding officer, and therefore I backed it up with a distinct battalion order, and now they either do what they are ordered to do, or they neglect what is ordered; if they neglect it I shall report it at once to the field officer who is the assistant inspector of the district; at the same time I find a general anxiety to carry out instructions when made clear.

1621. Is there not great difficulty in getting the arms properly inspected in such a case as that of No. 1 company, in which a man may not be a good attendant at drill, and his rifle cannot be inspected unless he brings it to headquarters and appears on parade?—Since the order was given the plan has been that the subaltern should name one or two days on which he would inspect the arms of the men who had leave to keep them at home, and if they did not appear on parade on one of those days, when he made out his report at the end of the month he named those men as not having produced their arms, and if the next month the same men did not produce their arms, then I instructed the captain to withdraw the permission to take them home from them, and told him that if I found he had not done so, I should perhaps take from him the power of giving the permission.

1622. (*Chairman.*) The captain is solely responsible for the arms being kept in proper order?—Yes, but I make his subalterns responsible to him. I may mention that I obtained permission from the War Office to retain the command of a company in a different county, which would otherwise have fallen entirely off for want of a gentleman to lead them.

1623. (*Viscount Hardinge.*) What do you pay for your armouries?—From 2*l.* to 3*l.* a year.

1624. (*Sir A. Campbell.*) In the case of the companies whose arms are kept in store are they cleaned by the men?—The arms are in that case taken charge of by the serjeant-instructor, but when the men go out to shoot for their classification, or for private practice, they are expected after that to clean their own arms, but they do not do it quite so well as the serjeant-instructor, he puts a little oil upon them afterwards. Then there are other men, artizans, who can only just get time to shoot late in the evening, and they have not time to clean them afterwards, and they would rust, and so the serjeant-instructor cleans them, and when he is on good terms with a company there is no difficulty about it.

1625. Does he receive any extra allowance for that beyond the Government pay?—Yes, he gets house rent in Berwickshire, we give him for house rent 5*l.* annually, and also for uniform.

1626. He receives nothing for keeping the arms in order?—All the materials are found for him; he gets 10*l.* a year, and he has to appear in uniform and to lodge himself.

1627. Do you find that the Government serjeants are generally well satisfied?—Yes, all but one man who came to me one day to complain, that he had too much to do. I threatened to report this man, and explained the War Office instructions. The man was silenced, and appeared to regret what he had said, and afterwards to be quite contented, and to realize that he has no more than proper duties to perform.

1628. Does your adjutant receive any extra allowance beyond Government pay?—Nothing.

L 3

Maj. G. Warrender.

6 June 1862.

1629. Do you think that the Government pay is sufficient generally speaking?—For the class of men who are best adapted for an administrative battalion I think it is; I think that the best class of non-commissioned officers are the best men. The adjutant of the Haddington battalion was colour-serjeant of the company that I was with, and after I exchanged into the Guards he became serjeant-major in the regiment for five years; he was then discharged with an excellent pension and went into a militia regiment. I recommended him to Lord Tweeddale, the lord lieutenant of the county, who named him to the War Office; there was no advantage in having such a man, he was perfectly satisfied with the pay, and he was willing to make himself useful at headquarters; if not absent with one of the other corps they never drill without his being present, and as he was a serjeant-major he understands squad drill better than any officer; he takes charge of the men and brings then on in drill in a manner that no gentleman who had never been a non-commissioned officer could hardly undertake to do.

1630. Have you never found any disinclination on the part of the captains to fall in under the adjutant when he inspects them, and you are not on parade?—I have made it clear that the adjutant's visits are not inspections, and on taking command of the battalion I said that until I made a change I considered them all under instruction, and therefore at drill they fall in.

1631. Do you think that an adjutant who has been appointed from the ranks would have the same authority over commissioned officers as an adjutant taken from officers in the line would have?—I should not desire that the adjutant should have any authority over the captains; he could not have, he is of inferior rank, and I have always put the captain in as high a position as possible.

1632. But there is such a thing as adjutant's drill?—Yes; I think that such men as I describe require to be very carefully chosen; I do not think as a rule that any serjeant-major would do, but I think that there are men, and a sufficient number of them probably for administrative battalions; I do not speak of a consolidated battalion, the case there may be different.

1633. With regard to battalion drill, I presume that each company being only five miles from headquarters, there is no difficulty in getting them together?—There is great difficulty.

1634. When they attend battalion drill do they, generally speaking, march in those five miles?—Yes, but when they come they have generally done a hard day's work beforehand. Those at headquarters only march in about half a mile, but those who are at outquarters generally come in farm carts.

1635. How is the hire of those carts and the railway fares paid for?—That is all arranged by the officers of each corps, out of their own finances; in the case of two companies the carts belong to Lord Tweeddale and Lord Wemyss.

1636. Are those expenses paid by the volunteers themselves, or are they paid by the finance committee?—By the finance committee, I apprehend.

1637. Do the expenses come out of the captain's pocket in any way?—In a great degree; when a captain is a farmer he has a certain number of carts, and he sends those carts in, they do not cost positive hard money, but he bears the expense; in the case of Lord Wemyss's company, I suppose that his Lordship's carts are used, and in the case of Lord Tweeddale's company the same.

1638. Who pays the railway fares?—They are paid either by the officers, or by some small subscription from the men.

1639. (*Lord Elcho.*) Do you know what the strength of the force in the county is?—There is a company of artillery in addition to the battalion of rifle volunteers, but I think the rifle volunteers, officers included, numbered last quarter about 407 or 408.

1640. Was there not a county fund raised at the commencement of the movement to establish this county force?—Yes.

1641. Did the sum so raised amount to 800*l.*?—About that.

1642. That has been expended has it not?—Yes.

1643. And a further sum of 200*l.* has been raised by the county?—Yes, for the current year.

1644. The sums so raised have been expended; the 800*l.* in the clothing required for a very large part of that force?—None of this sum was expended in clothing I believe, but in targets, drill instruction, and articles of military equipment, *exclusive* of clothing. When men did not clothe themselves, funds for the purpose were procured from friends and liberally disposed persons in the neighbourhood.

1645. The sum of 200*l.* has been raised to meet incidental expenses exclusive of clothing in this current year?—Yes.

1646. Of the force so raised what portion of it is self-supporting, that is to say, which has within itself the means of finding whatever sum of money is required for incidental expenses, and to renew the uniforms?—I do not suppose that there are above 100.

1647. There was an inquiry in the county into this subject, was there not?—Yes.

1648. Did not the result of that inquiry show that out of between 500 or 600 men there were only 100 who were self-supporting?—About that number.

1649. By self-supporting I mean finding their own clothing, and providing the necessary amount to meet all the incidental expenses of the company or the corps, such as an orderly room, a place for a rifle range, and such like expenses?—Yes, after the receipt of the assistance in kind which the Government already afford.

1650. You have stated that you command a company in Berwickshire, can you speak at all as to the position of the force in that county, and whether it is in the same condition as the force in the county where you command an administrative battalion?—It is very much the same on the whole; there are two companies that are composed of quite as low a class of men, if not lower, than any two in Haddingtonshire; on the other hand there is none that is quite so self-supporting as that one in Haddington, which entirely supports itself.

1651. You mean the artizans and labourers?—No; I mean there is none which supports itself so much as the No. 1, Haddington company. I think that there are three which support themselves more than any other company in Haddingtonshire, with the exception of No. 1. On the average, it is very much the same.

1652. No. 1 in Haddington is composed, is it not, chiefly of clerks of merchants?—Yes.

1653. Even in that company there has been some difficulty in getting the subscriptions, has there not?—Yes, there has; but at the same time one of them casually told me the other day that they were in doubt whether they would accept their portion of the 200*l.* which you alluded to just now, or whether they would not let it go to the other company. I believe that their pride was a little piqued by some questions that were asked them.

1654. Speaking generally of the battalion which you command, is it your opinion that, unless assistance of some kind is given, whether by the Government or from any other source, that battalion will fall away?—As a battalion, undoubtedly.

1655. Has it not the means of self-support in itself?—Distinctly not.

1656. From the knowledge which you have of the different companies in Berwickshire, are they practically in the same position as the battalion which you command?—I think that, if you struck an average, they might do a little more for themselves; but it is clear that they could not support a battalion in Berwickshire if they received no aid.

1657. Is there any extraneous system established in Berwickshire?—Yes, for one year; and it is understood that, in all probability, if the volunteers get no other aid, they might go on with it; and it was done with a view of not letting the thing go down with a crash, which it was apprehended that it would.

1658. Will you be kind enough to state what that system is?—That system is a voluntary assessment on the total rental of the county. I think it is two-twelfths of a penny; and the result has been that each commanding officer has been allowed to draw from this fund for the current year the amount of 10s. 6d. per effective volunteer. We sent in a return, and struck out of the return those that were non-effective, and they gave us the sum of 10s. 6d. per effective volunteer.

1659. You say by a voluntary assessment; by that you mean, do you not, an assessment upon the rental of each individual?—Yes, upon every person down to an income of 100l. a year.

1660. Does each individual contribute in proportion to his income whatever is required to maintain these companies?—I believe that there was one of our friends who declined to do so on principle.

1661. One who refused?—I allude to Lord Polwarth. He refused on principle, and I think some other very small proprietors did the same; but I think, on the whole, the assessment produced more than was expected by a few pounds.

1662. Was any similar proposition made in the county in which you command a battalion?—There was an inclination to do so, but it did not come to a positive proposal; there was a decided feeling against it.

1663. In that county there was an objection to a voluntary assessment?—Yes, principally on the part of the large proprietors; they did not wish to close their purses, but they objected to the mode of doing it.

1664. But they readily raised, as a temporary expedient, 200l. to meet the necessary expenses, did they not?—Yes, and there was a proprietor of the county of Haddington who would have had to give 9l. as an assessment, which he objected to, but he gave 25l. as a contribution.

1665. (*Chairman.*) The case of your Haddington battalion is rather an exception, is it not?— The case of my company that I have in Berwickshire is much the same also, and I know more about that than of the others, not having anything properly to do with the finances of the others. This corps has been almost entirely maintained by Sir Hugh Campbell, my father-in-law; he has spent, I believe, upwards of 300l. upon this company, both directly and indirectly, but the idea has always been, when the movement took place, that he was willing, as men came forward, to assist them until the experiment was proved, and then if the Government thought it worth while to go on with it, he having kept them going in the meantime, should feel that he had done a good thing, and then if the Government declined to go on with it, he should not feel called upon to make any further exertions.

1666. (*Lord Elcho.*) Am I right in saying that the inquiry which took place in the county of Haddington resulted in this, that it appeared that 500l. would be necessary annually to meet the incidental expenses of the force, amounting in numbers to about 600 men?—I think it was about that.

1667. Exclusive of the assistance then given by the Government, which included the serjeants and ammunition?—Yes.

1668. The number being 600 men?—No, I think it was 450 men, including the artillery. I think the force is now a little stronger.

1669. (*Viscount Hardinge.*) It included your battalion?—Yes.

1670. (*Lord Elcho.*) That estimate had reference to the whole force, including the artillery?—Yes.

1671. It came to something under 1l. a man, did it not?—I think so.

1672. Making no provision in that for clothing?—No. You will remember that we did not quite agree as to the difficulty of getting battalion drills. You thought that the men could march, and that if the volunteers were men in sedentary employments, it would be a very good thing for them; but to march five miles after a hard day's work and then to undergo a hard and long drill is a great deal to ask men to do, and indeed more than they will do; they must get some refreshment, and either they must pay for it, or the officers must pay.

1673. (*Viscount Hardinge.*) How often do you get your battalion together?—Last year we got the whole battalion together three times, and on two other occasions we got portions of it together. The whole battalion was inspected once by the assistant inspector and once by the lord lieutenant.

1674. I suppose that some of the members marched to the battalion drill ground?—I think not.

1675. (*Major-Gen. Eyre.*) You have five companies have you not?—Yes.

1676. Are they a considerable distance from each other?—No; there is a radius of about 5¼ miles from headquarters, and there is one 16 miles off, but that comes in by rail.

1677. They are some miles distant from each other?—Yes.

1678. The district inspector and adjutant can make their respective reports, if drill serjeants are necessary for squad drills?—Yes.

1679. Has each company a drill serjeant?—Yes.

1680. (*Lord Elcho.*) The subdivision has not, has it?—No; but at the same I think that economy might be effected in every administrative battalion throughout the country on that score, by having one instructor to two corps when circumstances and distance permit, and giving a higher rate of pay to such an instructor, but yet less than the pay of two instructors.

1681. (*Major-Gen. Eyre.*) Do you think that a drill serjeant is required for each company?—Yes; unless the plan I have just mentioned was found to work well.

1682. (*Viscount Hardinge.*) Will you be good enough to describe the class of men who principally compose the out-lying companies?—They are almost entirely agricultural, or else clerks and mechanics.

1683. (*Lord Elcho.*) Will you read from the Haddington report the analysis of the corps as to their professions?—" Lawyers', bankers', and merchants' clerks, 26; merchants and tradesmen, 94; " mechanics and artizans, 205; labourers, 89." The mechanics and artizans are men who are very often apprentices. The means of existence of a Scotch apprentice to a wheelwright or to a blacksmith are these; he is apprenticed for so many years, and he receives no pay whatsoever, but he gets some very coarse food and lodging, and he has given to him a certain number of days in the year for his own disposal during the harvest, during which time he earns what he can, and he requires what he earns to clothe himself; it is a bare subsistence, even putting volunteering out of the question. But at the same time he is made very amenable to discipline, and it keeps him in early life rather steady.

1684. (*Viscount Hardinge.*) Do you think that that is the sort of man you want?—I have had nothing to do with raising any corps. When first the corps that I had charge of was enrolled, I was asked to take charge of it as they wanted a man who knew something about it, and afterwards when the battalion was formed in East Lothian, Lord Tweeddale offered me the command of it, and I found as commanding officer that they were composed of very good material.

1685. Are they not men who would very likely enter the army on the militia?—I am now speaking from the experience I have had of my own company, and they will not go into the army or generally into the militia. I have never taken men from the militia, but I have given men to the militia.

1686. These labourers are clothed, are they not, out of the different funds of each company?—In some

Maj. G. Warrender.

6 June 1862.

L 4

Maj. G. Warrender.
6 June 1862.

instances they are; I believe that in the case of Lord Wemyss's men and Lord Tweeddale's men they were similarly clothed. I do not know that money was ever paid into the fund, but they were clothed by their employers; and in the case of my father-in-law, he paid 200*l.* into the fund, and it was spent by the committee; they were clothed to a very great extent. I think that in the case of my company in Berwickshire, 18 men clothed themselves, another 18 or 20 of them half-clothed themselves, and the remainder were clothed entirely as I have described.

1687. Do those who have been furnished with their clothing attend the drills as well as the other members who are in a better position?—Better. I wish to mention, with regard to non-commissioned officers, that I always prefer a non-commissioned officer who does clothe himself, for I think he has more stake in the company. Many of those men under the head of mechanics are mostly married, or else they are apprentices, and the latter cannot enlist.

1688. You have a subdivision in your battalion; that subdivision, I presume, according to the regulations, has not a Government serjeant?—No.

1689. Do you not think that, situated as subdivisions are, it would be a great relief to them if the Government gave them a drill serjeant?—It would be a great boon to them; but I think it would be a great tax upon the Government; it is 2*s.* 4*d.* or 2*s.* 7*d.* a day, according to the rate of the pension that a man gets, and I think that that would be a great deal for the Government to pay for a subdivision which is considered an effective subdivision with 30 men; it would be paying more than 1*l.* a man even for a drill instructor. In such a case the system of appointing a better paid instructor for two corps might succeed.

1690. Is it not a great tax upon that subdivision, as compared with a neighbouring company, that the one has a Government serjeant given to it and the other has not?—Yes.

1691. How does your subdivision obtain the advantage of a drill instructor?—It is generally obtained in this way: leave of absence is obtained for a soldier, and he comes for a certain period and is paid by them, and then he rejoins his regiment.

1692. Do you find that the subdivision is in as good order as the other companies are?—Yes; they happened to get the best drill instructor that we had.

1693. (*Lord Elcho.*) Is there any adjoining company or subdivision which might be joined to this subdivision for the purpose of instruction?—No; the nearest one is the artillery; then there is only the county of Berwickshire, where there is no battalion. If the men were put together, they must be attached to the company there, which is about 12 miles off. With regard to the expense of drill serjeants, I should like to state what actually occurred in the battalion; and this is a point upon which, I think, there might be economy effected. When I first had the command of the battalion, I found that the fund which has been alluded to, and which the county had subscribed, had been expended in finding drill instruction for each corps; each corps drew upon the lord-lieutenant, who had the administration of this fund, for the funds required for their drill instruction. I inspected those companies, and I was not entirely satisfied with the progress they had made. Some had got an indifferent drill instructor; there were only five companies, and on the average their instruction cost 5*l.* a week or 20*l.* a month. I then called the officers together and told them that I thought they might obtain better and cheaper instruction, but that I should require them to co-operate with me; and the first step that I took was to discharge all the men whom they had, with the exception of one, who was a good instructor; and I engaged one other good instructor as well. One man I made serjeant-major of the battalion, and the other I made musketry instructor; and those two men travelled from one company to the other, and as they did that, they received higher pay than the men employed originally, so that I reduced the expenses of the instruction to a little more than one-half, as the travelling expenses came to not two-thirds, three-fifths perhaps, and at the same time got better instruction insured, and also that each company was instructed on the same principles and by the same men. When the battalion was got together first, there were only those two men and an adjutant; but they have all been instructed on the same principle, and they have surprised me by the manner in which they have worked together; and I think that now we might do perfectly well with fewer drill serjeants, at higher rates of pay, if we received some assistance to cover the expense of a man to take charge of the arms, and the cleaning of the arms, which the drill serjeants now do for the pay which they receive from the Government. We get more drill serjeants in proportion than the consolidated battalions.

1694. (*Lord Elcho.*) You get one per company, and the consolidated battalions get three for eight companies, do they not?—Yes; and I think that we could do with fewer, at all events where the battalion is not very large. If the serjeants were reduced it would positively be necessary; indeed we could not do without some allowance to pay some old man to take charge of the armoury and keep the arms clean, which the serjeants have been in the habit of doing.

1695. Have you any suggestions to offer as to the best means of supporting and maintaining a battalion situated in the way that yours is?—They must get money; they cannot get it from the counties, I think, because the feeling seems to be that it was very well to start the thing and to see how it worked, but now that the experiment has proved successful, if the force is worth anything they think it is worth the consideration and support of the Government.

1696. (*Lord Overstone.*) Does that feeling amount to this, that if men volunteer their personal services it is the fair and proper duty of the Government to provide for the expense of keeping them in a state of efficiency?—That is their impression; there may be some men in each battalion who would prefer finding for themselves.

1697. You think that it is the opinion of respectable individuals in the district with which you are acquainted, that the volunteer force ought to be based on that principle, that the volunteers' personal services is sufficient to give on their part, and that the pecuniary burden ought to be borne by the Government?—That is distinctly the view upon which Sir Hugh Campbell, my father-in-law, acted in originally supporting these men, and having been mainly instrumental in equipping them, he thought that after that it should be left, as you say, to the Government.

1698. Can you give any opinion as to the extent to which the volunteer force could be maintained in that district by voluntary assistance, founded upon the opposite principle that the parties constituting the force should bear the whole of the expenses they incur?—I think that in the county of Haddington No. 1 company of volunteers would exist always if there were volunteers anywhere; but I think as to No. 2 company that Lord Tweeddale, who has borne all the expenses, would feel that if the Government did not think it worth their while to continue the thing, he would be absolved from any further obligation. Company No. 3 could not continue. Company No. 4 (Lord Wemyss's) could only continue on his lordship's liberality, and No. 5 could not, I think, continue. The subdivision would certainly fall to the ground, and in Berwickshire my own company would immediately evaporate. There is no corps in the county that is absolutely self-supporting; it is possible that Lord Home, who is a very liberal man, might support a corps.

1699. You are of opinion, making allowances for particular cases in which one individual might do a very liberal thing, that, as a general rule, the expenses incurred by the volunteer movement must be borne by the Government?—I think so. I think that the force in East Lothian and Berwickshire together amounts to 800 or 900 men, and that they would probably not amount to 160 if assistance be not given, as where half the number of a corps falls away that corps must collapse.

1700. Do you think that Government assistance could not be rendered thoroughly efficient if conveyed only in an indirect form, bearing a certain proportion of the expenditure connected with the force, or do you think it should be a direct pecuniary grant placed in the hands of the commanding officers?—If otherwise than a pecuniary grant I suppose it would take the form of clothing, and I think there would be a great difficulty about clothing if given in kind; men might come and go, and it would be a difficult thing to deal with when a man was to get a uniform; it would be almost impossible to work it.

1701. You are of opinion that the direct form would be the most practical, and the most efficient?—Yes, that is my opinion, but I must admit that it is opposed to the opinion of my adjutant, who writes to me in these terms:—"If we are to have volunteers in "the country they ought to be taken from all classes "of the people, and clothed at the expense of the "state. Clothing (not money) ought to be given, "as I am certain the division of money would be "a great trouble to officers, and it would be sure to "raise discontent in the force. There are many men "in every corps who do not attend more than 24 "drills during the year, and many of those drills in "plain clothes, but allowing that he attended 24 "drills in uniform, in four years he would only have "attended 96 times; say that he attended four field "days extra in each of the four years, that would "make 112 times for him to be in uniform during "four years. At that rate a suit ought to last eight "years, but then the men who have attended double "that number of drills would require new uniforms "every four years; then the men who did not "require new uniforms would claim the cash, and if "this was given it would be encouraging non-attend-"ance at drill."

1702. (*Lord Elcho.*) The writer of that seems to be under the impression that the money would be given to the individuals?—He thinks that it would be handed over to the finance committee, and I think that by the constitution of all rifle corps rules approved by the Government, there is to be a finance committee; but in my own corps I found that the finance committee is of no great assistance to the commanding officer. The responsibility rests on him, and the administration of the funds should be in his hands.

1703. (*Lord Overstone.*) Can you express any opinion as to what would be the necessary expenditure per head in the volunteer force generally to maintain its efficiency?—I wrote down this morning what I thought about that, in these terms. I should propose that, whatever assistance may be granted, and which should not be less than 1*l.* per head of effectives, be based on the minimum strength of a corps, so that the corps may be at least perfectly kept up; whilst it may swell its ranks, if possible, up to its maximum with such persons as may enrol on the conditions of equipping themselves completely. The simplest means of establishing the right of drawing the Government money by the commanding officer, would be to allow him to draw according to his return for the previous year on 1st August, and to leave the administration of such money solely to his responsibility and discretion. If cloth and accoutrements, and not money, are issued, there will be a difficulty in arranging its distribution, as men are constantly enrolling and leaving, and some are effective one year and non-effective another year. I think that it should be imperative on serjeants to provide their own uniforms, and therefore only 55 men should be drawn for. The 1*l.* a head should be only drawn for 55 men, the three officers would require nothing. Where a company is only 60 strong, you ought only to have three serjeants.

1704. Supposing the volunteer force of the kingdom to consist of 150,000 men, do you think that a subvention on the part of the Government to the extent of 150,000*l.* would be sufficient for maintaining that force in a state of efficiency?—I think that it ought to be done, but it would require economy and care on the part of the officers in many districts to do so. In other districts it would give them, probably, a considerable surplus.

1705. You think that the expense would, under different circumstances, and in different counties, vary; that the sum might be sufficient for some places, but not sufficient for others?—As to my own district, it would be barely sufficient; but I think that they ought to do with it.

1706. (*Viscount Hardinge.*) I gather from what you have stated, that this capitation grant should be expended principally in clothing?—No, not entirely. I suppose that the assistance which the Government have already offered, by enabling the clothing to be drawn at contract price, would not be withdrawn; and if it was not withdrawn, I calculate that 10*s.* a year should keep up a man's clothing.

1707. (*Lord Overstone.*) Upon the supposition that I have put that 150,000*l.* were contributed by the Government to support a volunteer force of the same number, can you form any opinion as to what would be the amount of pecuniary disbursements that would have still to be defrayed from other sources?—I think that in the rural districts to which they belong it would be such a very skimp allowance to get on with that, they must get some assistance.

1708. What proportion would the 1*l.* a head bear to the total expenditure?—Probably one-fourth more would meet all their expenses, except those of attending battalion drills.

1709. £150,000 in the case supposed you think would be rather short of meeting all the expenditure?—Yes.

1710. (*Viscount Hardinge.*) Supposing 1*l.* a head to be granted, should you propose to buy Government cloth, and to issue it to the men to be made up by their own tailors?—Probably the commanding officer would himself contract with some tailor at a fixed price; he would not allow the men to have the cloth delivered into their own hands; I should not advise that.

1711. How would you get over this difficulty? In a case of illness or resignation the clothing would be returned into store, I suppose?—The course that is pursued in my own company in Berwickshire is this. When a man joins, there is a book kept, and he has to sign the conditions under which he joins, that the clothes are not to be his own until he has served a certain time; and that rule might be carried out still further.

1712. But suppose a member becomes unfit for service through illness, what would you do with his clothing?—He would become a non-effective, and I think that I would have his clothes put into store during his illness.

1713. Do you think that you could get a man who took his place to wear his uniform?—Not in cases of illness, but in cases of retirement from other causes, frequently.

1714. (*Sir A. Campbell.*) You have stated that you thought it would be better to make a requisition with regard to the proposed grant on the returns sent in to the previous August?—That would be the simplest machinery, I think.

1715. Would it not make it more easy to do if the returns were made not in August, but later in the year, say in December, so that the requisition might be made at the beginning of a fresh year?—Yes; I think it might do better, because a man might become effective after August, as there are still long days left for drill.

1716. Do you think upon the whole that the period between January and December, is a better time to judge of the effectiveness of a regiment than the period between August and July?—I think that the 1st of August was an unfortunate day on which to make our annual returns.

1717. (*Lord Elcho.*) Might it be advisable that

Maj. G. Warrender.

6 June 1862.

M

Maj. G. Warrender.
6 June 1862.

the Government should give the accoutrements, as they do the rifle. I do not mean to the individuals, but to supply a certain number of accoutrements to a regiment?—I think that the corps would be much more efficient with the Government accoutrements; ours are not at all satisfactory.

1718. (*Viscount Hardinge.*) You stated that there was an artillery corps in your neighbourhood, do you find that the recruiting for the one interferes with the recruiting for the other?—No; in this case the artillery corps is six miles from the nearest volunteer corps, and they do not in the least clash.

1719. (*Sir A. Campbell.*) From your knowledge of the force in those two counties do you think it is desirable that the decision which may be come to on

the subject of this commission should be made immediately?—Yes; they are rather in a critical state.

1720. If the decision were not arrived at before the next session of Parliament do you think it would have a bad effect upon the permanence of the force?—A very depressing effect. At present it is difficult to obtain fit persons to accept commands and promotion of the expenses and the humiliations of asking for subscriptions. I wish to add that when I said that 55*l*. per company would keep up a company, I think that in all probability there would be more than the strength of a company, as it would encourage men who could pay for themselves to come forward, and I think that the corps would get considerably stronger.

The witness withdrew.

Adjourned till Friday next at half-past 12 o'clock.

Friday, 13th June 1862.

PRESENT:

Viscount EVERSLEY.
Earl of DUCIE.
Viscount HARDINGE.
Lord ELCHO.
Mr. BOUVERIE.
Lieutenant-Colonel BARTTELOT.

Lieutenant-Colonel Sir A. CAMPBELL.
Lieutenant-General Sir G. A. WETHERALL.
Major-General EYRE.
Colonel MACMURDO.
Major HARCOURT.

VISCOUNT EVERSLEY IN THE CHAIR.

Lord Lyttelton.
13 June 1862.

Lord LYTTELTON examined.

1721. (*Chairman.*) You are lord-lieutenant of the county of Worcester?—Yes.

1722. Have many volunteer corps been formed in that county?—Twenty-one; which, I think, for the size of the county and its population, is very good. Every town, and every populous district almost in the county, has its volunteer company, and they are now, all of them, full companies. One began by being a company on paper; but, after a short time, it became only a subdivision. It has now again increased its numbers, and it is a full company.

1723. Has there been no falling off in the volunteers in your county?—No.

1724. Do you think that the present state of efficiency amongst the volunteers can be maintained without assistance?—I think it is extremely doubtful. I should be sorry to express myself too strongly upon that point, but I think it is a matter of very great doubt whether, as a permanent thing, the force will be maintained as it is at present without further aid.

1725. Have those corps hitherto been supported by subscriptions amongst themselves?—They have been supported by subscriptions among themselves, including the members of the corps generally, and by very considerable contributions, although very unequal; but, upon the whole, considerable contributions, from the officers beyond what the others do; and by very handsome subscriptions from persons resident in the neighbourhood of each corps; and partly, but to no great additional extent, by a general county fund. The general county fund would have been, I think, very successful; but the answer that almost everybody gives is, "I am very willing to do "what I can; but what I can do, I do for the corps "in my own immediate district."

1726. What expenses have been principally defrayed out of those subscriptions?—That is a question which I do not think I can answer very particularly. Several of the captains could; but my impression is this, that the subscriptions have been given, with very little reservation or condition, by the subscribers, to the commanding officers of the several corps to do what they thought was best with them. With regard to the county fund, which I myself chiefly administer,

I have persuaded the subscribers, without the least difficulty, to entrust that fund to the colonels of the two battalions into which the county is divided to do what they think best with it; simply to diminish the expenses which fall on the members for battalion expenses.

1727. I presume that the money has been expended on rifle ranges and headquarters?—Yes, among other things; the local subscriptions.

1728. Has any part of the money been expended in providing clothing for the men?—No doubt the local subscriptions were, in the first instance, expended to a very great extent in providing clothing; but the general county fund is too small, and I do not think there is the least chance of providing clothing out of that. The local subscriptions, which were not permanent annual subscriptions, were either donations or subscriptions for a certain term of years; there were very few subscriptions, I think, that were given indefinitely; they were either donations or subscriptions for a term of years, and that they were at first very largely applied to providing clothing I have no doubt.

1729. Has this county fund been recently established?—Yes, very lately; I could not get it up till quite lately.

1730. At present you cannot say much as to the purposes to which it has been devoted?—We have only had it for one year: during that time I can say how it has been applied. It was divided into two sums of 110*l*. or 120*l*. a piece for the two battalions; being so small a sum, we thought that it could not go to local company expenses, and it has been applied to the expenses of the battalion drills, including the expenses of locomotion at a certain rate, according to the necessities of each corps and the distance that they were from the place of meeting.

1731. Have you heard much complaint made of the difficulty of bringing the distant companies together to take part in battalion drill?—I think very little; but it is owing to the public spirit and energy of the commanding officers, who make no difficulty about it. There is no doubt that it is a very considerable expense and labour to bring them together, but I cannot say that there have been any complaints.

1732. Are the battalion drills generally well attended?—Very well.

1733. Can you suggest anything that you think would tend to promote the efficiency of the rifle corps?—As far as I have been able to perceive, there is no difficulty of any kind, except the expense. I believe that in any event there would be very great efforts made in my county to retain the force as it is; but there is some apprehension that there will be difficulty in doing so; but, as far as I know, it is almost entirely on the subject of clothing. The clothing is a considerable charge; in my county it suffered a good deal from heavy rains in the first year, and in no great time, perhaps next year, or thereabouts, the clothing will require to be renewed. There is considerable apprehension, no doubt, on this point, but I do not doubt that if nothing is done, in the way of external aid, there will be a very great effort made to go on. The clothing is the chief thing, but some apprehension is also entertained on the subject that I mentioned just now, that the local subscriptions were not promised for more than a certain time; that time will be up this year or the next, and it is a matter of doubt whether the subscriptions will be renewed. But under both those heads I do not doubt that there would be very considerable efforts made to keep on, although there would be much uneasiness felt on the part of those connected with the movement. That is the only thing that I think requisite, some assistance towards the very heavy expenses which fall upon the members of the corps.

1734. Those principally relate to clothing, do they not?—That is by far the chief thing.

1735. Hitherto the volunteers have been wholly or in part clothed by the subscriptions which have been contributed by persons in the different localities?—Yes.

1736. May not those subscriptions be repeated?—I think there is great doubt whether they will be to the full extent. There are great differences in the companies; in some companies every member down to the lowest are persons of very fair means, and several of my companies have clothed themselves entirely; they have gone to every expense; but I have no doubt that the great majority of them have received great assistance from the local subscriptions.

1737. (*Viscount Hardinge.*) Should you say upon the whole that the county fund has worked well since it has been established?—As I stated before, it has been only established for a few months. We raised a very fair sum, which has been appropriated this year simply to the expenses of battalion drills, and that will be a great relief.

1738. This fund is solely applied to battalion purposes, such as meeting the expenses of the battalion drills?—Yes.

1739. But the money has not been spent for the purpose of giving prizes at any county meeting?—No; we have a clear feeling that prizes for shooting should come about the last of the objects of such a fund, because county meetings and shooting matches are the most popular, and most easily met of all the expenses; it is a great feast day and amusement for the whole county; and we can, without the least difficulty, get up such things. What the whole body of the officers wished was that such a fund as that to which I have alluded should be applied to meet the regular working expenses of the corps.

1740. There are two battalions?—Yes.

1741. Do you hand over a certain sum of money to the commanding officer of each battalion to be expended at his discretion?—Yes; the fund is administered by a certain council, of which all the commanding officers and captains are members. We propose to do this, to meet once a year, and receive reports from the colonels, setting forth, as well as they can tell, what the anticipated expenses of each corps under them will be during the twelvemonth coming, and then to reserve an absolute discretion to the council to appropriate this fund as they think fit;

and what we have done hitherto has been to entrust it to the colonels to be applied to the battalion drills.

1742. They send in an estimate?—Yes.

1743. Are they continued, to a certain degree, in the appropriation of the money which they receive by the instructions of the Council?—Entirely.

1744. (*Lord Elcho.*) Those instructions hitherto having limited the application of the money to battalion drills?—Yes.

1745. (*Viscount Hardinge.*) Has there been any difficulty in apportioning the money to each company for attending at battalion drills, or has it been done according to a system of mileage?—The aid towards the locomotion of corps would be given on a system of mileage.

1746. In point of fact, is not the expense of attending the battalion drills one which the rural corps find great difficulty in meeting?—It is a great burden upon them,—to distant corps.

1747. Have you formed any opinion as to the shape in which, if it is desirable to give further aid, Government aid should be afforded?—No, I have not considered that particularly; I thought that was a question for the Government and for parliament; but it is clear to me that there are heavy expenses, and very doubtful whether they can be met without aid if the force is intended to be maintained.

1748. Do you think that a direct capitation grant would be preferable to the system which you have sketched out, namely, that of each commanding officer sending in an estimate of the different expenses from which he may wish to be relieved, or which of the two would you prefer and think most practicable?—My impression is that the estimate plan would be the best. I think that the estimate should be carefully and fully framed, so that whoever had the administration of any fund might be able to judge fairly of it, and see that it was a satisfactory one; and that a full account should be rendered of how the fund had been applied. I should always be in favour of giving large discretion to the commanding officer as to the application of it.

1749. You would, I presume, object to placing a considerable sum of money in the hands of a commanding officer to be spent at his discretion?—Yes, at his uncontrolled discretion. I think that the manner in which it is to be applied ought to be very strictly defined.

1750. Is there in your county any rifle association?—Not in the ordinary sense of those terms, not for prizes. If we raised a very large amount by this county fund, we might so use it; but I do not see the least prospect of doing that.

1751. (*Lord Elcho.*) What amount has been raised by the county fund?—It has been only about 250 *l.* in donations, and I think 70 *l.* or 80 *l.* a year. I do not think there has been more.

1752. I suppose the greater part of the 250 *l.* has been spent?—The whole of it has been appropriated this year to battalion drills; we have spent all we had; we mean to provide for the occasion each year, and in each year to spend all we get.

1753. Is it at all likely that you will be able to raise by a county fund any such sum of money as would enable you to maintain these corps, clothing them, and meeting all their other expenses?—No, not the least; not by a county fund as distinct from the local subscriptions to each corps.

1754. Do you believe that local subscriptions are likely to be obtained for each corps, so that in that way a sufficient sum of money will be raised to clothe and maintain those corps?—I should have the very greatest doubt of that, but I will not speak positively; I can conceive this, that when the local subscriptions come to an end of their guaranteed-term, and when the necessity for renewing the clothing arises, which is by far the chief expense, then in the neighbourhood of each corps it will become a matter of serious consideration, and I think that great efforts will be made to repeat what was done before; that is, to raise, whether among the members of the corps or in

Lord Lyttelton.

13 June 1862.

Lord Lyttelton.
13 June 1862.

the neighbourhood, whatever may be requisite. I have no doubt of that, and I think that in many cases it might be successful; but I think it very unlikely that in every case it will be successful; in some I think it will be matter of very great uneasiness and uncertainty with those who wish to see the force a permanent one.

1755. Are the subscriptions in each corps paid by the members?—Yes; I will not be quite certain as to all, but I have no doubt that in a great majority of them there are regular contributions from them all.

1756. Are there many of the artizan class enrolled?—There are a good many in the populous places, but I think the smaller proportion of the whole.

1757. You perhaps cannot speak as to whether there are many artizans in Worcestershire, or as to the effect which volunteering has had upon them?—I can say pretty confidently that the artizans are the smaller proportion.

1758. (*Col. MacMurdo.*) Are there not at Kidderminster artizans?—There is one corps there which is almost wholly composed of artizans.

1759. (*Lord Elcho.*) What is your opinion as to how far it is reasonable to expect these men to give up their time and services, to pay their subscriptions, and clothe themselves?—I must confess that I have a very strong opinion upon that point. I think that in reason and fairness there is no ground whatever to expect any money contribution at all from the rank and file of these corps. I do not think that in strict reason there is any claim on the officers, but I do not doubt that the officers, and I might even include the non-commissioned officers, would always be willing and would feel a pride in contributing a good deal. I should be sorry to see anything done as a direct relief to the expenses falling upon the officers, although I do not think that there would be any actual injustice even in that; but in my opinion, as to the privates, there is no claim upon them whatever for any direct money payment of any kind; I mean such payments as can be brought to account, for there must always be expenses, actual money paid by the members of a force like this, which cannot be brought to account. Besides that it is obvious that to some of these men, indeed in almost every case, their time is money, it is not only time and labour which they give, but they incur actual expenses. They are volunteers as giving their services freely, and it seems to me that they would be just as much a volunteer force if they were not required to pay money besides. They are willing to undergo any amount of danger, risk, and toil; and besides that they must always be at an actual charge, which must be estimated at a very considerable sum of money, even if all the direct money payments were taken from them. I think it would be perfectly just if all their expenses were taken from them. As it is, as I understand, there are several expenses taken from them by the favour of the Government and by parliament, which I think is so far satisfactory; but there are several still left upon them, of which by far the heaviest is the expense of clothing.

1760. I think you stated that you did not anticipate that this force could be maintained in your county by private means, either by a county fund or private subscriptions?—I cannot say more than I have said before, that I should feel very great doubt about it. Although great effort will be made, I doubt whether it will succeed; of course it will be influenced by what is done elsewhere, and what may seem to be the intention of parliament, and the prospect of peace or war, but in any case I do not doubt that a great effort will be made, although in any case, I think, it is doubtful whether it will succeed.

1761. Do you think it is of great importance that the volunteer force should be permanently maintained?—Yes.

1762. (*Viscount Hardinge.*) Do you think it would alter the character of the force if their expenses were paid for them?—No.

1763. You do not think that they would rather approach to the character of a local militia, if all their expenses were paid for them?—No; I do not think so.

1764. (*Sir A. Campbell.*) Your lordship has expressed doubts as to the possibility of the expenses being met by the different corps or their supporters; have those doubts been entertained only recently, or was there reason when the corps were originally enrolled to suppose that they could not permanently maintain themselves?—I think that those who considered the subject and looked forward to events had sufficient reason to doubt that from the beginning, as soon as we saw the nature of the expenses that must be incurred, and their amount.

1765. Did you make any inquiries into that subject before you enrolled any corps that applied for enrolment?—No; in every case the first thing that I did was this, to ascertain the name of the proposed commanding officer, and then I made him give me his personal assurance, not as formally binding him, but his personal assurance that he would undertake that the corps should be maintained in a state of efficiency, whatever the expenses might be, for a certain number of years. I did not wish to make it too specific; the *subscriptions* were in many cases given for a term of years, say three years; but I required a man of responsibility and character and of some means, in every case, who should take the command of the force, to give me his personal assurance that he saw his way to maintaining the corps for a few years.

1766. Has your lordship any means of knowing whether such precautions were usually adopted by the lord-lieutenants of counties?—I do not know that.

1767. Were no instructions issued from the War Office as to the kind of men who should be enrolled in companies?—Not that I remember.

1768. Did you find it necessary to refuse the enrolment of any applicants on the ground of its being improbable that they would be able to maintain themselves?—No, that has never happened; there may have been once or twice a little apprehension that it might be so; but in the way that we have managed it it could hardly happen. I have never had a proposal from any gentleman to form and organize a company which was not satisfactory.

1769. Practically have you had corps organized through the officers, or have you had corps organized first, and appointed the officers afterwards?—It has been done through the captains alone. I have looked solely to the captains.

1770. (*Viscount Hardinge.*) You do not know probably to what extent in the different companies the captains have enrolled men who have not been able to provide themselves with uniforms?—I do not know upon what system that has been done. I know that in some cases the men have provided their own uniforms, and in some they have not; but I have not exercised any official interference in that respect.

1771. In those cases where the men have not provided their own clothing, I presume that the expense has been defrayed by the local finance committee of each corps?—The finance committee of each corps has generally administered the funds from whatever source they came.

1772. Do you think it desirable in these rural companies, which are not composed of working men, that men should be enrolled who cannot provide their own uniforms?—I do not see any objection to it, provided that those who undertake the responsibility of organizing these corps will engage that the expenses shall be met.

1773. But the men to whom I have alluded are not exactly the stamp of men of which it was originally intended the force should be composed?—I do not know how that is. I do not remember any instructions or limitations about that. We were told to get volunteers as well as we could.

1774. But it was always supposed that it was not desirable to take men who might be available for the line or the militia?—I believe that was said; but I do not think it was ever officially brought before me.

1775. I presume you would object to any system that did practically interfere with the recruiting for the line or the militia?—Yes.

1776. (*Lieut.-Col. Bartteelot.*) Are your corps all dressed in the same uniform?—Yes. I had no notions of my own upon that subject; but I understood that it was very desirable that the whole of the force in one county should be clothed alike, or nearly so, and in a very early stage of our proceedings I called together the captains, and said that it was necessary, before proceeding any further, that the uniforms should be agreed upon, which should be binding, not only upon them, but upon all those who came in afterwards; and they agreed upon a uniform which has since been enforced. The tendency of the opinions among all the officers and men has been since that time, I believe, still more in that direction; so that, as to the future, I have laid down a rule, although it is not in force yet, that the very slight difference which was allowed to exist before shall be abolished; so that, ultimately, we intend to act upon the opinion of the officers, that the clothing should be exactly the same throughout the county.

1777. Do you know the cost of the uniform?—I think it was somewhere between 3*l*. and 5*l*.

1778. (*Sir G. A. Wetherall.*) May it not be assumed that those who cannot afford to give their time to drill instruction, cannot afford to clothe themselves?—I think so.

1779. Have you any idea of the proportion of the men who have given a tolerable amount of attendance at their drill?—I cannot say with any accuracy. I am bound to say that I have heard frequent complaints of the somewhat irregular attention which has been given to drill. It varies according to the different periods of the year. I do not think that the captains see anything very serious in it; but they do complain, and they have to whip up the men a little.

1780. Supposing that it was thought expedient by the Government to grant some pecuniary aid, do you not think that it would be well to regulate it by some figure of merit, either by the numbers who attend drill, or by the rifle practice, or some other test of merit?—I have not heard that suggested before, but it seems to me that that might be a very excellent suggestion, and that some such check would be very desirable.

1781. (*Major Harcourt.*) With your present experience, do you not think that the volunteers might very considerably reduce their expenditure; is it not likely to be less now than it was a few years ago, from the experience which commanding officers have had?—I am not clear that it would be so; experience might enable them to diminish the duties and labours of the drill serjeants.

1782. I am referring now particularly to the cost of the uniforms; are they not now to be obtained at a lower rate than they were?—I am hardly aware of that, at all events I do not think it would make any material difference, for, put the price as low as you may, the cost of the clothing is always a very serious one.

1783. Do you suppose that if the subscriptions of the privates ceased, and the accoutrements were provided by the Government, the men then could generally provide their own uniforms?—I have very little doubt that they would do so in the majority of cases. I believe that it would be done, but I would not speak positively upon that point.

1784. Supposing that uniforms were found for the men, how should you propose that they should be given?—That is a point of detail upon which I do not think I can express an opinion that would be worth anything.

1785. Do you think there would be any difficulty in getting the men to wear second-hand uniforms?—I should not expect so; I do not think there would be, if they were substantial and good. Still that may be doubtful: the men might have some feeling against it.

1786. (*Viscount Hardinge.*) With reference to the expenses of the different companies, has not each company a band?—Very nearly so, I believe.

1787. Do you think that these companies could go on prosperously without a band?—Yes, they could certainly; but the band is a very popular thing. I would never for a moment advocate any public fund for the purpose of defraying such an expense as that, which is purely for pleasure.

1788. How are these bands supported in your different rural companies?—Just like all the rest of the expenses, out of whatever funds they have. I do not think that they have a special fund for the bands; they have a separate item for them.

1789. You do not perhaps think that you could get rid of that expense, and however anomalous the state of things may be you think that each company should have a band?—I think they would have it, unless you actually prohibit it. I do not mean to say that the companies would not go on without it, but I do think that they would not like it.

1790. If they were prohibited do you think that that would lead to a falling off in the numbers?—I hardly think it would; but I am confident that nothing would stop it but actual prohibition.

1791. (*Sir A. Campbell.*) Do you think it is important that the decision of the Government with respect to any relief which they might afford to the volunteer corps should be come to promptly?—I should hardly say that. I should say that before the end of next year it might be desirable; but I should not have any apprehension if it were postponed till next year.

1792. You do not think that it would affect the numbers if the decision were delayed?—Not in my county.

1793. (*Earl of Ducie.*) Have you found much difficulty in getting efficient officers?—There has been a little more difficulty in getting officers than in getting men when we have got officers. I cannot say that it has been a serious difficulty, but there has been often some little difficulty and delay in getting officers; in getting a captain, for instance, but very seldom, perhaps once or twice; and sometimes there has been a little delay as to subaltern officers, and perhaps as to staff officers, majors, and so on. On the whole I should say that there has been a little more delay and trouble in getting officers than in getting men, but nothing serious.

1794. Of the officers originally appointed have many left?—No; I think not many.

1795. There have not been many changes among the officers since the commencement?—I should say not many on the whole.

1796. Have the officers complained of the expense to which they were put?—They hardly complain; but I think I have been fortunate in every way, in the officers especially, for I have almost in every case been able to obtain men having very fair means of their own, and who were therefore not likely to complain. They mention the difficulty, but they have never made it a matter of personal complaint.

1797. Do you supplement the pay of your adjutants from the county fund?—No, we have not done that; the county fund was unable to meet it, and we thought upon the whole that it had better be applied to the battalion working expenses.

1798. Have you any heavy expenses connected with ranges?—It is very unequal, but I think it is not one of those expenses which press the most; there has been, on other grounds than that of expense, very great difficulty in *getting* ranges in some cases, but that I apprehend is a difficulty which is inherent in the case, and can hardly be removed. I think that in every case where a good range has been available, the expense has not stood in the way.

1799. Have you had a central or county range?—No, not in any formal way; they have not met in any fixed place.

Lord Lyttelton.

13 June 1862.

M 3

Lord Lyttleton.
13 June 1862.

1800. Are there any heavy expenses connected with the headquarters of the different battalions?—No.

1801. (*Major-Gen. Eyre.*) Upon the whole, your Lordship values the appointment of the adjutants as they are now appointed?—Yes, they are beyond all value.

1802. They could not be provided from the officers of volunteers?—No, that is totally out of the question; in any such force the adjutant is the backbone of the whole thing.

1803. (*Lord Elcho.*) Is the class of men who have volunteered in your county of the same class as would naturally go into the army or the militia?—No, I do not think they are.

The witness withdrew.

Lieut.-Col. G. Briggs.

Lieut.-Colonel GEORGE BRIGGS examined.

1804. (*Chairman.*) You command the 1st administrative battalion of the West Riding of Yorkshire?—Yes.

1805. Of how many companies does your battalion consist?—Eight companies and a half.

1806. I suppose the establishment is 100 men per company?—Yes, that is the maximum number per company.

1807. Are the companies full?—They average about 75.

1808. How often do you have battalion drills?—The battalion has two assemblies in each year, but we have battalion drills with the four companies at York every week during the summer.

1809. Are your companies situate sufficiently near together to enable you to bring them all to battalion drill?—Those which are at Knaresborough, Harrowgate, Wetherby, and Ripon, are sufficiently near together for wing drill, but we do not get all of them together more than twice a year.

1810. (*Viscount Hardinge.*) How far are the other four companies from York?—They are in York.

1811. (*Chairman.*) The other four companies are at some distance?—Yes, the other four companies and a half; two are near together.

1812. How often do you get them together?—They have been together twice this summer, and we shall have them together, I hope, four or five times more.

1813. I suppose there is railway communication for them?—Yes.

1814. The railway authorities, I suppose, take the volunteers at the same rate as the military?—Yes, they are fairly liberal.

1815. Have you a battalion fund?—We established one last year, which is beginning to work this year.

1816. What does it amount to?—150*l.* a year.

1817. Is that subscribed by the officers and men of the whole corps?—There are contributions from the staff officers of the battalion, and 12*l.* per company throughout the battalion.

1818. To what expenses do you apply this fund?—Chiefly to the assemblies of the battalion, and also to the expenses of the headquarters' office.

1819. Have all these companies separate funds of their own?—Yes.

1820. Are you aware whether the men have found themselves in clothing, or whether they have been assisted by local subscriptions?—I think that in every instance they have been assisted by local subscriptions. The first company of the York corps was entirely self-supporting, and found everything; all the others have been supported more or less.

1821. Have you any reason to apprehend, when the clothing requires renewal, that there will be any difficulty in renewing it?—I think so, certainly.

1822. Do you think that the subscriptions will fall off?—I do think so; I think there will be a difficulty.

1823. Are the companies resident in York provided with a rifle range?—Yes; the York corps is a consolidated corps, so far as it goes, and they have one range.

1824. Your battalion is partly consolidated and partly administrative?—Yes.

1825. The consolidated corps has its headquarters at York?—Yes.

1826. Are all the expenses borne by the four companies together?—Yes.

1827. Have you an adjutant attached to your corps?—Yes.

1828. Do you pay him anything more than the Government allowance?—No, nothing at all; except that he has a room at headquarters.

1829. You do not provide him with lodging?—Nothing, except the room.

1830. Do you find that his pay is quite sufficient?—I do not think so.

1831. Does he visit the four distant companies from time to time, and attend to their drill?—Yes.

1832. Do you find any difficulty in inspecting the different corps, particularly the distant corps?—There is no power of ordering a parade, and it is entirely a matter of people pulling well together.

1833. There are, perhaps, a certain number of men whom you do not see in the year?—I see all my corps. The only difficulty is in the York corps, and that is not with reference to inspection.

1834. Do you think that you ought to have more power?—I think that the position should be more defined than it is.

1835. (*Viscount Hardinge.*) Will you be good enough to state in what way you have any difficulty in summoning a parade for inspection?—I have never had a difficulty of that nature. The difficulties have been those which have arisen from a different source. The commandant of the York corps has been the principal cause of the difficulties I have had to encounter.

1836. Have you any difficulty in ordering a parade, say for the inspection of arms or the inspection of a company, referring now to the rural companies that are some distance away?—None whatever with regard to the rural companies.

1837. (*Col. MacMurdo.*) You stated that you considered the pay of the adjutant not sufficient?—Yes.

1838. Will you be good enough to state why you think so?—I think so because his work is more constant, and more difficult in many respects than that of an adjutant of militia or yeomanry, and his pay is less; he has no lodging money for one thing.

1839. (*Chairman.*) What is the pay of your adjutant?—The pay of my adjutant amounts to 182*l.* 10*s.*, exclusive of 4*l.* per company for stationery allowance.

1840. He receives 8*s.* per day, and 2*s.* for forage?—Yes.

1841. Has he a horse of his own?—Yes; he receives also 2*s.* a day for travelling expenses.

1842. Are you aware that a yeomanry adjutant receives only 6*s.* a day, and 2*s.* for forage?—I am speaking more of the militia. I believe yeomanry adjutancies average 300*l.* a year.

1843. (*Col. MacMurdo.*) Will you be good enough to state what instructions you give to your adjutant with regard to the inspection of the several corps of which the battalion is composed?—He visits them for the purpose of drill periodically, and whenever there is a review or anything of that sort approaching, he goes more frequently to them, and if necessary he stays with them a few days.

1844. I observe by the adjutant's diary for the last month, that the adjutant did not leave York from the 1st of May until the 30th, have you no systematic rule by which you require the adjutant to visit the out quarters?—Yes; he visits them certainly once a quarter, but practically it amounts to more than that. There must be some mistake, for the adjutant left York, and proceeded to Harrogate on four different occasions, and to Tadcaster once during May.

1845. There is one corps which is distant 9 miles, another which is at a distance of 15 miles, and a third which is 17 miles from headquarters, but if the adjutant has a horse is it not possible for him to visit them a little oftener?—I may mention that during the month of May, there was an investigation going on in York which required his presence, and he was engaged there the greater part of that time.

1846. Upon other occasions do you require him to visit these out-quarters more often than once a quarter?—Yes; during the summer months.

1847. (*Sir A. Campbell.*) Does the adjutant superintend any part of the musketry instruction of the corps?—Yes, and he has been to Hythe.

1848. Is the whole of the musketry instruction carried on under his supervision?—Yes, it is now, since his return from Hythe, *i.e.*, he exercises a general superintendence.

1849. (*Chairman.*) How many men of your battalion have passed through a course of musketry instruction?—I can hardly say without reference to the papers, but the greater part of the effectives, I think, have gone through a course of musketry instruction.

1850. (*Sir A. Campbell.*) I suppose that that occupies a good deal of the adjutant's time?—Yes, it does.

1851. (*Viscount Hardinge.*) Do you give your Government serjeant any extra allowance for cleaning arms?—Not in York; but the terms have been made by the commandants of the corps. I have had nothing to do with the terms upon which the Government serjeants are engaged.

1852. (*Chairman.*) Are they engaged by the commandants of the separate companies?—Yes.

1853. And paid out of the funds of the separate companies?—Yes; if any additional payment is made, it comes from that source.

1854. (*Viscount Hardinge.*) You do not know whether they do receive any extra allowance for cleaning the arms?—I do not.

1855. (*Sir G. A. Wetherall.*) Is there a register kept showing day by day how many men attend the drill instruction?—Yes.

1856. And the battalion drill?—Yes.

1857. How is the register of the target practice kept?—That is kept according to the form.

1858. Is that register kept strictly according to the form?—Yes.

1859. Do you depend upon the marker?—We depend upon the instructor on the spot.

1860. (*Lieut.-Col. Barttelot.*) I suppose with the exception of Knaresborough your adjutant can ride to all the out places?—Ripon is the farthest.

1861. With the exception of Knaresborough and Ripon, can he not ride to them all?—Harrowgate is as far as Knaresborough.

1862. If he cannot ride to all those places, what do you think would be the expense of his attending on the average once a month at each of the out stations, bearing in mind the 2*s.* a day which he is allowed for travelling?—He considers that every time he goes to one of those places his expenses average 1*l.*

1863. How many outposts have you?—We have five out-quarters; the fourth is a subdivision.

1864. Then it would cost 5*l.* a month?—Yes; I suppose so. My adjutant complains that the allowance is not sufficient; he considers that 2*s.* a day do not meet his expenses.

1865. Do you consider that a certain mileage rate for his travelling expenses would be better than the the 2*s.* a day which are allowed him?—He is nearly always obliged to stay all night, and that entails upon him a great amount of expense.

1866. (*Viscount Hardinge.*) For what reason?—Because you cannot get the volunteers to attend the drills except in the evening.

1867. When he visits these corps how does he go? By railroad.

1868. Do you mean that he never can get back by the train?—He cannot get back after half-past six, or some time of that sort. I know that there is no possibility of his getting back.

1869. (*Lieut.-Col. Barttelot.*) Is the allowance of 4*l.* per company for stationery more than sufficient?—I do not think it is more than sufficient; I think that it about meets it.

1870. (*Viscount Hardinge.*) With regard to the returns made by each captain of the number of effectives in each corps, I presume that you hold the captain responsible for the accuracy of the return which he makes to you?—Unquestionably.

1871. You have no reason to suppose that any of the companies are put down as effective when they have not gone through their 24 drills?—The difficulty that I have had in the York corps has turned very much upon that point. It was necessary to make an investigation of the muster rolls, when it was found that they had been very irregularly kept.

1872. (*Lord Elcho.*) Might you not have a volunteer who was thoroughly efficient, and yet who could not be returned as effective according to the requirements of the Act, that is to say, a man who had not attended 24 drills in the year?—I think it is possible that there might be so exceptional a case, but as a rule I think he must attend that number of drills.

1873. I do not mean in the first year, but I am supposing the case of a volunteer who has attended 24 drills, or twice that number, in the first year; do you consider that he could be passed as efficient with a fewer number of drills than 24 in the ensuing year?—I think that he ought to have that number of drills to keep him up to the mark.

1874. (*Sir A. Campbell.*) Do you think that from the 1st of August to the 31st of July is the best period that could be selected for making an annual return of the effectives?—I have hardly considered that point.

1875. If the period were more coincident with the actual year, from January to December, would not a more accurate return be given of the state of efficiency in each regiment?—I have really hardly considered that; I am not sure that it would, possibly it might.

1876. At what period of the year do recruits usually join?—I think they usually join during the spring and summer, so as to be in time for the shooting and the reviews.

1877. (*Viscount Hardinge.*) Have you any system under which the arms are inspected in the different companies?—The adjutant makes a point of seeing the arms when he visits the companies, and I see them when I have an opportunity.

1878. Has the adjutant had no difficulty in getting those members of the corps who keep their arms at their own residences to produce them for inspection?—I think not, as a rule; there may have been one or two instances.

1879. Do you think that you will be able to keep up your battalion, the rural companies and the town companies, in their present state of efficiency without further aid from the Government?—I think that further aid is required, certainly. I think that we require aid in the shape of a battalion fund, for the purpose of meeting the expenses of assembling for drill.

1880. In what shape would you recommend that aid from the Government should be given?—I think that some small grant might be allowed for each effective man in an administrative battalion in addition to what is given him, or on his account, as a member of a corps.

1881. What amount should you think would be sufficient?—I think that 5*s.* would do in my battalion.

1882. A capitation grant of 5*s.*?—I think so.

1883. Do you mean for travelling alone, or to meet all their expenses?—I mean to supply the place of the present battalion fund.

1884. You think that 5*s.* per head would be sufficient to keep the battalion in its present state of

Lieut.-Col. G. Briggs.

13 June 1862.

M 4

Lieut.-Col.
G. Briggs.

13 June 1862.

efficiency?—It would do as much as is done now by our 150l. a year.

1885. Would you require nothing more?—I mean that the 5s. should be in addition to what is given them as members of the corps, or as members of the battalion.

1886. But as companies?—I think they would require more than that.

1887. Will you be good enough to state to what extent you think the corps ought to be further assisted? Would you prefer that they should be aided in kind, that is, by each captain sending in an estimate of what he especially stood in need of, or would you prefer a direct capitation grant that should be given to the commanding officer for every effective man?—I think as a rule I should prefer money, because the wants of the different corps are so various; what was desirable in one might perhaps not be so in another.

1888. Would you propose that a capitation grant should be given to each commanding officer in money?—I think that it must come through him; I do not see how else it can be applied.

1889. But the question is whether it should be given directly or indirectly; whether he should send in an estimate of what his corps required in the way of clothing, ranges, and so forth, or that he should receive a direct capitation grant to be expended entirely at his own discretion?—I am disposed to think that a direct capitation grant, in proportion to the number of effective members in a corps, and to be accounted for, of course, annually, would be the best form in which to give assistance.

1890. Then what security would the Government have that a direct capitation grant would be properly expended? take, for example, bands and other expenses which are thought by some to have been most extravagantly incurred?—I should leave the bands altogether to corps subscriptions.

1891. (*Lord Elcho.*) Would it not be possible, supposing a capitation grant to be given to a commanding officer to be expended as he thought most advisable for the corps, to restrict that expenditure to certain heads?—Yes, certainly.

1892. Do you think it would be desirable, so far as respects the discretion of the commanding officer, that he should only so expend it?—Certainly.

1893. You think that there would be no difficulty in confining the items, whether for clothing, equipment, or ranges. or any purpose for which they have at present to find money, within certain rules and limits?—I think there would be none. I should limit the application of the money to certain objects, and I would limit the number of the men in the several localities.

1894. (*Lieut.-Col. Barttelot.*) When you say that the money should be entrusted to the commanding officer, do you mean that it should be given to him for each individual in the corps, or to you, for example, as the colonel commanding an administrative battalion?—I mean to the officer commanding the corps.

1895. Do not you think that you, as the colonel of an administrative battalion, would be able to make such a return of the effective men to the War Office as should ensure that the money which you received was properly applied, and only so far as those effective men went?—I think that the money might be perhaps better distributed if the order required the countersign of the adjutant and colonel of the battalion, but the commanding officer of the corps must be the person who knows the actual wants on the spot better than the commanding officer of a battalion.

1896. Do you not think that if the distribution of the money was confined to the effective men, it would put you in a better position with your battalion?—It would give me more power, certainly.

1897. (*Chairman.*) You would have an opportunity of communicating with the captains, and of ascertaining in what way the money could be spent most for the benefit of the corps?—Yes; but if that is done,

administrative battalions would require a different kind of organization, for at present the field officer commanding has nothing to do with questions of finance.

1898. In the case supposed, public funds would be supplied by the Government, and do you not think that you, as commanding officer, would be the proper person to whom those funds ought to be entrusted?—Yes, I do think so.

1899. (*Sir A. Campbell.*) If such a determination should be come to by the Government, do you think it is important that the decision should be arrived at at once, or do you think that the matter will admit of delay?—I think that the sooner the question is settled, the better.

1900. Do you think that delay will have the effect of diminishing the number of men in your corps?—I do not think it will for the present summer.

1901. (*Col. MacMurdo.*) You are increasing in numbers, are you not?—Yes, we have kept up our numbers very well, and I think we are increasing.

1902. (*Major Harcourt.*) Do you think that some assistance is necessary for the continuance of the force?—Yes; especially in the rural districts.

1903. Is it not your opinion that a great deal might be done in the different corps by reducing their expenditure, considering the large amount of expense which they have now to bear?—They know their wants better now, certainly, in every instance. I have endeavoured to keep the band funds entirely independent of the corps funds.

1904. (*Viscount Hardinge.*) Supposing the private subscriptions from the members to cease, do you think they would be in a position to pay for their own uniforms?—I think that a considerable portion of them would.

1905. Is it not very difficult to exercise any control over the financial questions that come before the committees of the different companies?—I have nothing whatever to do with their finances as commanding officer of an administrative battalion, except the battalion fund which has just been organized.

1906. (*Major Harcourt.*) Suppose that the men were provided with uniforms, should you find any difficulty in getting them to wear second-hand ones?—I do not know; I think so.

1907. (*Viscount Hardinge.*) You have stated that you do not think that the position of commanding officers of administrative battalions is satisfactorily defined; can you suggest any amendment in that respect?—As it is now, I think that it is not clear whether he is only to be a sort of occasional inspector, or the regimental head. My own feeling is, that it should be more regimental than it is at present. I do not see why an administrative battalion should not be on much the same footing as a yeomanry regiment.

1908. (*Lord Elcho.*) You have stated that you consider 5s. would be sufficient to defray the battalion expenses; I suppose you mean to cover brigade and field days as well?—Yes.

1909. What sum, in your opinion, would be required to defray the expenses of the different companies, in addition to what they now receive?—Our present battalion fund was formed with reference to that question; the subscription from each company is 12l., and the whole amounts to 150l. a year.

1910. You have stated that your battalion fund was used to defray the expenses of attending at battalion drills, but a further sum you think is necessary to keep up the companies themselves?—Yes.

1911. What sum do you think will be required per head to keep up the companies themselves in addition to the assistance which they now receive from the Government?—I am disposed to think that a guinea per head for each effective member would cover everything.

1912. Do you mean clothing and everything?—Yes, if it were properly managed; the clothing ought to last for two or three years.

1913. (*Sir G. A. Wetherall.*) How many effectives

have you in your battalion, and what do you call an effective?—A member who has attended 24 drills in a year.

1914. Is a man who attends and does nothing an effective?—No; I consider that a man who attends *bonâ fide* drill and musketry instruction an effective.

1915. (*Lieut.-Col. Barttelot.*) Are the uniforms of your battalion all of the same colour?—Yes, and they wear the same description of belts, but they all vary in the facings.

1916. Do you not think it essential that an administrative battalion should be all dressed in the same colour?—Yes, I consider it desirable and essential.

1917. (*Viscount Hardinge.*) If further aid is received either directly or indirectly from the Government, you must make the captains of the companies responsible for the returns which they send in to you as to the number of effectives in their respective companies?—Yes, certainly; I consider that they are responsible now.

1918. They are no doubt so now, but I dare say you are aware that irregularities have been found in these returns, and that members of the rural companies have been returned as effective members when they have really not gone through their 24 days' drill?—Yes; and in the town companies also.

1919. And consequently under any new system the most stringent rules would have to be laid down as to returning men effective or non-effective?—Certainly.

1920. (*Chairman.*) I understand you to say that you make a point of visiting all the distant companies in the course of the year?—Yes.

1921. On the occasions when you have visited them, have you found them muster well?—Not so well as I could wish.

1922. Have you found that half of the men borne on the rolls on the average have mustered?—Perhaps a little more than that,—perhaps two-thirds.

1923. What security have you that the absentees are properly drilled?—I have no power to enforce attendance.

1924. You have no security whatever that those who do not attend the company drills when you inspect them will be properly drilled?—All that I can do is through the adjutant; he looks after them when he goes round.

1925. But supposing he does not go?—He does go.

1926. (*Viscount Hardinge.*) Can you explain in what way the authority of an officer commanding an administrative battalion differs from the authority of a lieutenant-colonel commanding a yeomanry regiment?—The volunteer regulations say that the powers of the officer commanding an administrative battalion are given to him subject to the powers conferred on the officer commanding the corps by the Act of Parliament. The officers commanding troops in a yeomanry regiment are like the captains in any other regiment.

1927. Therefore when the yeomanry are called out for their eight days' duty, they are under the Mutiny Act, but in what other way do they differ; the colonel commanding a volunteer regiment on parade has the same authority as a colonel commanding a yeomanry regiment, has he not?—Yes; but I do not think he has any power off parade.

1928. (*Lord Elcho.*) They are independent of you, are they not, until you get them together for drill?—Quite so.

1929. (*Sir G. A. Wetherall.*) Do you think the volunteers would be better pleased if a stricter system of discipline were observed than there is at present?—I think they would now.

1930. (*Chairman.*) Would it, in your opinion, be desirable that parliament should give to the colonel of an administrative battalion the increased power which you seem to think he wants?—I think so; I think that the thing is unworkable without it.

1931. Do you think they cannot fairly be responsible for the whole battalion unless they have that increased power given to them?—They cannot be responsible for them unless on parade.

1932. (*Col. MacMurdo.*) To what extent would you give an officer commanding an administrative battalion increased powers?—I think he should be put in the same position as the commanding officer of a yeomanry regiment.

1933. A yeomanry regiment is called out for training, but a battalion of volunteers could not be called out for training without pay?—No, but I think they should be put upon the same footing to some extent.

1934. Will you define any power that you do not now possess, but which you wish to have?—I think that the officer commanding an administrative battalion should be more of a regimental head than he is now. At present he is only occasional inspector, and it is laid down in the volunteer regulations that he has charge of the discipline; and the question is, what do you mean by discipline? If an officer commanding an administrative battalion resides in the same locality with one of his corps, is he or not to allow gross irregularities to occur under his nose?

1935. You are aware that the regulations require the officer commanding a battalion to see that the regulations are carried out by those who are under his command?—Certainly, but when I did that I was accused of interference.

1936. The meaning of it is, that if you see irregularities occuring in a corps, you are to call the attention of the authorities to those irregularities?—Yes.

1937. But you have no power yourself to correct them?—At present I have none whatever, and I think that I should have.

1938. (*Lieut.-Col. Barttelot.*) Do you not further think that you should be able to give directions for the course of drill instruction that should be pursued by each corps under your command?—I think so, certainly.

1939. (*Lord Elcho.*) Have you at present the power to lay down any system of drill which each company must obey?—No; I may lay it down, but I have no power to enforce it.

1940. (*Sir A. Campbell.*) In case the system of drill which you laid down were not adhered to, what course would you take?—At the present time I see no power that I should have to enforce it.

1941. You would remonstrate with the captain, but you could do nothing further?—I see nothing further that I could do.

1942. (*Viscount Hardinge.*) The Government serjeants are under the authority of the adjutant, are they not?—Yes, but the captains of companies order their own parades.

1943. Have you known instances in which captains of volunteer corps have not carried out the system of drill which the adjutant may have recommended?—They may have done so at first, and they are very apt to take the bit in their teeth now.

1944. (*Chairman.*) Have you any power to assemble all the serjeants of the different corps in order to see that the men are all drilled according to one system?—I presume I may do that.

1945. (*Major-Gen. Eyre.*) Has each of your companies got a serjeant?—No, we have not been able to get them for all yet. Great difficulty is experienced in obtaining them.

1946. (*Lieut.-Col. Barttelot.*) Do you consider that you have full power to see when the battalion assembles together that each one of your corps is drilled according to the system laid down by you?—On parade I have.

1947. If they were not drilled according to that system you would reprimand not only the officer commanding, but you would call up the serjeant as well?—Yes.

1948. (*Viscount Hardinge.*) Do you find practically that the various companies do adopt a different system of drill?—I cannot say that I have had any difficulty of that kind.

1949. (*Sir A. Campbell.*) Do you consider it de-

Lieut.-Col. G. Briggs.

15 June 1862

N

90 MINUTES OF EVIDENCE TAKEN BEFORE THE COMMISSIONERS APPOINTED

Lieut.-Col.
G. Briggs.

3 June 1862.

sirable, in order to remedy the defects which you have pointed out, that a new Act of Parliament should be passed?—I think it is absolutely necessary.

1950. (*Major-Gen. Eyre.*) Your adjutant is also rifle instructor, is he not?—He exercises a general superintendence, but each corps has its own instructor, *i.e.*, a volunteer who has passed the course at Hythe or Fleetwood.

1951. Does he keep a register of the target practice?—In an administrative battalion it is stated that the adjutant has access to these papers, and in a consolidated battalion that he is responsible for them.

1952. (*Chairman.*) Have you any further suggestion to make to the Commission?—I think not beyond what is contained in the letter which I have addressed to you.

The witness withdrew.

Lieut.-Col.
D. Jones.

Lieut.-Colonel DOUGLAS JONES examined.

1953. (*Chairman.*) I believe you are inspector of the districts in Scotland?—I am inspector of the north-eastern division of Scotland.

1954. Have you been inspector of the whole division, or only a part of it?—At first I had the whole, but afterwards it was divided.

1955. How many corps have you under your inspection?—About 153.

1956. Do you consider that they are all in an efficient state?—No.

1957. In what respect are there any which are not efficient?—They are deficient in drill and in equipment; they are deficient in drill in consequence of want of proper instruction.

1958. Have they not serjeants allowed them who are paid for by the Government?—Some have, but not all; serjeants cannot be provided for all of them at present.

1959. Do those corps which are not in an efficient state and require instruction, form part of administrative battalions, or are they consolidated corps?—Some of them form part of administrative battalions; the consolidated battalions are better drilled.

1960. But they all have the advantage of having an adjutant to superintend the drill, or occasionally to visit them, have they not?—Some of them have.

1961. To what do you attribute their deficiency in drill instruction?—They are all very anxious to learn, but they have not the means of doing so, merely from want of serjeants; some of them get serjeants only for two or three months in the year, from the embodied militia; and they get on gradually, but they nearly forget it by the next year.

1962. Have you any suggestions to offer as to how these corps would be better supplied with drill instructors; it rests very much with themselves does it not?—I have found that those who have the best instructors are officers of the corps who have applied privately to regiments to know when serjeants will be discharged, and they get by that means the best instructors; they have their own friends in the army, and of course they hear a good character of the men, and some have very clever and good instructors indeed, but some have not.

1963. Is it not essential to corps of this description that they should have good instructors?—Most decidedly.

1964. They would be of very little use without them?—Of no use at all.

1965. In your visits of inspection do you find that the musters of the corps are satisfactory?—Not always.

1966. (*Viscount Hardinge.*) What should you say was the average proportion of the members present and of those absent?—I should say that not two thirds turn out as the average proportion.

1967. (*Lord Elcho.*) At your inspection?—Yes, I should say a little more than half.

1968. (*Col. MacMurdo.*) Is it your opinion that those who stay away cannot possibly attend, or that they stay away from indifference?—I think that those who stay away are either those who cannot possibly attend or those who are not sufficiently drilled and who are ashamed to show themselves. Many of the members of corps have kept away, because they are afraid to come before the inspecting officer, and those corps have generally had their serjeants recently, and the men have not had sufficient drill.

1969. You have stated that they were deficient in equipment, what is the deficiency?—In the whole of my division I do not think that there is a pouch fit to carry the ammunition properly.

1970. Is there anything else in the equipment that is deficient?—No; the pouch and the ball bag are the most essential things.

1971. Do you think it is necessary that the volunteers should be equipped with a knapsack at the present time?—No, I think that a good waterproof haversack would be by far the best.

1972. For present use?—Yes.

1973. (*Chairman.*) Are many of the men equipped with haversacks?—Very few of them; only three corps I think.

1974. What is the usual equipment of the corps under your inspection?—The equipment of the volunteers sometimes consists of a shoulder belt with a pouch, but rather a dandy looking thing, which I consider is of very little or no good; they also have a waist belt with a slung pouch which will hold about 30 rounds, but then it expands and consequently the ammunition could not safely be put into it, it would all go to pieces; all their pouches are bad.

1975. Do you find that their clothing is complete?—Not of all of them.

1976. Are they provided with great coats?—Not one.

1977. Merely with tunic and trousers?—Yes, and a cap.

1978. (*Lord Elcho.*) Some of them wear leggings, do they not?—Yes; and there are several Highland corps that are very well clothed, not well equipped, but they are remarkably well clothed.

1979. They have trowsers, have they not?—No.

1980. (*Sir A. Campbell.*) Is it, in your opinion, desirable that all the volunteers should have great coats?—No; I think that if they had a light cloak it would be better.

1981. It is desirable you think that they should have something in addition to the tunic?—Yes; I think so.

1982. (*Lieut.-Col. Barttelot.*) Have you heard any complaints made with respect to the pay of the adjutants not being sufficient in the district that you inspect?—No; no complaints have come to my knowledge.

1983. Have any complaints about the pay of the drill instructors come to you?—Yes; I have been very often asked by officers commanding corps what they ought to give to the serjeant instructor, and I told them, nothing; that the Government did not consider that they were to receive anything except the Government allowance. I also, at the same time, told them that I thought if they provided lodgings for them where there was a difficulty, particularly in a town, as to expense, it would be perhaps as well, if they were valuable men.

1984. (*Sir A. Campbell.*) You think that the present rate of pay is sufficient?—I think not; but I think that the serjeant instructor ought to be a different man from a common serjeant of a regiment; he ought to be a man of tact, and he ought to be a thorough good drill. At the same time you will not get the best non-commissioned officers out of the army for the pay which these instructors receive.

1985. (*Col. MacMurdo.*) Not in addition to their pension?—I think that their pay ought to be increased a little, and that the corps ought not to give them anything.

1986. (*Lord Elcho.*) Their pay at the present time is less than the pay of a militia serjeant, is it not?—Yes, in some instances; it all depends upon a man's pension on discharge.

1987. Take two men in the same position exactly; the pay that one receives as a volunteer serjeant is less than the other receives as a militia serjeant?—Yes.

1988. You think that a superior man is required in the position of a volunteer serjeant compared with a man in the position of a militia serjeant?—Yes, because he is all by himself; he is a man in whom you must place implicit trust, and he has nobody to overlook him; he must be a good man and a steady man.

1989. Do you think that much tact is required in dealing with militia recruits?—They are more under authority and they do not require so much tact.

1990. (*Viscount Hardinge.*) Is it your belief that these Government serjeants generally get extra gratuities from the corps?—Yes, I know that they do.

1991. I presume that that is for cleaning arms?—Yes, it is chiefly for that.

1992. (*Lord Elcho.*) Supposing all these drill serjeants who are now allowed to these corps, the allowance being one per company, to be good drills and efficient men, do you think that the allowance is more than is requisite, or that they can do with less?—I think that when there are two companies together in one place, one drill serjeant would be sufficient, but it depends upon their strength very much.

1993. Do you mean actually in the same place, or two or three miles apart?—They could not do it if they were that distance apart; they must be in the same place.

1994. (*Chairman.*) How many men could a drill serjeant attend to. 200?—Yes, but he would not, I think, get more than 50 together out of 200.

1995. (*Col. MacMurdo.*) Not for the ordinary drills?—No.

1996. (*Sir A. Campbell.*) Do you think that higher qualifications are required for an adjutant of a volunteer corps than for a militia corps?—No; I think that the adjutant in a militia corps is perfectly fit for the appointment in a volunteer corps, most decidedly.

1997. You do not think that the class of persons with whom the volunteer adjutant has to deal, from being less directly under his command than the militia are, requires different qualifications in the adjutant and therefore makes it more difficult to get a fit adjutant?—It is more difficult to get a fit adjutant, because I think that the pay is not good, particularly for an administrative battalion; he has to move about at an expense of 12s. a day, whereas the militia adjutant, I think, receives the same sum, and he is always stationary.

1998. (*Viscount Hardinge.*) Do you think that the adjutants of these administrative battalions visit their companies sufficiently often?—Some of them do; good adjutants do, but they are not all alike. I have seen a good adjutant visiting them perpetually.

1999. Have they ever excused themselves for not visiting their corps sufficiently often by saying that they are underpaid by the Government?—No, they have never complained to me about it, and I have known of several; for instance, I was up in the North of Scotland only a few weeks ago going round my inspection, and the adjutant accompanied me everywhere, and he had to go 50 and 60 miles across the country with me, and it must have been a great expense to him.

2000. Would not the position of the adjutant differ so materially in different parts of the country that in one administrative battalion he might visit every company by the rail, and not have to keep a horse, and in other battalions he must keep a horse all the year round, and ride many miles to visit the companies?—Yes.

2001. The circumstances are very different in different battalions?—Yes.

2002. (*Sir A. Campbell.*) Is it your opinion that the adjutants are sufficiently paid?—Yes, except the travelling allowance.

2003. Do you think that in the consolidated battalions the pay is ample?—By giving them more pay I think that you would get better adjutants, and I think that more officers in the army would come forward; there is a difficulty now in getting good adjutants.

2004. Of what class of men are the adjutants in the corps under your inspection mostly composed?—With the exception of two or three they are very good.

2005. Are they non-commissioned officers raised from the ranks, or are they officers from the army?—Taking the artillery and rifles, nine are non-commissioned officers raised from the ranks.

2006. But there are a good many officers?—Yes. Twenty from Her Majesty's European and East Indian army.

2007. (*Major Harcourt.*) In the artillery have the adjutants chiefly risen from the ranks?—Yes, in the artillery they have.

2008. (*Chairman.*) Do you think there will be any difficulty in maintaining the corps at their present strength when their clothing requires to be renewed?—Yes; I think there will be great difficulty. I do not think that the men who are effective, who are now useful men, and have been well drilled will come forward; there are several who will not unless some assistance is given to them towards their clothing.

2009. Can you state how that assistance ought to be given; do you think that it ought to be received from the Government through the commanding officers of the corps?—I think that if a man is effective his clothing ought to be given to him, but until then he ought to clothe himself. An allowance for each effective might be given to the commanding officer, who should properly account to the Government how it was expended.

2010. Who would you consider to be really an effective?—A man who thoroughly knows his duty in the ranks or in whatever position he is, either an officer, a serjeant, or a private.

2011. You would not consider a man thoroughly efficient, I presume, unless he had passed through a course of musketry drill?—Decidedly not.

2012. Do you find that a large proportion of the corps under your inspection have not passed through a course of musketry drill?—Yes, very few corps have gone through the whole course.

2013. Have the adjutants all qualified themselves by going to Hythe?—Not all of them.

2014. (*Major-Gen. Eyre.*) What steps do you take to ascertain the amount of target practice that has taken place in every corps; do you overhaul the register?—I look at the musketry drill and practice return; we cannot always do that, some corps do not produce it, the Government do not insist upon their producing it; it is only accidental, we cannot enforce it.

2015. They are not obliged to produce anything to you?—Nothing at all. The Volunteer Act does not enforce it.

2016. Then what evidence is there for you or for the Government as to the state of the corps in rifle practice; is there any proof at all?—None at all,

2017. (*Sir A. Campbell.*) I presume that most of the corps do send in returns of the practice they have gone through?—Some few do; but the regulations do not authorize the inspector to call upon them for it; if I asked any commanding officer for his target practice return, he could say " No; that is a private affair."

2018. (*Major-Gen. Eyre.*) But is not that a very rotten state of things with reference to the most essential part of their duty?—I must say that they pay great attention to their musters, and drill, and musketry instruction, and they do keep registers as far as they can.

2019. Who keeps the registers?—The serjeant instructors, those who have got them; other corps,

Lieut.-Col. D. Jones.

13 June 1862.

Lieut.-Col.
D. Jones.

13 June 1862.

who have not got serjeant instructors, have kept them very irregularly.

2020. Do you not think that the register should be subject to the supervision of some competent person, because it is open to a great deal of abuse from favouritism, and by entering men as qualified to be returned as effective who are not so?—Most decidedly. I think that the inspector ought to see the regular musketry drill and practice return.

2021. As an inspector of volunteers, is it your opinion that the use of the rifle in the hands of the volunteer is a most important part of his drill?—No; I would much rather have 20 well drilled moderate shots than 100 good shots badly drilled.

2022. But although a volunteer might be drilled in the ranks you would not consider him of much use unless he could use his rifle at the target?—No.

2023. (*Lord Elcho.*) They are thoroughly trained in the manual and platoon, and aiming drill, are they not?—Yes, their manual and platoon they generally do the best; they can work at that in the winter under cover, and they do it very well indeed.

2024. You have spoken of efficiency, what should you consider the best test of efficiency; should you consider the fact of a man having attended the statutory number of drills a good test of efficiency, or should you consider it a better test that he had passed some sort of examination either before his adjutant, or the serjeant-major, or the commanding officer?—I think that if his commanding officer considers him effective that the man should be returned as such.

2025. Irrespective of the number of drills that he may have attended?—Yes; some men would become effective after 50 drills, other men would not become effective after 100, and others would never become effectives, whatever number of drills they attended.

2026. You may have a volunteer practically efficient, but, according to the statute, ineffective?—Yes.

2027. (*Viscount Hardinge.*) Do you think that you could rely upon a volunteer officer using his discretion in passing a man or not as an effective?—He would have the assistance of his adjutant, who ought to be a competent judge whether a man was effective or not.

2028. Would there not be great difficulty in the case of a scattered corps; how would the examination be conducted?—Under the adjutant, I should say, most decidedly, he could prove them; he could always do that, by taking a dozen men; he could do it in five minutes.

2029. You would leave it entirely to the discretion of the commanding officer and the adjutant, and you think that no abuse of that power is likely to arise? I do not think so; I think that the commanding officer would take care of that.

2030. (*Sir A. Campbell.*) In case Government aid were made dependent upon the number of effectives in a regiment, do you think there would be any danger of commanding officers being tempted to return men as effectives who were not quite so?—It might be the case, but still I think that the inspecting officer, when he went round, could see whether the men had been drilled properly or not.

2031. You mean individually?—Yes; I would take a company and I could point out the men who had not been properly drilled.

2032. (*Lord Elcho.*) Is not the simple manual and platoon drill a good test?—No.

2033. It is part of the man's drill?—Yes.

2034. And it could be easily tested whether a man could go through the manual and platoon drill correctly?—Yes.

2035. Would the inspecting officer have any difficulty in the course of his examination in finding out whether any members of a corps who were supposed to be effective were inefficient in the rest of their drill?—If the inspecting officer saw the men moving as a company he would soon find out; I do not say

that he could pick out every man, but he could pick out certain men and say that they were not effective.

2036. (*Viscount Hardinge.*) Would it not be a very invidious duty for the inspecting officer to perform, to lay his hand here and there upon a particular man, and tell him to fall out, and tell his captain and adjutant that he had been improperly passed as an effective?—It certainly would; but still it would be a duty that a man must go through, and there is a way of doing it; you might smooth the thing over.

2037. Do not you at the same time think that a volunteer who has strictly completed his 24 days of drill is sure to have attained a certain amount of proficiency?—No.

2038. Why so?—Because I think that there are some men who go to drill merely for the sake of attending to get over the 24 prescribed drills; but they look to nothing but shooting, and these men will not learn their drills; some of them do not know how to learn, and they never will make soldiers.

2039. Would not the same observation apply to the militia who have 21 days' drill?—They have four and five or six hours in a day, and in four days they would have their 24 drills.

2040. (*Major-Gen. Eyre.*) Do those men of whom you spoke become very perfect in the rifle drill?—Yes, generally.

2041. They would do to put behind trees and in holes if they were good marksmen?—Yes, but they would require a certain amount of drill to bring them up to those trees; it would be rather dangerous with undrilled men.

2042. (*Major Harcourt.*) Is it not the case that these reports which are not required from the rifle corps are required from the artillery?—I do not know that.

2043. (*Lord Elcho.*) You have spoken generally as to the necessity of further Government assistance being given, from your knowledge of the state of the corps in your district in Scotland, which is confined to the north and to the east, what proportion of the force should you say was self-supporting?—I should say about one-third, not quite so much perhaps.

2044. I hold in my hand a report which you have written upon the Haddington report, you generally concur in the accuracy of that report do you not, as applicable to the rest of Scotland?—Yes.

2045. In your report upon that report you state that one-fourth of the corps in the rural districts are self-supporting, that about one-half contribute a portion, and one-fourth give nothing whatever towards the expense of their corps; is that generally a correct representation of the condition of the force in your district?—Yes; I took occasion in the first year to ask those questions of the different corps; I wanted to see how they managed, and I consider that that is about the average state of things in my division.

2046. Do you believe that unless further assistance is given these corps will cease to exist, or gradually disappear?—They will diminish in numbers; I do not say that they will cease, but they will become perfect skeletons.

2047. Do you believe that the assistance which is required can be obtained permanently in the district itself?—Not permanently; there are corps in which everything is paid by the gentlemen in the neighbourhood, and if those gentlemen left the country the corps would fall to pieces.

2048. Can those gentlemen be reckoned upon permanently to contribute the money required?—No, I think that they would get tired of it.

2049. They are getting tired of it are they not?—Yes, they are; there are several instances of corps where there have been regular contributions for two years, and the gentlemen in the country have stated that they thought their subscriptions would certainly cease.

2050. On what grounds do you believe they thought that their subscriptions would cease; do they disapprove of the volunteer movement and consider it unnecessary, or do they think that they ought not to bear a burden which ought to be borne by the community at large?—I did not enter exactly into their feelings upon the subject, but I imagine that it is partly from a feeling that they cannot afford it in some instances, and in other instances perhaps there is a little lukewarmness shown towards the movement.

2051. Does that lukewarmness arise from any other cause than the expense?—I dare say that that is the chief cause, but I cannot tell.

2052. (*Chairman.*) Did not those gentlemen come forward in the first instance when they considered that an invasion was imminent?—I think they did, it was a popular movement at the time, and everybody thought that they must give something.

2053. Feeling themselves more secure, and that there is less chance of invasion, are they less eager to subscribe to the movement?—I think that that feeling does exist.

2054. (*Sir A. Campbell.*) Was it not more in this direction, that they were ready to start the thing as an experiment; but now they think it is for the Government to judge whether it is a successful experiment or not?—I think that now every corps is looking to the Government for some slight assistance.

2055. But I am talking of the persons who contributed the money?—I dare say that that feeling may exist with them.

2056. Supposing that no assistance is given, to what extent do you anticipate that the volunteer force in your district will fall off?—It will fall off gradually. I should say that amongst the artizans, whom I consider the best drilled men, it will fall off very considerably; I hardly can say, but I dare say it will fall off about a fourth or something of that sort this year, according as the new clothing is required.

2057. Do you consider it of importance that a decision on the part of the Government should be come to speedily?—I think that as new clothing is required, the sooner they get assistance the better, if it is the intention of the Government to give them any assistance at all, it should be done at once.

2058. Has new clothing become requisite in many of the corps in your district?—Yes, there are several.

2059. In which new clothing is immediately required?—Yes; they have worn their uniforms very much.

2060. (*Viscount Hardinge.*) In what shape should you recommend further aid to be given?—I think that every volunteer on joining his corps should pay for his own clothing, and after he has become effective and continues effective for two years, let him have his clothing provided for him, for I think that he is worth keeping.

2061. Would you give aid in any other shape, or simply in clothing?—I would give him everything if he was effective.

2062. Do you mean clothing and accoutrements?—Yes; I would give him the whole of the volunteer's accoutrements, because they have not got a single pouch that is fit to hold ammunition.

2063. (*Major Harcourt.*) What security would the Government have that the man, after his clothes had been given to him, would not leave the force in a fortnight?—He must leave his clothes behind.

2064. Do you think you would find the volunteers ready to wear second-hand clothes?—Yes, they do that now in several corps.

2065. Tunic and trousers and all?—Yes; I am talking of course of the lower class.

2066. Of those who would wish to be provided for?—Yes.

2067. (*Viscount Hardinge.*) Do you think that in your district, referring both to the consolidated and the administrative battalions, clothing would be the most acceptable shape in which aid could be given?—Yes.

2068. You are probably aware that in the metropolitan corps clothing in many cases would not be considered a material assistance?—Yes, and in some of the corps in Edinburgh they would not accept clothing as they can afford to provide for themselves, but there are some of the companies composed of artizans, the labouring class, and some of the shopkeeping class, who would gladly receive clothing.

2069. If these corps received clothing and accoutrements from the Government gratuitously, you would not propose, I presume, that they should receive any further aid?—No, not at present.

2070. (*Lord Elcho.*) Do the corps in your district mostly pay subscriptions?—There are a certain number who do, but they vary in amount; there are some corps in which they pay a certain sum, 10s. a year, and even as low as 5s. a year; then there are other corps in which the subscription is 2l. a year, and a portion of them pay nothing.

2071. These subscriptions do not go to defray the cost of the uniforms but they go to meet the incidental expenses of the corps which are not now defrayed by the Government?—I do not know.

2072. You have stated that you think that Government assistance in the form of clothing would be sufficient, but are there not many incidental expenses such as ranges, targets, travelling expenses, armouries, drill sheds, orderly rooms, and headquarters which are at present defrayed, not by the Government, but either from local funds or subscriptions from the corps, and would not these expenses still have to be defrayed?—Yes; but I think, with regard to travelling expenses, that when the different corps of a battalion have been favourably reported upon by the inspecting officer, that the commanding officer of the battalion should be able to bring these corps together for battalion drill at least two or three times a year, and marching money should be given by the Government to defray all expenses. I am talking of administrative battalions whose corps are scattered.

2073. Do you calculate upon their still being defrayed from local resources or from subscriptions by the corps?—From both; but the orderly rooms are only in the consolidated battalions.

2074. But there are consolidated battalions in your district are there not?—Only seven; three of which are artillery.

2075. Each company has a place for its arms, has it not?—Yes.

2076. And that expense is now defrayed either by their subscriptions or from some local fund?—Yes.

2077. Assuming that clothing was given by the Government, do you think that the other incidental expenses could be met by the corps themselves?—In most corps they could, but I should like to see all expenses defrayed by Government for effectives.

2078. You have stated that the artizans are the best drilled men in your district, can you speak generally as to the good conduct and discipline of that class as volunteers?—I have heard from their employers that the men have improved very much in a social point of view, that there is more respect shown by the men to the masters, and to persons generally, than there used to be in former times.

2079. The result of volunteering as to that class you find, as inspector, to be that they are the best drilled, the most orderly, and that socially and in all other respects they are improved?—I do not know about their being orderly, but the masters decidedly say that they are very much improved.

2080. In the district which you inspect in Scotland what proportion to the whole force do you suppose that element bears, is it one-half?—I should say nearly a half.

2081. Without assistance being rendered in the shape of clothing to that portion of the force in your district, do you think there is any probability of its falling away and ceasing to exist?—It would gradually cease to exist.

2082. Do you think that some of them will renew their clothing?—Yes, a few; those who are good shots and are fond of it would make an effort to do so.

Lieut.-Col. D. Jones.

13 June 1862.

N 3

Lieut.-Col.
D. Jones.

13 June 1862.

2083. And continue to pay their subscriptions?—Yes, a few of them would.

2084. (*Major-Gen. Eyre.*) Some witnesses who have been examined have greatly condemned the system of extravagance which has been practised with respect to bands and balls, and unnecessary field days at a distance, which took money out of the pockets of the men; but those witnesses have belonged to corps in which the funds are in a very flourishing condition, owing to their avoidance of such extravagance, have you had an opportunity of forming an opinion upon that subject, and can you tell us whether you think there is great deal of unnecessary extravagance?—Most decidedly, it has come under my notice that there is unnecessary extravagance; I have seen it in the course of my inspection; for instance, there are two corps in one town, and each of them has its own band, and one of those bands must cost them, I think, about 130*l*. or thereabouts in a year, and the other about 150*l*. I thought that one band between the two corps, belonging to the same administrative battalion, would have been quite sufficient.

2085. Do you not think that by a little effort the volunteers might form for themselves bands at a very small expense?—Yes, they might.

2086. Can you recommend to the Commission any intelligent serjeants or men belonging to the volunteer corps, who should be examined?—I cannot; I could name officers.

2087. (*Col. MacMurdo.*) Referring to a former part of your evidence on the subject of musketry instruction, and bearing in mind that the drill instruction which the volunteers receive is purely voluntary on their part, and supposing that the Government had power to enforce the keeping of a register of musketry instruction, do you suppose that the instruction would be given in a better way in consequence?—I think that if the Government were merely to suggest that this should be forthcoming every year the volunteers would like it.

2088. You are aware that the Government did suggest that, by supplying them with forms to keep their registers in?—Yes, and I think that they will be kept, because several officers have asked me to receive these, and I am doing so now. I am receiving them from those corps that have gone through their course; they send me their returns, and I intend to compare them, and see which corps have produced the best shots, and see which battalion has produced the best shots.

2089. You are aware that the Government have no power to compel volunteer corps to keep musketry registers at all?—Certainly.

2090. Should you see any advantage if an Act of Parliament were passed to compel them to do so, or do you think that the inducements which are now held out to the force to practice firing, according to the regulations, such as the badges which the marksmen receive to encourage them to practice according to the Hythe regulations, are sufficient without any compulsion?—I think that if the Government were to insist upon an annual return being made of the shooting of every corps it would be an advantage, and I think that the corps would like it themselves.

2091. (*Major-Gen. Eyre.*) It would operate as a stimulus to them?—Yes, you would then see who were the effective men and who were not in this respect.

2092. (*Sir G. A. Wetherall.*) Would not the volunteers be more satisfied, and be better pleased with themselves if a stricter system of discipline were enforced than now exists?—Yes, but it must be done gradually.

2093. You think that they would have a better opinion of themselves?—I think they would.

2094. They wish, do they not, to be considered soldiers generally speaking?—Yes, I think they do.

2095. (*Lord Elcho.*) When you say that a stricter system of discipline should be enforced, will you be good enough to state in what respects you think the present system of discipline is inefficient, and how it might be improved?—I think that if the Government gave clothing, and gave everything, they would wish to know what the men really were, and whether they were effective or not, and the only way to arrive at that is to have these returns. I do not say that a stricter discipline should be enforced, but a good commanding officer should gradually instil discipline into his corps, which is not the case with some commanding officers.

2096. As to musketry, do you think it is desirable that there should be returns of the musketry practice, so that a book might be annually published as to the volunteers, similar to that which General Hay publishes as to the shooting of the army, or something of that kind?—No; I think that that would be rather too much, I think that it might be kept in the different divisions and submitted to the inspector-general.

2097. If it were to serve as an incentive to the corps you would have to publish annually some statement of the relative shooting of the different corps founded upon those returns?—Yes; it would take about two or three years before you could do that.

2098. Ultimately should you think that something of that kind was desirable?—I think so; I think that the volunteers would like to see the average taken and "figure of merit" given of each corps, and that it would excite emulation among them.

2099. (*Earl of Ducie.*) On the other hand, if you published a figure of merit, when it would be impossible that the firing should be compulsory, would there not be great temptation among commanding officers to confine the shooting to the men whom they knew to be good shots?—I think that every man should go through his course every year who can, and that commanding officers should certify that this has been done.

2100. But do you think you could enforce that?—Yes, I think so; if the Government gave them the ammunition they certainly ought to fire away a portion of it properly.

2101. (*Col. MacMurdo.*) But you are aware that they do not fire it away, and that every man in a corps does not fire?—Yes; I would not have an exactly similar course to that of General Hay, I think that it might be reduced to about three rounds, instead of five, for each distance, a reduction must be made; I would not have 60 rounds.

2102. (*Earl of Ducie.*) Is there not a large number of the men who do not fire at all?—Very few, I think; but there are a number who fire very irregularly; every corps, I believe, has received ammunition.

2103. (*Lord Elcho.*) Is it not the case that many of the ranges are at a considerable distance from headquarters, and that the corps, whether companies or consolidated battalions, have to pay for conveyance to the ranges?—Yes; but that is not so much so in my division; there are ranges to be had to any extent in Scotland, near small towns; but in the large towns they have to go some distance.

2104. (*Col. MacMurdo.*) Do not you think that the supervision which would be necessary to ascertain the figure of merit through all the corps in the country could not practically be exercised?—Not at present, not unless the volunteers wish it themselves.

2105. You cannot always make sure of the volunteers being quite right in their registers?—No, but I think that a reduction in the firing and a certificate at the bottom of the registers would ensure correctness. I think that something must be done, so that every man would feel that those who did not fire must not be considered effectives. I would only have effectives entered in these registers.

The witness withdrew.

Earl GROSVENOR examined.

2106. (*Chairman.*) You command the Queen's Westminster volunteers, consisting of two battalions?—Yes.

2107. It is the largest corps in the metropolis?—Yes; I believe so.

2108. Have you any suggestions to offer to the Commission?—With regard to the pay of the adjutants, I doubt whether they are not rather underpaid as compared with the adjutants in the militia. I think that there is a little feeling that that is so, because their duties are so much more severe, extending all through the year without intermission.

2109. The adjutants in the militia being provided with quarters, and the adjutants of volunteers not?—Yes.

2110. Do you think it would be desirable to increase the pay of the adjutants in the volunteers?—Yes.

2111. So as to put them on the same footing with the adjutants in the militia?—Yes.

2112. In the corps which you command is any increased allowance given out of the funds of the corps to the adjutant?—We did give 120*l.* to our late adjutant, but he has left us, and we now give 50*l.*

2113. (*Sir A. Campbell.*) Besides quarters?—No; including quarters.

2114. (*Chairman.*) Has he his own horse?—Yes.

2115. (*Sir A. Campbell.*) Have you found a difficulty in obtaining good officers to take the post of adjutant?—No; I have had innumerable applications whenever there has been a vacancy.

2116. I suppose the position of the corps in the West of London has been an attraction?—Yes.

2117. (*Chairman.*) With regard to your paid serjeants, do you consider that the pay allowed by Government is sufficient?—Yes; I think so.

2118. Do you give them no more?—They get fees for looking after the arms and other things, which, I think, make their pay sufficient, at all events, I have heard no complaints on that score.

2119. Have you any other suggestions to make as to the rifle force, in order to improve its efficiency?—There is one point with regard to the size of the companies, which I think is important. I think that they can hardly be too large, as they muster generally in so very small a number. I mean that a company consisting of 60 you never can work as a company, not above 20 of them attend; whereas if you had a company consisting of 110, you would probably have a workable company.

2120. So that at battalion drills it would not be necessary to break up the companies?—No; so many officers when we parade have to fall out, having nothing to do.

2121. (*Sir A. Campbell.*) How would you propose to meet that difficulty?—I really do not know how.

2122. Would you refuse to enrol new companies until all the companies in the district or in the corps had obtained their minimum?—The difficulty is to know what to do with the old officers.

2123. (*Colonel MacMurdo.*) You might absorb them as vacancies occurred?—Yes.

2124. What do you consider to be the proper minimum number in a company?—I should say 110.

2125. In cases where a district was thinly populated, it would be difficult to raise a company of that number?—Yes; but I was thinking more of a town.

2126. (*Chairman.*) Do you consider that any assistance is necessary from the Government to maintain the volunteer force in its present condition?—Yes; I think that it would be very desirable indeed.

2127. In what shape do you think it should be given?—I consider that 1*l.* a head would be the minimum to be given through the commanding officer on the guarantee of a certain number of attendances at drill.

2128. Would you limit the application of that fund in any way?—I should leave that to the discretion of the commanding officer.

2129. Entirely?—Yes.

2130. You would not restrict it to rifle ranges?—I think not.

2131. Would you approve of part of it being given to assist the men in the way of clothing?—I think not.

2132. (*Earl of Ducie.*) If you had such a sum at your disposal, how would you apply it?—We should get a longer range than we have, and which we cannot get for want of money; and we should get knapsacks, which we ought to have in store, and also cloaks, which we have not got.

2133. (*Chairman.*) Do you think that at the present time knapsacks are of importance?—Not at the present moment, except so far as it would be as well that the men should accustom themselves to wear them.

2134. (*Col. MacMurdo.*) Do you think that they would accustom themselves to carry them?—Yes, I think so, occasionally.

2135. (*Earl of Ducie.*) I presume that you have a sufficient income to carry on the ordinary affairs of the corps?—We want a longer rifle range; and then also I would defray the expense of the corps going down by railway to Bushy to drill, or to Wimbledon, out of those funds.

2136. (*Major-Gen. Eyre.*) Do not you think that if you paid those expenses, and the railway companies knew that the men were not putting their hands into their own pockets, they would increase the fares?—I suppose there is always some risk of that kind.

2137. (*Viscount Hardinge.*) Are you aware that in one of the metropolitan corps, the strongest and most efficient, no extra allowance is given to the adjutant?—I believe that in some cases there is no extra allowance.

2138. Do you consider it absolutely necessary to give an extra allowance to the adjutant?—I understand that there is a feeling amongst them that their salary is not sufficiently high, not so high as that of the militia adjutants, considering the work they have to do.

2139. Could you not obtain an efficient adjutant generally speaking, without giving him any extra allowance?—I think not.

2140. (*Lord Elcho.*) Your subscription is 1*l.* a year, is it not?—Yes.

2141. Is there any difficulty in getting the subscriptions in?—Yes; very great difficulty in some companies.

2142. Is that difficulty one which in the course of time you think will increase or diminish?—It will increase every year, probably.

2143. In order to meet the immediate expenses of the corps for headquarters and many other purposes, you are at present dependent upon your subscriptions?—Yes.

2144. That source might fail you?—Yes.

2145. Has the attendance of the men been good lately?—Not so good this year as it was last year.

2146. To what do you attribute the falling off in the attendance?—The men think that they know their drill; they have been pretty hard at it for two years, and they really think that they know it, and that it is not necessary to go on with it.

2147. Do you think that having great field days early in the year leads them to that belief?—I think so far it does.

2148. Has the attendance since the Brighton review been as good as it was before?—No; we have been obliged to give up some of our Saturday drills altogether.

2149. Would it not be more advisable to have great field days towards the end of the month of July?—Yes; I have no doubt of it.

2150. If they were given at the close of the season as a kind of reward for attendance at drill, to which

Earl
Grosvenor.

13 June 1862.

only those who were efficient should be permitted to go, do you think that that would have a good effect?—Yes, I think so.

2151. (*Chairman.*) Have you any other suggestion to offer?—I believe that a very strong feeling exists in the volunteer mind that some further aid than is now given is absolutely essential to the continued welfare, if not to the existence, of the force, and that this is really the main point which presses for consideration and decision. If the Government consider the force of real service to the country, the question remains, how that aid can best be given? I have a strong impression myself that a capitation grant of 1 *l*. per head upon effectives, according to, perhaps, a more limited regulation with regard to the minimum of attendances on parade, would be the most effective as well as the most simple way of meeting the difficulty; that this 1 *l*. should be paid to the commanding officer; that he should be responsible to the Government for the proper outlay of the grant; and that he should submit the balance-sheet of his corps to a Government Inspector when required to do so.

Those members of the corps who are rich enough would have the option of attending a sufficient number of drills to claim the 1 *l*., or would not attend so many, and in that case pay their usual subscription as before, while there would probably be an increase in the number of those who form the backbone of the system, namely, of clerks and small shopkeepers who have time at their disposal, but to whom the payment of 1 *l*., in addition to the expense of uniform, of accoutrements, and of travelling for battalion and brigade drill, is a heavy charge. I consider that, with regard to the corps I command, a capitation grant of 1 *l*. would be sufficient to defray the ordinary expenditure, which is estimated for this year at under 1,000 *l*. for a body of 1,480 men, while a part would also be available for the purchase of knapsacks and cloaks, for travelling fares, and for the enlarging our rifle range. I may perhaps add how difficult it is to enforce any "regulations" upon volunteers, and that, in my humble opinion, it is important that they should be as few and as simple as possible, for otherwise they become a dead letter.

The witness withdrew.

Maj. G. Warrender.

Major GEORGE WARRENDER further examined.

2151. (*Chairman.*) We understand that you have some further suggestion to make beyond what you stated in your evidence the other day?—There were one or two questions, and particularly one which Lord Hardinge addressed to me, which I was not prepared to answer then, but I have since taken means to ascertain the exact truth. With reference to the recruiting for the army and the militia, as far as we can ascertain in our rural districts, the recruiting for the army has never been very great at any time, but certainly has not been increased by the volunteer movement. On the other hand, we find that the recruiting for the militia has benefited, because we find that we have given men to it; we gave either six or eight men from one volunteer corps in the course of the last year; and further, that the officers of the corps think that if on any occasion the Government were anxious to increase the number of the militia, the officers could at all times help the militia very much.

2152. You do not, I suppose, allow men to belong to both forces?—Never, except officers; I believe that they bear commissions in both; not in either of the counties that I am connected with, but there are instances of that, I believe. Then I wish to mention with regard to the feelings of the men, if the corps were dissolved from want of money, that there would be the greatest regret felt amongst them all, and not only amongst themselves but amongst all their own friends; their general health from their improved cleanliness, and their steadier habits has decidedly improved, and therefore their friends would regret it as much as themselves. Then with regard to the comparative discipline between those men who have been entirely or mostly aided in obtaining what they wanted, and those who have entirely furnished themselves, the only difficulty that I have ever had, the only severity that I was ever obliged to put in force was against one man; there were several concerned, but it was the ringleader that I punished. They were volunteers who had entirely found themselves, and who considered themselves as the cream of the corps, and they were the most difficult to deal with; and the sense of the men who had been assisted was entirely against the offenders, and they entirely sympathised with the measures that I was obliged to take; and those men decidedly liked drill better, it was more amusement to them than to the others, as they had no other amusement except what they would have to pay for. Then with regard to two companies in one place; in many instances two companies have been, from the outset, placed under one commanding officer. At our headquarters there are two companies; but, unfortunately, the mode of consolidating them was not adopted at first,

and there have been, from the very first, the greatest possible rivalry and jealousies; and I have had more trouble in keeping the peace between those two companies than with all the rest. If the lord-lieutenant, at my suggestion or otherwise, had applied to this office to have them put together, they might consider it as some local job, and one company or the other might kick. But if the War Office were to determine that two corps or three corps in one place were always to be put under the command of one man, things would work far better as to ranges, and drill, and general discipline. They would not kick, I think, if it was done in that way. As it is, if one officer is slack and another officer is strict, it creates the greatest confusion between the two corps. Then as to the amount of assistance; I was asked the other day whether I thought 1 *l*. would be enough? I said at the time, that it was barely enough; but I forgot, at the same time, that out of that fund we should have to find belts, and to meet all the expenses of coming to battalion drills; and 1 *l*. I think, would be very bare work. I think it would be hardly possible to do it. I think that 25 *s*. would all be used up in the country. Then, as to the adjutants, I do not think that they are over-paid by any means; at the same time, in some districts I think that they might superintend more corps than those of a battalion of four or five corps. My own adjutant works very hard; but his whole heart is in it, and he likes work; therefore if he is at headquarters, and any drill goes on in either corps at headquarters, he goes and superintends; he goes to every corps twice in a month, but at the same time I think that the corps might do with perhaps a little less supervision, and it would be better I think to give the adjutant a little more money; and if one county can only raise one very small battalion, to put a neighbouring county in the same condition into the same battalion, I think that an adjutant with a little more money could perfectly do the work; that is to say, I do not think that the adjutant of a small battalion has enough to do, unless he does a good deal of serjeant-major's work, and therefore it would be economy if he had a little more pay; and if you threw four or five companies in a neighbouring county perhaps in the same condition all under him.

2153. (*Col. MacMurdo.*) You are aware, are you not, that that is done?—Yes; and I think that that is a very good thing.

2154. (*Sir A. Campbell.*) Does your adjutant superintend the musketry instruction of the companies?—He superintends generally and personally, as far as he can; but not entirely, as he cannot be present with each corps on each day of instruction.

2155. Does he see that the company instructors are fit to carry on the company instruction?—Yes.

2156. Do you think it would be desirable in case of any assistance being given by the Government, to make it a condition that all companies so receiving that assistance should consent to be battalionized?—I think that that is very necessary; and then it would create a disposition in the men to be put under more decided control, and I would not wish to see new corps raised in consequence of Government aid, as any persons thus enabled to volunteer can enter those corps which already exist in their own locality.

Where none exist, the raising of new corps might be permitted. Then with regard to the number of men who are likely to clothe themselves again, I have received a letter from an officer in the Forfarshire battalion, Sir John Ogilvies, although it is not from him, but from a gentleman of my own country living there, and they calculate that out of about 500 or 600 men 30 or 40 may reclothe themselves, but not more.

2157. (*Chairman.*) Are these all the points to which you wish to refer?—Yes.

Maj. G. Warrender.

15 June 1862.

The witness withdrew.

Adjourned till Tuesday next at half-past 12 o'clock.

Tuesday, 17th June 1862.

PRESENT:

Viscount EVERSLEY.
Viscount HARDINGE.
Lord ELCHO.
Lord OVERSTONE.
Lieutenant-Colonel BARTTELOT.

Lieutenant-Colonel Sir A. CAMPBELL.
Lieutenant-General Sir G. A. WETHERALL.
Colonel MACMURDO.
Major HARCOURT.

VISCOUNT EVERSLEY IN THE CHAIR.

Mr. WILLIAM LINTOTT examined.

2158. (*Chairman.*) I believe you are a private in the 7th Sussex Rifle Volunteers?—Yes.

2159. How long have you been in that corps?—Nearly three years next August.

2160. You are, I presume, well acquainted with the feelings of the members of that corps?—Yes, I think so.

2161. Do you think that the same spirit which gave rise to the volunteer movement in the first instance prevails now?—Yes; some men, perhaps, are getting a little tired of it, some few, but not many; we generally muster very well upon what we call great occasions, such as battalion drill days, or field days of any kind, we generally turn out then very well.

2162. You do not find your numbers diminish?—Not at all.

2163. When the corps was originally formed, did the members provide their own clothing?—No, they did not, at least only a small proportion of them did. I suppose that out of 80 men, at least 50 were provided with uniforms out of the money that we raised in the neighbourhood.

2164. Does your corps consist of 80 men?—Rather over that number; there are between 90 and 100 on paper, 80 effectives.

2165. Does your corps form one of an administrative battalion?—Yes.

2166. I suppose it has its fund separate from the battalion fund?—Yes.

2167. Was the clothing provided out of that fund?—Yes, it was.

2168. Do you have an account presented every year of the expenditure?—Yes.

2169. Is the balance in favour of the corps at the present time?—We have a very small balance indeed in hand.

2170. In what way is the money expended?—For the rent of the armoury, and the rent of the meadow that we use adjoining the butt, incidental expenses, tradesmen's bills, and cleaning rifles; until this year we have paid our drill instructor between 50*l.* and 60*l.* annually, which was the largest item.

2171. That will not occur again?—No.

2172. What is the annual subscription paid by the members of the corps?—We have hitherto succeeded in getting a little over 100*l.*, but I am afraid that this year the subscriptions will fall short; we have lost several very good friends in our neighbourhood.

Mr. Broadwood was one of those who supported our corps very liberally, and there were several others. I am afraid that many will not give so much, if they give anything at all this year.

2173. What is the annual subscription of each member?—In the first instance we never asked the members to subscribe at all, which was a mistake; there are very few who give anything towards the funds, not more than 8 or 10 of us.

2174. Is the fund principally supported by honorary members?—Yes, it is.

2175. When the clothing requires renewal, do you think there will be any difficulty in raising a fund to reclothe your men, or do you think they will be able to do it without?—I am afraid that we shall have very great difficulty; indeed, I am sure of it.

2176. Is the attendance at drill as good as ever?—Yes, it is.

2177. How often do you have your battalion drills?—About four times in the year.

2178. Is your muster good on those occasions?—It has been very good indeed; the other day in Petworth park we fell rather short, for so many men live in the country who are engaged at haymaking, and we fell certainly short on that occasion.

2179. The attendance is good upon the whole?—Yes, very good.

2180. Have you any great distance to go to the battalion drills?—They are held sometimes at one place and sometimes at another; sometimes at Hurstpier-point, which is about 15 or 16 miles from home, and the other day we were at Petworth, 18 miles from home; and we went to the review at Brighton, and sometimes we have them within a few miles of our own town.

2181. Looking to the future, do you see anything that is likely to interfere with the efficiency of the corps?—I see nothing but want of money.

2182. And especially, I presume, funds wherewith to supply clothing?—It is a question of uniform with us almost entirely; we have hitherto raised enough to meet our annual expenditure, which I am afraid we shall not quite do in future. I feel satisfied that we shall have the greatest difficulty in getting money to reclothe the men, and most of the uniforms are now completely worn out.

2183. If you had money, you see no prospect of the corps declining in numbers?—No; in fact we shall increase.

Mr. W. Lintott.

17 June 1862.

O

Mr. W. Lintott.
17 June 1862.

2184. (*Sir A. Campbell.*) From what class of men is your company recruited?—Mechanics principally, and young men holding situations in the town, and some dozen or so of gentlemen like myself, young tradesmen in the town, and young farmers in the neighbourhood.

2185. How was the uniform provided originally?—By the money that was raised in the neighbourhood. Some 20 or 30 of us found our own, and we also found uniforms for some of our own dependants; but for 45 or 50 we paid out of the funds that we raised for that purpose.

2186. (*Lieut.-Col. Barttelot.*) Your corps was one that first purchased their own arms?—Yes.

2187. Did not that throw you back very much in your funds to begin with?—Yes.

2188. I believe, from what I have seen lately, that it is the same with your corps as with many others, that after battalion drill the attendance of men is not so good for some time to come?—No, it is not.

2189. But at any battalion drill, or at any general or divisional field day, the attendance is always very good indeed?—Yes, very good.

2190. Have you sold your arms?—Yes; most of them have.

2191. To whom?—The major had the entire management of that, to dispose of them for us.

2192. The Government did not take them?—No. The London Armoury Company allowed us, I think, 2l. each for arms that we had paid 5l. for.

2193. Do you find that the attendance of the farmers, or of the artizans and mechanics, is the best at your drills?—The attendance of the artizans and mechanics, certainly, is the best.

2194. (*Viscount Hardinge.*) Is not that in some measure to be attributed to the fact, that they are upon the spot, whereas agricultural labourers have to come in from some distance?—That has a great deal to do with it, no doubt.

2195. (*Lieut.-Col. Barttelot.*) Are your arms all kept in store?—Yes; the members are not allowed to take them away.

2196. That is the reason, is it not, why you employ somebody to clean them?—Yes.

2197. Is not that a heavy expense on the corps?—No it is not.

2198. (*Viscount Hardinge.*) How are your travelling expenses defrayed when you go to battalion drill?—It all comes from the money that is annually subscribed, and that we collect.

2199. Do you give any extra allowance to the drill serjeant?—No.

2200. He has no extra allowance for cleaning the arms?—No.

2201. Have you heard any complaint made on that score, that he is inadequately paid?—No.

2202. How are the arms cleaned, by the serjeant?—Yes.

2203. What is the expense of your armoury?—We pay a rent of 16l. a year for the armoury itself, and then we have a serjeant armourer who is a gunsmith in our town, and to whom we pay 8l. or 10l. per annum for seeing that the rifles are all kept perfectly right, in addition to the cleaning; we give him that to inspect the arms.

2204. I suppose that some of the rifles are kept at the men's residences?—None now.

2205. Has any complaint been made on that score on the part of the men, that they dislike having their arms kept in the armoury?—None that I have ever heard of.

2206. Have you found no inconvenience result from that?—Not the least.

2207. Is the armoury close to the drill ground?—Yes, close, within 150 yards.

2208. Do you know what the expense of your butt has been?—I cannot call to mind; it was erected two or three years ago.

2209. (*Lieut.-Col. Barttelot.*) What rent do you pay?—30l. a year for the field in which the butt is erected.

2210. (*Viscount Hardinge.*) What is the expense of keeping that butt in order?—I should fancy it is 12l. or 15l. a year.

2211. Does that include a range keeper and a marker?—We have no range keeper, but we pay a marker extra.

2212. Have you anybody on the look-out when the men are firing?—Yes, invariably.

2213. Is he paid?—Yes.

2214. At what rate is he paid?—So much according to the length of time that we are at practice.

2215. Have you found in your corps that the material pressure has been the expenditure for uniforms?—Certainly.

2216. If you were relieved from that pressure, and if uniforms were given to your corps gratuitously, would not your funds be materially relieved?—Yes.

2217. In fact, you would ask for nothing more?—No.

2218. (*Lieut.-Col. Barttelot.*) Do you think that if the men were relieved from any expense as to battalion and other field days, it would tend very much to the permanence of the corps?—I think it would.

2219. The chief difficulty which artizans have to contend with is the money they are out of pocket?—Yes, it is.

2220. (*Lord Elcho.*) If you had clothing given to you, what annual subscription do you think would cover the other incidental expenses, such as for ranges, drills, armouries, and so forth?—100l. a year would do it well.

2221. Do you think it would require 100l. a year in addition?—Yes.

2222. What are your days for drill?—Tuesdays and Thursdays.

2223. Not Saturdays?—No.

2224. When the arms are brought in late of an evening, do the men before they go home clean their own arms, or are they handed over to the serjeant and put into the armoury and cleaned?—They are handed over to the serjeant.

2225. Has he any assistants?—Yes, he has a boy who is a bugler.

2226. It would take him a day or two to clean the arms, would it not?—Yes.

2227. (*Major Harcourt.*) Supposing that the uniforms were found for the men, would there be any difficulty do you think in getting them to wear second hand uniforms?—No, many of our men are wearing them now.

2228. (*Viscount Hardinge.*) How much do you pay your bugler?—5l. a year.

2229. (*Col. MacMurdo.*) You stated just now that the arms are cleaned by one man and a boy, do you not teach your men to clean them?—We have had several drills, and we have been teaching them to clean them, but they have not done so yet.

2230. (*Lord Elcho.*) Is it because they come in so late that there is not time to clean them?—That is very often the case.

2231. At what hours do you come in?—At battalion drills very rarely before 9 o'clock, from our company drills I suppose it is about 8.

2232. (*Col. MacMurdo.*) How often do you have company drills in a week?—Once a week; squad drill on one day, and company drill on the other.

2233. Are those drills well attended?—Pretty well.

2234. Does the adjutant warn you of the day when he is coming to see you?—He does.

2235. I see that on the 8th of last month you had 27 men present at drill, on the 20th you had 32 present, and on the 27th you had 12 present at drill; is that about your average?—Yes.

2236. (*Lord Overstone.*) Do I correctly understand it to be your opinion that the feeling in which the volunteer movement originated still remains unweakened?—I can hardly say; I think that the feeling is not quite so strong as it was at first.

2237. But still you think there is sufficient strength to inspire fair confidence in the permanency of the force?—Yes.

2238. You anticipate a great difficulty from pecuniary considerations?—Yes.
2239. Those pecuniary considerations affect principally the clothing of your men?—Yes.
2240. What amount per annum do you think would be sufficient to remove the difficulties which you anticipate?—150l. a year; I think we might manage to clothe them all with that.
2241. With 150l. so placed at your disposal, what number of efficient volunteers do you think could be maintained?—100.
2242. Then you think that about 30s. a head is the sum necessary to maintain the efficiency of your corps?—I think that that sum would do it.
2243. In what way do you think that sum could be best applied, by giving it in the form of material things, or placing it at the disposal of the commanding officer, or in what other way should you think it could be most properly applied?—By placing it, I think, in the hands of the commanding officers.
2244. If it were placed in the hands of the commanding officers, under what restrictions should you recommend that it should be so placed?—Of course there must be no mistake about the men being efficient.
2245. Do you think it would be a desirable course that the commanding officer should be called upon to give in an annual estimate, stating the purposes for which he requires the money, and to which he intends to apply it?—Yes.
2246. Do you think that a sum of money so placed at the disposal of a commanding officer would create a disposition on the part of the other officers or privates to interfere with the application of that money?—No, I think not.
2247. Do you think that the commanding officer would not be molested by the interference of subordinate members of the corps?—No.
2248. Do you think he ought to be placed under strict supervision by the Government office from which the fund emanated?—Certainly.
2249. (*Viscount Hardinge.*) Do you think that your muster rolls are now accurately and strictly kept, and that men are not returned as effective who are really not so?—I believe that our muster roll has been kept very strictly.
2250. (*Lieut.-Col. Barttelot.*) Can you not state honestly that your muster roll is very accurately kept?—I have not the slightest doubt of it.
2251. (*Viscount Hardinge.*) I presume that the greater proportion of the men who attend regularly and take an interest and pride in it attend a greater number of drills than 24?—Yes; we have many men who have attended considerably over their proper number of drills, a great number of them.

2252. (*Sir A. Campbell.*) Do you recollect a circular that was issued from the War Department, and which was afterwards withdrawn, intimating an intention to purchase from the men the rifles they had purchased with their own means?—Yes; I do.
2253. Would many of the volunteers in your company have availed themselves of that offer?—Yes; they would.
2254. The majority of them?—Yes.
2255. (*Viscount Hardinge.*) Does any portion of the funds of your company now go to providing prizes for the company to shoot for?—No portion whatever; the money for those purposes is raised in the neighbourhood, quite independently of the annual subscriptions.
2256. Have you not once a year a meeting, when the company's prizes are shot for?—Yes.
2257. Are not those prizes generally given either by the officers or by honorary members?—Yes.
2258. (*Lieut.-Col. Barttelot.*) Your corps, I believe, like many others, have a great difficulty about the band?—Very great.
2259. But I believe the expenses of your band are very small upon the whole?—Yes; very small indeed.
2260. What do you do for a band now?—We have a band, but we pay them so much a head when we want them.
2261. From what source is that money obtained?—I have the management of that entirely, and I collect it from the public in the town.
2262. It is not part of the funds of the corps?—It is not.
2263. Are any of your bandsmen effective members?—Some of them are, not all.
2264. Do they sometimes give up their instruments and go into the ranks?—Some of them do.
2265. (*Lord Elcho.*) Do you believe that there is a great readiness on the part of your men to give their time on service?—I believe there is.
2266. Is there any feeling on their part, that if they give their time on service they ought not to be called upon for more?—Yes.
2267. Have you heard that feeling expressed?—Yes, I have.
2268. Is that the general feeling amongst the men?—Yes, I know that that is the feeling.
2269. (*Viscount Hardinge.*) The individual members of your corps have not been put to any expense?—Very few of them; the greater proportion of them have not been.
2270. I think you stated that 8 or 10 provided their own uniforms?—25 or 30 of them provided their own uniforms.
2271. Then the accoutrements have been provided out of the company's funds?—Yes, for all the rest.

The witness withdrew.

Mr. *W. Lintott.*
17 June 1862.

Major NATHANIEL BOUSFIELD examined.

2272. (*Chairman.*) You are major of the 1st Lancashire Rifle Volunteer Corps?—Yes.
2273. Of how many companies does that corps consist?—At present it consists of 10, but we have applied to augment them to 13.
2274. Is yours a consolidated battalion?—Yes, it was originally an administrative battalion, but we broke it up and formed a consolidated regiment.
2275. How long have you belonged to that corps?—Nine years. I have been working at volunteering all that time; and I offered the services of the corps in 1857 to the Government. The corps was accepted on the 9th June 1859, and I was commissioned as captain on the 11th.
2276. You say that the corps consisted originally of 10 companies, and that it is now about to be increased to 13?—It exists now as a consolidated regiment. I was commissioned as captain of one company in 1859, and in May 1860 it was formed into a battalion, of which I was lieutenant-colonel.

2277. Of what class of men is your corps composed?—The 1st company was composed almost entirely of gentlemen, all pretty nearly equal in rank and position, merchants and brokers, and the sons of gentlemen connected with business in Liverpool; but now we have increased in numbers and we have taken in some of the better class of tradesmen, their sons and assistants also; we have so formed three companies of artizans.
2278. I presume that you have a regimental fund?—We have raised it entirely by subscriptions amongst ourselves of one guinea, which each man pays; originally we paid two guineas a piece each, and the honorary members do it now; but each man pays one guinea at least.
2279. Do you include the artizans?—Yes, they pay by instalments.
2280. Do they pay one guinea per annum?—Yes, they pay it in the course of the year; the captain

Maj. N. *Bousfield.*

Maj. N. Bousfield.

17 June 1862.

arranges how he will receive it; he receives it either weekly, or monthly, or quarterly.

2281. How is the money so raised expended?—In storehouse accommodation, band, and in a storekeeper; and until the Government gave us a drill instructor, in a drill instructor; a great deal of the drill instruction was given by a few old members of the drill club, who were competent to give instruction.

2282. Have you a rifle range?—Yes; we have one large range for the whole force, which Colonel Gladstone originally did a good deal for, and afterwards there was a subscription got up by friends in the town. It did not raise much, only 3,000*l.* altogether, of which Colonel Bourne's brigade of artillery received a portion, and the 15th received a portion, and a portion was allotted for a new rifle range, in which all regiments share.

2283. The rifle range was purchased?—No; Colonel Gladstone, I believe, spent 870*l.*, Major Tinley about 146*l.*, and the rest has been made up by subscriptions from gentlemen, and from the fund alluded to previously, about 800*l.*; but last year I am sorry to say that we found there was a little deficiency, and I am afraid this year there will be a larger deficiency.

2284. What is the annual cost of your rifle range?—I do not think we can keep it up much under 1,000*l.* a year.

2285. Do you give any additional pay to your adjutant beyond the Government allowance?—No.

2286. Nor to the drill serjeants?—No; except when we use them as storekeepers. We have two storehouses; we had three, but one company joined me in the neighbourhood and brought in a storehouse about a mile and a half out of town. It is used also for schools, and a very nice building it is. That was raised by the neighbourhood for 600*l.* or 700*l.*; that is our own.

2287. Is this storehouse the armoury?—Yes, and the storehouse.

2288. Are the arms all kept in store?—Yes; and we think that is a very bad plan to allow any to be kept out, as they get neglected.

2289. Do you pay men to superintend the cleaning?—Yes, and the men cost us on the average 15*s.* a week, and we have to find them quarters, coals, and gas.

2290. Are not the men drilled and taught to clean their own arms?—Yes, they are all instructed, but the difficulty is that we do not wish them to take them out of the storehouse, and I believe it is the wish not only of the officers but of the head constable and also the mayor that we should not let the arms get straggling about; we keep them in good storehouses and it costs us nearly 300*l.* a year.

2291. Are those storehouses in your own drill ground?—No, we have one general drill ground, for which we are indebted to Colonel Bourne, at Mount Vernon, within a quarter of an hour or twenty minutes' march from the storehouses; that is a large ground; about 2,000 men have been put into it.

2292. Are the storehouses in different parts of the town?—Yes. There is one in the south, one in the north, and one in another locality near at Fairfield.

2293. So that they are near the headquarters of the different companies?—Yes. I can assemble them in front of St. George's Hall without marching more than for ten minutes from any storehouse.

2294. Was any part of your funds expended in providing uniforms for the artizans?—None whatever. The artizan companies joining us have been principally clothed by their officers; there is an arrangement made among themselves as to paying by instalments, but of that we know nothing, we do not interfere with them.

2295. When the present uniforms are worn out do you anticipate that there will be any difficulty in getting the men to supply themselves with new ones?—In the artizan companies I think decidedly that there will be a difficulty, but none, I think, with regard to the others, and if we were assisted by Government in storehouses it would be everything; our guinea a year subscription is very heavy on the men. As to the clothing of the men who find themselves, I apprehend no difficulty in the renewal of that.

2296. You spoke of assistance to be received from the Government, in what way do you think that would be most beneficially applied for your corps?—In paying the rent of storehouses, or in something being done towards it; in the payment of arm cleaners, and in paying the rent of armouries, and in instruction of buglers, also a bugle major; I think that something ought to be done in the way of lodging allowance for the adjutant; he has to keep up his appearance as a gentleman. I also think that the practice range ought to be found, and, what is some consideration with us, an allowance made to meet the expense of transporting the men to and from the ranges. I also think that an increase in the allowance of ammunition is wanted. I believe that 110 rounds are now given, and if they were increased to 220 it would, I think, be sufficient. At present it is a very serious item the additional ammunition that is wanted, because the men shoot very much, and it is very serious for a man to give up his time and pay for his ammunition.

2297. Do you think that any assistance that might be rendered should be given to the colonel?—No, I should rather prefer that the colonel of each regiment should send in a statement to the Government authorities showing what he pays for his storehouse, and the Government should give so much for each man for that storehouse, and the yearly rent account should be sent up here.

2298. Do you mean that the Government should pay the actual cost?—Yes; I am rather against a capitation grant as to the men; we wish to retain our self-supporting and gentlemanly feeling; we would rather have some assistance by the Government giving us a good storehouse and a good drill ground, and a good practice ground, leaving the men to find their own uniforms and provide their own expenses for their bands and so on.

2299. Can you estimate the cost of keeping up these storehouses?—In Liverpool we think it is very necessary that any storehouses that we take should be near the Exchange, nearly all the men being engaged in the focus of business all round there; any storehouse that was remote would be of no use; we should want to get a house that was sufficient to accommodate a number of men, and I dare say that would cost us from 150*l.* to 200*l.* a year; and then as to cleaners of arms, we cannot get them much under 15*s.* a week. Wages are very high in Liverpool; a man can earn 3*s.* 6*d.* a day as a porter.

2300. What would be the expense for the whole of your regiment that you think ought to be defrayed by the Government?—At present the guinea a year for 700 men is pretty well spent, and I think to keep up our regiment the Government ought to give us between 400*l.* and 500*l.* a year.

2301. How much would that be per head?—About 14*s.* 6*d.*, we have 700 men, perhaps more than that we ought to have, including a practice range.

2302. (*Lord Overstone.*) You think that it would be desirable for the Government to advance a sum of 500*l.* for 700 men?—Yes.

2303. (*Lord Elcho.*) That is not to include any clothing, is it?—No, I think for an artizan fund it would be quite inadequate, or for any corps in which clothing was required.

2304. (*Lord Overstone.*) You think that clothing is not required?—Not for my regiment.

2305. (*Lord Elcho.*) But you have stated that it would be required by the three companies of artizans?—Yes.

2306. Those have been clothed by their officers?—Yes, and by the men to a certain extent.

2307. (*Lord Overstone.*) Of what number does your whole corps consist?—I think about 698.

2308. Do you think there is any ground to anticipate a falling off in their numbers except from pecuniary considerations?—No, certainly not.

2309. But from pecuniary considerations you do anticipate considerable difficulty?—Yes.

2310. Have I understood your evidence correctly that you think an advance of about 500*l.* by the Government would remove that danger?—Yes, yearly.

2311. That sum to include the cost connected with clothing as well as every other source of expense?—Not clothing.

2312. My object is to ascertain from you what advance of money by the Government would, in your judgment, be sufficient to place a corps of 698 men in a complete and satisfactory state, all things included?—Including clothing and everything, fully 30*s.* a man.

2313. In your opinion, what is the total of pecuniary amount which it would be necessary for the Government to advance in order to enable you to maintain your corps of 698 men in an efficient state?—By that question I suppose I am to understand you to include what I said about adjutants?

2314. Everything that you think should be included, but including nothing which you think ought not to be included?—To include everything, adjutant's allowance being part, I should say 30*s.* a man would be at least required.

2315. Our object is to ascertain exactly your view with respect to the management of your own corps of the cost necessary to maintain it, and do you think that an advance by the Government of 30*s.* per head would be sufficient to maintain your corps in a permanent state of efficiency?—No; in my own corps an advance of from 15*s.* to 1*l.* would do, as I should have assistance from the men.

2316. By your corps I meant the complete regiment to which you belong?—Yes, with the exception perhaps of three companies; the other men, I think, would support themselves.

2317. You have given the number of 698 men, and I understand that those three companies are included?—Yes.

2318. The object of my question is to ascertain what amount of advance by the Government would, in your judgment, be necessary to enable you to maintain a corps of 698 men in a state of permanent efficiency, understanding that number to include the three artizan corps which you have alluded to?—For 198 men I would require 30*s.* a man; the remainder to have 1*l.* to do it handsomely, that is for 500; 198 at 30*s.*

2319. I understood you to say that you think the form of capitation grant is objectionable?—Yes.

2320. You think that it would offend the feeling of independence in the members of your corps?—Yes, and they all desired me to represent that strongly, that they would rather find their own clothes, but that they wished to be assisted in the matter of the storehouse. I know very little of the views of the 198 men.

2321. Your general impression is that a capitation grant is objectionable?—Yes, very much so.

2322. And that assistance, if such be derived from the Government, should come in the form of bearing the expenses of certain branches of the service?—Quite so.

2323. Have you considered whether any branches of the service could be specified that would be applicable to the volunteer corps generally throughout the kingdom, or do you think it would be necessary to have separate regulations for each district or regiment?—I think separate regulations for each regiment are necessary as the regiments in my own town vary a good deal; there is a very fine regiment under Colonel McCorquodale, a very excellent and efficient regiment, and it is entirely composed of printers and artizans. What the colonel's views might be I cannot say, but I should think in his case it would be desirable that he should have a capitation grant.

2324. It is your impression that it would not be practicable or expedient to lay down any general rule either in favour of a capitation grant or condemnatory of it, and that you might resort to a capitation grant in some cases, and to a more indirect mode of supplying pecuniary assistance in others?—Yes.

2325. Can you lay down any general rule by which you think these cases might be distinguished?—I should distinguish them by making the commanding officer give a return stating the necessities of his men and what he wanted in one form or other, such as storehouse accommodation, arm cleaners, and so forth; he might state what he required, and send in an estimate for his regiment annually, draw the amount that was allowed from the Government, apply it to the purposes stated, and return the vouchers to the Government.

2326. Would it be a desirable course to put it to the discretion of each colonel commanding to say whether he wished to have assistance in the form of a capitation grant or in any other indirect mode?—I think it would be.

2327. (*Viscount Hardinge.*) Would you propose that if further aid were given, whether directly or indirectly, it should be calculated at so much a head for every effective man, or that it should be calculated at so much a head for the strength of the corps including non-effectives?—I think that non-effectives ought to be included, taking into consideration that many men become non-effective by their idleness, but many of such men would come forward at any time that you wanted them. I have many of that kind who are not included in what I have estimated; the number that I have given here is from the return of effective volunteers, that is 698. I have, I dare say, of honorary members and so on perhaps a couple of hundred more.

2328. Do these men fall in on the occasion of brigade reviews and so on?—Yes, except honorary.

2329. Do you find them tolerably efficient?—Yes; there is a great deal of musketry practice going on in our regiment, and we are very comfortable; we work very much *con amore*; the officers and men work very well together, and there is a great connecting link between them, as they are all men engaged in business.

2330. Have you ever heard any complaint made by the men who have attended upwards of 24 days of drill, that the non-efficient men come in on review days and brigade drills and throw the other men out?—Very often, but we generally work them in such a way as to prevent that, but it does happen to a certain extent; we always require the officers to use up those non-efficient men in such a way as to prevent it if possible.

2331. Did you not state that the range will cost 1,000*l.* a year?—Yes, to keep it up, but that is for the whole force in Liverpool; we all share in it.

2332. Is that 1,000*l.* a year paid for the rent of the ground?—Yes, and for the permanent staff on the ground, markers, a man to tell off the ranges, and a superintendent; we want a good superintendent; Captain Bushby was our superintendent last year, and we paid him 300*l.* a year, but he has resigned now.

2333. How many Government serjeants have you?—I am entitled to three, but I have not got three; I had only two; one died the other day.

2334. Cannot those Government serjeants be employed in cleaning the arms?—They refuse to do that as a general rule.

2335. When you offer them extra remuneration for it?—Without that they will not do it; they refuse to do it as part of their duty.

2336. Would it not be cheaper to give them some extra gratuity?—We have done that, and we have got old soldiers in our storehouses who do it, but as a general rule the drill instructors object to cleaning arms.

2337. Would it be possible or desirable for the volunteers to clean their own arms?—It is not possible, I think, for business men.

2338. They could not give the necessary time to

Maj. N. Bousfield.

17 June 1862.

Maj. N. Bousfield.

7 June 1862.

it?—No, they would never be in good condition. I have had them in camp for seven weeks, and they have cleaned their own arms.

2339. (*Chairman.*) How many corps make use of the rifle range which you say costs 1,000*l.* a year?—There are five regiments of artillery and engineers, and five regiments of rifles, besides some straggling companies.

2340. How many thousand men altogether?—I think there are somewhere about 4,000 men, cavalry, artillery, engineers, and rifles.

2341. (*Viscount Hardinge.*) Do you think that if any further aid were given, the volunteers would mind being put under stricter control?—I do not think that the control could be made more strict than it is, we are very strict in our corps: if a serjeant misbehaves himself on parade we reduce him on parade, and cut his stripes off, just as they do in the line.

2342. You mean the volunteer serjeants?—Yes.

2343. You have no difficulty in enforcing discipline?—I have had them in camp for seven weeks at a time and they have done sentry duty all through the night.

2344. How many men have you had in camp?—I had 220 in 1860, and in 1861 I had 150.

2345. For how many days did you have them in camp?—I had them in camp for seven weeks, and I lived with them myself under canvas.

2346. How could they afford to lose their time?—They did not lose their time; they went to business during the day; they got up at six o'clock in the morning, and went into town to business, and they were out again at six o'clock, and in bed at 10 o'clock.

2347. Did you find that answer?—Yes, very well, and a good many of the men want another camp this year; we found that there was a man in Liverpool who had a quantity of tents in his possession, and we hired them.

2348. (*Lord Elcho.*) How was the expense met?—The men paid the expenses themselves, 10*s.* a month, and four men slept in each tent; they paid 2*s.* 6*d.* a month for their tent, and four of them occupied a tent, except the officers.

2349. How did you furnish the tents?—We had several cart loads of stores taken out. We found a man in Liverpool who had a large quantity of india rubber Crimean sheets, and we lined the bottom of the tents with them after a medical man had inspected the ground, and we covered those with straw, and we used beds such as they have on board ships, and it cost us about 4*s.* a bed.

2350. Did they use a palliasse?—Yes, a little palliasse, and most of the men brought their own blankets and railway rugs, and the better part of the corps had got good military great coats with a cape.

2351. Had you any other fittings for the tents besides the beds?—They bought washhand basins.

2352. What were your washing arrangements?—We found that a tripod formed in this way (*describing the same*) with a tin basin, answered the purpose very well. There was one at the back of each tent, or at the rear of each line of tents. We had them in lines of four.

2353. How many basins did you have to half a dozen men?—They found them all themselves; we did not care how many they had, and the total expense was 10*s.* a man.

2354. That sum paid for the hire of the tents, the straw, and the carriage?—Yes.

2355. But it did not pay for the basins and those things, did it?—No; but it paid for a man watching during the day time, to see that nobody stole anything.

2356. Did the men clean their own things?—Yes, they cleaned their own. We contracted for a man to furnish a canteen; and they could get a breakfast or tea for 6*d.*, and on Sunday the dinner was 1*s.* 6*d.*, and the officers dined with the men.

2357. There being four men in a tent?—Yes.

2358. Could you have put conveniently 6 in a tent?—Yes; but we generally let them sort themselves; friends went together.

2359. Were they bell tents?—Yes; I slept in one.

2360. Did each officer have a tent to himself?—It was just as he liked. I slept with a brother officer.

2361. Did you find it inconvenient?—Not at all.

2362. What was the charge to the officers for fitting up their tents?—It was very much on the same scale as the men's, as Spartan-like as possible. I think that I had the worst tent in the camp. I set an example. We had visiting rounds and everything complete, and we sunk wells and built latrines; we were on sandy ground on the sea shore, and it was a capital place for it. I had only two cases of drunkenness, and I dismissed one man from the service; the other was a corporal, and I took his stripes off.

2363. Did the health of the men suffer?—No; it very much improved.

2364. Had you any bad weather while you were in camp?—We had only four fine days the whole of the time we were there; it rained nearly every night.

2365. Had you trenches dug round the tents?—Yes; and everything of that kind.

2366. Did the men pitch their own tents?—Yes; and they struck them by bugle sound.

2367. (*Col. MacMurdo.*) Had they been properly drilled for the purpose?—Yes; I drilled them myself.

2368. (*Lord Elcho.*) You had no staff to help you?—No; except the officers of the regiment. No military officers except the adjutant.

2369. (*Major Harcourt.*) You have stated that it might be desirable to provide some of the men with uniforms, how would you do that?—It should be done, I think, in cloth or something of that sort. An allowance of so much for a suit and for making up.

2370. What security would the Government have that a man who was so supplied with a uniform would not leave the regiment in a fortnight?—None. There is the difficulty, and I am strongly against anything that is not self-supporting.

2371. You are of opinion that it would be almost impossible to provide uniforms in any way for the men?—I am very much against anything but self-supporting volunteers, men who find their own clothes. Assistance ought to be given to the head-quarters of the regiment, but the clothes, I think, the men ought to find.

2372. (*Lord Overstone.*) You think that all that may be called personal to each man should be provided by himself; but that which applied generally to the regiment might be provided by the Government?—Yes.

2373. (*Lord Elcho.*) From your knowledge of the volunteer force, you are able to say that part of it is capable of doing what you say the whole ought to do?—Yes, there is Colonel Bourne's regiment, the 4th brigade of artillery, and my own.

2374. On your principle you would lose three companies in all probability?—Yes; but I do not find any good in these working men, except in such a case as Colonel McIver's regiment.

2375. Is that composed of artizans?—Yes; Colonel McIver and Colonel Clay are both large employers of labour, and the men who form these regiments are entirely in their own employ; consequently if a man should be disobedient he might lose 30*s.* a week good pay.

2376. (*Major Harcourt.*) If the uniform that was given remained the property either of the Government or the corps, do you think you would find any difficulty in getting the men to wear second hand uniforms?—Yes.

2377. (*Sir A. Campbell.*) Are the men to whom you have just referred officered by their own employers?—In the case of Colonel McIver's regiment it is entirely so; in the case of Colonel Clay's it is not so.

2378. In those cases in which they are officered by their own employers, do you think that in the case of strikes or disputes about wages there might be some inconvenience from such a mode of efficiency?—I should say not in Liverpool, the men not being mill hands we never hear of strikes much. The mill owners in Rochdale rather opposed the movement; spinners generally have been very much against it.

2379. Was the original enrolment of your regiment done by companies or otherwise?—By companies.

2380. You spoke, I think, of the proposed consolidation of the regiment into a smaller number of companies?—My plan would be this: we take them of course on the Government establishment; we return 13 companies, and there are many men who as we have gone on from the first have got into commissions who have no right to be there; who are totally incompetent as officers, not possessing the proper qualifications, and not being gentlemen.

2381. But they obtained their commissions?—Yes, they got 50 or 60 men on paper and they sent them in to the lord-lieutenant, and they were appointed captain, lieutenant, or ensign.

2382. (*Lord Elcho.*) They practically bought their commissions?—Not always.

2383. (*Sir A. Campbell.*) In case of the number of companies in your regiment being reduced, how would you dispose of the commissions of those officers?—I think that is a little matter which might be left to the colonel; we generally arrange that among ourselves.

2384. Should you anticipate no difficulty in transferring men from one company to another?—No; we had much difficulty at first, but we have broken that down; we equalize them in any way that we like.

2385. You said that in the original enrolment of the men they were got together on paper and officers were gazetted who were not proper persons to be officers?—Not in all instances.

2386. Was any inquiry made by the lord-lieutenants into the mode of the enrolment or the fitness of the officers for their posts?—I am not in the least aware; in my own case I was inquired into. Colonel Wilson Patten signed my commission. I attended before him in uniform, and I went through a regular examination by him.

2387. Practically were the officers elected by the men?—Practically they were in every case.

2388. Whoever was elected by the men was appointed without any trouble?—Yes, practically that was the fact.

2389. (*Viscount Hardinge.*) And that you think very undesirable?—Yes, I think that every officer should be subjected to an examination.

2390. (*Sir A. Campbell.*) Do you think that if the appointment of officers was placed in the hands of some other authority than that of the lord-lieutenant that that difficulty would be avoided?—No, I should say not. I think that lord-lieutenants have the power to fully examine every officer.

2391. (*Chairman.*) Is not that done in the militia?—Yes, and in the line too. In our regiment no man can be promoted until he has passed through an examination before his next step.

2392. (*Lord Overstone.*) Can you state shortly what course or system of measures you would recommend for the purpose of securing the permanent efficiency of the present volunteer movement?—First of all an examination of all officers as to efficiency, a monetary grant for a storehouse, drill instructors, and arm cleaners, adjutants with lodging allowance, instruction of buglers, practice grounds and transit to and from, and an increased allowance of ammunition.

2393. You think that all those things ought to be provided for by Government aid?—Yes; and especially that the examinations should be left to Government officers.

2394. Being so provided for, you think that the efficiency of the corps might be effectually maintained?—Yes.

2395. (*Lord Elcho.*) That answer is given, is it not, upon the assumption that it is a self-sustaining force?—Yes; I assume that if that is given by the Government, even though it was not entirely a self-sustaining force, the officers are willing to come forward; and we have not quite drained the towns dry.

2396. I think you stated with regard to a portion of your own regiment, three companies, that more would be required in their case than in the others?—Yes.

2397. In any requisition that you might make, you would have to ask for more for them?—Yes.

2398. If it should be proved that half or two-thirds of the force is in the condition of your three companies, would not those views which you have put on paper be modified?—Certainly, if that was proved.

2399. (*Lord Overstone.*) I understand the views you have just expressed to be your reply to the general question as to the system which you think it expedient to adopt to maintain the present efficiency of the volunteer movement?—Yes, my own opinion is that if the force is small no man should be a volunteer who is not self-supporting. I consider that the place of those men who require clothing and maintaining is in the militia.

2400. The heads already enumerated by you are those which you suggest to this Commission as being the proper ones to attend to in order to sustain the volunteer movement?—Yes.

2401. (*Lieut.-Col. Barttelot.*) What is the cost of your uniform?—5*l*. for tunic, shako, forage cap, belts, pouch, and trowsers.

2402. Any great coat?—Yes, but that is extra; there is a cape to take off, they all buy that.

2403. What is the expense of your band?—We give 100*l*. a-year to the band.

2404. Out of the funds?—Yes.

2405. (*Sir A. Campbell.*) In case your suggestion were adopted, what number of the 4,000 men in Liverpool could you maintain, do you think?—I should say most of them; they are all most of them self-supporting with us; many of them pay in instalments, but they all pay, and we rather think that that is the safety of it; if you gave them clothes they would be so dissatisfied; I have seen several instances of that, men will not wear second hand clothes.

2406. Do you think it is important that a decision should soon be come to on this subject?—I think the sooner the better; at present we shall get a little into debt, I am afraid, with the expenses of the storehouse and so on; and there is a difficulty in getting subscriptions from the men, although they do pay generally; at one time they were in arrear, and I went round myself, and got in nearly all the money.

2407. Do you think you shall lose numbers?—I think so; the officers have paid a good deal one way and the other, and I do not think they will stand it much longer; another thing is that the honorary members may not subscribe again; they did a good deal at first, but I do not think that they will renew their subscriptions so much as they did.

2408. (*Lord Overstone.*) Do you think that intervention by the Government in a pecuniary way, as you have suggested, is a matter of pressing importance as to time?—Yes, I do.

2409. Do you think that there should be as little delay as possible in coming to a decision?—Yes; before the expiration of the next three months, if possible; the half-year is always a trying time, and the falling off always occurs at Christmas; the men begin to resign then, but I really feel that the great source of any decay has been bad and inefficient officers.

2410. (*Viscount Hardinge.*) Have any officers in your battalion attached themselves to a regiment of the line to obtain instruction?—No, I do not think that any of them have. I have been two or three times with a regiment of the line.

2411. Do you find that there is a disinclination on the part of those officers, of whom you have spoken as having been elected by the men, to make themselves acquainted with their duties?—In some instances; not particularly in my regiment. I have had two bad officers, but they are both going.

2412. Does your adjutant report to your colonel those officers whom he considers inefficient?—I

Maj. N. Bousfield.

17 June 1862.

Maj. N. Bousfield.

17 June 1862.

always attend all the officers' drills and report to the colonel.

2413. (*Lord Elcho.*) How do you get rid of bad officers?—I find that the best and the safest plan is to work with your men.

2414. How do you get rid of bad officers; do you tell them that they had better go?—I call them out to the front and ask them to put the regiment through its manœuvres. I think that when a man has been a year in a commission and cannot move a company he ought to go.

2415. You have had nine years' experience in volunteering?—Yes, constantly.

2416. From your knowledge of the volunteers and their capacity for drill, what should you say would be a sufficient number of drills to constitute efficiency?—I think you cannot do with less than 24; they generally get a little more; a review perhaps is about to take place, and you coax them a little.

2417. When once a man has passed through his 24 drills, would not a smaller number than 24 drills be afterwards sufficient?—No, I think they require 24; we have 12 monthly musters, when we expect every man to turn out; we threaten fines, but we do not fine except in a very flagrant case, when a man comes on the ground in plain clothes, and stares at the regiment we do fine; good musters are best obtained by working amongst the men themselves; we take care that the serjeants are good men, and we have a very good feeling in the regiment.

2418. (*Viscount Hardinge.*) Do not you think that those men who are really heart and soul in the movement, generally would attend more than 24 drills?—Yes, I have 150 men who I think have drilled and been at rifle practice four or five times a week.

2419. Do not you think that if the Government gave aid they would have a right to say, we must have the regiments kept up as efficiently as they have hitherto been?—I do not see how you would enforce it. If you said to the officers we shall withdraw the grant unless you can do so and so, it would not be the fault of the field officers if they could not do it.

2420. Take the case of a capitation grant, might not a capitation grant be given for every effective member, or for every member who had gone through 24 days' drill?—I think it ought to apply to the non-effectives as well, because they work for us a good deal and they give us a good deal of money towards it.

2421. (*Lord Elcho.*) If the Government tried to apply more stringent rules, might it not happen that the men would stay at home?—Yes, and they would defy you then; the thing must be worked very delicately, it must be done by good nature more than anything else, and by the occasional use of a little badinage and sometimes by trying a little sterner method if a man is saucy; but it is quite a question as to the way in which the officer handles his men.

2422. It would be difficult, if not impossible, to attempt to use compulsion?—You could not apply it.

2423. (*Col. MacMurdo.*) What is your opinion as to the employment of the drill serjeants. You have two drill instructors in your corps, and you are entitled to three?—Yes.

2424. Are the two drill instructors that are attached to your corps fully employed?—They have nothing to do during the day; their work is done at night; they have to attend the rifle range twice a week, but very few of the men come, and they have had nothing latterly to do; they do nothing but walk about in the day time; they have plenty to do in the evening.

2425. Is their conduct generally good?—Yes; but a case occurred lately in which I had a good deal of trouble with a man; he strangled himself with a strap; he had been in the habit of drinking quietly, quite unknown to us; I saw him almost nightly, but I never saw this man drunk, but it turns out that he did drink.

2426. Do you think that the serjeants' having so much spare time is injurious?—Yes; it leads to drinking and general idleness.

2427. Could your regiment do with fewer serjeant instructors?—No; the difficulty is on account of the companies being scattered; we cannot get a storehouse big enough for us.

2428. Then you think no reduction would be advisable?—No, we want all three of them.

2429. Although they have plenty of spare time during the day?—Yes; they might be employed in cleaning arms, if ordered by Government as part of their duty.

2430. Suppose those men were allowed to enter into civil occupations, how do you think that would work; they might gain something by being so employed?—They would be the very worst men that could be employed by us.

2431. What do you think they could gain by such occupation?—If a man was accustomed to produce he might earn something, but these men are not at all accustomed to produce; they do not know anything about handling cotton or sugar; they come there and they are perfectly useless for a time, except for porters at halls, messengers, &c.; of those places there are few in Liverpool.

2432. What average wages do you think they could earn?—Probably at the rate of 3s. 6d. a day. I do not think that they would be able to keep up their appearance as they do, for men working amongst cotton must wear a mole-skin jacket, and get up at six o'clock in the morning and work till six at night, and that might disqualify them afterwards for drilling men; if they could get light work it would be very useful, but there is very little of that to be had in Liverpool; a warehouseman is as hardly worked a man as anybody.

2433. But you think it desirable that the serjeants should get some light employment?—Yes.

2434. It would not interfere with the discharge of their duties?—Except on Saturdays, and that is very often a busy day in Liverpool.

2435. You stated just now that the Government should aid the volunteers by making a larger allowance of ammunition. At the last inspection none of your men had had any shooting practice at all; no actual practice had been gone through in May?—I find that it is perfectly impossible to carry out the theoretical instruction laid down by General Hay; we have musketry classes, but the men do not care for them.

2436. Will you inform me whether every man in your regiment has had any ball practice?—I should say that every man has.

2437. Has every man fired his 90 rounds?—I should say not.

2438. What has become of that which is left?—We are keeping the annual allowance back; I suppose that we had no right to fire it until the men had gone through their courses.

2439. Then you have the residue to fire off?—Yes.

2440. Every enrolled member is entitled to 110 rounds in addition to the 90; have you fired away all that?—I should like to know this, whether we are allowed to fire that gratuitous ammunition for prize shooting.

2441. On what grounds do you require a greater allowance of ammunition than 220 rounds per man; you tell me that the whole of the gratuitous supply of 90 rounds per man has not been fired away?—I fancy not.

2442. You are not certain that every man in your battalion fires at all?—I am sure that they all fire; I do not think there is one who has not.

2443. Do you think that every man in the regiment has fired away his gratuitous supply of 90 rounds?—No; but I think of the total number in the regiment at least 200 have fired away four times that supply of ammunition supplied on repayment.

2444. Are there a certain number of men who have fired away four times that quantity, and a certain other number of men who have not fired away the 90 rounds?—The men there have nearly all taken their allowance on repayment.

2445. If those men have not fired away the 90 rounds given by Government, they certainly not touched the 110 rounds which they would have to pay for?—I think they have touched the 110 they have to pay for, but not the 90 which they have not to pay for. We have kept that back, in order to make the men go through their classes in accordance with what we consider to be the regulations. We sell the other to them at so much, and we put a little profit on, on account of the transit down, and the expense of escort.

2446. Do you not consider 200 rounds of ammunition for the enrolled men an enormous quantity to fire away?—Yes, it is; but we pay for a portion of that.
2447. But still you say that is not enough?—Yes; an increased allowance gratis, I mean; we only get 90 rounds given to us.
2448. But you say that all that is not fired away?—No, we are keeping it, according to the rules; we let them fire it only as they go through their classes.
2449. You want a larger gratuitous supply for prize shooting?—Yes.

Maj. N. Bousfield.
17 June 1862.

The witness withdrew.

Captain W. F. CAMPION examined.

Capt. W. F. Campion.

2450. (*Chairman.*) You command the 13th Sussex Rifle Volunteer Corps?—I do.
2451. Is your company part of an administrative battalion?—Yes, it is.
2452. It consists of one company?—Yes.
2453. How many men have you in your company?—Seventy-three of all ranks; 64 rank and file.
2454. Do you find that you keep up your numbers very well, or that they decline?—Very thirty. Some of the men of my company belong to a college near to us, and sometimes there are several of them who go away at once, and that of course reduces the corps considerably; but on the whole I think that we keep up very much to what they were, without increasing.
2455. From what college do you get the men you referred to?—St. John's College.
2456. Have you any artizans in your corps?—A very few.
2457. Have you any farmers?—Yes, I suppose that more than a third of them are farmers.
2458. You have a fund, I presume?—Yes, which is collected not from the men, but from any subscribers in the neighbourhood who will subscribe.
2459. Are these subscriptions from the honorary members of the corps?—Yes, they are.
2460. Out of that fund have you provided your men with uniforms or not?—No, they have provided themselves with uniforms, with this exception, that very often in the neighbourhood people will collect funds to clothe them.
2461. The clothing forms no part of the expenditure out of your fund?—None whatever.
2462. How often do you drill your men?—That is very uncertain, on account of the difficulty of getting them together; the company which I command extends over 12 parishes, and it is so very difficult, particularly in harvest time, to get them together, that it is always a matter of uncertainty; but, generally speaking, about once a week we get them together, but the attendance is more slack than it was.
2463. Do you get half of the strength of your company together then?—Hardly. If we get together 25 men we think it is very good.
2464. Do you have occasionally battalion drill?—Yes, we have battalion drills.
2465. How many have you assembled at those drills on the average?—I think rather over 40; perhaps over 50 of all ranks.
2466. (*Viscount Hardinge.*) Including the band?—Not including the band; that would raise us to about 70.
2467. (*Chairman.*) Have you a rifle range belonging to the corps?—Yes.
2468. Have all of your men gone through the courses?—No; a good many have; but there are some who, from different circumstances, find it difficult to get practice.
2469. They have not all passed through musketry drill?—No.
2470. You have a drill instructor, I presume?—I have been myself to Hythe, but we have no other drill instructors; we have a rifle serjeant, but he has not been to Hythe.
2471. (*Col. MacMurdo.*) His name is Waller, is it not?—Yes.

2472. (*Chairman.*) Is he competent to drill your men?—Perfectly.
2473. Is he paid by the Government?—Yes.
2474. Do you give him any allowance beyond what he receives from the Government?—Yes; we pay him 2*l*. a quarter to take care of the arms.
2475. Do you see any difficulty in maintaining your corps in its present state of efficiency?—I think not; I do not feel any doubt but what we could keep up the present strength.
2476. You do not require any assistance from the Government?—No, not beyond what we have now, the serjeants were a very great boon to us, both because we had always a difficulty in getting good serjeants, and because we can now have one uniform system of drill.
2477. (*Lieut.-Col. Bartlelot.*) When the present uniforms are worn out, shall you have any difficulty in renewing them?—I hardly know what to say about that, I have no doubt but what the men will all find them, but I am very averse to doing anything in the way of giving uniforms. I find that those men who have them given to them are the worst attendants at drill.
2478. Do you find that the tradesmen and that class of men attend better than the farmers, or the farmers better than the tradesmen?—I have not remarked any difference in the two, I should say not; the tradesmen are generally nearer to the spot, and therefore on that ground they are perhaps better able to attend.
2479. How do you provide for your travelling expenses when you go to battalion drill?—They are paid out of the funds of the corps.
2480. Your corps wears a different coloured uniform from that of many in any battalion, do you not think it an essential thing that they should all wear the same uniform?—Certainly, as soon as the uniforms are worn out, as in two years they will be, we shall be glad to do so, and in fact we have begun it already.
2481. Do not your men object, being in a different coloured uniform, and therefore conspicuous, to be taken away from your corps and put with another?—No, I do not think they do; I never heard anything said on that score.
2482. (*Viscount Hardinge.*) Do you see your way to clothing the whole battalion in one uniform colour?—I can hardly speak of any so well as of my own corps, and I do not think we should have any difficulty.
2483. Do you think that you and the other captains could agree as to the colour that it will be desirable to adopt when the uniforms require to be renewed?—Perfectly; I do not think that we should have any difficulty about it.
2484. How are your travelling expenses paid when you go to battalion drill?—Out of the funds of the corps.
2485. (*Col. MacMurdo.*) What does it cost you?—We have nothing but the travelling expenses to meet; the battalion meets at different places; we meet, perhaps, at Petworth, which is 40 miles off; and then at another place, close to where the corps belongs.
2486. (*Chairman.*) When you meet 40 miles off, have you railway communication in that direction?—Yes, we have.

P

Capt. W. F. Campbell.

17 June 1862.

2487. And the railway authorities, I presume, take you at a low rate of fare?—They take us at a regular price which is fixed for volunteers, which is a penny a mile; we should pay 3s. 4d. for 40 miles there and back.

2488. (*Viscount Hardinge.*) Your company can generally reach the place where the battalion drill takes place by railway?—Always.

2489. Therefore your travelling expenses are moderate?—Yes.

2490. (*Col. MacMurdo.*) It costs you 3s. 4d.?—Yes, to the most distant point.

2491. Supposing you went to battalion drill at Brighton, what is the distance?—Eight or nine miles.

2492. It would be much cheaper, would it not, if you belonged to a battalion there?—Yes, that is very true; but I should mention as to that that our men are particularly averse to that; we are in an agricultural district, and an agricultural district and a town district do not amalgamate so well. I am quite sure that if such a thing was attempted it would fail.

2493. (*Lieut.-Col. Barttelot.*) It would almost break up your company, would it not?—I hardly know that; for I hope that we are all too good soldiers to do anything of that sort; but I should be sorry to see it tried.

2494. (*Viscount Hardinge.*) Is there any subscription in your corps?—Not in the corps itself.

2495. Does not each member pay anything?—No.

2496. Have you a balance in hand?—Yes, 100l., which is invested in stock.

2497. Have you a band, and if so, what does it cost?—We have a band, but it is supported by a separate fund.

2498. Have you any members in your corps who are provided with clothing out of the company's funds?—None.

2499. Do you find a drum and fife band sufficient?—It is much better to march to than anything else.

2500. Have you heard any complaints among the members of the corps that the band is merely a drum and fife band, and they wish for a regular band?—No.

2501. (*Lord Elcho.*) What does your band cost?—I am afraid I can hardly tell you that; in the first place, their uniforms are found out of a separate fund, and those being found they cost us very little indeed, we have merely the expense of their being taught; and then we pay out of the funds of the corps their expense in going to battalion drills.

2502. They receive no pay?—No; only a labourer's pay for a day's work.

2503. Have you a drum major or somebody who teaches them?—Yes; there is a tradesman in the village who is competent to do that.

2504. Do you think that the incidental expenses of your company can be permanently met by subscriptions raised in the neighbourhood?—Yes.

2505. Viewing it as a permanent force?—Yes; I think so.

2506. (*Lord Overstone.*) Do your observation and experience lead you to entertain any serious apprehension as to the maintenance of the present volunteer force in a state of efficiency?—No, I think not, not from anything I have seen yet. If one looks back merely to what happened in the war at the beginning of the century, one might say that it might not be permanent, but I do not refer to any present facts that make me think so.

2507. Looking at the present times, do you entertain any serious apprehension as to the maintenance of the present volunteer force in its present state of efficiency?—No; I think not. I think it is very likely that many who have entered into it merely for pleasure and amusement may leave it; but I think we shall retain the efficient men, and those are the men that we really want to retain, and not those who have entered into it merely from caprice.

2508. It is not your impression that any special measures are now requisite for the purpose of maintaining the volunteer force in a state of efficiency for the purpose for which it was originated?—I think not; I do not see anything to make it requisite.

2509. (*Lieut.-Col. Barttelot.*) Have you found the adjutant most useful in drill and instruction?—Yes, very useful indeed.

2510. (*Viscount Hardinge.*) How often does he visit your company?—That depends a little upon how often I can get them together; our corps extends over 12 parishes, and it is so difficult to collect them together in harvest time; but the adjutant visits us whenever we are able to collect together a sufficient number, and generally speaking about once a month, or once in two months.

2511. Would you say that the average amount of his visits was once a month?—I think not.

2512. (*Sir A. Campbell.*) Does he superintend the musketry instruction of the company?—No, he does not.

2513. He has not been perhaps to Hythe?—I cannot answer that question.

2514. (*Viscount Hardinge.*) Have you ever heard any complaint on his part that he is inadequately paid?—No, I do not know him well enough to hear anything of that sort.

2515. (*Col. MacMurdo.*) Is the time of your serjeant instructor fully employed in musketry duties?—No, certainly not; he has a great deal of spare time.

2516. Do you think that his spare time might be occupied in private trade, or some occupation without detriment to the service?—I should doubt it very much, for as soon as he began anything of that sort of course he would not be so ready to give us instruction when he was required, and he is quite content to be as he is.

2517. That is to be idle?—He has a great deal of spare time certainly, but he is always ready to work.

2518. What employment do you give him besides that of actually drilling the men?—He drills the recruits and he keeps the arms clean, and he has to attend at all the parades and to keep the muster roll and books of the corps.

2519. Do you keep him in the orderly room at headquarters?—Yes.

2520. (*Chairman.*) Are your arms kept in an armoury?—Yes, but there are many of them that are out, and necessarily so, on account of the drill, and also on account of the musketry.

2521. (*Viscount Hardinge.*) Are your muster rolls accurately kept, or have you any reason to believe that men are returned effectives who are not so?—No; I know that every man who is returned is effective.

2522. Does your Government serjeant clean the arms?—He keeps the arms clean.

2523. Does he receive any extra allowance for that?—He receives 2l. a month in addition to the Government allowance.

2524. (*Col. MacMurdo.*) Have you not served in the cavalry?—I was a very short time in the cavalry.

2525. You are living now in a hunting country?—Yes.

2526. Is there any prospect of your raising any mounted volunteers or light horse in that part of the country; there must be a great many unemployed yeomen?—I can hardly answer that question.

2527. Are there not many men in that part of the country who would not enter into your corps, but who might do service on horseback?—There are plenty who might do it, but without there was some pressure I do not think there is any chance of it.

The witness withdrew.

JOHN LAIRD, Esq., M.P., examined.

J. Laird, Esq. M.P.

17 June 1862.

2528. (*Major Harcourt.*) If facilities were afforded by the Admiralty to any members of the volunteer corps on the coast for obtaining a knowledge of gun drill, are there any who would be likely to avail themselves of such an opportunity?—I think some of them might.

2529. Will you be kind enough to state the views which you may entertain on that subject?—I think it depends upon whether they would place gunboats at their disposal; referring to working men, at a time when they could get away from their work; if it were done in the summer evenings I think the men would be quite willing to go.

2530. If facilities were afforded, you think there are men who would avail themselves of the opportunity?—Yes; I think they would if it did not interfere with their work. Drill takes place now after working hours, and in my son's works the men always get off at 12 or 1 o'clock on Saturday, and longer drills take place on those occasions.

2531. Is there any reason to suppose that it would interfere with the Royal Naval Reserve, or that men would be likely to be drawn from it?—No; there are many men in Liverpool who would not join the reserve at all, and there are many men who would not go to sea again; I do not think that those men would bind themselves to go at any particular time without pay. If the Admiralty chose to give a special bounty to men of that class they might add very much to the naval reserve and get a very efficient class of men.

2532. Do you think there is a class of men who are willing to learn their drill on board ships on the same terms as other volunteers?—In our corps I think they would be very willing to go on board gunboats if it did not interfere with their regular work.

2533. (*Viscount Hardinge.*) How do the volunteer artillery now practise?—They practise at Rock Fort, about four miles down the river.

2534. How do they go down?—We generally hire a steamer to take them down, and march them back again, or take them by the usual ferry boats; they have guns in the works for drill, but they are not allowed to fire shot there.

2535. There is no difficulty about the guns in the fort being placed at their disposal whenever they choose to go there to drill?—No.

2536. The only advantage, I presume, of their being allowed to practise gunnery on board the gunboats, would be that they would be nearer to the gunboats than to the fort?—Yes, a gun-boat would come alongside the works and take the men to practice.

2537. You do not recommend that they should practise their drill on board a gun-boat, or do you recommend that they should practice it at the fort?—I think that the men would be very willing to go on board a gun-boat.

2538. (*Chairman.*) You have taken great interest in the volunteer movement?—I have.

2539. Although you are not member of any corps?—No, I could not give time to act as an officer.

2540. I believe you have given very effective support to the volunteers at Birkenhead?—Yes, as much as I could. I will give the Commission a short description of what has taken place at Birkenhead, and the present condition of things. We began in 1859, and the first four companies formed in Cheshire were started at Birkenhead, viz., Birkenhead, Claughton, Wallasey, and Rock Ferry. The four first companies were formed principally of the better classes, and there was a large subscription raised towards starting them. Since that time there have been five other companies formed within a few miles of Birkenhead, which are principally composed of working men, labourers, and farm servants; the four first of those companies found their own clothes and up to this time they have paid their own expenses, and they have in hand what remains of the contributions which were made for starting the movement. In those companies that are formed now, and I am now talking of the rifle companies in the outlying districts, the captains and the officers and some of the neighbouring gentry provide a large amount, and I believe that the expense will fall very heavily on some of the captains of these corps. They would have to pay a great bulk of the expenses for clothing and other expenses. Then, as to the artillery, they are formed on different principles; there is the first and second Cheshire artillery, they were started about the month of December 1859 in connexion with the Canada works at Birkenhead, the clothes were given to the men by Mr. William Jackson, M.P., and Mr. Brassey, but they belong to the corps. The officers and men were principally connected with the Canada works. The third company was formed at Wallasey and New Brighton, and I think it was formed partly of working men also. I believe they are either partially or wholly clothed by subscriptions. The fourth company was formed at Chester, and the fifth company is one that was formed in connexion with the works in which I was a partner, viz., the Birkenhead Iron Works. My eldest son is captain, and the other officers are young men in the establishment, or connected with it, but no one was admitted into that company who did not pay for his own clothes. Men wanted to come in, but I thought that if the men had not some stake in it the clothes would not be taken good care of, and that it would create in them a better feeling if they provided their own clothes. It was agreed when they joined that all the expenses connected with the corps should be paid by the firm, and that the accoutrements should also be found by the firm. That was the principle on which they were established, and it has been worked out in that way. I think that 77 men joined the first year, and there were many applications from others; but we refused to admit them till we saw how the thing went on, and at the end of a certain time an intimation was given that if others chose to join they might, and as the result about 140 men applied to join on the same principle of paying for their uniforms. The uniforms cost about 3*l*. and there was great difficulty in restraining the men as to the expense, they preferred to have the best quality of uniform, but we pressed them to be content with a cheaper kind, which cost 3*l*. and they were to repay that amount at one shilling a-week. There were many apprentices in the works, and in order to encourage them a proposal was made to them that if they would join the corps they should have the clothes at half-price, and if they conducted themselves well and attended drill for twelve months the money should be refunded to them; the object was to try to get them to attend and be steady, and that has worked very well. On the whole I think that the establishment of this corps in the works has produced very good effects amongst the men as setting an example to the others. The serjeants are generally the foremen and the better class of the workmen. I consider that the men paying for the uniform is a very important element in this movement. In the first company, consisting of 77 men, it is nearly all paid off, and as far as I can gather from a letter which I have received I think that the last two companies are paying up very well. Some men leave the works, but on the whole the payments are being made in a very creditable manner to the men, and the effectives this year will be about 160. If there is a great deal of overtime work, the men cannot give so much time to drill, and various circumstances may prevent them from making up their full time; we kept the men back and would not let them join until we found that the system worked out well.

2541. (*Lord Elcho.*) How many men are there employed in your works altogether?—2,500 altogether.

2542. Of whom about a twelfth are volunteers?—Yes, we would not take men in who were not likely to remain, who were not good workmen; many of the

P 2

J. Laird, Esq., M.P.
17 June 1862.

apprentices have paid very great attention to it, and that has had a good effect among the men. Another arrangement that we made was this, that all the expenses connected with going to practice shooting are paid by the firm, and they were promised, in case of any of them being able to shoot well, that they should be sent to the county meeting, and upon the last occasion there was a certain number selected, and out of three prizes given to artillery corps they won two; and when they came back, to show the feeling of the other men, they subscribed between 50*l.* and 60*l.* for prizes to be shot for by this company, and they went down to the practice ground and shot for it.

2543. You are referring to the men in the works generally?—Yes, they subscribed 55*l.*, which they placed in my son's hands to distribute in such prizes as he thought fit, and they went down and shot for them. I merely mention that to show that it produced a very good effect, for the other men were quite proud of what their fellow workmen had done at the county meeting. Then with regard to the expense of working out the corps, as far as I can make out now, exclusive of any loss upon the clothes, (which I do not think will be very heavy if anything,) the expense of working the corps is about 25*s.* or 30*s.* a man, and if working men give their time to it and attend to their drill, and pay for their own clothes, I think that you cannot expect them to go into the other expenses which follow. Very often they have to go down to our practice ground, which is about four miles from Birkenhead; they go down in omnibuses and march back generally; and then there are the expenses of going down to the fort, which is about four miles distant; they generally go down in a steamboat and march back.

2544. (*Chairman.*) They think that those expenses ought to be paid?—Yes; that is the arrangement made with them. You cannot get them to pay more than they do; they give up their time after their work during the week and on Saturday afternoon, and I think that that is as much as you can expect working men of that class to do; I should state that there is another corps which was established last year, an engineer corps, consisting of about 160 men, and the principle acted upon in that corps is that the men pay for their clothes by instalments, and they estimate that there will be a loss of 10 or 15 per cent. by those who do not pay; the members pay 1*s.* 6*d.* weekly, but the belts and accoutrements belong to the corps, and they are paid for out of the general fund; the preliminary expenses they expect will be paid by the public, and I believe the officers will have to contribute towards the preliminary expenses, amounting to 320*l.*; the public have subscribed 150*l.*, and 170*l.* will fall upon the officers; the annual expenses are estimated at 280*l.*, the band at 100*l.*; the subscriptions at 234*l.*, and 146*l.* will be the balance payable by the officers. The uniforms cost about 2*l.* 10*s.* each for 160 men, and they expect that that will be, with the exception of a per-centage and loss from those who do not pay, repaid by monthly subscriptions. I asked the officers what they thought would be the best way of meeting this, and they seem to consider that unless some grant is made by the Government they cannot go on; they suggest so much per effective man; and if that were granted, they would then be able perhaps to keep the thing going,—about 25*s.* or 30*s.* a man.

2545. (*Sir A. Campbell.*) Does that mean 25*s.* a head, exclusive of the cost of the uniform?—Yes, they find their uniforms.

2546. They would require 25*s.* or 30*s.* per effective, exclusive of the uniform?—Yes. Then with regard to officers, there is great difficulty in getting efficient officers; many men in our neighbourhood who are employed in the offices would make excellent officers, and give attention to their duties, but there is a great objection by persons of that sort to act as officers, because the officers, it is generally supposed, are bound to make up any deficiency that there may be;

if a man is a captain he is very often called upon; that has been the case in Liverpool, I know; and on our side of the water, if you get a corps composed altogether of men with good incomes, they would pay their subscriptions; but when you depend upon tradesmen and clerks in offices, they cannot be expected to find their clothes and pay their subscriptions. In one of the last corps which has been established in our neighbourhood at Upton, four miles off, I believe the captain will have to pay for the clothing of the men, and many large expenses.

2547. (*Lieut.-Col. Barttelot.*) What might those expenses be?—He is very near the shooting range, but still the expenses will be very heavy.

2548. Is it over 100*l.*?—Yes, and I think he will have to pay it, as far as I can learn; the feeling is, that it will require, in addition to the clothes that are found, but which will of course depend upon the condition in which the companies are, 25*s.* or 30*s.* to keep the movement in a state of efficiency in districts like Liverpool and Birkenhead.

2549. (*Chairman.*) Do you propose to spend any part of that in conveying the men backwards and forwards to the drill ground?—Yes; and there are storehouses wanted, extra pay to the serjeants, and a variety of other expenses which require to be met.

2550. (*Col. MacMurdo.*) Do you pay anything extra to the serjeants?—They have to find them a house. I think the Government now allow in the artillery and rifles the pay of the serjeants, but in the rifles they pay them extra, or they could not get them to stop.

2551. (*Lord Overstone.*) Is it your opinion that if working men and artizans are encouraged to join the volunteer movement, it is but reasonable that they should contribute only their time and labour, and that further pecuniary means should be obtained from other sources?—No, I think that they ought to find their own clothes, but as to all the other expenses, I do not think that the working men will join if they are asked to contribute anything more.

2552. If artizans and other working persons are encouraged to join the volunteers, you think it is reasonable that they should provide their own clothing, but that further incidental expenses should be met from other sources?—I think that you ought to have a class of men willing to do something towards the force, and if they find their clothes I think that is sufficient; the men take much better care of their own clothes, they have their own boxes for the uniform, and as to the working men, if the clothes last three years, it would cost them about 6*d.* a week, the money being advanced in the first instance.

2553. Your opinion is that the volunteer force as at present constituted, consists of a variety of classes, and according to the condition of those respective classes, it may reasonably be expected that a Government subvention in a pecuniary form should be more or less applied to it?—I think so.

2554. When you are dealing with the artizan and working classes, the pecuniary assistance from the Government may be larger than when you are dealing with companies composed of other classes?—Yes, I think that the others who can afford to pay would not ask for more than was necessary; but take the class of men to be found in a town like Liverpool, clerks, who do receive, perhaps, 50*l.* a year, they cannot afford to pay their subscriptions, and besides that give their time to it; they do not want any pay, but there is a practice ground to go to, and the distance from town makes that a great cost, and the drill sheds; I think my sons pay 50*l.* or 60*l.* a year for a drill shed.

2555. Upon the supposition that it was recommended to the Government to assist the volunteers by increased pecuniary advances, in what form do you think that those pecuniary allowances could be most appropriately made?—I believe that the simplest way would be so much per head for those who were returned as effective.

2556. To whom would you intrust the application

of that capitation grant?—I suppose to the commanding officers.

2557. Would you pay it over to a commanding officer, leaving it to his free and unlimited discretion, or would you require him to send in an estimate or statement of the specific purposes for which he required the money?—I think he should give in a general statement of what it was wanted for, and a similar account also of the expenditure.

2558. Do you think that that principle could be applied generally, or must it not be modified according to the condition and circumstances of the different class of persons of whom each regiment consisted?—I think that it must be modified, as some corps might not require assistance at all, and in others they could not do without it.

2559. May not there be various conditions; some corps not requiring it at all, and some requiring it to a very great extent, and many intermediate ones requiring it in a modified form?—All the parties I have consulted consider that the Government ought to find practice grounds and provide for drill sheds and fixed expenses of that kind; as to the expenses of going to and from the practice grounds there are many corps that would not accept anything of the kind.

2560. Would your suggestion assume something of this form, that the expenses connected with the persons of the volunteers should fall upon themselves, but that those which may be called general expenses, affecting a whole company or a regiment, should be borne by the Government?—That would be a very good definition in the cases of corps composed of the better classes, but I wish to encourage the working men to join who cannot afford to pay the expenses of going to and from the practice grounds.

2561. You consider that greater pecuniary assistance should be afforded to companies or regiments composed of the artizan classes than to those which consist of a different class of persons?—Yes; because if all the expenses of storehouses and practice grounds were paid, then those of the better class would not accept assistance to enable them to go from point to point; but the working men cannot afford that expense.

2562. Can you throw out any suggestion by which that distinction between advances to be made to artizan companies, and the more limited advances to be made to others can be carried out?—I am not prepared at present to do so.

2563. I think you stated that you thought the expenses which indirectly fall upon the officers have a very considerable tendency to prevent young men who would make good officers from undertaking that duty?—Yes; with regard to the artillery in Liverpool, I think that the officers had to pay an entrance fee of fifty guineas, and the uniforms cost them 50l. I was told that one of them has to pay 15l. or 20l. per annum, and he says that he does not know what his liabilities will be when the men's clothes are worn out. I think that in these working men's corps in towns the men should find their own clothes, as they would take greater care of them. There were large subscriptions raised at first to furnish uniforms to the men, and the difficulty now is felt when the uniforms want renewing.

2564. Do you think the volunteer movement was conducted on rather too extravagant a principle at its outset?—Yes; I think that the uniforms were at first most extravagant, and there are no people who require more checking in that way than working men. They are anxious to have expensive uniforms; that was one of our greatest difficulties; but I believe there is an end of it now, and they are all looking for economy. About from 50s. to 3l. is the outside price now.

2565. Has there been an unwise system of expenditure in other things, such as costly rifle prizes, and expensive entertainments, and so forth?—No, I think that the rifle prizes have done a great deal of good, but the cost has not generally come out of the funds of the companies.

2566. Are not the officers liable to considerable calls of an indirect compulsory character, but which are seriously inconvenient, to find prizes for rifle shooting?—In our neighbourhood they have not been, as the prizes have been quite voluntary; I do not think that in our neighbourhood there has been any compulsion on the officers, or that they are considered bound to contribute to prizes.

2567. Looking to the general prospects of the volunteer movement, and the danger to its efficiency which appears to arise from considerations of expense, do you think that we are proceeding upon a wise and prudent system in giving valuable prizes, consisting not solely in the honour of success but in their intrinsic value, calling your attention also to the system of entertainments and various other sources of expenditure?—I think it would be better not to give prizes of too high a value, and that they should think more of the honour of gaining them. I can give you an instance of that; after the Cheshire county meeting I gave 10l. to my sons to be divided into 50s. and 1l. prizes and so on, and the men were just as well pleased in gaining those prizes as if they had been of much greater value, and I believe that volunteers generally of the better class would look more to the honour of gaining the prizes; as to the entertainments I do not exactly understand what that refers to.

2568. It is pretty well known that a considerable amount of expenditure occurs throughout the country in connexion with the entertainments when volunteers assemble together, which, perhaps, partially falls upon each man, but in a larger degree upon the officers; and subscriptions are also raised from the surrounding public. Do you not think that those entertainments have been hitherto carried on on too expensive a scale?—As far as I know of the working men's corps, and of the parties originating them, we have agreed to pay all those expenses and have had to pay for them if there has been a review. Take Chester for example, to which the Cheshire volunteers go once a year. Lord Westminster said that he would only sanction one review a year, looking at the expenses of men going there. I do not think that there is any extravagance among the volunteers generally who pay their own expenses.

2569. Is it your opinion that the feeling in which the volunteer movement originated is as active and strong now as it was?—I think that if there was not a dread of being called upon for the expenses I have named there would be as many as ever, so far as I can judge in our neighbourhood. In the neighbourhood of Birkenhead they are much more efficient from the practice they have had, and there would be no difficulty in getting plenty to join if it was not for the expense.

2570. You think that the patriotic feeling in which the movement originated remains undiminished, but that its practical development is seriously checked by prudential considerations having reference to the cost incurred?—I think so; as to the officers that is a very important point; many men who go in as officers do not attend to it; men in business generally cannot do so, but the dread of expense keeps out many young men of character who would be very valuable officers.

2571. Can you form anything like an estimate of what amount per head defrayed from other sources would remove the difficulty you have spoken of?—I think about 25s. or 30s. per head. I have gone into the matter with the officers of some of the companies; two of my sons are captains, one in the men's corps connected with the works, and the other is a captain of a company in No. 1 Cheshire rifle company, and both of them seem to consider that about that amount would be sufficient.

2572. Considering your own well-known zeal in promoting the efficiency of this movement, and at the same time considering the duty which rests upon the

J. Laird, Esq., M.P.

17 June 1862.

P 3

J. Laird, Esq., M.P.

17 June 1862.

Government as to the administration of the public funds, is it your opinion that the Government would be justified in advancing 30s. a head to assist the volunteer movement?—I think they would be amply justified, and that it would be about the best expenditure that ever was made. From the communications that I have had with various classes of persons, gentlemen and tradesmen, with clerks and mechanics of all sorts, I am satisfied that among the working men the movement has had a beneficial effect; I mean in this way; instead of going, after leaving their work, about, not knowing what to do, they have had their drill to attend to, and it has excited a feeling of emulation among them when they went down to practice; when one man shoots a little better than another there is a little talk about it, and it has improved the men in the yard generally. Among the apprentices I have suggested the plan I have referred to; there are many apprentices who are very active and fine young men, and they are receiving 6s., 8s., and 10s. a week, and you cannot expect them to pay for their clothes; and I thought by giving them some encouragement of the kind, if they attended to their drill well for twelve months, and were steady, and conducted themselves well in their work, it would be a great boon to those young men, and it would be money not thrown away by the establishment to which they belong.

2573. Do you think that the discipline connected with the volunteer movement, exercises a valuable moral influence upon the habits of the parties who join it?—That is my own opinion. My son, who has the entire charge, as captain, of them and is more among the men than I am, quite concurs in that view.

2574. Do you think that it further exercises a beneficial influence upon their social relations and their respect for the institutions of the country?—Yes, I think that it has a very beneficial effect in that way; they seem to consider now that they are contributing their time and their money, and that they are doing something towards the defence of the country.

2575. I think I glean from you that the volunteer movement has been of great value beyond the fact of originating a means of protection against external danger?—Yes, I have always thought so since 1859, and I am the more impressed with that from being urged or rather forced into taking up this cause by the anxiety of the men themselves who were anxious to join a rifle corps or an artillery corps. I spoke to my sons about it, and we thought it better instead of going elsewhere to give them an opportunity of joining their own people in the works, about two years and a half ago, and I believe that it has had a very beneficial effect upon the men themselves, as it has set an example to the rest of the men in the works. If one of the corps became a drunkard or bad character they would not keep him in the corps.

2576. Upon these joint considerations you have no hesitation in recommending further Government aid in support of the volunteer movement?—I think it would be the very best laid out money that the Government could expend.

2577. In that case do you think that such further advance by the Government would necessarily carry with it an obligation on the part of the Government to look more closely into and interfere more directly with the organization and discipline of the volunteer force?—I do not think that there would be any objection to any assistance being given which should be in proportion to the efficiency.

2578. I am rather directing your attention to what would be the correlative duties of the Government, in case of their advancing largely for the support of the force, would it not impose upon the Government the obligation of looking more closely into and interfering more directly with the discipline and efficiency of the force?—I think if the corps were reported efficient when inspected, that would be quite sufficient without interfering any more. I should not like to see more interference with it; I think it would prevent parties coming forward to join.

2579. But you think it would be right for the Government to require proper certificates from the proper officers as to the efficiency of the corps?—Yes; but I should not like continual interference with it. If, at the end of six months' time it appeared that a corps requiring assistance was not efficient or up to its drill, I do not think that they ought to receive assistance, and what I want to see is assistance given to make them efficient.

2580. I understand your view to be that assistance from the Government and efficiency in a corps should be intimately connected and dependent one upon the other?—Yes, I think so; and I believe that by affording moderate assistance you may spread a very good feeling among the working classes in this country.

2581. Do you think that the volunteer movement thus supported by the Government would further extend itself?—Yes, I believe it would, and that is the opinion of other parties who are connected in the same way with mechanics. I cannot but think that if more assistance was given you might obtain any number of respectable mechanics.

2582. Is the opinion which you have expressed before this Commission concurred in by the best informed and most influential persons in the neighbourhood with which you are associated?—Yes, all whom I have spoken to and who are connected with corps of mechanics think that assistance to the extent which I have mentioned would tend very much to promote the permanency of the movement; but they all think that any assistance should be combined with securing efficiency. I do not say in detail how that is to be done, but that the two should be combined. I may state also that some few persons desire to have as little interference by the Government as possible, but then I do not see that the thing can go on for a long time without further assistance. Men are likely to remain, consisting of the middle classes, if they can only be relieved of these extra expenses.

2583. But further Government assistance in support of the volunteer movement would be much approved by the intelligent classes in that neighbourhood?—Yes, taking the bulk of them. I have communicated with many of the leading men there, and they are of the same opinion.

2584. (*Lord Elcho.*) You have stated that you think it is desirable that the artizans should find their own uniforms?—Yes.

2585. As a test of their sincerity, and of their earnestness in the corps?—Yes.

2586. Should you see any objection to this, that they should find their first uniforms, and that those who prove themselves efficient and conduct themselves properly, should, if they wish it, receive a second suit gratis?—If a man has conducted himself well for three years, and is willing to go on, that is a point for consideration, but the clothes would not belong to him in that case.

2587. Would you see any objection to such a course as that?—If a man has been three years in a corps, I think it is very desirable to continue him on, if you can do it; but I am afraid the amount required to supply uniforms would be larger than would be obtained from Government.

2588. (*Chairman.*) You think that 25s. per man would not cover that expense?—Yes.

2589. (*Sir A. Campbell.*) Are there any other items of expenditure besides the expense of conveyance to the practice grounds and drill grounds from which you would propose to relieve the artizan corps but not to relieve the wealthier corps?—I have stated before that with regard to the better classes I do not think that they would wish to be relieved from those expenses, but the working men cannot afford to pay for more than their clothes, in addition to giving their time.

2590. Are there any other items that you think the wealthier classes should still pay and the artizans not pay?—There are the expenses to and from the practice grounds, and refreshments and things of that sort; for instance, if the men were to go down to the Rock Fort, which is four miles down the river, in that case we always take a steamer.

2593. Do you consider that the expenses may be divided into three classes; one the expense of the uniform, which I think you said they would defray themselves; another, the expenses of travelling, which you think should be defrayed by one class and not by another; and a third, consisting of the remaining regimental expenses, of which you think your corps should be relieved?—Yes; we find accoutrements for our men, but it is a question whether the Government should not find them, as well as arms and ammunition.

2592. The third class of expenses, which you think your corps should be relieved from, would require from 25s. to 30s. per annum per effective man?—According to the best information I can get that would be required to defray the second and third class of expenses and to insure the permanency of the movement.

2593. Can you put before the Commission the grounds upon which you have formed that estimate, for it is higher than former witnesses have given?—I can make out a statement and show that.

2594. (*Viscount Hardinge.*) What do you suppose that in fact it costs a working man to belong to a volunteer corps, excluding the loss of his time, and the expense of his uniform?—I will prepare a statement in answer to that question.

2595. Do you think that a working man would prefer to be relieved from those incidental expenses rather than be clothed by the commanding officer or the Government?—I think that it creates a better feeling in the men when they find their own clothes; I do not think that as a general rule they like to be clothed.

2596. (*Lord Overstone.*) Suppose an artizan was to join the regiment in which you take an interest to-morrow, and his clothing was found for him, how much do you think at the end of six months he would be out of pocket?—I cannot go into the details of that, but I can obtain from two or three sources the details and send them to you.

2597. (*Viscount Hardinge.*) You do not think that the enrolment of these working men has in any way interfered with the recruiting for the line or the militia?—These men would have nothing to do with the militia; there was a great dread of these things in 1859, and there was a fear of having working men among the volunteers, but that has died away. Some of these men are getting 30s., 40s., and 50s. a week.

2598. What is the lowest rate of wages that they receive?—Perhaps 20s.

2599. Are you aware that there are working men in the militia in the county of Northumberland who earn 20s. a week?—I do not know that, but if you get men to join volunteer corps and find their clothes they are certainly quite above the class who join the militia.

2600. (*Chairman.*) You have spoken I think of two different classes of uniforms, one costing three guineas and the other two guineas?—I think that about 3l. or guineas is the cost of the artillery uniform. I spoke of the engineer corps in Birkenhead, and the engineer corps have a very good uniform; red tunic and blue trowsers, and exclusive of accoutrements they pay 50s. for it.

2601. (*Sir A. Campbell.*) Is it not the case that one of the corps at Birkenhead was armed by contract before the Government supplied arms, and that some of the men obtained arms for themselves and others did not?—At first they had to find them and then I think they were given out by the Government.

2602. Is it not the case that the arms were in store, and that they were issued upon two principles, one that the men took them to have the use of them, and the other that the remaining part of the corps paid for them to the commanding officer, and the rifles became their own property?—I think that they found them themselves; there were some corps that were found in that way, and then the Government found them all.

2603. Might not the same principle be applied to the clothing, if corps were clothed by contract and those who chose to provide their own might do so, while others might receive them as the property of the Government, the names of the two different classes of persons not being known except to the commanding officer?—I think it ought to be on one principle in the same corps, and not one class of men paying and the others not.

J. Laird, Esq., M.P.

17 June 1862.

The witness withdrew.

Captain JOHN MACGREGOR examined.

2604. (*Chairman.*) You command a company in the London Scottish Volunteers?—Yes; and I am musketry instructor of the corps.

2605. I believe you can speak to the moral effect which the volunteer movement has had upon the character of the men?—Yes.

2606. Has it had a beneficial effect?—Yes; with respect to all those of whom I have heard, and I have had a large correspondence on the subject with volunteers in England, Scotland, and Wales, and the colonies.

2607. Will you state to the Commission what you think the effect has been?—I think that the volunteers have been brought into association with classes they never would have met with otherwise, that they have had qualities in themselves developed that never would have else had play, and that they have had subjects placed before them that they never considered before, that discipline, cleanliness, order, punctuality, promptitude, and obedience have been imparted to them in such a manner as could not have been done by any other means whatever; but I might perhaps save the time of the Commission by handing a copy of a paper on this subject which I read last week at the Social Science meeting; it is to be found in the *Volunteer Service Gazette* (*handing in the same*).

2608. You put that paper in as representing your views upon the moral effects produced upon the men in the volunteer force?—Yes, upon the moral, social, and hygienic effects. The moral effect is produced by wearing uniform, by submission to another's will on parade, by forming good habits, and making new acquaintances, by restraint on time, temper, energy, and general behaviour, by emulation and speedy reward of good conduct, as well as rebuke of neglect, by the influence of educated men, by the sense of engaging seriously in a patriotic and manly movement for one's country, by intelligent admiration of the regular army, and a perception of the difficulties to be met by those who rule large bodies of men, by taking part in public business, by managing funds, rooms, halls, shooting ranges, and meetings. The effect is seen in volunteers who are less idle and dissipated, and more respectful to authority. It is seen in the public, who appreciate the necessity and advantage of armed defenders. The social effect is more various. Many relations and friends of the men reluctantly acquiesce in the loss of their society at home, and grudge the expense of time and money incurred by volunteering. The effect upon the volunteers' health seems to be very beneficial. In reply to about 300 letters on this subject, I find an almost unanimous testimony to the improved carriage, condition, appetite, and activity of the men. The parade drills give exercise to many who would otherwise be sedentary. The march out to country places gives fresh air; the shooting requires temperance, and even hard training of the body, which is further developed by the boxing, fencing, and athletic classes. Several

Capt. J. Macgregor.

P 4

Capt.
J. Macgregor.

17 June 1862.

instances are mentioned where casinos, dancing saloons, skittle alleys, billiard rooms, and similar places have been closed by the absence of the custom of men who once frequented them, but who now give their days to shoot, and evenings to drill, and find pleasure in band music or chorus singing.

2609. (*Lord Overstone.*) What is your impression as to the present state of the volunteer movement; do you anticipate any serious difficulty in maintaining it in a state of permanent efficiency?—I think that the force is more efficient than I could have expected, or than we ought to expect it to be at this period, and as to its permanence I am surprised that the force has not declined much more than it has, and I think that nothing would cause it to decline more rapidly than to fear that it is declining, any unnecessary fear or any unnecessarily expressed fear upon that subject would have a very prejudicial effect.

2610. By unnecessarily expressed fear I presume you mean an expression not founded on facts?—I mean any expression of fear which is not almost compelled by the circumstances.

2611. Do you not think that whatever may be the state of feeling as to the volunteer movement, the wisest course in the end will be to ascertain it accurately, to set it forth correctly, and to meet it, whatever it may be, distinctly?—I do most certainly; but first of all to arrange in one's mind, or begin in the minds of the country, a standard, and to say that everything that does not come up to that in numbers or efficiency amounts to a defalcation, would be, I think, rather to find the accuracy of a mistake than the accuracy of truth.

2612. I wish to know whether you think the present volunteer movement is at present declining, and if you think it is declining to what causes do you attribute it?—I think that the volunteer movement was impelled by several different forces, and that some of them have come to an end, and that others which were not fully recognized at first, and which are more permanent than the former, must and can be kept up for ever in England. I think there are two sets of purposes that bring men to volunteer; one is a desire to have a connexion with military efficiency and a soldier-like character, and the other is that part which may be called the amusing, social, and healthful recreation: the bands, the uniform, the marchings out, the parades, and the shooting; and I think that this latter part has to compete with other amusements, which may compete successfully when the novelty of volunteering has gone. But I think that the military part cannot be supplanted by any other amusement or engagement, that has the same features, in a like degree, and therefore will suffer little from competition. The military spirit I think has increased in England, and will continue to do so.

2613. You think that the volunteer movement had its origin in two sets of feelings, one of which was in its nature temporary and transitory, and the other set in motion by causes which were deep and permanent?—Yes.

2614. Do you think that the transitory causes are essentially transitory, and that it will be idle to make any attempt to give them permanency?—I think that the transitory causes are at any rate intermittent, and that they are of a different order from those which are permanent; they appeal to different feelings and to a different class of men.

2615. Do you think that there are any circumstances which are now apparent in connexion with the volunteer movement which make it desirable that any new or additional steps should be taken by the Government with respect to them?—Yes.

2616. What are they?—I think that in the first place the Government should look upon the movement, as the volunteers will have to look upon it soon, as one to be estimated by the number of enrolled men, men ready to serve, ready to drill, men who have shown that readiness by coming forward once at least to become efficient; neither the force nor the Government ought to look upon the movement as to be measured by the number of men who, after the excitement is subsided, continue to drill and maintain their efficiency; therefore I think that Government supervision and Government aid and the public approval should be given, not in proportion to the size of a battalion as it appears at present, but in proportion to the number of men attached to it, who have already once become efficient, and who could be summoned at any moment. I think that one of the most valuable things for the Government to do with regard to the public and the volunteers is to preserve those men who have once shown themselves patriotic and energetic in the position in which they are, and not to let them dissociate themselves from the corps and be in shops and places of business as if they had never connected themselves with the force. As far as recruiting goes, much will depend upon what is reported to their neighbours by those who have been once efficient volunteers, but who do not now come to drill, perhaps with sufficient or at least cogent reasons. To ignore those men because they are now absent would in my opinion be a great mistake.

2617. You are aware that this Commission originated in a considerable degree in the prevalent feeling that Government assistance, in a pecuniary form, beyond that which is now given, was desirable for the volunteer movement, are you of that opinion?—I think that men coming forward and giving time and energy for a national purpose, expect that those parts of the apparatus which they use in connexion with their duty, and which will not end with them or even with their successors, are to a certain extent national capital, and ought to be supplied by the nation.

2618. Will you specify a little more clearly what you mean?—I will begin with the butts, targets, and rifle ranges generally; then there is the rifle itself, which can be transferred to another, the orderly room or office, which is also a permanency, and the adjutant and paid serjeants, to connect the force with the Government through an official agency. Upon the question of supplying uniforms, I can only speak as to the corps I belong to.

2619. Will you state your impression upon this subject as to those corps of which you have had personal experience?—I think that a great number of men would leave the corps in which the clothes were supplied by the Government, but I think on the other hand that a great number would come into a corps in which they were supplied by the Government, and if we meet both those cases it must be by supplying those who wish for it, and not infecting as it were the whole corps with the appearance of being clothed by others. It appears to me that a man who has been effective for one year, and who is also effective in the second year, ought if he chose have assistance to a certain extent, 2*l.* or 2*l.* 10*s.*, for a new uniform, not his first uniform; I think that this plan would be recognized as a totally different thing from buying men's service by putting them into Government coats.

2620. (*Col. MacMurdo.*) You think that the men have earned that?—Yes.

2621. (*Lord Elcho.*) It would be a pledge that a man was earnest in the work if he was made to bear the first expense himself?—Yes, and by being effective he shows that he has bought his uniform, and has worn it out in public service.

2622. (*Viscount Hardinge.*) How do you define the term effective?—If I may be permitted to say what I think upon that I should divide our force as follows: We have effective men who are continually effective, and effective men who were once very valuable and effective, but who are not now connected with us, and thirdly, the recruits who are not yet effective. I think that those three require to be considered separately. There is at present nothing to encourage a volunteer in the ranks, after he has become an effective, to go any further forward in his drill, and therefore nothing to encourage him to attend to anything except the social and amusing part of it; many men in the ranks are unable to become officers, and unwilling to become serjeants. If such a one knows how to be a right or left file, and how to right and left wheel, and the manual and platoon exercises, he in fact knows all the drill of general battalion movements, so far as a private is concerned. When such a man finds that, however good he may become, he has men on both sides of him who drag down his excellence to the level of their mediocrity, no reasoning will convince him that he ought to spend valuable hours waiting until such persons become equally good drills with himself. There is a natural desire of the the nation, the Government, the volunteers, and especially of their commanders to represent at inspections two things which I think cannot be seen together in volunteers; the one is number, and the other efficiency. In the regular troops the men who are inspected can always attend, and their number and efficiency can be tested together, but with us, when our efficiency is tested at an inspection, our numbers are the most; and therefore our efficiency is the least, and unless we can exhibit our numbers and our efficiency separately, I think we never rightly test either of those qualities, and the men are not satisfied nor the Government informed. I should propose to the Commission this addition to our present system, that the inspection, which after all is the occasion that the volunteer commander labours for, should be only a drill of simple movements where the Government officer can see every enrolled member, not keeping away those who are bad at drill; but as tho regiment and the commander would not be content with that, there should be on certain occasions in the year, two, three, or four battalion drills, at which select companies of men, selected and formed into companies from each of the different corps, should be put into one battalion, and he supposed to come there ready to do everything, and without excuse for mistakes, so as to have every encouragement for firstrate drilling. These men so selected, say two companies from one corps, one company from another, and three or four from another, would have such a feeling of competition that it would inspire as shooting inspires, and encourage a great deal of practice. The other members of the several corps would look on, and would desire to be worthy to enter into such companies, and to be present on such occasions, and would therefore necessarily attend drill. This appears to me to be the most practicable manner in which, with a little change, a natural desire for excellence in drill must be encouraged. I beg also to add that some encouragement ought to be given to excellence in file and volley firing. Individual firing will always be sufficiently improved by private means, and associations supplying prizes; but so far as I am aware there have been as yet no regular competitions for file firing or volley firing, and while these would bring many inferior shots to practice, they would in fact encourage that kind of shooting which would be most required if the volunteers were ever called into active service.

Capt. J. Macgregor.

17 June 1862.

The witness withdrew.

Adjourned till Friday next at half-past 12 o'clock.

Friday, 20th June 1862.

PRESENT:

Viscount EVERSLEY.
Earl of DUCIE.
Viscount HARDINGE.
Lord ELCHO.
Lord OVERSTONE.
Mr. BOUVERIE.

Lieutenant-Colonel BARTTELOT.
Lieutenant-Colonel Sir A. CAMPBELL.
Lieutenant-General Sir G. A. WETHERALL.
Major-General EYRE.
Colonel MACMURDO.
Major HARCOURT.

VISCOUNT EVERSLEY IN THE CHAIR.

Captain JOHN GEORGE BLACKBURNE examined.

2623. (*Chairman.*) You command the 31st Lancashire Rifle Volunteer Corps?—Yes.
2624. Is that a consolidated battalion?—It is simply a corps without an adjutant, or without any connexion with other corps.
2625. I observe that you muster about 220 men?—Yes.
2626. Do you find that those men attend their parades regularly?—No; we muster, as a rule, about two-thirds.
2627. How often have you musters?—Every fortnight; every month we have a compulsory drill, and in the intermediate fortnight an undress or company drill; at which the three companies are sometimes worked singly, and sometimes together.
2628. What is the compulsory drill?—It is one that every member should attend, or pay a fine.
2629. Are those fines levied when the men are absent?—Yes, and they are enforced whenever a member leaves the corps.
2630. You have stated that you have no adjutant?—Yes.
2631. Have you a drill instructor?—We have one.
2632. Have you any assistance from the adjutant of another corps?—None.
2633. Have your men passed through a course of musketry drill?—Not the whole of them; our serjeant instructor is not qualified to put them through a complete course.
2634. I presume you can speak to the state of the volunteer force in Lancashire from your acquaintance with that county?—I think I can generally, but more especially as to my own town; because it is a matter which has occupied my attention considerably since I first entered the force; and I am very anxious that it should be put on a solid foundation.
2635. Do you think that at the present time it is not upon a solid foundation?—Yes.
2636. Will you state why you think it is not so?—In the first place I think that the volunteer force, in my district, certainly never can be placed on a solid foundation so long as you have to obtain subscriptions from the men in addition to the time they devote to drill.
2637. What is the amount of the subscription that you call for from the men?—In the first company we had an entrance fee of two guineas, and a guinea annual subscription. In the other companies the amount was 30s., including the first year's subscription, and the subscription at present is one guinea per annum in all the companies.
2638. Those subscriptions, I presume, constitute your regimental fund?—Yes, each company has its own fund, and each captain is responsible for the ordinary clothing and equipment of his company, and the three companies contribute in equal proportions to the regimental fund.
2639. What expenses are defrayed out of the regimental fund?—All the general expenses—every thing that may be termed regimental; for instance,

Capt. J. G. Blackburne.

20 June 1862.

Q

Capt. J. G. Blackburne.

20 June 1862.

the cost of the rifle range, the cost of the armoury and the drill room, as well as the extra cost appertaining to the instruction of the men, and the cleaning of their arms.

2640. Are the arms all kept together in the armoury, or are they left in the hands of the volunteers?—They are all kept together; I have never allowed them to be taken out, except by permission occasionally and in special cases.

2641. What expenses are defrayed out of the funds raised in each company?—The clothing, and other incidental expenses, which I can hardly enumerate; a variety of small matters appertaining to clothing, and accoutrements, and the keeping of the company generally in working order.

2642. The clothing is not paid for by individuals, but is paid for out of the funds of the company?—It is paid for entirely out of the funds of the company, and each company's fund has been assisted by subscriptions which were originally obtained from the public in the town. We had great difficulty in the first instance in establishing the corps at all on account of the opposition that was offered to the movement by those who are known as the peace party, and the chartists, who attempted to make it a political movement. I succeeded, by dint of sheer reasoning, to obtain the sanction of a public meeting, and for some time I laboured with one company under considerable disadvantages on account of the opposition of the above classes, who are numerous in that district.

2643. Has the same opposition to the volunteer movement prevailed in other parts of Lancashire?—It has not to the same extent. In Rochdale the same parties prevailed, and they refused the sanction of a public meeting for the establishment of a corps; but I believe that Rochdale was the worst place in Lancashire, and that Oldham was the next.

2644. Are you of opinion that these corps cannot be maintained unless they are assisted?—Certainly.

2645. Is that the case with other corps in the same county?—I think it is universally the case with the other corps in Lancashire, with one or two exceptions, one of which I will refer to. It is possible that the 1st Manchester corps might be able to maintain itself, inasmuch as that corps consists of a different class of men, upon the whole, compared with the Oldham men. They consist of a class of members who are more like some of the London corps, the Inns of Court, for example; some of them are certainly not composed of so good a class of members as the Inns of Court, but they are very much better than the ordinary corps.

2646. I think you stated that you had only one drill instructor for the whole of your corps?—That is all.

2647. Is he qualified to drill them properly in musketry, and to give them a proper amount of instruction?—I think not; I sent two serjeants down to Hythe for the purpose of obtaining instruction, and one of them went to obtain a certificate as serjeant instructor. Both of those serjeants distinguished themselves, one of them became the first marksman in the class (the ninth), and the other one, who was more fitted for serjeant instructor, became the best judge of distance in the class; he was a 1st class shot, but not a marksman.

2648. (*Major-Gen. Eyre.*) Are they volunteers?—Both of them, and at present I am in correspondence with the War Office on the subject of the latter one not obtaining a certificate, which we are all greatly surprised at, as he is a young man who has given a deal of attention to the subject, and seems to be perfectly acquainted with the whole theory and practice; but he has not obtained a certificate, which would enable him to do that by authority which he now does almost by courtesy.

2649. (*Viscount Hardinge.*) Do you mean a first-class certificate?—No; a certificate only as serjeant instructor; he only went for that, for he has been through two classes there; and when he first went the certificates were not then given on any terms to volunteers, but subsequently an announcement was made to

the effect that volunteers who wish to obtain certificates as serjeants might do so by staying after the expiration of any class, and undergoing an examination for the purpose.

2650. And to be entitled to draw the same amount of pay as that which is allowed to all the paid serjeants?—No, we do not want any pay; only a certificate. All that he wants is his certificate; we want no pay for him.

2651. (*Sir A. Campbell.*) It is a course, is it not, intermediate between the long and the short course?—It is termed, I think, the short course.

2652. (*Major-Gen. Eyre.*) What is the volunteer's name?—Serjeant John William Blackburne.

2653. (*Chairman.*) I understand you to say, that in order to place your corps and the corps in your neighbourhood on a solid foundation, some assistance is required from the public. In what way do you think that assistance ought to be given?—That is a matter upon which I have really not formed a positive opinion, i.e. as to the best way, and I therefore can give no answer to the question that would be any guidance to this Commission. I think, as I have stated before, that in order that the volunteer force should become a force of any value at all, and permanent, the men must not have to contribute anything; it is impossible to keep up a force like this upon the same plan on which you keep up a cricket club, or any similar kind of club. After the first enthusiasm of the men has passed away that is after the first year or two, and when they have learned nearly all they can learn, the only men who will remain in the force will be those who have become fair shots, and who consequently have a chance of entering into competition and showing themselves fit to compete for the various prizes. It is quite evident to me, that another great object with reference to the volunteer force at present, and one that is necessary in order to place it upon a better basis, is that the 14 days' notice should be done away with; I think that most of the men when they enrol themselves at first would enrol themselves for three years on certain conditions; those conditions being that if they could show to a board composed of their own officers that their circumstances were so changed, or that it was necessary in order to carry on their employment that they should go to other towns, or anything of a similar kind, showing that a complete alteration in their circumstances had taken place, which would justify them in withdrawing they would be released. If they knew they could do that, I think they would enrol themselves for three years, provided that they would not have to pay anything; but the 14 days is a very great objection, inasmuch as after a man has attended the requisite number of drills, and has made himself pretty perfect, and is then found fault with, perhaps, by one of the non-commissioned officers, or some other little disagreement takes place, he at once makes his bow and retires, and you have no remedy for it but to put a recruit in his place, and begin again.

2654. (*Lord Overstone.*) As I understand your evidence, the solid foundation upon which you think it necessary that the volunteer force should be placed means greater certainty as to their pecuniary resources?—Certainly.

2655. Supposing you were to receive a communication to-morrow from the War Office stating that, understanding you found a difficulty in maintaining the efficiency of your company, they were prepared to assist you, and wishing to know what you desired they should do, what answer would you give?—I should say, pay all the expenses that really belong to the instruction and maintenance of the force, and let the officers and honorary members meet all the expenses of the bands and other things which might be called unnecessary for the maintenance of the force. To the Government I should say, "You must pay "that which the men will otherwise have to pay, "or which will have to be paid out of their subscrip- "tions," or failing that will have to be obtained by going round with a collecting box, or having theatrical amusements or bazaars, and all those things which, I think, are degrading to the force, and to the state.

2656. I think you stated that your corps consisted of 220 men?—Yes.

2657. Do you consider that those 220 men are now in a state of good and efficient military discipline?— I do; I am satisfied that with a week's continuous drill at any time, the whole of the three companies could be put into any battalion or any brigade whenever they were required, and that they would go through the movements quite in unison with any other corps. I am not comparing them invidiously with the line, but in some points, for instance in the manual and platoon exercise, I have observed many regiments, and am quite satisfied of the efficiency of my corps in that respect; and know that the men thoroughly understand the bulk of all the movements and all that is necessary to be known by them. There is more difficulty with the officers and non-commissioned officers than with the men.

2658. Do you feel confident in case of the rifle volunteer force of the country being suddenly called out for public duty, that all the men would be capable of joining in general movements in an adequate state of general discipline and of capacity for the use of their arms?—Yes, as far as my experience goes.

2659. (*Major-Gen. Eyre.*) What is their efficiency in the use of the rifle as marksmen?—They have not yet undergone a complete course of musketry instruction; we have hitherto been restricted to a rifle range of 300 yards, but we have now obtained one that will be from 900 to 1,000 yards. My men are not as yet so perfect in ball practice as many others, but many of them have done very well.

2660. Have all the men passed through the third class?—They have not, they are now passing through.

2661. (*Sir G. A. Wetherall.*) Do you think they could perform their duty well and be useful if they were called out?—I wish to say distinctly that the volunteers and officers in my corps, without any desire to make a comparison, are as good as, if not above the average, but then I speak generally. I wish also to say that in my opinion the officers of volunteers should not have commissions granted to them so easily as they have now, and that before being granted to them they should pledge themselves to remain in the force for at least three years, and that twelve months after they have been in the force they should be bound to obtain a certificate of their fitness for the discharge of their ordinary regimental duties. I do not mean such an examination as officers in the army have to undergo on military subjects, but sufficient to ensure their fitness for the discharge of their duties on parade and in the field. I believe that if that was done the *status* of the officers would be altogether improved, and it would become, still more than it is at present, an honour to belong to the force.

2662. (*Lieut.-Col. Barttelot.*) Do you think that the officers have improved during the last year, compared with what they were when you first know them?—Very much so, and many of them are endued with a very strong sense of the responsibility of their position, and are gradually becoming what they ought to be and what the Government ought to expect them to be.

2663. (*Sir G. A. Wetherall.*) Of what classes are the three companies composed?—The great bulk of them are artizans. We could have a strong efficient and regular force in the town if the men had not to pay an entrance fee to begin with, and had not to pay subscriptions; they would willingly give their time and take a pride in belonging to the force, provided they were exempt from money payments.

2664. Have you observed any improvement in the social habits of the artizans since they became volunteers; do they attend more regularly to their work, and are they more sober and orderly in their conduct?—I cannot give a positive opinion upon that head, beyond what I have learned from some of their employers. Our late mayor spoke at a public meeting upon the subject, and he stated that at first he had objected to the volunteer movement, for fear it should lead men to contracting looser habits, but he was very glad to find that he had been mistaken, and I am happy to be able to say that I have not had, with one or two exceptions, any member of the force brought in any shape before the magistrates or the public.

2665. (*Major-Gen. Eyre.*) From the kind of assistance that you recommend to be given to the volunteer force, I conclude that you would disapprove of a capitation grant?—No; I reserved my opinion upon that point, and I stated that I was hardly qualified to give an opinion upon it: perhaps a capitation grant would be the easiest mode of giving it; but whether or not it would be the best mode of giving it I cannot say.

2666. (*Sir G. A. Wetherall.*) Are all your companies clothed alike?—They are.

2667. (*Lord Overstone.*) Is it your opinion that if the volunteer force were relieved from the pecuniary charge which they now have to meet the number of the force in the neighbourhood of Oldham would be largely increased?—I think it would.

2668. On what principle or motive do you think that that large increase would arise?—From the natural pride of belonging to the force, which cannot at present be gratified, and referring to the men who would join but do not on account of their inability and unwillingness to part with any money.

2669. By natural pride do you mean a feeling of superiority over those who are not in the force, and which is engendered by the fact of their being seen in a military costume, or do you allude to any other feeling?—I believe it is that to a great extent. At the time when the volunteer force was first organized there was then considerable reason for it; the whole feeling was a popular one, of banding together for the defence of the country. I believe that that feeling exists to a very great extent among the artizans in the manufacturing districts, and that it would be encouraged if they found themselves noticed more particularly; I do not mean by being flattered or praised for the manner in which they perform their evolutions, because that I very much object to unless they are really very good, but what I mean is that by making them a distinct class, and making them feel that their services were acknowledged and valued, and that they felt they became a superior class of men altogether to their fellows by being admitted into the corps. It should be a privilege and distinction to enter it.

2670. I understand you to mean that there is a spirit prevailing among the artizans in Oldham and the surrounding neighbourhood, and a desire to enrol themselves for the defence of their country in case of need, and that that spirit would be gratified if it were recognized by any acts of a complimentary kind on the part of the Government or the public?—Yes.

2671. They would feel a pride in being enrolled for the defence of the country?—Yes, and if the country was in danger our number would be quadrupled.

2672. Do you think that that feeling would be weakened or increased in proportion as the force was more and more intimately associated with the regular force of the country?—I think it would be increased the more that it was associated with the regular force of the country.

2673. Do you think that they would still feel a patriotic pride in the sense that they were becoming more and more identified with that regular force, and were being organized for the defence of the country? —I think they would; their importance and usefulness would be more evident.

2674. (*Major-Gen. Eyre.*) You have spoken of the strong feeling of opposition that you had to contend with at the beginning of the volunteer movement, is that feeling now worn out?—In twelve months after

Capt. J. G. Blackburne.

20 June 1862.

Q 2

Capt. J. G. Blackburne.

20 June 1862.

we had established one company, there came gradually a general change of feeling in our favour, and some of the influential men in the district gave in their adhesion to the movement, and we then raised two more companies, thus proving that such was the case; and also proving that the conduct of the first company had been such as the town generally approved of.

2675. The volunteers have reconciled the public to the movement altogether?—Yes, the volunteer force now is a popular force in Oldham, and any small thing that is done by way of recognition of it always meets with the support of the public.

2676. You stated that you would not allow the arms to be left in the possession of the men, although it is commonly the case that the men have them in their possession; why do you object to it?—I object to it for this reason, that the commanding officer has the responsibility of the charge of the arms, and I think that they are always kept in better order when they are under my control and when they are in the armoury. It is not with any invidious feeling against the men, but I think that it is an imprudent thing to allow the side-arms especially to be in the possession of the men, who like other men may sometimes get too much ale, and might sometimes get into a brawl; but when the arms are kept in the armoury I am quite satisfied that if there is any fighting going on it will not be with those weapons, which should be kept for other uses.

2677. (*Viscount Hardinge.*) Have you a range?—Yes, we have now got a range, which is nearly completed, by private arrangement. I have got one, and we hope to get about 900 or 1,000 yards in it; it has been inspected and approved.

2678. (*Col. MacMurdo.*) You have already got a range of 300 yards?—Yes.

2679. (*Viscount Hardinge.*) What has been the expense of the new range?—It has not cost much yet, but it will probably cost about 250*l.* to put up a butt and fence it in.

2680. Have you had nothing to pay for land?—Not yet; we are only able to obtain the land on lease for 14 or 21 years at an annual rent.

2681. Have you stated how the expense of the clothing in your corps is defrayed?—Yes, it is partly by public subscriptions, and partly by the entrance money and the subscriptions of the men.

2682. What is the entrance money and the subscriptions?—The entrance money and the subscription of a man who enters now when he takes one of the cast off uniforms, or the uniform of a man who has left the corps, is very little,—about 1*l.* or 30*s.*

2683. Not for a new outfit?—No, he takes another man's outfit, he supplies his vacancy; the original entrance money was, for the first company, three guineas, and for the other two companies 30*s.*

2684. Do you find no difficulty in inducing new recruits to take the clothing of those men who have resigned?—I have in my own company very few who have changed, in the third company many have changed, but there has been no difficulty in that company as the captain reports to me.

2685. Have you a balance in favour of the corps?—Yes, we have; with a great deal of care we have had a balance at the end of each year.

2686. Do you find that there is any falling off in the subscriptions and donations from honorary members?—Not with regard to the subscriptions hitherto, many of them have duplicated their donations and their subscriptions, but like most other subscriptions they are very precarious, and we have always to go to the same people for money.

2687. In what shape would pecuniary aid relieve your corps in the most satisfactory way, in clothing, or in meeting other incidental expenses, or what may be termed the regimental expenses?—The expenses of the corps consist in providing an armoury, and in providing a rifle range; those are the constant expenses, and in providing uniforms, which is only an occasional expense, and those are the three main items which I think should be provided for by the Government if they wish to keep this force as a permanent one, leaving the officers' subscriptions, which are considerable in my corps, and which accounts for the balance in hand, to meet all the other incidental expenses. The annual subscriptions of the officers in my corps are 25*l.* for the captain commandant, 20*l.* for each of the other captains, 15*l.* for the lieutenants, 10*l.* for the ensigns, 3*l.* for the serjeants, and 30*s.* for the corporals.

2688. (*Viscount Hardinge.*) Are you speaking of the annual subscription?—Yes; but besides that, of course the officers are called upon for a variety of other things, such as prizes and other matters; but I do not ask, on the part of the officers in my corps, to be relieved from any of these expenses; we are willing to contribute, but we cannot get in the subscriptions of the men, and we do not like to be always begging from those who have helped us heretofore.

2689. Do you propose that the Government money, if it should be advanced, should be expended in defraying the expenses of armouries, rifle ranges, and uniforms, which would relieve you from the necessity of calling upon the men to pay any subscriptions?—Yes, that is my proposition.

2690. (*Sir G. A. Wetherall.*) If the Government provided places for arms and rifle ranges, would your subscriptions enable you to keep them up without requiring any further assistance from the Government?—That would depend entirely upon whether those rifle ranges were purchased, or whether they were subject to an annual rent. In my case I shall have a rifle range subject to an annual rent, and with regard to the buildings we found that there was very great inconvenience in having to depend partly upon the generosity of some parties in lending us rooms to drill in, such as school-rooms; and the inconvenience at a variety of places, arising from our having to go there, that we got up a company among the officers chiefly, in order to enclose a parade ground, and to build a small armoury, and drill room. We raised about 900*l.* in shares for that purpose, and took a plot of land which we have enclosed, near the centre of the town. There will be an annual rent, therefore, for this also.

2691. (*Major-Gen. Eyre.*) If the volunteers obtained the assistance that you would recommend the Government to afford, I suppose they would readily meet the expense of going to and from the shooting grounds, and on field-days?—That, I think, the subscriptions of the officers would cover. I think when they are not summoned to any review by order of the Government, when it would be an official matter and form an exception to the rule, this is one of the things which the officers and honorary members would pay. I think that they should pay for all those things which are not really necessary for the efficiency of the corps.

2692. (*Earl of Ducie.*) You have stated that it was possible there would be a considerable increase in the number of the rank and file, if a certain amount of Government assistance were afforded?—Yes; but I did not mean to imply that I should encourage or wish for a great augmentation in numbers. I should seek rather to maintain something like the present force; and I would limit it to some fixed number, and not encourage a great influx of members. I think that every corps ought to have an establishment entitling it to the services of an adjutant, but beyond that I do not think it is desirable to increase the number of the force.

2693. In the event of any of the present officers being removed, do you anticipate any difficulty in supplying their places?—I do not.

2694. Although the expenses which fall upon them are rather unusually heavy according to your statement?—I do not know at all whether that is so or not; I cannot speak for other corps.

2695. (*Lord Elcho.*) Referring to the subscriptions which you require from the officers in your corps, do you think that has prevented you from getting better men than you have as officers, but who could not afford the expense?—I think not.

2696. You do not think that that has been a bar in any way to your getting good officers?—Not in the slightest degree in my case. Where I have had the option, I have chosen the officers by my opinion of their fitness for their posts, and I must say for them that they are quite as good officers as could be chosen in the town.

2697. Do you think that a supply of efficient officers ready to come forward and able to pay these large subscriptions will never be wanting?—The more permanency that you give to a corps, the better you will make the whole movement, and the more certain you will be to retain your officers; the enforcement of a certificate alone from the officers would so rouse their *amour propre* that they would be more attached to the force, and you would be certain to have more regular men in it than if you leave it in its present unsatisfactory position.

2698. (*Earl of Ducie.*) What is the population of Oldham, and the area from which you draw your men?—I should think the population of the area from which we draw the men is about 60,000.

2699. You draw from that number 220 men?—Yes.

2700. Therefore the number of men drawn, relatively to the population, is very small indeed?—Yes, very small.

2701. It is much smaller is it not than in other places?—Much smaller, and that arises partly from the reasons which I have given you, partly from the original opposition offered to the movement, and partly from the inability of the men, particularly at this moment, to pay any entrance money.

2702. Do you not think that the small proportion of officers and men to so large a population, enables you to find officers who are able to bear these very heavy expenses?—I do not think that the officers, as a body, consider that they do bear a very heavy expense; notwithstanding the amount, I think that they pay their subscriptions cheerfully, but they do not like, in addition to that, to have to take the trouble of sending round to the men, or of calling them out for their subscriptions time after time; that is a very annoying thing to the officers.

2703. (*Lord Elcho.*) Are you acquainted with any other corps in your district in which the same system prevails, and where such large annual subscriptions are paid?—Yes, many.

2704. And with equal success?—Yes.

2705. Can you give the names of them?—I am afraid I cannot at this moment, but I do know that there are several near to us who do so.

2706. (*Viscount Hardinge.*) I presume that these officers, according to your scale of subscriptions, are not called upon for any further expenses, such as giving regimental cups to be shot for?—Indeed they are; in the first year, when there was one company, we had no fixed subscriptions from the officers beyond the ordinary subscriptions and the entrance fee, but they subscribed for the band, and for certain other purposes they subscribed also. There were half-a-dozen different subscriptions, and in order to put an end to them all, and to enable a man to know when he came in what it would cost him, I laid down a scale, and the officers have all agreed to that scale, and most of them have come in having a knowledge of it and agreeing to it.

2707. What does it cost an officer now to hold a company in your corps?—I think it costs him about 50*l.* a year. I always consider that it costs me 50*l.* a year at the least, independent of uniform, horse, &c.

2708. (*Sir A. Campbell.*) If you do not obtain such relief as you have suggested, what amount of falling off in the number of your men do you anticipate?—I think it is very probable that my corps will be reduced, when the uniforms are worn out, to one-fourth or one fifth of its present number.

2709. Can you give the Commission any information as to the effect that will be produced in other corps in your neighbourhood, by the same cause?—I think that upon the average the same observation would hold good throughout a great proportion of the manufacturing districts.

2710. (*Lord Overstone.*) You have stated that you do not wish to see any large increase in the numbers of the volunteer force, but you rather contemplate keeping them at something like a fixed number?—Yes.

2711. Would you regard that fixed number in the light of a nucleus, round which, in case of a serious emergency, a larger number of volunteers would assemble?—Certainly; and it was for those reasons that I have defended the volunteer movement at public meetings, at which I have stated that that was one of my principal reasons for commencing the volunteer movement in Oldham, so that when an emergency did arise we should have any number of men ready to meet it; and I can say honestly that in the manufacturing districts of Lancashire men would enrol themselves rapidly, if there was any necessity for it; but there would be no use in their doing so unless there was a staff, and a nucleus round which the men could be rallied and made useful.

2712. Supposing it was known throughout South Lancashire that Liverpool was seriously menaced by an invading force, do you think, under those circumstances, that the artizan class, in common with others, would rapidly augment the numbers of the volunteer force?—I have no doubt of it, there are no more loyal men in the kingdom.

2713. Supposing under those circumstances that your corps, now consisting of 220 men, was augmented to 500, how long do you think it would be before those 500 men would become as efficient as the present corps of 220 are?—If they could be brought together and worked continuously, I should say, giving a rough estimate, perhaps six weeks or two months; it might possibly take less.

2714. (*Col. MacMurdo.*) The time depending upon the amount of assistance afforded by the Government for instruction?—Yes.

2715. (*Viscount Hardinge.*) In all probability under such serious circumstances as those, the new recruits who would join the volunteers would be kept to drill every day, as the old volunteers were in the time of the war, and consequently you would in all probability be able to bring your new recruits into a state of efficiency in a smaller space of time than you have mentioned?—I think so. It was for that reason that I qualified the opinion which I gave when I said that it might take less.

2716. (*Lord Overstone.*) I understand your opinion to be that a certain number of the volunteer force, kept in a high state of discipline now, would be a nucleus round which, in case of a sudden emergency, a very large number might be rapidly collected, and brought rapidly to a state of efficiency?—Yes.

2717. You believe that the spirit and feeling which pervades south Lancashire would facilitate that operation?—Yes.

2718. (*Major Harcourt.*) You would prefer in a time of peace to have a small efficient nucleus, but you would also retain a larger number of men less effective?—Yes, I should. I think it is far better that this force should be regular in its numbers and that it should become a privilege to belong to it, so that every member connected with it, whether in the ranks or holding a commission, should feel himself honoured by belonging to such a force. There is one point that I have not yet alluded to, but which I think is a very important one, and it is that all members of the force, when effective, should be exempted from serving in any civil office. Upon a recent occasion, since I have held a commission, I was summoned to serve as a special constable, upon the occasion of a religious riot; it was a serious matter, and I went before the magistrates, who had called out a considerable force of special constables. I employed a solicitor; but although he could find me no real exemption, the magistrates after hearing me, not only exempted me from serving as a special con-

Capt. *J. G. Blackburne.*

20 June 1862.

Q 3

Capt. J. G. Blackburne.
20 June 1862.

stable, but all the other volunteers as a matter of equity and courtesy. I think that the volunteers ought to be exempted from serving any of these civil offices while they are performing their duty in a military capacity.

2719. (*Col. MacMurdo.*) You mean that they should be exempted from serving as constables?—I mean that they should be exempted from all civil duties, such as juries, constables, overseers, and the like. We all seek to make the force permanent;—when I say we, I speak of myself, and those especially who promote the force;—we all seek to give permanency to it by offering inducements, in addition to the ordinary one of patriotism, to men to join the force and to remain in it. If a man was exempted from performing these civil duties in the same manner that a soldier is exempted from them while performing his duties as a soldier, it would be no cost to the country, while there could be no harm in allowing an exemption among so large a population. It is a very great hardship to a man engaged in a small business to have to go, say, to the Manchester or the Salford sessions, and remain there for a week at his own expense, or to go to the Liverpool assizes for a like time. If a man, by being exempted from these duties when he was serving as a volunteer, and if, after 10 or 12 years' service, he was exempted for life, he would have a great inducement to join the volunteers, and to remain in the force, in order to obtain that permanent exemption. There are innumerable things in manufacturing towns to which men are liable, but which are not felt in large towns; for instance, a man is called to serve on a coroner's jury, or he is sent to the assizes, and all these things are a very great loss to him.

2720. (*Major-Gen. Eyre.*) If all the population were to become volunteers, how would you get those civil duties then performed?—I stated specially, before I expressed that opinion, that I would limit the number of the volunteers; I would say, for example, in to take my own town, suppose that I had 400 men enrolled, what difference would it make out of a population so large, consisting of say 60,000 people including women and children? It would be nothing, while it would be considered a great boon to the volunteer force.

2721. (*Lord Elcho.*) You have stated that you thought the force ought to be limited to its present numbers?—Yes, I think that is desirable, because I wish it to be made a permanent nucleus, and not an uncertain force moving up and down and influenced just by the whim of the moment.

2722. Your view is, that if a man volunteers to perform military duties, he ought to be relieved from civil duties?—Yes, during the time that he performs his duty as an effective volunteer, and then after his service, for a certain number of years, I think he should be exempted for the remainder of his life.

2723. (*Lord Overstone.*) You think that if he is called upon to protect the country from external danger he should be exempted from the duty, which is common to all of us, to preserve internal peace?—I think that it is quite inconsistent with the duties of a volunteer to act as a special constable. He cannot obey two authorities.

2724. (*Chairman.*) Are you aware that he is already exempted from that?—I am informed that it is not so. I do not think that he is exempted from serving as a special constable, and I should like to allude further to the subject of serving as special constables. As I understand it, the volunteer force is not to be called upon to suppress ordinary riots; it is only to be called out to defend the throne of Her Majesty, or to assist in repelling invasion; and I think that as that is so, and as it is precluded from being called upon to suppress any internal riots, it is very important indeed, to prevent them from being classed with a very useful body of men, and to prevent them from incurring the risk of participating in the unjust odium attached to that class, I mean the yeomanry. I think that it is a very unfair thing to take a man and strip off his uniform, and make him serve as a special constable, and it is not right to put him in that position; he does not feel himself in his own place when acting as a special constable; he feels a sort of degradation in being made a special constable, while he is apt to be pointed out as a volunteer by the populace, and his duties in the two cases associated together. Every care should be taken to prevent such a result and to prevent even the most ignorant of the population from viewing the volunteer force as a civil force.

2725. (*Major-Gen. Eyre.*) Do you think that the volunteers at all interfere with the recruiting for the militia?—I think that the volunteer force do not interfere with the militia at all, as they are drawn from quite a different class of men; the militia are drawn by bounty and by pay, and they are drawn from a very much lower class than the volunteer force could be under any circumstances. I cannot conceive, therefore, how the two forces could be in opposition, for that reason.

2726. (*Col. MacMurdo.*) Is the time of your serjeant instructor fully occupied?—I think not. I was asked whether we had only one serjeant instructor, and said that one was sufficient with the exception of musketry instruction. That I think is quite a different branch; one serjeant instructor for three companies is plenty in all other respects.

2727. That is the regulation?—Yes.

2728. I wish to know whether the time of your serjeant instructor is fully occupied?—It is not.

2729. What spare time has he?—He has the bulk of the day time to himself except on Saturdays when the parades occur.

2730. Do you think it would interfere with the discharge of his duties to the corps if he were allowed to engage in any other trade or occupation?—I think that that would be very undesirable he should do so.

2731. For what reason?—I think he ought to be perfectly independent of any trade, and should not be in such a position that a volunteer might go to him for anything whatever, that is to say to purchase as a customer; I think he should be perfectly independent of that.

2732. You are of opinion that such a principle as that would be wrong?—Yes; and I think the present one is quite right.

2733. You think that if a serjeant instructor were allowed to engage in any trade or occupation it would be liable to abuse?—I think so.

2734. (*Major-Gen. Eyre.*) Do you feel yourself armed with sufficient authority as a commanding officer?—I do.

2735. (*Col. MacMurdo.*) Do you find any difficulty in controlling the serjeant instructor?—I have experienced none.

2736. Some witnesses have stated that they desired to see one uniform system of discipline, do you find any want of that?—I entertain the opinion that the present system is amply sufficient to keep up the force if the commanding officers will only pay attention to their duties, and exercise those duties with discretion and enforce the rules of their respective corps.

2737. Are not the duties of commanding officers defined?—I am not aware that they are specially defined, but I find no difficulty, and I see no difficulty in the organization of the corps at present.

2738. You think that the power of the commanding officers, and the code of discipline are sufficient for the force with its present constitution?—Yes; with the 14 days; you have no hold upon the men beyond that, and you must rule the men with judgment, or you cannot rule them at all.

2739. (*Sir A. Campbell.*) You would propose to substitute three years' enrolment?—Yes.

2740. How would you apply that to the members of the existing force?—I think that if the Government gave assistance to the force, they ought to have in return a force for giving that assistance, and that is why I say that they ought not to be called upon to incur great expenses per head for these men, unless there was a certainty that they would have these men as a nucleus, and that such nucleus should not consist partly of old volunteers and partly of recruits.

2741. How would you get the men to be attested for a longer period?—They can leave at 14 days' notice as it is, and if there was a new law, it should be quite optional to them either to remain as they are, and find their own accoutrements, or enter for a longer period; I should make it a condition that those men who enrolled for that time should not be called upon for subscriptions, and that certain exemptions from civil offices should be extended to them, as I have before stated.

2742. (*Earl of Ducie.*) You would then have two classes in the service; the short service men and the long service men?—Yes; take, for instance, the 1st Manchester, which I happen to know; they might, but I do not say they would prefer remaining under the short service, and find everything themselves.

2743. (*Col. MacMurdo.*) Do you think that you would have a greater hold over the volunteers if they served for a longer period?—Yes, I think so.

2744. You would not have any greater power as commanding officer over a volunteer who served for the longer period than over the others?—No power certainly in addition, but he must obey orders; and if enrolled for the longer period he must not leave on any freak of his own while I think that his pride would induce him to remain in the force and become efficient, but at present, if a man happens to be lazy, or disinclined to do this or that, and thinks the discipline too severe for him, or the parades too frequent, or something of that kind, he leaves at 14 days' notice.

2745. If he were lazy under the shorter period of 14 days, he would probably not be more diligent under the longer period?—I think he would; when a man may be called to the front for negligence in his manual exercise, or for any of those things, such as non-attendance, and reprimanded, you would have, I think, a much better hold over him. Most men court praise among the class from which volunteers are drawn.

2746. If it were a case of non-attendance, how would you call a man to the front if he did not choose to attend the parades?—You could not in that case, and there will be always some difficulty of that sort in connexion with a volunteer force. I do not see any way to placing the volunteer force under such a state of discipline as you can enforce in the regular army, or in the militia, whom you pay. I think that is impossible.

2747. You think that you would have a greater moral hold over a volunteer whose period of service was long rather than short?—Yes; I think that rules might be made and adopted which would place them on a sound foundation in this respect.

2748. (*Lord Elcho.*) By rules adopted by corps do you mean fines for non-attendance?—Yes, partially.

2749. Do you at present impose fines in your corps?—Yes.

2750. Do you enforce them?—Yes, we do.

2751. Are they heavy?—They are rather heavy, 6d. in the 2nd and 3rd. companies, and 1s. in the 1st, for non-attendance every fortnight.

2752. If a man does not attend parade once a fortnight, he is fined 6d. or 1s. according to the company in which he happens to be?—Yes, it is always booked against him, and sometimes the fines are collected. We have never brought any man before the magistrates, but whenever a man leaves the corps he is called upon to pay all his fines.

2753. Are those fines effectual?—No; sometimes they are not, but they are a considerable advantage nevertheless. I can give you an example: I had a lazy man in my company who never kept his uniform in order; it was the worst in the corps, and he seldom attended parade. I fined him, and his fines amounted to 1l. 19s., which he paid up before he left the corps.

Capt. J. G. Blackburne.

20 June 1862.

The witness withdrew.

Lieut.-Gen. EDWARD PERY BUCKLEY, M.P., examined.

2754. (*Chairman.*) You command the Wiltshire Rifle Volunteers?—The South Wiltshire.

2755. Is that an administrative battalion?—Yes.

2756. Of how many companies does it consist?—Nine.

2757. How many men do you muster altogether?—There are about 700 on the list, but we never get that number together.

2758. How often do you have battalion drills?—Last year we had three, but this year we have only had one.

2759. Can you muster all the men at the battalion drills?—By no means. I have never mustered 400, and the reason will be readily seen; it is owing to the very extensive area over which the battalion is scattered; there is the whole of the south, Trowbridge and Bradford in the north, in order to equalize the numbers, and the consequence is that when they meet they have to come by railway, and when they do meet some of them who are at a considerable distance have to travel both by road and by railway, and the expense of coming to any one point is large, and it is a consideration to them; then, again, they like to meet at different places and not always at the same place; and if I assemble them at Salisbury, those from Bradford and the north have a long way to come; and it is not only the expense, but the short time that can be allowed for them; the railway companies make no very great difference in the fare for taking them backwards and forwards, and the consequence is that I have never had more than 400 assembled together. I think it is more important that the battalion should meet for battalion drill than to have 7,000 or 8,000 assembled for a great review.

2760. Have you many opportunities of seeing your companies?—I have occasionally visited some of them separately; but the companies are so completely corps, under the commanding captains, that I have nothing to do with them as companies; they are entirely under the dominion of the captains. When they are together I command them, and I have a great deal of correspondence to carry on.

2761. Have you calculated what the expense is of bringing your men together?—Yes; it varies, and depends upon the place at which they meet; but, taking it at the most central place, which is Warminster, the last time that they came there, it cost them about 46l. in different expenses, calculating it at so much a mile, and supposing each company to have mustered 50 men.

2762. (*Viscount Hardinge.*) Was that money expended for refreshments?—No; merely the expense of the journeys, they probably took refreshments with them. I do not think that they can be calculated; they ought to take them in their haversack. If they came to Salisbury, which is an extreme point, or Trowbridge, or Bradford, it would be more.

2763. (*Major-Gen. Eyre.*) Does each man pay for that himself?—Yes; but occasionally the captains have made it up, as they do not like the men to be at that expense.

2764. (*Viscount Hardinge.*) Is it not the practice in your battalion to defray these expenses out of the local funds of each corps?—They do that sometimes; some of the companies have not attended, and they think that it ought not to come out of that fund. Lord Edward Seymour's company did not attend on the last occasion, which is one of the most efficient companies. He said that it ought not to come out of the fund, and they did not come.

2765. Do you think that is a legitimate way of spending the funds of the corps?—I think that there

Lieut.-Gen. E. P. Buckley, M.P.

Lieut.-Gen.
E. P. Buckley,
M.P.

20 June 1862.

ought to be some provision for it. I think it is hard to expect every man to pay each time, for they are not like the corps in London, who are well to do; they are little tradesmen. Some are very efficient men, but they do not like to pay the expenses of their journeys three or four times a year.

2766. (*Chairman.*) Have you any battalion fund?—No.

2767. Do the men in your battalion clothe themselves?—I think they did in the first instance, but now the clothing is getting rather shabby, and that is a difficulty, and they rather make it a grievance that it is an expense to them.

2768. When the clothing requires renewal, do you think there will be any difficulty in renewing it?—I think they will do that, but I think they are rather holding back now in the hope that something will be done.

2769. Are all the companies provided with ranges?—Yes, I think they are; that they do themselves.

2770. Are those all paid for out of the funds of those companies?—Yes, except what is allowed by the Government; some of the captains pay, one does not know what, but some of them pay for a drill instructor, and they are at considerable expense individually.

2771. Did you ever hear complaints made of the expense of those ranges?—No complaints have been made to me.

2772. (*Earl of Ducie.*) I believe that the geographical conditions of your district enable you to obtain ranges rather more easily than in other counties?—Yes, from the nature of the country, being very open.

2773. (*Lord Overstone.*) You have stated that your corps consists of about 700 men in round numbers?—Yes.

2774. But you seldom or never get 400 men together?—I think I have never had 400 men together.

2775. These men are drawn from a very extensive area throughout Wiltshire?—Yes.

2776. What, in your opinion, would be the efficiency of a corps consisting of 400 men, whom you draw from a very extensive area, in case of a sudden demand for their services to resist invasion?—I think they would be very efficient; the chances are that they would be got together a little time before, and when they were together I think they would be very efficient.

2777. Do you anticipate any difficulty in bringing together to one point those men?—The railroads are so convenient that there would be no difficulty in assembling them in the county at a very short notice.

2778. Upon the supposition that either Liverpool, or Portsmouth, or Bristol, was suddenly and seriously menaced by a foreign invading force, do you think that your corps could be brought to the assistance of the regular army to protect those places expeditiously?—They could be in a very short time, owing to the railways, say in a few hours.

2779. Your opinion is founded on your military experience, that that body of men would be useful and valuable for the purpose of internal or national defence?—Most decidedly so.

2780. Are you able to extend that opinion more widely, and to pronounce it generally with respect to the effect and character of the volunteer movement?—Yes, I should say that the force would be very efficient, and could be got together in a very short time. I think you might get very valuable assistance from them; but I have had no experience in my own battalion, for I have not seen it out more than once or twice. I was only appointed at the beginning of last year.

2781. Can you express any opinion as to the present state of efficiency of the volunteer force generally as to their discipline and their capacity to use their arms?—There was a review the other day at Bristol of about 8,000 men, and the report that I received from my adjutant was that the men were exceedingly efficient, and went through their manoeuvres very well; that their discipline was everything he could expect.

2782. What is the largest number of the volunteers that you have personally seen together?—Except in London I have never seen a large number together.

2783. Then you cannot, from any personal observation of a large number of the volunteers brought together, pronounce an opinion as to their fitness to act as a combined body?—No.

2784. But you think that the discipline, so far as it has come under your notice, is sufficient to enable them to render valuable service in case of external danger?—I certainly think so.

2785. (*Viscount Hardinge.*) Would it be possible or advisable to put the volunteers, in the event of any further aid being given by the Government, under a stricter system of discipline or a greater amount of military control?—That, I think, is rather a difficult question to answer; for I think if you attempted too much discipline, or put them too much under the control of the military authorities, you would, perhaps, lose a great number of men.

2786. Do you think that the authority of the colonel commanding an administrative battalion is sufficiently defined?—It is hardly defined at all. I believe they have very little power.

2787. Your authority as colonel commanding a battalion is, in a great measure, confined to your being on parade yourself?—Yes, I am told that I have not the power to punish a man, supposing a necessity should arise, and that it must be done entirely through the captain of the corps.

2788. Do you see your way to giving the colonel a greater amount of authority?—No; I think that when they are together the colonel exercises such a degree of influence that they are all perfectly ready to be amenable to any wish that he has.

2789. That would, of course, depend upon the good feeling that existed between the colonel and his captains?—Yes.

2790. Do you think that the returns of the effectives and the non-effectives in each corps, as far as you are aware, have been correctly made?—Yes; I think they have.

2791. You do not think that men are returned as effective, who are really not so?—I think not; they are those who have gone through a certain number of drills.

2792. Do you think that if further aid was given by the Government a fewer number of drills than 18 or 24, as now prescribed by the Act of Parliament, would be sufficient?—Perhaps they might, if the men could meet oftener than they do now.

2793. You are aware that at the present time 18 or 24 drills are necessary to constitute an effective?—Yes.

2794. Would a fewer number of drills be sufficient?—I can hardly speak to that point; I do not think they would attend very regularly the whole of them, for their time is so much taken up; I can hardly say.

2795. Might not the Government fairly say, if we give you further aid we may fairly expect you to continue as efficient a force as you are at present?—Yes.

2796. (*Chairman.*) Is there any mode which you can suggest by which you think the efficiency of the volunteer force can be maintained or improved?—I think, as far as my experience has gone, that if the travelling expenses of going backwards and forwards were defrayed to a greater extent by a fund given to captains of corps to be used for that purpose, making them render an account of how it was expended, and in certain cases to clothe some of the men, it would be a good thing.

2797. Do you mean a capitation grant to be given to the commanding officer of each company, or each battalion, and that it should be limited to certain expenditure, and that the officer to whom the money was entrusted should render an account of the way in which it had been spent?—Yes.

2798. Would you limit that grant to the number

of efficient men on the roll?—Yes; and I think it would be a good thing to do it, as it might cause a certain number to attend oftener, and thereby increase the number of the effectives.

2799. What should you consider the best test of the effectives?—The number of times they had attended at their drills.

2800. And a certificate, I presume, that they could perform the manual and platoon exercise?—Yes.

2801. And that they had passed through a course of musketry instruction?—Yes; they are obliged to do that now before they can be returned as effectives; they must go through a certain number of drills.

2802. How many drills do you think it is necessary to enforce upon the volunteers?—I can hardly say, but I think that what they go through now is sufficient for that purpose.

2803. Are they not rather more than sufficient for the purpose?—If they attend every one of them perhaps they might do with fewer, but I think that if they attended a fewer number of times more regularly that might do.

2804. (*Major-Gen. Eyre.*) To entitle them to be called effective, do you not think that a certain amount of target practice should be made a *sine qua non*?—I think so.

2805. To go through the 3rd class, at all events?—Yes.

2806. (*Viscount Hardinge.*) In your companies, I suppose the attendance at target practice counts as a drill?—Yes, I suppose so, but I have very little to do with it; that does not come under my notice; that is attended to by the captains of the companies.

2807. (*Lord Elcho.*) You have stated that you think your men are now holding out'with reference to renewing their clothing, in the hope that something will be done?—Yes.

2808. Is there a feeling on the part of your men that their clothing ought to be provided for them?—I think there is a sort of feeling that something more ought to be done for them; I think they have a disposition to make a little growling until something is done, and I was obliged to check a little feeling of that kind. I reminded them that they had enlisted as volunteers, and that they must not look too much to the country for assistance.

2809. If this Commission should recommend that a certain sum of money should be given to the commanding officer, of which he might expend a portion at his discretion in clothing, do you think that the men would think it at all derogatory to receive clothing in that way?—No, not in the country battalions, if it were done judicially; some would not accept it, but others would be glad of it.

2810. (*Lord Overstone.*) Do you think that the demand for assistance from the Government arises from a feeling that the present cost is troublesome to the volunteers, and that it does not emanate from a feeling amongst them, that if they give their personal services they are entitled to expect the country to meet the expenses?—I think that they have got to know their own value a little, and that the country looks upon them as very useful, and therefore they think that something ought to be done for them to repay them for their services.

2811. Do you think that the demand for pecuniary assistance proceeds to a considerable degree from the feeling that they are entitled to an equivalent for their services to the country?—Yes, to a certain extent, but not entirely an equivalent; they expect that certain things will be given to them that they may not be entirely out of pocket.

2812. (*Viscount Hardinge.*) Do you think that the allowance made to the adjutant is, generally speaking, sufficient?—No, certainly not; he has a great deal to do, and I think that he is very ill paid; he is always going about, and he stated that if it were not for the hospitality of the different captains he should be out of pocket; but when he goes to visit the different companies and he cannot get back that night, they take him in, but except for that his expenses would be very considerable.

2813. Does he keep a horse?—No; I think he hires one.

2184. Can he reach his companies principally by railways?—Mostly, and his horse is of very little use to him in visiting the companies, except one or two of them.

2815. Can you state whether he visits the different companies once a month, or is that not the average?—He visits them, I think, certainly once a month; he is obliged to make a return as to how often he visits them; a quarterly return, showing how many times in the course of a quarter he visits them.

2816. He cannot receive his pay without making that quarterly return?—No, and he is always visiting them; he constantly writes to me, telling me where he has been, and in what condition he finds the different companies.

2817. (*Sir A. Campbell.*) Does he give the musketry instruction as well as attend to the drill?—Yes, he has been down to Hythe; he takes the general superintendence. There is great difficulty in getting the companies to wear a uniform of the same colour; every company differs from the rest. I have had two meetings, and at the first meeting they agreed to my proposition, that at the end of three years they would adopt the same colour. At another meeting, which had reference to what that colour should be, there was a small majority in favour of its being a uniform colour; but they do not seem to like to abide by that; having begun with one colour, they are very jealous of being made to take another; and again, a man now joining a company does not like it, and selects a different colour from that which the rest of them wear, as he will be singular.

2818. Would it be possible, do you think, for the lord-lieutenant to take up that matter, and decide what the uniform colour of the company or battalion should be?—I think that that is the only way in which it could be done, if it were done judiciously; after ascertaining in the first instance what colour they liked, then to say that that should be the colour worn. I do not think they like the idea of changing. I believe Lord Winchester, in the first instance, looked into the thing, and he ordered one colour to be worn.

2819. Are you aware how that has worked, and whether there has been any dissatisfaction expressed at the decision?—I fancy not; I have not heard of it.

Lieut.-Gen. F. P. Buckley, M.P.

20 June 1862.

The witness withdrew.

Lieutenant-Colonel EDWARD MOSELEY PERKINS examined.

Lieut.-Col. E. M. Perkins.

2820. (*Chairman.*) You command an administrative battalion?—Yes, I do.

2821. In Durham?—Yes.

2822. Of how many companies does that battalion consist?—It consists of 10 companies, actually.

2823. What number do you muster together?—Our last quarterly return shows a strength of 770 effectives, the maximum establishment being 1,105; with 11 companies, but there is one corps of four companies, which consists, in point of fact, only of three.

2824. Do you find that you muster anything like that number at the battalion drills?—We muster very well on certain occasions, but our corps are too far apart to muster in great strength frequently; for instance, at the review which took place at Lambton park the other day, we mustered 620 men, but that was a great occasion; our average attendance, I see, is about 200.

2825. Do you visit these separate companies and inspect them separately, as well as drill them together in battalion?—Yes; the adjutant goes once a week, and I go to visit them as frequently as I can.

2826. Do you find that you have sufficient autho-

R

Lieut.-Col. E. M. Perkins.
20 June 1862.

rity as commandant of the battalion?—Quite so; I never have my authority disputed for a moment in any way.

2827. Have you a battalion fund?—We have not; There is no battalion fund, but the expenses of battalion meetings have hitherto been defrayed by the officers of that corps at or near whose headquarters the assembly takes place; with the exception of the expenses of the transport of the corps to the place of meeting, they have always been defrayed by the officers of the respective corps.

2828. You mean the officers of each separate corps?—Yes.

2829. Are you aware whether they have a fund in each of the separate corps?—In two of the corps they certainly have what may be called a public fund, but in the other corps the expenses fall almost entirely upon the officers, and their more immediate friends. The 7th corps in the city of Durham has many honorary members in it, I believe so many that they get a good deal of money. I do not know what their financial condition is precisely. The Beamish corps is the 10th, and that is maintained almost exclusively by the officers and their immediate friends. The Chester-le-Street corps have a public subscription, and the other corps are almost entirely composed of workpeople employed in the manufactories in the neighbourhood of the Tyne, and the proprietors of those works, and the officers and their more immediate friends, pay whatever deficiency there is short of the subscriptions.

2830. Are the men clothed principally at their own expense?—Some of them are clothed at their own expense, but in the artizan corps I have always found that whenever they are clothed nominally at their own expense eventually there is a public subscription required to pay for the clothes; the men start in debt, and they have no opportunity of ever getting out of debt again.

2831. Has each of these corps a rifle range of its own?—Yes.

2832. And an armoury?—Yes.

2833. Are those paid for out of the funds of the corps?—Yes, out of the general funds of the corps.

2834. When the clothing of your men requires renewal do you anticipate that there will be any difficulty in renewing it?—I anticipate very great difficulty in all the artizan corps, for it will throw too great a burden upon individuals and the men cannot afford it.

2835. The individuals to whom you allude I presume are the officers?—Yes, and their immediate friends. Sometimes they get up amusements, and they beg of the public in one way and another; by a return that I have received to-day I perceive that one corps has made a great deal of money in that way, but it is not a very pleasant thing to turn one's self into a temporary publican.

2836. Do you think that you lose the services of a great number of efficient men who would act as officers, owing to the great expense that they would be liable to?—I think that it does deter many persons from joining who would otherwise join, but I think that we have an ample number of officers, if they would only learn their duties; I think that the question of expense deters the men more than the officers.

2837. Have your officers put themselves under the orders of any military authority, or have they been attached to any regiment to learn their duties?—I do not think that any officer in my battalion, except myself, has ever been attached to any regiment of the line; I was attached to the 1st battalion of the 60th rifles, but none of the others have been. We have an adjutant and a drill instructor to each corps, and as a rule, I consider that the officers in our battalion are a very good average sample.

2838. Do you pay the adjutant more than he receives from the Government?—Nothing.

2839. Or your drill serjeant?—The drill serjeants receive a small pay in addition to what they receive from the Government and rather more than we expected, because we thought that they were to have billet money, which has since been deducted by some subsequent order.

2840. Do you think that the corps under your command require assistance from the public to enable them to maintain their present state of efficiency?—I do not hesitate for one moment to say that it is of vital consequence to them to receive such assistance. I do not think that they want a very great deal more than they have, but they want something, and I think that they are entitled to it; I think that if they receive it you may have a permanent and very efficient force, but without that assistance I am afraid, with some exceptional instances, that the force will dwindle.

2841. To what extent, in your opinion, ought that assistance to be given and in what manner?—My experience has been obtained entirely in the working of an administrative corps, and not a consolidated corps; each has its own peculiar advantages and disadvantages, but my remarks will apply entirely to an administrative regiment; I think that if the volunteer force is to be made permanent, the whole of the equipment should be provided.

2842. (*Viscount Hardinge.*) Do you mean including the uniform?—Yes, I think that they ought to have a dress suit for great parades, and on great occasions, and the only way by which you can arrive at anything like a uniformity of colour is to have a colour fixed upon by the Government, and to say to the men "you must have that and no other, or else provide "your own." I think also that every man should have a fatigue suit, for we knock our uniforms about by learning drill in them frightfully, and have a great coat, or something of that sort, and a sufficient supply of ammunition. In an administrative regiment I think that there should be an allowance of some sort to meet the expenses of getting the corps together, for it is a very great expense to bring a corps together.

2843. (*Chairman.*) On all battalion field days?—Yes; in page 66 of the volunteer regulations, there are two letters, one written by the late Lord Herbert, and the other written by Sir James Yorke Scarlett, referring to the necessity of getting the men together; and if there is a necessity to get them together they are practically debarred from it by the expense of attending, and the organization in battalions is, so to say, rendered of no avail. I do not think that it need be very much. I have gone into the matter as nearly as I can so as to arrive at what it might be estimated at in an administrative battalion; and I think that there should be an allowance made for the expenses of assembling together, (which do not fall upon consolidated corps) of about 1s. 6d. per man on parade for eight battalion drills during June, July, and August, one of which should be the official inspection, provided that at least a certain proportion of the enrolled strength is present on the ground; that it should be paid to the commanders of the various corps comprised in the battalion by the commanding officer and the adjutant through official channels; I am satisfied that it costs 2s. a man, every time we assemble at battalion drill, on the average, for mere transport.

2844. (*Viscount Hardinge.*) How do you calculate that?—First, I take the railway fare and the expense of conveyances of one sort and another; I do not include any time in that calculation.

2845. Would it not be very difficult to fix upon any definite sum for different battalions, as they are so differently situated with regard to the radius of the distance from headquarters?—Yes; I think that ours are as well situated as any are.

2846. (*Col. MacMurdo.*) Your companies are all within 10 miles?—Yes.

2847. (*Viscount Hardinge.*) The sum that you would suggest for each effective would be applicable to your own battalion; but not to battalions generally?—There are some battalions that I think can hardly be got together at all; for example, there is the Northumberland battalion, of which Lord Tankerville is the commander, and I believe that some of those corps are an enormous distance from headquarters, with no railway communication for their accommodation; but the railway company, with us, will put on one special train at Durham, and that will go along the line and pick up all the corps at the various stations at an average of from 1s. to 1s. 6d. there and back.

2848. (*Lord Elcho.*) Has Lord Tankerville's corps ever been brought together?—I believe it has never been brought together. His inspection is coming off next month, and I think I heard him say the other day that he did not expect that the corps which was raised at Mr. Beamont's works, would be present on account of the distance from the point of assembly.

2849. (*Viscount Hardinge.*) What is the greatest distance from headquarters of any of your companies?—The greatest distance is nine miles; but as regards most of the corps we can assemble four, or five, or six companies always with very little notice, but they have to march some two or three miles. The corps that I am more particularly connected with, and which has been raised under my own eye, I think has only been by railway twice. They have marched on most occasions to the ground, on other occasions they have gone part of the distance in carts.

2850. What is the average distance that those companies who travel by railway have to march to the railway?—With regard to those companies at Washington and Felling, the railway goes within 200 yards of the armoury.

2851. Then those men have only the expense of their railway tickets to meet?—Yes.

2852. The other companies in your battalion are at the expense of going in carts?—Yes.

2853. How would you appropriate any aid that might be given, so much per effective to the different companies?—I think upon an average; for instance, when the battalion parade is near to the railway, the corps in the battalion which are situated on the line of the railway have little further expense beyond the railway fare out, when we have a battalion meeting in another direction, and the railway is not available, then they have to travel five or six miles, either marching or in carts so that the average expense of each corps would be about the same.

2854. You would arrange your battalion drills so as to make it equally fair to all?—We endeavour to do so. I have never had a full battalion parade near my own residence on that very account.

2855. Your calculation for each effective, the longest distance that any of your companies are from headquarters being nine miles, could only be made to apply to your own particular battalion?—Yes. I have no data to go by so as to form an opinion in respect of other battalions. The North-eastern Railway Company have been tolerably liberal with us; they take us at a single fare and they will put on a special train, which is a great convenience. I am speaking now entirely of my own battalion and other artizan corps. I think that as the men give their time that is all that can be expected of them.

2856. (*Chairman.*) You spoke just now of the equipment; what sum would you suggest as necessary to cover the expense of the equipment?—I think, as far as I can judge, although it is rather difficult to get at it, that the dress suit would average about 10s. 6d. a man per annum; and the fatigue dress about the same; it would, of course, be cheaper, but it would not last so long. A great coat or a cape would cost about 4s. a year per man, the belts would cost about 3s.; the ammunition is now supplied by the Government. But we should have more. Each enrolled member should have 150 rounds of ball cartridge, and 150 rounds of blank cartridge supplied to them per man, for I know the keenness with which the men go to target practice, and they attend ordinary parades very much better when they are going to fire than when no blank ammunition is served out. The adjutant costs about 6s., and if there is a drill allowance, it would come, I think, to 15s. per effective; we are found the serjeant instructor, and I think that in a large corps we ought to have a serjeant armourer. These two would cost about 15s. per man per annum. I think that it would save expense by having a man to attend in the armoury to clean the rifles; that at present is entirely done at the expense of the corps; and where men of that class take their rifles home with them, it is utterly impossible to keep them under proper supervision; a man, perhaps, does not come to drill for two or three months, and his rifle becomes as rusty as a gas pipe; most of the corps in my battalion, have all their rifles lodged every night when they come home, whether it is 10, or 11, or 12, or 1 in the morning; the whole expense of the above items is about 3l. 12s. per man per annum.

2857. (*Sir A. Campbell.*) Including what is already given?—This includes a good deal of what is given; the only thing that is left out is the rifle, and we know that the cost of that is about 4l. or not quite so much, and it lasts about 12 years, I believe. I do not think that our rifles will be effective so long, for we shoot so much more at the target than they do in the service, that the grooves of the rifle would get worn out sooner.

2858. (*Viscount Hardinge.*) How long do you calculate that your pouch belts will last?—I think they will last for from 6 to 8 years, depending, of course, entirely upon the care of the individual; some will last longer than others.

2859. What do you put them at with the waist belt?—15s. a set, that is what we paid for them; they are made of common leather and the pouches are made to hold 60 rounds.

2860. (*Chairman.*) Three shillings a year would about pay for them?—Yes.

2861. (*Sir A. Campbell.*) In what form would you suggest that this assistance should be given; in money, or in kind?—For the purposes of carrying on the affairs of the corps, I think it would be much better if it were given in materials, because then there would be some security that the money was applied to the purposes for which it was voted.

2862. (*Viscount Hardinge.*) Would you have the cloth issued in a piece?—I would have the clothing issued.

2863. (*Major Harcourt.*) What security would you have in that case that the men would not leave the corps in a fortnight, and take their clothes with them?—The same security that we have now; we should go after them, and take them before the magistrates, if they took that which did not belong to them.

2864. The clothes would remain the property of the Government, I presume?—Yes, the same as the rifles.

2865. Do you think that you would have any difficulty in getting the men to wear second-hand clothing?—No; they are frequently so clothed, speaking now of the artizan corps.

2866. You are speaking of the persons likely to require a uniform to be given to them?—Yes.

2867. (*Viscount Hardinge.*) If Government supplied the volunteers with clothing and accoutrements, do you think that would generally satisfy the wants of the force?—If the Government gave us clothing and accoutrements, and made some arrangement to provide for the expenses of getting the regiment together at battalion drills, I think it would. There is great difference of opinion as to the colour, but the feeling in our neighbourhood is so strongly in favour of scarlet that if the Government were to put us into that colour, and to provide the things I have enumerated, I think the difficulty would be to keep men out of the volunteers and not to get them to come in.

2868. (*Sir A. Campbell.*) If no such assistance is given, do you anticipate that there will be a falling off in your numbers?—Yes, I am sure of it; I should think that some battalions would become entirely extinct in a short time.

2869. But I am referring particularly to the battalion under your own command?—I think that

Lieut.-Col. E. M. Perkins.

20 June 1862.

R 2

would depend very much upon some few individuals, of whom I am one myself.

2870. You mean that it would depend how long their liberality would last?—Yes, and their general enthusiastic support.

2871. Do you think it is desirable that some prompt decision should be come to by the Government on this question?—I think that if a prompt decision were come to it would do a great deal of good, I think that if the men knew what they had to rely upon next year it would be of very great service indeed to the force, and I believe that if eight battalion drills were provided for in this way, or if a fixed number were provided for in this way, there would be a great many others provided for in some other way. I have a return from a little rural corps about five miles west from our head quarters, and I see that on two occasions they have had what they call a soirée in our part of the world, and perhaps the Commission would hardly believe that two soirées realized a profit to them of 137*l*. 18*s*., and a third 75*l*.

2872. (*Sir A. Campbell.*) But do you think you could reckon upon that sort of inducement being successful again?—No, it is only very exceptional where you can get that sort of thing done.

2873. (*Lord Elcho.*) Is it desirable, in your opinion, that the force should be dependent upon such a source as that?—Unquestionably not.

2874. (*Lord Overstone.*) Your corps consists of 770 effective men?—Yes.

2875. Am I right in understanding that the term "effective" is a technical term, meaning a man who has attended a certain number of drills, and that it does not necessarily follow that an effective is an efficient soldier?—It does not necessarily follow; it means a man who has attended a certain number of drills; I believe it also means that it exempts him from the militia ballot.

2876. The word "effective" is merely a short term implying attendance at a certain number of drills, without any reference to the effect of those drills on the particular individual?—Quite so; but the service has taken a deep hold of the people, and it has now become very popular, so that I have no doubt of every effective being efficient. In the first instance we had great difficulties to contend with, for the female part of the population was very much against the movement; they thought that all the men were going to be drafted off to India or to China; but I think that that feeling is entirely removed now, and I have no hesitation in saying that if some liberal assistance, the exact nature of which it is difficult to specify, is afforded, and a uniform colour adopted (and I attribute a great deal of the success to having a uniform colour), great satisfaction will be felt.

2877. Supposing that the coast of Durham was seriously menaced by a foreign invading force, and an appeal was made to the volunteers of the country, do you feel confident that you could bring up your 770, efficient as well as effective for the defence of the coast?—Yes, I think I could.

2878. Is it your opinion that you would be able to bring up the whole, or what proportion of those 770 effectives, in a really efficient state to support the regular force in resisting invasion?—I should say everyone who was not bedridden.

2879. You are of opinion, speaking generally, that those 770 men might be relied upon as capable of being brought up to the shores of Durham for their defence?—Yes, I am quite satisfied upon that point.

2880. Do you think that they would be in an efficient state for military purposes?—It might be presumption in me to offer an opinion upon that point, but I think that they have made great progress, and only want the opportunity of meeting together more often than we can do from want of funds, and if they did that I should have no hesitation in saying that they would act under a proper commander very efficiently indeed.

2881. May I take the purport of your evidence to be this, that as they exist at this moment you would speak with some hesitation as to their efficiency if they were suddenly called out for the defence of the coast; but, if certain further measures which you recommend were adopted, after a short time you feel confident that they would be efficient when called out?—Quite so. With regard to some battalions I would venture to allude to a report which I expect Col. MacMurdo will have received from the north from Col. Harman as to our operations on a recent occasion; and I think that if they can do what they did then they will very soon be able to do something better.

2882. You clearly understand that the object and duty of this Commission is to ascertain from the commanding officers of the different corps their opinions as to the present state and efficiency of those different corps, and the extent to which reliance can be placed on that efficiency in case the emergency with respect to which they have been organized should suddenly occur?—Yes, I think that many of the battalions would be able in a very short time to take their places with the regular troops and militia; but with regard to others I should not like to speak with the same confidence; I do not think that they are quite so efficient as they might be if they had better opportunities of assembling together.

2883. Do you think that military discipline and training are requisite to give them that efficiency which they ought to possess to justify full reliance upon them in a case of emergency?—Quite so.

2884. What measures do you think ought to be resorted to, to accomplish that result?—Merely providing their necessary equipment, and giving them an opportunity of assembling together for the purposes of drill.

2885. The necessary equipment has not hitherto failed them, nor has it caused an absence from the necessary drills?—No; but it is now wearing out.

2886. You think that a continuance in training, which is requisite to give them efficiency, will not be kept up unless new clothing is found for them, which cannot be found by the men themselves?—I should say so.

2887. But you think that if that new clothing is found for them from other sources, and the present training continues for some further length of time, the desired result will be accomplished?—Yes; I am quite sure of it.

2888. Within what period do you think it could be accomplished?—From what I know of the volunteers I should think, speaking of the bulk of the corps, that another 12 months' or 18 months' training would make them all very efficient; some of them are very much better than others.

2889. Supposing the danger to which I have alluded was showing itself on the shores of Durham, and developing itself on the southern coasts of England, do you think that your corps could be carried to the south of England in an efficient state for the purpose of aiding in the military defence of the country?—I am sure of it; but we have no field equipment, no knapsacks, or tents, or cooking apparatus.

2890. In your present state you could not be relied upon as an efficient force for operations at a distance from your present quarters?—Not unless we had those necessaries which I have specified provided.

2891. (*Col. MacMurdo.*) If the troops took the field, are you not aware that they would be furnished with a camp equipment?—No, I am not; but, if so, then they would not know what to do with it, a good many of them.

2892. (*Lord Overstone.*) May I understand the purport of your evidence generally to be this: that in the present state of the force, its efficiency for national defence is limited and imperfect; that with certain aid from the Government, it might be rendered much more efficient; but that for distant operations still further training, and the habit of using the things which must be provided for the movement of troops at a distance, would be still requisite?—Yes.

2893. In the present state of the force, it would not be efficient for operations in a distant part of the country?—No; certainly not, unless those necessaries were provided for them in anticipation of such operations.

2894. I understood you to say that not only the requisites must be provided, but that the men must be accustomed to the proper use of them?—Yes; it you put raw troops into camp life, they would, of course, be wanting in experience.

2895. (*Lord Elcho.*) That remark would apply equally to the militia, or to any regiment of the line, which had never been in camp?—Yes; but not so much, because from their habits, and being subjected to barrack discipline, they are taught many things which the volunteers are unaccustomed to.

2896. If the articles to which you have referred; viz., tents, cooking apparatus, great coats, and knapsacks, were provided for them, you think there would be no difficulty?—Yes.

2897. Those are the portions of the equipment for the field to which you refer, and which they have not now?—Yes; and without which they would not be efficient.

2898. You have heard from Col. MacMurdo, that these things would be supplied when they were called upon to do duty in the field?—Yes.

2899. So that with regard to the field equipment, although the volunteer corps have it not now, they would have it furnished to them when called out into the field?—Yes.

2900. Judging from your experience of the volunteer corps, to make them thoroughly efficient as separate companies in drill, what time should you think it necessary to have them together?—That depends a good deal upon who takes them in hand.

2901. I will assume that they were properly taken in hand?—Then I do not think there is a corps in our part of the country that within, say a fortnight, could not be very well up indeed in its work.

2902. Is it probable that any army could be landed on the shores of this country, without the Government of the country receiving at least a fortnight's warning?—I should think it was utterly impossible.

2903. Your corps is chiefly composed of artizans, is it not?—Yes.

2904. What effect has the volunteering had upon the artizans, physically and socially; has it improved their appearance?—It has produced a marked improvement in every way, both in their health, in their habits, and in their demeanour to others.

2905. Do you hear their employers speak favourably of the movement, as to its effect upon the men?—I have never heard hardly a complaint; and on a recent occasion we had an assembly for rifle shooting in the county of Durham, at which all the corps attended; and the police superintendent told me that it was the only meeting of that size that he had ever known in the county of Durham, at which the police had not a complaint to make; not a single police case arose during three days' contest, and a large review, which afterwards took place in Lambton park.

2906. I think you stated that you were of opinion that the volunteers who give their time and services should not be called upon to contribute in other ways?—I think so.

2907. Do you think that that feeling exists among the volunteers themselves?—I am quite sure of it. I think, moreover, that some little favour might be shown; for instance, I think that field officers ought to be exempted from service on juries, and such little calls upon their time as that. If a man was called upon to serve on a special jury at the time when he had to parade his regiment it would be very inconvenient.

2908. (*Chairman.*) Would you confine that privilege to the field officers?—I think that that would be sufficient.

2909. (*Lord Elcho.*) Do you think that if that principle was extended to exempting the men from civil duties in consideration of military service voluntarily rendered to the state, it would be an inducement to men to enter the force and remain in it?—Not materially.

2910. Are the men of whom your corps is composed not frequently called upon to act as jurymen or special constables?—No, it is principally the officers.

2911. (*Sir A. Campbell.*) Do you find that the nature of the employment of the artizans in your corps makes it difficult for them to make arrangements to receive rifle instruction?—Yes, I think that the course of instruction as laid down in the regulations is almost inapplicable to rural corps, or to any other volunteers; I think that they cannot go through the course.

2912. Do you think that they can be properly instructed in the use of the rifle without going through the course?—I think they can be made to hit a target every time at from 400 to 600 yards; I saw a man the other day shoot off a tie against a Henry rifle with an ordinary Enfield, and it took three shots afterwards to decide it; they divided because the owner of the Henry had not sufficient confidence to fire it off.

2913. (*Major-Gen. Eyre.*) Was that a man who had not had actual practice?—No; he had had such practice as we could give him at his own range.

2914. (*Lord Elcho.*) But he had not gone through all the position drills as laid down in the illustrations?—No.

2915. (*Major-Gen. Eyre.*) Had that man had practice at the target?—Yes, principally.

2916. (*Lord Elcho.*) Do the officers of your corps pay a higher annual subscription than the men?—Yes, the officers pay every deficiency almost, whatever it may be.

2917. We have been informed that there is a corps in which the captain pays 25*l.*, the lieutenant 15*l.*, the ensign 10*l.*, and the corporals 3*l.* annually, and that the incidental expenses of the corps are in a great measure covered by the subscriptions on the part of the officers; do you think it desirable that such a system should be general, and that the officers should be called upon to contribute such large sums annually?—I think not; for you would then get for a commander a man with the most money in his pocket and not the most sense in his head.

2918. Do you think that there would not be a sufficient demand for officers' commissions to enable you to select good men if such a tax were imposed?—I think not; not in the rural districts.

2919. (*Major Harcourt.*) You have stated that you think the men ought to be supplied with uniforms and accoutrements; have the expenses of storing those uniforms and accoutrements entered into your calculation?—Yes.

2920. And the hire of a room to keep those stores in, and a quartermaster-serjeant to look after them?—That would be the armourer's duty; the uniforms would remain in the possession of the men as long as they remained in the corps.

2921. Do you think that the same man could also perform that duty?—Yes; he would not have above ten or a dozen suits in a company, if so many, to look after; I think not beyond that if the national colour were adopted.

Lieut.-Col.
E. M. Perkins.

20 June 1862.

The witness withdrew.

Adjourned to Tuesday next at half-past 12 o clock.

Tuesday, 24th June 1862.

PRESENT:

Viscount EVERSLEY.
Earl of DUCIE.
Viscount HARDINGE.
Lord ELCHO.
Lord OVERSTONE.
Lieutenant-Colonel BARTTELOT.

Lieutenant-Colonel Sir A. CAMPBELL.
Lieutenant-General Sir G. A. WETHERALL.
Major-General EYRE.
Colonel MACMURDO.
Major HARCOURT.

VISCOUNT EVERSLEY IN THE CHAIR.

Captain GEORGE DARBY examined.

Capt. G. Darby.
24 June 1862.

2922. (*Chairman.*) You command the 3rd Sussex Artillery Volunteer Corps?—Yes.

2923. Consisting of two batteries?—Yes.

2924. And of 160 men?—No; I have about 108 on the roll; I think there will be about 125 actually on the roll the first time that I go down.

2925. You have taken a great interest in organizing a mode of conveying artillery to the coast?—Yes. When first I formed the corps I had that in contemplation, for I thought that the time would come when you would both have to move guns and other stores, and I happened to have some communication with His Royal Highness the Duke of Cambridge, and I told him that I had had the idea of this scheme from the formation of the corps, and I asked H.R.H. whether he thought there would be any use in it, and he said that if I could succeed in doing it he thought it would be a most desirable thing. In consequence of that I sent down with the view of carrying out the scheme, and in two days I got above 300 draught beasts volunteered, and I have now I think between 600 and 700. This is the original map (*handing in the same*) which was signed by those who volunteered to provide the draught beasts, and I have never had any difficulty whatever since that time; they drew the heading of it themselves; it was done in a hurry as if in contemplation of a possible invasion. I have had occasion to move 18-pounders to Brighton, and I have never had the least difficulty in getting the number of draught beasts I wanted.

2926. Do these persons who undertake to supply the horses, also undertake to move the guns without any charge?—When I was going to the Brighton review I asked leave to take four 18-pounders, as I did not like going without guns; and it being thought desirable to test the reality of the movement, leave was given to me to take the guns; I then sent round to know what horses I could have, and they said 100; I said I wanted only 30, and they supplied them, and two men to each team of horses; they supplied the horses, and the whole of the forage for nothing, and, I believe, gave something to the men, who behaved well, when they came back.

2927. Did they convey the guns belonging to your battery only?—I changed the position of some other guns, but only conveyed my own guns from Blatchington to Brighton, over Newhaven Bridge, and up by Red Hill near Oving-Dean, which I have had measured, and is an incline of 1 in 6; we marched past with the guns, and back to Blatchington, a distance altogether of about 30 miles, and we parked the guns that night, getting back at 25 minutes past eleven; we placed sentries over them, and the next morning six of the horses took the four guns up the hill to the shed, wheeled them, and reversed them; the same team had been over to Brighton the day before.

2928. Do the persons to whom you have referred belong to your corps?—Some of them, and I believe that they will all be honorary members of it; one of the rules of the corps is that, with the sanction of the commanding officer, those furnishing draught beasts are entitled to become honorary members of it.

2929. You would be able to command those horses in case of invasion and at other times, I suppose, if it were necessary?—Yes; the plan was carried out very suddenly, because I wanted to see the shortest time in which I could get a number of draught beasts supplied; I did not draw up this paper myself, but this is the form of it: "We, the undersigned, Sussex farmers residing within a few miles of the South Coast, viz., between Beachy Head and Newhaven, do hereby pledge ourselves in case of an invasion by a foreign enemy to supply for the use of Her Majesty Queen Victoria, the following number of horses and oxen whenever we may be called upon so to do. Witness our hands, 30th day of July 1860." The object was, first to obtain a register of the number of animals to be obtained, and next to make use of them; and upon any occasion when I have asked for them they have supplied them most readily; guns of position have in fact been sent down to the batteries, so that the horses became actually serviceable; and four of those guns of position I took to Brighton with me. There were originally only breeching rings to the shafts, and I could not, except by some shift, harness my horses to those shafts, and we then contrived a plan which would do either for artillery or agricultural harness, and after some contrivance I had a set made at Eastbourne. I forwarded them to the Horse Guards, and they were kind enough to send Colonel Cuppage, R.A., who came down and saw them tried with both sorts of harness, and reported, I believe, that they answered perfectly well. In consequence of that the fittings of the shafts have been altered all along the coast, and we can now in a moment change from the artillery to the agricultural harness.

2930. That contrivance has made the whole of the artillery along the coast perfectly efficient?—Yes; but another thing was required to be done; for, although it answered for the counties of Sussex and Kent, it was suggested that it would not do for other counties, and upon that I sent for drawings and information from all the Eastern and Southern counties, and got returns, from which it appeared that along all the Eastern and Southern counties the harness is suitable for the new fittings.

2931. All the appointments and equipments necessary for the artillery are furnished, I believe, by the Government?—Such as the ammunition, that is furnished, and the carbines are furnished.

2932. (*Col. MacMurdo.*) And the small stores?—Yes, all those; everything is furnished for the guns. I was not aware that the carriage of the small stores was furnished, or of the drill-guns; at least, I paid for it.

2933. (*Chairman.*) Have you any company fund formed of subscriptions amongst yourselves?—None among non-commissioned officers or gunners, and only about 10*l.* or 12*l.* by persons who are not members of the corps.

2934. Have your men found their own clothing?—I have different ways of finding it; some persons found substitutes, and they found the money for the uniform of their substitutes, but they submit the men to me in the first instance for approval.

2935. When that clothing requires renewal, do you think they will renew it?—I hope at least that some of them will. I should think I may have, out of the funds of the corps, to clothe about 30 men wholly, and 19 in part.

2936. (*Major Harcourt.*) Do you send in quarterly practice returns to the officer commanding the Royal Artillery in your district?—Yes.

2937. Do you send returns of stores to the same officer?—Yes.

2938. Is your practice carried on under his superintendence?—Yes.

2939. Are you inspected by him or by some one whom he appoints?—I believe the inspector is appointed on his recommendation; I have just been inspected by Colonel Aylmer, R.A.

2940. So that your organization is rather of a more military character than that of the rifle volunteers?—I imagine so.

2941. Do you think that the artillery volunteers dislike this organization?—No; I think they like it.

2942. Do you think that they would dislike being placed even more under the superintendence of the officers of the Royal Artillery than they are at present?—Not the least. I believe they would like it; and so they ought, because there is no possible assistance that we do not receive from the officer commanding the district, and from all in the service, even down to the gunners. They seem to take a great interest in us; but, of course, I can only answer for my own corps. I am quite sure I may speak for them as well as for myself.

2943. Speaking for your own corps, do you think that they would not dislike being placed more under the district officers of Royal Artillery than they are at present?—I do not think that they would in any way dislike it.

2944. Are there any rifle volunteers in your district?—Yes, at Eastbourne.

2945. Does the recruiting for the one arm interfere with the recruiting for the other?—Not materially. Some of those who joined the rifles would probably have joined the artillery had no rifle corps been formed. I think the formation of that corps may have very much diminished the funds which might have been raised for the artillery.

2946. Which arm do you consider it is of most importance to encourage on the sea coast?—Certainly, when I formed this artillery corps, all the authorities gave me to understand that the artillery was of the most consequence.

2947. Have you any regular course of drill?—Yes.

2948. Is every man obliged to go through a course of marching drill before he is allowed to go to gun drill?—Yes, every man is obliged to go through company drill. I should not think him steady enough to go to the guns, unless he had gone through company drill.

2949. Is every man obliged to go through gun drill before he is allowed to go to carbine drill?—Yes, in my case they had all gone through the gun drill before I had carbines. I kept out the carbines as long as I could.

2950. Do you attach any importance to the use of the carbines?—I cannot bear them; I think they are of no use.

2951. Do you consider file firing, or firing in square safe with the artillery carbines?—Do you mean the rear rank firing?

2952. The third and fourth ranks firing?—No; I never heard an artilleryman say that it was so; in file firing the front rank kneels down.

2953. (*Lord Elcho.*) Is that ever done?—I have asked many artillerymen, and all the men who have seen service that I have asked in the artillery have said that they do not consider it a safe thing in square to fire from the third and fourth ranks with carbines, as they are so short.

2954. (*Major Harcourt.*) Then of what use are they to the volunteer artilleryman?—If they go on garrison duty at any time; I strapped mine to the limbers when I went to Brighton, but I never un-

strapped them again, they do for mounting guard; the carbine is a very neat little weapon without the sword bayonet, but with it, it is a most top-heavy thing.

2955. Have you been at any expense in storing the carbines, or paying an armourer?—Yes, and that is one of the things that I think we ought to be relieved from; my carbines have only just arrived, or not very long ago. I have a paper drawn up which every man, before he takes his carbine, signs; and that paper is to the effect that he is to produce the carbine so often for inspection, and be answerable for any damage done to it, and that he is not to fire it without leave from the commanding officer; subject to those regulations, they may take the carbines, the rest are kept in store. We pay 8*l.* 10*s.* a year for looking after those belonging to the second battery, which are, I think, at present in a room in one of the batteries.

2956. Has your corps ever had any battalion drill?—Not a great deal, but they have had sufficient company drill.

2957. Do you attach much importance to battalion drill for artillerymen?—I think that anything which makes a man steady is a great thing, in order to do their work neatly at the guns; if they cannot do their company drill neatly, they cannot do it at the guns; and after all battalion drill is only company drill extended.

2958. Do you think that divisional field days are of any advantage to artillery volunteers?—That depends upon how far they go, and for what purpose they go. I do not think too many meetings are desirable; and I do not want to go at all to them if I go with carbines; I think it is a great nuisance.

2959. (*Col. MacMurdo.*) Are you aware that the carbines were furnished to the artillery volunteers at their own request?—Certainly; I am quite aware of that, and not only that, but I kept out of them as long as I could; but we went to Brighton, and the men saw the artillery there with carbines and the rifles with their rifles at Eastbourne, and then I found that there was a great desire to have them, and the colonel of my corps told the men that he wished them to have them, and then I yielded, but not till then. I should not now, however, attempt to get rid of them.

2960. Is it not the fact that some of the corps were about to resign, and would have resigned if the carbines had not been issued to them?—My corps did not.

2961. (*Lord Elcho.*) Do the men shoot much with the carbines at a mark?—No, I have, as yet, declined to have any blank cartridges.

2962. But the other artillery corps?—I really do not know.

2963. (*Earl of Ducie.*) Do you not find that if you have no ammunition, some dissatisfaction is expressed by the men as they cannot join in the matches?—That time may come; but I have always tried to turn my corps against it. I have said it is of no use your doing what everybody can do; you must do something more. There are many things which relieve the artilleryman from monotony in his work, for it is that which annoys volunteers. It may be necessary for the rifles either to attend field days or go to this place or to that for a change; but when you have your repository work going on, and the men are learning the use of the gyn and sheers, and to mount and dismount guns, there is a very great change in their work, and it prevents the monotony which is felt from constant company and battalion drill.

2964. You are not of opinion that rifle matches and county meetings are a great means of holding the volunteer system together?—I really cannot speak from myself with respect to the course that the rifle volunteers take; I know very little about them, but I think I could hold the volunteers together without them in the artillery; but I have no doubt that if prizes are given away for artillery practice the volunteers would be very glad to compete for them.

2965. (*Viscount Hardinge.*) Do you know of any instance in which prizes have been offered for the best artillery practice?—Yes.

Capt. G. Darby.

24 June 1862.

R 4

Capt.
G. Darby.

24 June 1862.

2966. Where corps have met together and competed for the prizes?—Yes, there are prizes given in Sussex.

2967. I mean prizes for artillery practice?—Yes. The way it was done in Sussex was this,—so much money was given to the 1st, 2nd, and 3rd corps of artillery, but the competition was between each of those corps among themselves; the corps were not brought together for the purpose of competing with one another, but the one, two, or three batteries of each corps competed among themselves for the particular sum that was allotted to that corps; I think 20*l.* to the Brighton corps, 10*l.* to mine, and 5*l.* to the Fairlight corps.

2968. You might carry that still further, might you not, so as to give the artillery volunteers the same interest in competing for those prizes as they do at county meetings in competing for rifle prizes?—There is more difficulty in it; I do not like anything that unnecessarily takes men often away from their occupations; I think that the best rule is never to get your men together except for duty; some might like it well enough, but men in business and fathers and the masters do not like it, and the less you can take them away from home, the more permanent the force will be in the end, I am certain.

2969. (*Major Harcourt.*) With what kind of guns are you supplied for drill and practice?—I drill with 32-pounders, 68-pounders, 24-pounders, and 18-pounders.

2970. Have you been put to any expense in building drill gun sheds?—No. We hire one or two.

2971. How many drills do you consider that a gunner should attend to, to entitle him to be considered an effective after he has passed out of the list of recruits?—He should attend to his drill once a month.

2972. Do you think that 12 drills a year would be sufficient?—Yes, provided he knew his work previously.

2973. Do you find that the attendance of your men is better at gun practice than at gun drill?—Yes, I think it is.

2974. (*Viscount Hardinge.*) Do you mean 12 days gun drill only?—Yes, but there is a great deal that has to be learned besides.

2975. What is the minimum number of days' drill which you think is necessary for a volunteer artilleryman to go through to render him effective. Take the second year. You are aware that in the rifle volunteers a man is considered effective who has gone through 24 days' drill?—Yes.

2976. I presume that that would also apply to artillery volunteers?—That is rather a difficult question to answer, for it depends upon what battery you are in, and the facilities for the different kinds of drill; we have a great advantage in that. I can always teach the men a certain amount of repository drill—knotting, shifting the guns, gyn drill, &c., and whenever you have that change of work there is much less difficulty in getting the men down to drill.

2977. Do you return every man as effective who has gone through 24 days' drill?—Yes; I think it is 24.

2978. Do you think 24 days are sufficient, or would you recommend an extension of that time?—I do not think that I should recommend an extension of the number of days to make a man effective; you always will have some men more efficient than others. In the artillery some of them cannot learn the repository work so quickly as others, and there are others who are very clever at it, but you cannot expect to have them all alike.

2979. (*Major Harcourt.*) Do all your men go through a course of theoretical instruction in boring and fixing fuses, trajectory, and the science of artillery generally?—Yes.

2980. Is the possession of such knowledge in any degree necessary to a man before he is competent to be made a non-commissioned officer?—Yes.

2981. How are your non-commissioned officers selected?—I select them.

2982. How are your officers selected?—I recommend them.

2983. Have any of your officers been attached for instruction to the Royal Artillery, if not have they all gone through such a course of instruction as you think sufficient?—I have been attached to the Royal Artillery and Scots Fusilier Guards, and my second captain, who is a capital mathematician, is an excellent artillery officer; he has worked very hard at it; he has always been in the battery and he lives close to it.

2984. Are the fuses with which you have been supplied generally good?—Yes; I think I have hardly had a bad one.

2985. Have you ever had any accidents during practice?—Never.

2986. At what distance is the magazine from the battery at which you practise?—We have no magazine of our own; there are Government magazines at Eastbourne, at Blatchington, and at Newhaven.

2987. Are you put to any expense in the conveyance of ammunition every time you practise?—No, the magazines are close by.

2988. (*Col. MacMurdo.*) Are you ever put to any expense for the carriage of stores at all?—Yes, and I am going to send a bill in; it is but a small one.

2989. (*Major Harcourt.*) Were you not aware that that is an expense which is undertaken by the War Office?—No, they told me at the railway that I was to pay it.

2990. Have you the charge of any large amount of Government stores?—I am responsible for them.

2991. Are you put to any expense in storing them?—No.

2992. Do you not think that varying the drills as much as possible secures a much better attendance at drill?—Yes, the less monotony the better.

2993. Do you think that such a variety in drill as would be afforded by repository exercises to the extent of moving heavy ordnance without a gyn, would be appreciated by the men?—They cannot be artillerymen without repository drill. I had to get one of those nasty cast-iron carriages out of a truck at Berwick, and I had not a handspike, or a rope, or a skid, and had not a crane that would lift it. I had to get it out with my own men, and we got it out without any trouble.

2994. (*Col. MacMurdo.*) That gave you excellent practice?—Yes, but then we were afraid of mounting that gun without a gyn; we should probably have broken the carriage. Then came in use the volunteer horses, who brought a gyn, and my second captain put it together. The gun and carriage were taken away to Berwick and mounted, there my second lieutenant drills all the men; he has done it all himself; one of his detachments was at Brighton at the review.

2995. (*Major Harcourt.*) Have your men ever given any assistance to the coast brigade of Royal Artillery?—I have a general understanding with Lieutenant Robinson that whenever he wants men he shall have them, and he tells me that they are perfectly efficient.

2996. Have you ever given such assistance when the coast brigade of Royal Artillery would have been otherwise too weak-handed to have done the work themselves?—Yes; they fill up their numbers with our men.

2997. Do you think that the arrangement you have spoken of, by which you can obtain a supply of volunteer cattle for moving guns on travelling carriages, might be generally extended?—Certainly. I have received a letter from the colonel of the 1st brigade of Yorkshire artillery, asking me to give him the whole account of it, and I think he had some idea of attempting to carry out the same scheme. I see no difficulty in it. Mr. Turner, a serjeant in my corps, who is a very large agriculturalist, assisted me in carrying out my plan, and whenever I want horses I send to him to make arrangements. When I went to Brighton, I never allowed a man to fall out during the whole time. I had a sort of petty commissariat, everything was supplied, and the men had tickets for beer, and they could only obtain the quantity to which those tickets entitled them; all the provisions went in my store cart.

2998. Do you think that your corps, generally speaking, is in a healthy condition?—Yes.

2999. Besides what you have mentioned, do you consider that Government aid is necessary to ensure the permanency and efficiency of your corps?—I do not say the corps would go down without it, but we are pressed, and I think that if the Government gave us drill sheds and took care of our arms, paid for getting out targets and the entire cost of one instructor, it would be desirable. Where there is a battery with non-commissioned officers of the Royal Artillery, an arrangement might be made causing little loss to the Government by which our carbines might be taken care of.

3000. (*Col. MacMurdo.*) Do you think that the carbines should be taken care of at the expense of the Government, bearing in mind that they were supplied to the volunteers at their own request?—Major Harcourt has asked me what I thought should be done with a view to the permanency of the corps. Everybody knows that the volunteers are not rich, and I have gone upon the most economical plan that any person can go upon. I have never allowed any lace to be worn in my corps; the serjeant's badge of the crown and gun is alone in silver; and we all wear the same cloth, and the expenses have been in every way as small as possible; the only exception was that at Eastbourne the rifle volunteers had a band, and my men pressed me very much to let them have a band to be composed of those who volunteered their services, and after a long time I subscribed, but I soon after disbanded them. Therefore I think that if we supply all the clothing, those things for which I ask might be conceded, and would be little expense to the Government.

3001. (*Major Harcourt.*) Supposing any damage was done to the carbines, I suppose the loss would fall upon the Government and not upon the volunteers?—I consider it would fall upon me.

3002. Then supposing that assistance were afforded by the Government, you would prefer it in the form you have described, to receiving aid in money?—Yes, assistance in money might, I think, lead to accounts and to difficulties, out of which I do not see my way.

3003. (*Viscount Hardinge.*) Does your corps wear busbies?—No, I will not have them.

3004. It is not at all necessary to have them, is it?—I think it is very unnecessary: in the first place, if it is a shabby busby it is a horrible looking thing, and if it is a good one it is very expensive.

3005. It is also very expensive for the officers to provide it?—Yes; I believe that my uniform cost only about 9*l*. Our uniform is blue with scarlet facings; the trousers have scarlet braided cord instead of a broad stripe of scarlet cloth, as the former wears better and remains cleaner; the belts are of brown leather.

3006. (*Sir A. Campbell.*) You have expressed your opinion in accordance with high military authority, that on the coast the artillery volunteer corps are of greater service than the rifle corps?—Yes, immediately on the coast.

3007. What view do you take with respect to the corps in the inland districts?—I should imagine that in the inland districts the rifle would be the best, and for this reason I think it would be absurd for volunteer corps to attempt to use light field guns, and to horse them; if you have horses for light field guns, you must have them always at your command, and always trained, and they must not be changed, whereas my object is not to train the horses and not to train the carters, for if you attempted to drill them you would puzzle them; but they are first-rate fellows to drive, if you do not puzzle them. I think that if the volunteers attempted to deal with lightfield artillery it would be a very great mistake.

3008. (*Viscount Hardinge.*) Is it not the fact that if the services of the volunteer artillery were ever required in the case of an invasion, they would be required, generally speaking, to man the existing batteries and forts on the coast?—Yes, and in my view to move guns of position and heavy stores.

3009. (*Lt.-Col. Bartelot.*) Have you made up your mind as to what sum of money will find you in gun sheds, and the necessary things that you think the corps requires to keep up its permanence and efficiency?—The nearest calculation that I have made brings it to about 5*s*. a head.

3010. (*Sir A. Campbell.*) Is it your opinion that the enrolment of volunteers as artillerymen should mainly be encouraged on the coast, but that in the inland districts they had better be enrolled as infantry?—That is a military question, and I am not a military man; but what I mean is this, that if by inland artillery field artillery be meant, I think light field artillery would be a mistake; and I should be very sorry to engage in it, for you must have a permanent staff in that case, and horses perfectly trained; and my object has been not to have that, but to know where I could lay my hands on draught beasts to move heavy weights, and I believe that some artillery officers are of my opinion, that our horses are especially calculated for this purpose, because they are trained constantly to drag heavy weights. I will undertake to pledge myself to move guns or anything out of the sheds on the coast anywhere where wheels can travel.

3011. (*Viscount Hardinge.*) Should you say that the artillery service amongst the volunteers was generally popular?—Decidedly, in our part of the country.

3012. Do you think that the rifle volunteers could in certain districts be converted into artillerymen, or that they would willingly give up their particular branch of the service?—That is rather a delicate question. I dare say some of them would, but that would depend upon how they liked their captain; they might not dislike the artillery, but they might like their captain better.

3013. Is there a company of rifle volunteers near you?—Yes, Mr. Frederick Thompson's.

3014. Are the guns which you took to Brighton in charge of your company?—No; the Duke of Cambridge let me have them to try the horses with.

3015. Are you allowed a drill-serjeant to each company by the Government?—I have only one drill-serjeant detached at head quarters at Hailsham; for the rest there is the master gunner at Blatchington, a non-commissioned officer at Newhaven, and there is Serjeant Barnard at Eastbourne; Lieutenant Robinson has given me the greatest assistance. I have 16 or 17 men at Alfriston, and they are drilled entirely there until fit to come into the batteries; that has been done by one of my lieutenants, company drill and everything.

3016. Have your officers instructed the volunteer serjeants in each company?—Of course we began with instructors necessarily; but I may say this, that with the exception of one or two officers who last joined, and who I hope are going to Woolwich or Dover, my officers are very good artillerymen, and they do a great deal themselves.

3017. In fact your non-commissioned officers are entirely volunteers?—Yes, I have no non-commissioned officer that has been in the artillery, they have learnt their work as volunteers.

3018. (*Lord Overstone.*) How many men have you under your command?—I have a few who have not put their names down, with these I shall have about 125.

3019. From what classes of the community are they principally drawn?—I have master blacksmiths, carpenters, farmers, and a considerable number of the principal tradesmen in Eastbourne. I have also four

Capt.
G. Darby.

24 June 1862.

S

Capt. G. Darby.
24 June 1862.

superior labourers, especially useful if I have any earthworks to throw up, and then I have skilled artizans, shipwrights, and a number that belong to the Custom House at Newhaven.

3020. In case your corps was called out for actual service, have you considered what would be the probable effect upon the surrounding community of drawing from it persons engaged in those various occupations?—I take it that if they were called upon for permanent duty, it would be in case of some danger of an invasion, and I think that everybody then, whatever their occupation was or their business, would do the best they could.

3021. My question was not directed so much to the duty as to the probable effect upon the public interests, and to what extent the order of society and the ordinary course of transactions would be interrupted and thrown into confusion by drawing from it so large a number of men engaged in such very important pursuits?—With great submission, my idea is that, if such a case should arise for everybody who was, from his knowledge and skill, able to aid in the defence of his country that would be his best occupation for the time; I think he ought to be called out, and I think that the greatest security which he could give to all those occupations, would be to take care that there was not any invasion.

3022. Do you consider that your corps is at the present moment in a state ready for actual service?—Certainly.

3023. The meaning of my question is this: in the case of a sudden emergency occurring, do you consider that your force is at this moment, with regard to equipment of every kind, in a state ready for actual service?—Of course the equipment for service; the principal equipment, namely the guns and all the material of war, are found by the Government; as to everything else, uniforms and so on, they are perfectly fit for it, and if even they wanted a commissariat to take their provisions, although it would certainly be in a very small way, I think I could provide for that immediately.

3024. The purport of my question is this: in the general regulations it is stated that the volunteers should be at all times prepared for actual service?—Yes; I suppose that the returns have come in. I can only add that the other day I practised at Eastbourne, when Colonel Aylmer, R.A., made his inspection, and I think he would say that my men were steady at their guns and their practice very good.

3025. You think then, speaking in the ordinary sense of the word, that in case of an emergency arising, your corps would be prepared for actual service?—I certainly do. I have received the greatest kindness from the artillery officers; and if you take the greater proportion of my men, I think it is not too presumptuous in me to say that they could go into the battery, bring out all the stores, fill their shells, bore and fix their fuses, and prepare all the guns for action; and I believe that their practice would be found, generally speaking, to be such practice as they need not be ashamed of.

3026. Upon the supposition that the volunteer force was left to support itself in the way in which it is now doing, do you anticipate any serious difficulty in maintaining the efficiency of your corps?—As far as my own corps is concerned, I should hope not, because I will not let it go down, if I can help it; but at the same time my only difficulty is in respect of funds, and I certainly have heard from various sources that there is a difficulty in maintaining corps. Of course, one must inquire what are the excrescences that have grown up, and which must be lopped off, in order if possible to reduce the expenses; that will be a matter for inquiry; but at least you have this to say, that this has been a magnificent movement; and if even a certain number were to fall off, you would still have a nucleus, and I have no doubt that if the occasion arose, you would have an immense number who would form round that nucleus again, and who would very soon become efficient. I do not think that anything will destroy the volunteer force as a force, which is now completely established in this country; in particular places it might be so.

3027. (*Viscount Hardinge.*) How often do you practise with shot and shell?—That depends entirely upon circumstances; we practise at targets placed out at sea.

3028. Take the year round, how often do you practise during the year?—We always fire off the quantity of ammunition allowed.

3029. You always do that?—Yes; and I do not complain of the quantity allowed.

3030. Do the Government provide for you floating targets?—Yes, though we have ourselves got one out; but I ought to mention, we always have to get our target out, and every time it is taken out it costs 7s. 6d.

3031. (*Col. MacMurdo.*) Do you think that that ought to be defrayed by the Government?—Yes; that is one of the things that I should like to see defrayed by the Government.

3032. (*Viscount Hardinge.*) Who takes charge of your storehouse?—The ammunition is under the Royal Artillery; all our practice is from the regular batteries. My Eastbourne detachment practise at Eastbourne, all the Blatchington men practise at Blatchington battery, and the Newhaven men, who muster above 30, practise at Newhaven battery. I never have any firing from the drill guns.

3033. All the small stores that you use are royal artillery stores, I presume?—I cannot say all.

3034. (*Major Harcourt.*) Are not all the stores in your own charge?—Yes, all of them. Whenever I have drills, the small stores are actually in my own charge. The stores that are in the charge of the Royal Artillery are only the stores of ammunition which are in the batteries, the rest are in my own charge.

3035. (*Viscount Hardinge.*) Who takes charge of those stores for which you are responsible—have you a gunner in charge?—No; I have a lieutenant or serjeant-major, and he is responsible to me for them. I go over them and have them checked every now and then.

3036. Are the shells with which you practise the same kind of shells that the royal artillery make use of?—Yes; they are the common shell.

3037. Do you give your adjutant any extra allowance?—We have only an adjutant of brigade; the adjutant is at Brighton, and I very seldom see him. We are necessarily separated from Brighton.

3038. With regard to the standard of height, have you any limit, so that you refuse men under a certain height?—With our present guns we must have men of a certain height, they have to load the 32-pounders, and a very short man cannot do it; my corps average about 5 feet 9.

3039. When you practise with shot, do the men take it in turns to do the duty of No. 1?—They change rounds every time. No. 1 lays his own gun, and the officer looks over it; it is never allowed to be adjusted; he must take the chance of his own shot.

3040. (*Chairman.*) After that No. 6 takes his turn?—They change rounds regularly.

3041. (*Major Harcourt.*) Then the only charge from which you wish to be relieved is the charge for taking the floating target out to sea, and also the charge for the conveyance of ammunition?—We do not pay for the conveyance of the ammunition, but for the other small stores. My difficulty is this, if you once clothe the men,—I do not individually object to being brought under the Government,—but if once the Government say, we will clothe the volunteers, and they do that, they will have a right to say, you shall come out so many times a year; they would have a right to have an inspection with regard to the clothing, and to have a general control, and it is possible that such a control might be thought necessary which you could not enforce upon volunteers, and I question whether the line of demarcation between the militia and volunteers might not become inconveniently indistinct. I may mention that I have a drill shed at Hailsham, a very large room, the market room, at present, through the kindness of the landlord, I have the use of it free ; at Newhaven 5l. is paid for a drill shed. In a corps with no income it would be very convenient to be relieved from the following payments ; and I do not think it would cost the Government a great deal. I should be very glad if there was any extra expense for the instructor that that should be paid ; that drill sheds, which are absolutely necessary, should be found; that accommodation for storing the carbines should be furnished, and that they should be looked after by a non-commissioned officer R.A., and that the targets should be got out for us. I think these expenses would be very little to the Government, and it would be an assistance to the volunteers.

3042. (*Lieut.-Col. Barttelot.*) Do you know sufficient of the other corps in the county, to be able to say that 5s. a head would be sufficient for them?—No, I have said that 5s. would be a great help to us ; but of course that would leave us with a considerable amount to pay. In my instance, I think we had about 180l. subscribed originally, but there is no doubt about this, that whatever deficiency there may be at last, the officers must bear the brunt of it.

Capt. G. Darby.

24 June 1862.

The witness withdrew.

Captain ALEXANDER INNES examined.

Capt. A. Innes.

3043. (*Chairman.*) I believe you command the 1st Kincardineshire artillery volunteer corps ?—Yes.
3044. How many batteries are there ?—Two.
3045. How many men ?—There are 120 men at present enrolled ; 160 being the establishment.
3046. Have you 100 effective men ?—Yes.
3047. Are you attached to any brigade ?—No.
3048. Do you have regular company and battery drills ?—Yes, regularly.
3049. Is your corps within reach of any batteries of Royal Artillery ?—We are within 14 miles of Aberdeen where there are two batteries with a detachment of Royal Artillery.
3050. Are the guns that you practise with your own, or do you march to practise with the artillery guns ?—We have a private battery quite close to my head-quarters.
3051. How many guns are there in the battery ?—I have three guns at present ; three 32-pounders. We have very recently been at Aberdeen, to which place I took two detachments for the purpose of instructing the men in the 68-pounder drill in addition to the 32-pounder drill for the purpose of enabling them to compete with heavy guns.
3052. Have you any drill instructors allowed by the Government ?—I have.
3053. Are those men permanently attached to your corps or not ?—There is only one and he is permanently attached to the corps.
3054. Is he in the receipt of regular pay ?—Yes.
3055. Do you pay him anything in addition out of the funds of the corps ?—Not to my knowledge. I know that the members of the corps are in the habit of contributing something for his assistance in superintending and cleaning their arms, but I insist upon every member of my corps being responsible for the state of his own arms.
3056. Are the men armed with carbines ?—Yes.
3057. Are they kept in an armoury or do they remain in the possession of the individual members of the corps ?—I have always insisted upon their being kept in the armoury, and being kept under the superintendence of the officers of the corps.
3058. Were your men originally clothed at their own expense ?—A small proportion of them ; a very considerable proportion of them were clothed by private contributions.
3059. Did those contributions come from honorary members, or from gentlemen living in the country ? —One of the batteries consists entirely of seafaring men, fishermen on my own estate, they were very zealous in erecting the earthworks of the battery, they expressed a desire to enrol, and on condition that they enrolled themselves I gave them a dress or uniform, such as seafaring men generally wear, or as worn by the Royal Artillery when they are in the Mediterranean, a blouse, the same as the Cinque Ports men, but not of such an expensive description as that of the other battery, which consists of the regulation uniform similar in pattern to that of the Royal Artillery.

3060. Was the expense of that uniform defrayed by yourself entirely ?—Yes.
3061. How many drills have you in the course of a year ?—80 or 90 ; we have had very irregular attendance at drill, the drills have been very constant throughout the winter, but in consequence of the expense of hiring a hall to drill in during the winter, until very recently we have had very little drill.
3062. How many drills do you consider necessary to make a man effective ?—I consider that a great many more than the statutory number of drills are necessary. I find a difficulty in this way, there is a very general impression, not only in my own corps, but all over the country, that it is only necessary that 24 drills should be attended to entitle a man to receive his certificate of efficiency. I have always resisted that myself, for I consider, as the commander of the force, that we are compelled to see that the men are efficient in their duties before granting any such certificate.
3063. Are your guns in position ?—Yes, all of them.
3064. (*Viscount Hardinge.*) At whose expense was the battery erected ?—It is erected entirely on my own property, overlooking the sea, the platforms were provided by the Government, and a certain proportion of the expense of the magazine, all the rest, such as accommodation for gun stores and other accommodation has been provided very much at my own expense.
3065. Is it an earthwork principally or is there any masonry ?—It is a regular battery with merlins, stone revêtments, and stone platforms; it is very complete in its formation.
3066. (*Col. MacMurdo.*) Were the platforms laid down at the expense of the Government ?—Yes.
3067. (*Viscount Hardinge.*) Was the other expense borne by the corps ?—They contributed the labour ; the expense of the stonework and everything of that sort, being on my own ground, I defrayed.
3068. I presume that you have a magazine ?—Yes, for about, I think, 80 cases.
3069. Was that also built at your own expense ?—I received a certain allowance, which assisted in the construction of that magazine ; I think it was about 10l. from the Government.
3070. Have you to pay one of your gunners to take charge of the stores ?—No, I have the assistance of the Government instructor.
3071. Is he in charge of the stores ?—Yes ; the guns and all the artillery stores ; that of course has nothing to do with the small arms.
3072. (*Col. MacMurdo.*) He is a corporal of the coast brigade, is he not ?—Yes.
3073. (*Viscount Hardinge.*) Have any of your officers been to Aberdeen to receive instructions from the artillery there ?—No one but myself. I placed myself at the disposal of the Government when I first received my commission, and I was attached, therefore, for two or three months at Woolwich.
3074. I suppose you and the drill instructor have

S 2

Capt. A. Innes.
24 June 1862.

instructed your officers?—I am sorry to say, that I have now only two subalterns. I have always resisted the applying for or recommending any officer until he was efficient, consequently I am very shorthanded in officers.

3075. Have you a range in front of this battery where you can practice with safety?—Yes; there is a very excellent range out to sea.

3076. Have you ever practised with shot and shell?—Yes.

3077. How often in the year have you so practised?—I do not suppose I have had it above eight or 10 times.

3078. Is there any shape in which further Government aid is, in your opinion, desirable?—I have a very strong opinion that Government aid would tend very much to our efficiency; at the same time I consider that at the present moment my corps is upon a better footing than it was at the beginning—the people better understand the nature of our relations than they did at first—and I consider that although we do not keep up to the same number, that we stand upon a more firm foundation. There is no doubt that Government aid would tend very much to our efficiency, and the manner in which I should humbly submit that that aid should be given would be in the way of contributing, not in small sums annually, but I think that if the Government gave us any assistance, it should be, say, for five years, so as to keep those, who are really efficient in the force, and not allow them to go. A man, after he has been drilled, of course is of far greater value to us than a raw recruit, and consequently if any Government aid was given that would enable men to withdraw from the force, the public money would be very much thrown away.

3079. How would you propose to carry it out?—I should say, that in order to entitle any recruit to any aid from the public purse, he ought to be at least of five years' standing, and then according to the amount that might be appropriated by the Government for that purpose, I should retain a certain proportion for the purpose of improving our administration—for instance, to assist in providing a house to contain the stores, and then to apply the other half as a reserve fund to be appropriated for the pay of the volunteers —say, after five years' service, 3l. perhaps in five years. I think that less than that would not have much effect.

3080. What do you mean by the pay of the volunteers after they have served five years? Do you mean that they should be entitled to some sort of remuneration?—Yes. I am satisfied that if we give them something, however small it might be, if we make them aware that for the time they spend they will receive something from the Government, we shall ensure their attendance in such a way as you cannot possibly expect at the present time.

3081. Do you think there would be any delicacy on their part in receiving pay?—I think that a great many would not receive it; but that there are many very valuable members to whom it would be of very great importance.

3082. (Chairman.) Of what class do your men consist generally?—I think that I have almost every class; there is a large number of fishermen, who are the very poorest class of the community; but they are the most valuable men that we have for artillery corps.

3083. (Major Harcourt.) Did you find those men in uniforms yourself?—Yes.

3084. What was the expense of that uniform?— Very small indeed; I think I clothed 60 men for 30l., about 10s. a man.

3085. Do you send quarterly practice returns to the officer commanding the Royal Artillery in your district?—Yes.

3086. Do you send returns of stores to the same officer?—Yes.

3087. Is your practice carried on under his superintendence?—Yes.

3088. Do you find that the artillery volunteers dislike this organization?—No; I find, on the contrary, that there is no complaint, and I think that we are on a better footing with them than we were at first.

3089. Do you think that if your artillery volunteers were placed under the district officers of Royal Artillery even more than they are at present, they would be better pleased with it?—I think so.

3090. You have, I suppose, a regular course of drill in your corps?—Yes.

3091. Commencing with marching drill?—Yes.

3092. And going on to gun drill?—Yes.

3093. And at last carbine drill?—Yes.

3094. Do you attach any importance to the use of the carbine by artillerymen?—I consider that it is one of the greatest standby's that we have, and the rifle range; for nothing is so great an inducement to the volunteers to enrol and to maintain themselves as the annual competitions which take place about this time, and the desire to distinguish themselves.

3095. Are your seafaring men armed with those carbines?—Not at all; it does not apply to them; I spoke of the other battery.

3096. Do you find that it makes any difference in the enrolments, or that the men would just as soon enrol with the carbine as without it?—Only as to the seafaring men.

3097. Is there any organized association for prize firing with great guns amongst the artillery in your district?—Yes, both with great guns and with carbines; we have two.

3098. Which is the most popular?—As far as the great gun competition is concerned, I cannot speak from experience, for we are only going to commence just now, but the men are looking forward to it with a very great deal of pleasure, and they seem to take great interest in it.

3099. Have you ever had any battalion drill?—No. I have endeavoured to induce my different batteries occasionally to parade with a neighbouring rifle corps, with the assistance and superintendence of the adjutant who has been appointed there, but they assume that provided they attend 24 drills we are not entitled to insist upon their attending any further.

3100. When a man is no longer a recruit, how many drills do you think are necessary in the course of a year to keep up his efficiency?—If he has once been effective I think 24 statutory drills and parades would be perfectly sufficient.

3101. Do you think that that is the largest number that would be requisite?—If he has once been efficient I think that would be quite sufficient.

3102. You think that 24 drills is the largest number of drills that would be necessary—gun drills?— I mean for both marching and gun drill.

3103. How many gun drills do you think would be sufficient after a man has once become effective?— When you speak of gun drills you mean merely, I suppose, loading and firing the 32-pounder, without reference to other duties, such as mounting and dismounting guns, &c., of course that is a very different matter, but if a man is an effective gunner I think that he might recollect perfectly everything by turning out twelve times in the year. I think that would be quite sufficient.

3104. What kind of guns are you supplied with? —With 32-pounders. I have also provided at my own expense a considerable amount of tackle, skids, and gyn for repository work, to give the men every possible inducement to attend.

3105. Have you found the attendance of the men better at gun practice than at gun drill?—No, they generally come together. I always make it a rule to give them a good deal of gun drill with the gun practice.

3106. I suppose you only have the gun practice in summer?—No; we have had it in a very desultory manner, at different times.

3107. Have you ever had any gun practice in the winter?—Not in the depth of winter, but very early in the spring.

3108. Have you any rifle corps in your neighbourhood?—Yes, we have two very near to us.

3109. Do you find that the recruiting for the one arm interferes with the recruiting for the other?—No, not in the least; I do not think that it has any effect now.

3110. Do all your men go through a course of theoretical instruction in boring and fixing fuses, trajectory, and the science of artillery generally?—Yes.

3111. Do you make it a *sine quâ non* that a man should be up in all those subjects before he is elected a non-commissioned officer?—Yes.

3112. How are your non-commissioned officers elected?—They are not elected; they were originally, but I completely upset their plan, for I found the principle of election was a very bad one, and that it created a great deal of evil in the corps.

3113. You have taken that matter into your own hands?—Yes, entirely.

3114. Have any of your officers been attached to the Royal Artillery for instruction besides yourself?—None.

3115. Have the fuses with which you have been supplied by the Government been generally good?—Very good, indeed.

3116. (*Viscount Hardinge.*) Are they the old wooden fuses?—They are Boxer's fuses, the most improved kind for land service.

3117. (*Major Harcourt.*) At what distance is the magazine from the battery at which you practise?—About 400 yards.

3118. Then you are at no expense for conveying ammunition from the magazine to the battery?—No.

3119. You have stated that you constructed the battery, what was the expense of the construction of that battery?—I cannot tell you, it was so desultory, a great deal of the construction was done with the aid of my own farm horses and farm servants, as well as some considerable assistance which was rendered by the volunteers.

3120. Have you been put to any expense for the conveyance of stores?—I believe that the officer commanding the district has undertaken to reimburse the expense.

3121. Have you the charge of any large amount of Government stores?—At times we have a very considerable amount of ammunition in the magazine; we have got all the ordinary side arms and other things in store.

3122. Can you state what the expense of erecting your magazine and store rooms was?—No, that is all in stone buildings, which I have appropriated for that purpose.

3123. Were those buildings previously used for other purposes?—Yes, they were generally farm buildings.

3124. Can you set a value upon them?—No.

3125. Do you think that varying the drills as much as possible is beneficial to the men, and secures a better attendance?—Yes, decidedly.

3126. Do you not think that such a variety in drill as would be afforded by repository exercises would be very salutary?—Decidedly. I have been very desirous to induce the Government to see the advantage of bringing my drill instructor out of the small town where he resides, where he is mixed up very much among the population there; it would be a very great advantage for the service, and a great advantage with respect to keeping the stores, if we were allowed to have his quarters close to the battery. If we had the gunner's quarters close to the battery of three guns, considering the great value of the stores under his charge, and the small arms as well, it would be a very great benefit.

3127. Suppose facilities were afforded by the Admiralty to any members of volunteer corps on the coast for obtaining a knowledge of gun drill at ships' guns, do you think that any would be likely to avail themselves of such facilities?—I can speak very much upon that point. I began in the year 1854, and I assisted, as far as was in my power, to induce the fishermen and the seafaring population to enrol in naval coast volunteers, and for a long time they persevered and attended during the month, which they had to spend on board the "Edinburgh," but I found that it had so very bad an effect in breaking up the different crews of my fishing boats, and throwing a certain number of people idle, that I recommended to the Controller of the Navy to permit the drill which was taking place on board the ship to be transferred to the coast; that was some years before the volunteer movement took place, and I found that the only objection against it was the expense, for it was undeniably a much better plan. If we want to have the benefit of the seafaring population we must bring it to their doors; we cannot take them away from home for a month.

Capt. A. Innes.

24 June 1862.

3128. Is the class of men to whom you allude likely to enrol in the royal naval reserve—are they eligible for it?—There is a proportion of those men who are now in the volunteer force, who have been drilled on board of one of the ships in that reserve.

3129. I am not talking of naval coast volunteers, but of the royal naval reserve; a man must be rated as an A.B., are there many of the men to whom you have referred likely to be so rated?—I should think so.

3130. Are there many men who would be likely to enrol themselves in the royal naval reserve?—No, I am afraid not, for these fishermen are extremely prejudiced as to their own mode of life.

3131. Still you think if they had facilities afforded to them to learn drill on board ship, they would avail themselves of such facilities, if placed on the same footing as other volunteers?—I am not so sure of that; I have no reason to say that they would not, but I have no reason to think that they would. I have tried to induce them to carry out their deep-sea fishing by means of a vessel that I brought down for that purpose, but I could not get them away, they are so wedded to the practice of fishing in small boats.

3132. But if you brought the means of learning ship gun drill to their own doors, do you think they would avail themselves of it?—Yes.

3133. Is your corps generally in a healthy condition?—Yes.

3134. Do you think that Government aid is necessary to ensure its permanence and efficiency?—I think that Government aid would very materially assist it, at the same time I do not think it absolutely necessary.

3135. If Government aid were given, will you be good enough to say in what form you would like it to be given?—I may remark, that I have no desire as the result of experience in the administration of the funds of the corps, to show that the permanence of our force must depend on additional aid from the public purse. I see no reason to anticipate the break down on this account, and I consider this to establish our best claim for public favour and support. Some additional aid from Government would promote our efficiency and relieve some private individuals of unequal expense, which has to be provided. But the most rigid economy in our financial arrangements is more absolutely necessary, and should be extended to the supplies and furnishings by Government; and I have reason to think there is room for improvement in the arrangements by which a saving of arms and stores may be effected with considerable advantage to the service. For instance, in the case of two or more amalgamated batteries it would be of great advantage that the gunner, in charge of the guns, stores, magazine, and small arms, should have his permanent quarters close to the gun battery and head-quarters, with every detail under the close inspection of the commanding officer, so as to obviate the present inevitable inconvenience and disorder resulting in

S 3

Capt. A. Innes.
24 June 1862.

much unavoidable deterioration of public property, and such private contributions would be readily afforded for the purpose as Government should see fit to demand. With regard to the question of Government aid, I conceive that there is no sort of aid which the Government can bestow, that must not come in the shape of a pecuniary contribution to the force; that contribution, I consider, should come in the shape of a fund, which should not be bestowed upon the volunteers annually, but should be extended over five years, because I think I see great evil in it otherwise. I have had a good many recruits pass through my hands, and they have given us the trouble of drilling them, and they have put the Government to the expense of much ammunition; and after we have had the trouble of making them effective, I consider that the Government aid should have the effect of inducing those men to remain with us at least five years; so that whatever the sum may be which is contributed for that purpose, it should be looked forward to as a bonus after a certain number of years probation.

3136. (*Lord Overstone.*) Do you consider that your company is at this moment in a state capable of rendering efficient service in working the guns in position?—The battery which is composed of sea-faring men, particularly so. I have given them such instruction in the use of the different tackle, and the different appliances, and in what we call repository work, as would enable them to be very efficient in mounting and dismounting heavy ordnance. I have been also trying to induce them, by going to Aberdeen, to keep up the practice with the 68-pounder, in addition to the 32, and they have had the opportunity.

3137. Speaking of your corps generally, do you think that, in case of a sudden emergency arising, they are in a state fit for actual service, and are capable of rendering efficient assistance in working guns in position?—I think that a very considerable proportion of them are in that state, but there are some men in whom I should not have that confidence.

3138. Your company is limited to the duty, if I understand your evidence correctly, of working the guns in position, and it does not in any way enter upon the duty of working moveable guns?—No, no field gun duty.

3139. (*Major Harcourt.*) What is the average height of your men?—There is one battery in which I should say they average perhaps 5 feet 7, or 5 feet 8; I have been in the habit of enrolling in the corps a number of very small boys, who are growing rapidly out of their clothes, and I conceive that they are by far the most valuable recruits that we have, as they are always learning their drill better, and consequently their number would bring down the average very considerably; they are employed in the band, but they are all drilled as gunners.

3140. (*Major-Gen. Eyre.*) What has prevented your establishment being completed?—I have never been very anxious, seeing that they are not self-supporting altogether, to make the corps so large, but to what I could manage to do to keep it up on a permanent footing; the funds at my disposal are, of course, very small indeed, coming from other sources, and I have been very anxious to avoid having officers appointed, and placing the corps in such a position, that if there was any failure we should be forced to go down. I consider that from the system which I have adopted of keeping everything as moderate as possible, both with regard to numbers, and in other respects, we are in a much more substantial position than otherwise we should have been.

3141. Could you obtain recruits if you wished for them?—Yes, easily.

3142. (*Lt.-Col. Barttelot.*) What is the expense of your band?—I really know very little about the band, I do not recollect; all the band are gunners; but I really know little or nothing about their ac-

counts, it is simply a flute band, a good many have been instructed.

3143. Have you no men in your band who are not effective artillerymen?—No.

3144. (*Col. MacMurdo.*) You mentioned a short time back, that your magazine was a building that was formerly used for another purpose?—No, that was the stores, I have built it according to the plans I received from the officer commanding the engineers in Edinburgh.

3145. Has that been inspected and passed?—Yes.

3146. Have you got three 32-pounders in a battery that was built by the volunteers?—Yes.

3147. Have you got a corporal of the coast brigade attached to you?—Yes.

3148. Are you satisfied with that man's conduct?—I am very much satisfied with him; I consider that he is very satisfactory in every way, and I have been very anxious, as he has, like all old soldiers, very little to do, to have him nearer to me, both for the sake of his own family and himself, for the temptations in a small county town are not at all desirable.

3149. You are aware that the regulations require that the accommodation in the way of residence for the gunner to take charge of the battery, and proper storage for the amunition, should be provided by the volunteers?—I beg your pardon, that was our original understanding, but that is taken off; we are relieved from that expense; we used to provide accommodation for the gunner down in the town, but there has been a change made and the Government now provide accommodation for him.

3150. The Government allow fourpence a day for lodging money, but you stated that you were desirous that the gunner should live near the battery?—Yes; I should like to have his quarters attached to the battery.

3151. Are you aware that by providing those quarters near the battery you would be entitled to receive 4d. a day as lodging allowance, which is now paid to the man for providing his own?—I was not aware of that. I thought that the volunteers had nothing to do whatever with the question of the Government supply to the coast brigade.

3152. Who cleans your guns?—That is a question which has just been mooted by Colonel Maclean and myself for the first time.

3153. How are the guns cleaned?—The guns are not cleaned; but, do you not mean new lacquered and put into good condition?

3154. Yes; to be kept in good condition.—Immediately after firing I always insist upon the men washing out the guns; but that is not what I mean by cleaning; the guns are very much in want of being scraped, and they require to be lacquered. It requires a certain amount of anti-corrosive paint, and everything which has not been supplied is very much wanted. We have not tompions, and the guns are deteriorating from being constantly exposed to the sea.

3155. Have you made any application to have your guns lacquered?—Yes.

3156. What answer did you receive?—That it is about to be done.

3157. I wish to know who has the charge of the guns generally, to keep them in order, and also the side-arms?—The gunner in charge belonging to the coast brigade, a non-commissioned officer of the Royal Artillery is entirely in charge of that duty.

3158. (*Major Harcourt.*) Are you not responsible for him?—Yes, I am responsible for him; he is under my orders.

3159. If anything went wrong you would be held responsible?—Yes, I conceive so.

3160. Is it not the case that you cannot fire more than 100 rounds without the gun being examined by an officer of artillery?—I never heard that; it is not yet carried out.

3161. Is it not part of the drill that the gun should be cleaned every time it is used?—Yes; one means of saving a considerable expense to the Government is in our ammunition. Unfortunately just now, not being a brigade, I have no adjutant, and I am obliged to send to Aberdeen for a lieutenant of Royal Artillery whenever I have practice with shot or shell. That is not the case where we fire with blank, and I do not exactly understand the object of it, because really the practice with blank cartridge is more dangerous than the other, and it would be very desirable, when an officer has made himself efficient at head-quarters at Woolwich, that he should be allowed to superintend his own practice, which would save much to the Government, because when I bring an officer there it is always blowing great guns by some accident, and we lose all our practice from the very wild manner of firing from the high elevation of my battery—firing at a long range—it is hardly possible to make anything like correct practice, and where you do not get that you do not instruct the men.

3162. Have you ever made any application through the officer commanding the Royal Artillery in your district to practise the corps under your own command?—I felt that I should be placing him at a disadvantage, because it is a very serious responsibility that I should be placing him under.

3163. (*Col. MacMurdo.*) Are you not aware that such applications are received at this office, and that upon the recommendation of the artillery officer of the district such applications are allowed?—I made such an inquiry within the last few weeks, and I learned that that was the case in very rare instances only; I was not aware that it was the general practice.

3164. In the case of an officer who has passed through a course of gunnery at Woolwich, he ought to be perfectly competent to do it, ought he not?—Yes; and indeed for twelve months I conducted it entirely myself; but I had an order at the end of that time to the effect that it should no longer be so; and the consequence was this, that very great inconvenience resulted; we always expend much more ammunition than is necessary. I should prefer firing only four or five rounds; but when you bring an officer a certain distance, you like to have some amount of practice, and not bring him back so frequently.

3165. (*Major-Gen. Eyre.*) From whom did you receive the order?—It is the regulation. I felt great difficulty in asking anyone to say that I was competent. I think that it was for them to find it out.

3166. (*Chairman.*) Have you any further suggestions to make to the Commission?—Experience shows that the spontaneous action of a close population may easily take the form of volunteer corps, and for a time maintain its number on the muster roll, receiving the support of the public by considerable contributions. But it is evident that its constitution as a useful and available military body must depend on its organization and superintendence by competent and qualified officers. I have had frequent occasion to observe the advantage we derive from the able and zealous instruction and assistance afforded us by the superior officers appointed by Government to inspect and superintend the force, greatly contributing to confirm and support the inexperienced volunteer officer in his new command. In the case of a small county, with rural population, the want of a sufficient number of resident proprietors taking an active interest in public affairs is much felt; and for the opinion that no measure would tend more to support and confirm our establishment than to make it be felt that the force is under the more active encouragement and superintendence of those holding Her Majesty's commission as deputy-lieutenants. It appears to me that the duties of commanding officers of volunteer corps can only be adequately performed by those possessed of certain qualifications, some natural and some acquired, and with a due regard to the public interest these appointments should on no account be too lightly bestowed. If Government wish to see men of station and education filling such appointments with zeal and efficiency it seems absolutely necessary that they shall find themselves associated with and supported by men of similar characters and qualifications. In the appointment of subalterns the same rule holds, with the exception, that some of the qualifications of the commanding officer may be dispensed with, provided his time may be sufficiently at his disposal for the due discharge of his duty. If the above requirements were better complied with and the duties, authority, and standing of the officers more completely defined and vindicated, the right men would soon take their right place. While it is absolutely necessary to provide leading strings for those who have neither time nor opportunity to procure instruction, it is equally necessary to stimulate and encourage efficient officers by allowing more exercise of their discretion, which would save much inconvenience, and the useless expenditure of ammunition, and the demoralizing effect of subverting authority. Where it can be accomplished without expense, great advantage is derived by affording our gunners more extended instruction of learning their drill in mounting and dismounting heavy ordnance, by practice with guns of different calibres, where they are to be found in the neighbouring stations, by mutual interchange of ammunition, of which we have already the successful experience, and advantage should be taken of such opportunities of the assembly of neighbouring corps for the purposes of inspection. For most classes of volunteers I find no sort of encouragement more effectual to promote regular attendance at drill and parade than the facilities for practice at a good and accessible rifle range, and no duty and responsibility of a commanding officer can be more important than to provide against accidents as far as possible, and, in many cases, on private property the precautions and regulations to be established with this view should be left to his report and suggestion, in preference to the crude and impracticable conditions recommended by inexperienced inspectors; for while the system of inspection is right, and ought not to be dispensed with, the best interest of a corps may be sacrificed by the result of an ill-digested report.

Capt. A. Innes.

24 June 1862.

The witness withdrew.

Lieut.-Col. JAMES BOURNE examined.

Lieut.-Col. J. Bourne.

3167. (*Chairman.*) Do you command the 4th Lancashire Artillery Volunteer Corps?—I do.
3168. Is it a brigade?—It is.
3169. Of how many batteries does it consist?—Of eight.
3170. Have you any suggestion to offer to the Commission, with respect to artillery corps?—I am scarcely prepared to offer any suggestions; I rather expected to have been examined particularly as to finances.
3171. Have you any fund that is raised for brigade purposes?—We have a fund that has been raised by the officers and by the subscriptions of the men, and we had in 1859, when the brigade was first established, a large donation from the town, amounting I think, in round numbers to 1,200*l.*; which sum was entirely appropriated to the clothing of the regiment in general.
3172. Was the clothing entirely paid for out of that fund?—The clothing was paid out of that fund, with the addition of an equal sum that was subscribed by the officers, and another sum that was subscribed by the men, amounting altogether in round numbers to about 3,500*l.*
3173. Of what class were the men who were so clothed?—The class of men in my brigade, I may say, are entirely clerks. I have 50 or 60, but not more, mechanics or artizans of the higher class.

S 4

Lieut.-Col.
J. Bourne.

24 June 1862.

3174. You mean clerks in merchants' houses?—Yes.

3175. Have you any standard as to the height of men you admit?—There are none now admitted less than 5 feet 8 in., I may say that the average height is very little short of 5 feet 10 in.

3176. Do you apprehend when the clothing requires renewal that a fund will be raised to clothe those men who require it afresh?—I have very great doubts about it; we have in hand about 25 suits of clothing, some few of them have been issued, and some have not; we have also in hand about 90l. as a reserve fund, applicable to the renewal, or to the refitting of the clothing.

3177. Are you supplied by the Government with guns and gun sheds, or are the expenses defrayed out of the funds of the brigade?—The Government have found us with the short carbine and sword-bayonet, and they have also supplied us with eight garrison guns, small 24-pounders, which we use for drill purposes; but we were at the expense of making platforms for those guns.

3178. (*Viscount Hardinge.*) Are the platforms of wood or of stone?—Of wood.

3179. Was not the cost of the wood defrayed by the Government?—No.

3180. Is not that generally so?—It has never come under my observation.

3181. (*Major Harcourt.*) Are you not aware that the platforms are supplied by the Government, being made by the Royal Engineers for artillery volunteers when asked for?—I was not aware of that.

3182. Have the corps under your command ever had any battalion drill?—Yes.

3183. To what extent?—We have battalion drill during the summer months, once every week.

3184. Do you attach much importance to battalion drill for your corps?—I attach importance to it as a means of employing and giving occupation to the men when they are assembled, inasmuch as we have not any means of giving them gun drill to the extent of the numbers in the brigade at one time.

3185. Do you think the divisional field days are of any use to artillery volunteers?—I am afraid I must say no.

3186. (*Viscount Hardinge.*) I think you have stated that you have not facilities for drilling more than a certain number of your men at gun drill; I presume you mean that your guns being limited in number you cannot put the different companies through the gun drills as often as you would wish?—That is so.

3187. Have you a gun range?—Yes.

3188. Can you practise with shot and shell at that range?—Yes; we have practised.

3189. Do you see your way at all to erecting another battery, or having facilities afforded to you for mounting more guns, and thereby increasing the opportunities for drill?—No; the fort which we practise from is about four or five miles distant from head quarters, the North Fort; we march the men down there by batteries in succession during the summer months, and we have boarded the men there for certain periods, say for ten days or a fortnight at a time, and during the period that those men resided at that fort we had two gun drills per day, or practice very early in the morning and very late in the afternoon, the men returning to their daily avocations in the town and coming back to sleep at the fort at night.

3190. Where were those 24-pounders mounted?—On our parade ground, close to the storehouse.

3191. Did you say that you had a range from the parade ground?—No, only from the fort, where we carry on the practice.

3192. Could not you mount more guns on your parade ground?—Yes, we could cover it with guns and make a park of it, there is space enough.

3193. Would it not be an advantage to you if you were able to put a greater number of the men through their drill and if you had a greater number of guns mounted on your parade ground?—No; I think that it would be no great advantage, as we have now at our storehouse what we call a dummy gun made of wood, with which we put every man through a preliminary course of drill, and after he has gone through a certain course there he is taken to the parade ground and is there put through a drill with a 24-pounder; but that is done almost every evening.

3194. (*Chairman.*) Is that done by separate batteries?—Yes, in fact it is done by separate detachments of batteries.

3195. (*Major Harcourt.*) Do you not think that if artillerymen were allowed the use of guns, where practicable, on the occasion of divisional field days, with a special allowance of blank ammunition, and they were placed under the command of an artillery officer, it would do them more good, and please them better, than being brigaded with infantry?—Yes, it would do them very great good and afford them great pleasure; or even with siege guns.

3196. Have you any organized association for prize firing with great guns in your district?—No.

3197. Do you think that something of that sort would generally be of advantage to artillery corps?—Of very little advantage to artillery corps. I do not quite understand your question as to prizes; I was referring to rifles, we have no organized association for great guns.

3198. Do you think that something of the sort would be an advantage to artillery corps generally?—Yes, but not much.

3199. You are only supplied with garrison guns?—With garrison guns only.

3200. How many drills per annum do you consider that a gunner should attend to entitle him to be considered an effective after he has passed out of the list of recruits?—I should say from 15 to 20.

3201. With regard to gun drills, how many gun drills do you think should entitle a man to be considered effective after he has become a competent gunner?—I should say about the same number, 15 to 20, or perhaps less.

3202. How many should you consider necessary, including company drill, carbine drill, and gun drill altogether?—Thirty.

3203. Do you consider the present number not sufficient?—Not sufficient for the artillery.

3204. Do you find the attendance of your men better at gun practice than at gun drill?—Much better.

3205. Does that refer to firing blank cartridge?—It alludes to blank cartridge, but more especially to shot and shell practice.

3206. Do your men go through a course of theoretical instruction in gunnery, and in boring and fixing fuzes?—A very superficial one.

3207. Is not such instruction necessary for artillerymen?—Most necessary.

3208. Particularly for one who aspires to become a non-commissioned officer?—Most necessary.

3209. In what way are your non-commissioned officers selected?—I can scarcely tell you in what way they were selected on the formation of the corps, but now, when there is a vacancy, the captain of the battery is requested to send the names of a certain number of men who attend most regularly at their drills to the adjutant, and generally that number consists of about six or eight; the adjutant then examines those men and reports to me as to the man who he thinks is most eligible for promotion, and I invariably adopt his suggestion.

3210. Have you been put to any expense for the carriage of stores?—Yes.

3211. Were you aware at the time that that was an expense which is undertaken by the War Office?—No.

3212. Are you aware of that now?—Yes, I am.

3213. Have you the charge of any large amount of Government stores?—No, because we are so near the place where the ammunition is kept.

3214. You are put to no expense in storing it?—None.

3215. Have any of your men ever been through any repository drill?—Very few of them.

3216. Do you think that such a mode of varying the drill would be advantageous to the men?—Most advantageous.

3217. And particularly so to garrison artillerymen?—Yes, particularly so.

3218. Is it not so considered in the Royal Artillery?—Most decidedly.

3219. Have you no guns on travelling carriages?—None at the fort where we drilled; there were some at the storehouse.

3220. Have you any organized means of moving guns on travelling carriages when necessary?—They were in the storehouse under the charge of an officer of the Royal Artillery militia.

3221. Do you consider that the corps under your command generally is in a healthy condition?—Very much so.

3222. Do you think that Government aid is necessary to secure the permanence and efficiency of your corps?—I do.

3223. In what form should you prefer that aid to be given?—I think that the Government ought to give proper instructors, ammunition, and storehouses, and meet the expenses incurred for the custody of the arms; in fact, all the expenses that a volunteer is out of pocket for drill purposes.

3224. Are not instructors provided at the expense of Government?—Yes, to a certain extent.

3225. Do you mean that a larger number of instructors ought to be provided by the Government?—Yes, we have had to pay lodging money for them.

3226. Is that generally so in your district?—Generally so; at the commencement of the volunteer movement we paid as much as 120l. or 130l. for instructors.

3227. Who are your instructors?—They belong to the Royal Artillery.

3228. The Coast brigade?—Yes.

3229. You have stated that you wish for Government aid to meet certain items of expense, should you prefer that aid being given in the way you have suggested to having a money grant?—I should prefer a money grant.

3230. To what extent?—To the extent of 1l. 5s. or 1l. 10s. per head.

3231. Why should you prefer a money grant?—Because it would leave the commanding officer more control over it; he might save on one head and loose upon another.

3232. How would you recommend that it should be applied?—I would apply it to the rent of storehouses, the custody and repair of small arms, headquarters, and the carriage of ammunition.

3233. (*Chairman.*) Is not that already paid for?—We have paid for our own 60l. in the last three years. I would apply it to the providing of a drill ground, the expense of attending parades, and, where it was necessary, for the men to go by rail for drill purposes, to the expenses incurred; as I have said before, to the custody and repair of arms, to headquarters, the serjeant-major, to the carriage of ammunition, to a rifle range, and to moving the targets, which is rather a heavy amount with us. It costs 15s. or 1l. every night or morning that we go out to gun practice.

3234. (*Major Harcourt.*) Have you been supplied with floating targets?—Yes.

3235. Should you not be satisfied to be supplied with the other items which you have named, on the terms upon which you have been supplied with floating targets; that is to say, that the Government's specification should be adhered to, with a maximum price, trusting to the commanding officer to reduce it as much as possible, but defraying it up to a certain amount?—Yes.

3236. And leaving it to the commanding officer to provide himself with the targets, the money being refunded by the Government if they are provided according to a certain specification, and the cost not exceeding a certain amount?—Yes; I may say, by way of explanation, that our great expense is more for mooring and re-covering the targets than for the target itself. Our practice is carried on in a very crowded river, with a very strong tide, and the target has to be towed out by boatmen, and when the practice is over it has to be towed back again, costing each time 15s. or 1l.

3237. (*Lord Elcho.*) You have stated that all the uniforms were found for the men from a general fund, which had been collected?—Yes.

3238. By what means do you expect to re-clothe them?—I can scarcely answer that question; we have, in round numbers, clothes and money to the extent of about 200l. in hand. The income of the brigade is about 800l. a year; the expenses in round numbers are about 650l. a year, leaving a balance of 150l., which may or may not be applied to the renewal of the clothing.

3239. Those expenses coming under the heads which you have just enumerated?—Precisely.

3240. In your calculation of 25s. or 30s., which you think ought to be given to the commanding officer to be spent at his discretion, you do not include clothing?—No.

3241. Do you mean that the expenses of your artillery corps, which are not now met by the Government, would require 25s. a head?—I think they would; they have done so hitherto.

3242. Under the heads you have mentioned?—Yes.

3243. And you do not see any way in which provision can be made in the way of clothing for the maintenance of your corps?—No, unless the Government were to relieve the men and officers from the expenses which they are now liable to. From the class of men that form the brigade I have no doubt that they would clothe themselves.

3244. What do they now subscribe?—18s. a year.

3245. Do you believe that if the Government relieve you of the expenses to which you have referred your brigade would in that case probably clothe themselves?—I think they would; I think there is no doubt about it.

3246. (*Lord Overstone.*) Do you consider that your corps is now in a fit state for actual service?—Certainly, in a fit state for garrison service.

3247. Do you think that if Liverpool was menaced by an invading force your corps is now in a state in which it could render valuable service in working the guns?—Most valuable.

3248. Do you think that the efficiency of your corps is now exposed to any serious danger arising from pecuniary difficulties?—Not very serious danger.

3249. I therefore understand your opinion to be that your corps could be maintained without further aid from the Government, but that aid from the Government would materially strengthen your confidence?—Precisely.

3250. It is your judgment upon the whole that that aid ought to be rendered?—It is so.

3251. (*Lord Elcho.*) Do you say that your corps can be maintained without further aid from the Government?—I anticipate some difficulty as to the renewal of the clothing without some aid from the Government.

3252. Is not the clothing an essential part of the business?—Most essential.

3253. So that either the clothing must be found by some means or other, or the incidental expenses must be met or curtailed, in which the men would probably find, if they had no subscriptions to pay, what was requisite for the clothing?—Yes.

3254. But without the one or the other you do not think that your brigade can be maintained at anything like its present strength?—I think not.

3255. (*Major-Gen. Eyre.*) You have stated that you have a certain number of artizans in your brigade; have you found them very orderly, well disposed and amenable to discipline?—Very much so.

3256. As much so as the others?—Quite as much

138   MINUTES OF EVIDENCE TAKEN BEFORE THE COMMISSIONERS APPOINTED

Lieut.-Col. J. Bourne.
24 June 1862.

so as the others. I may state that the artizans are principally in the band, and those do not contribute to the general fund, they are paid by the corps.

3257. The artizans are actually paid?—Yes, several of them, those in the band.

3258. So that the band is really not a volunteer band?—No; it costs the officers at least from 160l. to 180l. a year, which is not included in these expenses. I may be, perhaps, allowed to state to the Commission, that I can speak most favourably of the great moral effect which this movement has had upon the volunteers. I am a magistrate in the neighbourhood of Liverpool, and take a very active part in the local administration of justice, I can speak most confidently as to the very good effect that the volunteer movement has had both in Liverpool and in its neighbourhood. I have observed that many young men who before were lounging and idling about and spending their evening in places of questionable resort are now quite changed. They come to drill, and they induce others to come, and the effect has been of a very beneficial character to the neighbourhood; and I think that the money would be exceedingly well spent, if for no other purpose than that.

3259. Have you any other suggestion to offer to the Commission?—No.

The witness withdrew.

Capt. H. Boys, R.N.

Captain HENRY BOYS, R.N., examined.

3260. (*Chairman.*) You are a captain of the Royal Navy?—Yes.

3261. You are the 1st lieutenant of the 2nd Cinque Ports Artillery Volunteer Corps?—Yes.

3262. How many men have you?—It is a battery.

3263. Of how many men does it consist?—Sixty-four.

3264. Do you drill all your men at the batteries of the Royal Artillery, or have you guns of your own?—We have guns of our own.

3265. (*Viscount Hardinge.*) Where are they?—Two are mounted at Sandwich; two on the coast near Sandwich, at No. 2 battery (north of Deal).

3266. (*Chairman.*) Is that an old battery which has been given up to you?—It is an old battery, but there are no guns in it at present except two that have been sent for our gun drill practice.

3267. You have not erected it at your own expense?—No; we do not use it, except as a magazine.

3268. How often do you get your men together for drill?—I should say eight or ten times a month in the summer months, and three or four times a month in the winter months.

3269. Do you find them pretty perfect in their garrison gun drill?—Yes.

3270. Are they armed with carbines?—Yes.

3271. What value do you attach to the possession of carbines by artillery volunteers?—For service none whatever; but as artillery at present have no guns with which they can attend at volunteer reviews and assemblies they would not be satisfied without their carbines.

3272. How often do you drill them at the small arms drill?—Three or four times a month.

3273. Are you provided with drill instructors?—We have a drill instructor.

3274. Is he paid for by the Government?—Yes; we have to pay his travelling expenses from Sandown to Sandwich.

3275. Does he belong to the coast brigade of Royal Artillery?—Yes, he is master gunner at Sandown Castle.

3276. He is only attached to your corps for the purposes of instruction?—That is all.

3277. And you pay his expenses in going and coming?—Yes; it is 6 miles from where he resides.

3278. (*Major Harcourt.*) Do you send your quarterly practice returns to the officer commanding the Royal Artillery in your district?—Yes.

3279. And also returns of stores?—Yes; the master gunner sends in returns of stores also.

3280. Is your practice carried on under the superintendence of the officer commanding the Royal Artillery in your district?—It is carried on under my superintendence, being myself a naval gunnery officer, by sanction of the officer commanding the Royal Artillery in the district.

3281. Are you inspected by the artillery officer commanding in the district, or by some one appointed by him?—Yes.

3282. Have you any reason to think that this mode of organization is objectionable to the artillery volunteers, and that they dislike being placed under the officer commanding the Royal Artillery in the district?—I have not, nor do I think they dislike it.

3283. Do you think that if they were placed even more under the control of the district officers of Royal Artillery they would dislike it?—I think that they would like it; I think that they are always glad to be commanded by regular officers.

3284. Are there any rifle volunteers in your neighbourhood?—Several.

3285. Does the recruiting for one arm interfere with the recruiting for the other?—It has interfered with both.

3286. Which arm do you consider the most important?—On the coast, certainly the artillery.

3287. (*Viscount Hardinge.*) In what way has it interfered?—When the corps was first established there was a sort of rivalry whether it should be artillery or rifles, and there was a complete canvassing throughout the town of Sandwich as to whether the eligible men would join the rifles or the artillery, and it interfered materially with the establishment of the two corps; at the present time I think it does not interfere so much, as there are very few recruits to be had for either.

3288. Should you say that the artillery volunteer service was popular or not, or that the men generally preferred the rifles?—The men generally prefer the artillery.

3289. (*Major Harcourt.*) Have your corps ever had any battalion drill?—Yes.

3290. To what extent?—I should say eight or ten times a year.

3291. Do you attach much importance to that?—Not for the men, but I think the officers should know something of battalion drill.

3292. Do you think that divisional field days are of any advantage to artillery volunteers?—I think that all field days are good for them.

3293. Do you not think that if artillerymen were allowed the use of guns where practicable, on the occasion of divisional field days, with a special allowance of ammunition, and were placed under the command of an officer of Royal Artillery, it would please them better than being brigaded with infantry?—I certainly think it would, or if they were placed under the command of one of their own officers.

3294. Have you any organized association for prize firing with great guns in your district?—We have.

3295. Do you think that something of that sort would be of advantage to artillery corps generally?—Yes I think so, judging from the advantage which they seem to derive from that in the Cinque Ports.

3296. What are the advantages to which you refer?—I think that it creates emulation amongst the volunteers, and teaches them to notice and to find out their respective faults at their drills.

3297. You have stated that you consider the gathering together of artillery volunteers for the sake of competition prize firing with great guns very advantageous; and you found your statement upon your own experience in the matter. Have the kindness to tell the Commissioners how the prize association with which you are connected is worked, and what you consider the chief points to be attended to in such associations in order to secure success?—Each battery of Cinque Ports artillery subscribes annually a sum to provide prizes. Once a year the competition firing takes place at the most convenient battery for practice in the district; each battery sends two detachments, each subdivision one, which ensures having drilled men. The detachments fire five rounds each at two targets at different distances, alternately at one and the other; points are given for elevation, and direction of each shot, and the exact time taken. The greatest number of points made in the shortest time wins the prize. The result is arrived at by allowing 20 seconds of time to be equivalent to one point, or by adding 20 seconds to the time the five rounds are fired in, for each point short of the greatest number of points gained by any detachment. The chief things to be attended to are, I think, that only one detachment should fire at a time, and there should be strict supervision in the sponging and loading; the whole to be carried on under an officer of the Royal Artillery.

3298. With what guns are you supplied?—Two 24-pounders, garrison guns for drill purposes, and two 18-pounder field guns of position on the coast for shot practice.

3299. Have you been put to any expense in making gun sheds?—We have not erected any, but we have been put to expense for platforms for them.

3300. Are you not aware that those platforms are supplied by the Government?—We expected that they would have been supplied by the Government, and we applied for the expenses, but they were refused.

3301. On what ground were they refused?—We erected them, I believe, before the order came out.

3302. They were not erected, perhaps, according to a specification?—No.

3303. Was that the ground on which payment was refused?—I do not know.

3304. How many drills per annum do you consider necessary for a gunner to entitle him to be considered an effective after he has passed out of the list of recruits?—For each description of gun drill; I should say for a fairly intelligent man, 10 drills a year.

3305. Do you find that the attendance of the men at gun practice is better than at gun drill?—I think it is.

3306. Do your men go through a course of theoretical instruction in the science of artillery, such as boring and fixing fuzes, trajectory, and other things?—All our men have been instructed in boring and fixing fuzes, and they have also received some instruction in the general principles of gunnery from me in the winter months.

3307. Before a man is selected as a non-commissioned officer in the artillery, do you not consider it essential that he should be acquainted with these subjects?—Certainly; he should be acquainted with everything that has to do with shells and fuzes.

3308. How are your non-commissioned officers selected?—By the commanding officer.

3309. Have any of your officers besides yourself been attached for instruction to the Royal Artillery?—No.

3310. I believe you were on board the "Excellent?"—Yes.

3311. As gunnery instructor?—Yes; I was doing duty as a gunnery instructor for some months.

3312. (*Viscount Hardinge.*) Your commanding officer has served in the line, has he not?—Yes, for some years — Major Thompson. He was in the King's Dragoon Guards.

3313. (*Major Harcourt.*) Have you ever had any accident occur during practice?—No.

3314. At what distance is the magazine from the battery at which you practise?—20 or 30 yards; it is in the old fort in which we practise.

3315. Have you been put to any expense for the transport of ammunition?—We have had to pay for the carriage of it sometimes from Dover, where it is supplied from, and from Sandown Castle, a distance of three or four miles.

3316. Are you not aware that that is an expense that would be borne by the War Office?—They demanded it; they sent an account in to us from the garrison at Dover, and we paid it.

3317. Have you been put to any other expense for the carriage of stores?—Yes; we have been put to expense for the transport of a gun carriage from Dover; and we have had to pay for the transport of carbines, and ball cartridges for them.

3318. You are not aware that that is an expense which is undertaken by the War Office?—No; I am not.

3319. Have you been at any expense in the construction of a battery?—No; the guns are mounted on a mound.

3320. Have you the charge of any great amount of Government stores?—No, very few.

3321. Do you think that varying the drill as much as possible secures much better attendance on the part of the men?—Yes, I think it does; the men, when once they have learned a drill, and think that they know it, will not be so likely to come again as when a new description of drill is to be learned.

3322. Do you think that such a variety in drill as would be afforded by repository exercises would be appreciated by the men?—Yes.

3323. Do you consider such drill necessary for garrison artillerymen?—Yes.

3324. It is so considered, is it not, in the Royal Artillery?—Yes, I believe so.

3325. Would it not be convenient that volunteers provided with guns on travelling carriages should be able to shift the wheels for the sake of greasing them, to dismount the guns in case of accidents happening to the carriages, and other simple repository services of a like nature?—I think it would be advantageous to the artillery volunteers to know how to shift everything belonging to a gun or carriage, the wheels and so on.

3326. Have you ever been called upon to move guns from a railway?—Yes, but not for more than a few hundred yards.

3327. If it were necessary to move guns on travelling carriages, are there any organized means by which that could be done in your neighbourhood?—No.

3328. Is it not possible to organize such means?—I think it would be, on the system that I have heard of, which is organized in Sussex. I believe that the farmers in the neighbourhood would horse the guns to go certain distances, provided they were not required too often, or at a time when they were very busy in their agricultural pursuits.

3329. Suppose facilities were afforded by the Admiralty to any members of volunteer corps on the coast for obtaining a knowledge of gun drill at ships' guns, do you think any of your men would be likely to avail themselves of such facilities?—I think some would, but I can not speak of my own battery, as we have no seaboard and no seafaring population.

3330. Will you be kind enough to state any views that you may have on this subject?—I think that gun-boats or floating batteries should be stationed at various ports on the coast, to be in charge of the coastguard at the station with ship keepers on board, the same as they have now; that they should be manned by seamen from the naval reserve in the neighbourhood, and that the volunteer artillery should provide marines for these vessels when they should be called out; that those artillerymen should be still attached to their batteries on shore, but merely told off to march on board a certain vessel in case of actual service, to form the crew of that vessel in conjunction with the naval reserve.

3331. Do you suppose that obtaining men of that class would interfere in any way with the naval reserve?—I think not, because you would not require seamen.

Capt. H. Boys, R.N.

24 June 1862.

T 2

Capt. H. Boys, R.N.

24 June 1862.

3332. You have stated that you are supplied with siege guns or garrison guns, in your opinion is it desirable that the volunteer artillerymen should be provided with guns of any other class?—I think it would be a great advantage to them if they were provided with light 6-pounder guns, or 12-pounder howitzers. I think they would be very effective in repelling a landing from an active enemy's cruisers or privateers. I think they would be particularly useful against boats coming up winding rivers.

3333. How would you move them?—With drag ropes in action, and to go any long journey I have no doubt that the farmers would horse them.

3334. How many men would it take to move a 6-pounder?—15 men is the establishment. I speak of the drill that is established in the navy.

3335. Do you consider that your corps generally is in a healthy condition with reference to its finance?—I think it is. Perhaps I may be allowed to hand in a statement of our finances for the last year (*handing in the same*).

3336. Do you consider that Government aid is necessary to ensure the permanence and efficiency of your corps?—Yes, it will be, but I do not think it is at present.

3337. Supposing any aid were afforded, in what form should you prefer to receive it?—I should prefer an allowance of so much per head; a money allowance to be made to the commanding officer for the purpose of paying the travelling expenses of the volunteers in going to reviews and meetings, which at present fall very heavily upon them or the officers, also to establish gun-sheds.

3338. (*Viscount Hardinge.*) How far are your men from their batteries?—From the drill batteries, about five minutes' march; from the practice battery, between two and three miles; and over bad roads.

3339. Where is the drill battery?—It is just outside the town of Sandwich, on a mound, which was given to us.

3340. Have there been any earthworks thrown up?—None whatever.

3341. Merely a platform?—Merely a platform; we had the mound levelled, and the platform laid on it.

3342. When your men go to gun practice at the battery on the seacoast, how do they go; do they march?—Yes, generally.

3343. They never go by railway?—There is no railway communication; they march through the sand hills; or some of them may take their own conveyances.

3344. What class of men are enrolled in Sandwich?—We have various classes; we have some medical men, some lawyers, farmers, men in business, tradespeople, and apprentices.

3345. Do none of the seafaring population join you?—There are very few of that class at Sandwich.

3346. Have you any men from Deal or Walmer?—That is entirely another district; there is a large seafaring population there.

3347. But that is rather out of your district for recruiting?—Yes, there is another corps there, and also a rifle corps; but I think the latter is falling to ground.

3348. In the event of that rifle corps breaking up, do you think that the men would join the artillery corps?—Ultimately they may, but not at present; there would be a sort of feeling that they were deserting from the rifles to the artillery.

3349. Are your men clothed by the funds of the corps at Sandwich?—Yes; some partly, and some altogether.

3350. What proportion of them should you say are so clothed?—From one-half to two-thirds.

3351. Two-thirds are clothed by the funds of the corps?—No; I should say half altogether, and another portion partially finding their own belts; one third clothing themselves entirely.

3352. (*Chairman.*) Have you a good many honorary members belonging to your corps?—Yes.

3353. And subscribers?—Yes.

3354. Have you subscriptions?—Yes; the honorary members pay a guinea a year, which goes towards our fund.

3355. (*Viscount Hardinge.*) Do you apprehend that your present subscriptions from the honorary members will fall off?—I do not think that the subscriptions will fall off. I am afraid we have got in all the donations.

3356. (*Chairman.*) I perceive that the officers of the corps subscribe very largely?—I think they do; but they are not called upon for many other expenses.

3357. (*Viscount Hardinge.*) Have you been formed into a brigade?—No.

3358. (*Lord Overstone.*) Do you consider your corps to be at this moment in a state efficient for actual service?—Yes, I do.

3359. In case of a sudden emergency arising, do you feel confident that your men could render real and valuable assistance?—Yes, I certainly think they could. If they had repository drill more so, as I think that their services would be as much required to mount the guns in the different batteries as to work them.

3360. (*Major-Gen. Eyre.*) What expenses do the poorest men in your corps feel to be the heaviest, and complain of the most?—I think they most feel the expenses of moving about to their different meetings.

3361. (*Chairman.*) I perceive by the account you have handed in, that you have a balance in hand?—Yes, we have funds in hand; but we have had our uniforms now for two years, and we must look forward to renewing them in another two years.

3362. The other expense to which the individual members of your corps are put, is 10s. 6d. entrance fee?—Yes.

3363. Do you not call upon them for any annual subscription?—Yes, there is an annual subscription of 10s. 6d., and most of them pay their travelling expenses.

3364. (*Major-Gen. Eyre.*) What rate of wages do you think the poorest class of your corps receive?—We have some apprentices, and I think that they feel the expense the most; most of the rest are tradesmen; I cannot tell exactly what their means may be.

The witness withdrew.

Maj. Harcourt.

Major EDWARD W. V. VERNON HARCOURT examined.

3365. (*Chairman.*) Have you been in communication with the Admiralty in reference to the questions which you have put to the last witness?—Yes.

3366. Have you received any answer from the Board of Admiralty upon that subject?—I wish a little to explain the reasons that I had for putting the questions that I did to several witnesses belonging to the artillery force, and with that object I wish to hand in this letter.

The same was handed in as follows:

"4 Cinque Ports Artillery."

"SIR, "War Office, Nov. 7, 1861.

"WITH reference to your letter of the 11th ultimo, a copy of which was forwarded in a communication addressed from this office to the Secretary to the Admiralty, I am directed by Secretary Sir George Lewis to inform you that the Lords Commissioners of the Admiralty have intimated that they will be glad to appropriate occasionally one of Her Majesty's ships to the service of drilling the corps under your command when a vessel can be spared for the purpose, but that at present there is no vessel available, and the great demand for ships to drill the Royal Naval Reserve force, and the Royal Naval Coast Volunteers precludes them from leading you to expect an early compliance with your wishes. I am to request that you will state whether, under these circumstances, you are disposed to proceed with your scheme for the formation of an artillery volunteer corps of a new description, provided that the other proposals contained in your letter of the 11th ultimo meet with the approval of Her Majesty's Government.

"I have, &c.
(Signed) "GEORGE ERSKINE,
Colonel.

"To Officer commanding
"4 Cinque Ports Artillery
"Volunteer Corps, Hastings."

Maj. Harcourt
21 June 1862

Captain HENRY THOMAS LAYE examined.

Capt.
H. T. Laye.

3367. (*Chairman.*) Do you command the 3rd North Riding Artillery Volunteer Corps?—Yes.
3368. Where are your head-quarters?—At Scarborough.
3369. Of what does it consist?—Of one battery.
3370. How many men?—80 is our full compliment.
3371. Do you form part of a brigade, or are you a single battery?—We are part of a brigade. We are brigaded with the East York.
3372. Are there any batteries belonging to the Royal Artillery at which your men are drilled, or have you your own guns?—We have our own guns; we formed a battery in one of the old places at the castle, which we did at a small expense, and then we were supplied with guns.
3373. Have you found garrison guns there?—Yes; two 32-pounders, 49 cwt. guns.
3374. Are your drills regularly carried on there?—Yes; our gun drills.
3375. I presume the men have carbines?—Yes.
3376. Have you also small arm drills?—Yes; when it is wet we drill in the town hall, and when it is fine we go into the castle yard. The War Office has given me the privilege of going in there, and also of excluding the public if necessary.
3377. Is your battery supported by any fund raised in the neighbourhood?—Yes.
3378. Do the men annually subscribe any sum?—Yes; 10s. each.
3379. Do the officers subscribe more than the men?—Yes.
3380. Is that fund applied for the purpose of clothing the men?—No.
3381. In what way is that money expended?—There are various things. I can hardly tell you, the carriage of ammunition; and we provide ammunition for shooting for prizes. The Commission sent questions to me, and I sent our balance sheet. I thought that was the simplest way of seeing how the money was spent.
3382. Do the men clothe themselves?—Yes; we had a few, I think about 10 or 12, whom we have half clothed.
3383. To what class do your men belong?—They are artificers, builders, and architects. I have several men in my battery worth 5,000l. or 6,000l. a piece.
3384. They are men of a sufficiently independent class to clothe themselves?—Yes; it costs them 5l. each.
3385. When the clothing requires renewal, do you anticipate any difficulty in renewing it?—I think not.
3386. Do you think that you will require any assistance from the public to enable you to maintain your corps in an efficient state?—It would be a great assistance to us if we had money; I have to beg for money, or I find it myself at present.
3387. Do you think that your corps will fail altogether if you do not receive assistance from the Government?—I support my corps by the honorary members, and, of course, those are liable to fluctuation.
3388. (*Major Harcourt.*) Have you any rifle volunteers in your district?—Yes.
3389. Does the recruiting for the one arm interfere with the recruiting for the other?—I think not; indeed the rifles were established before my corps was formed; they had a bazaar, and brought in a number of people who, I think, would have been perhaps better in the militia, and that has caused a little dissatisfaction among some of them, but it makes my corps the more popular having to pay a little.
3390. Do you find any difficulty in getting your men to drill?—No.
3391. What number of drills have you in the course of a month?—We have two every week regularly, and then there is a recruit drill besides; but I have men in my corps who, in the course of a year, have attended, to speak within bounds, 170 drills, and I have been astonished at their zeal.
3392. What kind of drill do you have?—Both carbine drill and the big gun drill.
3393. Do the men attach much importance to the carbine?—Yes, we could not do without it; in the first place it teaches them to shoot and to use the sight, then I think it is an amusement, they march, and with our busbies we cut quite a figure.
3394. But do you consider it is of any assistance to them as artillerymen?—It makes the corps popular.
3395. Have you ever had any battalion drill?—Yes.
3396. Do you attach much importance to that?—The greatest; but the difficulty is we want money to move.
3397. Have you any organized association for prize firing with great guns in your district?—No, we devote the money that we get to prizes.
3398. For carbines?—We give prizes for both if we can.
3399. Have you prize firing with the great guns?—Yes.
3400. You say that you have 32-pounders?—Yes.
3401. How many drills per annum do you think a gunner should attend to entitle him to be considered an effective?—I think we want a few more than 24.
3402. How are your non-commissioned officers selected?—That is a difficult question, in the first instance I selected them, and I endeavoured as much as possible, to hold that power in my own hands, but still you must have a certain amount of popularity in bringing in a man, you would have a difficulty, for example, in making a young recruit a bombardier before an older man who had been in the corps a long time.
3403. I presume you consult the feelings of the corps as well as look to the efficiency of the man?—Yes, I endeavour to manage that, but it requires the greatest tact to get the non-commissioned officers right.
3404. I believe you are in the royal navy?—Yes.
3405. Have any of your officers besides yourself received any instruction or been attached to the royal artillery?—No.
3406. Are they in your opinion competent officers?—Yes, mine have only been a short time appointed, but they have been most zealous in attending drill.
3407. Do your officers receive any instruction from the adjutant of your brigade?—We have a master gunner, who is drill instructor, and he is quite a better sort of man; we have also an adjutant, and he is very willing to give us instruction, but the master gunner is the person who has drilled my corps.
3408. I suppose you give them considerable instruction yourself?—The gun drill is different; the shore drill and the ship drill.
3409. At what distance is the magazine from the battery at which you practice?—500 yards. I have

Capt.
H. T. Laye.
4 June 1862.

had a moving magazine built, in which I bring the cartridges.
3410. At what cost was that constructed?—About 1*l*. 10*s*.
3411. Have you been put to any expense for the conveyance of stores?—Yes, certainly.
3412. Were you not aware that that is an expense to be borne by the War Office?—Yes, but still we are put to expense.
3413. What have you paid for the carriage of stores?—I cannot tell you without the accounts.
3414. Have you been put to any expense which has not been paid for you?—Yes.
3415. Have you in charge any great amount of Government stores?—Only our own for the battery.
3416. Are you put to any expense in storing them? Yes, it costs us money; we had this storehouse to build where we keep our side arms, and the other stores belonging to the guns.
3417. (*Col. MacMurdo.*) Is there not a side arm shed built by the Government?—Not for us; it cost us, I think, 17*l*.
3418. (*Major Harcourt.*) Have any of your men been through any course of repository drill?—Yes; they all go through the fuse drill.
3419. And for shifting, mounting, and dismounting guns?—I think not; we mount our own guns; we have got a gyn to do that.
3420. Have you any guns on travelling carriages?—No; not belonging to us.
3421. If it were necessary to move guns, have you any organized method of moving them by horses?—No.
3422. Would it be possible do you think to establish such a system among the farmers in the district?—I do not know that they would volunteer the use of their horses; it would depend, I think, upon how the land owners influenced their tenants.
3423. If facilities were afforded by the Admiralty to any members of volunteer corps, for obtaining a knowledge of gun drill on board ship, would any of your men be likely to avail themselves of such facilities?—I asked my men on parade about that; there were 27 present on the occasion, and six or seven of those men said that they would learn the drill in a gun-boat.
3424. Do you consider that your corps is financially in a healthy condition?—Yes; we have money in the bank.
3425. I think you stated that you did not consider Government aid necessary to insure its permanence?—If we could have 1*l*. a man it would set us up well.
3426. Is that the form in which you would prefer Government aid to be given?—Yes; and the commanding officer to use it to the best of his judgment. I have a committee formed of the men; they choose the committee, and I never do anything of any moment without consulting them; but then I always

manage to guide the committee my own way; it is all management.
3427. Why should you prefer receiving Government aid in the shape of money?—Because we could do as we liked with it, and apply it where most wanted.
3428. You have a floating target at the expense of the Government, have you not?—Yes; we are supplied with a floating target, but we have to find a boat, and it costs us 10*s*. every time we fire at that target, for a boat to go out; we must have a range party, and we are not paid for that.
3429. Supposing you were supplied with the different things of which you think you stand in need, on the terms upon which you are supplied with the floating target, would that satisfy you, supposing that a Government specification was issued, and you were bound not to exceed a certain estimate, and the Government refunded the money expended?—I would rather have the sovereign; remember the letters there would be to write.
3430. (*Col. MacMurdo.*) You mentioned just now that you had a side-arm shed, which was provided by the corps; if you refer to appendix B. in the code of regulations you will find this paragraph, "Where no " other convenient place for the side-arms can be " procured, a small box shed, not less than 12 feet " long, with a row of pegs for the rammers, &c., as " shown on shed C., may be provided, or a larger " shed, also of wood, with two rows of pegs and " space for tackle or other stores." Perhaps you were not aware of that?—No; one of the men in my corps is a builder, and a very zealous man; and there are a number of carpenters in the corps; and with the aid of these men we built it at prime cost.
3431. (*Major-Gen. Eyre.*) What are the daily wages of the poorest men in your corps?—I have one or two jet turners in my corps, and I think they would receive, perhaps, 4*s*. a day.
3432. Are they valuable men?—Yes.
3433. Are you desirous that they should remain with you?—Yes.
3434. What expense do you think those men feel the most?—They feel most providing their clothing; it costs every one of my men 5*l*.
3435. How long does the clothing last?—We bought the best. I advised them to have the best strong cloth.
3436. How long will it last?—We have had it a year already, and it looks very nice; a coat after a year's wear begins to look seedy; but we have got good stuff.
3437. Does that include the busby and accoutrements?—Yes.
3438. The busby will last more than a year, I suppose?—Yes; we found the belts also, and they last for a long time. I think the busby might last for 10 years.

The witness withdrew.

Adjourned till Friday next at half-past Twelve o'clock.

Friday, 27th June 1862.

PRESENT:

Viscount EVERSLEY.
Viscount HARDINGE.
Lord ELCHO.
Lord OVERSTONE.
Lieutenant-Colonel BARTTELOT.

Lieutenant-Colonel Sir A. CAMPBELL.
Lieutenant-General Sir G. A. WETHERALL.
Major-General EYRE.
Colonel MACMURDO.
Major HARCOURT.

VISCOUNT EVERSLEY IN THE CHAIR.

Maj.
T. Brooks.
June 1862.

Major THOMAS BROOKS examined.

3439. (*Chairman.*) You are major of the 3rd Manchester Rifle Volunteer Corps?—Yes.
3440. What is the strength of your corps?—We are now 731.
3441. Is your corps composed of 10 companies?—Yes.

3442. Is it a consolidated battalion?—Yes.
3443. Do you hold the rank of major in the corps?—Yes.
3444. Of what class is your corps composed?—We have 347 artizans, principally consisting of mechanics in the foundries, and men of that de-

TO INQUIRE INTO THE CONDITION OF THE VOLUNTEER FORCE IN GREAT BRITAIN. 143

scription. We have also 21 labourers, 124 tradesmen, 62 clerks, and 77 gentlemen.

3445. Do you raise a subscription in your corps from every man in it?—Yes; 10s. 6d. per man. The colonel pays 75l., the major 50l., the captain 20l., the lieutenant 10l., the ensign 5l., non-commissioned officers 15s., privates 10s. 6d., and honorary members one guinea.

3446. In what way is that fund expended?—It is expended in the expenses of the orderly room, the re-clothing, the expenses of the drill grounds, and storage for arms principally.

3447. Do you find that the fund is sufficient to cover those expenses?—Up to this time it has; the captains have paid very largely out of their own purses.

3448. No part of the expenses of the band is defrayed out of that fund?—I am sorry to say that it has been up to this time; in the year of 1860 and 1861 we expended nearly 300l. on the band.

3449. How will the band be supported in future?—We have a special subscription for the band separate from the regimental fund.

3450. How often have you battalion drills?—Every fortnight in uniform; we have two battalion drills every week, on Wednesdays and Fridays out of uniform, and every other Saturday we have a general battalion drill in uniform.

3451. And company drills besides?—At present not; we find that we get an equally good muster at the battalion drills out of uniform, and we do not get more men go to drill at battalion drills than in the separate companies.

3452. All the recruits, I presume, have a certain amount of preparatory drill before they join in the battalion drills?—Yes, they assemble every Monday morning; but they do not join in the battalion drills until they have had a month's preliminary drill, and have been passed by the serjeant-major.

3453. Is your corps increasing or diminishing in number?—We have decreased 58 men this year, owing entirely to their being unable to pay their subscriptions; we have at present great distress in Lancashire; they would otherwise be very willing to come. They are still good volunteers, but they could not pay the subscriptions which before they did, and we cannot keep up the battalion without.

3454. Do you attribute the failure of the subscriptions to the distress which prevails in Lancashire?—Partly so.

3455. Do you think that in good times there would be any difficulty in maintaining the force at its present strength?—I am afraid that the subscription of 10s. 6d. is too high for them; the majority of our men receive upon the average 1l. a week wages, and they have their families to keep; and it is rather hard upon them to have to pay the 10s. 6d. and other expenses at all the reviews; up to this time they have paid their own expenses.

3456. Has your corps a rifle range?—Yes, of 900 yards, at Barton Moss, about eight miles from Manchester.

3457. Is there railway communication to that rifle range?—Yes; and the railway company takes us there and back for 6d., all of which money is paid by the men themselves, with the exception of the markers, and that is paid out the regimental fund.

3458. Have all your men passed through a course of musketry instruction?—Yes, all of them; we took 600 men through nearly the whole of the three periods last year.

3459. Have you a regular inspection of accounts in your corps?—I myself inspect them twice every year, the colonel inspects them once every year, and the captains of the companies every month and send in a report.

3460. Are the arms in good condition?—Yes, they are; allowing for fair wear and tear, almost as serviceable as when we first had them.

3461. Are they generally kept by the men, or have you an armoury?—We found it very inconvenient to insist upon their being taken into store after every drill, and therefore on certain conditions we allow the men to take them home.

3462. Do you find that the men take good care of their arms?—I think that we have certainly not had a dozen cases in which they were found to be in a bad state.

3463. (*Viscount Hardinge.*) Do you give the men a written permission to take them home?—Yes.

3464. (*Chairman.*) What are your average musters at battalion drills?—To give you an example of coming out of uniform, when the men would be hardly supposed to come, they have come so well that in the last three or four battalion drills we have had an average number of from 250 to 300 out of 731, that is, on the week days; on the Saturday battalion drill, when they come in uniform, they march through the town with the band, and we have from 550 to 600; we average 500 men.

3465. I suppose in the course of a year every man passes through several battalion drills?—Every man must make himself effective, or he must leave the regiment.

3466. (*Sir A. Campbell.*) What number of your men have passed through the remainder of the course; take the last year for example?—I should say that 600 of them went through nearly the whole, if not the whole portion of it; we have had great difficulties in getting the men to pass through all the periods regularly, because it will happen with the casuals that a man will go down once upon a Saturday and fire away his ten rounds, and then perhaps we do not see him again for months.

3467. As a casual he would get through his 10 rounds?—Yes; 600 have passed through a portion of the musketry instruction.

3468. The whole of the musketry instruction and a portion of the practice?—The whole of their musketry instruction, and a portion of their practice; about 250 or 300 have passed through the whole of the musketry instruction, and the whole of the practice. I must except the judging distance drill, which they have not been able to do at all.

3469. (*Lieut.-Col. Barttelot.*) How are your officers appointed?—They were appointed first of all by names being sent to Colonel Egerton.

3470. Who recommended the names to him?—In the first instance there was hardly any recommendation; we met together, and as I may say organized the regiment.

3471. Were your officers elected or selected by the commanding officer?—Hardly; a certain number of gentlemen met together to organize the regiment, and they took upon themselves the organization of certain companies, and names were sent into the colonel through the major, and he approved of them; the whole of the names are sent to the orderly room through me, and I inquire whether they are properly qualified persons, and send the names to the colonel with a report. I am responsible to the colonel that they are proper and fit persons.

3472. Who appoints the non-commissioned officers?—The captains of the companies.

3473. Irrespective of the commanding officer?—No; it is always with the consent of the commanding officer for the time being.

3474. (*Viscount Hardinge.*) Is it your opinion that your regiment cannot remain long in its present efficient state without further aid from the Government?—Apart from the question of the clothing, I believe that we could maintain eight companies at present; the officers would certainly have to make a great sacrifice, but I believe that we could maintain a battalion of eight companies irrespective of the clothing.

3475. Would you recommend that assistance should be given to the battalion in the shape of clothing?—Not in kind.

3476. What way do you mean?—I should prefer the assistance being given in money for clothing, rather than the clothing itself being given.

3477. How would you propose that that money

Maj.
T. Brooks.

27 June 1862.

T 4

grant should be calculated, at so much per head?—Yes; so much per head for every effective man.

3478. To be placed in the hands of the commanding officer, and spent at his discretion?—Yes; he being responsible to the War Office.

3479. Would you tie him down to spending it upon clothing, or would you permit him to spend it in other ways, with a view to defraying your regimental expenses?—To defray all the regimental expenses.

3480. In his option?—Yes; at his discretion.

3481. What security would the Government have if such a proceeding were to take place, that this money might not be spent on bands and other expenses, which might not be strictly regimental expenses, such as armouries, targets, and ranges?—I am hardly able to give an opinion upon that, but I think that an order from the War Office to the effect that it must not be spent upon bands or going to reviews would prevent his doing so.

3482. Would it not equally answer your purpose if the commanding officer of the regiment were to send in to the War Office an estimate with certain heads under which the money should be granted?—That would answer our purpose equally well, speaking of my own battalion.

3483. You would be equally satisfied with respect to your own battalion?—Certainly.

3484. (*Sir A. Campbell.*) Would you be equally satisfied to receive assistance in articles instead of money; for instance, that you should be provided with an armoury, and a range, and so forth?—Equally so.

3485. (*Viscount Hardinge.*) Would you be equally satisfied if the Government were to issue to you so many yards of cloth per man to be made up by your own tailors?—Do you mean that we should have the expense of making them?

3486. Yes?—It certainly would not be so satisfactory as if we had the clothes given to us ready made.

3487. Would you approve of complete suits of clothing being sent down to you from the Government stores?—Hardly; I think that many members of the corps would not like putting on such clothes; in my own battalion we should not mind, as the members consist of artizans, and the men would not object; but there are many other battalions consisting almost entirely of gentlemen.

3488. Supposing you had a money grant to expend at your own discretion, and you thought that the best way would be in clothing the men, you would have to make a contract, would you not?—Yes; but each man would be measured.

3489. In the case of the Government issuing so many suits of clothing from the stores, the uniforms would be fitted to the men, as they are now in many regiments of the line, the cloth being equally good, and perhaps better than you would get from your own contractor?—Yes.

3490. (*Sir A. Campbell.*) Do you think that if uniforms were given out by the Government, or obtained by contract with money provided by the Government, you would have any difficulty in inducing a man to wear a uniform that was the property of a retired member?—We have done that every day.

3491. Would there be any difficulty of that kind, do you think, in the other battalions?—Yes, great difficulty.

3492. Are those other battalions in the same financial difficulties as your own?—Not quite, and for this reason, that their members, consisting principally of gentlemen, can make greater efforts than we can. In case of a financial crisis they would make a call upon every member, who would respond to it; but we could not do that.

3493. Does your evidence go to this, that there are some volunteer corps in which the men cannot afford to clothe themselves, but they would be willing to accept uniforms if issued by the Government; while there are others in which they would not consent to receive such uniforms, as they could afford to clothe themselves?—Exactly so.

3494. (*Lord Overstone.*) Beyond your experience and knowledge in detail of the condition of your own corps, have you a general knowledge of the condition of the volunteer movement in South Lancashire?—I have.

3495. Is it your opinion that that movement is subject to any serious danger as to its present condition?—It is not; I believe that the movement is rather increasing than decreasing in South Lancashire. We can get now a better class of recruit than we could a year ago among the artizans, whereas a year ago I could get a common man as an artizan, now I can get a foreman.

3496. The first object to which this Commission is instructed to direct its attention, is the present condition of the volunteer force. As far as your knowledge and experience go, you can say that you think that condition is satisfactory?—Yes, certainly.

3497. The three main points which affect the condition of the volunteer force must of course be the pecuniary considerations, the discipline and organization of the corps, and, thirdly, the condition of their arms and accoutrements. How far do you think you can say that the volunteer force is now in a satisfactory condition with regard to those three heads?—As to the financial part of the question, I do not think that they are in a satisfactory condition.

3498. Do you think that the pecuniary pressure upon the artizan class in your corps, threatens considerable danger to the maintenance and efficiency of the corps?—I do.

3499. Do you think that that danger may be materially relieved or alleviated by pecuniary aid from the Government?—I do.

3600. With regard to discipline and organization, do you consider that the corps is now in a satisfactory state?—I do; I consider it in a highly satisfactory state.

3601. I understand you to say, also, as to the condition of their arms and accoutrements, that you feel confident they are in a satisfactory state?—I feel every confidence.

3602. Supposing that South Lancashire was suddenly menaced by the approach of a foreign force, say in the neighbourhood of Liverpool, do you think that your corps could turn out in a state capable of rendering real and effectual assistance to the regular army?—I do.

3603. Do you think that it would turn out, under such circumstances, without hesitation?—I feel convinced of it.

3504. Do you think that, under such circumstances, there would be an increased and extended disposition to enter the force?—Yes, I do.

3505. Do you think that the men so brought into the force, and amalgamated with the existing corps, would be rapidly rendered efficient?—I do.

3506. You think that the volunteer movement, as it now exists, is a valuable nucleus for the further augmentation of the force which would take place if the danger of the emergency was sufficient to require it?—I do.

3507. With regard to the probable continuance of the present volunteer movement at its existing strength, am I correct in inferring it to be your opinion that that strength can be efficiently maintained, and that, in a case of emergency, it would be largely augmented?—Yes; that is my opinion.

3508. Do you think that the certainty of that opinion may be increased by limited pecuniary aid on the part of the Government?—I do.

3509. Are you prepared to suggest to this Commission any measures which you think might be usefully adopted for the purpose of increasing the efficiency of the volunteer force, and so enable it to act as a valuable auxiliary to the regular army in a case of emergency?—With the exception of a grant of money I am hardly prepared to say.

3510. Do you think that the volunteer movement is

in a satisfactory condition both as to its present efficiency and its probable permanency, reserving only the opinion which you have already given, that some pecuniary aid to relieve the pressure on the poorer classes of the volunteers should be obtained from the Government?—I do.

3511. (*Major-Gen. Eyre.*) Were the men who you say you have lost in consequence of their poverty men whom you valued and desired to keep?—Three or four of them I personally knew, from their having been privates in my company, and I should have very much liked to have kept them.

3512. It was simply their poverty that obliged them to leave you?—Yes, not being able to pay the 10s. 6d., and a few incidental expenses, such, for instance, as the 6d. for the railway fare every time they went down to shoot.

3513. Is there anything in particular that presses upon them more than another, that you can mention?—No, I think nothing more than the subscription.

3514. (*Major Harcourt.*) How many drills do you think it is necessary that a man should pass through to render him effective?—I think 24 are not enough.

3515. How many should you consider sufficient?—We have 35.

3516. Do you think that that is the minimum number of drills that a man should pass through?—It depends very much upon the man.

3517. (*Viscount Hardinge.*) What do you mean when you say you have 35 drills?—We return a man as effective, but we do not consider him effective, or able to undergo inspection, nor do we let him join the battalion movements.

3518. (*Lord Overstone.*) You think that 24 drills will make a man technically effective, but that 35 are requisite to make him efficient?—Yes.

3519. (*Sir A. Campbell.*) Do those 35 drills include musketry instruction?—No.

3520. Do you think that on the average 35 actual drills are necessary to keep up the efficiency of a man who has once passed through his drills?—I think so.

3521. (*Lt.-Col. Barttelot.*) Do you not think that it would be a great hindrance to the movement in the manufacturing districts if you said to a man that he must pass through 35 drills in order to make him efficient?—We do not find it so.

3522. (*Viscount Hardinge.*) What proportion of your corps have gone through a course of 35 drills?—More than two-thirds of them up to this time who have joined.

3523. Have you been obliged to strike many men off your list in consequence of their not having completed their 24 days' drill?—No, I do not know a case. I might mention in illustration of that, that only a week or two ago a company sent in a requisition to be allowed to attend eight consecutive drills in order to learn light infantry movements, and out of a company of 62 we never have less than 59 to attend those drills.

3524. That being the satisfactory state in which your corps is, do you consider that other corps are in a similar condition, generally speaking, as to their attendance at drill?—Many that I can mention are; there is one at Bury which is in an equally efficient state.

3525. (*Lord Overstone.*) You have had abundant means of becoming well acquainted with the state and feelings of the artizan class throughout South Lancashire?—Yes.

3526. Is it in your opinion, a just and wise course to draw the artizan class largely into the present volunteer movement?—I have up to this time seen no objection to it.

3527. But looking forward, and guiding yourself by your knowledge of the state and character and feelings of the artizan class in South Lancashire, do you consider it expedient on the part of the Government to draw largely upon that class to assist in the volunteer movement?—I have never heard or seen anything to make me think that they should not be drawn upon largely.

3528. In case there was immediate danger of foreign invasion, what do you think would be the effect upon the condition of trade and all the complicated machinery of the productive operations throughout South Lancashire of drawing from it for military purposes a considerable portion of the artizan class?—I presume that in case of invasion, business would be at an end.

3529. Do you give that answer after full consideration? Is it not probable that there might be a menace of danger to our shores of such an extent as to make it necessary to call out the military resources of the country, but at the same time it would be very expedient and desirable that the ordinary processes of society should not be violently or unnecessarily disturbed?—I believe that in case of a menace, were the Government to call out my own battalion, more than two-thirds of them would assemble.

3530. My question was not so much directed to the question of whether the men would obey the call, but what would be the effect on the productive industry of South Lancashire of a large number of men being drawn from the various occupations which are there in a state of great activity?—In case of a menace only?

3531. I wish generally to obtain your opinion, after a little consideration, as to what would be the practical effect under a state of alarm for the safety of the country, not carried to its last extremity, but assuming a serious aspect, which would lead the Government to call forth all its military resources, and amongst the rest the volunteer force, that volunteer force consisting to a considerable extent of persons engaged in the various industrial pursuits of South Lancashire, and, therefore, necessarily drawn away from those pursuits to discharge a military duty?—I should think that the masters and the mill owners would permit their men to go, and that they would receive them back again when they were no longer wanted.

3532. In that case, how far do you think that the operations of the mills generally would be suspended and thrown into confusion by drawing away a certain and not an unimportant portion of their hands?—Generally, I think the masters would not oppose it.

3533. Your opinion therefore is, that in case of an adequate emergency, a large volunteer force, including a considerable part of the artizan population might be safely relied on for the discharge of their military duties?—Yes.

3534. Directing your attention to internal considerations of this kind, are you quite satisfied as to the prudence and safety of training a large portion of the artizan class in military discipline and placing in their hands arms?—I am convinced that it would be quite prudent.

3535. Is that answer given with a full consideration of times different from those which now exist; but bearing in mind the state of things which has existed in former times in the manufacturing districts?—Yes.

3536. You, being interested largely in the peace and good order of your district, feel no apprehension as to the effects of the volunteer movement from teaching an important portion of the artizan class military combinations and the use of military weapons?—Not the least.

3537. (*Sir G. A. Wetherall.*) Do you think that the social habits and general conduct of the volunteers have been improved by the volunteer organization, and that there is now, in consequence of that, less chance of those *émeutes* which formerly agitated the country?—I do; it is so, invariably.

3538. (*Major-Gen. Eyre.*) It has had a good moral effect upon them?—Very great indeed.

3539. (*Sir G.A. Wetherall.*) Do you find that the artizans are the most efficient men in your corps, and that they attend more regularly to their drills?—Yes.

Maj. T. Brooks.
27 June 1862.

U

Maj.
T. Brooks.
27 June 1862.

3540. (*Major-Gen. Eyre.*) Do you consider that you have sufficient power to enforce discipline under the rules?—I think so.

3541. You have spoken of your corps as being in an exceedingly satisfactory state, and you have also some knowledge of the volunteers generally in that part of England. Do you think that the same endeavour is made to maintain the efficiency of the corps generally?—Yes.

3542. I mean as to the musketry instruction?—Yes; but in South Lancashire we have experienced great difficulties in getting the rifle ranges. Many regiments last year could not go through the musketry instruction for want of a range.

3543. I presume that you consider that practice of the first importance?—Of the very first importance.

3544. (*Major Harcourt.*) How far is your range from head-quarters?—Eight miles; but there is a railway there and the railway company takes them for sixpence there and back.

3545. (*Major-Gen. Eyre.*) You have stated that you have sufficient power to enforce discipline; by what code are you guided, is it a regimental code, or simply this book?—Simply that book.

3546. You find that that is sufficient?—We find it sufficient.

3547. (*Viscount Hardinge.*) Do you think that the enrolling of artizans has in any way interfered with the recruiting for the line or the militia?—I do not think it has at all interfered with the recruiting for the line or the militia; I think that the men we get in the volunteers would not be likely to enlist in either.

3548. I suppose their wages are good?—Their position is better than that of the men who usually enlist in the line or the militia.

3549. (*Sir A. Campbell.*) What number of volunteers do you think there are in Manchester?—About 3,000.

3550. Of those, what proportion are artizans?—Perhaps 2,000 or more of them are artizans.

3551. (*Viscount Hardinge.*) You stated, I think, that your officers had had to make large contributions in order to meet the expenses of the corps. Have you found any difficulty in filling any vacancies which may have occurred in consequence?—We have experienced a difficulty in this last year; but I should say that it is not entirely in consequence of the subscriptions. The subscription of the captain, as I stated before, is but 20*l.*; but the gentlemen whom we wish to get as officers would not give themselves the trouble to attend the drills.

3552. (*Sir G. A. Wetherall.*) Do you consider that your captains are competent to command their companies?—We endeavour to make them so, and I think they are.

3553. (*Major-Gen. Eyre.*) Have your officers shown any dislike to military supervision, in the common acceptation of the term?—On the contrary, I am convinced that the Lancashire volunteers would prefer much to feel, if I may so say, the reins from the War Office more than they have done yet. That is a feeling which has been generally expressed; we have felt ourselves too much left alone.

3554. Then you would rather have more military supervision than less?—Certainly.

3555. (*Col. MacMurdo.*) Referring to that part of your evidence which related to the probable effect that the calling out of the volunteer force would have upon trade, and the disinclination that the mill owners would have to allow the men to go for any lengthened period to be embodied, are you aware that the Act only contemplates that the volunteers should be called out for actual service in case of actual invasion, or the appearance of an enemy in force on the coast of Great Britain?—Yes.

3556. And therefore it is not probable that for any lengthened period before such invasion took place the volunteers would be called out for actual service?—No.

3557. That being so, the mill owners or any other employers could not have any objection to the volunteers being enrolled as they are now enrolled in any number for the purpose of being drilled preparatory to being called out?—None whatever.

3558. And no stoppage of trade or manufactures need necessarily take place?—No, not at present.

3559. You are also probably aware that during such a crisis the regular army and the militia would be called out to form what may be considered the first line of defence, and that it would only be when an actual invasion took place that the volunteers would be called out?—Yes.

3560. Do you not think that that arrangement could be made without inconvenience to trade?—Yes, I think so.

3561. (*Sir A. Campbell.*) Is there considerable anxiety in your neighbourhood to know the course which the Government intend to adopt in consequence of the proceedings of this Commission?—Very great anxiety indeed.

3562. Do you think it is important that that anxiety should be allayed without much delay, or that time may be taken for consideration?—I think that time may be taken for consideration.

3563. (*Lord Overstone.*) What do you mean when you say that there is very great anxiety upon the subject; is it anything more than that which would naturally arise to know what may be the decision of the Government, acting under the advice of the Commission inquiring into this subject?—I think there is a feeling that our corps cannot go on for another year without being reclothed, and that is the question perhaps more than any other that presses on commanding officers.

3564. You think that a decision as to the mode of meeting the expenditure in the next twelve months is important?—Yes.

3565. What do you think would be the effect of nothing being done?—I am afraid we should lose a great many more men.

3566. What do you mean by a great many; what proportion?—I cannot give you the proportion.

3567. Do you think that there would be a loss arising from a sense of disappointment and vexation, or a real *bonâ fide* loss arising from pecuniary pressure?—A real *bonâ fide* loss arising from pecuniary pressure.

3568. (*Viscount Hardinge.*) You have spoken about military supervision. Can you suggest in any way how any greater amount of military supervision could be exercised over the volunteers?—No, except that I may say I have heard opinions once or twice expressed to this effect, that they wished an order would come down for us to assemble to be inspected, the whole Manchester brigade, and not to be left to ourselves to arrange our own battalion days.

3569. (*Col. MacMurdo.*) Is it your opinion that such an arrangement could be carried out?—Certainly, by giving us, say, a week's notice. For instance, if we knew that Colonel MacMurdo was coming down on Saturday week next, we should turn out 2,000 men certainly, if not more.

3570. Would that be because you would like to be inspected?—Yes; we wish to show you what we are able to do. We wish it.

The witness withdrew.

Lieut.-Col.
F. W. Knight,
M.P.

Lieut.-Col. Frederick Winn Knight, M.P., examined.

3571. (*Chairman.*) I believe you command the 1st Worcestershire Rifle Volunteers?—I do.

3572. That is an administrative battalion, consisting of 11 corps?—Yes.

3573. How many men have you?—936, the establishment being 1100; there are about 85 men per company.

3574. Have you a battalion fund as well as a company fund?—We have no battalion fund, but we have a share of a small county fund which was established last year, and which amounts to 11l. a company.

3575. Of what classes is your battalion composed principally?—It is composed of all classes; there are only two companies which are exclusively formed of the middle class; there may be two or three in which the majority are working men; but in most of the companies there are men standing in the ranks in quite an equal position to the officers as well as working men.

3576. Did most of the men in your battalion clothe themselves?—When the volunteer movement was first proposed in Worcestershire it broke down; meetings were called in the different towns by the deputy lieutenants, and the terms proposed were that every man was to clothe himself, but they failed; in some cases they got together 16 or 17 men, but they failed in raising anything like a company. Mine was the first company that was raised, and it was raised on the principle that the clothes would be found for every man who was accepted, and who did not choose to clothe himself; that was taken as the rule in my part of the county, and I think in a good deal of the rest of the county. Mine is a village corps; all the rest are town corps; there is no small town in Worcestershire without a corps, and they were formed chiefly on this principle: a certain number of the most wealthy and influential inhabitants, on both sides of politics, formed themselves into a committee called the organization committee; they put their names down for subscriptions, and they raised donations and subscriptions in the neighbourhood; the subscriptions were all given for three years certain, so that each district engaged to establish and keep a corps for three years, and we said, "We shall see at the end of " that time whether the country thinks us worth " anything." There was, I should think, 400l. or 500l. raised in each corps for the first year, and in some cases much more. The clothing, except for such men as chose to clothe themselves, was provided out of that fund. A great many men who could perhaps have afforded to clothe themselves had clothing supplied by the fund, and they might not have joined if it had not been for that fund.

3577. When the time comes for reclothing the men, do you anticipate that there will be much difficulty?—I am quite sure, from what I know of them, that they will not reclothe themselves; they think that the country ought to do it. I do not mean to say that a certain number of the men would not do it, but I mean that the companies cannot be kept up.

3578. You do not anticipate that any subscriptions will be raised in the future, such as were raised before in order to establish the corps?—There was great alarm felt at that time; people thought that their property was not secure from invasion, and many rich people were willing to subscribe at that moment; but they feel, I believe, now much greater security, (perhaps partly on account of the volunteer movement,) and I am sure that we shall not get the subscriptions again; besides which, Government aid has been so much talked about, and is so absolutely expected, that I am sure people will say, they have done enough for the country individually. There will have been spent in the three years at least 1,000l. from each district for each company, taking the rifle ranges, the uniforms, &c., altogether.

3579. Has each company its own rifle range?—Yes.

3580. And a drill serjeant?—Each company has a drill instructor.

3581. Have you an adjutant?—Yes.

3582. Do you pay him anything beyond his ordinary pay?—He was an officer whom I was very anxious to have; he was particularly recommended by a distinguished officer under whom he had served; he was a young man who had been adjutant of two regiments, and was very fit for the position. He would not come to us at all for the first pay that was offered by the War Office, and I had refusals from several other men. I could have got abundance of adjutants, but not one who had a high character as the adjutant of a regiment. This officer came to us upon an increase of pay being given by the War Office; but when he had been with us a year and a half, he said he could not live on his pay, and must give it up, and go somewhere else. A meeting of officers was held this spring, and we agreed to make him an allowance in these proportions: the field officers 10l. each, and 10l. from each of the companies, making 130l. a year more than his pay. This matter has been very much discussed, and we think it very hard that our adjutant's pay should be less than that of an adjutant in the disembodied militia. I think that there is something like 70l. difference in their pay; the adjutant in the disembodied militia receives lodging money, has a servant provided, and training allowance of 3s. 9d. a day while his regiment is in training. There is another point with respect to our adjutant. I think he ought to have a serjeant-major allowed him. The militia adjutant only works one month in the year, while our adjutant works almost every day in the year. I may safely say that, because he writes letters on Sundays, and sometimes comes to see me on Sundays; but he has no clerk, while the militia adjutant has one or two, and a serjeant-major besides. I think that all battalions of eight companies or more, which are capable of being divided into two battalions and of having two adjutants, should have a serjeant-major. The adjutant is constantly wanted and written to to visit two or more companies on the same day, which he cannot do. A serjeant instructor of a company has no authority over the other companies if appointed acting serjeant-major, and if the serjeant instructor of company A were sent to company B, they would be in arms in a moment; you cannot make him an acting serjeant-major except on field days; you cannot send him to do anything. It would be of great assistance to an active adjutant to have a serjeant-major under him. When an order has to be sent to the 11 companies, of course there are 11 sets of circulars to be written, and the adjutant and his wife are constantly kept writing. He wants a clerk, and the serjeant-major could perform the duties of clerk, besides taking the adjutant's place at any drill or practice where he might be wanted.

3583. Does the adjutant attend the drill of all the companies separately?—He is constantly at work; last year, during the summer, he saw five of the corps once a week, three of them he saw together every week; five of the corps once a fortnight, and one, which was a long way off, without railway communication, he saw once a month. In the winter he saw them not quite so often, but very frequently. He is obliged to keep two horses to do his work.

3584. Has he satisfied himself that the men have all gone through a proper course of musketry instruction?—I wrote to him to ask him that question, and whether all the corps had sent in musketry returns, and he informs me that they did, but that they varied very much in completeness.

3585. Do you ever inspect the arms of the regiment?—When I go to visit a company I do.

3586. You do that occasionally?—Yes.

3587. Do you also inspect the arms?—Yes.

3588. Are they all in good order?—I have known them sometimes in bad order, but that has been when they have not had a serjeant instructor whose business it is to keep the arms in order.

3589. Are the arms kept in an armoury all together?—Yes, generally; in some of the companies a portion of the men are allowed to take their arms home, and these are usually well taken care of. When I have found them not so well taken care of, it has been when there has been an armoury, and no serjeant instructor in charge of it; when they come in after it has been raining, and there is no person whose business it is to take care of them, they soon get into bad order.

3590. What is the average attendance at battalion

Lieut.-Col.
F. W. Knight,
M.P.

27 June 1862

U 2

Lieut.-Col. F. W. Knight, M.P.

27 June 1862.

drills?—Our battalion drills are generally wing drills, or drills of two, or three, or four companies, and they are generally well attended; a company seldom comes out with less than 40 men.

3591. Then you get about one half to attend?—I think, when I send for a battalion drill, we get more than one half, or quite a half; I think that generally on equalizing them there are from 20 to 25 files in a company.

3592. You have nothing to do, I presume, with the appointment of the officers to these companies?—The lord-lieutenant does not now recommend any officer except through me.

3593. Do you satisfy yourself that the officer is competent beforehand?—I may say that I have not one officer who has been in the army; what I think the most important point in forming these town companies is, that the officers should be persons whom the rest of the town will follow and like to serve under; I think that that is of much more importance than any special qualification. At the first forming a company in a little town there are, perhaps, not more than two or three persons whom it would be possible to choose as captains; they must be men with a considerable amount of energy and activity, willing to attend to their duty, and such men as their fellow townsmen will follow. The lord-lieutenant made the appointment of captains generally on the recommendation of the organization committees; after that he put the appointments of the other officers in the captains' hands. In some cases the men have had a choice, but not recognized by the lord-lieutenant. There was a sort of feeling that the head people in a town must be at the head of the corps. I have known several instances of persons who would not have been able, perhaps, to have formed a corps at first, having since been selected by acclamation as captain, because they are now known to be thoroughly good officers.

3594. Do you think upon the whole that the subaltern officers are competent to discharge their duties?—I think that many of them are now very competent. I have seen a great difference in them this year; they have taken great pains with their duties, and most of them attend their drills very regularly. Some are able to learn much more quickly than others. I find with both officers and men that some of those who take the most pains have less absolute capacity to learn quickly; but by taking pains they pick it up after a time.

3595. You have stated in a former part of your evidence that you are of opinion there must be some assistance given to the force to enable them to be maintained in their present state of efficiency?—Yes, I am quite certain that it cannot go on much further without. We only decided upon establishing the corps and carrying them on for three years, and these three years will begin to run out next October. After that I am sure that unless the country think them worth something they will fall to pieces.

3596. In what way do you think that assistance ought to be given?—I think that there are three heads under which it ought to be given; the first head is the increase of the efficiency of our permanent staff. As I said before, the adjutant wants more pay, and then, in large administrative battalions, a serjeant-major is wanted. The second head comprises the uniforms, which I divide into two parts; the first consists of that which is absolutely necessary for the men to enable them to appear on parade, viz., tunic, trousers, shako, cap, belts, and pouches; after that come leggings, great coat, havresack, or knapsack, and these most of the men in my battalion have not got. My notion is, that 1 *l*. a head per annum would enable us to provide the necessaries; that is, the tunic, the trousers, the shako, the cap, the belts, and the pouches. I do not think that they can be provided much under 3 *l*. 10 *s*. The difference of cost between the highest and the lowest priced outfits in my battalion is quite ridiculous; and I think that 3 *l*. 10 *s*. is a very reasonable estimate. I find that in the yeomanry the clothes are estimated to last seven years: I do not think that ours will last above half that time, as we are out very much oftener than the yeomanry are. I do not think that they will last above three years, or three years and a half at most.

3597. How many drills do your men have in a year?—They are always drilling. I have received a return from my own village company. I wrote to them to know what drills they had this year, and I am informed that, on the average, there has been 74 attendances per week from the first week in January until now; each drill takes an hour, and they have all sorts of drills; bayonet exercise, and all the musketry exercise comes into it. There are generally in every company a few men of whom the captain complains that they do not come to drill often enough; but they are often men who think that they know their drill; they knew it very well last year, and therefore they will not give so much time to it now. Some of the most constant attendants at drill last year are some of those who are rather deficient this year.

3598. The established number of drills is 24 per annum?—Lord Elcho informs me that it is 18; but as I understand the Act of Parliament it is 24.

3599. You were just now going to enumerate the different items which you thought ought to be supplied?—The first head is the increase of strength in the staff; the second head is the uniform. A uniform, without great coat, leggings, or havresack, might be provided for 1 *l*. a year. The third head embraces another class of expenses—a sort of contingent expenses that should be allowed for; they are expenses that must be paid by some one. I will read a list of items which I have taken out of the accounts of the different corps, and the Commission will determine whether the officers or the country ought to pay for them. I must premise that each item has to be multiplied by 11 for the 11 companies. First, there is the rent of headquarters or orderly room; then the rents of the armoury, drill ground, shed, or school room for winter drill, and rifle range. Then there are payments for targets, flags, hurdles, &c. Then coal, gas, lighting and cleaning the rooms after drilling; repairs of uniforms; serjeant armourer for repairs of arms, and some one must be paid for cleaning them; a bugler,—he is, generally speaking, paid; stationery, printing, books, postage, advertisements, travelling and other expenses to brigade and battalion field days, carriage of stores, parcels, &c.; Grant's pontoon kettles, canteens, and expenses incurred for feeding the men on field days. We generally feed them on the field; that is an expense which appears in some of the accounts, but not in all of them. It occurs about four or five times a year, on field days, when we are out the whole day.

3600. (*Viscount Hardinge.*) How often can you get the men together in that way?—Four or five times a year. Then there would be sundry payments for stores of different sorts. Petty cash disbursements, and then extra pay for the adjutant, and extra pay and allowances of different sorts for serjeant instructors. Some of these have extra pay, as they were engaged before. They were allowed pay by the War Office; at that time there was something like 1,000 or 1,200 serjeants wanting at once, and they were not forthcoming. We were then obliged to give them extra pay, which we now continue if they are good men.

3601. (*Col. MacMurdo.*) You do not give anything to those whom you have received under the regulations?—We give uniforms extra to all those whom we receive under the regulations; and some men who have served 18 or 19 years in the army come to us, taking the pay allowed to them; and then we make up the amount of the pensions which they will have at the end of their service to them until the pensions become due; so that we have extra pay and allowances to provide.

3602. (*Viscount Hardinge.*) You have mentioned stationery and advertisements, are they not paid for by the adjutant out of his allowance?—No, I am not speaking of the adjutant's stationery; it is the company's stationery. There are also prizes for company shooting; that the officers have to find. Among these items I include feeding the men on the battalion field days. An exceedingly good meal, with beer, costs about 1s. 6d. a man, and taking each company to consist of 50 men, at four battalion drills, the sum would amount to 15l. a company per year. All the things I have named cannot be done for less than from 80l. to 100l. per company; I think there ought to be an allowance of 1l. a man for these expenses.

3603. You would then allow 2l. a man?—Yes, and I find that that is the new allowance made for the dress and the contingent expenses of the yeomanry, who have not these 11 sets of miscellaneous payments to provide for. We think (barring the pay, which we do not any of us want,) that a company of riflemen costs quite as much as a troop of yeomanry; and we hope that we shall receive the same allowances that the yeomanry receive. You may depend upon it that clothing the men and finding all these necessary expenses cannot be done for less; it will cost that much to somebody, and the only question is, how much is to be thrown upon the officers, and how much the Government will take off their hands.

3604. (*Chairman*.) Your men do not provide themselves with horses or appointments?—No; but we have all the contingent expenses I have named, multiplied by 11, to be provided in lieu of the horses.

3605. I understand you to propose that there should be an allowance of 2l. per man to cover all the expenses, excepting, of course, the band?—Yes; I have nothing to do with the band. I think that the bandsmen's uniform ought to be paid for, if the men are effectives, but not otherwise.

3606. In addition to what is at present paid for the staff of the corps?—Yes.

3607. (*Viscount Hardinge*.) Is the 15l. per company for dinners which have been paid for by the captains and subalterns of each company?—I think that the two companies which are entirely composed of tradesmen or of middle-class men have paid for themselves, all the others have been paid for by the officers or out of the local fund.

3608. The expense of these dinners has not fallen on the officers individually?—In some cases it has done so, and in some not; in some cases it is charged in the accounts of the company, and in some cases it is not charged.

3609. How was the battalion fund raised, and to what purposes was it to be applied?—It is not a battalion fund, it is a county fund for the two battalions, which was raised at a public meeting called by the lord-lieutenant. It has been applied to travelling expenses for field days.

3610. Do you think that your returns of effective and non-effective members are accurately kept?—I have not the least doubt of it; I think that the captains are thoroughly to be trusted in that respect.

3611. You would not reduce the number of drills that are required to make a man effective?—We have no difficulty about effectives in my battalion; I wrote to my adjutant, to know how many drills he thought necessary, and he says certainly not less than 24 for recruits, but he thinks that a man should learn to march and to understand the manual and platoon exercises before he comes in; afterwards he thinks that not less than two drills per month in summer, and one per month in winter, exclusive of musketry practice, should be required.

3612. That would be for the second year?—Yes; and any subsequent year.

3613. (*Sir A. Campbell*.) Does that mean exclusive of musketry exercise as well as target practice?—I think it does.

3614. (*Viscount Hardinge*.) In returning a man effective do you make musketry drill count?—In returning a man effective every drill of at least one hour's duration counts; when a man attends a squad, a company, or a battalion, and does one hour's drill under the command of his officers or the instruction of the serjeant instructor, we count that as a drill.

3615. Have you or your serjeants ever gone round to the men at their houses to drill them?—They have not done so. The principle on which our corps are formed, and which I believe to be the only principle on which they can succeed is, that the men should have a central drill ground close to their homes, and that every man should live not further than a mile from it, so that they can lounge on to the drill ground for an hour instead of lounging somewhere else. If you make an afternoon's work of every drill, I do not think that men will come often enough to learn their drill.

3616. What is the average distance of your companies from headquarters?—I think that the men generally live within half a mile of their parade ground.

3617. Is it absolutely necessary in an administrative battalion that the adjutant should have a room in which to carry on the orderly room correspondence?—It is absolutely necessary that he should have some sort of office, and it must be at his own house. I think that he ought to be allowed the rent of a house, and then he would find a room to carry on the business in. He has at present to provide an orderly room for the battalion out of his pay, and we have one to find for each of the 11 companies besides.

3618. Have you a headquarters orderly room?—No; there is no battalion orderly room.

3619. In nine cases out of the 11, cannot the adjutant conveniently transact his business in his own house?—I think that his own house must be the orderly room for the battalion business.

3620. In fact, you wish to increase the adjutant's allowance by giving him the rent of a house?—Yes; 50l. a year is the rent he pays for his house.

3621. (*Sir A. Campbell*.) In case your suggestion were not adopted, to what extent do you anticipate a falling off in your numbers?—I do not think that the battalion will exist at all unless something is done for it.

3622. Supposing your suggestion were adopted to the extent of relieving the men of all their expenses except the uniform, what do you think would be the result?—I am quite certain that they will not find their uniforms.

3623. You think, that unless they are relieved of the whole expense, they will practically sink?—I think that they must be relieved of the expense of the uniforms; I believe that they would still continue to pay something towards other expenses, but they must have their uniforms; we have no subscriptions from the men in most of the companies; unless a man chooses to subscribe to the fund, he is not called upon as a volunteer to do so.

3624. (*Viscount Hardinge*.) What proportion of the men clothe themselves in the different companies who would not require to be clothed at the expense of the Government?—I think, if there was an allowance made, that every man would take the allowance towards the clothes, unless they were very rich men.

3625. I think you stated that there were a good many gentlemen in the ranks?—Yes, in some of the corps. There are some men in all of them, perhaps, who would not take it.

3626. Do you think that the greater proportion of them would take it?—Nine-tenths of them would certainly.

3627. (*Sir A. Campbell*.) You have said that they must be supplied with clothing; is that on account of pecuniary necessity, or because they have a feeling that they have a right to expect it from the country?—I think that many of them could pay for it if they liked to do so; but they look upon it that this Commission is certainly going to give them clothing, and they feel that they have done enough in providing it at starting. The inhabitants of the districts feel that they have clothed the companies and sup-

Lieut.-Col. F. W. Knight, M.P.

27 June 1862.

U 3

ported them for three years, and that they have done enough as individuals.

3628. Do you think that an immediate decision upon this point is important?—I think that by the time the three years' subscriptions have run out, and they will begin to do so next October, we ought to know what we have to expect; after that I think there will be a great falling off, and great disappointment felt if nothing be done.

3629. (*Lord Overstone.*) The feeling to which you refer as to the clothing is, that they think it reasonable the clothing should be provided, rather than a feeling that they cannot go on if they are subject to that charge?—I think that some of the corps, for example, two of the Kidderminster corps, could not go on. I think that there are men in all the corps who could not go on.

3630. Is that the larger or the smaller proportion?—In some of the corps it is a very large proportion; in some of the corps men who could provide themselves with clothing do not choose to do so; they say, "If we give our time, that is all that ought to be required of us."

3631. How many volunteers are there in Worcestershire?—There are 10 companies besides my own battalion, I have 936 men, the other battalion consists of more than 700.

3632. Should you say that the condition of the volunteer force in the county of Worcester is at the present moment satisfactory?—I think it is so far perfectly satisfactory: there has been no falling off, we can get plenty of recruits, and we have no difficulty at all in getting fit and proper men for officers.

3633. Do you think that it is without doubt in a satisfactory and proper condition as to the arms and accoutrements?—Certainly quite so.

3634. Do you think it is in an equally satisfactory and efficient state as to the discipline and organization of the men?—Colonel MacMurdo made a good report of us last autumn, after he had inspected us.

3635. Supposing that an emergency occurred, rendering it necessary on the part of the Government to call out the aid of all the volunteers in the kingdom, do you think that the Worcestershire volunteers would be prepared to render efficient service?—I am quite sure of it; we have had in every corps some men who have gone through the drill and have left us, that is to say, we have more drilled men in each parish than we have got in the ranks; and I have not the least doubt that I could take the field with 1,100 men in case of sudden alarm, having filled up the companies to 100 from the men who have been already in the corps, and we should be as efficient as Colonel MacMurdo reported us to be; they can go through their battalion days very fairly well, and they make mistakes very seldom.

3636. You feel confident that in a case of emergency, with respect to which the force has been organized, suddenly occurring, the county of Worcester would furnish something like a body of 1,200 men?—I think it would furnish a great many more. I think that every company would be near 100, and we have 21 companies. I have no doubt that we should send out 2,000 drilled men in case of invasion, and leave our parade grounds occupied by three or four times that number of recruits.

3637. (*Col. MacMurdo.*) Do you think that they would fight?—I know they would fight; and the way in which they are now recruited is such as to take in just the cream of the young fighting population. During the late war you forced a lot of middle-aged men into the volunteers to avoid the militia ballot; but these are nearly all young men, all active and high-spirited fellows, who go into the volunteers to fit themselves for fighting, and I will answer for their fighting.

3638. (*Lord Overstone.*) Do you see any ground for doubting the continuance of the force at its present strength and efficiency, setting aside the question of numbers and pecuniary considerations?—I am confident that they will go on if the allowances I have named are made by the country, judging from everything that I see and know.

3639. You feel confident that the existing force may be maintained, and rather increased in numbers and efficiency, provided pecuniary assistance of the kind you have already alluded to is given?—I think that if the assistance which I have already alluded to is given, and if you wanted, in case of emergency, to raise more corps in Worcestershire, you would find no difficulty in doing so; the chief difficulty would be to officer them properly, there would be plenty of men.

3640. Do you think that there is considerable difficulty in finding proper officers?—We have found none as yet. Of course the supply of officers is shorter than the supply of men; but we have found no difficulty hitherto.

3641. Do you think that the officers of the Worcester volunteers are now fully competent to the discharge of all their duties?—I think that they are fully competent to command their companies on a battalion field day.

3642. Do you think that the efficiency of the force would not be seriously impaired by any defects in that respect if they were called into real service?—I think not; I think that by the time we had been out for three weeks we should be very fair soldiers.

3643. What would be the condition of the volunteer force in Worcester upon the supposition that things were left as they are now; do you think they will go on for another twelve months?—I think there would be great disappointment if they heard that this Commission had broken up without doing something of them; but until our three years are run out, I think there will be no falling off; we have from the first expected that we should get assistance from Government.

3644. Supposing this Commission had never been appointed, do you think that the Worcestershire volunteer force would have suffered severely in its efficiency and numbers from want of pecuniary aid?—I think that if the Government refused, with or without a Commission, to give us new uniforms, we should fall away.

3645. You think that that would have been the case, supposing this Commission had never been appointed?—Yes; some time next spring the thing would be getting very slack indeed.

3646. Having stated that some pecuniary aid from the Government is essential for maintaining the efficiency and permanency of the volunteer force, are there any other measures which you think should be adopted for the purpose of maintaining or increasing its efficiency?—One of the things that has been pressed upon me very much, is the exemption of volunteers from serving on juries. There are a number of gentlemen in the corps, and many of them are manufacturers, and they think that if they give their time, and they do sacrifice a considerable amount of time to the service of the country as volunteers, they ought to be exempted from serving on juries.

3647. Do you mean that their opinion is that those who, either from indisposition or incapacity, cannot serve in a volunteer force ought to take upon themselves those civil duties from which the volunteers should be exempted?—Yes.

3648. Is it your opinion, upon a full consideration of that question, that that is a reasonable expectation?—I think it is a very reasonable expectation indeed.

3649. (*Chairman.*) Do your men principally belong to the class who would be called upon to serve on juries?—Many of them do.

3650. (*Major Harcourt.*) Do you find any difficulty in enforcing the orders that you think it necessary to give in the separate corps?—I have never found any difficulty.

3651. What do you conceive to be your present position as colonel commanding an administrative battalion?—I do not quite know what it is, but I think that the position ought to be that of a lieutenant-colonel of yeomanry; that force has gone on for many years very satisfactorily, and I think that the relation between the colonel and other officers and non-commissioned officers and privates ought to be the same as that in the yeomanry. As long as there is a good feeling between officers, there never can be the least difficulty, but supposing that there is not that good feeling, then the thing could not go on. It is impossible that it can go on. If the officers were on bad terms, such as would render it impossible for them to serve in the regiment together, then I think the War Office ought to interfere.

3652. Do you wish any change to be made in your position as colonel commanding an administrative battalion, and to have further powers given to you?—I do not feel that any further powers are necessary. If on any disputed point I have the power of appealing to the War Office through the lord-lieutenant, and if the War Office gives a proper support, I do not feel that I want more power.

3653. (*Col. MacMurdo.*) On the contrary, you have reason to think that you are well supported?—Thoroughly.

3654. (*Sir A. Campbell.*) Do you found your opinion on the general principle of the thing, or upon the terms which you are with your own officers and the personal character of your lord-lieutenant?—You cannot force men; all these men are volunteers, and can leave the force at once. I think that if an officer chooses to oppose his superior officer in any matter concerning the drill or anything of that sort, the lord-lieutenant would immediately represent it to the War Office, and I have no doubt that it would be sufficiently taken notice of. I think it ought not to be considered whether an officer is in uniform or not, and that anything ought to be taken notice of that concerns the discipline and well-being of the battalion. I cannot imagine any more power that I want personally.

3655. (*Major Harcourt.*) Do you conceive that you have any power at all as colonel commanding an administrative battalion when you are not assembled for the purposes of battalion drill?—I have no direct power; but from the position I am in with the officers under my command, I feel certain that anything I said would be attended to. The relation of officers in volunteer battalions to each other ought to be the same as in regiments of yeomanry.

3656. (*Col. MacMurdo.*) You will remember that an officer behaved disrespectfully to you as colonel of the battalion when you were out of uniform?—Yes.

3657. And that the circumstance was brought to the notice of the Secretary for War through the lord-lieutenant?—Yes.

3658. Do you remember that that officer was called upon to resign his commission?—Certainly.

3659. Although neither he nor you were in uniform at the time, it was considered by the Secretary at War that your relative positions at the time were well understood to be that of a commanding and a subordinate officer, and the Secretary of State decided that the officer who behaved disrespectfully to you, although out of uniform, was culpable?—Yes; but it must be remembered, that he was summoned by a battalion order to attend a certain meeting, although it was not ordered in uniform, and the question only arises whether, if he had not been summoned by that battalion order, the War Office would have taken the same notice of it. I think that it ought to do so. I think that if an officer chooses to offend or insult his superior officer when he meets him out of uniform, it is impossible they can go on together. I think that there should be full power in the War Office upon the recommendation of the lord-lieutenant to take notice of such a case, whether the individual was summoned by a battalion order or not at the time; if not it is quite clear that a couple of officers could drive a lieutenant-colonel out of his regiment. It would be quite impossible for him to challenge or to strike an officer under his command, and therefore, as he could not right himself, it is necessary to have full authority in the War Office to deal with a case of that sort.

3660. (*Major Harcourt.*) Suppose that in any one of your companies you wished any alteration made in the drill, I suppose you would hardly feel yourself empowered to give directions to that effect?—The drill itself is laid down by the army regulations, and cannot be altered; with regard to time and place of drill, &c., I think it would be very imprudent to make any general orders, because the circumstances of each company and the circumstances of the men are quite different. I am sure that the captains in command would always select those occasions for drills that were most suitable for their companies. We are not men who have been forced in by the militia ballot, and who mean to do as little as we can; we mean to make ourselves efficient; and the object of the captains is to have such drills as are most suitable for their men, and to get as much drill as they reasonably can out of them. I do not know the habits of their men, and if I were to give any general order, I should probably make a great mistake.

3661. (*Major-Gen. Eyre.*) From your knowledge of the feelings of the volunteers generally, do you think as a body they would have any objection to be placed under the superintendence occasionally of a military officer, or do you think on the contrary they would like it when they were ordered for great parades, or were assembled together in any numbers?—I think they are a little jealous of their own position; that an officer who is competent and ready to pass an examination would not like to be put under command more than he could avoid.

3662. What rank do you allude to?—I mean that if two or three battalions were brought together and put into brigade, the senior lieutenant-colonel should take the command of the brigade; but I think it might be right to call upon him to be examined before he was put in command; he would feel considerable disappointment if a stranger were sent to command his brigade if he was competent to do so himself, and had proved himself to be competent.

3663. (*Col. MacMurdo.*) You have mentioned the subject of the repair of arms; how are they repaired now?—Generally in every town there is a gunsmith or an ironmonger who understands repairing guns, and, perhaps, the son of the ironmonger is acting in the capacity of serjeant armourer, and some allowance is made to him per annum to keep the arms in repair.

3664. What descriptions of repairs are executed by such a man?—I do not know, but they do repair them; I know that there is a charge for serjeant armourer in every company; I have not personally seen their work.

3665. You are probably aware that when arms require to be repaired, they should be repaired by Her Majesty's officers at the small arms factory, and should be reported and sent into the factory?—I am not capable of giving an answer, but any orders that are issued from the War Office we shall of course obey them.

The witness withdrew.

Adjourned to Tuesday next at half-past 12 o'clock.

Lieut.-Col. F. W. Knight, M.P.

27 June 1862.

U 4

Tuesday, 1st July 1862.

PRESENT :

Viscount EVERSLEY.
Earl of DUCIE.
Viscount HARDINGE.
Lord OVERSTONE.
Mr. BOUVERIE.
Lieutenant-Colonel BARTTELOT.

Lieutenant-Colonel Sir A. CAMPBELL.
Lieutenant-General Sir G. A. WETHERALL.
Major-General EYRE.
Colonel MACMURDO.
Major HARCOURT.

VISCOUNT EVERSLEY IN THE CHAIR.

Lieutenant EDWARD EDWARDS examined.

Lieut. E. Edwards.
1 July 1862.

3666. (*Chairman.*) I believe you are adjutant of the first administrative battalion of Warwickshire Rifle Volunteers ?—Yes.

3667. How many corps are there in that battalion ? —Nine corps and a subdivision.

3668. Are there nine corps of 100 men each ?— No, they are just companies, numbering 639 of all ranks.

3669. How often have you battalion drills ?—We had nine last year, and we have had three this year already; one will take place at Coventry to-morrow afternoon, which will make four battalion drills this year, but they cannot be often got together.

3670. How many men do you generally muster at a battalion drill ?—Between 400 and 500 as a rule, about two-thirds of the total strength of the corps.

3671. Do you visit the other companies occasionally ?—I resolve my work into a system; I have got one company at Rugby, and I go there every Monday; I have three companies at Coventry, and I go there every Tuesday; I have one company at Stratford-upon-Avon, and I go there every Wednesday and devote the whole of that day to them; then I have another company at Warwick, a company and a subdivision at Leamington, and I devote the Thursday to them; except the first Monday and Wednesday in each month. I take the Monday from Rugby and the Wednesday from Stratford-upon-Avon in each month, and I devote that to Warwick and Leamington, so as to equalize the number of drills in every corps. Friday I give to Nuneaton, and Saturday to Saltley.

3672. Have you an opportunity of seeing every corps belonging to the battalion ?—Yes; every corps and every man in them. I drill every corps, and get them together for battalion drill as often as they can come.

3673. Do you allow the men to join in battalion drill before they are perfect in company drill ?— No. I am sure they are correct before they do that, because I drill them myself before they join the battalion.

3674. Are there drill instructors attached to each company ?—No. Coventry has none; it has three companies.

3675. Those companies are all in one town, and therefore one drill instructor is sufficient ?—By the regulations of the volunteers, there is one drill instructor allowed to three companies.

3676. (*Col. MacMurdo.*) That is if the three companies happen to be in one place or within a radius of one mile ?—Yes.

3677. Beyond that radius there is one drill instructor to every corps ?—Yes.

3678. (*Chairman.*) Do you find that these companies have all passed through a course of musketry instruction ?—No; not above two-thirds of them on the average; as nearly as possible there is one-third of every corps who are so employed; their duties calling them away that you cannot get them to judging distance drill and position aiming drill or target practice. I find that they are chiefly employed in the drapers' shops, and their masters cannot spare them till about 8 o'clock at night and after that for drill; they cannot be spared out during the morning to go through the judging distance drill and position drill and target practice.

3679. Do you consider the musketry instruction a very important part of the drill ?—That is everything in the volunteers.

3680. (*Major-Gen. Eyre.*) Would they be of any use without it ?—Not the slightest. What is the use of a man who cannot shoot ?

3681. (*Viscount Hardinge.*) You can put them through position drill at those hours, can you not ?— Yes; you can teach them position drill, but you cannot give them target practice, it is generally getting too dark.

3682. (*Chairman.*) I understood you to say that there are not above two-thirds of this battalion who really are thoroughly drilled ?—They are all thoroughly drilled as far as regards their drill as a battalion. I believe that every man could turn out and go through his drill with the battalion, and you would not find out who were the absentees; but I know who they are, because I drill them myself.

3683. (*Major-Gen. Eyre.*) You mean that they are thoroughly drilled barring the shooting ?—Yes, barring that. I cannot guarantee that.

3684. (*Sir A. Campbell.*) By whom is the rifle instruction in the companies carried on ?—By the serjeant instructors of the companies.

3685. Are those serjeant instructors previously examined and passed by you ?—They are Hythe men. Every one of them has to go to Hythe, and to go through a long course at Hythe, *vide* Volunteer Circular, No. 5, 22nd August 1861, Article 153.

3686. With regard to the musketry instruction, your functions I presume are confined to general superintendence ?—Yes.

3687. What work have you to do in the orderly room ?—Having an administrative battalion, there is very little to do, because the captain of every company is the *bonâ fide* commanding officer of his own corps.

3688. I presume that the captain of each company keeps Colonel Scott informed of the system of drill pursued, the times of the drills, and of the manner in which the whole instruction is carried out ? — No; I keep him informed upon these subjects. I make out and send to him by every Sunday night's post a detailed statement of what the battalion will do next week, with the companies on the left hand side for Monday, Tuesday, Wednesday, Thursday, Friday, and Saturday; for instance, Rugby company drill at such a time on Monday, and target practice, or what ever it may be; then Coventry, Tuesday, so and so, so that Colonel Scott knows on the Monday morning where I shall be employed every day, and at what time during that week. Then, on the reverse side, I send to him the number of men who actually were present at that particular parade last week, so that he can see what I am going to do next week, and what I did last week.

3689. My object in asking you these questions is to ascertain the amount of official duties as distinguished from drills and instruction which falls upon the adjutant, correspondence, and so forth ?—There is none, except making out the monthly diary and quarterly returns.

3690. Do you mean that in conducting the arrangements of the drill for the different companies, and in making the commanding officer acquainted with them, there is no correspondence and no office work?—It is very little; I do not know how it is with other battalions, but you see that I have resolved the thing into a system, and it works as I have told you; every day does its own work, and the colonel is informed of this. Then each officer commanding a corps in an administrative battalion is really and truly the commanding officer himself; and, in fact, the commanding officer of a volunteer company in an administrative battalion has the same power as a captain commanding a battery of artillery, and those are superintended by the colonel, *vide* Regulations for the Volunteer Force, page 52, art. 190.

3691. Referring to your last answer, do you consider that the commanding officer of an administrative battalion has sufficient control over the management of the different corps?—I very much question whether he has, in fact the control is so little, that I scarcely know what it is. He certainly has, I believe, so far that all the promotions of the officers must go through him. I believe that when the battalion parades for general battalion drill, he has authority to order it, but how far the officer commanding the administrative battalion can interfere with the interior economy of a company, I cannot say; I do not think he can interfere at all.

3692. Considering not only what may or may not have happened in your own battalion, but what might happen, do you think it would be an advantage to the service if an alteration should be made as to the power of the administrative lieutenant-colonel?—No, I am not afraid not.

3693. Do you think that he could be placed in the same position as the lieutenant-colonel of a yeomanry regiment?—Not being aware what the powers of a lieutenant-colonel of a yeomanry corps are I cannot answer the question, but I should imagine that the colonel of a yeomanry corps has greater power over the yeomanry cavalry, which are assembled for a certain number of days, during which days they are, I presume, subject to some law, when assembled under the orders of the commanding officer; whether they are subject to the Mutiny Act during those days I am not quite sure.

3694. (*Viscount Hardinge.*) Have you ever known any inconvenience to arise from the present state of things, or from the colonel not having sufficient power?—No, I have not.

3695. All the promotions go through you, do they not?—No; all the promotions in an administrative battalion are worked by the clerk of the lieutenancy, the commanding officer of the battalion, and the lord lieutenant. The adjutant has nothing whatever to do with them in my battalion.

3696. In a case where the captain of a company recommends a member of his corps to fill a vacant ensigncy, does he not send his recommendation to you in the first instance, and do you not then forward it?—No; I have nothing whatever to do with it.

3697. Then the captain forwards it direct to the colonel?—Yes; I am not allowed to interfere.

3698. (*Chairman.*) Is there railway communication to all the places which you have enumerated where there are companies?—I place myself in the centre so as to get it; there are two railways coming to Leamington, and by placing myself there I get by the Great Western railway to Stratford-upon-Avon, and by the North-western railway to Rugby, Coventry, Nuneaton, and Saltley.

3699. Your expenses are not so large as those of other adjutants, who have to go over a great extent of country without the aid of railways?—I do not know that.

3700. (*Earl of Ducie.*) Have you any supplemental allowance besides your pay?—Nothing more than is allowed to the adjutant of an administrative battalion, 8s. a day pay, and 2s. a day for travelling allowances.

3701. I mean from the corps?—Not a farthing; and if I was not a pensioner in the receipt of 2s. 6d. a day pension, I could not do the duty. I ought to save my pension every year, but I cannot do it. I have 65l. 12s. 6d. a year (20l. for distinguished conduct in the field, and 45l. 12s. 6d. pension) otherwise I could not do the duty.

3702. (*Viscount Hardinge.*) It appears that you visit your companies more frequently than other adjutants?—Not being aware of what other adjutants do, I cannot answer that question.

3703. (*Sir A. Campbell.*) Do you think that the drill instruction of the volunteers could be carried on satisfactorily without a drill instructor?—Certainly not.

3704. (*Col. MacMurdo.*) Have you ever estimated the loss you sustained in travelling?—No, but it is considerable; I can give you the amount of each day's expenses, that is, what it should be, not what it is, because I am forced to tramp to be able to do it. I start from Leamington to Rugby on Monday, the company at Rugby cannot drill until half-past 7 or 8 o'clock in the evening, consequently I must stop there all night, and there are hotel charges for the night and railway fare for a distance of 15 miles, the 1st class fare would be 2s. 6d., and both ways the railway fare would amount to 5s.

3705. You travel as an officer?—Yes, in uniform.

3706. Do you get an officer's ticket?—Yes; then come the hotel charges, and we cannot do it for less than 5s. to sleep there at night and to have supper and breakfast the next morning, and you may put down the fair expenses for Monday at 10s. Then on Tuesday I go to Coventry, a distance of nine miles; they drill there in the afternoon at various times between two and six, but I can always get back from Coventry the same night; nine miles there and back would be 18, and the railway fare would be 3s. No expenses are incurred more than simply the railway fare, as I get my dinner before I start, and get my supper when I come back. On Wednesday I go to Stratford-on-Avon, and that should be the same sum as to Rugby, because I leave home at about five o'clock in the afternoon, and the company at Stratford-on-Avon drills from half-past seven until dark in the summer time, in the winter time they have the use of the Corn Exchange. I have to stop there all night, and the fair charge for that is 10s. On Thursday I am at home, either at Leamington or at Warwick. They are so close together that they need not entail any expense; I may walk to Warwick, the distance being only two miles and a half; there is a railway, but that is no reason why it should be taken. On Friday I go to Nuneaton, and the distance there is just the same as to Stratford and to Rugby, fifteen miles. At Nuneaton the company cannot drill until after 7 o'clock at night; the last train leaves Nuneaton for Coventry at 5 minutes before 7, and the consequence is that the captain of the company sends me to Coventry, a distance of nine miles, in his dog cart, so that I save so much; to go to Nuneaton the railway fare would be for 15 miles 2s. 6d., and if I had to stop there all night would make it 10s. exactly, the same as in the case of Rugby and Stratford, or were I to take a dog cart, and pay for it, at Nuneaton to bring me back to Coventry I should get it for 8s., and 2s. 6d. would make it 10s. 6d., 6d. more than if I stopped there all night; therefore if I was not dependent upon the kindness of the captain of the company in sending me back the expenses ought to be 10s., the same as in the other cases, as I must stop there all night or take a dog cart at my own expense to come back to Coventry. On Saturday I go to Saltley, which is close to Birmingham, the distance is 18 miles from Leamington by railway, and then to come back again from Snow Hill station to Saltley College is three, and the question is in making this estimate whether you would allow cab fare for the three miles there and the three miles back, together six miles. At Birmingham they charge you 1s. a mile for a cab, and then the

Lieut.
E. Edwards

1 July 1862.

154 MINUTES OF EVIDENCE TAKEN BEFORE THE COMMISSIONERS APPOINTED

Lieut.
E. Edwards.
1 July 1862.

railway fare would be 12s. to go to Saltley and back. Then it would be Monday, to Rugby, 10s.; Tuesday, to Coventry, 3s.; Wednesday, to Stratford-on-Avon, 10s.; Friday, to Nuneaton, 10s.; and Saturday, to Saltley, 12s.; making together 2l. 5s., for which I get allowed 14s.

3707. You do not keep a horse?—No, Colonel Scott very kindly keeps one for me.

3708. Then the 2s. for forage are supposed to go to travelling expenses?—Yes; making 28s.

3709. You are therefore at a loss of 17s?—Yes.

3710. And that you pay out of your pension?—Yes, it would take about 40l. of my pension to pay my travelling expenses.

3711. (*Lord Overstone.*) I think you stated that once in every week you have personal communications with every company of volunteers throughout the county of Warwick?—Yes; once in every week.

3712. In your opinion are the volunteers generally throughout Warwick at the present moment in an efficient state?—I never could get them all together at one time so as to be able to give a fair answer, but I should say certainly from what I have seen of the other volunteers that they are quite up to anything else that is to be found.

3713. I wish you to give your answer with reference to the duties the volunteers will have to discharge in case of their being called into active service and not with reference to the comparative state of other volunteers?—I have no doubt for one moment that if I had them all together for about one week I could make them all as efficient as the best of them are now.

3714. You think that with a short notice of a few weeks in case of a great emergency the Warwickshire volunteers would be an efficient force?—Quite so.

3715. Capable of rendering valuable assistance to the regular army in defence of the country?—Quite so.

3716. Is their condition at the present time satisfactory with regard to the state of their clothing?—No, it is not.

3717. Will you have the goodness to state to the Commission in what respects you think the clothing is deficient?—The clothing has been in wear for two years, or rather more, and a great number of the men require new clothing, or will very shortly require new, and they are not prepared to pay for it themselves, they require some assistance.

3718. Do you think that assistance with regard to the clothing will be necessary to preserve them in a state of efficiency?—I believe that upon that simple question hinges the existence of the corps.

3719. Do you think that they are in an efficient and satisfactory state as to their arms and accoutrements?—Decidedly so.

3720. In all respects you think that their arms and accoutrements are in that state in which they would be fit for service if suddenly called upon?—Perfectly so. I can answer from my own knowledge for every arm and every accoutrement.

3721. Are their pouches in a satisfactory state?—Yes.

3722. Are they provided with knapsacks?—They are not.

3723. Do you think that they are necessary?—Most decidedly, if they were going to take the field.

3724. Is it not the fact that the Guards lived three months in the Crimea without knapsacks?—I beg to inform you that I was one of them that did exist during that time without, but hardly lived.

3725. Considering the difference of circumstances, and the facility for communication in this country, do you not think that havresacks without knapsacks might be sufficient?—No; not to keep a man in any sort of comfort, or as he ought to be efficient; a man will breed vermin in no time without clean shirts and socks, just the same as the British army did in the Crimea.

3726. The knapsacks you consider as essential for anything like prolonged service; but might they not be dispensed with for a short time?—Yes, I think so; but only for a very short time.

3727. Passing on to the question of discipline and drill, do you think that the Warwickshire volunteers are now in a state sufficiently advanced as to discipline and drill to turn out forthwith as an efficient auxiliary to the regular army?—Yes, I do.

3728. I believe you have already stated that as to the use of their musket there is still a deficiency?—Yes, in about one-third of the corps.

3729. Have you observed that there are any clear indications of danger in maintaining the Warwickshire volunteers in their present state of efficiency?—I have.

3730. Will you have the goodness to state the grounds of that apprehension?—As I stated before, I think the whole efficiency of the Warwickshire volunteers depends entirely upon the question of clothing; so I am informed by the captains commanding companies, and so it appears to me as far as I can judge.

3731. Supposing the difficulty as to clothing to be met, do you think there any other circumstances calculated to excite apprehension as to the efficiency of the force?—None.

3732. I infer, therefore, from that last answer, that you cannot suggest to this Commission any measures which you think desirable for giving greater certainty to the permanence and efficiency of the force, saving always the question of the clothing?—Yes, there are two other questions. I think there are three headings under which the Government may assist the volunteers, and I think there are three only.

3733. Will you have the goodness to state them?—First of all comes drill instructors. The Volunteer Circular, No. 3, dated 22nd August 1861, is, I am afraid, a failure.

3734. Do you think it would be of valuable assistance to the volunteer movement if some arrangement was made within the army for the supply of good drill instructors, or some arrangement for constituting a staff of drill instructors for the use of the volunteer force?—Yes.

3735. Can you suggest any particular form in which that could be advantageously accomplished?—Yes.

3736. Will you have the goodness to do so?—The Volunteer Circular of the 22nd August 1861, I am afraid is a failure. The pay is not sufficient for a good drill instructor, and I do not think the Government will give a higher rate of pay to a drill instructor of volunteers than they give to a serjeant of militia. I think so, because they are both exactly one class of men, consequently an intelligent serjeant who is good for anything will not on his discharge join either the militia or volunteers, but will obtain some other employment that pays him better.

3737. Is it your opinion that an increase of pay should be awarded by the Government?—Yes. The question then arises, could not the Government establish a corps of instructors from out of the army, and let their service with the volunteers count for pension, in the same manner as if they were still serving in the army. Something of this sort will have to be done, as I do not think it would answer to detach good non-commissioned officers from their regiments for any length of time, as they get into loose habits, and are rarely ever good for anything on rejoining the regiment.

3738. (*Col. MacMurdo.*) Do you mean that those men should be detached from the army?—I mean simply to form a school for volunteers, the same as the school of musketry at Hythe is for the army.

3739. But the men to be non-commissioned officers?—Yes.

3740. And simply to be detached from their regiments, and attached to the volunteer force?—No. First of all a school must be established, the same as the school at Hythe, where men are taken from their regiments and put into the staff of the Hythe school, and they belong to Hythe, and they have nothing to do with anything else; and I think that the same must be done for the volunteers; and to have a school of volunteer instructors, the Government must form a school in the first instance, and have a central school the very same as that at Hythe, and then they must detach instructors from that school to all the volunteer corps, but you must be able with regard to the men that you detach to the volunteer corps to send them back to the school in case of misconduct, and if the commandant of the school disapproves of their conduct, send them back to the regiment by way of punishment. Then you would establish a school of instruction for the volunteers, the same as the school of instructors at Hythe for the army, allowing a man's time to count for his pension, exactly the same as the time of the serjeants counts, who are attached to the Hythe school.

3741. (*Major-Gen. Eyre.*) But you say the difficulty of obtaining them is on account of the insufficiency of the pay?—I was alluding, in that case, to the men who have served their time and are discharged; you cannot really get serjeant instructors who are good for anything.

3742. (*Col. MacMurdo.*) The volunteers have had a good many serjeant instructors; in your own case you have already four serjeant instructors to eight companies?—Yes, we have, and the proportion is fair enough; but then the question arises, what is the quality of those instructors.

3743. You do not think that they are good?—They are good for nothing, or next to it; they have been old soldiers, and they can give the volunteers a few ideas; they are very steady men themselves, in fact they are rather too steady.

3744. One of them was a colour-serjeant in the 28th regiment, and three of them had been serjeants in their respective regiments?—Yes; but if they had had that amount of ability and activity that they ought to have had, they would have found some employment that would have paid them better.

3745. Do you not think that when a soldier has served for 21 years in the army, whatever his trade might have been before, he must have got rather rusty in it?—There are so many different branches of employment in this country, that if a man chooses to look about he can always find employment.

3746. What is your opinion as to the circular which is now about to be issued from the War Office, providing for a second class of serjeant instructors for the volunteers, not requiring them to have been non-commissioned officers, but soldiers who have been discharged with sufficient testimonials of good character, capable of imparting instruction to the volunteers, to be examined by an adjutant or inspecting officer, such soldier to receive from the Government 1s. 6d. or 1s. 4d. a-day, with permission, under the sanction of the officer commanding the volunteers, to work at any trade or any occupation in addition to his duties as serjeant instructor of the corps; do you think that will work?—Yes, I do; I do not see any objection to that.

3747. It then provides for that class of non-commissioned officers who have occupations or trades, but who have not got pensions, but who might impart instruction to companies of volunteers and at the same time attend to their work in the day-time?—There is no reason for one moment why a serjeant instructor of volunteers should not work at his trade just as much as the volunteers, for it must be observed that nearly the whole of our volunteers are men engaged in business and they can only come to drill in odd hours.

3748. (*Major-Gen. Eyre.*) As an old soldier thoroughly well acquainted with the service, and I dare say knowing something of the militia, do you think that the serjeants of disembodied militia who are doing nothing all the year round, with the exception of 28 days, could be turned to any account?—No, and for this reason: I have had dealings with these militia serjeants, and I find very few of them who have got much in them as to drill, and if they are asked to drill a corps of rifle volunteers the remuneration they want is something alarming.

3749. (*Viscount Hardinge.*) Would you propose to give them a higher rate of pay than they now receive?—Most decidedly, they must have it; not higher than at the school of musketry at Hythe, but a penny a day or something like that less, just sufficient to keep the musketry school at Hythe No. 1, and the volunteer instructors No. 2.

3750. But there are different classes of serjeants at Hythe?—Yes, and I would have the same in the volunteers; the same rules and regulations.

3751. (*Chairman.*) Then they would only be temporarily attached to the volunteers?—Yes, so far; so that if there was any complaint made of misbehaviour or inefficiency they could at once be sent back to the school to the commandant, who would be their real commanding officer; he would settle all cases of complaints.

3752. (*Viscount Hardinge.*) How would they be employed at the school when they were not on duty with a volunteer corps?—I should not have more than I could employ, and just occasionally to rub them up a little.

3753. Then there would be hardly any serjeants at headquarters?—Very few indeed, never certainly more than a section. I would have a regular school established upon the Hythe principle for the volunteers to go to and be drilled, and the same as they are at Hythe taught musketry.

3754. How long would a serjeant draw pay at this school?—That must depend entirely, I should think, upon his intelligence; not long.

3755. He should be attached at once?—Yes.

3756. Of what would the staff at the school consist as to officers?—I should have them belonging to the royal army.

3757. How many would you have?—Perhaps a couple, a commandant and an adjutant. The Hythe school is very small, but particularly efficient. I do not see why you should not have a small school for volunteers.

3758. At Hythe the serjeants are employed all the year round?—Yes, and I will employ the others all the year round. There are plenty of places round the coast where you could establish a school and have classes of volunteers to go and shoot there under the serjeants, only a number of volunteers instead of belonging to the royal army.

3759. (*Lord Overstone.*) You have stated that there were three points to which you wished to draw the attention of the Commission with a view to increasing the efficiency and organization of the volunteer movement; you have mentioned the first, will you now proceed to the second?—The second would be by defraying the railway expenses of the volunteers.

3760. (*Chairman.*) You mean when going to battalion drills?—Yes; but the second head, I think, will require some little consideration, because I should not feel disposed to encourage too much riding; for instance, if the company (properly armed and in charge of its officers) had to proceed a distance less than five miles, I would not allow them their railway fare, as marching will do them much more good than riding; but I do think if the distance exceeded five miles their railway fare ought to be allowed them. It would be much easier to get companies of an administrative battalion together for battalion drill, and also to attend reviews at a distance. The third head would be by assisting to clothe them, and the third, I think, is the most difficult question of the three to deal with, and will, I think, require to be based upon some general rule. The fourth rule of the Warwickshire rifle corps is as follows:—" The annual subscription of the officers " and enrolled members shall be as follows,—captains " and superior officers five guineas annually; non- " commissioned officers and members 10s. 6d.;" and those subscriptions, together with the subscriptions

Lieut.
E. Edwards.

1 July 1862.

X 2

received from the honorary members, defray the whole expenses of the company.

3761. (*Chairman.*) Not including the clothing?—No; they defray the whole expenses of the company, and if the Government were to allow each corps a sum of money equal to the amount of the subscriptions from its effective members, the expenses of the company could not be increased, and it would relieve the effective members in such a manner that they ought to be able to pay for their own clothing. There is a report in circulation to the effect that the Government are about to issue cloth to the volunteers at contract price. One moment's reflection will, I think, put an end to that idea. Will the Government issue it in single suits, if not, how much at a time? Who is to be responsible for it, and who is to make it up into suits? It is a matter of fact that neither tailors nor dressmakers care about making clothing for either men or women, except they find the materials. I have spoken to several tailors on the subject, and each of them says, that they can get cloth as cheap as the Government can, and that in making the volunteer clothing they get their profits out of the cloth. If the volunteers find their own cloth, the tailors will charge such a price for making it up that the volunteer will save nothing by having his cloth from the Government.

3762. (*Lord Overstone.*) The result of your evidence I take to be this, that making proper provision for the three heads you have alluded to, namely, the clothing, the drill serjeants, and the payment of travelling expenses, in all other respects you consider the volunteer movement in Warwickshire in a satisfactory state?—I think so.

3763. And you think that they would in a case of emergency be found to be a useful and efficient force?—Yes.

3764. (*Viscount Hardinge.*) You have stated your objections to the Government issuing cloth to the volunteers; what is your opinion with regard to the advisability of receiving the clothing already made up?—That is what it must be; made up into suits, one uniform suit; and I would beg to suggest one colour for the whole of the volunteer force.

3765. Do you think that the volunteers would object to receiving made-up clothing from the Government from any feeling of delicacy?—I think not, providing it were made up into suits. I would have all the volunteers in England clothed in one colour, and for this reason, which I think is a very strong one; we have lost a great number of men who have gone out of the county and obtained employment in other towns; and a great number of those men have not joined the volunteers in other towns to which they have gone to work because they could not afford to pay for another suit of clothing; but had the volunteer force in the county to which they went been clothed as they were, they would have become volunteers there. I have asked several men who have come into our county, and they have said, "I can-"not afford to pay for another suit of clothing."

3766. Do you think that a recruit on joining would object to wear the cast-off uniform of another member who had resigned, or who no longer belonged to the corps?—I should think that would depend a good deal upon the class to which that recruit belonged; an artizan, for instance.

3767. But that is a difficulty that you might meet with?—No doubt of it; but I believe now that that is carried out in my own battalion, because the men in several companies are clothed partially by the funds that the captains have got, and when the members become non-effective, they keep the clothing, and put it on to other recruits.

3768. (*Sir A. Campbell.*) Are there any to whom the wearing of a suit of clothes which had previously been worn would be objectionable, and who could not afford to supply their own?—Certainly not.

3769. You think that the volunteers with whom you are acquainted might be divided into two classes, one of which would wear the uniform prescribed to them, whether it had been worn before or not, and the other would provide their own?—I think so; I find that in my battalion there are 198 artizans and 12 labourers, and I am quite sure that in those two classes there would be no objection to wear clothing which had been previously worn; but I find that there are 225 tradesmen, men who are holding a good social position, and who can afford to pay for their own clothing. The Saltley company is composed of students in training for national schoolmasters, and consists of 60 members; that company is clothed by donations, and the tunics, belts, &c., remain the property of the corps. In this company one half goes out every spring, and you cannot have a man belonging to that company for more than two years. The clothing is not worn out, and it belongs to the college, and the belts, so that 25 will be coming in next Christmas, and the senior 35 in the college will go out next Christmas; they will leave their clothing, and the other 35 coming in will take their clothing, the belts belonging to the college, that is, with respect to one company.

3770. (*Major-Gen. Eyre.*) Have you any preference for colour?—None whatever; I should not care what the colour was, supposing that all the volunteers were dressed in one uniform colour. If it were possible to get all the lord-lieutenants—for I believe those are the only gentlemen with whom the matter rests—together for five minutes, and ask them to decide what the colour of the clothing should be, and admit no other into their counties, I think the question would be decided in an instant.

3771. (*Mr. Bouverie.*) Do you contemplate the clothing being given to the men, or a money contribution to be given to the corps towards clothing?—That I think is a very grave question, but I should be very sorry to recommend either; I think it is very nearly balanced. I look upon it that a suit of volunteer's clothing ought to last for about four years; for I do not think that a volunteer wears his clothing above one-fourth as much as a man in the royal army does, who has a new suit every year; and as the volunteer's subscription is 10s. 6d. towards the funds of the company, if the Government was to grant a sum of money equal to that subscribed by every effective member, that would give him two guineas for a new suit of clothing.

3772. But would you give the allowance to a man in money?—No; I should give the money to the officer commanding the corps to pay all his expenses with, and start a clothing fund. Why should we not have a clothing fund, the same as I have no doubt many gentlemen here know of,—little clothing clubs in their own parishes? The Nuneaton company has started one, and according to the rules the members pay 2s. a month, and as soon as the clothing gets worn, if they have attended a certain number of drills in the twelvemonths, they are allowed to have a new suit of clothing.

3773. (*Chairman.*) What is the amount of the individual subscription?—2s. per month.

3774. (*Mr. Bouverie.*) Do you find any indisposition on the part of the artizan or labouring class to pay that 10s. 6d. subscription?—That is the class that are backward in paying; but the best volunteer is by far an artizan; he is a man that you can drill, a man that will work, and who understands you; but if you get hold of tradesmen, very fine gentlemen, they are so thin-skinned that you cannot do it; but you can order an artizan to do a thing, and he will do do it like a man; but drill does not really go down with those to whom you have to say, "if you please, sir?" Captain Caldecott got up a company of watchmakers at Coventry; there are about 80 strong; the company is composed entirely of watchmakers, working watchmakers, and they are the best company in the county; they always turn out the best for drill, and they always muster the strongest; they shoot the best, and they seem to do everything the best; in fact they do it in that style that a soldier does it; the men seem to understand it, and they do everything in a workmanlike sort of way.

3775. Is there any difficulty in obtaining their subscriptions?—The captain of the company, I expect, has to make up a good deal; I know that he took 14 members into his company a month ago, and he clothed every one of them.

3776. Do you find that the volunteers come in pretty readily?—The Commission will be able to judge from what was the number of the members on the muster roll on the 1st of August 1860, 1861, and 1862. In 1860, on the 1st of August our strength was 346; on the 1st of August 1861 our strength was 604; and on the 1st of April 1862 it was 656, so that it will be seen we are increasing.

3777. (*Major-Gen. Eyre.*) That does not look like great distress or that the men are unable to pay?—When you come to look at the number of the unpaid subscriptions it will be seen that there are arrears of subscriptions, and I will state to what extent. In Coventry, 48*l.* 10*s.*; in Warwick, 30*l.*; in Leamington, nothing; in Stratford-upon-Avon, 16*l.* 12*s.* 6*d.*; Nuneaton, 17*l.* 3*s.*; the total amount being 112*l.* 5*s.* 6*d.* subscriptions not paid.

3778. (*Chairman.*) Is that a copy of the return that has been sent in that you hold in your hand?—This is an analysis of the whole battalion, in fact, just the same as if it were a consolidated battalion. I have an account of every company here and what it has cost.

3779. (*Viscount Hardinge.*) Did you say that you would recommend the volunteers, in time of peace, to be provided with knapsacks?—No, I think not in time of peace; I think they would be in their way.

3780. (*Major-Gen. Eyre.*) Are your arms kept in a central depôt, or are they in the custody of the individual members?—Each corps has got an armoury, and each armoury is in charge of an individual, and every arm is kept in that armoury.

3781. You have spoken of a considerable proportion of the corps not having had musketry practice; supposing your corps to be used as light troops, to take out-post duties and to be marksmen, which would be almost the only duties of the volunteers in a case of necessity, what would you do with those men who had not received musketry instruction?—I presume that it would be impossible to take those men into the field without some short warning sufficient to make them equal to the best in the battalion.

3782. What time would it take do you think to do that?—A couple of months.

3783. (*Sir G. A. Wetherall.*) Do you think that the facility with which your men can leave their corps at all affects them?—Nothing of any consequence; we have had some men leave, but very few, except for the purposes of going to other places to work; in fact, I think there is a sort of feeling among the population generally that the men should not go. I think that a man would lose caste to a great extent among his fellow townsmen.

3784. (*Col. MacMurdo.*) In your military experience in drilling men, do you consider, bearing in mind that the Enfield rifle is a very modern invention, that musketry instruction is absolutely necessary for a soldier in the field?—Most decidedly.

3785. How came it then that we fought our battles with muskets?—Because we got to close quarters; but they will now fire at much longer ranges than they used to do, and the party that does not will suffer most fearfully before they can get to the point of the bayonet.

3786. Suppose that an army took the field composed of men all instructed in musketry, and that, as in the Crimea, in the course of a few months about two-thirds of that army pass through the hospitals, and that the army had then to be recruited from home by what are called in the army 40 days' drill men, you cannot suppose, I presume, that those men could have passed through a course of musketry instruction in that time?—Yes, they would; they would get them through a short course. Even a corps of militia that is now embodied only for 28 days get, most of them, through a short course of musketry instruction even in 28 days.

3787. Does that short course of musketry instruction make a man what you consider he ought to be in the field?—No, certainly not.

3788. Do you think that a volunteer in two months could be sufficiently instructed in musketry to take the field?—I believe that any man ought to be. I believe that any drill who professes to be a drill ought to take any men and make them in two months fit to do anything from the plough-field.

3789. Fit for the line of battle?—Fit for anything, in two months; I do not mean one drill a day, but to make them work six hours a day, as if they were recruits in the army.

3790. Adverting to that part of your evidence which had reference to a report that the Government intended to issue cloth at contract prices, did you receive a circular from the War Office, or does Colonel Scott receive them?—He receives them all; I rarely see them.

3791. You are not aware perhaps that that circular was issued on the 15th of May?—I do not know the date, for I have not seen it; but I saw the cloth in Birmingham, several sorts of cloth.

3792. Is your opinion with respect to the working of that circular derived from actual facts, or from the opinions of the tailors?—From the opinions of the corps at large, the captains of companies, and the whole of the officers, non-commissioned officers, and men of the corps.

3793. But they were merely opinions, not facts?—Yes.

3794. You are not aware, perhaps, that as far as the facts have been gathered by my inquiries, I find that the privates' tunics are made up by the tailors for only 2*s.* more than the Government pay; in 1857 the Government paid 8*s.* 7*d.* for making up privates' tunics, and in Liverpool the tailors will make up privates' tunics for volunteers at 10*s.* 6*d.*, and the other parts of their garments in the same proportion. Do you think that your informants were correct in what they stated?—Our suit costs 4*l.* 6*s.* 6*d.*

3795. What does the tunic cost, for example?—The tunic, trousers, and cap cost 4*l.*, leggings, 6*s.* 6*d.* They are always furnished in suits. I do not think that any man has required to have any one garment.

3796. From information obtained by me before this circular was issued, it appeared that the tunics cost upon the average from 32*s.* to 2*l.*, and a good cloth tunic, according to this circular, could be supplied to the volunteers for 22*s.*?—Yes, I should think that it ought to be given out in suits; not in cloth, exactly the same as in the army, the army clothing is all made by a scale. A regiment requires new clothing, and the tailor sends in a return for so many suits for men five feet six, and so many suits for men five feet seven, and so on; each suit to measure certain dimensions round the breast, and certain dimensions round the waist by sizes.

3797. Your evidence as to the working of this system is not given from actual experience, but merely from the opinions of others?—Yes.

3798. (*Viscount Hardinge.*) You would propose, I think, that the commanding officer should make a contract in the same way that the War Office does with a regimental contractor to furnish so many suits of clothing to his corps?—No, not for the commanding officer to do it.

3799. Then, who should make the contract?—The commanding officer with the Government, and keep a debtor and creditor account between every corps and the War Office.

3800. Do you mean that the commanding officer should obtain the suits of clothing from the Government factory, at Pimlico?—Yes; for the whole of the volunteers, exactly the same as for the royal army; and a debtor and creditor account should be kept with

Lieut.
F. Edwards.

1 July 1862.

158   MINUTES OF EVIDENCE TAKEN BEFORE THE COMMISSIONERS APPOINTED

Lieut.
E. Edwards.

1 July 1862.

every corps in England, and they should send there for everything; a suit would come down, and with a little alteration it would be made easily to fit, and then charge the commanding officer so much, and send the bill in every quarter.

3801. You think that that plan would be preferable to the commanding officer of the corps providing the clothing himself?—Yes; it would be the simple practice of the army.

3802. (*Maj.-Gen. Eyre.*) Do you consider that your corps is one that at all interferes with the recruiting for the militia?—No, not in the slightest degree whatever; I think that General Wetherall will bear me out in that, for it was remarked at Warwick, at our inspection, by the lord-lieutenant, there being present the yeomanry cavalry, two regiments of militia, and two regiments of volunteers, it was generally understood that out of the whole of the volunteers there was not a single man in the militia that had ever been in the volunteers, and on the other hand, there was not a man in the volunteers who would ever have been in the militia; they are so distinct a class; the only people that we are likely to clash with are the yeomanry cavalry; but it is very good naturedly when it happens.

3803. (*Chairman.*) Do they interfere with the volunteers?—Farmers would make capital rifle volunteers.

The witness withdrew.

Lieut.-Col.
R. Luard.

Lieut.-Colonel RICHARD LUARD examined.

3804. (*Chairman.*) You are assistant inspector of the south-eastern division?—Yes.

3805. Do you find the corps of volunteers in that division in a perfectly efficient state?—It would be using strong language to say so; I should like to see them in a more efficient state. I am afraid that they are rather more slack in their attendance at drill than they used to be. It is a rural district, and there is a difficulty in getting them to attend.

3806. They are more slack, you think, in their attendance?—I think they are a little.

3807. Do you find that more than one half of the strength of the corps assemble at your own inspection?—Certainly more; I should say about two-thirds. If there is a company of 60 I should say that about 40 attend. I do not say that they alway do so, but it is generally so. I should say that that was about the rule, and if I get 40 to attend I consider it is very fair.

3808. Do you inspect the corps once a year?—Yes.

3809. Do you find in an administrative battalion that there are any companies which fail in their attendance altogether?—I do not think that the companies do, but some few subdivisions do; at least, I may say, that one or two subdivisions of an administrative battalion do not attend battalion drill, and I think the reason of that is the expense.

3810. Do you inspect the subdivisions separately?—Yes, I do; I had to inspect one subdivision some time ago. I went a long way to do so, and I found nine men present, or some number like that.

3811. Have you any return of the number of men who have passed through a course of musketry instruction?—No, I have none. I have not anything statistical with me at all. I came up from Wimbledon, and I did not know what I was to come here for; but I have not kept anything as to musketry instruction; everything that I know about it I have sent into the War Office.

3812. You can only speak of the efficiency of the volunteers from what you have seen of them in battalion drills?—Yes, and company drills.

3813. How many corps are there in your division?—I cannot tell you exactly, but I have roughly about 9,000 men. As I said before, I have not any statistics with me.

3814. In the course of your inspections do you hear complaints made that the corps will not be able to go on?—It must be remembered that I am particularly cautioned not to inquire into their financial affairs; but from quietly talking with people upon the subject, I think I may say that in the district which I inspect they feel that the expense is greater than they expected; in the rural districts it is so.

3815. Do you find that there is a difficulty in keeping up the number of officers in consequence of the expense?—I have not found that as to the officers, for people like to be officers. I think that the captains of corps find that it is expensive, and that they have been put to more expense than they expected; they are always putting their hands into their pockets. I think it is with regard to the men that the expense is felt the most. The captains also find it expensive, but I do not think that they object to that; I think that they like to be officers, and the desire to be officers overcomes the expense except when they cannot afford it.

3816. Do you think that occasional meetings at division and brigade drills are of use?—Yes, I think so; but I think that a battalion drill is of far more use. Where they have a good commanding officer, the battalion drill is very important; they can learn more in a battalion drill than they can in a brigade drill. In a brigade drill the niceties of the thing cannot be looked to so well.

3817. If it were thought desirable to assist the volunteers, would it be possible to insist upon every man who received assistance attending, at all events on the day of inspection, at battalion drill, besides other days?—If you give assistance in kind, I think you may do a great deal of good, but I think that assistance given in money will be bad.

3818. How do you think the assistance should be given?—First of all I would give assistance to the subdivisions, which are not now allowed non-commissioned officers as drill instructors. I would give assistance by giving them a drill instructor, and I would allow travelling expenses for every *bonâ fide* man of an administrative corps who attended a battalion drill, because these things come very unfairly upon them. Take, for example, Hampshire, the first battalion; the first corps belongs to Winchester, where there is a capital drill ground. All the other corps have to come to Winchester, and that is a very heavy item of expense to them, for they have to pay their travelling expenses, and I think it would be fair for the Government to pay the *bonâ fide* travelling expenses of those who attend a battalion drill.

3819. (*Viscount Hardinge.*) What do you mean by a *bonâ fide* man?—I mean every man who has absolutely attended drill on parade that day, and who is not a bugler or a bandsman; a man in the ranks or a non-commissioned officer, or other officer.

3820. Whether he was effective or not according to the interpretation of the Act?—He must be effective, or he would not be fit to go to his drill. I would not have bandsmen counted, but I would have a bugler per company.

3821. Is it not frequently the case in rural corps that men attend battalion drills who are really not effective, and not fit for the drill?—I am afraid that some few do; they attend drills not so efficient as they should be—if they are recruits we hope they will become more efficient.

3822. Would you pay the expenses of a man who joined only once or twice a year, and was really not effective?—I would pay the expenses of any man who had attended at a battalion drill, and had managed to keep up with the ranks. I would not discourage the volunteers in any way.

3823. (*Chairman.*) It has been suggested to the Commission that the expenses of no man should be paid who does not come a distance beyond 5 miles?—I think that that is fair enough. I think that they may very well walk five miles. I think that the volunteers would not mind that.

3824. What amount per mile would you allow?—I would give them a penny a mile, the same that you give the soldiers.

3825. You would propose that there should be a certain sum allowed for travelling expenses to every man who lived beyond five miles from the battalion drill ground?—Yes; not for company drill.

3826. (*Lieut.-Col. Barttelot.*) When you say a certain sum per man, do you mean that the money should be paid to the commanding officers of the corps?—Yes; because they have to pay all the expenses, and they do it as cheaply as they can by railway.

3827. (*Major-Gen. Eyre.*) Early in this inquiry I asked a commanding officer whether his men would object to receive their travelling expenses, and he scorned the notion of it, and said that they would not do it?—Perhaps in some corps they would rather not; but I am sure that a great many of the corps would like to get anything they could.

3828. (*Lieut.-Col. Barttelot.*) From your experience in your south-eastern district, do you not think that out of the 9,000 men that you have, over 8,000 of them at any rate would take the money?—I think that the majority of them would; I do not say 8,000, but the majority of them would; they would be very happy to accept any travelling expenses, or any other expenses, that you could give them. I think that there is also another way in which they might be helped, and that is as to ranges. You have helped them in some way, and I think that all the expenses of ranges might be fairly paid, because the unfairness of the thing is, that some people get benefits and some do not; for instance, some corps are in the neighbourhood, perhaps, of a Government range, or they are on the sea coast, or near some place where they have a fine high hill, where they can make a range without expense; whereas another corps has to go to great expense, and the poorest corps are often those which have to go to the greatest expense. I think that you might fairly pay the expenses, and do the work either by sending down sappers or in some other way. I think that every corps should come equally into the field to shoot without the range costing them anything.

3829. (*Viscount Hardinge.*) Do you think that the Government should also defray the charges which are now paid by volunteers for targets?—Yes.

3830. (*Sir A. Campbell.*) With regard to the rent paid for the ranges themselves, do you think that the Government should relieve the volunteers from that also?—Yes, I think so; I think that every volunteer should go and have his shooting on equal terms; that is to say, for nothing; the Government should then do it as cheaply as they can, whether they will have this range or that, or whether they will have a range for 10*l.* a year, or 100*l.* a year.

3831. Do you not think that when a Government officer goes to make an arrangement as to the rent, that a very much larger sum would probably be asked of him than of the captain of a volunteer company?—I cannot give an opinion upon that, but of course that is human nature, and it would be a Government arrangement.

3832. (*Viscount Hardinge.*) With regard to assistance to be given in the way of clothing, would you recommend that the clothing should be made up, and should be issued by the Government?—I think that if you could give the volunteers assistance in all those other ways, it might occur that they would not require clothing. If you gave clothing, I think you should give it to all those who would receive it; but I think that many would reclothe themselves; and if you once gave it, you must give one uniform to the whole. I would suggest that a blouse and a cap, and a pair of trousers should be given.

3833. You would not leave it to the commanding officers to provide them?—No.

3834. You would prefer that the clothing should be issued by the Government?—Yes. I do not know whether it would not make it necessary to increase the Pimlico warehouse tremendously, and therefore it would be better to say, there is so much a suit, and you must clothe yourselves.

3835. Do you think there would be no difficulty in getting recruits to wear the clothing of those members who had left the corps, or had resigned?—I do not know about that; but I should not think so. If it was a good dress, I think there would be no difficulty in that case if it were made sufficiently loose to fit all comers. I think it must be a blouse.

3836. Do you think that the drill instructors are sufficiently paid?—I have not heard any complaints from them.

3837. Have you heard no complaints about their being required to clean the arms without receiving any additional allowance?—No, I have not; they have not told me anything of that kind. I know one serjeant who drills a corps at a distance, and he wants more money.

3838. Do you think that the officers in your district, generally speaking, are efficient, and up to their work?—I think that the officers are the weak point of the volunteer movement.

3839. Do you see your way to making them more efficient?—I cannot say that I do much; there are some to whom I give the greatest credit, who seem to know as much as if they had been in the line for years, but there are others in the regiments who do not know their drill.

3840. Does your observation apply to captains and subalterns, or generally to field officers as well?—More to the captains and subalterns than to the field officers. I think that the field officers are generally more zealous, that is my notion about it.

3841. You do not think that it would be possible to have some sort of examination in particular districts to be conducted by a board, in the same way as in the militia?—I do not know how that would do; I do not know how it is done in the militia. I did not know that they were ever examined.

3842. Do you think it would be possible to introduce any such system for the volunteers?—I think there would be a good deal of difficulty about it. I have not turned my attention to that before; but it seems to me that local reasons might prevent anything of that sort; a man may get on very well with his corps by putting his hand into his pocket, and it may go on very well, although he is not a very good officer.

3843. Do you think that the number of days' drill which constitute an effective might be reduced or increased?—I have heard many say that they thought they might attend a fewer number of drills. I think that the number is few enough to make them drilled soldiers; whether it interferes with their occupations more than it should is another question, but I think before a man is declared to be thoroughly efficient the drills should not be less than they are now, and if every volunteer were to go through an examination before he finished his attendances at drill, I think they are more than would be sufficient; you might say once every half year.

3844. Do you think that the drill instructors, generally speaking, are up to their work?—As a rule I think they are. I have not had to find any fault with them, taking them as a whole; some are, of course, better than others.

3845. (*Sir A. Campbell.*) You appear to think that after a volunteer has once become thoroughly acquainted with drill, he might be allowed to pass through a smaller number of annual drills than he does now?—Yes.

3846. Can you suggest any means by which the efficiency of a man should be ascertained?—That is a very difficult question; it is very difficult to carry that out unless the volunteers themselves will consent to it. If every volunteer would say before he becomes a volunteer, "I will attend a sufficient number of " times to enable me to pass an examination in order

Lieut.-Col. R. Luard.

1 July 1862.

160   MINUTES OF EVIDENCE TAKEN BEFORE THE COMMISSIONERS APPOINTED

Lieut.-Col.
R. Luard.

1 July 1862.

" that afterwards I may attend less often," then it would be all right, but it is delicate ground, I think.

3847. Supposing they consented, with whom would you lodge the power of passing them?—I think with the adjutant of the battalion; I think he would be competent to decide whether a man should remain in the ranks or not.

3848. For that purpose would the adjutant be responsible to his commanding officer or to the assistant inspector of the district?—I should make him responsible to his superior, and as long as he is responsible to the War Office he would be responsible to his superior; his commanding officer is his superior, and the commanding officer of the battalion would have nothing to do with the commanding officers of the different corps; I am talking now of an administrative battalion.

3849. Are you of opinion that the powers of the officer commanding an administrative battalion are at present sufficient?—They have not got much power, I think.

3850. Do you think that they require more?—I do not know what sort of power you could give them; if you could give it to them, I think it would be good.

3851. (*Col. MacMurdo.*) You say that they have not got power; have they not got power to command on parade?—Yes.

3852. If anything occurs there contrary to the duties of the volunteer under the Act of Parliament, has he not power to call upon the officer commanding that volunteer to put the law in force?—Yes.

3853. Is not that power?—Yes; but he cannot act as a commanding officer of a regiment would; the power is very different.

3854. You are aware that the object of the Government, in appointing an officer to command an administrative battalion, is for purposes of drill, and not for the formation of the corps?—No; that is under the commanding officer of the corps.

3855. It is merely for the purpose of imparting military instruction to an aggregate number of corps?—Yes.

3856. (*Chairman.*) He has no power over the non-commissioned officers of any company belonging to his administrative battalion, except on parade?—The commanding officer then steps in.

3857. Supposing the colonel of an administrative battalion visited the companies separately, and he saw a non-commissioned officer who was not efficient, would he have any power to dismiss him?—I think that he could put it so strongly to the commanding officer of the corp, that he would have to make the man efficient or dismiss him.

3858. Ought he not to have power to dismiss him?—I do not know.

3859. (*Lord Overstone.*) Is it not the fact, that the principal power which a commanding officer of an administrative battalion has must be exercised through a subordinate officer?—Through the officer commanding the corps very much.

3860. Do you think that a power can be so efficient which must be exercised through the medium of another officer as a power that is exercised directly?—Not so efficient; but I am not sure that the volunteers would put up with an authority with whom they had nothing to do. I mean, that a man goes and volunteers to serve under Captain Smith, but he does not wish to be under Colonel Jones' thumb.

3861. Your opinion, I think, is this, that the power vested in the colonel commanding an administrative battalion is defective, but you cannot suggest a mode by which that evil might be remedied?—Yes.

3862. (*Viscount Hardinge.*) A lieutenant-colonel has complete control over the drill instructors, as they are under the Mutiny Act bound to obey him as their superior officer; is not that so?—I think there has been some clashing as to the drill instructors being under the command of the commanding officer of the battalion, or under the officer commanding the corps.

I think it has been maintained that the drill instructor is under the officer commanding the corps, and under him only.

3863. But being subject to the Mutiny Act, he must be subject to the lieutenant-colonel's authority, he being his superior officer?—That may be right, but I do not think that that is thoroughly understood; indeed I think that many commanding officers of corps consider that the drill serjeant is under them independently of the commanding officer of the battalion; that is the idea of some of them.

3864. (*Sir A. Campbell.*) Independently of the adjutant also?—The adjutant can only report to the officer commanding the corps that the drill serjeant did not do so and so.

3865. (*Major-Gen. Eyre.*) What power would you have in that case?—I should merely report it to the War Office and put the man under arrest if there was anything serious.

3866. (*Col. MacMurdo.*) Bearing in mind the organization of an administrative battalion, and that companies are sometimes 20 and even 40 miles distant from headquarters where the officer commanding the volunteers is, the operation of the authority of the commanding officer would be more direct if that authority were vested in the officer commanding a company?—I think I have stated that I thought it would be very difficult to carry out that as a volunteer who volunteers to serve under Captain Smith would not wish to serve under Colonel Jones.

3867. But from geographical considerations he could not have the means of exercising that power directly?—He could if he visited the place and saw that a man did anything wrong.

3868. But that would necessitate his continual visits?—Yes; and some colonels might do so.

3869. (*Major-Gen. Eyre.*) Do you mean to say that a volunteer enrols merely that he shall serve under a particular captain?—I think there is a great deal of feeling of that sort amongst them.

3870. (*Viscount Hardinge.*) Supposing a case, which probably would rarely occur, that the lieutenant-colonel goes to inspect a company, and the captain being on parade supersedes his adjutant, and that a man who is insubordinate in the ranks insults the lieutenant-colonel, the lieutenant-colonel has no power to dismiss that man on the spot?—No lieutenant-colonel in the army has power to dismiss a man on the spot; he must put him under arrest.

3871. But the captain of a company has power to dismiss him on the spot if he thinks fit?—That is a greater power than is accorded to any officer in the army, and I should say it is a power which ought not to be in the hands of the commanding officer of a corps.

3872. (*Lord Overstone.*) You have stated, I think, that about 9,000 volunteers come under your inspection?—Yes, speaking roughly.

3873. The first duty imposed upon this Commission is to ascertain the present condition of the volunteer force, what is your opinion as to the present condition of the volunteer force that comes under your inspection?—I should say that it has attained a very fair state of efficiency.

3874. Do you think that it would be in an efficient state for useful service in case it was suddenly called into active operations?—I do; I think that a very few days, if they were actually called together, would make them very efficient.

3875. What is your opinion of the condition of the volunteer force, as to their clothing?—I think that the clothing is very much worn out, and that they want new clothing.

3876. Do you think there will be any difficulty in getting the clothing renewed?—Yes, I think they will find a difficulty in renewing their clothing.

3877. Do you anticipate such a difficulty in renewing the clothing as might make it expedient to consider the propriety of affording some assistance on the part of the Government?—If you gave them assistance in the other respects which I have pointed out, perhaps that may be unnecessary. I look upon that as the last thing that I would give them assistance in kind in. I would try all the other things before I gave them that.

3878. Do you believe that the arms and accoutrements are at the present time in a satisfactory state?—Yes.

3879. Evidence of a contrary character has been given by some of the witnesses examined before the Commission?—I have not found anything to find fault with in the arms as a rule; as to the accoutrements, some are better than others; I mean some are better for service than others.

3880. Do you think, generally, as to the arms and accoutrements, that the volunteers would be able to turn out for useful service?—Yes, I do, most thoroughly.

3881. As to their discipline, do you think that that is now in such an advanced state as to enable the volunteers to act as an efficient body in actual service?—I think it will improve constantly, and I think that a very little more practice would improve it. I do not mean that they would be perfect if they went into the field to-morrow.

3882. Supposing they were suddenly called out, do you think that within a short time, say two or three weeks, the force under your inspection would be in a state of efficiency as to their discipline and as to their arms, and their capacity to use them?—I think they would be ready to fight the enemy in three weeks.

3883. Does your experience lead you to think that there are any causes seriously menacing a deterioration in the efficiency of the volunteer force?—I think they are a little slacker than they were in their attendance, and I think that the expense has to do with it; and I think also, that their having arrived at a certain degree of efficiency, leads them to think that they know more than they really do know, and that is their reason for attending drill less.

3884. You think that there is some little diminution in the active feeling which led to the organization of the force, and some little diminution of efficiency arising from over self-confidence?—I think so.

3885. Are you prepared to suggest any measures or steps that might be taken to obviate these dangers?—I have heard already of something.

3886. You refer, I presume, first of all, to pecuniary assistance in some form or other?—I think that if you give assistance at all, assistance in kind is what you should give.

3887. I think it is your opinion that some further assistance as to drill instructors, and as to travelling expenses when going to battalion drills, and also for the purpose of providing ranges is necessary?—Yes.

3888. With those aids, do you think that the efficiency of the volunteer force may be satisfactorily maintained?—I think so; and I should rather hope with such aids it would not be necessary to give them clothing. I consider clothing the last thing that ought to be given to them.

3889. Do you not think that the question of a more organized system of providing drill instructors is one of great importance?—It depends upon the system. I think that it would be a great improvement on the present system to put all the serjeants of a battalion under the adjutant, to let them be directly under him, be drilled at first by him at his headquarters,

so that all the companies of one battalion may drill exactly alike; and to let them be sent by him to the different corps of the battalion at his and the commanding officer of the battalion's discretion. By this means fewer serjeants might suffice; but some little travelling expense would be incurred.

3890. Do you not think it very desirable that by some means a more ready and complete supply of efficient drill instructors should be provided?—I have not heard of many complaints of the difficulty of finding drill instructors. I have heard a few; but that is the only way in which I can answer the question; in my district I do not find that many people complain that they cannot get drill instructors, but a few have.

3891. (*Major-Gen. Eyre.*) In your position, have you any difficulties to contend with?—I think I get on pretty smoothly.

3892. Have you all the power that you think you ought to have?—If they were a little more liberal in their allowances for travelling expenses and those sort of things I should be better pleased; they treat me very shabbily on that score.

3893. (*Sir A. Campbell.*) Your functions, I presume, consist in receiving, verifying, and forwarding returns, and in inspecting the various corps in your district once a year or oftener?—I cannot say that I verify the returns. I receive and forward them, and I make inspections.

3894. I suppose you see that they are in the proper form?—If I see anything glaringly wrong I return them, but I have no means of verifying those returns; they are merely numerical returns. I have nothing to do with the nominal returns; they come in once a year to the War Office.

3895. Has an assistant inspector any other duties besides those I have enumerated?—He has occasionally to visit the ranges, and so on; if there is any row I am sent down.

3896. (*Major Harcourt.*) You think that it would be more desirable to give assistance to the volunteers in kind?—Yes.

3897. For what reason do you think so?—Because if you gave the money, the means of spending that money must be investigated; and if I had, as inspector, to investigate that matter, I think it would be much more than I could do.

3898. Do you say this chiefly with reference to yourself and to the work at the War Office rather than with reference to the volunteers?—I think it will affect the volunteers very much, for you must lay down the rule whether they shall wear feathers and expensive uniforms or not, and whether they shall have a band or not, and I think it would so much hamper the volunteer movement that they would say, "We cannot allow all these rules, we must have some "little way of our own," and I think it would thus interfere with the movement.

3899. (*Lieut.-Col. Barttelot.*) Supposing aid was given to the volunteers, do you not think that if certain things were recognized by the War Office, certain legitimate expenses, that it would be the best way to give the money to the commanding officer, making him responsible for the money being applied in the way that was specified by the War Office?—No. I do not like money at all; I should like assistance, if given, to be given in kind, but no money.

The witness withdrew.

Lieut.-Colonel JOSEPH HUDSON examined.

3900. (*Chairman.*) I believe you are superintendent of the Royal Army Clothing Factory at Pimlico?—I am.

3901. You have been consulted about the issue of cloth to the volunteers?—Yes, by Mr. Ramsay, and, I believe, by the wish of Lord de Grey.

3902. If cloth is issued by the Government, do you intend to confine the issue of that cloth to particular colours, or shall you issue all colours that may be required?—It is intended, I believe, by the Secretary of State to confine the issue to four colours, one grey, one scarlet, one rifle green, and blue.

3903. Do you consider that there would be a considerable saving if that cloth was issued at cost price

Lieut.-Col. J. Hudson.

1 July 1862.

to the volunteers?—I think that the volunteers would get a better material and more durable clothing, and, I think, a little cheaper.

3904. We have been informed by several witnesses that if that issue of cloth is made, the persons who make up the clothing would charge a considerable sum in addition for the making up as a profit, and that in fact the volunteers would not gain much if cloth were issued by the Government?—I think at first they might not gain much advantage, but I believe that the competition in this country is so great that the volunteers would eventually find they could get their clothing made at a very reasonable price.

3905. You issue clothing from your department for the army made up?—Yes; for the army only.

3906. What do you think that the volunteers' clothing would cost, if issued by the Government made up in a complete set?—I have a return here of the cost of the four cloths, the patterns now worn by the volunteers vary very much, and the cost of the clothing would vary a little with those patterns.

The witness delivered in the same, which is as follows:—

	TUNICS.											
—	From Scarlet Cloth at 8*s.* 11¾*d.*			From Rifle Green at 9*s.* 2*d.*			From Grey at 6*s.* 1½*d.*			From Blue No. 3 Cloth at 8*s.* 5¾*d.*		
	£	*s.*	*d.*	£	*s.*	*d.*	£	*s.*	*d.*	£	*s.*	*d.*
1 12/36 yards tunic cloth	0	11	11¾	0	12	2¾	0	8	2	0	11	3¾
5/36 yard facing cloth at 7*s.* 3*d.*	0	1	0	0	1	0	0	1	0	0	1	0
¾ yard silver cord at 1*s.* 9*d.*	0	1	3¾	0	1	3¾	0	1	3¾	0	1	3¾
20/36 yard drab jean at 8*d.*	0	0	4½	0	0	4½	0	0	4½	0	0	4½
1 21/36 yards selesia at 6*d.*	0	0	9¼	0	0	9¼	0	0	9¼	0	0	9¼
1/36 yard buckram at 7¼*d.*	0	0	0¼	0	0	0¼	0	0	0¼	0	0	0¼
1/36 yard canvas at 6½*d.*	0	0	0¼	0	0	0¼	0	0	0¼	0	0	0¼
Twist	0	0	1¼	0	0	1¼	0	0	1¼	0	0	1¼
Silk	0	0	2½	0	0	2½	0	0	2½	0	0	2½
Tape, stay	0	0	0¼	0	0	0¼	0	0	0¼	0	0	0¼
Thread, red	0	0	1	0	0	1	0	0	1	0	0	1
Thread, white	0	0	0½	0	0	0½	0	0	0½	0	0	0½
Hooks and eyes	0	0	0¼	0	0	0¼	0	0	0¼	0	0	0¼
Making	0	3	6	0	3	6	0	3	6	0	3	6
Cutting	0	0	6	0	0	6	0	0	6	0	0	6
Establishment	0	0	2¾	0	0	2¾	0	0	2¾	0	0	2¾
	1	0	2¼	1	0	5½	0	16	4½	0	19	6¼
If with silver braid	1	2	5¼	1	2	9	0	18	8	1	1	9¾

	s.	*d.*
Great coat made from grey cloth at 4*s.* 1½*d.* per yard	19	8½

	s.	*d.*
Trousers, grey, from cloth at 6*s.* 1½*d.* per yard	11	2¾
Do., green, from cloth at 9*s.* 3¾*d.* per yard	15	8¼
Do., blue, from cloth at 7*s.* 11¾*d.* per yard	14	8
Do., grey, from cloth at 4*s.* 1½*d.* per yard	9	5¾

3907. Upon what ground is it wished to confine yourself to four colours?—It was so decided by the Secretary of State.

3908. Are those the four colours predominant in the clothing of the volunteer force?—Yes, I think so, excepting the greys. Of the greys I think there are upwards of 9 or 10 different shades.

3909. (*Sir A. Campbell.*) The grey that you allude to is the grey selected by the committee which sat here?—Yes; I think it is Lord Elcho's colour.

3910. (*Chairman.*) How long ought these uniforms to wear, four years?—Not so long as that if they wear them frequently. The cloth that we give to the army only lasts about a year, or a year and a half. In the foot guards it lasts two years, but I think not more than two years.

3911. (*Major-Gen. Eyre.*) But the army are employed every day; the volunteers are supposed to have only a small number of drills in the year?—They do not work so hard as the army, but still the clothing wears out by dust and moth, even if it is put by.

3912. (*Viscount Hardinge.*) How long does the clothing of a militia man last?—Five years.

3913. He has 21 or 28 days' drill in a year?—Yes.

3914. An effective volunteer has 24?—Yes; but I think he does more work than that; the volunteers in many instances drill nearly once a week.

3915. (*Col. MacMurdo.*) If clothing was issued to the volunteers, is it your opinion that the cloth and the trimmings should be issued, and that an allowance should be given to the volunteers to make up the clothing?—Yes; but the cost of the establishment and labour would be so great, that it would be a matter of consideration whether it would not be better to make an allowance to cover the cost of the trimmings.

3916. The Government do not find the cloth now, but they will issue it at a certain price?—Yes; they will provide it on payment being made.

3917. Does the cost that you have calculated include 5 per cent. for establishment?—Only on the cloth.

3918. Is that 5 per cent. sufficient to cover all the expenses?—Yes, and that is the usual per-centage.

3919. (*Chairman.*) Does the cost of the different coloured cloths, enumerated in the return you have handed in, include the 5 per cent.?—I think that the scarlet cloth actually cost 8*s.* 8*d.* I see it put down in the Government return at 8*s.* 11¼*d.*, so that in that case it includes the 5 per cent.

3920. (*Major-Gen. Eyre.*) Is not 5 per cent. a very large per-centage?—That rate was determined upon by the clothing department in Pall Mall, with the approval of the Secretary of State; and it is difficult to say, without further experience, whether it could be done for less.

3921. (*Viscount Hardinge.*) What would be a fair allowance for making up?—3s. 6d. for making the tunic; that is the price we pay at the Government factory; a contractor would have to put his profit on all those prices that I have put down.

3922. What would a contractor charge?—I think he would expect fully 12 per cent. as his profit; the prices I have put down are exactly what it would cost the Government if the clothes were made at the Government factory.

3923. (*Col. MacMurdo.*) You do not suppose that the volunteers could get a tailor to make their tunics up for 3s. 6d.?—I think that Mr. Taite, of Limerick, would do it at that price.

3924. (*Chairman.*) You have put down the trousers at different prices; do those prices include the making up?—Yes, everything.

3925. (*Col. MacMurdo.*) Would it not be better to issue the cloth for clothing, and make an allowance for the trimmings and making up?—Yes.

3926. Is that the better system, or that the Government should issue the trimmings with the cloth?—I think that the Government would have a difficulty in doing that, as all the volunteer patterns would require different trimmings for almost all the different patterns of uniform.

3927. You think that the cloth simply should be issued, and an allowance made for trimmings and making up?—Yes.

3928. (*Lord Overstone.*) I understand you to say that the Government, should this Commission be disposed to recommend it, would be prepared to issue cloth, but not made up into clothing?—The clothing establishment could not at present undertake to issue the clothing made up.

3929. (*Viscount Hardinge.*) Would there be any difficulty in the War Office, supposing it were deemed advisable, contracting with certain houses to provide the uniforms made up for the different corps until your premises at Pimlico were enlarged, if they should ever be so enlarged?—I think that the Government could contract as they do for the army, but this is a question which could only be settled by the clothing department at Pall Mall.

Lieut.-Col. J. Hudson.

4 July 1862.

The witness withdrew.

Colonel CHARLES BINGHAM examined.

Col. C. Bingham.

3930. (*Chairman.*) You are Deputy Adjutant-General of Artillery?—Yes.

3931. (*Major Harcourt.*) Do you find any difficulty in obtaining reports from artillery volunteers, or do you know of any difficulties being found by the commanding officers of districts?—None that I know of.

3932. On the occasion of divisional field days, would the authorities be disposed to allow the use of guns, where practicable, to artillery volunteers, with a special allowance of blank ammunition, and place them under the command of royal artillery officers?—This has been done on several occasions; viz., at Brighton, Bristol, in Devonshire, and I think some other places. The War Office has always sanctioned an increase in the number of rounds of ammunition on these occasions.

3933. Will the authorities be likely to recognize the value of the volunteer cattle movement for moving guns of position on the coast?—Yes; and I am satisfied His Royal Highness the Commander-in-chief thinks that the power of making use of all the horses in the district is one of the best arrangements that could be made. Captain Darby has organized Sussex in that way, and it is, perhaps, the most useful organization that could be made.

3934. Would it be desirable that that should be extended as much as possible along the coasts?—Yes, undoubtedly; and also as to bullocks; all the 18-pounder batteries in the counties where bullocks are to be had have been fitted with pole draught for the purpose.

3935. Do you think that the artillery volunteers might fairly ask for the carriage of ammunition for practice where the magazine is unavoidably at a great distance from the battery?—I do not quite understand the question; the magazines ought properly to be in the batteries.

3936. I mean in cases where there is no provision made for expense magazines?—Then I think it should be the same as in the Royal Artillery; it should be brought to them free of expense.

3937. Do you think that the artillery volunteers might fairly ask for the construction, where practicable of expense magazines, to save the inconvenience and danger of such carriage?—I should say that they ought to have expense magazines, or that all ammunition be conveyed free to the volunteers. In almost all the districts, as far as I know, these magazines are in the batteries, and the ammunition is deposited in them.

3938. Is not that where the batteries are the property of the Royal Artillery?—No; it is so in the volunteer batteries too.

3939. Do you think that the artillery volunteers might ask for the construction of store-rooms for Government stores where store-rooms of the Royal Artillery are not available?—Yes; there was a question some time ago, and it was arranged by the War Office that where the volunteers built their own batteries they were to provide magazines and store-rooms, and a residence for the gunner in charge.

3940. Do you think that the volunteer artillery might fairly ask to be relieved from that expense?—Undoubtedly it would be for the good of the Government that these stores should be preserved.

3941. As well as for the good of the volunteer?—Yes.

3942. Do you think that the artillery volunteers might ask for the erection of gun sheds for the protection of guns on travelling carriages and for purposes of gun drills where guns or travelling carriages are supplied to them?—We have never given any 18-pounder field moveable guns to any volunteers unless they have guaranteed to protect them from injury.

3943. Do you think that the volunteer artillery might fairly ask to be relieved from that expense?—There again these guns, &c., are Government property, and deteriorate very much if sheds are not built.

3944. You are aware that this Commission is engaged in inquiring into the constitution of the volunteer force, and in what way it may be assisted, do you think that that is a species of assistance that they might well ask for?—Yes.

3945. Where many Government stores are in charge of a corps, might not the artillery volunteers ask for a paid quartermaster serjeant or, better still, the appointment of a non-commissioned officer of Royal Artillery with a slight increase of pay to perform the function of quartermaster serjeant, such non-commissioned officer to be distinct from the drill instructor?—I do not understand how the volunteers can have charge of any stores, because the drill instructor is the Government custodian of all the stores entrusted to the volunteers, and it is his business to keep an account of them, and he is responsible to the commanding officer of artillery in the district, for their being at all times in good order.

Y 2

Col.
C. Bingham.

1 July 1862.

3946. Properly speaking the volunteers ought not to be put to any expense as to the custody of the Government stores?—Certainly not; they are entirely military stores, and in charge of the commanding officer of artillery in the district.

3947. Do you know who takes charge of the artillery small arms?—No; I know nothing about them.

3948. Whose property are they?—I do not know.

3949. They are not in charge of the Royal Artillery?—No.

3950. Might not the artillery volunteers ask to have the expense defrayed of sending out their targets for practice?—I always thought this was done. I think it ought to be, certainly, as regards the boating charges, the same as for the Royal Artillery; the volunteers themselves would assist in laying out the targets, but the boat hire for taking the targets out to sea, and bringing them back again, I think should be defrayed.

3951. Might not the artillery volunteers be supplied with skidding, luff tackle, ground and other rollers, scotches, selvages, straps, drag ropes, &c. for moving heavy ordnance without a gyn, where such articles are not obtainable from the royal artillery stores?—Where the volunteer artillery make use of royal artillery guns, the commander-in-chief has desired that commanding officers of artillery would afford every facility in teaching them and training them to the use of artillery machines of all kinds; but it has not been thought expedient to incur the expense of sending all these stores to small volunteer batteries at out-stations.

3952. But to such inexpensive stores as those I have enumerated, you see no objection?—If you multiply them into a great number, the expense will be great; still, if it is with the object of considering what it would be good to allow the volunteers, I think it would be a very good thing.

3953. Is it not one very important point with reference to the artillery volunteers on the coast that they should be able to assist the royal artillery when short-handed?—There is no doubt about it.

3954. Without these appliances they could not do it?—They could not, nor without a very good knowledge of them.

3955. Do you not consider that a most important consideration?—Most important, far more than the mere firing the guns.

3956. Can you inform the Commission whether any great extra expense is incurred by the district offices of Royal Artillery or at the Horse Guards in consequence of their having to receive reports and pass accounts of artillery volunteers?—No, in each district office where there are large numbers of volunteers, an extra clerk is temporarily employed at 1s. a day. In my office I have only one extra clerk at 1s. a day for volunteer purposes. Of course it increases the work very much, and at first it was very heavy, but after it had once got organized it became comparatively easy, and the whole of the stores belonging to the volunteer artillery are taken up on the store returns of the commanding officer of artillery.

3957. Then it is a mistake to suppose, according to the present practice, that commanding officers of volunteer artillery are considered to be in charge of the guns and the stores?—Yes, they are not at all so considered.

3958. It is a mistake?—Yes, quite a mistake. The Horse Guards authorities have no control nor can they give any orders or directions to the volunteer officers.

3959. (*Major-Gen. Eyre.*) Are the artillery volunteers organized in districts under the officer commanding the Royal Artillery in the district?—Yes; as far as their matériel and practice are concerned.

3960. Then they are different from the rifle volunteers?—I do not know what their organization is; if the commander-in-chief is asked to name an officer to inspect the artillery volunteers, the district commanding officer is generally selected; but in large districts, such as the northern district, or Scotland, where the volunteer artillery are so numerous, it takes five or six officers to inspect them.

3961. (*Sir A. Campbell.*) But the system is different from that pursued in the rifle volunteers, is it not?—I do not know.

3962. (*Lord Overstone.*) I presume you are of opinion that the artillery volunteer force along the maritime counties of England is about the most valuable of all the volunteer corps?—They will be most valuable auxiliaries to the Royal Artillery, I have no doubt.

3963. You think that they would be of very great importance as a force auxiliary to the Royal Artillery?—Of the greatest possible importance.

3964. Do you think they ought to receive all possible encouragement from the Government?—Yes I do, and as far as I can see they have every possible assistance.

3965. You have expressed your concurrence as to the propriety of many requests being made to the Government for aid to the artillery volunteers. Are the Commission to understand that in the cases in which you have expressed that concurrence, you are aware that the Government are prepared to grant those requests?—I cannot say that; the Horse Guards have nothing to do with money.

3966. You have simply expressed a professional opinion that the requests are reasonable, but you can say nothing as to the intentions of Government?—Nothing whatever.

The witness withdrew.

Adjourned till Friday next at half-past 12 o'clock.

Friday, 4th July 1862.

PRESENT:

Viscount EVERSLEY.
Viscount HARDINGE.
Lord OVERSTONE.
Lieutenant-Colonel BARTTELOT.
Lieutenant-Colonel Sir A. CAMPBELL.

Lieutenant-General Sir G. A. WETHERALL.
Major-General EYRE.
Colonel MACMURDO.
Major HARCOURT.

VISCOUNT EVERSLEY IN THE CHAIR.

Lieutenant-Colonel THOMAS DYKE ACLAND examined.

Lieut.-Col.
T. D. Acland.

4 July 1862.

3967. (*Chairman.*) You command two bodies of volunteers in the county of Devon; a Mounted Rifle Volunteer Corps, and also an Administrative Battalion?—Yes.

3968. Does the mounted rifle volunteer corps consist of more than one company?—It consists of one company, with a certain number of dismounted men; they are either a section of a company, or they are a section attached. I do not think that that point is quite settled. The original intention sanctioned by the War Office was to make the mounted corps a nucleus, to which sections of artisans in various villages should be united.

3969. Are your mounted men all drilled to act as infantry?—Yes; they are all drilled on the ordinary principles of infantry with the dismounted men. They are also drilled in the instructions for mounted rifle volunteers, issued by Colonel Lysons, under authority of the Secretary of State, and in some additional movements suggested by Colonel Bowers, of Hampshire.

3970. Was there any fund raised for that corps in the first instance?—Yes; a considerable fund.

3971. Was the clothing of the men paid for out of that fund?—It is a fundamental rule that no clothing is to be paid for out of the fund; every man clothed himself, or was clothed by private friends.

3972. Do you call for subscriptions from every member of the corps?—Yes; 5s. annually, which they are not very willing to pay.

3973. Out of the fund so raised, can you pay for all the rifle ranges, and everything else that is necessary?—Two ranges, with butts, &c., have been all provided for by my father at no cost to the corps; there is also a liberal annual subscription from honorary members.

3974. Then we may consider that your mounted corps is well provided for?—Yes.

3975. And does not require any assistance?—No; beyond that already given for ammunition and drill instruction.

3976. You also command an administrative battalion, of how many corps does that consist?—Of eight corps, and two mounted corps attached. There are six companies and two subdivisions of rifle volunteers, and two attached mounted corps, No. 1 and No. 3.

3977. Are those mounted corps able to support themselves?—You mean the second one; that is No. 3.

3978. Yes?—It does not support itself very well, for it leans a good deal upon individuals; it consists of a certain number of small hill country farmers, who are very zealous and intelligent, and I am very desirous to keep up the corps; they have been entirely dependent for drill upon my drill instructor, who goes a distance of 16 miles once a fortnight to drill that corps, but that has been done by private arrangement, they having no drill instructor.

3979. Are you speaking of the drill instructor who is attached to the mounted corps?—Yes, to the corps No. 1, of which I am captain.

3980. On principle, those corps should be self-supporting, if possible?—I am very strongly of that opinion; I think it is desirable that all volunteer corps should be self-supporting.

3981. Supposing it were necessary to give them Government aid, on what conditions do you think that Government aid should be given?—I think that any assistance that may be given by the Government should be subject to strict conditions as to the efficiency of the corps, either as to its numbers or as to the attendance of the men at drill, or, which I think still more important, as to their proper knowledge of their drill, and also as to certain special conditions with regard to keeping up the practice of systematic shooting; of course also as to the state of their arms and accoutrements, and whatever belongs to the Government.

3982. You do not consider that attendance at a certain number of drills is any proof of a man being an effective soldier?—No, and I think it is most desirable that the definition of an effective should be altered.

3983. A man ought to have passed through a course of musketry instruction to be an effective?—Yes.

3984. And through all the preliminary drills?—Perhaps he ought; but it is difficult to enforce all the preliminary drills.

3985. Supposing that it was made one of the conditions before any assistance was given that the men should have passed through a course of musketry instruction, and all the preliminary drills, how would you obtain that sort of information?—I have very great difficulty in getting information as to the corps under my command. I have been trying to get information; but I am not in a position to state officially, as to any one of my corps, whether they have fired in file and volley, and I consider it important that the colonel of a corps should have the power of ascertaining what progress is being made in the corps for whose drill he is responsible.

3986. Are these corps all provided with ranges?—I believe they all are; indeed, they were not formed until their ranges had been inspected; but there has been a great difficulty in some parts of Devonshire in getting ranges. The Exeter corps has had a great difficulty about a range. The arrangement now made is, that they have a very good range on the sea coast, which they reach by a sixpenny fare from Exeter. That is just one of those local cases in which it is desirable that the suggestion, with regard to the nature of the assistance required, should come from below, and not from above. What they want is to be relieved from the expense of getting to their rifle range.

3987. (*Major-Gen. Eyre.*) What is the actual distance that they travel?—About 10 miles.

3988. (*Chairman.*) You are of opinion that the officer in command of an administrative battalion should have rather more power than he has now?—I think that he should have more responsibility, and more discretion in matters of administration, if I may draw the distinction. He has a means of persuasion and of inquiry which cannot possibly exist here. Most of the administrative field officers, from their former military position, or from their local property, or their connexion with property, have a certain public character to maintain, and I think the War Office might rely on information derived jointly from the adjutant and field officer.

3989. If any assistance were given to an administrative battalion do you think it should pass through the hands of the commanding officer?—I should be very sorry to have the money passed through my hands. I should be prepared to investigate the circumstances of each application for aid, and to report upon them; but I should not like to have to spend the money.

3990. Do you think that the colonel should be made responsible for all the wants of the corps?—I think he should be held responsible for making the War Office thoroughly aware of the state of the circumstances, and for suggesting the course most likely to ensure efficiency and the willing co-operation of all parties concerned.

3991. (*Viscount Hardinge.*) As to the efficiency of the men in drill, such as file firing and volley firing, the colonel of an administrative battalion has power, has he not, to go and inspect the different corps, and ascertain how far they are proficient in their drill?—Yes; but I am speaking not of the actual proficiency of those on parade, which can be judged of by inspection, but of the regularity and system brought to bear on the course of drill and musketry.

3992. Have you a difficulty in ascertaining from the captain of each company the exact routine of the drill that the company has gone through?—Yes.

3993. (*Chairman.*) Could not a return be called for by the colonel of an administrative battalion, which should be signed by the adjutant and the drill instructor, and the captains of companies, that would show exactly what drill every man had gone through?—There is a great dislike to paper work among volunteers. Any returns called for should be very simple, and not too frequent. I have taken much pains to prepare such a return in a form which will give as little trouble as possible, but I do not feel sure that I shall get it filled up for all the corps. I think it is clearly the duty of the adjutant to keep the field officer regularly informed of the progress of the corps under his command, and if the returns are not

Lieut.-Col.
T. D. Acland.

4 July 1862.

Y 3

Lieut.-Col.
T. D. Acland.
4 July 1862.

sent to him by post, that he ought to go and obtain the information on the spot. I should, however, suggest that some allowance should be made for an orderly clerk, or a serjeant-major, because I think that such a man, having a recognized position in the service under the adjutant, would be able to get returns systematically kept, and execute orders which can hardly be given to an officer who has left the army at a certain time of life.

3994. Do you think that the allowances made to the adjutant are sufficient?—I hardly like to give any opinion as to their pay, but I believe that adjutants of volunteers do not consider themselves properly paid in comparison with adjutants of militia.

3995. What is your opinion as to the allowances for travelling expenses?—I think that the allowances for travelling expenses are made upon an extremely bad principle, as I have already stated officially. I will put two corps side by side, Lord Mount Edgcumbe has his corps all close together in Plymouth, Stonehouse, and Devonport, except one, and that one is at Tavistock. That one is, I believe, over the required distance, and his adjutant gets the same allowance per diem as my adjutant receives, who goes down two lines of railway, a distance of 20 miles, and at the end of one journey by rail has to hire a conveyance for five miles, and at the end of the other journey to hire for seven miles. I should be glad if he could visit the distant corps more frequently than some of the others, but every time that I send him I take from 15s. to 1l. out of his pocket. I therefore strongly disapprove of the plan of compounding for travelling expenses, because it hampers a commanding officer, and taxes the adjutant in proportion to the zeal with which he does his duty.

3996. You spoke just now of the drill instructor of your mounted corps doing duty with other corps?—I have been obliged to lend him to another mounted corps attached to my own battalion, and to two mounted corps in another battalion. They could not get a drill instructor, and that is a point which I wish most earnestly to press upon the attention of the Commission. I think that the present mode of appointing and paying drill instructors should be entirely altered. The practice of attaching a man permanently on a yearly salary to a corps which only gives him work to do once a week, or twice a week, and at certain seasons in the course of the year no work at all, is in my opinion a waste of public money, and I think it of the utmost importance to keep down all the charges on the public purse for the volunteer force. I entertain that opinion very strongly. A serjeant attached to a volunteer corps is in a totally different position from a serjeant in a good regiment. In his regiment he is under all the influences that keep a man up to his work, whereas the serjeant in a volunteer corps is under influences which tend to make him get slack, unless he is a very conscientious and active man. I have 10 corps to deal with; the corps of which I am captain is extremely well served, therefore I do not complain on personal grounds; but practically out of the 10 corps there are only two besides my own that have any aid from the Government towards drill instruction; all the others have been doing their best to engage serjeant instructors on the terms of the regulations, but they cannot succeed, and that is the case with many other corps in Devonshire.

3997. Would not those two drill instructors have a great deal of leisure time and be able to give the necessary instruction to the whole of the corps in the battalion, if placed under the command of the colonel and the adjutant?—That is the plan which I strongly urged on the Government before they decided to give separate instructors to each detached corps, and I think it would have worked much better than the present arrangement; but now that the officers of the separate corps have been led to think they can have serjeants at their own command, and I do not think that they would like the drill instructors to be transferred from them to the colonel and the adjutant. I think the most convenient course would be to give a money payment to the officers of each corps to be spent either on the payment of an occasional drill instructor or of a resident orderly, or for both purposes.

3998. (*Lord Overstone.*) Do you mean a money payment from the public purse?—I mean instead of giving 2s. 4d. a day or 2s. 7d. to a permanent drill instructor, that a smaller sum of money than that should be placed at the disposal of the captain of a corps, to enable him to engage a serjeant, with the concurrence of the field officer, on his own terms.

3999. You do not contemplate an increased charge upon the public purse?—No; I think that less money would do; I consider the present a very improvident arrangement, and that a smaller sum of money spent in a different way would do the work a great deal better; nearly all my corps have been drilled by engaging a serjeant from the staff of the disembodied militia; they are excellent drills; they are very much improved in my opinion as volunteer drills by their experience; they have learned how to drill volunteers, and do their work very well. They are willing to go out as often as they are required at 5s. a day; the cost of the arrangement I suggest would be from 15l. to 25l. a year.

4000. (*Col. MacMurdo.*) Are you aware that the serjeants of the permanent staff of the militia constitute a class of drill instructors for the volunteers at the rate of 1s. a day?—I am aware of that regulation. But you cannot get them to work on those terms as permanent instructors; they will not come; but they are willing to come if you deal with them on the basis of the market value of their services.

4001. (*Viscount Hardinge.*) Does each company in your administrative battalion give gratuities to those militia serjeants?—They pay them regularly for the work done; they make a private engagement with them, and they pay them for the work done.

4002. That is, I suppose, for the number of drills they attend?—Yes; at so much per drill.

4003. You are probably aware that you can have the services of a militia serjeant throughout the whole year if you like?—I am aware that that is upon paper; but I do not believe that they can be compelled to leave their quarters or to undertake the extra duty unless they are properly paid for it.

4004. (*Lord Overstone.*) Is it the result of your experience that practically you can not obtain the services of these militia serjeants?—Yes.

4005. (*Chairman.*) You cannot secure the services of the militia serjeants when you want them, or when they are secured they are paid at the rate of 5s. a day?—Yes; that is by a private arrangement, which I think works very well; some of them are first-rate instructors. They have a standing engagement with some of the corps that they shall go once a fortnight, in other cases once a week, and I think that that is all that is wanted, or can practically be done, for drill in rural districts. The drill of volunteers is an employment which requires very high skill, and should be dealt with as skilled labour. The men who can drill well are exceedingly few in number, and they know their own value. If it is convenient to have a man on the spot to take care of the arms and to attend on parade to mark points, and to give a certain amount of military steadiness to the volunteers, perhaps the fittest kind of man would be a pensioner, whose services would be obtained at a very much lower rate if he were allowed to fill up his time and to earn money in other ways; a skilled drill instructor will not work at the same low rate of remuneration.

4006. (*Viscount Hardinge.*) At what rate per week, supposing you received a money payment from the Government, do you think you could obtain the services of a discharged soldier or pensioner from the line to act as your drill instructor?—I do not mean as drill instructor, but a person to perform certain orderly duties at the headquarters of a small corps. I may, however, answer the question by mentioning that in connexion with my own company I have employed one of my father's woodmen whose wages are about 10s. a week for half his time to clean arms, to act as marker at target practice, and occasionally as assistant drill instructor. The expense may be estimated at 5s. or 6s. per week. The man was a serjeant in the line.

4007. Would such a discharged soldier occupy the place that is now occupied by the drill instructor?—He would do part of his duty, and that which would be the least costly, clean the arms, for instance, and take care of the armoury, act as marker, and he might possibly keep books.

4008. Would it not be advisable in a rural company, where, perhaps, neither the captain nor the subalterns had served in the line, that they should have an experienced drill instructor to refer to upon any disputed point in the details of the drill?—No, I do not think so, I think that they ought to refer to the adjutant.

4009. But suppose the adjutant is not present?—I think the officers had better rely upon themselves, and learn their own work. I do not approve of volunteer officers leaning on the drill instructors, I do not think that any good comes from that.

4010. (*Lord Overstone*.) Do you think that the officers could practically carry out the drill and discipline of the corps without the aid of a drill instructor?—I think they want the assistance of a skilled drill instructor periodically, perhaps, in certain cases once a week, and in other cases once a fortnight.

4011. The occasional presence of a drill instructor you think ought to be sufficient to enable the officers to carry out the instruction practically in the intervening periods?—Practically the men do not meet much in the intervals between the weekly or fortnightly drills.

4012. (*Viscount Hardinge*.) Under your plan would these men be detached from the militia to visit the corps periodically?—No, not detached.

4013. Should they come from any line or militia regiment that was within reach?—Yes, they would come by rail and return the same day or the next day.

4014. (*Chairman*.) Have you any difficulty in assembling a good many of your men at battalion drills?—It is very much a matter of expense. I hope to get about one or two assemblages of the whole battalion in the year. With some encouragement and assistance we might have several meetings for combined company drill, varying from two to four companies.

4015. Do your men who come from a long distance require assistance, and if they received assistance do you think you could assemble a larger number together?—I think that some of the corps would find assistance a very great relief, as all these expenses are apt to fall on the officers. There is one corps in another battalion, the Chudleigh subdivision, composed of artizans and others, in which they have adopted a very good system, the men pay a penny a week towards an excursion fund which they manage themselves. But as a general rule the expenses incurred when travelling to battalion drills fall on the officers, and of course this circumstance imposes a limit on attendance, and also on the appointment of officers.

4016. You had a great brigade day a few days ago, had you not?—Yes.

4017. Were the expenses of the men paid on that occasion?—The arrangement was this. The corps travelling less than 12 miles had no allowance, the corps travelling more than 12 miles had an allowance of three farthings per mile per head one way, that is for the whole distance minus 12 miles, so that all the men were put upon the same footing, as the men who lived at Exeter and the men who lived at Torquay, each being distant about 12 miles from the stations near the rendezvous. To those who had to come by carts or other conveyance, to get to the station near their own headquarters, if they came less than two miles, we allowed nothing; but if they came more than two miles I think we allowed them 2s. for every 10 men per mile, and the practical result was that for railway expenses and road expenses of infantry and artillery on foot we paid 135l.

4018. How many men assembled on that occasion?—Including the mounted corps, 2,700. For the mounted corps we allowed to those who came over 20 miles and under 30 miles 7s. 6d. per horse; to those who came over 30 miles we allowed 10s. per horse; and the total expense for the horses was 42l. 17s. 6d. We also allowed to a field battery, bringing 60 horses, 30l. We also gave beer on the ground, which, perhaps, will not be done again. The total expense of the review, including printing and other sundry expenses, was about 300l. on the part of the association; but individuals incurred considerable expense besides.

4019. How was that money obtained?—It was raised by the Devon County Volunteer Association, the rules of which I have here, and which was founded generally for the purpose of assisting the volunteer force in all respects. It began by considering the question of clothing, ranges, and local organization. It was called upon by the lord-lieutenant to report on the division of the county into battalions, and it provided for a course of musketry instruction given to a class of 40 officers and noncommissioned officers. We have since had two county rifle meetings, which we have given up for the present year. We are now engaged in promoting the average shooting of companies and battalions, and in assisting the volunteers to assemble for the purpose of brigading. We do not give money for battalion drills, but only for brigade drills.

4020. (*Col. MacMurdo*.) Why have you given up the prize meetings of the county rifle association?—Because we found that they were putting money into the pockets of a very limited number of good shots, and not giving satisfaction even to those few who complained that our prizes were of too small amount for the expense of attending the meetings. We are now turning our attention to the average shooting of companies and battalions. It is proposed to encourage a high figure of merit by giving battalion prizes, to be held as challenge prizes between the companies. The arrangement is that the figure of merit is to be made out on the range of the corps under the responsibility of its own officers. The companies are to produce their registers, and out of ten companies a certain number, to be fixed at the discretion of the field officer, are to be selected as the competing companies. But as the shooting of companies on their own ranges would not be a basis that would give public satisfaction with regard to the award of the prize, the prize is to be awarded at a public competition on the shooting of sections proportioned to the strength of the companies selected to compete. If 10 men represent a company of 60, a company of 90 would be represented by a section of 15. A subdivision of 30 by a section of 5.

4021. (*Chairman*.) How will the fund be raised?—It will be granted out of the county fund. The sum of 100l. has been voted for challenge bugles, to be held in each battalion by the company which shows the highest average of shooting. I attach the greatest importance to this plan, for I think the present system of merely promoting a few crack shots has no effect in raising the military efficiency of the corps. The badges sanctioned by the Government, the prizes of the National Association, and private matches, offer sufficient stimulus to the best marksmen. The majority of volunteers cannot afford the time or money required to attend rifle meetings at a distance from home. What is required, is to give them encouragement to persevere in regular class shooting on their own range. I have found the good effect of this in my own company.

4022. Do you find any difficulty in keeping up the companies at their proper strength?—They are all, I think, keeping up nearly the same strength, some have increased lately; there is a difficulty, no doubt, but I think that difficulty may be overcome by good local arrangements. Whatever can be done to give

Lieut.-Col. T. D. Acland.

4 July 1862.

Lieut.-Col.
T. D. Acland.
4 July 1862.

them a more definite object to work for, and when that object is attained, to give them credit for having done well, will keep up the spirit and reputation of the corps. Therefore I attach very great importance to the authorities encouraging those who are willing to make an effort to go through what is called "setting " up drill." I do not mean by that term extension motions, but beginning at the first page of the book and going to the end of company drill once a year. One of my neighbours, acting on my suggestion, took an average of 52 men a week out of 60 through a regular course of company drill before Easter, on the understanding that after that time they should not be required to attend drill, except for musketry, or for combined company drill, in the nature of field-days.

4023. I suppose that no man can compete for any of the prizes who has not gone through all these preliminary drills?—Such a rule was laid down as regards the setting up drill. With regard to the preliminary musketry drills, I confess that I do not think it necessary to enforce all the details of the Hythe system. I have heard that in one distinguished London corps the colonel has required all the men to go through the preliminary course annually, there being in that corps very intelligent university men who are quite as capable of giving a lecture on the theoretical principles of musketry as their instructors. I think this very unreasonable and impolitic. I have been at Hythe myself, and although I have much injured eyesight, I passed into the first class, and I have conducted a musketry class, with the assistance of some of my friends at Exeter. I have the very highest opinion of the good effects produced on the army by the Hythe school, but I think that to require our volunteers to listen to theoretical lectures with which they are familiar is a waste of time without an adequate object. Position drill is another question.

4024. (*Viscount Hardinge.*) You think it would be almost impossible to carry out the Hythe system in small rural corps?—They have a great dislike to judging distance drill, but I am endeavouring to overcome this dislike by giving a mark of distinction to first class men on condition of their being passed by the adjutant in judging distance. I think that if a man thoroughly understands what is meant by elevation and direction, and has a moderate theoretical knowledge of the principle of the trajectory, position drill and practice alone are required to make him a good shot.

4025. Why do they dislike the judging distance drill?—Because it takes up a good deal of time.

4026. (*Lord Overstone.*) You have stated that in your opinion, it is a matter of the greatest importance to keep down the charges upon the public purse, with reference to the volunteer movement?—I do think so.

4027. Do you think that the volunteer movement can be maintained in its present state of efficiency, without further pecuniary aid from the Government?—I am afraid that several corps are in great pecuniary difficulty. The disposition to subscribe privately is very nearly exhausted in many cases.

4028. Does your opinion as to the inexpediency of increasing the public charges, in connexion with the volunteer movement, go to this extent, that it would be inexpedient for this Commission to recommend any further charges being made on the Government account?—No.

4029. What charges do you think, with a due regard to your feeling, could be most properly recommended to the Government?—I should think that every corps should be allowed to state its own wants, and that the field officers of those corps should be held responsible for giving detailed opinions upon such applications, and that the greatest facilities should be given, consistently with official rules, for the corps to be aided in the way in which they most require it.

4030. Your opinion is that the requirements of the different corps would necessarily assume a different character, and that Government aid, under one rule, would not be applicable to the majority of cases?—Yes.

4031. And that it must be, to a certain extent, discretionary aid, to be exercised through the judgment of the commanding officer in each case?—I think there should be the exercise of the judgment of the office too, on the reports made to it; when I said field officers, I meant subject to the special report of the assistant inspector.

4032. You mean that a final judgment should be exercised by the War Office; but that they should receive the reports and opinions of the commanding officers of each corps?—Yes, with that of the assistant inspector, for I think really that the mode of dispensing the fund is more important than the amount of it.

4033. What do you exactly refer to?—I refer especially to what I have already said as to the drill instructors; the Government have already promised to pay for our drill instruction, and we do not get the help. I think if more were left to local discretion, a smaller amount than that proposed for the pay of permanent serjeant instructors would provide amply for the efficient drill of an administrative battalion. It has been well said, "We can make a pound go much " further than the Government can."

4034. (*Major-Gen. Eyre.*) You have spoken of having a yearly subscription of 5s.?—Yes.

4035. And that your corps is a good deal composed of little hill farmers?—Not my corps; my corps is composed rather of a higher class of farmers or their sons, and they pay their own expenses entirely.

4036. Surely the little hill farmers do not feel a contribution of 5s. so inconvenient as to make it difficult to contribute it?—I cannot answer for them, but I can say that the larger farmers in my neighbourhood are very unwilling to pay it; they say, " We clothe ourselves, and we give our time which " is very valuable, and we think that we ought not " to be called upon to subscribe."

4037. But in that case it is not from want of means?—No; they say that there is a certain portion of the public who do not volunteer, and that they should subscribe, or if they will not, then if the services of volunteers are wanted the Government ought to provide the necessary expenses.

4038. (*Lord Overstone.*) What is your opinion as to the expediency of Government intervening to assist in providing clothing for the volunteer force?—I very much wish that all volunteers should clothe themselves, but I believe that there are cases in which it is impracticable to retain the services of very good volunteers without public assistance for clothing. I may, however, state to the Commission the experience of a friend of mine, who is a very efficient officer, Mr. Poole, of Bridgewater. I asked him his opinion a few days ago, and he said that he had a strong opinion in favour of keeping up the self-clothing system; that all the men who had been clothed at the expense of others had gradually left his corps. The whole of his corps now clothe themselves, and he said that they had got on better in consequence.

4039. Do you think that that case could be taken as illustrating a general class of cases, or were there not peculiar circumstances which might have enabled that gentleman to accomplish his object, which would prevent that case being taken as a general rule?—I think it might be taken as a very common case in towns where the volunteer movement is sufficiently popular to enlist the sympathies of what are called the respectable classes of the community. There are cases in which, from indiscretion in management or other causes the respectable middle class are not willing to be volunteers. The cases in which the demand for clothing is most urgent are those in which the members of the corps are composed of working men earning wages; there are such cases in my battalion. I confess that I do not think it very desirable, as a general rule, that the corps should be very largely recruited from that class, but some of them, I am bound to say, are very good volunteers, and take a pride in clothing themselves. They are very practical men, thoroughly in earnest about what they undertake, but who cannot afford to contribute money. Every drill that they attend involves a loss to them of money out of their pockets, much greater in proportion than the loss to men who are engaged in business, making a profit on capital, and having time at their own disposal.

4040. Can you form any estimate as to what number of the volunteers in the county of Devon could be expected to continue permanently in the force, without any further Government aid as to clothing or otherwise?—I cannot answer that question without inquiry.

4041. (*Col. MacMurdo.*) You have stated that there is a difficulty in obtaining the services of militia serjeants as drill instructors; you are probably not aware that there are at the present time 163 militia serjeants employed in the instruction of volunteer corps, and that many others who have been so employed have discontinued that employment in consequence of the appointment of permanent instructors to the volunteer corps?—I am not.

4042. (*Sir A. Campbell.*) You have given your own experience of the difficulty you have found in your own county, where you find that you can not get them to come?—Yes; that is my opinion; and besides that I have reason to know that several of my friends have made provisional engagements with serjeants to come to them, and then, owing to various official restrictions and requirements, they have been disappointed. I do not speak now of militia serjeants only, but of men from the line.

4043. (*Chairman.*) Is there any other point that you wish to bring before the Commission?—Yes; I wish the Commission particularly to consider the position of the subdivisions. Supposing the present arrangement with regard to drill instructors to be continued, something should be done for them. I may have misunderstood the intentions of the office, but I certainly did understand that it was my duty to order one of the serjeant instructors attached to two of my companies to drill a neighbouring subdivision gratuitously, and I was prepared to give the necessary order, but the officer commanding the subdivision said to me, "I think both of the serjeants so " inefficient that I would rather have neither of them: " I would rather pay a militia serjeant per drill at " my own expense." I, therefore, did not raise the question as to my authority to order one of the serjeants to do duty with the subdivision. I have since been informed by another officer of a subdivision, not in my own battalion, that after he had obtained the consent of his colonel to make an arrangement with a drill instructor of a neighbouring company, that the arrangement with regard to the drill of his subdivision was not confirmed by the office. I think that the subdivisions should be specially considered, as it often falls upon two or three individuals to maintain them, and it is very hard that they should not have [that assistance which is offered freely to others. The small money payment which I have suggested would remove all difficulty. There is another matter of small detail, which is this, I think that upon inspections taking place, all rifles ought to be seen, not only those in the hands of the men on parade, but every rifle in the possession of the corps ought to be produced.

4044. (*Col. MacMurdo.*) By what means would you carry that out?—By ordering every rifle to be brought on to the ground to be inspected.

4045. But supposing they are not brought to be inspected?—Then, I presume, there would be a report made to you.

4046. You have 218 rifles in the possession of the individual members of your corps, how would you enable the assistant inspector, on making his inspection, to call them in?—I presume that that is a matter for the captain of each corps to attend to.

4047. Do you think that those rifles could be brought in for the inspection of the assistant inspector, every one of them?—I do not see why they should not be brought in.

4048. Suppose, for example, that the men did not attend on parade, there is no compulsory power. It is true, that you may punish a man by ordering his rifle to be kept in the armoury afterwards?—I think that if the captain knew that his credit was at stake if he did not have all the rifles produced on parade, that in most cases he would get it done. I do not wish to press my suggestion; I only intended to call attention to the fact that if only a fraction of the men are on parade, the inspector may not know what condition some of the rifles are in. The inspection of volunteers at the present time partakes very much of the character of a review or an exhibition, and the volunteer officers, of course, wish to set their corps in the best possible light, not only before the inspector but before the public, and there is great unwillingness to have ill-drilled men in the ranks. I think that all the rifles could be brought in in carts for inspection, if they could not be brought otherwise. I have boxes for all my rifles, and I could bring them all for inspection. It happened to me at the last inspection that one rifle escaped my notice, owing to my not being obliged to account for the whole number. This called my attention to the point.

4049. (*Sir A. Campbell.*) Would it meet your objection if staff armourers were appointed in Government pay to inspect periodically the rifles, and, if necessary, to repair the rifles of the different corps?—I have not considered that plan; I am very much for throwing the responsibility on the individual officers, and leaving them to make their own arrangements, provided that the result is satisfactory to the inspecting officer. On the subject of field officers I may mention one principle that was brought before me by a very intelligent yeomanry officer, who explained to me the reason why corps of yeomanry, and volunteers especially, require field officers, namely, that the captain of a volunteer corps is essentially a recruiting officer, and he cannot always afford to be unpopular; it is therefore a great thing to take unpopular measures out of his province by enabling him to say "That is not my wish, but it is the wish of my " field officer. I am not carrying out my own wishes, " but I am carrying out the orders which I have " received from a superior authority." I may also mention another subject. One very active member of our volunteer association begged me to express to this Commission his own belief, and in his opinion some other gentlemen seem to concur, as to the importance of camp instruction. I made considerable efforts last year to establish a camp, and I met with much discouragement, and am not disposed myself to renew the efforts at present. I do not think that many of the best volunteers can spare time for continuous service, being busy men; the busy men make the best volunteers, but they are just those men who cannot afford to be away from home for many days at one time. Many a man who is willing to do his duty and give his time or even his life for his country, if necessary, is not willing to run the risk of interrupting his business by illness, except in the direct course of duty.

4050. (*Col. MacMurdo.*) You have stated that the inspection of a corps partakes too much of the nature of a review?—I did not, I believe, say "too much;" I intended to say that it necessarily partakes of that character.

4051. Have you any suggestions to make as to the mode of proceeding on those occasions that you think would be more agreeable to the volunteers, as to testing their efficiency?—No.

4052. You are aware that it is the duty of the inspecting officer to examine the arms and accoutrements, the clothing, and general appearance of the men on parade very minutely, allowing the commanding officer of the corps, when present, to do whatever he pleases, but not requiring him to do things which he might not be able to do, in order to show the

Lieut.-Col. T. D. Acland.

4 July 1862.

Z

Lieut.-Col.
T. D. Acland.

4 July 1862.

efficiency of the men in military exercises?—I think that that is quite enough.

4053. He then visits the headquarters, examines the system of books, and also the arms and the armoury; he also examines the registers of the firing and muster rolls; are there any other duties that you would suggest he ought to attend to?—No, I am sure that in our case the duties are very judiciously done by Colonel Hume. The main point which I suggest is that the inspection should carry practical consequences to the funds of the corps.

4054. (*Major-Gen. Eyre.*) Do your volunteers like being mixed with the regular troops?—I do not think we have any opportunity, except in the neighbourhood of Plymouth. I have no doubt that they would feel it to be a great compliment, if they were encouraged to do so; under our present general I am sure that every encouragement would be given to them. There is one other point that I should be glad to allude to, which is the plan adopted by Lord Mount Edgcumbe, and which I think of very great importance. He requires every man to be examined in company drill, in the manual and platoon exercises, in light infantry, by the adjutant, and in musketry by the musketry instructor, and he gives them that card once a year (*handing in the same*); if I may venture to speak for him in his absence, I believe that he entertains very strongly the opinion, that a man should be judged to be effective by the results of his work, and not by the time he has spent upon it.

4055. (*Viscount Hardinge.*) I suppose you have no idea what proportion of the men in the regiment to which you refer have those cards?—I cannot state the proportion in the battalion. But I can state an important fact in reference to Lord Mount Edgcumbe's subdivision, consisting of 30 men, at Maker, near his own residence: 25 or 26 out of 30 men passed into the first class, which I look upon as a very great test of the general state of their efficiency. I am sure that if we are assisted in promoting a short annual course of setting up drill and in keeping up the average rate of firing in our corps, if we are supported in that direction, by certain results being the condition of receiving pecuniary aid, that the greatest benefit will result.

4056. (*Lord Overstone.*) When you say if you are supported in carrying it out, to what do you specifically refer?—That which I have already mentioned, that the aid of the Government should be conditional upon certain results being attained, and that the report of the adjutant and field officer confirmed by the assistant inspector should be required before gratuitous ammunition is served out, or pecuniary aid for drill instruction, travelling expenses, or any other military purpose be paid. I may, perhaps, be allowed in conclusion to refer to a letter addressed by me to the Secretary of State for War on the 11th April, and which I understood would be referred to this Commission, for a more precise statement of the regulations which I would propose for the grant of aid towards drill instruction, and of my reasons for objecting to the present regulations.

The witness withdrew.

Lieut.-Col.
Harman.

Lieut.-Colonel HARMAN examined.

4057. (*Chairman.*) I believe you are Assistant Inspector of Volunteers in the Northern Division?—Yes.

4058. How many corps have you under your inspection?—There are 107 corps.

4059. How many men do you muster altogether?—I believe 15,000 and 16,000 is the amount of the whole force in the north. I cannot tell you exactly the number because they fluctuate. I have not seen the returns of this present quarter.

4060. Do you consider that the condition of the corps under your inspection is satisfactory?—I think they may be considered so generally, excepting in point of finance.

4061. Have you heard any complaints from those corps that they are unable to meet their expenses?—I have heard such complaints very generally. I think that up to this time the majority of them have met their expenses, but now the uniforms are getting shabby, and in fact in many places they are nearly worn out; I know now of no instance in which any preparation has been made for renewing them. The greater part of the corps in the north are composed of artizans who have been clothed almost entirely from the funds of the corps.

4062. Do those artizans contribute to the funds of the corps by annual subscriptions?—They did at the commencement, but I think that has been discontinued; the men generally state that they consider that giving their time and attention is sufficient.

4063. Do you find that the corps muster well when you go to inspect them?—I find on the average that the corps in the towns muster about one-half of their enrolled strength; in the agricultural districts they muster better, generally about two-thirds.

4064. Are the corps in the agricultural districts principally administrative battalions?—They are.

4065. Do you hear any complaints of the difficulty of bringing the distant companies together on those days?—Very great complaints; in fact I think that the administrative system as it is at present is very defective. I do not think that it works well; certainly not in battalions under my supervision.

4066. In what respects do you think it does not work well?—I consider that the position of both the commanding officer and of the adjutant is most unsatisfactory, and that neither of them can carry out their duties in the manner they ought to do, or as it is desirable that they should do. The commanding officer has no real authority; he cannot call a parade. If he sees anything going on amiss he has no power of immediate interference, and the consequence is that I find the commanding officer in most of the administrative battalions in the north interferes in no way whatever. If the corps wish to meet together, he will go and take the command of them; but as it entails expense upon them, he is diffident in asking each of the corps to assemble.

4067. Do you find that they visit each of the corps separately?—I do not think they do.

4068. If they did I presume they would have very little authority?—None whatever; they cannot order them to parade.

4069. Are their arms generally in good condition?—Generally speaking they are, but the regulations of the War Office as to the arms are not strictly carried out. In very few instances are the arms all kept in store where it is directed they should be, unless by special authority from the commanding officer. Men living at a distance are allowed to keep them at home. When I complain of this, I am told by officers in command of corps, that they have no means of keeping the arms in store; they ought properly to provide stores, and persons to look after them, but they let the men take them home to their own residences, and say that they find them in better order in that manner, but I think that those in stores are always better kept.

4070. When they are kept in store I presume there is some one to clean them and look after them?—Yes.

4071. Are you enabled to report upon the arms which are in the hands of the individual members of the corps who do not attend?—I always before inspecting a corps give as much notice as I can, generally a month or more, of my intended visit, and then I think they generally work up for inspection, which perhaps does good, and they get the arms generally in, with few exceptions I generally see all the arms when I inspect a corps either in store or on parade.

4072. (*Sir A. Campbell.*) Do you find that the officers of volunteers on the average are qualified for their work?—They are, generally speaking, very deficient; the men know twice as much as their officers, and consequently they do not like to come to parade. I find that in many of the administrative battalions the commanding officers have no opportunity of learning their work; unless they attach themselves to some regiment, I do not see how they can become qualified.

4073. Are you speaking of commanding officers of corps?—I am speaking now more particularly of commanding officers of battalions. The commanding officers of corps in company drill generally know their work moderately well; and in some instances they know it very well indeed.

4074. (*Chairman.*) Are they provided with drill instructors?—In the majority of the corps they are.

4075. (*Sir A. Campbell.*) You have stated that the commanding officers of administrative battalions are not in the practice of visiting their various corps; do the adjutants do so?—Yes, the adjutants are in the habit of doing so, but the corps do not turn out well when the adjutants go to see them, and I think in many instances the corps dislike turning out for the adjutant; they do not like his visits. I think that in this case it is very important that some different arrangement should be made. I am sure that if an administrative battalion in my district was called out by the adjutant, you would see that the general attendance was ridiculously small.

4076. Do you think that that arises from any neglect on their part to give due notice of their visits?—No, I think that the adjutants feel that they are in a very difficult position with respect to the corps; in some places, where the adjutants are liked by the men, they turn out for them well, but in other instances I cannot tell why they do not turn out well.

4077. Do you think it would obviate those objections if the administrative battalions were put in the same position as regiments of yeomanry with regard to the relations existing between the commanding officers and the officers of the different companies?—I cannot answer that question. I do not sufficiently know the system pursued in the yeomanry.

4078. Can you suggest any mode by which an improvement might be effected?—I think that a very great improvement might be made by requiring a different system to be pursued in order to render a man an effective; I think that the present system works very badly in my district; I think that instead of a man being rendered an effective member by attending so many drills, (a course of 24 drills,) it would be much better he should attain a certain standard of efficiency, and I think in that way you would get a better class of men into the volunteer force who would be equally efficient. I have been thinking the matter over, and I should suggest that if any capitation grant be made, or if it is the intention of Government to give any additional money to the volunteer force, instead of it being given for every effective member, it should be given for every efficient member. I do not believe that the corps in the north will object to that system, and I should therefore propose that before a volunteer is allowed to participate in any capitation money he should have attained a certain standard of efficiency; on joining he should be drilled in musketry and platoon and manual instruction, and in the general course of company drill, and then he should pass an examination before the commanding officer and the adjutant, and after having done that he should be reckoned as an efficient and allowed accordingly any advantages that an effective member may be entitled to. Then I should propose that instead of a man attending a certain number of drills he should have all the advantages of constant drill whenever he chose to attend, but that on two occasions in the year he should be required to be present, unless some very good reason were given, and that on those occasions the commanding officer and adjutant should be present, and then if a man passed muster and showed that he possessed a certain knowledge of his work he should be allowed to continue as an efficient.

4079. (*Viscount Hardinge.*) Do you mean that he should be present in battalion or in his company?—In battalion would be more desirable if it could be done without expense, but with his company. At the present time the adjutant very often does not see many of the men; many never attend drill except on some special occasions, or a review; and moreover, parades that now are called drills, really are not drills. I have had occasion to look into the attendance rolls of some of the corps in the north, and I find that the church parade is reckoned as a drill, or somebody invites the corps out to some entertainment, and that is reckoned as a drill; the men march out to the entertainment, and, perhaps, fire their five rounds of ammunition and march home again, but they have no drill; and I think that it would be much better to have a standard of efficiency rather than to require that the men should attend so many parades in a year as at present.

4080. Then you would be practically giving the capitation grant to every man who attended twice a year?—No, I would give it to every man who was passed as an efficient; he should be seen twice a year by the commanding officer and the adjutant; the adjutant should keep a roll of every man in the corps, and at the end of those parades he should notify against the name of every man whether he was an efficient member or not; if not, he should be cautioned that he must work up, and then if a second time it happened that he was not efficient, he should not be entitled to the benefit of the capitation money.

4081. (*Sir A. Campbell.*) You would depend entirely upon the adjutant, and throw upon him the responsibility of returning a man as efficient or non-efficient?—I would leave that with the commanding officer of an administrative battalion. I think that he might visit his battalion twice a year, and then when the assistant inspector came round I think that every member ought to be obliged to attend at the annual inspection, unless he could give some good excuse for not doing so.

4082. (*Viscount Hardinge.*) In a question affecting money, do you not think that that would be liable to abuse, and that the adjutant might pass a man who was really not efficient?—No; I think again that that the inspector should have to see these corps once in a year, and if he had reason to think that the standard of efficiency was too low, he should report that to this department, in order that it might be seen whether the adjutant had carried on his duties properly or not.

4083. And if the standard was too low the Government money should be withheld?—Yes.

4084. (*Col. MacMurdo.*) This has no reference, I suppose, to the class of men who are termed effective by the Act of Parliament, do you mean that all efficients are to be legally considered effectives?—Efficients in my view should be legally considered effectives.

4085. And be exempt from the ballot?—Yes; at the present time in most of the corps in the north there are certain men who have been very regular in their attendance at drill, and who are well drilled, men who like the thing; but then there are about one fourth of the members of the corps; who at the annual inspection, or upon any occasion when the corps has been invited to go to any gentleman's park, come in and destroy the general appearance of the corps to the annoyance of the men who have been working hard, and who perhaps leave the corps in consequence in disgust; under the present system there is no difference made between a man who learns his work well, and a dull man to whom 40 drills are of no use.

4086. (*Viscount Hardinge.*) But would it not be a very invidious thing for the captain of a company to tell a man to fall out, because he was unfit?—Yes; when I go to inspect a corps I usually find that

172 MINUTES OF EVIDENCE TAKEN BEFORE THE COMMISSIONERS APPOINTED

Lieut.-Col. Harman.
4 July 1862.

the commanding officer says, "You must remember that there are now many men in the ranks who have not been in the ranks since you were here last year."

4087. (*Major-Gen. Eyre.*) Do you think it would be a good plan to define in detail what a volunteer ought to know in order to be considered an effective?—Certainly; I do not think there ought to be too high a standard required; but that a man should have a general knowledge of platoon exercise, and preliminary musketry instruction and company drill. The adjutants at the present moment are in a most difficult position; they go to corps to impart instruction, instead of which, perhaps, if there is a pretty good muster, whoever is in command of the corps very seldom gives it up to the adjutant, and several adjutants have told me that they have not drilled their corps half-a-dozen times. The senior captain, if the field officer is away, is only too delighted to step out and say, "I shall command the parade," and in consequence of that the men are badly commanded, and they learn nothing, but they lose what they have learned, and they are annoyed, and the adjutant is annoyed, and every one is annoyed but the captain. I think myself that the position of the adjutants ought to be bettered with respect to the volunteers.

4088. (*Col. MacMurdo.*) But does not the same thing happen in other services sometimes, and is it not an inconvenience which every service is liable to?—Yes, but I would propose that the adjutants should have another title affixed to them besides that of adjutant, in the event on their having to report on the efficiency of the men. I think that an adjutant should be called an adjutant, and, say, "Deputy assistant inspector," or an "Assistant inspector," for a certain district, and that he should have authority to inspect the arms and report upon them quarterly. I think that he ought to inspect the arms quarterly, and report upon the general state of the corps quarterly.

4089. How do you think that authority would do in his relations with his commanding officer?—It is merely with reference to what the adjutants should do as to the arms; I think that the adjutant should be held responsible for seeing every arm that has been issued to a corps once a quarter, and at the present time I am convinced that in many corps the arms are not seen perhaps for six or eight months at a time; the adjutant says that it is not his duty, and he does not interfere with the arms.

4090. The arms being the property of the corps vested in the commanding officers?—Yes.

4091. (*Lord Overstone.*) I understand it to be your opinion that drills are merely a means to an end, the end being the efficiency of the soldier?—Yes.

4092. You think that some better standard of efficiency in the soldier might be established than the present one of attendance at a certain number of drills?—Yes, I do.

4093. Do you think that the efficiency might be examined into, and pronounced upon by some competent officers in the same way that the efficiency in scholarship is examined into, and pronounced upon at the universities?—I think it might be so done; I think that there should be more than one officer.

4094. A competent board?—Yes; I should leave it with the commanding officer, and the adjutant or the inspector of the district.

4095. I think you have stated that in your opinion the whole of the volunteer force which comes under your inspection is in a satisfactory condition, saving the question of pecuniary pressure?—There are some instances in which unanimity does not prevail in the corps, and where the commanding officers are unpopular, which, of course, tends to work badly; beyond that I think that, generally speaking, the volunteer force in the north may be considered in a satisfactory condition.

4096. Are they in a satisfactory condition with regard to their discipline, the condition of their arms and accoutrements, and their capacity to make an efficient use of them?—I think that, taking them generally, I may say yes. Some of their accoutrements are not of a serviceable description; they would not do for service; a great many of the corps have copied the accoutrements worn by the Victoria rifles, whose pouch slings in the centre of the back, so that no knapsack could be worn with it. The arms generally are serviceable certainly, and the discipline of the volunteers I think I may consider good. But there is no real discipline in the volunteer movement, and no discipline can be enforced; for example, if a man is annoyed, and you say something to him which he does not like; he simply gives 14 days' notice and resigns.

4097. As a practical test of their efficiency, upon the supposition that the Government found it necessary to call out all the volunteers for active service, do you think that the volunteers who have come under your inspection would be found in a state competent to render valuable assistance as auxiliary to the regular army?—Most decidedly. I am confident upon that point.

4098. Can you go further, and state whether you think they would be competent to act as a separate and independent body with safety and efficiency?—I think that they would not, on account of not being properly officered; that refers to their acting independently.

4099. You think that that deficiency which you have already alluded to, in the knowledge of the officers, would not be so serious as to impair the efficiency of the volunteer force, if acting in co-operation with the regular army, and as a supplement to it; but that it would be a serious consideration, if they were called upon to act independently?—I think that it would be a serious consideration under any circumstances; but I think that if they had the advantage of being with the regular forces, it would not be felt to the same extent.

4100. Can you suggest any practical mode, by which the difficulty which you have alluded to as to the condition of the officers, could he remedied?—It is a most difficult matter. I think it would be desirable that all officers of volunteer corps should have to show a certain standard of efficiency at a general annual inspection.

4101. You think that something like the same test of efficiency that we have already alluded to as to be applied to the volunteers generally should be specially applied to the officers?—I think so, most decidedly.

4102. (*Viscount Hardinge.*) How would you carry it out? Sometimes an inspector has not much time to inspect?—It would be impossible in my opinion to carry it out if we had to perform the same duties that we have to perform at the present time. I may say that my district is so large; I have so many corps to visit that I find it is perfectly impossible to carry out my duties in the way I think they ought to be; for example, during the last month I never passed one day at my own headquarters, which are at York. I am constantly travelling, and I have an immense deal of correspondence to carry on, I am allowed no clerk, and my duties are greater than I consider I can properly carry out. I think, therefore, that if the officers had to undergo an examination before the inspector, that he would have to devote more time to it than he has now at his command.

4103. You think that it would necessitate the appointment of a larger number of officers?—I think that if the adjutants were named deputy assistant inspectors they might inspect the men in single companies, excepting perhaps in particular instances; and if a company was not reported satisfactorily of, I think the district inspector might be directed to visit that company; but at the present time I go all over the north of England, seeing single companies averaging about 40 rank and file on parade, and I think that with regard to the inspector, it would be sufficient if he could see those companies when they meet for purposes of battalion drill.

4104. (*Col. MacMurdo.*) How do you think it would do to give the adjutants of administrative battalions the authority of deputy assistant inspectors under the orders of the field officer commanding the battalions?—I think it would work in some instances, but unfortunately I do not consider that all commanding officers commanding administrative battalions have a sufficient knowledge of what is required of them, or that they pay sufficient attention to become qualified.

4105. You are aware that at the present time the duty of the adjutant of an administrative battalion is to visit the component parts of that battalion?—Yes.

4106. He visits each company very much in the character of an inspector, although not with the authority of an inspector?—He has no authority whatever.

4107. Suppose that authority were given to him as inspector in his battalion, under the authority of the field officer commanding the battalion, how do you think that would work?—I think it would be a very great improvement on the present system.

4108. (*Viscount Hardinge.*) Are the adjutants in your opinion as efficient as they ought to be?—They all pass an examination before they are appointed.

4109. (*Sir A. Campbell.*) Do you think that the adjutants are all equally efficient, or that they vary?—They are certainly not all equally efficient.

4110. (*Lord Overstone.*) Upon the supposition that the volunteer force was called out to act as auxiliary to the regular army, do you think that in any case it would be most important that they should be clothed similarly to the regular troops?—I think it is very desirable that they should be all clothed alike, or nearly so.

4111. You think it important that they should be clothed like the regular troops, so that when called out in front of an enemy there should be as little means as possible of distinguishing one force from the other?—I think that the present equipment is too varied.

4112. (*Sir G. A. Wetherall.*) Do you think the volunteers would be efficient auxiliaries to the army in the field?—As they are at present I should say no in consequence of their equipment. I consider that the men generally have attained to efficiency in drill very near to the present disembodied militia, and that as riflemen they would form a very efficient body indeed.

4113. (*Lord Overstone.*) I am desirous of ascertaining your opinion upon this point, whether upon the supposition that the Government found it necessary suddenly to call out the whole of the volunteer force for the protection of the kingdom, you think that the volunteers who come under your inspection would at once turn out capable of rendering valuable assistance as a supplement to the regular army?—They could not do so at once, on account of their equipment not being complete; they have no knapsacks or means of taking the field.

4114. Do you think that knapsacks for the short service which the volunteers would probably have to render are essential?—Most decidedly.

4115. (*Lieut.-Col. Barttelot.*) Would not the havresack answer every purpose?—They want some description of knapsack; a man must have a change of clothing.

4116. (*Lord Overstone.*) Do you think that the volunteers who have come under your inspection are at this moment in such a state that if suddenly called upon to act as a supplement to the regular army in protecting the integrity of the country, they would be efficient for that purpose?—No.

4117. Will you have the goodness to state as distinctly as you can in what respect they would be deficient, and by what means you think their deficiencies could be remedied?—They would be deficient in their general equipment, and in some instances their accoutrements are not calculated for service; I refer to the corps that have their pouches made to fit midway between the shoulder and the waist, that sling across the back; they are elastic pouches and I consider that they are unfitted for general service; they have no great coats, and in fact no means of carrying any change of clothing, and as yet they have not been taught the duties of a camp. The volunteers in the north have never been encamped, and they have no means of looking after their cooking, &c. or of conveying their luggage and stores.

4118. Will you be good enough to enumerate the deficiencies that you think would disqualify them for effectual service at home?—I think they may be embraced in this, that the volunteer wants everything in the shape of the general equipment of the soldier except his arms and accoutrements, which are the only things he has now to enable him to take the field.

4119. (*Chairman.*) And those accoutrements are not in all instances quite what they ought to be?—No.

4120. (*Lord Overstone.*) Is it your opinion that the volunteer force, if immediately called out, would be very inefficient for the purpose of offering material resistance to the enemy?—Yes; unless they could be immediately provided with knapsacks and necessaries for taking the field.

4121. You think that as regards discipline and their capacity to use their arms they are in a satisfactory state?—I think so generally, except as I have already said as to the officers.

4122. (*Viscount Hardinge.*) With regard to greatcoats and knapsacks, supposing that in the case of an emergency the Government were to issue those articles to each volunteer, would your objections as to their efficiency in those respects be removed?—Yes.

4123. They would then only labour under this difficulty, that they had not been taught to march in heavy marching order?—There would be that and also this, that they have no staff at the present moment qualified to look after those matters; no qualified quartermaster who would be indispensable in case of taking the field.

4124. (*Major-Gen. Eyre.*) I suppose you consider their present equipment sufficient for peace time?—Yes I do.

4125. (*Lord Overstone.*) Your opinion with regard to the general condition of the volunteer force does not include the artillery volunteers, or do they come under your observation?—No, they do not generally.

4126. (*Col. MacMurdo.*) You cannot speak to the scientific part of their arms, but you can speak of the artillery volunteers in your division with reference to their establishment, their general appearance on parade, their arms and equipments as they stand on parade?—Yes. I have not had any opportunities of seeing their arms on the coast, for I have not visited many places where there are artillery volunteers.

4127. (*Major Harcourt.*) When you refer to their arms do you mean the great guns or the carbines?—I speak now of the great guns.

4128. (*Lieut.-Col. Barttelot.*) You have said a great deal about the inefficiency of the officers, do you think that the officers have improved since the formation of the volunteer force, or do you think that many of them joined for the purpose of obtaining a certain rank and position, and having done that they have taken no further trouble in the matter?—I consider that they have greatly improved, but they have very great difficulty in learning their duties.

4129. (*Sir A. Campbell.*) Does your observation as to the officers of administrative battalions apply equally to consolidated battalions?—Not so generally; my observations were meant to apply more to administrative corps.

4130. But there are, I believe, consolidated battalions in your district?—Yes, 16.

4131. Are they in a higher state of efficiency?—I think the officers are, certainly.

4132. (*Major-Gen. Eyre.*) If it were made a condition, before any officer was gazetted, that he should be attached to a regiment of the line for a month or six weeks, do you think that would tend much to prevent them coming forward?—Yes; I think it

Lieut.-Col. *Harman.*

4 July 1862.

Lieut.-Col. Harman.
4 July 1862.

would. I do not think that it could be carried out. In some parts of the north of England large landed proprietors are generally the persons who have taken up the volunteer movement very warmly; they are most valuable men at the head of the corps on account of their position, but at the same time they can neither find time, nor, perhaps, have they the inclination to qualify themselves for their appointments, but they are men who would be only too happy at any moment to relinquish their commands if any more efficient men could be found.

4133. Do you think it could be carried out in the junior ranks?—I do not think it could be carried out, for I do not think they could find the time.

4134. (*Viscount Hardinge*.) You are aware that there have been instances of volunteer officers being attached to regiments in the line, particularly in large towns where troops are in garrison?—Yes, in many instances, but in the district to which I am attached it happens that there are no regular troops, except two companies, which are at Newcastle. I mean infantry. With regard to the drill serjeants, I may say that I think it would be desirable that they should be placed more immediately under the control of the adjutant; at the present time those men have little or nothing to do, and I think that in some of the administrative corps they would do equally well, or better, with fewer non-commissioned officers, if the drill serjeants could be placed under the adjutants and sent about to the different corps, where they might be most required.

4135. (*Lieut.-Col. Bartletot*.) Do you think that the travelling allowance for the adjutant is sufficient?—No, in some instances it certainly is not, and it happens that the adjutant, who does the most work, is the worst paid man. In some instances the adjutants have a large circuit to visit; there is one in Northumberland where the distance is 240 miles round his district, and yet there is no difference made between the pay of that adjutant and the pay of a man who has only a distance of 7 or 8 miles to go.

4136. (*Col. MacMurdo*.) Referring to your suggestion about the serjeant instructors, do you propose that they should be kept at the headquarters of an administrative battalion, in the way of a depôt or a school of instruction, and that the men who were sent out to the corps requiring instruction should be under the orders of the commanding officer of the battalion?—I think it would be better. I think at the present time that the serjeant instructors have not sufficient to do to keep them employed. May I refer to the duties which fall upon inspectors. Last year I was travelling from the 21st of February until the 4th November, and during all that time I was constantly on the move. I inspected 88 distinct corps, I had to organize three reviews, and I had to attend at different places to make certain investigations. To do all this my expenses were very great indeed, and I consider that the pay of an assistant inspector is quite inadequate to meet these expenses. Although I am a substantive field officer I am not placed on the same footing as other officers in the army who are holding the rank of field officers. I am not allowed the same money for lodging as surgeons are who rank as field officers or paymasters, or other field officers on the staff. I have to keep two horses, for I have to appear mounted on the parades, and I frequently take a horse with me sometimes for a week, travelling from place to place; to meet that expense I am allowed a bare fare for travelling, and 1*s.* a day to cover all the expenses of a servant; and the consequence is that I am obliged when I go away to put one horse out at livery, and if I take my servant,—I have no servant nor clerk, nor anyone to forward my letters, or anything else, and I think that at the least we should be allowed the same advantages that other field officers have who are on the staff, namely, two servants, and an additional allowance for lodging money.

4137. (*Major-Gen. Eyre*.) You do not speak with reference to reckoning your time towards promotion?

—I am under the impression that that is allowed to reckon.

4138. But at the present time you are speaking only of the expenses?—Yes.

4139. (*Col. MacMurdo*.) You are allowed 6*s.* a week for an office?—I am now allowed that sum.

4140. And there is a certain allowance made for a clerk when you are making arrangements for great reviews?—Yes, I am allowed 2*l.* a quarter for a clerk.

4141. And 6*s.* a week for an office?—Yes.

4142. Do you find that that is not sufficient?—I find that it is totally inadequate; and if I employed a clerk temporarily for a few days it would take me more time to teach that man his duty than to do it myself.

4143. Do you think you would have employment for a permanent clerk?—Yes, for a permanent clerk during the summer months.

4144. What would his employment be?—His employment would be to open any official letters during my absence, and to make copies of letters, which I cannot now have done; to forward correspondence to me during my absence; and to assist me in making out my reports, &c.

4145. (*Major-Gen. Eyre*.) Are you satisfied with your present powers?—I consider that I have no real power in connexion with the volunteers: but I have found no difficulty in carrying out my duties in consequence of not having more power; hitherto I have always met with the greatest courtesy, and anything that I have suggested has generally been followed or been taken notice of.

4146. You say, as an inspecting officer, that you have no power?—I have so far no power that I cannot command a parade.

4147. When you go to inspect what do you do?—I always write some time beforehand to ascertain from the commanding officer about what time will suit his convenience for the inspection; and so much is this the case that many of my engagements to inspect volunteer corps are already made for next month, and the month after that, which were made as long as two months ago.

4148. When you are present at an inspection, and you see things that you consider are wrong, or you perceive deficiencies in the officers, have you no power to point those matters out, and to find fault?—I point out to the officers any deficiencies that I observe.

4149. I infer, from what you have stated, that you are merely to look on, and not to say a word?—When I inspect a corps, I remark upon anything that strikes me as objectionable. I always notice anything I see wrong. Referring to the deficiency of the officers, I do not wish it to be inferred that the officers of volunteers in the northern district are more deficient than in other parts of England. I think that they are not so efficient as the men.

4150. Can you not say, I perceive so and so, and all that is very wrong, and I request that that may be rectified by the next inspection. Would not that be received as an order; and have you not the power of ordering that such things should be rectified, and do not the same rules govern every administrative battalion?—The same rules do, and the rules for my guidance are in the red book.

4151. (*Lord Overstone*.) Your power, I conceive, consists in inspecting, commenting, suggesting, and reporting?—Exactly.

4152. But you have not the power of ordering?—Exactly so.

4153. (*Chairman*.) Are your remarks generally attended to?—I think they are generally. I hope so; but I only see the corps once a year.

4154. (*Sir A. Campbell*.) At all events, do you find that they receive your remarks in good part?—Always.

4155. (*Viscount Hardinge*.) Do you find, generally speaking, that a uniform system of drill is carried out; for example, take the administrative battalions?

—Yes; at the present time the whole of the volunteer corps in the north are drilled according to the field exercises which are laid down for the army, they adopt those as their guide.

4156. I presume you consider that the field officers and the adjutants are responsible for that uniform system being carried out as far as their powers go?—Yes.

4157. (*Col. MacMurdo.*) Referring to your statement that you have no power; suppose you saw a corps practising at a range that you considered unsafe, should you have no power to stop their firing?—An instance of that kind occurred not long ago in which a farmer in the north wrote to me complaining that the volunteers were in the habit of practising at a place that endangered his safety and that of his cattle, and he appealed to me for a remedy. I informed him that such and such a place was the authorized range, and that if the volunteers practised in other places he must appeal to the civil power, but that I had no power to interfere.

4158. If you saw a volunteer corps in military formation skirmishing over a field with ball practice, would you not order them back to their quarters?—Yes, decidedly; if I saw the Government arms being misapplied, I should consider that I had authority in that respect.

4159. If you saw any gross irregularity take place on parade when the men were under arms, you would stop it, would you not?—Certainly.

4160. (*Major-Gen. Eyre.*) I understand from you that you have no defined powers?—No.

4161. (*Sir A. Campbell.*) Have you found any difficulty occur from the want of those defined powers?—I never have in my district.

Lieut.-Col. Harman.
4 July 1862.

The witness withdrew.

Captain PHILLIP STAPLETON HUMBERSTON, M.P., examined.

4162. (*Chairman.*) What corps do you command?—The 6th Cheshire. I am captain commandant.

4163. We understand that you have some suggestions to offer to the Commission?—I wish to mention what I have thought we required to keep the force on a proper footing at Chester. Chester is a place of about 30,000 inhabitants, which I think may be taken as a fair specimen of many of the country towns. I propose to show what we have done, and what I think is necessary to keep the corps together. We raised three companies of rifle volunteers in Chester, and one company of artillery; they were partly equipped by subscriptions, amounting to about 1,200*l.*, contributed voluntarily by the inhabitants. Of that sum about 150*l.* was expended in fitting up a drill-room and store for arms, about 100*l.* upon a range and targets. Then there were the drill instructors and various other expenses, and of the remainder about 2*s.* 3*d.* was applied to the clothing of the rifle volunteers, and about 1*s.* 3*d.*, or not quite so much, to the artillery company. We have been in existence about three years. We have paid our current expenses partially from the subscriptions in the corps, the subscription being 10*s.* 6*d.*, from each officer and man, and partly from contributions from the general subscription of 1,200*l.*, which was managed by a committee independent of the corps. The subscriptions in the corps I find to be very objectionable; they have the effect of keeping the men away from drill. About one-third of the rifle corps are mechanics and labourers, who cannot fairly be asked for a money subscription, the others are chiefly men who equip themselves. A certain portion of the men have paid their subscriptions regularly, another portion of them have got regularly into arrear; asking for subscriptions was a great hindrance to the attendance at drill. I used to represent to the corps that the subscriptions were in arrear, and must be paid; but I found that they were not paid; and then the only alternative was to proceed against the men before the magistrates, which I did not choose to do. This last year we came to the conclusion that we must have some other means of raising funds, and I said that during the year 1862 I should require no subscriptions to be paid, and I found immediately that the attendance at drill improved. As a substitute for the subscription, we raised funds by an amateur dramatic performance, and by a volunteer ball, but I consider it derogatory and objectionable that a great national movement should be dependent for funds upon such sources. Then, with regard to what we require for our future purposes; our total number is 243 rifle volunteers, who are, or should be effectives. I am not quite certain what our return was last year, but there were from about 50 to 60 who were non-effective, that is, who had not qualified by attending the requisite number of drills. My impression is, if an allowance could be made of 1*l.* per effective man would pay our current expenses, (exclusive of the armourer,) that is, the rent of range, the rent of drill shed, markers, targets, repairs of arms, gas, coal, water, taxes, repairs, and incidentals. About 170*l.* a year would pay all those expenses very readily, and if an allowance of 2*l.* a year was made, we might keep up our number, and clothe the same number of men that we now have, who are clothed by means of the subscriptions. At present we do not receive any men who do not equip themselves, but we have kept up our numbers; and if an allowance was made, having reference to the effective men only, it would be a great stimulus to attendance at drill; the men would feel that they were earning their money, and that although they paid no subscriptions out of their own pockets they were in fact contributing to the welfare of the corps, by earning the money allowed to them as effectives. With regard to clothing I think it would have a beneficial effect in this way, I do not think that the volunteers would like receiving clothing direct from the Government, and that they would object to it; I think it would be considered that they were not wearing their own clothes, but if an allowance was made for the effective men they would in fact have earned their money, and to a certain extent they would consider that they had paid for their clothing.

4164. What do you call an effective man?—A man who has attended a certain number of drills and is returned as an effective in the ordinary returns.

4165. You mean in the parliamentary sense of that term?—In the War Office sense, because a man is required to attend a certain number of drills, and unless he does so attend he is not returned as an effective man to the Inspecting officer when he inspects the corps or to the Government.

4166. He is not necessarily efficient?—No, but a man who attends eight drills every four months, generally attends a good many more, as a rule. I should say that in my corps, and I merely speak of that, they are efficient, because all the effective men are reported to be efficient by the inspecting officer. Of course some are not so good as others, still they were reported to be efficient, and I believe they were all of them quite efficient.

4167. Have you any other suggestion to offer to the Commission?—I cannot suggest the equivalent, but I think it would be desirable to give to the volunteers something like a *quid pro quo.* They give their services and their time, but they virtually receive nothing for it beyond the feeling of satisfaction that they have discharged their duty. At the same time, there is another feeling which exists, which is, that many men in the same position do not join the volunteers, and do not equip their men, and allow them to join, and that leads to a feeling of dissatisfaction, amongst those who do. They say, "I give " my men's time, or my own. I equip myself and my " men, but Mr. Somebody, who lives near me, and

Capt. P. S. Humberston, M.P.

Z 4

Capt. P. S. Humberston, M.P.

4 July 1862.

" is equally well able, does not do either." Therefore I think that if anything like an equivalent could be given it would tend very much to strengthen the volunteer movement. If it were determined by Government to ballot for the militia, I think you would then at once have an equivalent in an exemption; but as to whether the Government, should or should not enforce the ballot, I give no opinion. I think also that facilities should be given for shooting by allowing ammunition, and providing rifle ranges; the shooting is a great inducement to men to enrol themselves in a corps where the ranges are within reach, and if facilities for obtaining ranges were given it would do good, for there is great difficulty in obtaining them; we have a short range of 200 yards about four miles from Chester; there happens to be a railway near, and we can get to it without much difficulty, but it takes time and costs money; we have also another range of about 600 yards, which we have obtained very much by personal favour, and for which we pay a rent of 25l. a year, that is two miles and three-quarters from Chester, and it takes up a good deal of time to go there and return, but we cannot get another, for the roads interfere nearer to Chester; a public road interferes at a place where we might have an ample range, but we cannot stop the road; I think that it might be protected by placing men upon the road.

4168. (*Col. MacMurdo.*) Is that a point which you wish to press upon the Commission, that power should be given to the volunteers to stop a road?—I think that some power should be given to stop roads which are not much used whilst the firing is going on; in this case the road is very little used, it is a township road, and I think that if a man was placed upon the road, there would be no difficulty or danger in stopping it. There is another thing that I should mention; it is very desirable to give facilities for officers to become acquainted with their drill by either being attached to some regular corps, or being allowed to drill with them; there is a depôt at Preston, I believe, and other places, and if officers had the power of going there without much difficulty, or of drilling with the regular troops if quartered near, I think they would avail themselves of it; and the men as well as the officers would have an opportunity of becoming better acquainted with their duties.

4169. (*Chairman.*) Would you insist upon it before an officer received his commission, that he should have been attached to some regular regiment?—I think that that would create great difficulty in obtaining officers.

4170. (*Major-Gen. Eyre.*) You have spoken of the volunteers receiving a *quid pro quo*, would they in that case be volunteers?—I think so; they are exempt now from the militia, and you would then be giving them an effectual exemption; now it is nominal only, as every one is exempt; there is no ballot; but I think you would be giving them a fair *quid pro quo*, and they would still be volunteers. I think it would be gratifying to the volunteers if some privilege could be conferred upon them.

4171. (*Chairman.*) Have you any other recommendation to make?—Yes; as to the adjutants. It is very desirable to have a man of experience as an adjutant—I mean a man of some standing in the army. I think the adjutants should have the same pay and allowances as adjutants of militia, the men would look up to them. Senior captains who had seen service, or a major, or lieutenant-colonel, might, I think, be very glad to take such an appointment, as it would keep them at home.

4172. (*Col. MacMurdo.*) One of your adjutants in Cheshire is an officer who commanded the 25th Borderers?—Yes, he is adjutant of the battalion to which I belong, and a very valuable officer he is.

The witness withdrew.

Lieut.-Col. E. Maberly.

Lieut.-Colonel EVAN MABERLY examined.

4173. (*Chairman.*) You are an officer in the Royal Artillery?—Yes.

4174. Have you inspected a great many of the artillery volunteer corps on the south coast?—Yes, during the last year.

4175. Will you be good enough to state in what condition you found them?—In every variety of condition; it would be scarcely possible to describe the whole of the artillery volunteer service in Devon and Cornwall in one word, except by saying that their condition is very creditable to the individuals composing the corps. As far as regards their efficiency as artillery they are in every stage of efficiency.

4176. Upon the whole were they in a satisfactory condition?—They are very satisfactory corps indeed; but there are cases of doubtful use of public money.

4177. The public money which they receive now, I suppose, is in the shape of an allowance of ammunition?—In plant, in ordnance, carriages, and batteries, ammunition, instruction, and arms.

4178. When you find corps that, in your opinion, are wasting the public money you report that, I presume, to the authorities?—I should hardly use so strong a term as that in a public report; but speaking truthfully before a Commission like this I have no retreat.

4179. (*Sir A. Campbell.*) You would report such a corps as inefficient?—I should report their drills in a backward state, and it is for those who receive the report to judge of the meaning of it; each corps has been reported upon separately.

4180. (*Col. MacMurdo.*) Did you report any of the corps that you inspected last year as inefficient?—I have not any copies of my reports with me; but there must have been reports tending that way. Some corps, I think, offered no drill of a certain kind, and in that respect, therefore, they must be inefficient.

4181. Were the other corps that you inspected efficient?—As efficient as they could possibly be; they had made as good use of the means entrusted to them by the Government as it was possible they could have done.

4182. (*Viscount Hardinge.*) Have all the corps in your district facilities for gun-drill and practice?—I think they all have now; some scarcely had at the time of my inspection, and, so far, they necessarily must have been inefficient.

4183. What proportion of the corps in your district have got ranges and facilities for gun-practice with shot and shell?—I believe all now have facilities that are on the sea-board. I have not inspected them this year, another officer has been appointed to perform that duty.

4184. Have the companies which are inland no facilities for practice?—They go down to the sea-shore and practice there, but they are, of course, at a disadvantage.

4185. What distance have many of those corps to travel in order to do so?—From Exeter they would travel to Exmouth; the corps on the upper plateau of Cornwall would come down to Marazion or to Penzance.

4186. Which is the longest distance that a corps would have to travel to get to the nearest range?—12 or 15 miles.

4187. Can they get to those batteries by railways principally?—From Exeter to Exmouth they would go by railway, and from the Lands' End and Saint Buryan, and thereabouts, to Marazion, they would not.

4188. What facilities have the inland corps for gun practice; have they guns mounted on their parades?—Yes; scattered about. They have guns at different places, but they collect the men there with extreme difficulty.

4189. Were the platforms erected by themselves?

—They may have been erected by themselves; the Government have made them an allowance for them. I believe that every other corps now, except Exeter and Saint Buryan, has a range; they fire at rocks at sea, or targets.

4190. Every company has a certain number of guns mounted at headquarters?—I think they have.

4191. (*Col. MacMurdo.*) Some of the batteries have 18-pounder iron guns, mounted on field carriages, have they not?—Yes.

4192. And they horse them occasionally, do they not?—They do.

4193. Do you think that those batteries, so equipped, are likely to be more efficient than the batteries which are supplied only with garrison guns?—Certainly; if you mean by efficient, useful to the country.

4194. On account of their being able to move the guns?—Yes; a battery having two garrison guns is nailed to the spot; but a battery having moveable ordnance is available for service elsewhere.

4195. (*Sir A. Campbell.*) To what do you attribute the difference in the efficiency of the various corps?—The great difficulties which the members have to contend with; the mere fact of distance is one.

4196. Can you offer any suggestions to the Commission by which the worst corps might be brought to a higher state of efficiency?—Not categorically, in answer to a question; on the spot one might recommend something; it is perhaps a matter of temper in the people that command them, and it is a want of zeal, perhaps, in those who are commanded; it is a matter of distance; the difficulties have been very great; it is a matter of the nature of their employment; when they happen to be sea-going people, they are liable to be away, and when they are fishermen they labour under very great difficulties in some stations. Perhaps there has been too much zeal at starting, and they have established a corps where they need not have been established, and their zeal has gone beyond their means of keeping them up.

4197. In those cases I presume you would recommend that the corps should be allowed to drop?—It requires more knowledge of the circumstances than I have to justify me in making such a recommendation. When inspecting a corps you can only speak of it as you find it, that it is inefficient; and you say that in the mildest words that you can, for great allowances are to be made; perhaps the greatest allowances for the most inefficient corps. The best security for progress and efficiency appears to me to be the appointment of active and good officers as adjutants of brigades. It would be better to lend an officer from the regular service than to let an artillery brigade of volunteers work on without one. Some amount of military knowledge is almost essential to direct the zeal of volunteers profitably. If the commanding officer, or anyone else in the corps, can supply time and experience, that will do, if not the drill instructors alone are not a sufficient guarantee of system and order. There are cases of great efficiency where no officer has assisted, but they are rare.

4198. (*Major-Gen. Eyre.*) Do you not ascertain the causes of the inefficiency?—It is not by the regulations within the province of the inspector, he does so as far as he can. The business of the inspector is first to take a note of the number of men actually present; then of their physical stamina; then of the condition of the arms and accoutrements which the Government have given to them; then of the state in which their exercises and drills are, and so forth, and then to pronounce on the whole; and when all breaks down you can only say that there are corps which are inefficient.

4199. But we are rather at a loss to know the cause of their inefficiency, whether it is physical difficulties that they have to contend with, or apathy, or neglect on the part of the individuals concerned?—It is impossible to describe it in one word. Sometimes it may be want of tact in the officer commanding; sometimes it may be distance.

4200. (*Viscount Hardinge.*) In case of an invasion, what proportion of the corps in your district do you think would be fit to go into garrison and fire with shot and shell; is it two-thirds, or a half, or what proportion?—I think you might say that a half would cause the Queen's service no embarrassment whatsoever if incorporated with them to-morrow; but I would rather say a third; personally I should not hesitate to take over one half.

4201. (*Major Harcourt.*) Does that refer to your experience this year on the coast?—No; I have had none this year.

4202. Then it refers only to your inspection of last year?—Yes.

4203. (*Major-Gen. Eyre.*) You have stated that they would cause no embarrassment to the Queen's service; but would they be of any actual use?—Certainly, in defence.

4204. (*Col. MacMurdo.*) With reference to that part of your evidence, in which you say that some of the corps are wasting the public money, I think it is very important that I should read to you some short extracts from your reports:—"There is no "ammunition or charge, nor have the volunteers "fired for want of a range and of time to do so. "The corps is remarkable for its fine appearance, "and steady movement upon parade." "The artillery "enthusiasm of the district is great; the members in "some instances come from six to eight miles to the "drills, after the days' work in mines. One section "are miners, another are agriculturists, but all are "of a superior class in intelligence and social "standing to the majority of the volunteers in the "ranks as privates elsewhere. Hence the peculiar "necessity of influence and discretion in their "command, which the captain seems to exercise so "well. The arms have been only lately supplied in "part. There are still 10 stands wanting. A plat- "form on the coast for gun practice is very de- "sirable. I recommend the grant of the regulated "allowance to the volunteers themselves to do the "work, and to erect a wooden store and magazine in "the neighbourhood, by which their labour and "difficulties will be greatly lessened." "The members "who attended the inspection were creditable in "appearance, young men in the prime of life, "well appointed, and fairly drilled. Everything "indicates a start made in a right direction, with "no fault to be found, and nothing wanting but "perseverance on the part of members in attend- "ance at drill." "This corps is in a very promising "and creditable state, having made great progress "during five months, existence. I recommend that the "volunteers be allowed to put down their own "practice platform, and conduct their gun practice "forthwith. They are quite fit to fire." "The "condition of this corps is most creditable to the "officers commanding and all concerned. The mem- "bers have no service ammunition or charge. This "is the first year of their formation. The gun "practice was witnessed by me on a previous oc- "casion, and was extremely good." "This is a very "promising corps, and in very good hands. The men "all fired in their turn, at a target 1,200 yards off, "steadily and well. The instruction of the four "corps of this brigade is essentially well conducted, "and reflects great honour upon the officers and men "concerned." "The corps is well trained to gun "drill, and much interested therein, and is said to be "capable of augmentation." "The drill to which "most notice seems to have been given is the gun "drill. This exercise is creditable." "This corps is "in the highest order, and, together with the other "corps would cause no confusion if drafted into the "ranks of the royal artillery to-morrow." "The in- "struction of this corps is good as far as it goes, and "seems to be progressing." "The corps reported "upon is in very superior order to any corps seen

A a

Lieut.-Col. E. Maherly.
4 July 1862.

"hitherto; except the dockyard corps. They have carried their training so far as to pass inspection as perfectly as regular troops would do." "The corps is in a very creditable order, reflecting honour upon all concerned. Good use has been made of the instruction and means of training furnished by Government. The men only just stop short of fitness to be incorporated with regular artillery." "This corps is in a most creditable and efficient state, due, without doubt, to the zeal and intelligence of the captain, and to the spirit and perseverance of the officers and men. The battery is quite fit to occupy the place of a battery of regular artillery whenever called upon to do so. As far as an inspection such as this goes, the corps may be reported thoroughly effective and disciplined." "This corps is in very good hands. The officers are very competent and active, the men are young and are very zealous, and attend drill well. The carbine exercise has been allowed to stand over to perfect the gun drill during the summer. The latter has been well learnt, but is a little slurred over for speed sake; nevertheless the corps deserve great credit." "This corps has made creditable and fair progress." "The men are quick and smart at gun exercise." "The training has been good and systematic, the corps marches and performs the carbine exercises better than most corps, and is progressing with the gun drill, nearly mastered satisfactorily." "This corps appears to be in a very hearty and flourishing state and in good hands. The gun drill is quite mastered and well performed." "This corps is in fine order and in excellent hands; the drills have all been well learnt, and the corps is very little, if at all, short of being perfect." "This corps is composed of very fine men, averaging about 26 years in age, 5 feet 7 inches in height, and weighing probably nearly 12 stone per man. The corps has derived the greatest benefit from the residence of the major in the neighbourhood, by whom the battery was raised. It is now in excellent hands and in full vigour. The chief attention has been given to the gun exercise." "The battery paraded with two 18-pounder guns, horsed by means of farm horses provided by the officers and farmers adjoining, and with officers and serjeants mounted, forming a very effective division of a battery of position; the remaining men were formed on foot under arms. The trouble and expense incurred in bringing this corps to its present state reflects the highest credit." I must say that I am a little surprised that you should say that any of those corps are wasting the public money after the receipt of your reports?—I scarcely know how I can answer you without particularizing, and I do not wish to do an invidious thing; I should gladly be excused from doing so; I can only say that I have no copies of my reports, and if I have reported incorrectly in the case that is in my mind, then I have done so; but I hold in my hand my own notes made upon the spot. The reports are made from the notes, and must and do agree with them. I can read the notes, if permitted, without naming corps.

4205. (*Lord Overstone.*) I presume your intention in speaking of a waste of the public money was to express an opinion that, speaking generally, the artillery volunteers under your inspection are in a tolerably satisfactory condition, but that there are some exceptions to that statement?—Certainly.

4206. And you feel some delicacy in stating specifically what those exceptions are, as they would then appear upon the minutes of evidence?—Yes, for the sake of encouraging the volunteer force generally, one has caught at everything that was susceptible of praise.

4207. (*Col. MacMurdo.*) There are only two cases in which your reports are different from those which I have already read, which are these: "This corps has been unfortunate, and is behind all those hitherto inspected in efficiency; the reason alleged for backwardness is want of regular attendance amongst the members at drill. The appearance of the men upon parade is satisfactory, and the state of their arms is creditable. The district is agricultural, and the distances which are travelled by the members to the evening drills, after their day's work, are often great. It is in contemplation to bring a gun into the village under cover, and exercise the men there in winter." The next is: "The arms are not in good order; the practice adopted of allowing a remuneration to the drill instructor to keep them clean has not answered here. There may be valid objections to the entrusting of arms to volunteers' private custody, but in the interest of the arms themselves it seems to me desirable to do so, as well as to teach the art of keeping arms in order to every man reputed to be a soldier, as the first duty required from him. But in any way some more frequent purview or other precaution is needed for the protection of the arms here?"—I thought that a reference to my official reports would show that there were two cases in which I had reported unsatisfactorily.

4208. Is it your opinion, with reference to the efficiency of the volunteer artillery, supposing it progresses favourably, that in the event of war they would be good troops for the purpose of manning the fortifications of the country?

4209. (*Viscount Hardinge.*) With a certain proportion of trained gunners with them?—With or without, taking only the best corps. There are many corps of which too much cannot be said in praise.

4210. (*Lord Overstone.*) Do you look upon the artillery volunteers as a force likely to be of considerable value acting as a supplement to the regular troops?—Yes; unquestionably.

4211. (*Viscount Hardinge.*) Do you mean to say that you would trust the forts, in the event of an invasion to be garrisoned by the volunteer artillery, and to be commanded by their own officers and non-commissioned officers, without any portion of trained men with them?—Yes; there are corps fit to be thus trusted in a case of emergency; there might be a danger of accidents to themselves from want of the habit of caution, which they can only acquire by usage.

4212. (*Chairman.*) In all other respects you would trust them?—Yes; as far as efficient service of their guns goes, in manipulation, and mechanical efficiency, I do not think it is possible to give them too high credit. I speak of the positive condition of those corps at my inspection of last year.

The witness withdrew.

Lieut.-Col. J. Bower.

Lieut.-Colonel JOHN BOWER examined.

4213. (*Chairman.*) You command the 1st Hampshire Light Horse Volunteer Corps?—Yes.

4214. Of how many men does your corps consist?—44.

4215. I believe all the men ride their own horses?—Yes, with the exception of the serjeant instructor and the trumpeter, they do not ride their own horses; the two farriers do not ride their own horses, but they ride their masters' horses; they are gentlemen's servants.

4216. Will there be any difficulty in providing your corps with clothing when it requires renewal?—I do not think there will be any difficulty in that respect, for they are all persons capable of clothing themselves; the paid members of the corps are clothed from the funds of the corps, that is the serjeant instructor and the trumpeter.

4217. Should you require any assistance whatever from the Government?—We are not above accepting assistance from the Government if they like to give it to us; of course our existence somewhat depends upon our income, and our income prospectively will certainly not meet our expenses; they can only be met by making appeals from time to time to the community around us, and we must help ourselves; but if the Government are disposed to assist us they could do it in this way: they give us a serjeant instructor who is paid for by the Government, but a serjeant instructor without a horse is only half a serjeant instructor; he cannot move about without a horse; and if the Government would find us forage for the serjeant instructor's horse it would be a relief to our funds; we bought the horse out of our own funds, but that is a thing done, and we hope it will last some time, but the current expenses of keeping a horse are a considerable drain upon our funds. I do not know that there is anything else that we could ask the Government for.

4218. Is your fund raised by private subscriptions from every member of the corps?—By private subscriptions from the community around; the effective members give a donation, at least most of them do; about half of us are gentlemen, who can afford to give a donation to the fund which formed the capital upon which we started, and most of which is exhausted now; besides that, we have an annual subscription, which, by the regulations sanctioned by the Government, is 10s. or 10s. 6d.; that is the minimum, but by a bye-law of our own, we do not limit the annual subscription to 10s. 6d., but it suits some of our members to content themselves with giving that support to us, whilst others who can afford it give a guinea, and this keeps us going a little; but before another year is out we shall have to make a special appeal to our honorary members.

4219. Have you many honorary members?—I think about 50.

4220. They raised the subscriptions originally, I presume, which formed the fund of the corps?—The honorary members and the effectives jointly raised a fund of some 400l. or 500l., which we have been living upon as our capital, and, in fact, at the present time. Our original expenses were disposed of in the first year, that is to say, our targets, and the expense of a range, and all that sort of thing came out of our capital, but they are disposed of, and there is an end of them; they are not likely to be repeated.

4221. Were the horse appointments supplied by yourselves?—Yes, but the horse appointments did not come to very much, because we use the common hunting saddle and bridle, and by a very little alteration it is rendered serviceable for our purposes.

4222. Do you carry the short Enfield rifle?—Yes, at the present time we do, and if we could by any means get a lighter weapon from the Government, but at the same time as efficient, we should be very thankful for it. A breech-loader is what we ought to have, and for this reason: we never ride with our arms loaded, and consequently it takes a little time, and of course any military man will know that a very rapid fire is not very desirable, as it encourages people to waste the ammunition; but with intelligent people like ours, they can learn to reserve their fire, and you can trust them better than you can the common soldier, because they see the object of taking care of their ammunition; and therefore to enable us in our rapid mode of working, to deliver our fire a little more promptly, a breech loader would be a very valuable weapon, if we could get a thing to suit us. I asked the Government whether they would assist us, as we were then disposed to provide ourselves with Westley Richard's breech-loading carbine—we were willing to buy them for those who cannot do it for themselves. I put the question officially to the Government, whether, in that event, they could supply us with ammunition, because we could not depend upon any private source for that; and the reply was, that they could not—therefore we abandoned it. Since then, the Government having given arms throughout the volunteer force, we only hope, if at any time they have a breech-loading rifle to suit us, we may have it. It is not desirable, according to our system of carrying the rifle in our bucket, to have a very short weapon, there is no advantage in it; the short Enfield rifle answers our purpose perfectly well in that way; we carry it in what we call a nomaqua bucket; it is so called after a Caffre tribe, at the Cape of Good Hope.

4223. (*Major-Gen. Eyre.*) The Cape mounted rifles use it, do they not?—I believe Colonel Sutton tried it, it has been persevered with; by a little perseverance, any one who takes the trouble will succeed with it. Carrying the rifle in that way, there is nothing gained by having a short barrel: on the contrary, it is an objection.

4224. You cannot offer any suggestion that any assistance should be given to a corps of mounted rifles like your own beyond what you have mentioned, namely, forage allowance for a horse?—That would be acceptable; but there is another thing that we ought to have. We are a peculiar corps; I do not believe that there is anything of the same sort on the earth; it is quite an experimental thing, and it has been worked out by the farmers and people of our description; and I think at the same time it answers very well; but we want a proper designation; we are not mounted riflemen, because we are cavalry; we are not light horse, we are a kind of irregular cavalry; and I think that if some other designation were applied to us, such as volunteer dragoons, it would be better.

4225. (*Lord Overstone.*) In what respect do you call yourselves a peculiar corps?—Because we carry the rifle. My object is this: we are called cavalry, and I do not think we are quite cavalry, but we are given the cavalry allowance of ammunition, and the cavalry allowance of ammunition for a corps of the description that I command is not sufficient.

4226. (*Chairman.*) You do not adopt cavalry drill when skirmishing, do you?—No, because we are riflemen; our weapon is the rifle, the cavalry weapon is the sword; and our system of drill is not for mounted riflemen, because mounted riflemen work on foot; we do not work on foot, beyond this, that we dismount to fire; but we do all our skirmishing on horseback.

4227. (*Major-Gen. Eyre.*) So far as your wants are concerned, they appear to amount to this, that you would take all you can get; but you are not really in want of anything?—We are not in absolute want of anything; but if we do not get some kind of assistance, I cannot answer for the corps going on; it is a very disagreeable thing to have to go round to the community and say, we want a little help; our neighbours tire of that sort of thing. If our annual expenditure could be relieved a little, it would be a great help to us; and the other thing is the ammunition; what we want is a mounted rifle allowance of ammunition; we are expected to go through a mounted rifle course of military practice, and we are allowed cavalry ammunition for that purpose. I think it simply wants to be explained, and then it would be set right; it is a matter of expense, for if we do not get the ammunition that I ask for we must buy it; we must go through our course of instruction and practice at our own expense, or else we shall not fulfil the duties that we undertake.

4228. (*Col. MacMurdo.*) Have you expended the last year's supply of ammunition?—We are going on with our course now; it is almost finished. I have applied for the quantity that is allowed by purchase, which will enable us to go on with our practice; but it gives us no opportunity whatever of practising ourselves.

4229. Have you got the current year's gratuitous supply?—Yes; that is 50 rounds, and if you do not give the men something to practice with besides their annual course, they have no opportunity of mending their shooting. The people at Hythe say you learn position drill, and you come to the target ready made

Lieut.-Col. J. Bower.

4 July 1862.

A a 2

180 MINUTES OF EVIDENCE TAKEN BEFORE THE COMMISSIONERS APPOINTED

Lieut.-Col. J. Bower.
4 July 1862.

marksmen; but that is all nonsense. You have to learn the power of your rifle, and a thousand things that you can only learn by burning powder.

4230. (*Chairman.*) You think that you ought to have a much larger allowance of ammunition?—I think that we ought to be put on the same footing as mounted riflemen.

4231. With a new designation you think you should have an increased allowance of ammunition annually, and also forage for a horse?—Yes.

The witness withdrew.

Adjourned to Tuesday next at half-past 12 o'clock.

Tuesday, 8th July 1862.

PRESENT:

Viscount EVERSLEY.
Lord OVERSTONE.
Lieutenant-Colonel BARTTELOT.
Lieutenant-Colonel Sir A. CAMPBELL.

Lieutenant-General Sir G. A. WETHERALL.
Major-General EYRE.
Colonel MACMURDO.
Major HARCOURT.

VISCOUNT EVERSLEY IN THE CHAIR.

Major L. L. Dillwyn, M.P.
8 July 1862.

Major LEWIS LLEWELLYN DILLWYN, M.P., examined.

4232. (*Chairman.*) I believe you command the 3rd Glamorganshire Rifle Volunteers?—Yes.

4233. Of how many companies does that corps consist?—Four companies.

4234. How many men?—I have sent in a return; I forget the exact number.

4235. You are acquainted with the rifle movement in Wales?—Yes; I was one of the first who was called upon, and I believe mine was the first corps that mustered in Wales.

4236. If you have any suggestions to offer to the Commission upon this question, we shall be glad to hear them?—I think that some assistance should be afforded.

4237. Do you think that assistance is absolutely necessary?—Yes; I think it is absolutely necessary, both in respect to clothing for the privates and assistance towards the regimental expenses in some way. I would suggest that for the privates should be by giving them clothing. I do not think that giving the cloth at Government prices would be any assistance whatever to them, and for this reason, that the cloth at Government prices which I have seen will not wear anything like so well as the cloths that we furnished to our own men. The cloth that I have used is a brown cloth, and it has worn so well that although I have had the men out very constantly for a considerable time, indeed, since the first movement took place, and they have been out in all sorts of weather,—and it has been very bad weather since the movement was first instituted, —you cannot now tell the new recruits from the men who have worn their uniforms from the first. Thus with regard to my own uniform, I have made it a point of not changing it, and when I am out the men cannot tell whether it is a new one or an old one. I chose it for this reason, that the men should not feel ashamed to come out to drill when the clothes begin to look shabby as compared with the clothing of the new recruits, and that has worked very well. I am quite sure that it is better to pay double the price, or even more than that, rather than get the grey cloths, which begin to look shabby in no time, and if they are to buy them at all, there would be very little saving by having the Government cloth at Government prices. I do not think it would be any great privilege to give them that cloth at the Government price. I am in favour of giving them clothing, and of one colour, red, if it were thought advisable. I would suggest that if it is to be given it need not be made up. I feel sure that the privates require some assistance. My corps principally consists of mechanics and shopkeepers and respectable people, but who can very ill afford to give more than their time for the movement, and meet certain other expenses to which they are liable. I do not think that they can afford to give very much more; and I do not think they ought to be asked to give any more.

4238. In what way do you think they ought to be assisted. Do you mean that their travelling expenses should be paid?—No; I would give them the cloth for the uniform. I think that would be sufficient. I think that the Government ought also to relieve the officers from the great expenses which they are now put to.

4239. (*Lord Overstone.*) Do you mean that the cloth should be given to them, or that the uniform already made up should be given to them?—I think that if you gave them the cloth for the coats and trousers it would be sufficient. I think I could manage with that in my own corps. Of course I assume that the rifles are to be continued. I certainly think that you ought to relieve the officers from the regimental expenses which fall now so very heavily upon them. I do not see upon what principle we are called upon to bear them. I do not want to relieve the commanding officers of all expenses, but I think they ought not to be put to such very heavy expenses as they are now; for instance, for ranges, armouries, the rent of ranges, and the rent of armouries, buglers, and for cleaning the arms.

4240. When you use the word "armouries," have you any persons to take care of the arms?—Yes, and the expenses are something very considerable, as in my own case. I bear the greater portion of them with the other officers, but I think that you ought to enable the other officers to be relieved of all expenses. I hardly like to ask my officers, and I think that they ought not to bear the proportion that they have to bear, and the fact of there being any regimental expense connected with the commission to some extent might prevent me from selecting some of the best men from the corps for officers. I know many men who would be most popular, and who are some of the most efficient in the corps, but who would not feel justified in undertaking an undefined expense, particularly as it was in the starting of the corps in the early days of the movement. It is somewhat modified now, but there are still many unsettled accounts and expenses. Relieving officers from these expenses would have this effect, I think, that you would be able, in the first place, to get the best men for officers if you relieved all except the commanding officers from them; and if you could relieve the commanding officers of some part of the expenses which they are at present liable to, I think it would further assist the movement very much, because they would then feel themselves enabled to assist their corps by giving prizes, and in many other ways which would give other inducements to the volunteer force to muster better, than they are now able to give. The necessary expenses are so heavy that they are often obliged to economize, and to be stingy in many things when they would not like to be so. If you could relieve them from the heavy burden which they have now to bear in the shape of expenses, I think that they would readily give fêtes and give prizes, and offer little inducements which I think are of great importance in maintaining the volunteer movement. Of course all these things would require a larger amount than is required at present, and when we came to ask parliament for it we should probably be met with the reply on the part of some of the economists who do not like the volunteers (although I do not think that there are many of them): It is very well to ask for this amount, but if the volunteer force has arrived at this great strength of 170,000 without any assistance, or with only limited assistance, subject to all the disadvantages and expenses and burdens which are now thrown upon them in the present case, what would it be when assistance is given? You are asking parliament for an undefined and not a fixed quantity; you do not know what you are asking. This is the argument which would probably be used, and with some truth, as with the increase that we are now asking for you will find, I think, that the volunteer force will go up to 250,000 instead of 170,000. I would therefore suggest, as the first thing to be done, to limit the force. I would ascertain, as well as I could, what the normal strength of the volunteers ought to be, and then would come whatever assistance the Government might think proper to give them. I do not think that parliament would very much grudge it in respect of a fixed quantity; at least that is my own notion about it. I think that if you so limited the force you would increase its efficiency very much. I do not suppose that 170,000 is the normal strength at which you wish to keep it up; and I will suppose that we reduced it to 120,000, and then you would get rid of all the corps that are inefficient, and which have neither efficient officers nor regular drill, nor anything else; and then, instead of constantly seeking to increase the force, you would say, no, you are to stand where you are, or you are to be reduced from four companies of 90 men each to four companies of 80 men each, or as the case may be. I am assuming that you would give all the advantages and power to commanding officers to assist their corps more than they do now, and that you would relieve the other officers from the expenses which they now bear; and if in addition to that the men had their clothing provided for them I believe you would find that there would be a great rush into the volunteers, and you would turn the tables upon the volunteers, if I may use that expression. At the present time you are asking men to come in, and it is rather a sort of favour on their part to join volunteer corps, but by giving these privileges and inducements I think you would turn the tables upon them, and you would then make it a favour to let them become volunteers. The commanding officers would then be able, I think, to insist upon more regular attendance at drill than they now can do, which clearly is so very desirable; and directly it was felt it to be somewhat of a privilege it would be more sought after, and you would get a better class of men in the force; you would get rid of all the inefficient men; you would be then obliged to say, I cannot have more than this maximum establishment to which I am limited, and I must therefore weed out those who are the most inefficient.

4241. You say that you would first give some assistance towards the clothing, next that all the ordinary expenses, such as rifle ranges and regimental expenses, should be defrayed by the public?—Some portion of them.

4242. How would you propose that the clothing should be given to the men; is it to be made up by the War Office, and issued in that way, or do you propose that a certain sum should be given in aid of the clothing?—That depends upon whether you wish to have a uniform colour for the volunteers to be clothed in; if you allow them to clothe themselves in any colour, as at present, I think it would require a fixed sum of about 2l. a year.

4243. I understood you to say that you would object to cloth being given?—No; I object to it being given at Government price, I should consider that as no assistance at all, or next to none, for it would be so small; I would not take the Government colour (grey or red) at the Government price. If you insisted upon a uniform colour, I think the Government ought to give the cloth altogether. I do, however, think they ought to give some assistance as to the clothing.

4244. Do you think, if the officers were relieved to a very large extent of their present expenses, that you would get a more efficient class of officers?—No doubt about it.

4245. I presume you would not give any assistance to a corps unless the privates were thoroughly efficient?—Certainly not.

4246. Unless they were thoroughly efficient in musketry drill, and unless they had attended, I presume, a certain number of drills in the course of a year?—Precisely so.

4247. Unless a man could be certified to have gone through those drills, and to be an efficient rifleman, you would not give any assistance to a corps for that man?—Certainly not.

4248. (*Major-Gen. Eyre.*) You propose that the volunteer force should be limited to a certain number? —Yes.

4249. Say 120,000 or 150,000?—Yes.

4250. Would not your object be attained at once by withholding the aid and by contenting yourselves with such volunteers as were *bonâ fide* volunteers, and who would require no aid?—No; because in that case you would not be able to come to parliament for a certain assistance, and without aid I think the force would soon fall away to an insignificant amount.

4251. But you would not want to go to parliament in that case at all, you would have a sufficient number of volunteers who could afford to be volunteers, and who would not require any aid?—I do not think that would do; with us I can assure you that they cannot afford it, they require aid.

4252. A certain proportion of the present numbers do; but if you were satisfied with a nucleus of 120,000 men, would not the object to which you have referred be at once attained, without going to parliament for anything?—No, I think you would soon lose some of the most efficient corps; and in many districts the force would entirely disappear.

4253. (*Col. MacMurdo.*) Do you think it would amount to a prohibition of the volunteers in certain parts of the country where the classes only exist who require assistance?—Yes, and some of the best classes; you would get very often clerks and many respectable people; but the class of mechanics I think to be the very best, they are the most regular attendants, and the most amenable to their drill, and you would lose them, for they cannot afford it.

4254. (*Lord Overstone.*) Is there, in your judgment, any reason for limiting the force, except pecuniary considerations?—I should rather refer to general officers for an answer to that question.

4255. Is that your opinion that the volunteer force ought to be limited in its numbers?—Perhaps I ought not to give that opinion; but I think that a normal force of 120,000 men would be sufficient.

4256. I understand the very basis of your evidence to be, that the volunteer force ought to be limited in numbers?—I have heard that opinion very generally expressed.

4257. Is that your opinion?—Yes, as far as I am qualified to give an opinion.

4258. Is that opinion founded upon pecuniary considerations exclusively, or upon any other considerations combined with that?—I want to know what you say is requisite for the defence of the country, be it large or be it small; I think that parliament would cheerfully grant it, if it was a fixed quantity, but

Major L. L. Dillwyn, M.P.

8 July 1862.

that they would object to an undefined and uncertain quantity.

4259. When you speak of an undefined and uncertain quantity, do you mean an uncertain pecuniary charge?—Yes.

4260. Do you think that the limitation of the volunteer force would be sufficiently accomplished by more stringent regulations as to the amount of discipline and efficiency which should be required to constitute a volunteer, in the technical sense of the term, "an effective?"—If you do not give the volunteers aid, they will soon dwindle away altogether.

4261. I want to ascertain whether you think that the limitation of the number which you seem to think desirable would be sufficiently accomplished by means of increased strictness in the requisitions as to discipline and efficiency, compliance with which should constitute an effective volunteer?—No, I think not; I think you must recollect that if you give them aid it would operate as a great stimulus to volunteering, and that you would have a great increase to the force.

4262. Assuming that aid is given to those only who are declared to be effective, and that the requisitions laid down to constitute an effective were more stringent than they are now, do you think that that would accomplish a sufficient limitation of the numbers?—No, I think you would increase your force if you gave aid, and still make them effective.

4263. Do you think, with the pecuniary aid that you suggest, the force would still increase in numbers, notwithstanding that the aid was given only to those who were declared to be effective, and that the qualifications were considerably raised?—If you give the pecuniary assistance that I suggest, I think you may increase the force, and unless you limit that force to some fixed quantity, it would increase it to a great extent.

4264. Your opinion is that with some additional pecuniary aid from the Government the present volunteer force might be largely augmented in numbers, and their efficiency largely increased?—Yes, that is my opinion decidedly.

4265. Do you consider the volunteer force at the present moment under your command in an efficient state?—Yes, I do.

4266. Is it your opinion that the volunteer force throughout your county is in an efficient state?—Yes, I do, so far as I have means of judging.

4267. But speaking generally, do you think that they are in an efficient state?—Yes.

4268. Do you give your opinion as to their efficiency with reference to their discipline and to the condition of their arms, and their capacity to use them?—Yes, I do.

4269. Do you see any ground to apprehend diminished efficiency in the force, assuming that the pecuniary pressure to which you have alluded was sufficiently met?—No; I think that by reducing the force you will increase the efficiency of it very much; and by making it a sort of privilege to become a volunteer, and not to let any man who thinks he may join this or that regiment enter it and make it a favour that he should come; I would make it a matter of scrutiny in order to get men of good character into the force, and to make it a favour to let them come in.

4270. When you speak of making it a favour, do you mean that you will examine into their general character and condition?—To a certain extent I do that now; I do not allow an habitual drunkard or a man of notoriously bad character to come into the corps.

4271. Do you think that the examination into their character and condition ought to be more searching than it now is?—It necessarily would be so if you seek to increase them; but I have no right now to say that I can refuse a respectable man to be a volunteer; I have no instructions that I am to limit my corps to a minimum battalion, which is its present strength.

4272. I wish to ascertain whether you contemplate diminishing the numbers and increasing the efficiency of the volunteers by greater stringency of examination into their character and condition, and how you would work that principle?—I think that if clothes were given to them, and you held out to them certain other inducements, there would be an anxiety on their part to be retained in the corps, and I should insist then upon more punctual attendance at drill, and as to many other little matters.

4273. You would rely more upon increased strictness in the regulations with regard to attendance at drill and the military requirements generally than you would upon an examination into their character and condition?—Yes; I should not go much into the character of the men, but I should be a little more particular than I am now.

4274. Have you formed any opinion as to the effect of the volunteer movement upon the moral and industrial character of the people of your county?—Yes.

4275. What is that opinion?—That it has had an extremely good effect; and I may mention one case. There is a person who is a large manufacturer in Swansea, and a number of his men joined my corps; after they had been in it for some time their employer told me that they had been, generally speaking, much better conducted and steadier men since they joined.

4276. Do you think that the volunteer movement has a tendency to promote the moral and industrial training of the community?—Yes. I have seen it in very many instances with respect to young men about town, who used to hang about billiard rooms and the bars at public houses; they now go to drill and shoot at the rifle ranges.

4277. (*Lieut.-Col. Barttelot.*) Do you think that you have enrolled in your corps the class of men who in your part of the country were likely to enlist in the army or in the militia?—No.

4278. Are they of quite a distinct class?—Yes.

4279. Do you not think that if your men were relieved from any pecuniary expenditure they would be willing at all times to give their time to the volunteer service?—Yes, at all times if they could possibly do so; but they cannot always, for in large towns there are so many works going on that you must consult their employers; I cannot insist too much upon it even with the men I have. I have to consider the interest of the employers, who will suffer if I take the men out too much from their work.

4280. It is only to the money out of pocket, as far as you know, that they object?—That is all.

4281. (*Sir G. A. Wetherall.*) Would not the same difficulty exist, in the event of a war, in getting all the men together?—No.

4282. Why not; would all the works stop?—I suppose in the case of an invasion most works would stop, or be only at half work, and every one, employers and all, would willingly make every sacrifice required of them for repelling it.

4283. (*Major-Gen. Eyre.*) Suppose that the Secretary of State informed you that your corps should receive a certain amount of pecuniary aid for every man whom you could certify to be effective, and that the term effective referred principally to the man's proficiency in the musketry course, with some little knowledge of company drill, should you be able to give such guarantee, or what means would you have of ascertaining it?—I should inspect the men in order to ascertain it. I have a regular adjutant, a gentleman who has been in the line, Captain West; and I have a serjeant, the best serjeant I could get from the line; and with their assistance, consulting with them, I should take care never to give a guarantee unless I was satisfied that it was an honest one.

4284. It appears to me that it is not so easy to ascertain the state of the musketry instruction, because, although in some corps a register is kept, in some it is not kept, and it does not appear to be obligatory upon you to keep a register?—I know that Captain West

TO INQUIRE INTO THE CONDITION OF THE VOLUNTEER FORCE IN GREAT BRITAIN. 183

has insisted very much upon the musketry instruction and the regular drill, and he has had my full concurrence in so acting.

4285. But still it is rather a vague knowledge of it that you have, is it not?—Yes, no doubt, as I have not been myself in the army; I should be very much guided by my adjutant and the serjeant, who have been in the army; the serjeant was a serjeant-major in the 3rd battalion of the rifle brigade. I have got the best men that I could.

4286. It appears to me that the arrangement is not sufficiently defined to enable you to make this return?—I do not see that; we have regular drill books and regular drill returns, and regular entries as to every man and the drills they have attended. My returns are sent up every month. I have lately fitted up an armoury at considerable expense; it is a very large room, 70 feet long, where they meet every night, and there are squads of recruits always drilling there; they like to come down there, and they are drilled in musketry and in every other branch of volunteer drill according to regulations.

4287. (*Chairman.*) Have you any further suggestion to make to the Commission?—No.

Major L. L. Dillwyn, M.P.

8 July 1862

The witness withdrew.

Mr. Sheriff GLASSFORD BELL, Lieutenant-Colonel STIRLING CRAWFORD, Lieutenant-Colonel WILLIAM STIRLING, Captain ALEXANDER B. MCGRIGOR, Mr. JAMES LOCKHART, examined.

4288. (*Chairman.*) The Secretary received a letter a short time ago, dated 2nd July, enclosing a copy of a resolution which I believe was agreed to at a meeting of the committee held in Glasgow, in which it was stated, "That in the opinion of this committee " it would be of great importance to the interests of " the volunteer movement in this quarter, that " Colonels Stirling Crawford and Stirling, who " are presently in London, and Mr. Sheriff Bell, " who is to be in London shortly, should be examined " as witnesses by the Royal Commissioners; as, also, " that Captain A. B. McGrigor and Mr. Lockhart, " the secretary, should be asked to attend and give " evidence." In consequence of that letter, you have been invited to attend here to day. I believe you have been made acquainted with the purport of Colonel Dreghorn's evidence, which was considered by the Commission very satisfactory, and we shall now be glad to know whether you have anything to add to that evidence, or if you in any way dissent from what Colonel Dreghorn has stated?—(*Mr. Sheriff Bell.*) I believe I may say, for myself and the other gentlemen who accompany me, that we concur generally in the evidence given by Colonel Dreghorn; we think that in many respects it is very sound and important evidence, but there are one or two matters upon which we desire to be permitted to give a little additional explanation. One or two questions were put to him, which would seem to point to a difference of opinion having at one time existed in the Glasgow committee as to the best mode of applying the fund which was collected there for the aid of the volunteer force. But the committee came to a unanimous resolution on the subject. That committee originated from a very great public meeting of the citizens of Glasgow, which was held on the 23d November 1859; it was one of the earliest public meetings on the subject of the volunteer force which took place in Scotland, if not the very earliest meeting. It was held in our largest hall, and was very crowdedly attended, and the resolutions that were moved there were moved by all the most eminent gentlemen connected officially with Glasgow; a committee was then appointed of 138 individuals, the committee consisting of citizens, field officers, and captains; that committee appointed a sub-committee of 32 citizens and officers, and that sub-committee again sub-committed to Sir James Campbell, the present Lord Provost, myself, Sir Archibald Campbell, Colonel Dreghorn, Captain Taylor, and Captain Murray, to report as to the objects to which the fund that was to be collected, under the superintendence of this committee, should be applied; and that committee unanimously reported that they considered the object of the fund should be first to afford facilities for the formation of volunteer corps, especially among the artizan and working classes, and generally among those who were unable to defray entirely their own expenses, and to make grants in consideration of the necessities and the number of effective members of each corps. The second object was to promote the efficiency of the corps after they were formed, by affording pecuniary assistance to defray the expenses of ranges, targets, &c., the custody of arms, and if necessary the pay of instructors. I may say that that committee prepared its report very carefully; there was some discussion in the committee as to whether it would be proper to vote as our first object a proportion of the funds for the formation of artizan corps; but after full consideration of the subject, the committee unanimously reported that such ought to be the primary object, and they were influenced in coming to that conclusion by this conviction, which I believe all the gentlemen present with me entertain too, that without introducing the artizan element into the volunteer movement you might have a small and excellent body of volunteers, but you could have nothing like a national army. Artizan is a wide word, but we understand it to cover all persons who have limited incomes, varying perhaps from 30l. or 60l. to 100l. or 120l. per annum. The committee thought that unless we included that class of people it would be impossible to give the volunteer movement a wide diffusion; the result was successful in Glasgow, because in consequence of the fund being a good deal applied towards the aid of the artizan companies, we have succeeded in establishing a highly respectable force, numerous in proportion to the other bodies of volunteers in Scotland.

4289. Are there any other points that you wish to refer to?—Yes; I wish to refer to the question of the restrictions that should be placed on the application of a grant amounting to 30s. a man, if such a grant were made. Of course, all those who want the assistance are prepared to take it, and our impression is, that if put as a general Government measure, there is nobody at all who would refuse it. We think, however, that if there happened to be, or if the Commissioners receive evidence that there are certain corps who do not want it and would rather be without it, they could easily be put on that footing, and that the Government might determine to give as a maximum a certain sum, and that if any corps intimated that they did not want it, or that they wanted less, or that they wanted nothing more, of course they would not get it, but our impression is that if it was put on such a footing it would be taken as a national grant, and that every volunteer would take it. I may take the liberty of calling the attention of the Commission to this. The Glasgow officers have unanimously affirmed it to be their opinion that the Government grant should not be under 2l. a man. This was affirmed by them, not only by resolutions passed at public meetings of their own, but it was affirmed upon a broader basis at a meeting which took place at the Thatched House Tavern here on the 23d of February 1861, when it was stated that the expenses which were absolutely required would amount, including clothing, to 2l. 3s. 0¾d. There were full details given showing how that sum was arrived at. It included 4s. 4¾d. for drill serjeants, who have now been supplied, but I think that that is the only thing that has been supplied since that resolution was passed; of course that would diminish the amount and bring it a little under 2l., but since that there has been an additional expense thrown upon the volunteers in the shape of capes and leggings, which probably

Mr. Sheriff G. Bell, Lieut.-Col. S. Crawford, Lieut.-Col. W. Stirling, Capt. A. B. McGrigor, Mr. J. Lockhart.

A a 4

Mr.
Sheriff G. Bell,
Lieut.-Col.
S. Crawford,
Lieut.-Col.
W. Stirling,
Capt. A. B.
McGrigor,
Mr. J.
Lockhart.

8 July 1862.

brings up the sum very nearly to what it was stated at before. At that meeting the gentlemen who came up to attend it from various quarters, both of England and Scotland, were anxious to have the Glasgow resolution for 2l. a man affirmed, but we found that in London there was considerable diversity of opinion, and the feeling seemed to be that if such a large sum was asked, nothing might be got at all, and so, as a compromise, the resolution that was passed at that meeting was to ask only for 1l. a man. I would next refer to the public subscription raised in Glasgow, with respect to which there may be some misapprehension. I am authorized to say that whilst the funds subscribed and placed at the disposal of the committee amounted only to 3,618l., one cause why it was not a great deal larger was, that very large sums were subscribed by individuals and bodies of individuals who took an interest in the formation of particular corps, and they considered it unnecessary to subscribe to the general fund, as they had done all they could out of their own funds in support of particular corps in which they were interested; and it was for this reason also that some of the corps in Glasgow have abstained from asking assistance from the central fund, as they have been supported by funds from parties who were interested in them, such as the ship-building companies, and the shipowners in Glasgow. The leading merchants and a number of others had companies, and they subscribed largely to aid them; and a great many of those companies were really called into existence by subscriptions from the leading men in those different departments of trade. Some of the companies that asked for relief from the central fund committee were refused on the ground that they had large assistance given to them from those sources to which I have alluded. It is also unquestionable that the honorary members have contributed a considerable sum, taking them as a body, in aid of the volunteer movement, so that I think, from local sources, I may say safely that the fund was three or four times larger on the whole than the fund that was placed at the disposal of the central fund committee. We quite concur in the opinion that that source of assistance is now at an end, and that we cannot collect any fund for our local committee now; nor will those parties who have strained their efforts to the utmost to support particular corps be able to renew those efforts, except, perhaps, in two or three instances. As a general rule, we believe that assistance from private sources is substantially at an end in Glasgow.

4290. You presided, I think, at a meeting that was held on the 2nd July, where the resolution was passed which led to your examination here to day?—Yes.

4291. Did Colonel Dreghorn move that resolution?—He did.

4292. And he is perfectly aware that you differ from him in some respects as to the evidence that he has given, and that you have come to day to give evidence on the points concerned?—I have not had an opportunity of communicating with him since I saw his evidence; I have not seen him since; and we wish to be understood as not coming here to criticize his evidence, but to concur in it generally with two or three explanations.

4293. You do not, I believe, concur with him in thinking that the grant should be 30s. per man?—I have already stated the opinion of the Glasgow officers to be that 2l. per man should be granted. I do not know whether the Commission will receive it as a piece of evidence, but our secretary holds in his hands a petition to the House of Commons signed by 261 officers praying for aid to that extent.

4294. All belonging to Glasgow?—Yes, and Lanarkshire.

4295. (*Lord Overstone.*) Has that petition been received by the House of Commons?—It was never presented to the House; it was proposed to have been presented; but in consequence of the appointment of the Royal Commission it was thought better to delay its presentation, as the matter had been referred to the Commission in the first instance; but our secretary can lay that petition on your table.

4296. (*Sir A. Campbell.*) Was it not also delayed in consequence of a doubt arising as to whether it would be proper for the officers of the force to petition parliament collectively, instead of making their representations, each through his lord-lieutenant, to Government?—I am not aware of that.

(*Col. Crawford.*) I rather think it was.

(*Mr. Sheriff Bell.*) I know that one of the members for Glasgow, to whom I spoke upon the subject, consulted an officer of the House of Commons for the purpose of ascertaining whether he thought there was any incompetency in the presentation of the petition, and he was informed that he did not think so.

4297. (*Chairman.*) The petition could not have been presented to the House of Commons, it being a petition for money, without some recommendation from the crown?—It was thought proper at all events not to present it as matters turned out. If the Commissioners are anxious for specific information with regard to the present number of the volunteers at Glasgow, there are one or two gentlemen here who can give them the precise numbers. I believe that there are in Lanarkshire somewhere about 7,000.

4298. (*Col. MacMurdo.*) I do not suppose that Colonel Dreghorn was very far out in stating the present number at Glasgow to be some 6,000 or 7,000?—No; I may be permitted, however, to say that it is the opinion of Colonel Dreghorn, of myself, and the other gentlemen here that the continuance of those numbers cannot be relied on, except to a very limited extent, unless some general measure of assistance is extended to the volunteers in Glasgow. I may say that we are all of opinion that the issue of clothing in kind would not be satisfactory, and would not be a popular measure with the volunteers in our district; but we believe that by placing at the disposal of the officers a grant of money to relieve the volunteers of personal expenses, both as to clothing and other expenses, it would be perfectly agreeable to almost the whole of the volunteers in Glasgow, if not the whole.

4299. How would the issue of cloth be received not made up?—I think it would be thought to be an imperfect measure.

4300. (*Sir A. Campbell.*) Imperfect in what sense?—As not meeting the necessity; the real necessity is either to keep up the volunteer force to a larger number, or to let it fall to a much smaller number; we think that you cannot keep it up to a larger number merely by giving cloth for uniforms; we think that more must be done than that.

4301. The meaning of Colonel MacMurdo's question was that the cloth should be given gratis?—Yes, I am aware of that, and I spoke under that impression.

4302. (*Col. MacMurdo.*) You have stated that the volunteers would object to receive the clothing made up; why would they object, simply because it would be an objectionable way of distributing a fund intended for the volunteers, or because an issue in kind would be objectionable?—I think that the issuing of cloth not made up would be more generally liked by them than issuing it made up; but I think, whilst of course it would be accepted as a boon, that it would not be considered generally so satisfactory a mode of dealing with the question.

4303. (*Major-Gen. Eyre.*) In point of fact they would rather have the money?—I think so. May I be permitted now to state to the Commissioners what we think would be the number remaining of the volunteers in Glasgow if the artizan element was left out?

4304. Certainly?—Our belief is, understanding by the word "artizan" not merely a mechanic, but such persons as clerks and young men employed in warehouses, and persons whose incomes do not exceed about 100l. a year, that if that element was left out of the number of the Glasgow volunteers, there would not be more than eight or ten companies left.

4305. (*Lord Overstone.*) You mean 100*l.* a year in receipts, not income from realized property?—Yes, receipts; we wish very strongly to state our concurrence in the opinion that the admission of that class of people into the volunteer corps has greatly tended to improve their social tone. I must say, as a magistrate myself of a good many years' standing in Glasgow, that I feel it very strongly, and therefore concur entirely in what Colonel Dreghorn has stated upon that subject. In connexion with that subject, I may state that we do not exactly understand what is meant by self-supporting. There are in Glasgow properly speaking very few self-supporting corps, for even those who have not received assistance from the central fund committee have received assistance and have been almost called into existence, I may say, by assistance from other sources. If the term self-supporting corps signifies those who have received no assistance whatsoever, those who have entirely supported themselves from beginning to end, then in Glasgow those are very few. I am not prepared to tender any further suggestions, but I shall be happy to answer any questions upon the various details. Some of the gentlemen with me can speak from more practical knowledge of the subject than I can. I may say that it would be very satisfactory to the Glasgow volunteers if these gentlemen were allowed to make some statements to the Commission.

(*Col. Stirling.*) I should like to make a few remarks as commanding 10 companies of pure artizans; and, first, I would say that even supposing the Government were to issue cloth, and that the men were thus clothed and accoutred, I require 30 officers, and if there is no money grant made by the Government, the other expenses, which I believe the Commissioners are aware of, would fall entirely upon those 30 officers and myself. I find it impossible to get 30 officers to pay the money that is required for the battalion expenses. I could do so just now, but I am well aware that if nothing is done this year my officers will begin to resign; many of them have done so already, as their income will not allow them to bear the expenses which fall upon them. I have sent in a report very fully stating those expenses. I think that what I have to raise now is equal to 400*l.* or 500*l.* a year.

4306. (*Sir A. Campbell.*) Does that cover the whole expense of the corps, except as to clothing and reclothing?—Yes, it does. I have reported very fully upon that point.

4307. (*Lieut.-Col. Barttelot.*) Is part of that expense for butts?—Yes, and for the range and all the et ceteras.

4308. Do you make the men clean their own arms?—No, we call them in once a year, and clean them.

4309. Who pays for the cleaning of the arms?—The officers do.

4310. Whom do you employ to clean them?—We employ a pensioner or the serjeants, who are paid by the Government. We cannot insist upon their cleaning the arms, and they do not do it.

4311. (*Col. MacMurdo.*) Is there one half of your arms in the possession of the members, and do they clean them?—Yes.

4312. The other half that is in the armoury are cleaned at the expense of the officers?—Yes.

4313. (*Lieut.-Col. Barttelot.*) What does it cost per annum to clean the arms; you have 10 companies?—I have commanded the battalion for two years, and I called in the rifles at the end of the last year, and they were thoroughly cleaned. I could not say exactly, without reference to my report, what the cost was.

4314. It would be quite impossible to make the men clean their own arms entirely, I suppose?—We do make them clean them as long as they are in their own possession. It is necessary, as I am responsible for the arms of the battalion, that I should see them once a year, and it is also desirable that I should have them thoroughly cleaned and taken to pieces.

4315. (*Col. MacMurdo.*) It appears that one-half only of your members are clothed; is that the case?—A great many of them do not come to inspection, as their uniforms are very shabby.

4316. (*Chairman.*) Have they got uniforms?—Yes. I suppose they could show their coats and trousers; they are still in existence.

4317. (*Sir A. Campbell.*) The real difficulty is as to reclothing them?—Yes.

4318. (*Major-Gen. Eyre.*) How long have they had their clothing?—A great many of my companies are of different ages.

4319. Which is the oldest?—It is three years old.

4320. Unless they have used their uniforms for every-day purposes they ought not to be worn out. Do they attend the drills very often?—The company drills are very numerous; we have battalion drills once a fortnight.

4321. (*Sir A. Campbell.*) If uniforms were supplied to the men by Government, either in clothing made up or not made up, or money was granted for the purpose of purchasing them, what security would you propose that the Government should have as to the care of that clothing, and as to the men not leaving the regiment after a fortnight's notice, taking the uniforms with them?—It has struck me that it might be done in this way, that when the clothing was given to them by the Government, should a man not attend a sufficient number of drills, the uniform might be taken from him, and he be legally compelled to pay a certain sum of money.

4322. (*Major Harcourt.*) Would there be much difficulty in getting a man to wear a uniform after it had been taken away from another?—Considerable difficulty; I know that in the Lanarkshire yeomanry we have got many of the men when the clothes were not much worn to wear them; but I think there would be a difficulty with us.

4323. In point of fact it would be a dead loss to the Government if a man left at the end of the 14 days, taking his clothes with him?—Yes; if you could not insist upon his paying for that uniform; but suppose that he got clothes at the value of 3*l.* 10*s.*, and he went away at the end of the year, I should consider that if he paid 2*l.* 10*s.* and took away his clothes, the Government would have a very good bargain with him.

4324. With respect to the mechanics, do you think that there would be any difficulty in recovering the price of the uniform if they left in that way?—If they ran from the country, there would, of course; there is all the risk of that; but if a man was known, and he was still to be found, and he did not attend a sufficient number of drills, there would be no difficulty.

4325. (*Col. MacMurdo.*) Suppose that at the end of one year he gave notice to leave, how would you recover two-thirds of the amount from him if he were an artizan, and not able to pay except by instalments?—I have had two cases occur in the regiment of the men pawning their rifles, and I immediately took steps and obtained a sheriff's warrant, and put the man in gaol. I got the value of his rifle immediately if I did not get the rifle itself.

(*Mr. Sheriff Bell.*) There are two matters which have occurred to me upon this question; and one is, that if the uniform supplied were a uniform uniform, and a volunteer left a district, supposing that he was not leaving the country altogether, he could take a letter from the Government officer of that district, and he would very likely continue as a volunteer in the new district to which he had gone, from having a uniform uniform. Another matter is this, we think, in Glasgow, that if Government aid was given a longer period of notice as to resignation might be demanded.

4326. (*Major Harcourt.*) Do any of your men now pay by instalments?—(*Col. Stirling.*) I have one company the members of which are all in one factory now, and these men are still paying.

4327. Do you find any difficulty in getting in the payments?—Yes, considerable difficulty, without you have a hold upon them through the party who pays their wages.

Mr. Sheriff G. Bell, Lieut.-Col. S. Crawford, Lieut.-Col. W. Stirling, Capt. A. B. McGrigor, Mr. J. Lockhart.

8 July 1862.

Mr.
Sheriff G. Bell,
Lieut.-Col.
S. Crawford,
Lieut.-Col.
W. Stirling,
Capt. A. B.
McGrigor,
Mr. J. Lockhart.

8 July 1862.

4328. Would not the difficulty be equally great in recovering the value of uniforms supplied by Government (supposing them to be supplied), if these men chose to leave the corps a fortnight after receiving the uniforms?—These men have houses containing furniture.

4329. (*Lord Overstone.*) What number of artizan volunteers do you consider are connected with Glasgow?—I should say that four-fifths of the volunteers in Glasgow are artizans.

4330. What number do they represent?—I should say 4,000.

4331. With what feeling do you conceive that the artizan volunteers of Glasgow would contemplate a discontinuance of the volunteer movement?—With considerable disgust.

4332. Disgust, of what nature; based upon what grounds?—That they had sacrificed a great deal in themselves; that they had sacrificed their time and their money, and that they had met with no support from the Government.

4333. For what reason would they desire a continuance of the volunteer force?—On account of a certain trust, which they feel has been given to them by the Government; that they have been considered worthy of that trust, and they have taken considerable pride in it; and I believe that they would be too happy, speaking of a large portion of them, to continue.

4334. You consider that their feeling is that serving in the volunteer force is an honourable trust reposed in them?—I do.

4335. What do you think would be the effect, supposing that the volunteers of Scotland were called upon to act in Lancashire, of the withdrawal from Glasgow of 4,000 artizans?—I could trust implicitly in them.

4336. My question is not directed to the confidence to be placed in those artizans; but to what would be the effect upon the industrial system of Glasgow if a sudden withdrawal from Glasgow of 4,000 artizans took place?—I should presume that if occasion required it their position would be such, as artizans, that they would be too glad to go, and would feel it their duty to go.

4337. Do you think that the withdrawal of so large a number as 4,000 artizans from Glasgow would in any way derange and throw into disorder the industrial system of that great city?—Not under the circumstances under which it would arise.

4338. How would the circumstances under which it would arise affect the question?—I believe that it would be in the case of an invasion or civil war, when the disorganization of the industry of Glasgow would be complete.

4339. Suppose some serious menace upon a distant part of the shores of Ireland caused the withdrawal from Glasgow, otherwise in an undisturbed state, of 4,000 of the most active and respectable artizans, do you think that that would create confusion by disturbing the industrial system of Glasgow?—I consider that there would be a panic in Glasgow, and that there would be disorganization in consequence of any invasion in a distant part of the country.

4340. Do you think that the withdrawal of 4,000 efficient artizans at a moment of panic would increase and intensify that evil in Glasgow?—Rather the reverse. I think it would show that the parties holding property in Glasgow could depend upon the mechanics or the lower orders of the city.

4341. Do you consider that the volunteer force in Glasgow is now in an efficient state for real service?—I am only a volunteer myself, and I am not capable of judging as men in the army would be.

4342. Supposing you, as commanding a portion of the volunteer force, received an announcement from the Government that it was necessary to call for the services of that force, should you feel that the Glasgow volunteers were in a condition of efficiency as to their discipline, the state of their arms and accoutrements, and their capacity to use them?—I can speak for my own battalion, and I consider that we are in a state of efficiency if we have the adjutant that we have now.

4343. Do you feel confident that your volunteers could, upon a sudden emergency, render valuable assistance in supplementing the regular force of the country?—I do.

4344. (*Sir A. Campbell.*) I think I understood Mr. Sheriff Bell, or one of the gentlemen present, to suggest an alteration in the time of the enrolment, or a prolongation of the notice?—(*Mr. Sheriff Bell.*) I suggested a longer notice.

4345. At present a man is only enrolled for a fortnight, and you would suggest that he should be enrolled for a longer period. How would you apply that to the present state of the law?—I presume that this Government measure, if it is carried through, will have such conditions annexed as the Government may think right. If a supplementary Act of Parliament were required it could easily be obtained.

4346. A man being enrolled already under the Act, by the provisions of which he can quit the service on giving a fortnight's notice, it would require, would it not, that each individual volunteer should re-enrol himself for a longer period of service in order to place himself under the new Act?—In point of form there might be something of that sort necessary.

4347. How would you apply that practically to the corps at present existing, in which some of the members might be willing to re-enrol themselves for a longer period and others might not be willing to enrol for a longer period?—If they were not willing to re-enrol for a longer period, and a longer period were thought desirable, it might be necessary that they should resign.

4348. (*Col. MacMurdo.*) Do you think that you would have a greater hold upon the volunteers on account of the period of time being extended?—I think that Government aid being afforded to the volunteers would give a much greater hold over them; as they would feel bound in honour to discharge their duty still more efficiently and better than they have hitherto done.

(*Col. Crawford.*) And the Government would require more from them.

4349. My question has reference to the extended period of time. I do not clearly understand what greater hold we should have over the volunteers by making the period six weeks or six months?—(*Mr. Sheriff Bell.*) I would like to guard myself by saying that I do not think a very long period of enrolment could be demanded, but certainly I think that it might be materially increased some weeks beyond the present period.

4350. What solid advantage do you think the Government would derive from extending the period?—It would at all events bind the volunteers for a longer period; it would indicate an expectation, it they accepted all these benefits from the Government, that they would be permanent.

4351. But what would it bind the volunteers to do?—To continue as volunteers.

4352. Enrolled?—Yes.

4353. It would not compel a volunteer to go to drill, and I do not see what better hold you would have over a volunteer by extending the time?—An extension of the time would only be in connexion with the grant, and we think that the grant would put such a spirit into the men that it would cause them to attend more regularly at drill and make them much more permanent volunteers.

4354. (*Sir A. Campbell.*) You are aware that at the present time there are no means of compelling an enrolled member to come to drill; how would a longer period of enrolment give commanding officers more power to enforce it?—It would give more power, as it would require a longer notice of resignation.

4355. But a man having received aid from the Government might remain on the roll for a year and yet not come to drill?—Yes.

(*Col. Crawford.*) I think that such a man ought to be turned out altogether.

(*Mr. Sheriff Bell.*) It would be for the consideration of the Government whether the aid, if granted, should be given in advance, or at the end of a year, and whether there should not be certain regulations as to the men who were to be entitled to receive aid with reference to the amount of drill they had gone through.

(*Capt. McGrigor.*) I should wish to mention that there is a considerable drawback under which many of the corps labour, as I believe, not only in Glasgow but in the kingdom generally, and which is pretty much in the ratio of their activity in coming forward, namely, that the Government did not grant a full allowance of rifles at first, and those corps, my own company, for example, were in a manner obliged to purchase their own rifles. The practical result of that was, that we were saddled with a sum of something like 430*l.* for rifles, which, at the present time, may be said to be a dead loss, as the Government now have granted rifles to the full amount of the enrolled strength of corps.

4356. (*Chairman.*) What was done with the old rifles?—We have drilled with them up to a very recent period; but seeing that other companies were being armed with the long Enfield, and all competitions were being carried on with them, it was thought desirable that we should be also armed with them.

4357. (*Sir A. Campbell.*) You are aware that a circular was issued at one time proposing to purchase those rifles?—Yes; they offered to give 3*l.* 2*s.* 6*d.* per rifle, whereas they cost us 5*l.* 15*s.* and 5*l.* 10*s.*

4358. Would many of your men have availed themselves of that offer if it had been carried out?—The rifles belong to the company, and at that time we thought it better to keep them; but the feeling has much changed, in consequence of the universal use of the long Enfield in competitions, and if an offer were renewed it might be accepted; the matter was brought up at one of our meetings lately, and we then thought that we could not afford to part with these rifles under 4*l.* With reference to the self-supporting companies in Glasgow, I think that there are 97 rifle companies in the county, of which about 80 are in Glasgow; and if by self-supporting companies is meant companies the members of which exclusively pay their own expenses, I do not think that there are half a dozen of them.

(*Mr. Sheriff Bell.*) May Mr. Lockhart, our secretary, now hand you the petition of the Lanarkshire officers to which I have before referred?

(*Chairman.*) After the direct evidence we have had that will now be unnecessary.

The witnesses withdrew.

Captain CHARLES WHITWORTH RUSSELL examined.

4359. (*Chairman.*) You are adjutant of an administrative brigade in Devonshire?—Yes.

4360. To what brigade are you attached?—The 2nd brigade of the Devonshire Artillery Volunteers.

4361. We understand that you have some suggestions to offer to the Commission as to the artillery volunteers?—The chief point that I wish to recommend is that the volunteers should have a knowledge of every gun and carriage that they are likely to be called upon, in case of service, to work. The volunteer artillery at present are confined to standing gun drill, I think that is the word in the instruction now; one of the corps in my brigade happens to be placed where the only fort is armed entirely with the present modern gun, the smooth-bore 68-pounder solid shot, and an eight-inch shell gun, both mounted on dwarf traversing platforms, which is a drill in itself, perfectly separate from the standing gun drill, or from the 18-pounder or 24-pounder on travelling carriages. It is of course easy to learn, but there is something in it which volunteer artillerymen, however perfect they might be in the manner of serving ordinary garrison guns, would be useless at for a certain time, and in case of mere shot practice at inspections or for prize firing they would probably hurt themselves from not understanding the use of that gun. At Dartmouth, the place that I speak of now, they practise across the river Dart, firing into a ploughed field, and it is impossible to fire shell at all. I should like, if it could be done, that my men might have permission to learn the drill of these guns, and there is an open range seaward where shell practice might be conducted; we are allowed for instruction a certain number of shells every year, and in the course of a year and a half we have not fired one shell, having no range.

4362. (*Major-Gen. Eyre.*) Are your batteries inland batteries?—No; we are at the estuary of the river and we fire across the river; but if we could use this fort, which is only three-quarters of a mile from the town, we could fire seawards.

4363. (*Major Harcourt.*) Are you not aware that in the south-eastern district the artillery volunteers receive regular instruction in drill at guns on dwarf traversing platforms, guns on travelling carriages, and siege guns?—I was not aware of that. I have applied through the colonel commanding the district, and it has not been in his power yet to give permission for the wear and tear of the materials.

4364. Have you applied to the War Office?—No.

4365. (*Col. MacMurdo.*) You have mentioned a fort three-quarters of a mile from the town of Dartmouth?—Yes; from the centre of the town.

4366. That is a royal artillery fort, is it not?—Yes.

4367. And armed?—Yes.

4368. Is practice ever carried on from that fort?—No, it is a new fort.

4369. Is it intended for practice?—No, the fort has been built since the guns were supplied to the volunteers, and my object is to try to use this fort, as it is the arm they (the corps) will probably be called upon to use in action or time of war, and that permission should be given to the colonel of the western district to permit practice to be carried on with that gun.

4370. Are you aware of any objection to practice being carried on there, on account of the inconvenience to the public?—On the contrary, for I think that it would be better than where it is, and where it is carried on at great inconvenience to the public. I have had to change the range from 1,000 yards to 800, to suit the convenience of the public; I found the corps firing over a floating ferry, and I refused to carry on the practice there as it was not safe.

4371. (*Major-Gen. Eyre.*) Is not this a matter entirely for the local authorities to settle with the War Office?—Yes, but the difficulty I fancy would be the expense between the ammunition for a 68-pounder and a 24-pounder, which is the gun usually given to volunteers in our district.

4372. (*Major Harcourt.*) Are there any other things with which you think the artillery volunteers in your district ought to be supplied?—I think it very important that they should be supplied with all the appliances for repository drill.

4373. (*Chairman.*) Are the volunteer batteries under your control in a perfectly efficient state?—That is rather a difficult question for me to answer, as far as I am concerned I am perfectly well pleased.

4374. (*Col. MacMurdo.*) Do you think that the volunteers would be fit to man the fortifications in the event of a war?—I think so perfectly.

4375. (*Chairman.*) Have you any other suggestion?—Only what has been spoken of before, viz., the recommending triangle gyns and skidding to be supplied for mounting and dismounting guns, of which I spoke to Major Vernon Harcourt.

The witness withdrew.

Major Sir GEORGE DENYS, Bart., examined.

4376. (*Chairman.*) You are the Major, I believe, of the 1st administrative battalion of the North Riding of Yorkshire Rifle Volunteers?—Yes.

4377. Of how many companies does that battalion consist?—There are 12.

4378. What is the present strength of the battalion?—About 750; it varies between 700 and 750.

4379. Of what classes are the corps composed?—They vary very much in the different districts; for instance, in three or four of the corps they are composed almost entirely of working men, of men who are earning probably from 10s. to 20s. a week; in others, such as at Richmond, most of the men are respectable tradesmen, who provide their own accoutrements and clothing, but they vary a good deal, in some one or two corps they are mostly farmers' sons; but on the average of the 750, I do not think there would be more than one half of them who pay for their own clothing.

4380. Did those men upon the first enrolment of the corps provide themselves with clothing?—Not in my corps.

4381. How was that supplied?—By subscriptions.

4382. Was there a subscription to a battalion fund?—There was a general fund in the first instance, and it was divided amongst those corps who stood most in need of it; those who could do without it drew nothing from it, and those who wanted it divided it between them. Since that time there has been no general fund; it was merely to start the thing at first.

4383. Some of the men, I presume, are entirely clothed and equipped from this fund?—Yes, completely; in my own corps, of which I am captain, I think out of 60 men only seven paid for their own clothing.

4384. (*Major-Gen. Eyre.*) Did the other members contribute no part whatever towards their clothing?—No.

4385. (*Chairman.*) Are any subscriptions annually raised to support the corps?—There is a subscription, viz., captain 5l., lieutenant 4l., ensign 3l., and there was, of 5s. per man annually; but there was great difficulty in raising that 5s.; it was then reduced to half-a-crown; but there has been equal difficulty in getting that from a great majority of the men.

4386. Is the clothing at all wearing out?—It is looking very well, considering that it has been in use for three years; it will do very well till next year.

4387. When it requires renewal, how do you suppose it will be paid for?—There is no money to pay for it whatever, and there are 25 of my men, recruits of this year, who have no clothes at all.

4388. Do you think that any assistance is necessary from the Government to enable the corps to go on?—I think that one half of the corps in the battalion to which I belong will come to an end very speedily unless there is material assistance afforded more than has hitherto been given from the Government.

4389. There are, of course, other expenses connected with the corps beyond the clothing?—Yes.

4390. Have you a rifle range for each corps?—Yes.

4391. Are the men well drilled in the use of the rifle?—The men are, upon the whole, tolerably well drilled.

4392. Do the arms remain in the possession of the men, or are they lodged in an armoury?—My own arms are in the armoury; they are only allowed upon particular occasions, for the convenience of the men, to take them home, and they bring them back to the armoury at the next parade.

4393. Who takes care of them in the armoury?—A serjeant.

4394. Is he paid for out of the funds of the corps?—No, he takes charge of the armoury; I have a regular armourer serjeant who belongs to the militia, who comes once in six weeks to examine and clean the arms, and for which he is paid the Government price of 2d. or 3d. for each rifle each time that he comes.

4395. Have you an adjutant?—Yes.

4396. Does he receive any extra pay?—None whatever.

4397. Can you say the same as to the drill instructors?—As to the drill instructors, it is impossible to say what they have; they are generally overpaid; I know one instance of an instructor getting 3s. 6d. a day, others get watches, &c., in addition to their pay.

4398. You are speaking now of the serjeants in the permanent militia staff?—Yes; who go out as drill instructors for six weeks or two months at a time.

4399. Do the subaltern officers know their duty in these corps?—I think the great defect in the volunteer force is the inefficiency of the officers generally, and the non-commissioned officers; neither the officers nor the non-commissioned officers, as a general rule, know their duty. I do not mean to say that there are not exceptions, but as a general rule they are inefficient; take them away from the drill instructors, and they are done for directly.

4400. Can you suggest any mode by which they could be made more efficient?—That is a very difficult point, for it very often happens that the most inefficient officers are those who pay the greatest amount of money towards keeping up the thing, and if you were to enforce discipline or to enforce an examination, and said that no officer should be appointed to a corps, either as a subaltern or as a commander, unless he passed a certain examination, it would have the effect, I have no doubt, of driving out a vast number, and therefore you would lose men who are contributing more than any others to support the movement.

4401. (*Major-Gen. Eyre.*) Supposing the thing were possible, and that such Government aid was given as would make the volunteers independent of donations, or anything of that kind, would you not then recommend that the officers should be subjected to some test?—I should recommend this, that if the Government decide upon recommending to the House of Commons to make a grant of money, and the House of Commons agreed to give the money, then having paid the piper, the Government ought to choose the tune; that is to say, if you give money you ought to stipulate strictly, looking at the mass of evidence that you have been collecting, as to how that money ought to be expended, otherwise I think the money might be squandered, and the country put to very great expense, and have very little to show for it. The great want, next to the want of discipline, is the want of power in your officers to carry out that discipline; in my battalion there is Lord Cathcart, the lieutenant-colonel, myself, his major, and 12 corps, and those 12 corps are 12 *imperia in imperio*, 12 separate War Offices with one Horse Guards, with no power whatever; each captain of a corps is totally and entirely independent of the major and the colonel. If you read the orders of the lieutenant-colonels commanding you will find they are to this effect: If it is agreeable to the captains to meet on such and such a day he will make things pleasant, and if there is plenty provided to eat and to drink, you can get a certain number of men to come; but instead of having 700 men at his battalion drills, he has perhaps only 200.

4402. (*Major-Gen. Eyre.*) Does a picnic count for one of the 24 parades?—No; that is a battalion affair altogether. And the fact is that no commanding officer can enforce a battalion parade, because of the expense incurred in bringing the men together. It is all very well in small counties, but in Yorkshire, take, for example, these 12 corps, some of them are perhaps 70 and 80 miles asunder, and how can you bring them together for battalion parade without incurring great expense. Who is to pay for that battalion parade? The commander wishes to have a battalion drill, and his captains may be equally anxious to have a battalion drill, but who is to pay for bringing the men to the place, if they are put to an expense of 4s. for each man. That must come out of the funds of the corps. Then there is the eating and drinking, which probably comes

TO INQUIRE INTO THE CONDITION OF THE VOLUNTEER FORCE IN GREAT BRITAIN. 189

out of the lieutenant-colonel's pocket, and then there are a certain number of men to be paid for their day's work as well, for if they are labouring men they cannot afford to lose four or five days' work in a year, and unless there is a fund out of which to pay for the battalion expenses, there is no other way to do it except out of the pockets of the officers.

4403. (*Lord Overstone.*) In case of the volunteer force being suddenly called out, is it your opinion that the volunteers in Yorkshire would be able to render effectual aid in assisting and supplementing the regular army?—That would depend very much upon what you want the volunteers to do. If you were to ask me, supposing that you wanted the volunteers for field service, whether I would rather have 10,000 efficient regulars, well officered, with the non-commissioned officers and men well drilled and ready for immediate action in the field, or 100,000 volunteers, I would say give me 10,000 regulars, but if they were wanted for garrison duty, I should say they are perfectly fit for that. In three months' time, if embodied, I have not the slightest doubt that they could be made equal to the militia.

4404. (*Sir A. Campbell.*) Do you mean the embodied or disembodied militia?—The disembodied militia. The great strength of the militia lies in their officers, and in their regular staff. They have a regular staff of old, experienced, picked men ;– of pensioned men from the regular army, and that is a nucleus to begin upon. Take a man who has been in the service, and give him 30 good non-commissioned officers, and he can make a regiment in a short time. Our non-commissioned officers are not to be compared with the staff of a disembodied militia regiment, who are always kept together, where they are under the eye of the commanding officer and the adjutant. But it is a great advantage to the country no doubt to have 150,000 or 200,000 men who are to a certain extent drilled, and who have a certain knowledge of military matters, who can handle the rifle, and who, if they were embodied, would be made equal to a militia regiment.

4405. (*Lord Overstone.*) Is it your opinion that the existence of the present volunteer force does tend to strengthen the power of the country for defending itself against invasion?—Most certainly ; but I think we have flattered the force a great deal too much. The officers have been too much flattered ; the officers and non-commissioned officers and men go away from these great reviews and battalion parades laying the flattering unction to their souls that they are equal to the regulars.

4406. You think that the volunteer force properly estimated and accurately weighed might render material assistance in preserving the security of the country, but great danger may arise from over estimating the value of that force and misunderstanding its real efficiency?—Yes ; I should like to see the volunteer force more Horse-guarded, that is, more put under the control of the authorities, because I think that having 12 *imperia in imperio* in each battalion having a large force of armed men in the country, subject to no control whatever except that of their own officers, they might become very dangerous ; but the more they are assimilated to the regular army or to the militia, and the more the officers commanding corps are made subservient to their field officers, and the field officers to the War Office, the more use they will eventually be to the country.

4407. Does that amount to anything more than this, that the more nearly the volunteer force assumes the character of the regular army, the more efficient it will be?—No.

4408. (*Major-Gen. Eyre.*) You spoke of their handling the rifle ; do you find that that very important branch of the instruction to be given to volunteers is in a satisfactory state?—Yes ; I think that the men generally go through the manual and platoon exercise very well.

4409. I refer more particularly to actual target practice?—Of course the efficiency of a corps in practice depends very much upon the amount of money that each individual private can spend in the purchase of ammunition ; a man may be a very good shot, but a very slovenly man in the ranks, as far as his rifle is concerned.

4410. (*Col. MacMurdo.*) The corps in your Riding all consist of separate companies, do they not?—Yes.

4411. You have not, I believe, had many opportunities of seeing them together?—There have been several attempts made at battalion drills, but Lord Cathcart has never succeeded in mustering more than 300 men at one time.

4412. Have you ever had an opportunity of observing closely the drill of the consolidated battalions of volunteers?—Except in London I have not.

4413. Does the opinion which you expressed broadly a short time back as to the efficiency of the volunteer force refer to those consolidated battalions?—Certainly not.

4414. You rather referred to the state of the corps under your own particular observation?—Yes ; the administrative battalions in general. I think it would be very unfair to compare the administrative battalions with the metropolitan battalions, for instance ; they are totally different. I am quite astonished to see the efficient state at which the metropolitan battalions have arrived.

4415. (*Major Harcourt.*) With reference to the powers of the colonels commanding administrative battalions, have you any suggestions to make?—I think that the thin end of the wedge might be introduced, in the event of the Government giving an allowance of money to the force, for a general keeping of accounts in every individual corps in the same way that they are kept in the regular army, and making the captains of corps responsible to the colonel ; in fact, that the colonel himself should be held responsible to the War Office for inspecting the books of every individual corps, and seeing that the money granted by the Government was expended in the way that Government intended, and in no other way ; and I think that the inspecting officers should make a particular point of looking into the books to see the way in which the money has been expended, when a corps is inspected, just the same as a general officer does when inspecting a regiment. Then the captains would feel that they could not spend the money for bands or other follies, which they are very much given to do.

4416. Would you propose that the colonel of an administrative battalion should have any control over the drills of the individual corps composing that administrative battalion?—Yes, certainly, and enforce a uniform drill.

4417. (*Sir A. Campbell.*) You have stated that you consider the system of drill instructors does not work satisfactorily in administrative battalions?—Yes.

4418. Do you think that if the drill instructors were under the control of the officer commanding the district, in the same manner as master gunners of the artillery volunteers are under the control of the artillery officer, it would be an improvement?—In the first place the majority of the drill instructors are primarily under the control of the officer commanding the militia battalion to which they belong, and if they were subject also to the officer commanding the district, they would be in the position of having two commanding officers, and I do not see what you would gain by it.

4419. (*Sir G. A. Wetherall.*) You get inefficient instructors to the volunteer corps, and you say that they are spoiled?—I did not say they were inefficient, but they are spoiled by being overpaid.

4420. In the artillery all the instructors of the volunteers belonging to the coast brigade of artillery and the whole of that coast brigade are under the immediate orders of the general officer commanding the district. If any man happens to instruct an outlying company of artillery, and misconducts himself in any way, the officer commanding that district has power

Major Sir G. Denys, Bart.

8 July 1862.

B b 3

Major Sir G. Denys, Bart.
8 July 1862.

to order him to headquarters. Would it not be advantageous if the same power were given to the officer commanding the district over these drill instructors, who are many of them pensioners from the line?—Yes, there is no doubt that anything that would facilitate the removal of a man charged with misconduct would be a desirable thing. The more immediately you can place him under the authority of the general commanding the district the better; but I apprehend that no officer commanding a corps, if he is in the slightest degree fit for his situation, would keep a man for one hour who had been guilty of misconduct. I think that, generally speaking, drill instructors conduct themselves well as a body, but I should say, knowing what soldiers are, that they have too much idle time on their hands. Of course there are only certain hours in the 24 when they can be employed; that is to say, perhaps for two hours out of the 24 they are employed, and for the rest of their time they are not employed, and they must get into idle habits. Generally speaking I believe they behave themselves well, but what I complain of is, that the officers have spoiled their own market by bidding one against the other, and by paying these men so extravagantly they have become above their work.

The witness withdrew.

Adjourned till Tuesday next at half-past 12 o'clock.

Tuesday, 15th July 1862.

PRESENT:

Viscount EVERSLEY.
Earl of DUCIE.
Viscount HARDINGE.
Lord ELCHO.
Lord OVERSTONE.
Lieutenant-Colonel BARTTELOT.

Lieutenant-Colonel Sir A. CAMPBELL.
Lieutenant-General Sir G. A. WETHERALL.
Major-General EYRE.
Colonel MACMURDO.
Major HARCOURT.

VISCOUNT EVERSLEY IN THE CHAIR.

Colonel W. M. S. MACMURDO, C.B., examined.

Col. W. M. S. Macmurdo, C.B.
15 July 1862.

4421. (*Chairman.*) We shall be obliged to you to give us an explanation of some of the evidence that we have heard. One of the recommendations, I think by Lord Radstock, was that there should be certain brigade districts, and that no person should be allowed to recruit out of his own district. That would appear to be almost impossible, and we should like to know what your opinion is upon that point?—I think with regard to country districts, that the recruiting would naturally assume the form of local corps; but in such a place as London, I consider that that is impossible. London has changed very much from the time when the old volunteers were formed according to districts; then people lived within their districts; but now, in consequence of railways, London has become extended far beyond its former limits, and the people who properly belong to certain districts and wards in London, actually live now out of town after their business hours, and that has been the cause perhaps of a certain large class of corps having been formed in London, without reference to localities, and of the system of district local corps having fallen generally into disuse.

4422. With regard to the colonels of administrative battalions, do you think it would be possible to put the drill instructors of the corps included in an administrative battalion under the orders of the lieutenant-colonel commanding the battalion in the same way that the adjutant is, so as to form the staff of the battalion?—It might be possible to do so, and I dare say it would work well, but it must be done I think by a special Act of Parliament, for the drill instructors are enrolled volunteers, and we are therefore obliged, in distributing the drill instructors to the different corps constituting an administrative battalion, to cause them to be enrolled in the several corps to which they are attached as volunteers. Hence, if you take them from those corps and form them as part of the staff of an administrative battalion, they are no longer volunteers, but they are a part of the staff in the same way that the adjutants are. I think that the system would work well, supposing that you mean that their non-commissioned officers should belong to the staff of a battalion, and be distributed to the corps at the discretion of the commanding officer of the battalion.

4423. Are the drill instructors at present subject to the articles of war or not?—Yes, they receive pay, and they are consequently serving under the Mutiny Act, but a special provision would be necessary with regard to those men if they were formed into a staff, because they would be serving under conditions different from the present Act.

4424. What is the exact position of the lieutenant-colonel commanding an administrative battalion; when he goes to inspect a corps included in his battalion, has he any power or authority as he would have if he were present at a battalion parade?—He has the power of an inspecting officer, that is all; and if any irregularity takes place when the men are under arms on parade, or at any time indeed, he has the power then of calling upon the officer commanding the corps in which that irregularity takes place, to carry out the provisions of the law; he requires him to do so, and if he does not do it, of course the matter is then referred through the lord lieutenant to the Secretary of State for War.

4425. If the officer commanding the corps does not do what the lieutenant-colonel thinks right, he reports the matter to the lord lieutenant, who forwards the report to the Secretary of State for War?—Yes; in establishing the system of administrative battalions it was apparent that the powers which, by the Act of Parliament, belong properly to the officer commanding a corps could not be given to the officer commanding a battalion composed of corps according to the administrative organization, but the Secretary of State for War put it in the power of the officers commanding a battalion to call upon any officer commanding a corps to carry out the provisions of the Act in punishing any offender.

4426. (*Lord Overstone.*) Do you think that the authority of the colonel commanding an administrative battalion can be advantageously increased or extended?—No; the administrative battalion is simply a provisional arrangement, and might not last; for instance, if war threatened, the probability is that the corps of which it was composed would increase themselves so as to become separate battalions, consequently there would be no necessity then for the administrative organization to be continued; and I see no necessity, therefore, to increase the power of the colonel commanding an administrative battalion.

4427. (*Major-Gen. Eyre.*) Not so long as the present organization of the administrative battalions exists, as that could always be altered if the corps swelled so much as to become separate battalions?—I do not see any necessity for it.

4428. (*Sir A. Campbell.*) In case the commander of an administrative battalion is not satisfied with the mode in which the muster rolls are kept, or the returns are made, what course must he adopt?—He has at all times access to the muster rolls of the corps composing his battalion, and if he finds that any one of those muster rolls is improperly kept, it is his duty to point out the irregularity to the officer commanding, and if he neglects his duty he would naturally report him through the lord lieutenant to the Secretary of State.

4429. Then it would require, first, an inspection to find out the fault; secondly, an examination to see whether it had been corrected; then a report; and then a court of inquiry?—A court of inquiry need not be the consequence, but you must consider the situation of the several corps composing a battalion; they are geographically scattered, and it would require a personal inspection in the first instance, under any circumstances, by the officer commanding the battalion.

4430. (*Viscount Hardinge.*) Is it your opinion that the muster rolls of the different corps are, generally speaking, correctly kept, or that volunteers are returned as effectives who really are not so within the meaning of the Act?—I have no reason to suppose that the muster rolls are irregularly kept, or that inaccurate returns are made of men as nominally effective who are non-effective; the returns are all made to the lord lieutenant, and abstracts of those returns are sent to this office.

4431. What I mean is this, that in one of the circulars issued by the War Office, an order was issued that no volunteer should be returned as effective who was not present at the annual inspection?—Yes.

4432. Do you believe that, generally speaking, volunteers are returned as effective who have not attended at the annual inspection, and where no excuse has been given for their absence?—I have no reason to believe that that circular is not attended to; it is the duty of the commanding officers of corps who certify to the correctness of their returns.

4433. (*Chairman.*) Does not the Secretary of State for War require a nominal return to be made from every corps?—No.

4434. (*Sir A. Campbell.*) Have the assistant-inspectors the power of examining the books and muster rolls?—Yes.

4435. Do they exercise that power?—Yes.

4436. (*Chairman.*) The assistant-inspectors also inspect the arms, do they not?—Yes; they inspect the arms of the corps, and a return is given in not only at every annual inspection, but every quarter, of those arms that are in the possession of the members, and of those that are deposited in the armouries.

4437. (*Lieut.-Col. Barttelot.*) I think you stated that in the case of an invasion the rural corps would so increase in numbers that they would most likely become consolidated battalions, and therefore that the officers now commanding them would be done away with?—I think I said that in some districts they might increase, and that consequently we considered the administrative organization a provisional one.

4438. But do you not think, from your knowledge of the administrative organization, that most of the corps are now nearly as strong as they will be?—No, I think not; for example, at East Grinstead, according to the census, the effective volunteers are calculated at 1 in 10 of adult males, and there would be 330 in a time of war in East Grinstead alone.

4439. Supposing you do away with the officer commanding an administrative battalion in a time of war, do not you think that he would be a man the most likely to know his duty?—Certainly; unquestionably he would be the first person employed.

4440. (*Lord Elcho.*) You did not say, I think, that you would do away with him?—No.

4441. (*Lord Overstone.*) Did you not state, in reply to my question as to the present sufficiency of the authority of the colonel commanding an administrative battalion, that it was your opinion that his present authority ought not to be extended or strengthened in consideration of the probability that the authority of the officers commanding the several companies in that battalion would, in case of war, become more important than it is now?—Yes.

4442. Upon the supposition that the respective companies now forming an administrative battalion became so augmented in numbers that the authority of the officer commanding each company became necessarily more important, and so important as to make it inexpedient now to augment the authority of the colonel commanding the full battalion, what would be the condition of the authority of the colonel commanding the administrative battalion?—The colonel commanding the administrative battalion, if he were an efficient officer, would be the very first person to be employed to command one of those corps so augmented to the establishment of a battalion.

4443. If that be so, how does the objection to extending his authority now apply?—Because he would then become, according to law, the commanding officer of one large corps of the establishment of a battalion, and not the commanding officer of an administrative battalion composed of several small corps.

4444. Will you have the goodness to explain the difference between the position of the commanding officer of a corps, and that of the commanding officer of an administrative battalion?—According to the Act of Parliament, a volunteer corps is to have a commanding officer, and that commanding officer is given by that Act of Parliament certain powers, and no limitation is put to the establishment of the corps; therefore, the corps may consist of one subdivision of 30 men, or one large battalion of 10, 12, or 20 companies, but the officer commanding a subdivision of 30 men has the same power given to him by the Act of Parliament as commanding officer of a corps as the officer who commands the 20 companies, being commanding officer of a corps also. When the volunteers were first raised a few years ago, many of the corps in the country districts consisted of separate companies, and it was deemed expedient to bring those corps into what we term administrative battalions; but the Secretary of State for War was not able to give officers who were to command those administrative battalions the powers which were given by the Act to the officers commanding corps: the only power that he could give to them was that of commanding the corps upon parade, and attending to their military instruction: that was all. He could not confer upon the officers commanding administrative battalions the powers given by the Act to the officers commanding the corps of which his battalion was composed.

4445. Then I understand it to be your opinion that the authority now vested in the colonel commanding an administrative battalion is, in your judgment, sufficient for its present purpose, and that the objection raised to it would not constitute any formidable impediment to extending the authority of that officer in case the volunteers in his county became far more numerous?—I think not.

4446. (*Major-Gen. Eyre.*) You say that the Secretary of State cannot give more power than he has already given to the commanding officers of administrative battalions?—Yes.

4447. But he can give to you or to me, or to any officer he chooses, power to go and inspect these corps, and to give any orders that he may think it necessary to give, and, in fact, to interfere. If so, why can he not in the same way give to the officers commanding administrative battalions a similar power?—The inspecting officer is a functionary provided for by Act of Parliament, and every volunteer corps that is raised

Col. W. M. S. Macmurdo, C.B.

15 July 1862.

Col. W. M. S. Macmurdo, C.B.

15 July 1862.

under that Act is required to be inspected by a field officer once a year; therefore a field officer goes down and appears upon parade with certain powers given to him by the Act of Parliament and not by the Secretary for War; but I question very much whether I, as an inspecting officer, should have power to interfere, except in cases where I saw a positive dereliction of duty and a departure from the regulations of the service.

4448. (*Sir A. Campbell.*) The inspecting officer has no power off parade, has he?—Inspecting officers have a power deputed to them by the Act of Parliament in the name of the Secretary of State within the scope of the regulations to require officers to comply with those regulations.

4449. (*Viscount Hardinge.*) You have stated that in the event of a war the commander of a corps or a company would become much more important than at the present time. Will you be good enough to explain what you mean by that?—I said it would be so when they were augmented to battalions.

4450. Assuming that three or four companies were expanded in the event of a war, and became a battalion, say of 1,000 men, would the senior captain necessarily command that battalion, and is it in that way that you mean that the command of a corps would be more important in a time of war than in a time of peace?—It would depend upon the recommendation of the lord lieutenant, whether a captain should be promoted to the rank of a lieutenant-colonel in command of a battalion.

4451. Then how would the command of a corps become more important in a time of war, than in a time of peace if the commandant of a corps was to be superseded and have another officer placed over him?—Because, if he was competent, he might command ten companies instead of one.

4452. All those companies that now form administrative battalions might be increased to battalions?—Yes.

4453. The same authority which embodied the company I suppose would increase it and embody it into a corps?—A company may be a corps.

4454. A captain might be made a lieutenant-colonel?—Yes, if considered competent.

4455. But still the officer commanding an administrative battalion might be appointed?—Yes.

4456. Would those companies, if increased into battalions, submit to be commanded by the person appointed by the War Department, in preference to the person who had enlisted them, and whose tenants they might be, and to whom alone, as it has been put, they owe allegiance?—The War Department appoints no one, Her Majesty approves on the lord-lieutenant's recommendation.

4457. (*Lord Overstone.*) Is not the effect of your view this, that the officer now commanding an administrative battalion would not necessarily, in the case of war, be the officer commanding that regiment?—Yes; not without the recommendation of the lord lieutenant and a special appointment.

4458. A new recommendation and a special appointment must necessarily precede the transition of the authority of the colonel now commanding an administrative battalion into the colonel commanding the corps under special circumstances?—Yes.

4459. (*Sir A. Campbell.*) Am I to understand you to say that the companies which have been united in administrative battalions are not intended, in time of actual service, to act as integral parts of a larger corps, but that each of them is to be a nucleus in itself of a corps with augmented numbers into which it will grow?—Such would be the natural result of war, because by referring to the state of things in the time of the old volunteers you will find that one in ten of the population capable of bearing arms took up arms, and there is no reason to suppose that the spirit is less active at the present day; and, consequently, there would be the same proportion, if not a greater proportion, of the population who would take up arms in the event of a war, and arrangements would be made by causing all the small corps now brought into administrative battalions to be so many *points d'appui* for the increase of the volunteer force generally, and they would form the nuclei of larger battalions.

4460. On the supposition that the same increase of numbers would take place under the same circumstances in places where consolidated corps of considerable strength existed, how would the new recruits be organized?—I should imagine by forming fresh corps and transferring part of the staff of the already consolidated battalions to form the nucleus of fresh corps.

4461. (*Lord Elcho.*) They might be formed, might they not, into second battalions?—Yes.

4462. (*Sir A. Campbell.*) Then in case of a war you would have three classes of corps, one composed entirely of the old, and for volunteers well drilled men; another in the country composed of a nucleus of well drilled men with an *entourage* of raw recruits; and a third composed of new men in the towns who would be entirely raw recruits?—Yes, that would be the natural process of expanding the force into a war establishment; the present force numbers about one-third of what it would be in a time of war, and the natural mode of increasing that force with reference to efficiency would be by increasing all the smaller corps now constituting administrative battalions into larger battalions, and also in raising new corps in districts where they do not now exist.

4463. From what you have seen of the small corps, is it your opinion that they are now sufficiently well drilled not only to go upon active service, but to form a basis for each of these full corps of three or four times their number, of which all the new men should be raw recruits?—I have seen very many of the small companies so far advanced in efficiency as to be very useful nuclei for their expansion, but up to the present moment they are not generally in that state of efficiency, although they are progressing very rapidly.

4464. (*Chairman.*) If the commanding officer of an administrative battalion was an efficient officer, the lord lieutenant would take care, would he not, to place him in command of one of these larger corps?—He would be only too glad to avail himself of his services, and the adjutant would be the adjutant of the battalion.

4465. If it were thought necessary, so long as an administrative battalion continues in that state, to give him more authority, it must be done by Act of Parliament?—I do not see much necessity for disturbing the Act.

4466. Several of the witnesses who have been examined have complained that the adjutants of volunteers are not so well paid as the adjutants of militia regiments, are you aware of what the duties of an adjutant of militia are?—Yes; the duties of an adjutant of militia are those of paymaster as well as of the adjutant, and he is reponsible for many duties which are not applicable to the adjutants of volunteers, hence the pay is larger.

4467. The pay is larger on account of those increased responsibilities?—Yes; I assume that to be the reason.

4468. Would there be any difficulty, if it were thought desirable to assist the volunteers by a money grant, in employing the adjutants of volunteers in that manner?—None. I may say that I think, under any circumstances, the travelling allowances made to the adjutants ought to be increased.

4469. (*Lord Overstone.*) Supposing you had now a regiment of 1,000 volunteers in a high state of discipline in every respect, efficient in every sense of the word, and war was to break out, and the effect was that you mingled with those 1,000 efficient men another 1,000 undrilled raw recruits, do you think that the efficiency of that corps would be increased by that augmentation in numbers, or otherwise?—If I commanded a corps of 1,000 well trained volunteers, and another 1,000 was about to be added to them, I would do it by forming a second battalion; by drawing from the several companies of the well-formed battalions, a staff of officers, non-commissioned officers, and drilled men, to form a nucleus for the instruction and leading of the new battalion; I would then let my efficient battalion take the field with reduced numbers, leaving the others at home to be formed, and to follow afterwards.

4470. Do you think that the general result of that operation would be a greater increase of strength from an augmentation of numbers than there would be loss of strength by diminishing the numbers of the efficient battalion?—Unquestionably, because I believe, that the intelligence of the volunteers is so great, and their aptitude in acquiring a knowledge of their duties so quick, that they would become efficient troops in a very short time.

4471. (*Major-Gen. Eyre.*) That is if they had officers?—Yes, trained officers, non-commissioned officers and men.

4472. (*Viscount Hardinge.*) How would you proceed in the rural districts, would you make a small company of 60 men a nucleus for a corps which might be expanded to 500 or 600 men?—Yes.

4473. Do you think that the rural companies are fit to form such nuclei?—I have already said that some of them are fit, but I have seen others that are not fit; but, as I said before, they are progressing satisfactorily in acquiring a knowledge of their duties, which will fit them for such a purpose.

4474. What interval of time would you allow for the purpose of attaching so many raw recruits to such a company, and to render it fit for service in the field or in garrison?—I should say 20 days.

4475. (*Earl of Ducie.*) That is if they worked all day long?—Yes.

4476. (*Lord Elcho.*) And assuming that the officers and non-commissioned officers understand their duty?—Yes.

4477. (*Sir A. Campbell.*) Do you anticipate, if war were apprehended, that the increase in the numbers in the country districts would be something like five or six times their present numbers, but that in towns the increase would only be about twice as many?—I have made no calculation to that effect. I calculate upon one in ten in the population, and the increase would be according to the density of the population.

4478. (*Lord Elcho.*) Have you thought of any other way in which the force could be increased?—No.

4479. (*Viscount Hardinge.*) Do you see any grave objections to giving the colonels of administrative battalions more authority even as a temporary organization?—No; there are no objections to it.

4480. It would merely require another Act of Parliament?—Yes; but they can work very well according to the present system.

4481. (*Lord Elcho.*) To what extent would you increase those powers?—I do not recommend it.

4482. (*Chairman.*) Several complaints have been made by witnesses examined before the Commission as to the inefficiency of some of the serjeant instructors coming from militia regiments, and one witness suggested that there should be a drilling school established similar to the schools for rifle instruction at Hythe?—Yes.

4483. Do you think that there is any force in that?—Yes; I think there is something. A modification of such a plan was suggested by yourself, that these drill instructors of administrative battalions should be collected at headquarters, and be at the disposal of the officer commanding the battalion. Something might be done, I think; they would be immediately under the eye of the adjutant, whose duty it would be to drill them during the day.

4484. A man so drilled and always kept up to the mark would be more qualified to drill recruits than men who were drawn from militia regiments?—Yes; but the system at present pursued of drawing the drill instructors from militia regiments is only a provisional one; the paucity of drill instructors to be obtained from the line is very great indeed, on account of the number of drill instructors that has been sent out to the volunteers in Canada.

4485. (*Major-Gen. Eyre.*) Your intention, I believe, is to bring forward privates, which plan will a good deal supply the present deficiency?—Yes.

4486. (*Lieut.-Col. Borttelot.*) Supposing the plan just referred to were adopted, and that drill instructors were assembled at the headquarters of administrative battalions, you would have to increase their pay, would you not?—No, I do not think it would be advisable to increase their pay; you may increase their allowances.

4487. I refer more particularly to their lodging-money?—That might be increased.

4488. If they were placed under the command of the commanding officers, the officers commanding the different corps would not be so likely to find them lodgings as if they chose the drill instructors themselves?—No.

4489. (*Viscount Hardinge.*) Where a company is 20 or 30 miles distant from headquarters, the drill instructors under such an arrangement would have to attend that outlying company whenever it was drilled?—Yes, and I think there would be an advantage derived from changing the drill instructors occasionally. I am of opinion that that would prevent the petting and spoiling of them, which we find by the evidence so often takes place.

4490. But you must make some allowance to the drill instructors for travelling expenses?—Yes.

4491. (*Chairman.*) We have heard from some of the artillery volunteer officers, that they make their returns to the artillery officers commanding the districts; will you be good enough to explain why it is that there is that difference between the artillery volunteers and the rifle volunteers?—There are at present 347 batteries of artillery scattered all round the coasts of Great Britain, and the Secretary of State for War has found it convenient to place these batteries under the inspection of the officers commanding royal artillery in the districts, because we could not furnish a sufficient number of assistant inspectors of artillery to do the duty, the batteries being so much scattered; but the reason for making use so largely of the royal artillery officers is on account of the stores and guns, which are furnished to the volunteer batteries, remaining still in the charge of the royal artillery. The superintendence of the royal artillery officers is limited only to the disposal of those stores, and to the practice with the guns; the returns of the practice only are furnished by the officer commanding the volunteer artillery corps to the officer commanding the royal artillery in the district; but they eventually reach this office.

4492. Does the War Office appoint officers to inspect the artillery volunteer corps?—The Secretary of State requests the commander-in-chief to appoint royal artillery officers to inspect certain corps in certain districts, but they have only to inspect the gun practice in those corps, and not in any other respect; in all other respects they are under this office as other volunteer corps are.

4493. (*Viscount Hardinge.*) The returns go to the Horse Guards, do they not?—The returns of the artillery practice are transmitted through the Horse Guards to this office.

4494. And the returns also of the number of days' drill?—No, that is essentially a volunteer return, but every return of artillery practice naturally goes through the officers commanding the artillery in the districts, because the stores are in their charge.

4495. (*Lord Elcho.*) Many of the guns are in Government batteries, are they not?—Yes, they are arms which require special inspection by artillery officers.

4496. (*Major Harcourt.*) Were not great expenses incurred by persons travelling about the country to inspect them?—Yes.

Col. W. M. S. Macmurdo, C.B.

15 July 1862.

Col. W. M. S. Macmurdo, C.B.

15 July 1862.

4497. And was it not found less expensive to employ district inspectors?—Yes.

4498. With regard to the returns sent in by the artillery volunteers, I believe the payments, or rather the repayments, are all sent to the officer commanding the district?—Yes.

4499. All the accounts are passed through him?—Yes.

4500. An officer of the artillery volunteers is not permitted to send his accounts to this office, but he is told to send them to the officer commanding in the district?—Yes, because the stores are in his charge.

4501. (*Viscount Hardinge.*) Is it not the fact that the assistant inspectors have so much work to do that they cannot inspect all the companies in their districts?—Yes.

4502. Do you see your way to remedying that state of things?—I believe from the corps being formed into administrative battalions so much more now than at first that the inspections will be more easily carried out from year to year than they have been.

4503. Do you see any reason why field officers of the line should not be occasionally employed in inspecting volunteer corps as they do the militia and yeomanry?—No; I see no reason against it; and we have employed them.

4504. To whom do they report under those circumstances?—They report direct to this office.

4505. And also as to the militia?—Yes.

4506. (*Sir A. Campbell.*) I presume that the duty of a field officer of the regular army so employed would be the same as that of an assistant inspector?—Yes; he is given a form of confidential report, which he is required to fill in.

4507. (*Major Harcourt.*) An adjutant of Devonshire artillery stated to the Commission that his men were not allowed to practise from 68-pounder guns, although they were very near at hand. I understood you to say that an order was issued from this office that the artillery officers commanding in the districts should restrict the artillery volunteers as much as possible to guns of the lowest calibre, on account of their burning only a small quantity of powder?—Yes; the ammunition is very expensive for the larger guns.

4508. I suppose that the view taken by the War Office is that the artillery volunteers should be made practically acquainted with the calibres which they would be likely to work in a time of war?—The Secretary of State would be prepared to consider any recommendation coming from the Royal Artillery officers commanding districts as to the calibre of guns with which the volunteers should practice.

4509. And against that, of course, would not be set the expense of a few pounds of powder?—I do not know.

4510. Practically that question is very much left to the discretion of the officers commanding the artillery districts?—Yes.

4511. When you asked Colonel Harman, one of the inspectors, the other day, whether he could speak to the artillery volunteers as far as their arms and accoutrements were concerned on parade, you did not mean, I suppose, that he had anything officially to do with the artillery volunteers as inspector?—His first duty is to inspect the rifle volunteers, but the artillery volunteers ought, if he has time, to come under his inspection also; that is, with regard to their general state, not as to their artillery practice, but the state of the muster rolls, the establishment and the state of efficiency of the corps in company drill, and the arms.

4512. Is not that now done by an assistant-inspector of royal artillery?—Generally in their observations they make a note of the appearance of the corps.

4513. (*Viscount Hardinge.*) The volunteers generally are, in your opinion, very much improved since last year?—Yes; very much improved indeed since last year.

4514. So that a report made of the inspection of last year would hardly apply to the present state of the volunteer force?—No; I should hope that they have reported this year an increase in efficiency.

4515. Therefore the only inspector of artillery who has given evidence before this Commission can hardly have given a fair account of the present efficiency of the artillery volunteers from his own personal knowledge, not having been employed since last year?—That is quite possible.

4516. (*Lord Elcho.*) With regard to brigades, you said that you did not think it was desirable that the recruiting should be limited to certain districts, because many persons, if their business was in one part of London, live out in the country; irrespectively of limiting men to a certain district, do you think it advisable that London should be mapped out into brigade districts, I mean for command?—I do not think it would be advantageous.

4517. You have been asked some questions as to effectives; what in your opinion, according to the Act of Parliament, is the proper definition of the word "effective;" how can a commanding officer return his "effectives"?—There was a question put to the law officers lately, as to how many drills would constitute an effective in point of law; and the answer was 18, and that the man should also have attended the annual inspection of the corps.

4518. So that supposing the annual inspection was the 19th drill, those men who had attended 18 drills, but who were not present at that inspection, could not be returned as effectives?—No.

4519. Then it must be 18 drills plus the inspection?—Yes.

4520. What description of drills should they be?—That depends upon the Secretary of State's regulations. The distribution of drills is laid down in the 60th article of the regulations in these terms:—
"The authorized drills, in virtue of which the
"enrolled member is reckoned as effective, need not
"take place on consecutive days. One half of them
"must be musters of the whole corps; the remain-
"ing half may consist, in the case of a corps of more
"than one troop or company, of troop or company
"drill, or instruction in musketry, ordered by the
"commanding officer, under the command of one of
"the company officers; and in the case of the
"scattered rural corps, the squad drills ordered by
"the commanding officer, and attended by the officers
"of the corps, provided that authority for such an
"arrangement has been previously obtained from the
"lord lieutenant of the county, who should be
"guided in granting it by the local difficulties
"experienced by the volunteers in assembling for
"drill, and in the case of the artillery corps of any
"gun drill ordered by the commanding officer, and
"attended by the officers of the corps. In all these
"cases, the volunteers must be properly armed and
"accoutred."

4521. So that with reference to the consolidated battalions in towns, according to the law, 18 drills are required; one half of them may be simply turning out to drill, no matter in what form, provided the men are under the officers, so that one-half or nine of those drills may consist in the men coming out and beginning their setting up, the squad drill counting as one; but the other nine drills must be drills of the whole corps?—Yes.

4522. From your knowledge of the degree of efficiency which the volunteers have attained, and from your knowledge of the aptitude which they show in acquiring a knowledge of their drill, do you think that the present statutory number of drills, divided as we have just supposed, could be diminished without prejudice to the force, in the cases of men who have been trained, and have once been passed as efficient?—Yes; I think that nine drills would in such cases be sufficient for a man who had already passed under the adjutant's observation, three of them to be elementary or company drills, and six of them battalion drills.

4523. Do you think that this would be a reasonable proposal, that there should be a certain number of setting up drills, 3, 4, 5, or 6, every year, through which every man should pass; but if a volunteer had passed through them he might at once be passed into battalion drill, and then fix the number of those battalion drills at whatever figure might be thought necessary?—You allude, I presume, to efficient men?

4524. Yes; I allude to men who are efficient?—I conceive that three elementary drills would be enough, and six battalion drills.

4525. Exclusive of brigade drills and field days?—Yes.

4526. Do you lay great stress upon every volunteer annually passing through a course of setting-up drills?—Yes; those three drills which I have already mentioned.

4527. Do you think it desirable that a uniform system as to those setting up drills should exist throughout the volunteer force; for example, suppose that the commander of one of the corps obliged every man in his corps to go through at a certain period of the year those setting up drills, and assuming that the principle was sound, should you think it advisable that that should be extended in order that comparisons might not be drawn, and that a man might not say, "You force me to do this, "whereas in such and such a regiment it is not done, " and therefore why should I do it?"—I do not think that the system of drill ought to be made more compulsory than the present regulations require.

4528. Would it be advisable that there should be a sort of understanding that every volunteer should go through those setting up drills and should pass through a certain examination, after which he should be entitled at once to step into a battalion and then pass through a smaller number of drills?—Yes.

4529. At the present time, according to the Act of Parliament, you may have efficiency in a man without his being effective?—Yes.

4530. Is not that an anomalous state of things which you think ought to cease?—I know that many of the non-effective members are the best soldiers.

4531. Do you not think that the Government should endeavour to find out the efficiency of a man irrespectively of whether he was effective according to the meaning of the statute?—Certainly, and therefore a test of efficiency would be advisable.

4532. Have you at all considered what would be the most advisable test of efficiency?—We base our estimate of the efficiency of the volunteer force very much upon the artillery and musketry instruction, and upon the knowledge on the part of the members of company and battalion drill, a certain amount of which we think is sufficient.

4533. Supposing there was any recommendation from this Commission, or supposing the Government thought it well to propose certain grants or certain assistance based upon a certain condition, that condition being efficiency, irrespective of the statutory number of drills, have you considered at all what test you would apply in that case?—No, I have not; but I think it would be very easy to do so.

4534. You cannot suggest anything at the present moment?—No, it requires a little reflection, looking at the various classes of which the volunteer force is composed; you must consider all those classes, and all the various circumstances connected with them.

4535. You apprehend that there will be no difficulty in finding and applying such a test?—I think there would be none, and I think it is very desirable.

4536. You think that you could apply such a test as would, irrespectively of the statutory number of drills, give security to the Government that the public money was not wasted on inefficiency?—Yes.

4537. (*Earl of Ducie.*) You think you could apply a more practical test than is applied at present?—Yes.

4538. (*Lord Overstone.*) Do you think that the test of efficiency to which you refer could be such as would not only be sufficient to satisfy your own irresponsible judgment, but also be such that you could found upon it a public measure that you could defend and justify?—Yes; and that test should also be the certificate of the officer commanding, signed by the adjutant, to the effect that the member had passed through a certain course of drill; and upon that alone should the aid be given if aid is to be given at all.

4539. Does not that answer proceed upon the assumption that the test of efficiency after all must be the having passed through a certain number of drills, or process of discipline, and not the fact of a man's actual competency as the result?—No, I think not; I think that the certificate ought to be given with reference to the man's efficiency, as well as to the number of drills he had passed through.

4540. I thought your preceding answer was that there must be a certificate from the officer commanding, signed by the adjutant, as to the man in question having passed through a certain number of drills?—I meant a certificate that he had passed through a certain number of drills with a satisfactory result.

4541. The object of the question, as I understood it, was to ascertain whether you might not arrive at a test of efficiency in the volunteer without a certificate of his having gone through a certain number of drills, that is without reference to the process by which the efficiency was accomplished, and that you should direct your attention in giving your certificate solely to the result, that is the fact of the efficiency?—According to the present law a man is considered effective who has passed through a certain number of drills; but it does not follow that the man who has passed through a certain number of drills is efficient, and I therefore recommend that there should be a test of efficiency given in the form of a certificate, and signed by the commanding officer through the adjutant, that a man has passed through a certain number of drills as required by law satisfactorily, and that he is an efficient volunteer.

4542. Your test of efficiency, therefore, would be a double certificate, certifying to the fact of his having gone through certain forms, and the further fact that having passed through those certain forms the desired result had been accomplished?—Yes; if the Government contemplate giving further aid to the volunteers it must be grounded on the efficiency of the volunteers. The other return as to making a volunteer effective should merely relieve him from being balloted for the militia.

4543. The final test of efficiency must be the private judgment of the certifying officer as to the qualifications of the man in question?—Yes; he should be responsible.

4544. (*Lord Elcho.*) After the examination?—Yes.

4545. You might assume such a case as this, that a man had attended 28 drills instead of 18, and yet had not a certificate?—Yes.

4546. On the other hand he might obtain a certificate after attending only six drills?—I do not know that, but that a man had passed through the prescribed number of drills satisfactorily.

4547. (*Lord Overstone.*) Your certificate, if I understand it, would be strictly analogous to a university degree, in which it is required that you should have resided a certain number of terms, and have attended a certain number of lectures, but in addition to that, you must have gone through a direct personal examination, to show that the result of those attendances had produced a knowledge of the subjects which you had been inquiring into?—Yes.

4548. (*Lord Elcho.*) What I gathered from you was this, that under the present system you may find a man efficient without being effective, that there are many who attend the 18 drills, but who do not become efficient, while other men in nine drills would become efficient, and therefore it was advisable to apply a test, in order that a man might pass at once. In that case a man would not have to go through 18 drills, but receive his certificate of efficiency at once?—Yes. I said that nine drills would be sufficient, three of them to be elementary, or company drills, and six battalion drills; but I understood you to ask me

Col. W. M. S. Murmurdo, C.B.

15 July 1862.

Col. *W. M. S. Macmurdo, C.B.*

3 July 1862.

whether the number of the drills required by law might not be reasonably reduced. I said that I thought they might be reduced to nine, and in that case it would bring the two together.

4549. (*Sir A. Campbell.*) How would you bring this new system of testing efficiency by the results under the present Act?—The grant would be given by the Act of Parliament, and it would be given under certain conditions.

4550. You contemplate a new legislative enactment to enable this test to be applied?—Yes; if a grant is made it ought to be given under certain conditions.

4551. (*Viscount Hardinge.*) But they ought to be more stringent, ought they not, than they are now? —Yes, in point of efficiency. I do not mean discipline.

4552. (*Sir A. Campbell.*) Article 60 states that one half of the drills for the effective members must be musters of the whole corps, from what part of the Act of Parliament does that come?—I think that the Act of Parliament leaves a discretion to the Secretary of State as to the distribution of the drills, and what they are to be.

4553. (*Chairman.*) We have been speaking of the efficiency of the men, is there any mode that you can suggest of testing the efficiency of the subaltern officers and non-commissioned officers of volunteer corps?—I do not think it desirable to have any test of that kind. The volunteer officers are of course much more difficult to form than the men, and there is no doubt that in the earlier stages of this movement our great weakness was the inefficiency of the officers, but I have been very much satisfied lately by seeing the very marked improvement that has taken place in the efficiency of the officers, and I really believe that as time goes on the officers will improve themselves and become efficient in the discharge of their several duties.

4554. Does that observation apply also to the non-commissioned officers?—Very much so. I have been lately greatly pleased at seeing both officers and non-commissioned officers acting with a knowledge of their duties far beyond what I expected to see.

4555. (*Lord Elcho.*) Would there be any objection to making every officer, whether he commands a battalion or a company, put his battalion or his company through battalion or company movements before the inspecting officer. I do not mean a book examination?—It would be very desirable indeed to do so; but I would not press it, because we know very well that many of the volunteer officers are useful to the movement in bringing their services to bear, and they may not be exactly of the stuff out of which you could ever form good officers in the field; but at the same time they are of extreme use to the Government in bringing men in, and maintaining them in a state of efficiency in other ways. I think it would be undesirable to press upon those men duties that they could not perform, and thus get rid of them and the men too.

4556. Do you think that they would object to it? —I am sure that they would in many cases.

4557. Have you any doubt that there are many men in the rural districts in that position, possessing local influence?—No.

4558. Is it not likewise the case that nothing tends so much to keep up a battalion as the conviction on the part of the men that their officer knows his duty? —Yes, the influence possessed by a good officer over his men is very great.

4559. And the attendance at drill is, perhaps, worse in those companies where they are the worst officered?—Yes, frequently.

4560. Setting one against the other, do you not think that a practical examination as to a man's knowledge of his duties in the field would rather tend to do good than harm in keeping the men together?—I think it would be inexpedient to establish an arbitrary test to officers at present. It is inconsistent with the principles of the volunteer force, but if any circumstance should arise, such as a war, to require a special looking into the condition and state of efficiency of the officers, I have no doubt that a thorough sifting of such men as were incapable would then take place.

4561. Would it not be a great help to the commanding officer of a battalion who had inefficient officers, and who perhaps did not attend, to have some such power as that?—When an officer is non-effective he is removed according to the present system.

4562. You may have an officer effective as to his attendance at drill, but who is thoroughly inefficient?—You must deal leniently with them, and see what time will produce. I have seen very marked improvements in officers who I did not expect would turn out well; and really I think that we ought not to establish any arbitrary rules of that kind; I think it would tend much to damage the service. When an officer is pronounced to be thoroughly inefficient it is time then for the lord lieutenant to place the circumstances before the Secretary of State for War, and then that officer may be induced to resign his commission.

4563. On account of his inefficiency?—Yes; he might be induced to resign, but even in the army it is not often possible to get rid of inefficient officers.

4564. (*Earl of Ducie.*) Your opinion is that officers in rural districts, and where they are the only available officers, if called upon to perform duties for which they were not competent might resign, and the corps might fall to pieces?—Yes.

4565. In town districts, possibly, such a test might be enforced, as there would be plenty of others to take their places?—Possibly.

4566. (*Viscount Hardinge.*) If so important an improvement has taken place in the efficiency of the subaltern and company officers as you have described, why do you think that they would object, generally speaking, to such a test in the field as Lord Elcho has sketched out?—I think that those officers commanding rural companies, to whom Lord Ducie has just referred, would be the first to object, for they have not the means of acquiring a knowledge of their duties that the officers in town corps have.

4567. They have as good an opportunity of learning their duties as an officer commanding an independent company, have they not?—Yes.

4568. (*Chairman.*) Are you not aware that the officers commanding squadrons and troops of yeomanry are called out and made to put the squadron and troop through certain movements in order to prove that they are up to their duty?—Yes, and we do so frequently in the volunteer service at inspections, but if an officer is not able to put his company through their work there is no immediate pressure put upon him as a necessary consequence of his inefficiency; he is cautioned to make himself more acquainted with his duties, and if, after a time, the lord lieutenant pronounces him to be inefficient, then the Secretary of State would recommend him to resign, but I do not think that any arbitrary pressure should be put upon him at first.

4569. (*Sir G. A. Wetherall.*) What is the strength of the rifle volunteer force at present?—The return to the 1st of April of the present year is now at the printer's, but on the 1st of August 1861 there were 133,918 rifles.

4570. How many of those, do you suppose, have gone through a course of rifle instruction, that is, *bonâ fide* firing at the target?—I think about two-thirds of them. I questioned an officer commanding a corps in Edinburgh the other day as to the number of men who had gone through that course of instruction, and he said that 1,000 men had passed through it.

4571. It strikes me that the masses do not fire at all?—The number is increasing.

4572. (*Lord Elcho.*) With regard to the administrative battalions, you have said as to giving further power to the officer commanding the battalion that, although you did not recommend, you did not object to giving an increase of power; what increase of power would you not object to?—I have no proposal to make.

4573. Do you think, supposing what has been suggested was carried into effect, namely, that these administrative battalions had an administrative staff attached to the headquarters, and not as now attached to the different local companies, that there would be any danger of insubordination or of disrespect towards the captain of a local company on the part of the drill instructor?—I think not; the captain would still be his superior officer and have power to put him under arrest and report him to the officer commanding the battalion, who would take steps to withdraw him.

4574. (*Lord Overstone*.) What is the total number of the volunteers at the present time?—162,700.

4575. What number of those are returned as effectives?—142,000.

4576. Can you give any estimate of the pecuniary charge annually incurred by the Government in connexion with the volunteer force?—160,000*l*.

4577. Do you think that the pecuniary charge now incurred by the Government annually is about 1*l*. per head?—As nearly as possible.

4578. For the total number, not for effectives only?—Yes.

4579. (*Chairman*.) Is that exclusive of the cost of arms?—It includes the cost of ammunition; but not the cost of arms.

4580. (*Lord Overstone*.) Do you think that the items not included in that estimate are of serious amount?—If the arms are not included that is of course a very serious amount.

4581. (*Major Harcourt*.) When you stated that the artillery volunteers were liable to inspection by the War Office inspector as well as the Horse Guards inspector in the course of a year, which of those inspections is the one which is made a test of a man's efficiency?—The artillery inspection. Lord Overstone has several times asked whether certain battalions were ready to go into the field at once; and if I may be permitted I think it would be as well to explain that the object of the volunteer service does not require that the volunteer corps should be prepared to take the field at once; the object is that they should be prepared at a time of danger, and I am of opinion that there would be time before a war actually broke out to render the volunteer corps efficient for the field. With regard to equipment, I should explain also that the tents and field equipments of that kind are not usually furnished even to the regular troops, until the moment when they are required for the field.

4582. (*Lord Overstone*.) It is your opinion that the volunteer force, although not ready in the strict sense of the word for immediate and efficient action in the field, are in an advanced state of efficiency; and therefore, the time that might be reasonably expected to elapse after serious warning was given, would be sufficient to enable them to render efficient service to the regular army?—Yes; and I think it is one of those points that ought to be understood, that time will certainly be given to the volunteers to be prepared. It is true that the advances of science have tended to make the operations of war more rapid and destructive than formerly; but at the same time I consider, that although science has overcome the natural obstacles to the invasion of this country, human nature has not undergone any change; and I think that Governments would hesitate before incurring the risks of such a war as would then take place, and that that hesitation would be just in proportion to the rapidity and destructive nature of the means employed on both sides, and therefore that the usual warnings would precede the coming war.

4583. Setting aside the moral considerations, upon which you rest your anticipation of notice previous to an invasion, do you think that the material considerations would oppose certain obstacles to an instantaneous invasion?—If political and moral considerations were not sufficient to warn this country of its danger, material considerations would certainly not be wanting. So vast an enterprise as the invasion of England could not be undertaken without preparations in provisions, forage, and transport, upon a scale which would leave little doubt as to their object. No invader would be justified in speculating upon finding supplies for his army in this country; he must calculate upon nothing, and be prepared, therefore, to supply his army from its own base; to do this will require vast accumulations of provisions and forage, and the indications thus afforded would not be disregarded by the Government. I repeat that straws, political as well as material, must move before the storm breaks, and it would be at this juncture that the volunteers, without causing any disastrous check to the commercial system of the country, would train in earnest in their own localities, and be equipped for the field.

4584. Would it not be impossible for any foreign power, however highly organized its army might be, at once, and without any warning, and without the attention of the country being called to it, to land a very large force on the shores of this country?—That is my opinion.

4585. It is your opinion, founded upon your knowledge of the present condition of the volunteer force, that that warning which circumstances would render inevitable would be sufficient to correct what might otherwise be deficient in the condition of the volunteer force?—Yes. The accoutrements are very generally defective, and ought to be changed as soon as possible. I have scarcely seen one corps that has got accoutrements fit to carry ammunition in the field, and I believe that if they took the field those accoutrements must be changed. They will also require great coats, knapsacks, and blankets. I have made inquiries upon this subject, and if you will allow me I will read what has been communicated to me from the store department in answer to my inquiries. "We "are required to keep a store of 100,000 great "coats and 40,000 knapsacks, but in the event of an "emergency, these would be required for the army "and militia. The difficulty in procuring a large "quantity of great coats is, that no cloth can be "manufactured in less than six weeks, but if we take "different patterns of cloth (adhering to one colour), "I have no doubt that from 100,000 to 150,000 yards "of cloth could be brought up within a week in the "cloth districts, which would be sufficient for about "40,000 great coats. Within two months from the "date of order, we could get enough cloth to make "500,000 great coats. With regard to the making "of the coats, we could make about 40,000 a week. I "think, therefore, that upon an emergency we could "get 100,000 great coats made in two months, 40,000 "of which would be delivered within one month of "date of order, and the remainder in weekly deliveries; after the first two months we would supply "40,000 a week in regular deliveries, and as we "should be in full working order, I have no doubt "we could do more. During the Crimean war "almost all the great coats for the French army were "made in London, and this was before the sewing "machines were used in making army clothing; with "regard to the knapsacks, the difficulty is in the "preparation of the cloth, which takes at least two "months to dry, and as skilled labour is required to "manufacture these articles, I much doubt if 100,000 "could be procured in less than six months, but I "think there would be no difficulty in getting a substitute, which would take less time to make. We "had very great difficulty in procuring knapsacks "during the Crimean war, and had to purchase large "quantities on the continent." I think that this is a very important question, considering the difficulty of procuring knapsacks in the event of a war, and that we should provide the volunteers now with knapsacks; but such a provision would entail, I apprehend, the appointment of quartermasters to corps of volunteers.

4586. (*Lord Elcho*.) Is it advisable in your opinion

Col. W. M. S. Macmurdo, C.B.

15 July 1862.

W. M. S. McMurdo, C.B.
July 1862.

4587. Do you think it is possible?—No; the volunteers consist of such a variety of classes that they would not submit to one colour.

4588. You would recommend an adherence to the present arrangement, which is four colours, red, dark green, Government grey, and blue?—Yes; recommending to the lord lieutenants that the corps in their counties should be clothed in one uniform.

4589. As has already been done in Staffordshire?—Yes; and in Surrey, Hampshire, and several other counties.

4590. (*Viscount Hardinge.*) What difficulty would there be in the Government keeping the requisite number of great coats and knapsacks in store?—Because they are perishable.

4591. But if they keep in the store department 100,000, there is no reason why they should not keep another 100,000 for volunteers?—That depends upon the annual consumption.

4592. (*Lord Elcho.*) Do you think it advisable that all the adjutants, and the drill instructors, and the staff of the volunteer corps should have staff uniforms, and that they should not wear the uniform of their corps?—Yes; I think that some uniform should be fixed for them.

4593. (*Chairman.*) What is your opinion of the present state of the volunteer force as regards its efficiency?—With reference to the objects for which the force is raised, I consider it to be in a satisfactory state of efficiency. But the term has a very wide signification when used in a military sense, and is liable to misconstruction when applied to volunteers. A regiment of the line is known to be efficient when the inspecting general is satisfied that every man is on parade or is otherwise accounted for; that the men composing the regiment are physically fit to serve in any climate, and to carry between 60 and 70 pounds weight under any circumstances of service; that officers, non-commissioned officers, and men are perfectly armed, equipped, and trained to undertake any service in any quarter of the globe at an hour's notice, and that the system of interior economy in the regiment is perfect in all its branches. But with volunteers the standard of efficiency is, in my opinion, altogether different. 1st, the objects of the force are limited to service at home, and then only in the event of invasion; 2nd, the constitution of the force is consequently regulated by these special objects of service, hence it is composed of all classes of the community, the majority of whose occupations do not admit them to undergo more than a partial training during peace. Thus corps arrive at various degrees of efficiency according to their circumstances, and some corps are prevented by local and temporary causes from becoming as efficient as others possessing superior advantages. But without reckoning much upon the actual present efficiency of a portion of the force, a most important step has been taken in the establishment of cadres upon which the population of the country can be organized for its defence in the time of danger. It appears to me as if the people are gradually preparing themselves for this contingency. Thousands, after passing through a course of drill have left their corps and have been succeeded by others in increasing numbers, while tens of thousands habitually attend every muster of volunteers as spectators. The unflagging interest exhibited by the latter in all the proceedings of the volunteers is remarkable, and I have often been made aware, by casual remarks in the crowd, that the people are insensibly acquiring a knowledge of military exercises, which the increasing use of the rifle throughout the country will enable them to turn to good account if their services as volunteers are hereafter required. The number at the inspection of a corps generally falls far short of its enrolled strength; an inspecting officer must therefore exercise his judgment in forming his opinion of those who are absent by the progress in drill exhibited by those who are present, and must accustom himself in estimating what the real value of the corps might be in case of invasion, by the rapid progress which it has made under many disadvantages in time of peace. Generally speaking—from this point of view—I estimate the efficiency of the whole volunteer force—that is to say, not so much by its actual state as by what it is capable of becoming at very short notice. But I should not be doing justice to the volunteers if I did not place on record that a very considerable portion of the force is already in an advanced state of efficiency in all that is most essential for the objects of its service. There are many corps at present which, in point of numbers, drill, and the use of the rifle, may be esteemed at once and in every respect admirable troops. About 48,000, or more than a third of the rifle volunteer force, are already organized in large corps or consolidated battalions, and would require little more to fit them to take their place in a line of battle. I have had opportunities of exercising many of these corps in brigade movements, under circumstances sufficiently trying to young troops, such as darkness and difficult ground for manœuvring upon, and I have generally found them perfectly steady and manageable; and I may add that His Royal Highness the General Commanding-in-Chief was pleased to express to me his satisfaction at the progress made by the volunteers generally who were manœuvred lately at Wimbledon in considerable bodies and over very intricate ground. The remainder, or about 85,000, are in corps composed of one, two, or three companies each, and are, generally speaking, scattered throughout the rural districts. For the most part, these are formed into provisional or administrative battalions under field officers as already described, and although they all labour more or less under various disadvantages the proficiency in drill of the volunteers composing these small corps is generally speaking and all things considered—satisfactory; some indeed, are really good, and may soon be depended on as so many nuclei for future expansion. The state of efficiency of the artillery volunteers is in most cases highly satisfactory, and the importance of this branch of the service cannot be overrated. Whatever difference in opinion there may be among military men as regards the real value of the volunteer rifle force, as troops intended for immediate service in the open field; none ought to exist with reference to the artillery force whose efficicucy is more mechanical in its character and calculated to be made immediately available in manning the fortifications of the country. The volunteer artillery force numbers 350 batteries, and is composed chiefly of engineers and workers in iron, peculiarly qualified for the service. The efficiency of a force formed out of such materials cannot therefore be a matter of doubt. For the same reasons the engineer volunteer corps are of extreme importance to the country, and the progress made in their efficiency is quite satisfactory. It would not be in the performance only of the ordinary works of military engineers in the field that the chief importance of the volunteer engineers would be found during an invasion of this country. A glance at the railway map shows that, unlike any other country, a war in England would be carried on principally upon railways, and that even a field of battle would be considered as ill-chosen that had not several lines converging upon it. To render, therefore, these railways completely available for the operations of an army in the field, a vast number of engineers would be required in the construction of temporary platforms alone at points where none now exist, and the class of men which compose the present force of volunteer engineers, and the knowledge which they display in their duties, make me believe that they would in the event of invasion constitute a valuable aid to the engineers of the regular army.

The witness withdrew.

The Earl de Grey and Ripon examined.

Earl de Grey and Ripon.

15 July 1862.

4594. (*Chairman.*) Will you be kind enough, in the first place, to give the Commission some idea of the course which has been taken by the Government, with respect to the volunteers?—You are probably aware, that in the spring of 1859, the late Government, when General Peel was Secretary for War, put out two circulars, the first of which indicated that the Government were ready to accept the services of volunteer corps, offered under the old volunteer Act, and the second of which laid down, in somewhat greater detail, the principles upon which the Government intended to act as to those corps. When the present Government came into office, those were the only two official documents which had been issued to the public upon the subject, although in regard to one or two other points, office decisions had been given. The principle upon which the services of the corps were originally accepted was, that they should occasion no cost whatever to the public; that no pecuniary assistance was to be given to them, but that their services were to be accepted under that Act. It appears to have been the intention of this circular to limit the formation of the corps to companies; though there is an indication, I believe, in some of the office records, that an organization in counties under field officers might have been contemplated about that time; but I think the general intention was, that the corps should be formed as separate and independent companies. When the late Lord Herbert became Secretary of State for War, a certain number of corps had already been formed besides those two corps, the 1st Middlesex and the 1st Devonshire, which, as the Commissioners are aware, had been formed some years previously. At the end of June 1859, when the present Government came into office, there were in existence, including those corps, 13 volunteer corps; that is to say, 11 corps of one company each had been formed under the new arrangement; but the public being aware that the services of the volunteers were required by the Government, and that the services of corps of that description would be accepted, we received, as the previous Government had been receiving, numerous applications, increasing almost daily in number, from corps that were being formed under the original circular, the principle then being that no assistance whatever from the Government was to be given to the corps. Lord Herbert took the subject under his consideration, and abiding in the main, in the first instance, by the principles which had been adopted by his predecessor in office, he, however, so far departed from them as to indicate his readiness to supply a portion of the rifles required for the corps, 25 per cent. being the amount originally given. Very shortly after that he also adopted the battalion organization, that being, in certain instances, substituted for the company organization, which had been originally contemplated. Those battalions, however, were to be formed on the principle of what is now called consolidated battalions; that is to say, that the corps originally formed as one company increasing under the same commanding officer to a greater number of volunteers were allowed to divide themselves into different companies and to form themselves into one consolidated battalion. As time went on it was found that there was considerable practical inconvenience, not only to the volunteers but to the Government itself, arising from the fact that they were not supplied with arms. It was found that the great demand that was springing up for arms for the volunteers was creating a very inconvenient competition with the Government, both in London and in Birmingham; that is, the arms that were purchased by the volunteers were much less strictly examined, if they were examined at all, and were consequently of an inferior description; the workmen, therefore, greatly preferred working upon the arms for the volunteers than upon the arms to be supplied to the Government. Partly for that reason and partly for the purpose of affording more encouragement to the volunteers, and also from the conviction that it was not altogether sufficient to secure what General Peel originally contemplated, namely, that the bore of the rifle should be the same as the Government rifle, and the nipple the same, but that it was desirable that the rifle placed in the hands of the volunteers should be the same as that used in the regular army, so that it might be replaced on an emergency without difficulty, Lord Herbert determined ultimately to supply 100 per cent. of rifles to the volunteer corps, entirely superseding the original arrangement, and giving them assistance which originally they had not been entitled to. The matter rested mainly in that position for a considerable time, the corps increasing very rapidly in number, but with the exception of the consolidated battalions, which were chiefly formed in towns, they consisted entirely of scattered companies. It was then thought desirable to take farther measures than had been previously taken, to make sure that the corps were sufficiently and properly drilled; it was found that they had not the means of providing themselves with either adjutants or drill instructors of a satisfactory character, and the first step taken in that direction was to supply the corps with adjutants. Of course as the adjutants could only have been given to battalions, they could only have been supplied to consolidated battalions, if it had not been for the adoption of that organization which has been called the organization of administrative battalions, which was originally devised for the purpose on the one hand of having commanding officers to bring together and to exercise a certain general supervision over the various companies, and on the other hand to enable the Government in the case of those rural companies to supply them with adjutants. When that step was taken the Government had supplied rifles, and afterwards a portion of the ammunition, gratuitously, and they had also given paid adjutants to battalions. The only other step with respect to assistance afforded by the Government to the volunteers which has since been taken, was at the end of the Session of last year; the Government then took a supplementary estimate for the purpose of supplying drill serjeants, it being found that there was great difficulty in the corps getting them for themselves unless they paid very exorbitant prices, and after all there was no control over them, as they were not men who were properly under the command of the commanding officers of the volunteer corps, and if not actually soldiers they were not men under martial law. With a view to removing that difficulty, the Government supplied the corps with serjeants, and at the present moment, with regard to Government assistance, we stand in this position:—A volunteer comes forward and offers his services, and provides himself with everything except arms and ammunition, and the persons required for his drill and instruction, and the principle upon which we have limited our assistance up to this time is, I think, a perfectly intelligible one. I do not give any opinion as to whether it is one upon which we can rest; but it is, at all events, a perfectly intelligible one. We gave arms and ammunition because it was desirable and necessary for their utility in the field that the volunteers should be armed with a weapon similar to that of the regular troops, and because we found that the great demand for arms on the part of the volunteers actually interfered with our own supply; we gave them drill serjeants and adjutants, because the Government alone, in fact, had the power of supplying efficient adjutants and drill serjeants, and at the same time keeping them under effectual control, because, even if it had been possible that the volunteers could have done it, it would have been undesirable that persons coming under the Mutiny Act, and receiving pay, should be dependent on any one, except, directly and immediately, upon the Government. At the present time that is the only

C c 4

Earl de Grey and Ripon.
15 July 1862.

description of assistance which has been given; the Government, up to this time, have contemplated that the volunteers should in all other respects provide themselves with whatever might be necessary, to maintain their efficiency. That, I think, is the present position of the matter.

4595. Have you ever considered whether it was desirable to give a more military character to the force?—Do you mean as to military discipline?

4596. Yes; placing them under military authority?—I conceive that to be practically impossible, without entirely altering the character of the force, and without completely changing the basis upon which it now rests. You are aware that at the present time, until a volunteer is called out for actual service in the cases contemplated by the Act, you have no power of compelling any volunteer to do anything, except such power as you may derive from being able to tie him under the rules of the particular corps; there is no punishment which you can award to any volunteer officer or man except the punishment of dismissal or of censure, except in the single case when corps are actually assembled under arms, when by a clause in the Act of Parliament the commanding officer can put any volunteer who misconducts himself under arrest; but you could not enforce, as it seems to me, anything beyond that which we have always determined to enforce in regard to discipline, unless you took power under an Act to punish men by imprisonment or fine or by some other legal means for disobedience, and to compel their attendance. When I say that you cannot do more than we have done hitherto, I would explain that the principle that we have gone upon has been this; as to volunteers, when not actually assembled under arms, we require no military discipline, except an adherence to those general principles of subordination to the Government, and to their own officers, and to all those in authority above them, without which it would not be safe or proper that any armed body should exist in the country; in regard to the force when actually on parade, we have always thought it right to require that they should then, officers and men, strictly obey the orders given to them by their military superiors; but, except in those two respects, we have no power to enforce any discipline; and I think it would be impossible so completely to change that state of things as to take any effectual power to enforce any more extended discipline; and I certainly think that nothing would be more undesirable than to pretend to enforce discipline by your regulations which you could not enforce by law.

4597. You have referred to administrative battalions. The power and authority of the commanding officer of an administrative battalion appears, sometimes, to be hardly sufficient; he has power, when the battalion is on parade, the same as any other commanding officer; but if he visits a company belonging to his battalion to inspect it he appears to have no power, for in the case of an officer misconducting himself he can only recommend the officer commanding the company to dismiss him, or visit him with some sort of punishment. Do you think it is possible to increase that power?—I do not think it possible to increase the power without some alteration in the Act of Parliament; as I have stated before, the organization of the administrative battalions grew up from the circumstances connected with the development of the movement in the country; we had to deal with separate companies, each possessing various rights given by Act of Parliament to a corps and to its commanding officer. We had, in the name of Her Majesty, accepted the services of those companies as separate corps, and it was not competent to us, after having entered into certain engagements with them, to insist upon any arrangement that was inconsistent with those engagements, and to deprive them of the position to which, by the act of the Government, they had been admitted. Therefore, when we wanted to have something more of a united organization in those companies, and to be able to give them adjutants, all we could do was to appoint over them an officer who should have such general powers of inspection and of command in the field when the companies were called together as were not inconsistent with the power that had been conferred by the Act of Parliament upon each separate corps when its services were accepted. But although I do not think that you could do what I see has been suggested by some of the witnesses, namely, that you could put commanding officers of administrative battalions precisely in the position of commanding officers of yeomanry regiments, yet I think that you might, if you took power to do so by an Act of Parliament, give a somewhat more extended power of command to the commanding officer than he now possesses. The case of the yeomanry is not parallel, because they are called out for eight days; they are brought together generally in one town, and they are therefore precisely in the position in which a volunteer administrative battalion is when it comes out for drill; but they are not constantly at drill in their own particular district, with a separate local organization and with a separate fund. I do think it is desirable to give the commanding officer of an administrative battalion distinct authority over the captains of the companies under him when he is present at their parades. I see that the question has been raised about the power of ordering of a parade; the real fact is that nobody can effectually order a parade; that is to say, if the men do not come there is no means of enforcing their attendance, and all that the commanding officer of a battalion could do would be to say to the commanding officers of the companies, I wish to see your company on such and such a day; but it would be very unwise if he did that without consulting the local convenience of the corps. I believe, generally speaking, that nothing of that kind has been thought of; but that he should have, when they are actually under arms, full power to act as commanding officer if that power is wanting, I think is very desirable. I think also that a new arrangement as to the drill-serjeants of the administrative battalions might be made with advantage.

4598. You give an adjutant now to an administrative battalion, and he is under the orders of the colonel?—Yes.

4599. Would there be any objection to placing the drill-instructors also under his orders?—I think that, generally speaking, it would be a most desirable arrangement, and I have always been of that opinion. It was too late in the last session, when the determination to supply drill-instructors was taken, and a supplemental estimate was voted, to pass an Act to carry out this arrangement, although an Act is necessary, as you cannot bring the drill-serjeant under the Mutiny Act, through the operation of the twenty-first section of the Volunteer Act, without attaching him to a particular volunteer corps; if there had been time in year 1 should have thought it most desirable.

4600. Several of the witnesses who have been examined by the Commission have recommended that there should be one set of rules laid down for the whole force; do you think that that could be carried out?—Meaning by one set of rules that which the Act of Parliament intends by the word?

4601. Yes?—I think not; it would certainly have been impossible under the Act of Parliament. Some opinions have been given that it ought to have been done, but the Act of Parliament gives the initiative as to rules to the corps themselves, and the corps devise their own rules, and submit them to the lord lieutenant, and if he approves of them he submits them to the Government, and if they are not disallowed on the part of Her Majesty within a certain time they become actually good rules, and are enforceable by law. Therefore the Government have no power of enforcing rules on anybody, they could only lay down certain general regulations as to the principles which they would permit to be adopted in those rules. A body of model rules was drawn up, and those model rules have formed the basis of the vast majority of the rules which have been adopted by volunteer corps since they were published, and the principles upon which the rules submitted have been altered in this office are thoroughly well understood in the volunteer branch. They required a good deal of attention and care at first, but the principles are now thoroughly understood, and it is completely a matter of routine. I do not think that it would have been possible or wise to enforce strict uniformity, as those rules related so much to the private affairs of corps when they supported themselves entirely.

4602. In any amendment of the Volunteer Act, do you think it would be desirable that the rules should be sanctioned by the Secretary of State, and not that the non-disallowance of those rules after they have been laid before him for a given number of days should be in effect a legal sanction of the rules, it being so difficult to prove before a magistrate, for example, that those rules had been a given number of days before the Secretary of State; whereas, if he was called upon to approve of them, his signature would be sufficient evidence of the rules having been sanctioned by him?—I think that theoretically it might be a better arrangement; but I do not think that any inconvenience has arisen in practice, and upon the very ground that you have just mentioned, that it is so difficult to prove that the rules have not been disallowed. Indeed we have now thought it necessary to adopt a system by which the signature of the Under Secretary of State is appended to each copy of the rules, stating that they have been not disallowed, our solicitor having advised us that that was the only authority that a court would be likely to admit.

4603. Supposing that an invasion was imminent, and it was necessary to place the volunteers under military discipline, I presume that the course of the Government would be still to allow them to remain in their own districts, until they were actually wanted in the field?—I should think that the wisest course would be to permit them to remain at their own homes until the very last moment, to require them to drill regularly and steadily when danger was imminent, but not actually to move them from their own homes, until the time had arrived when, remembering the great facilities that there now are for moving troops by railway, it was in the opinion of the military authorities necessary to concentrate the force on a given point.

4604. They would not be necessarily withdrawn from their industrial pursuits until they were wanted in the field?—No, except perhaps in the case of some of the richer corps that it would be easy to deal with, and that might be placed in camp as circumstances might arise.

4605. Supposing it was thought desirable that the volunteers should have some assistance from parliament, would it not be necessary to have some test of efficiency beyond the mere test of their being effectives?—Reserving to myself the right not to give any opinion upon the question whether such further assistance is required or not, I should say unquestionably it would be necessary. I do not think that the Government could consent to incur any expenditure of the kind I imagine you to allude to, without taking proper security on behalf of the public that the men receiving such assistance were efficient in the degree that it may be possible to obtain from corps of this kind.

4606. (*Lord Overstone.*) Was any such test applied as that which you have alluded to as a necessary condition before assistance was given in the former volunteer movement?—As far as I am able to judge from the information in regard to that movement which I have been able to obtain, and which is very imperfect, I should say that it was not so; but then it must be borne in mind that the old volunteers, invasion being imminent during the main part of the time they were on foot, were being drilled continually, and that there was very little doubt that they were becoming as efficient as the nature of their service rendered possible.

4607. (*Chairman.*) With regard to the duties of adjutants of militia, are they not employed to a certain extent under the Secretary of State as paymasters when they are attached to corps?—The adjutants of disembodied militia act as paymasters for their corps.

4608. And they receive remuneration accordingly?—Yes, a certain allowance accordingly; and they have also their pay as adjutants. If you were to propose to disburse any considerable sum to each corps in the shape of money, I do not see how it could be possibly done, except by some arrangement of that description; you must make somebody accountable to the public, and from that person you must take whatever security you may find necessary. I think that there are obvious objections to entering into relations of that description with commanding officers of volunteer corps, whereas the case of militia adjutants affords a very good precedent that might be adopted, and I do not think, under any circumstances, that aid of that description should be given to any volunteer corps unprovided with an adjutant; that would be one means by which you could apply your test of efficiency.

4609. He would be responsible to the Government for the proper expenditure of the money, and for its being applied to the objects for which the Government intended it to be granted?—Yes, the adjutant would be responsible, I should imagine, to the Government for not expending any part of that money except for the purposes that might be sanctioned by regulation, or by the special sanction of the Secretary of State; but the adjutant must pay on the orders of his commanding officer; all he could say would be this, and he must have the latitude of saying it to his commanding officer, " I cannot apply the money for these purposes, as it " is not within the regulations, without the special " sanction of the Secretary of State," and you should certainly, in any case of that kind, lay down very decidedly what are the objects for which such payments are to be made.

4610. Would it not be desirable, in case it were thought right to afford assistance to the volunteer force, to limit the number of the force in a time of peace?—Yes; I think so decidedly. I do not think that you would get parliament to consent to spend a large sum of money on the force, irrespectively of its size; the House of Commons would say, tell us what amount of this force you mean to maintain; practically that must be the case, because you take your estimate, and you could not spend more than your estimate.

4611. Have you ever considered how a limitation of the force could be best arrived at?—That depends entirely upon what amount of force you mean to keep up; if you took an amount of force considerably less than the existing force, you would have a very difficult process of reduction to go through; and, although it might be done, it would, of course, be an invidious and disagreeable process. If you took a force something like the present, then the object would be not to permit any more corps to be formed, unless the old corps died out.

4612. (*Lord Elcho.*) If a great part of the evidence that we have received is to be relied upon, the force will soon limit itself if the Government do not give what is asked for?—I do not wish to give evidence upon that point; but it seems that it would limit itself very largely indeed by a process of dissolution.

4613. (*Lord Overstone.*) Is it your opinion that this Commission should look at the volunteer movement as a means of organizing a fixed body of men to be always in a state of readiness and efficiency for action, having, in a case of emergency, a certain fixed amount of men prepared for that purpose, or that it should be looked upon as a present nucleus of an expansive character, capable of being enlarged when more serious apprehension of danger shall pervade

Earl de Grey and Ripon.

15 July 1862.

D d

Earl de Grey
and Ripon.

July 1862.

the public mind?—I am inclined to think that you must regard it, to a certain extent, from both points of view. If you were, as has been suggested just now, to limit the force, and were to take measures for increasing gradually its efficiency, you would then, if a sudden attack upon this country were made, have a large body of men whom you could immediately bring into the field, and who would be instantly available. But, on the other hand, if you had a foreign war, for instance, which did not involve the immediate invasion of this country, but which made the Government of the country think that a great increase to our military force was required, you might then use the volunteers that you had as a nucleus with a view to raising a very much larger force, such as existed during the late war.

4614. Of course a limitation and an expansion of the volunteer force is necessarily involved in the granting or withholding Government aid; that is to say, in proportion as the Government withholds or extends its aid to the force, the numbers of the force will be restricted or expanded?—Certainly.

4615. (*Viscount Hardinge.*) In the event of further aid being given to the volunteers do you see any difficulty in carrying out the relations of the volunteer corps with this office as to the examination of their accounts?—No; I do not. Of course that depends upon the nature of the aid that you recommend should be given, and the purposes to which it is to be applied; but speaking generally, and, of course, in ignorance of the views of the Commission, or their intentions on that subject, I should say that there would be no difficulty in regard to the arrangements of this office, supposing aid to be given of the general description that I have seen sketched out in the questions and answers in the evidence before this Commission.

4616. Should you see any difficulty in carrying out such a system if a capitation grant were made, to be expended, as some of the witnesses have recommended, at the discretion of the commanding officers?—I should think it unwise that any grant of money that might be made should be expended at the absolute discretion of the commanding officers.

4617. Would there be any difficulty, in your opinion, in the Government granting aid to the volunteers in the shape of a capitation grant, to be expended under certain regulations?—Putting entirely aside the question of the propriety of making any farther grant to the volunteers, I do not think there would be any practical difficulty in the adoption of such a system.

4618. Can you form any rough estimate of what the additional expense would be to this office in the pay of additional clerks for the examination of such accounts?—That would of course depend upon the nature of the accounts to be rendered; but, speaking generally, as far as I have been able to form any idea of the sort of plan contemplated, I think that a very small addition, if any, would be required, for I believe that accounts of that description, such as I allude to, would be very much less troublesome to examine than the training pay lists of the militia; and having consulted those in this office who are better judges of that than I am, I believe that they would be very easily examined, and dealt with, as a mere matter of official routine.

4619. From your experience of the way in which the adjutants of disembodied militia act as paymasters, have you every reason to believe that the adjutants of the volunteers would be as efficient as they are, if they are efficient in the examination of the volunteers' accounts?—It seems to me, if I understand the nature of the accounts that you contemplate, and of course it all turns upon that, that the duties of the volunteer adjutant as to the accounts would be infinitely less complicated and difficult than those of the adjutant of militia, who has to pay men individually, to pay or to strike off bounty here, and to consider what is the amount due to a man there, and to take care that the account of each individual in the regiment is accurate, and in accordance with the regulations of the service. I imagine if any such aid was given to the volunteers, as appears to be contemplated by some of the witnesses, that all an adjutant would have to do would be to pay a certain number of bills once, or twice, or three times, in the course of a year; but those bills he would pay only if consistent with the orders of the Secretary of State; if they were not consistent with those orders, he would not pay them until the sanction of the Secretary of State had been obtained; that appears to me to be a very simple matter, both as to the adjutant and as to the question of accounts in this department. With regard to the character and reliability of the adjutants, they are gentlemen who have served in the army, and in whom perfect reliance, speaking generally, as to matters of account may be placed quite as much as in the adjutants of militia, who are drawn from the same class of persons.

4620. The vouchers in such a case would have to be sent to this office?—Yes.

4621. With regard to the drill instructors and the subdivisions, in cases where a company is reduced to a subdivision from want of pecuniary aid, do you think that that subdivision might be permitted to retain its Government instructor?—If drill instructors were attached, not to individual corps, but to an administrative battalion, I think in that case the services of a drill instructor—I do not mean the whole exclusive use of the drill instructor—might be obtained for subdivisions, and that instruction might be given to those corps which are now deprived of it by the existing regulations. I certainly would not give any further Government aid to any corps that were not in some battalion.

4622. (*Chairman.*) All corps would either be in a consolidated battalion or form part of an administrative battalion?—Certainly.

4623. (*Viscount Hardinge.*) If the drill instructors were under the orders of the adjutant and the colonel of an administrative battalion at headquarters, would it not be necessary to give those drill instructors a travelling allowance to enable them to visit the different companies and to drill them?—That is a question for the consideration of the Commission.

4624. (*Sir A. Campbell.*) I think you stated that when the present volunteer force was first organized it was contemplated that the whole of the expense should be borne by the corps, and not by the Government?—Yes.

4625. Were any indications or suggestions of that intention made to the lord-lieutenants, through whom the offers of enrolment of volunteers were forwarded?—I have the original circulars here; and I think you will find that that principle breathes throughout the whole of the two first circulars. One of the provisions of the very first circular dated the 12th May 1859 is, that the members of a volunteer corps undertake to provide their own arms and equipments, to defray all expenses connected with the corps, except in the event of its being assembled for actual service: and as each step in advance in the direction of increased Government aid has been taken by the Government, successive declarations have been made in parliament, if not in circulars, that they were not going to give any further assistance than that which was given at that moment. I am quite aware that in consequence of the successive steps which have been taken, any belief in the determination of the Government to adhere to those declarations may have been somewhat shaken, and I may, perhaps, be permitted to say this to the Commission, that while, as I said before, I think the position in which we now stand is a perfectly intelligible and clear position in regard to aid, it seems to me most important, whatever may be the result of the labours of this Commission, or the decision to which the Government may come when they receive the report of the Commission, that that report, and the result of it, should be such as to put an end to the expectations of the volunteers, that the arrangements which may then be adopted will be liable to revision, for whatever those arrangements may be, the sort of agitation which has existed on this subject should be put an end to, so that the corps may hereafter be placed on a permanent basis, whatever may be the amount of the force that you can obtain upon that basis.

4626. I suppose it is within your knowledge that numerous enrolments have been forwarded from many parts of the country, when it was perfectly well known in the locality that those corps could not maintain themselves beyond the first start?—I could not state that of my own knowledge. I gather it from the evidence which has been given before the Commission, and from what I have heard from others.

4627. Do you not think it would be desirable that something like a code of suggestions should be issued to the lord lieutenants of counties, so as to secure uniformity in the manner of enrolment and the mode of appointing officers, and all the other functions which appertain to lord lieutenants in making their recommendations to this department?—That is a difficult question, because there are very great differences in different localities; the whole foundation of the volunteer force, as at present organized, is that it is a force raised locally; and we look to the lord lieutenants, in accordance with the general instructions which they may receive, to raise such corps as they may think fit and proper within their own districts. It might be possible to put out upon the subject of enrolments some more strict regulations than have hitherto been put out, but I very much doubt whether there would not be very considerable difficulty the moment you departed from the few general principles which have already been laid down in those circulars in devising further rules on this point. As to the appointment of officers, the Government have, at the present moment, as far as I know, no legal authority, except the general supremacy of the Government to make regulations binding upon lord lieutenants. The lord lieutenants are entrusted with the power of granting commissions to officers, subject to the disallowance of Her Majesty, and there is not in the Volunteer Act the powers that there are in one of the recent Militia Acts for issuing regulations as to that matter. It is a point, perhaps, as to which it is desirable to obtain fresh legislation; but you must leave the main responsibility, both as to the corps to be raised and the officers to be nominated, with the lord lieutenant; he has local knowledge, and you must enable the Government to hold him responsible for all the steps that are taken and appointments that are made.

4628. (*Lord Elcho.*) If any assistance is recommended by this Commission, and it is granted by the Government, the Government will naturally expect that it is only given for men who are thoroughly efficient?—For men who are efficient within the meaning which the Government may think fit to attach to that word.

4629. At present that measure is in accordance with the wording of the Act of Parliament, which prescribes a certain number of drills, namely 18, half of which are to be of one description, and the other half of another description. Are you of opinion, from your knowledge of this matter, that you may have efficiency without a man being effective in the present state of things?—I should say that you might possibly have efficiency without a man being effective, and you might, certainly, have an effective without the man being efficient; the two cases are entirely disunited.

4630. Is it advisable that those two cases which are at present disunited should be united?—I think so.

4631. Do you contemplate a new Act of Parliament?—I think that if such changes as have been discussed before this Commission are to be carried out, there must be a new Act of Parliament.

4632. (*Major Harcourt.*) I believe it is the wish of the Government specially to encourage the artillery volunteers on the coast?—Yes.

4633. It appears that the Government had intended to pay for the carriage of all artillery stores?—Yes.

4634. From the evidence that has been given before this Commission, it appears that that has not been clearly understood amongst the commanding officers of artillery?—Yes.

4635. Would it be possible, in the shape of a Government circular or memorandum, to make them aware of that?—Yes; nothing would be more easy. If it results from the evidence that there is any doubt upon a point of that kind, we should be ready to clear it up immediately without any recommendation.

4636. (*Viscount Hardinge.*) Would it not be very desirable to increase if possible the numerical strength of the artillery volunteers?—Certainly.

4637. And not in any way to limit that branch of the force in numbers, if it were thought advisable to limit the strength of the rifle volunteers?—I think that you must limit the total strength of the force, because that is the only mode by which you can limit the expense. I mean that you must limit it upon the supposition that more aid is given. You cannot limit it in one part, and let it expand indefinitely in another.

4638. Considering the great value of the artillery volunteers as auxiliary to the militia and royal artillery, would it be desirable to limit the numerical strength of that force?—I think that a limit must be put; you might say that the total strength shall not be beyond so and so, or you might say if the total strength reaches only so and so, we will allow a further addition of such and such a number of artillery.

4639. (*Lord Overstone.*) Would not the limitation be sufficiently accomplished by laying down more stringent regulations as to the qualifications of those who received the assistance?—That is entirely a matter of experience. I do not think that you could very well decide upon that until you had seen how the new scheme, whatever it might be, would work. I do not suppose it is intended that any limitation should be put into the Act of Parliament, or that there should be any limitation of that absolute description, but that the Government should annually state to parliament that they took an estimate for such and such a number of volunteers, and that it should be understood that the force was not to be increased beyond that number.

4640. (*Chairman.*) Without that limit you would hardly be able to obtain a vote from the House of Commons?—I should imagine not.

4641. Is it desirable, in your opinion, that the volunteer corps should be placed under the command of the general officers commanding in districts, somewhat after the manner that the artillery corps are so placed under their command?—I think there seems to exist in the minds of some of the witnesses who have been examined before the Commission, as far as I can judge from the evidence, considerable misconception as to what really is the connexion between the officers commanding the royal artillery and the artillery volunteers, and I am glad that your question gives me an opportunity of endeavouring to clear up that point. The connexion between the officers commanding the royal artillery in the Districts and the artillery volunteers relates exclusively to instruction and practice; the artillery volunteers are dealt with in a different manner from the rifle volunteers in this respect, that from the beginning guns and ammunition have been supplied to them gratis, and from a very early period bombardiers and non-commissioned officers of the coast brigade have been given to them as drill instructors, but those drill instructors have remained in the coast brigade, and have not been attached to the volunteer corps by any direct connexion; they have been detailed to do duty with those corps, and therefore they have remained of course under the general supervison and orders of the commanding officers of the royal artillery. On the other hand, the guns and stores, for obvious reasons, have also remained in the charge, theoretically at all events, of the officers of royal artillery; that has worked very well, and has been

D d 2

Earl de Grey
and Ripon.

15 July 1862.

admirably managed by the officers of royal artillery, and from those two circumstances there has grown up the present special connexion between the artillery volunteers and the officers of the royal artillery in the different Districts. I confess that in time of peace I think it would be undesirable and indeed inconsistent with the character and constitutional nature of the force that it should be placed under the command of the general officers commanding Districts; it would be certainly inconsistent with the obvious intention of the Act of Parliament, because it says that the volunteers shall come under the command of general officers only when called out for actual service, and that obviously points to their not being under their command at any other time, and, indeed, they could not be in any military sense under the command of any officers in the army, as they are not under military discipline. The general commanding a District is the officer in command of Her Majesty's troops in the District; the lord lieutenant, on the other hand, is the officer in command, or, as it is called, the commander-in-chief of the militia, yeomanry, and volunteer forces within his county; that is his constitutional position, and to place anybody else in that position would be an innovation not consistent with the Act of Parliament, and not consistent, I think, with the nature of this force, and would not be acceptable, I should imagine, to the lord lieutenants. The drill instructors and adjutants of the rifle volunteers, and the adjutants, be it remembered, of artillery volunteers also, are all under the direction and command of the commanding officers of the volunteer corps, subject to the orders of this department; they are under martial law, and they are liable to be tried by court-martial; but not by a court-martial composed of military officers, for the Act says distinctly that the court-martial is to be composed of volunteer officers, and, therefore, it seems to me that it would be quite inconsistent with the nature of the force to attempt to place it under the general officers commanding Districts in time of peace. I do not think it would be desirable to alter their present relations to the general officers commanding Districts. We have always received from the general officers commanding Districts the greatest assistance in all matters relating to the volunteers; they have shown great interest in them and a desire to afford them every assistance, advice, and instruction that it was in their power to give; but I think it is desirable, both for the army and for the volunteers, that in a time of peace their relations should be of that friendly character, and that they should not be brought into closer connexion, it being always understood that the moment they are called out for actual service they come *ipso facto* under the orders of the general officers appointed by Her Majesty to command Her forces under those circumstances, and that then they would be entirely and completely under the direction of such general officers.

4642. Is it not the case as to the yeomanry that they are only under the command of the commanding officer of a district, or the officer in command of a garrison or town in which they are placed, when they are on permanent duty under military law, and, in fact, under the articles of war?—Certainly.

4643. (*Viscount Hardinge.*) Is it not the fact that the placing the artillery volunteers under the officer commanding the artillery in the district has rather given satisfaction than otherwise to the volunteers?—No doubt it has; but they are not under the officer commanding the royal artillery in the sense that the volunteers would be if under the general officer commanding a District. The officer commanding the royal artillery in a District has nothing to do with them, except as to their practice and drill, and he has to do with them as to their practice and drill, because their drill instructors are royal artillerymen, and their guns and their ammunition are in charge of the royal artillery.

4644. Would it be possible, do you think, to put the rifle volunteers under the general officer, in the same way that you put the artillery volunteers under the officer commanding the royal artillery in the district?—I think not, as the cases are not parallel; their drill instructors are not soldiers remaining in their regiments; in some cases they are soldiers who are transferred under a peculiar regulation, but they are not soldiers actually liable to be withdrawn at any moment, another man being sent in their place, as in the case of the artillery; neither are there any stores in any way in charge of any officer of the army; they are in a totally different position. I do not see how you could carry it out.

4645. But still they are under martial law, that is, the adjutants and the drill instructors?—They are not under ordinary martial law, they are under the Mutiny Act and the articles of war, but they are not liable to be tried by officers of the regular forces.

4646. (*Major-Gen. Eyre.*) Some two or three witnesses have maintained that the volunteer force ought to be a perfectly independent force, and talked of their having a complete staff of their own, does not it appear to you that to accustom the volunteers to work with those with whom they must necessarily be intimately associated in case of actual operations in the field, would be a desirable thing, as often as it could be done?—Certainly, most desirable.

4647. Is it not great folly to suppose that they could be, under any circumstances, allowed to act as an independent force, or that they would be of any use as such?—In my judgment it would be impossible; certainly, I think most undesirable.

4648. Would they not be under the command of the commander-in-chief of the army in the field and his generals?—Yes.

4649. Would not any such system in a case of war only render them an obstruction instead of valuable auxiliaries to the regular troops?—I cannot conceive a system of that kind being adopted by any Government.

4650. Does your lordship entertain any doubt that the more intimately the volunteers are associated with the regular troops the greater will be their efficiency and discipline, and the more cordial the feeling existing between the two bodies?—Certainly not.

4651. Does your lordship believe that the volunteers as a body, although there may be some objections on the part of individuals, would not only like it, but in point of fact, would like it very much?—I have every reason to believe so.

LETTERS AND MEMORANDA.

CONTENTS.

	Page
(1.)—Memorandum relative to Government Aid given to the old Volunteers	205
(2.)—Enrolled Strength of the Volunteer Force on the 1st of April 1862	206
(3.)—Copy of Reports from the Assistant Inspectors of Volunteers	224
(4.)—Copy of a Letter from Lieutenant-Colonel Acland, on the Provision of Drill Instructors, &c.	228
(5.)—Copy of a Letter from the Hon. F. C. Curzon, on Cadet Volunteer Corps	229
(6.)—Letters addressed to the Chairman of the Commission	229

(1.)—MEMORANDUM RELATIVE TO GOVERNMENT AID GIVEN TO THE OLD VOLUNTEERS.

(Furnished by the Secretary of State for War.)

The great body of volunteers commenced in 1803, their numbers were (including yeomanry):—

1803	463,134	1810	299,860
1804	449,140	1811	299,000
1805	429,165	1812	206,062
1806	420,310	1813	203,528
1807	406,869	1814	133,669
1808	413,464	1815	111,153
1809	200,983		

The votes for volunteers and local militia were (including yeomanry):—

	Volunteers.	Local Militia.
	£	£
1803	899,169	—
1804	2,590,568	—
1805	1,600,000	—
1806	1,738,806	—
1807	1,490,301	—
1808	1,293,487	—
1809	1,060,820	1,219,803
1810	869,569	643,650
1811	566,022	704,827
1812	531,169	720,078
1813	475,400	636,623
1814	312,804	636,623
1815	*167,038	360,000
1816	*110,113	†50,000

The volunteers received from the public:—

Pay for a permanent adjutant.
 Do.   do.   serjeant-major.
 Do.   do.   drill serjeant.
Clothing, &c., as an outfit. A clothing allowance of 20s. per man once in three years.
6s. 8d. per head per annum for repair of arms.
When called out for duty or exercise, pay, &c., at various rates, about equal to the pay of the regular army.

* Nothing included herein for volunteers in Great Britain, the votes being confined to English and Irish yeomanry.
† This was the last vote taken for the local militia.

The average cost per man per annum was nearly 4l., exclusive of arms and ammunition.

*The local militia established in 1809 appears to have taken the place, to a great extent, of the volunteers, of which there was a reduction in that year of 212,000 men.

Encouragement seems to have been given to the volunteers to enlist into the local militia, and whole regiments transferred their services to that force.

The chief part of the volunteer infantry of Great Britain were reduced in 1813, on which occasion a circular letter was sent from the Secretary of State for the Home Department to Lords Lieutenant, in which the following occurs:—
"I have it in command from the Prince Regent to acquaint "your Lordship that as the establishment of the local "militia precludes the necessity of continuing, under pre-"sent circumstances, the services of the greater part of the "volunteer infantry," &c.

In three years afterwards, the war having terminated, the local militia also ceased to exist.

On the introduction of the Bill for local militia in 1808, the reasons given by Lord Hawkesbury for the creation of the new force, and the reduction of the old, were that although the volunteer system was not objected to so far as it went, yet that it could not altogether be depended upon, because its efficiency entirely rested upon the spirit which might prevail at the time, and which might dwindle and evaporate.

The local militia, being a more permanent and compulsory force, would remedy this defect.

That the volunteers had not become unpopular appears from the following:—Lord Palmerston, in 1814, "pro-"nounced a very animated eulogium on this meritorious "body of men, who had boldly come forward to defend "their country when it was threatened with invasion." (Hansard, 27th June 1814, v. 28.)

The thanks of the House were voted to the volunteers on July 6, 1814. (Hansard, v. 28.)

The Secretary of State for the Home Department, in circular letter of 17th March 1813, to Lords Lieutenant, passed a very high eulogium on the volunteers in the name of the Prince Regent.

(Signed)   W. O. MARSHALL.

War Office, 27th March 1862.

* Acts 48 Geo. 3. c. 3, 1808 (Great Britain), and 48 Geo. 3. c. 150, 1808 (Scotland).

(2.)—ENROLLED STRENGTH OF THE VOLUNTEER FORCE ON THE 1ST OF APRIL 1862.

(Given in by Colonel MacMurdo.)

County	No. of Corps	Organization	Light Horse		Artillery		Engineer		Mounted Rifle		Rifle		No. of Arm in each County	Total 1862.	Total 1861.	Total 1860.
			Troops.	Enrolled Members.	Batteries.	Enrolled Members.	Companies.	Enrolled Members.	Companies.	Enrolled Members.	Companies.	Enrolled Members.				
ABERDEEN	1, 3, 4, 5, 6, 7	1st Adm. Brig.	—	—	6	404	—	—	—	—	—	—	404			
	3, 4, 7, 8, 10, 11, 14, 21	1st Adm. Batt.	—	—	—	—	—	—	—	—	9	504				
	2, 6, 13, 15, 16	2nd Adm. Batt.	—	—	—	—	—	—	—	—	6	398				
	5, 9, 17, 20	3rd Adm. Batt.	—	—	—	—	—	—	—	—	8	428				
	12	. . .	—	—	—	—	—	—	—	—	—	48				
	18	. . .	—	—	—	—	—	—	—	—	—	80				
	1	. . .	—	—	—	—	—	—	—	—	11	695				
	22	. . .	—	—	—	—	—	—	—	—	1	40				
	23	. . .	—	—	—	—	—	—	—	—	1	60	2,253	2,657	2,507	1,947
ANGLESEY	1	. . .	—	—	1	49										
	2	. . .	—	—	2	113										
	3	. . .	—	—	1	54							216			
	1	. . .	—	—	—	—	—	—	—	—	—	229	229	445	385	
ARGYLL	1, 3, 4	1st Adm. Brig.	—	—	4	284										
	2	. . .	—	—	1	65										
	5	. . .	—	—	½	32										
	6	. . .	—	—	1	60										
	7	. . .	—	—	1	78										
	8	. . .	—	—	1	63										
	9	. . .	—	—	1	51							633			
	2, 3, 7, 11	1st Adm. Batt.	—	—	—	—	—	—	—	—	5	301	301			
	6	. . .	—	—	—	—	—	—	—	—	2	53				
	8	. . .	—	—	—	—	—	—	—	—	2	61				
	10	. . .	—	—	—	—	—	—	—	—	1	111				
	12	. . .	—	—	—	—	—	—	—	—	1	71	296	1,230	1,305	939
AYR	1, 2, 3, 4	1st Adm. Brig.	—	—	5½	320	—	—	—	—	—	—	320			
	5, 1, 2, 3, 4, 5, 6, 7, 8, 9, 10, 11, 12, 13	1st Adm. Batt.	—	—	—	—	—	—	—	—	12½	971	971	1,291	1,329	1,034
BANFF	1, 2, 3, 4, 5	1st Adm. Brig.	—	—	5	280	—	—	—	—	—	—	80			

Enrolled Strength of the Volunteer Force on the 1st of April 1862—*cont.*

County.	No. of Corps.	Organization.	Light Horse.		Artillery.		Engineer.		Mounted Rifle.		Rifle.		No. of Arm in each County.	Total 1862.	Total 1861.	Total 1860.
			Troops.	Enrolled Members.	Batteries.	Enrolled Members.	Companies.	Enrolled Members.	Companies.	Enrolled Members.	Companies.	Enrolled Members.				
BANFF—*cont.*	1,2,3,4	1st Adm. Batt.	—	—	—	—	—	—	—	—	4	215	215	495	747	452
BEDFORD	1,2,4,5,6,7,8	1st Adm. Batt.	—	—	—	—	—	—	—	—	7	449	449	449	504	297
BERKS	1,2,3,4,5,6,7,12	1st Adm. Batt.	—	—	—	—	—	—	—	—	10	975				
	8	. . .	—	—	—	—	—	—	—	—	1	64				
	9	. . .	—	—	—	—	—	—	—	—	1	75				
	10	. . .	—	—	—	—	—	—	—	—	1	62				
	11	. . .	—	—	—	—	—	—	—	—	1	74	1,250	1,250	1,008	589
BERWICK	1	. . .	—	—	1	51	—	—	—	—	—	—				
	2	. . .	—	—	1	50	—	—	—	—	—	—	101			
	1	. . .	—	—	—	—	—	—	—	—	1	81				
	2	. . .	—	—	—	—	—	—	—	—	1	70				
	3	. . .	—	—	—	—	—	—	—	—	1	59				
	4	. . .	—	—	—	—	—	—	—	—	1	66				
	5	. . .	—	—	—	—	—	—	—	—	½	37	313	414	382	407
BERWICK-ON-TWEED.	1	. . .	—	—	2	104	—	—	—	—	—	—	104			
	1	. . .	—	—	—	—	—	—	—	—	1	61	61	165	164	In Berwick.
BRECKNOCK	1,2,3,4,5,6	1st Adm. Batt.	—	—	—	—	—	—	—	—	7	484	484	484	406	271
BUCKS	1	. . .	—	—	—	—	—	—	—	—	½	56				
	2	. . .	—	—	—	—	—	—	—	—	1	69				
	3	. . .	—	—	—	—	—	—	—	—	½	32				
	4	. . .	—	—	—	—	—	—	—	—	1	73				
	5	. . .	—	—	—	—	—	—	—	—	1	72				
	6	. . .	—	—	—	—	—	—	—	—	1	54				
	7	. . .	—	—	—	—	—	—	—	—	½	48	404	404	418	271
BUTE	1	. . .	—	—	—	—	—	—	—	—	1	86	86	86	85	80
CAITHNESS	1	. . .	—	—	1	61	—	—	—	—	—	—				
	2	. . .	—	—	1	41	—	—	—	—	—	—				
	3	. . .	—	—	1	58	—	—	—	—	—	—	160			
	1	. . .	—	—	—	—	—	—	—	—	1	61				
	2	. . .	—	—	—	—	—	—	—	—	1	86				
	3	. . .	—	—	—	—	—	—	—	—	1	78	225	385	415	161
CAMBRIDGE	1	. . .	—	—	—	—	—	—	½	28	—	—				
	2	. . .	—	—	—	—	—	—	1	42	—	—	70			
	2,4,5,6,7	1st Adm. Batt.	—	—	—	—	—	—	—	—	4½	309				
	1	. . .	—	—	—	—	—	—	—	—	1	113				
	3	. . .	—	—	—	—	—	—	—	—	6	595				
	8	. . .	—	—	—	—	—	—	—	—	1	102				
	9	. . .	—	—	—	—	—	—	—	—	½	34				
	10	. . .	—	—	—	—	—	—	—	—	½	28	1,181	1,251	1,188	90

Enrolled Strength of the Volunteer Force on the 1st of April 1862—*cont.*

County.	No. of Corps.	Organization.	Light Horse.		Artillery.		Engineer.		Mounted Rifle.		Rifle.		No. of Arm in each County	Total 1862.	Total 1861.	Total 1860.
			Troops.	Enrolled Members.	Batteries.	Enrolled Members.	Companies.	Enrolled Members.	Companies.	Enrolled Members.	Companies.	Enrolled Members.				
Cardigan	1	.. .. ..	—	—	—	—	—	—	—	—	½	30				
	2	.. .. ..	—	—	—	—	—	—	—	—	1	56				
	3	.. .. ..	—	—	—	—	—	—	—	—	1	66	152	152	151	180
Carmarthen	1															
	2															
	3	1st Adm. Batt.	—	—	—	—	—	—	—	—	6	427	427	427	423	406
	4															
	5															
	6															
Carnarvon	1	.. .. ..	—	—	1	54	—	—	—	—	—	—	54			
	1															
	2															
	3															
	4	1st Adm. Batt.	—	—	—	—	—	—	—	—	7	542	542			
	5															
	6															
	7													596	524	535
Chester	1															
	2															
	3	1st Adm. Brig.	—	—	8	525	—	—	—	—	—	—	525			
	4															
	5															
	1	.. .. ..	—	—	—	—	2	196	—	—	—	—	196			
	1															
	2															
	3															
	4	1st Adm. Batt.	—	—	—	—	—	—	—	—	9	683				
	11															
	14															
	30															
	34															
	6															
	7	2nd Adm. Batt.	—	—	—	—	—	—	—	—	6	456				
	23															
	24															
	12															
	15															
	22															
	25	3rd Adm. Batt.	—	—	—	—	—	—	—	—	8	568				
	26															
	28															
	32															
	9															
	13															
	17															
	18															
	19	4th Adm. Batt.	—	—	—	—	—	—	—	—	9	660				
	20															
	21															
	29															
	31															
	5															
	8															
	16	5th Adm. Batt.	—	—	—	—	—	—	—	—	7	524				
	27															
	33													2,891	3,612	3,565	2,836
Cinque Ports	1a	.. .. ..	—	—	2	86										
	1b	.. .. ..	—	—	1	68										
	1c	.. .. ..	—	—	½	59										
	2	.. .. ..	—	—	1	62										
	3	.. .. ..	—	—	1	61										
	4	.. .. ..	—	—	4	221										
	5	.. .. ..	—	—	½	40										
	6	.. .. ..	—	—	½	38	—	—	—	—	—	—	635			
	1															
	9															
(Sussex)	16	1st Adm. Batt.	—	—	—	—	—	—	—	—	4½	339				
"	17															
"	19															
	2															
	4															
	5	2nd Adm. Batt.	—	—	—	—	—	—	—	—	5	358				
	6															
	7															
	8													697	1,332	1,142	In Kent.
Clackmannan	—	Attached to 1st Adm. Brig, Stirling, R.V.	—	—	—	—	—	—	—	—	—	—	—	—	224	219

Enrolled Strength of the Volunteer Force on the 1st of April 1862—*cont.*

County.	No. of Corps.	Organization.	Light Horse.		Artillery.		Engineer.		Mounted Rifle.		Rifle.		No. of Arm in each County.	Total 1862.	Total 1861.	Total 1860.
			Troops.	Enrolled Members.	Batteries.	Enrolled Members.	Companies.	Enrolled Members.	Companies.	Enrolled Members.	Companies.	Enrolled Members.				
CORNWALL	1,2,3,4,5															
	7,8,9,10,11,12	1st Adm. Brig.	—	—	10	616	—	—	—	—	—	—	616			
	1,2,3,7,11,12,15,17,18,20,21	1st Adm. Batt.	—	—	—	—	—	—	—	—	10½	884				
	4,5,6,9,10,13,19	2nd Adm. Batt.	—	—	—	—	—	—	—	—	8	562				
													1,446	2,062	2,073	1,814
CROMARTY	1	-	-	-	—	1	36	—	—	—	—	—	—	36	36	55	
CUMBERLAND	1,2,3,4,5	1st Adm. Brig.	—	—	4½	270	—	—	—	—	—	—	270			
	1	-	-	-	—	—	1	72	—	—	—	—	72			
	1,2,3,4,5,6,7,8,9,10,11	1st Adm. Batt.	—	—	—	—	—	—	—	—	12½	910	910			
														1,252	1,196	1,011
DENBIGH	1	-	-	-	—	—	1	37	—	—	—	—	37			
	1,2,3,4,5,6,7,8	1st Adm. Batt.	—	—	—	—	—	—	—	—	8½	441	441			
														478	572	267
DERBY	1	-	-	-	—	—	—	—	1	55	—	—	55			
	1,4,5,12,13,15,16	1st Adm. Batt.	—	—	—	—	—	—	—	—	8	634				
	2,8,10	2nd Adm. Batt.	—	—	—	—	—	—	—	—	4½	233				
	3,7,9,11,17	3rd Adm. Batt.	—	—	—	—	—	—	—	—	5	389				
													1,311	1,366	1,429	1,050

Enrolled Strength of the Volunteer Force on the 1st of April 1862—*cont.*

County.	No. of Corps.	Organization.	Light Horse.		Artillery.		Engineer.		Mounted Rifle.		Rifle.		No. of Arm in each County.	Total 1862.	Total 1861.	Total 1860.
			Troops.	Enrolled Members.	Batteries.	Enrolled Members.	Companies.	Enrolled Members.	Companies.	Enrolled Members.	Companies.	Enrolled Members.				
Devon	1	—	1	54	—	—	—	—	—	—	—	—	54			
	1,2,3,4,5,7,8,9,11	1st Adm. Brig.	—	—	9½	685	—	—	—	—	—	—				
	6,10,12,13	2nd Adm. Brig.	—	—	8	524	—	—	—	—	—	—	1,209			
	1	—	—	—	—	—	—	—	1	60	—	—				
	3	—	—	—	—	—	—	—	1	28	—	—				
	4	—	—	—	—	—	—	—	1	53	—	—				
	6	—	—	—	—	—	—	—	1	58	—	—				
	7	—	—	—	—	—	—	—	1	50	—	—	249			
	1	—	—	—	—	—	—	½	29	—	—	—	—	29			
	5,8,11,13,14,20,25,27	1st Adm. Batt.	—	—	—	—	—	—	—	—	7	568				
	2,3,16,22	2nd Adm. Batt.	—	—	—	—	—	—	—	—	7	579				
	4,6,18,21	3rd Adm. Batt.	—	—	—	—	—	—	—	—	5	476				
	9,10,17,23,26	4th Adm. Batt.	—	—	—	—	—	—	—	—	4	432				
	1	—	—	—	—	—	—	—	—	—	11	762	2,817	4,358	3,838	3,205
Dorset	1	—	—	—	1	68	—	—	—	—	—	—				
	3	—	—	—	1	87	—	—	—	—	—	—				
	4	—	—	—	1	62	—	—	—	—	—	—	217			
	1,2,3,4,5,6,7,8,9	1st Adm. Batt.	—	—	—	—	—	—	—	—	10	797				
	10	—	—	—	—	—	—	—	½	29	—	—				
	11	—	—	—	—	—	—	—		26	—	—				
	12	—	—	—	—	—	—	—		45	—	—	897	1,114	1,225	1,031
Dumbarton	1	—	—	—	1	56	—	—	—	—	—	—				
	2	—	—	—	1	54	—	—	—	—	—	—				
	3	—	—	—	1	53	—	—	—	—	—	—	163			
	1,2,3,4,5,6,7,8,9	1st Adm. Batt.	—	—	—	—	—	—	—	—	10½	804	804			
	10,11,12														967	1,010	923
Dumfries	1,2,3,4,5,6,7,8,9	1st Adm. Batt.	—	—	—	—	—	—	—	—	8½	570	570	570	594	526

Enrolled Strength of the Volunteer Force on the 1st of April 1862—*cont.*

County.	No. of Corps.	Organization.	Light Horse.		Artillery.		Engineer.		Mounted Rifle.		Rifle.		No. of Arms in each County.	Total 1862.	Total 1861.	Total 1860.
			Troops.	Enrolled Members.	Batteries.	Enrolled Members.	Companies.	Enrolled Members.	Companies.	Enrolled Members.	Companies.	Enrolled Members.				
Durham	1	· · ·	—	—	2	196										
	2	· · ·	—	—	5	258										
	3	· · ·	—	—	1	76										
	4	· · ·	—	—	5	365							895			
	7, 10, 11, 13, 14	1st Adm. Batt.	—	—	—	—	—	—	—	—	11	770				
	4, 12, 17, 18, 20	2nd Adm. Batt.	—	—	—	—	—	—	—	—	7	407				
	8, 6, 9	3rd Adm. Batt.	—	—	—	—	—	—	—	—	6	399				
	1, 15, 16, 19	4th Adm. Batt.	—	—	—	—	—	—	—	—	7	419				
	3	· · ·	—	—	—	—	—	—	—	—	5	296	2,291	3,186	3,098	2,003
Edinburgh	1	· · ·	—	—	9	564	—	—	—	—	—	—	564			
	1	· · ·	—	—	—	—	1	64	—	—	—	—	64			
	1	· · ·	—	—	—	—	—	—	—	—	21	1,801	1,801	2,429	2,509	3,688
Elgin	1	· · ·	—	—	1	53	—	—	—	—	—	—	53			
	1, 2, 3, 4, 5, 6	1st Adm. Batt.	—	—	—	—	—	—	—	—	6	439	439	492	564	366
Essex	1	· · ·	—	—	1	54										
	2	· · ·	—	—	1	68										
	3	· · ·	—	—	1	55							177			
	1	· · ·	—	—	—	—	1	77	—	—	—	—	77			
	1	· · ·	—	—	—	—	—	—	½	30	—	—	30			
	4, 6, 10, 11, 12, 13, 14, 16, 23	1st Adm. Batt.	—	—	—	—	—	—	—	—	9½	715				
	5, 9	2nd Adm. Batt.	—	—	—	—	—	—	—	—	12	970				
	1, 2, 3, 7, 15, 18, 19, 21, 24	3rd Adm. Batt.	—	—	—	—	—	—	—	—	11	651				
	8	· · ·	—	—	—	—	—	—	—	—	4	294				
	17	· · ·	—	—	—	—	—	—	—	—	1	68				
	20	· · ·	—	—	—	—	—	—	—	—	1	91				
	22	· · ·	—	—	—	—	—	—	—	—	½	107	2,836	3,120	3,107	1,848
Fife	1, 2, 3, 4, 5, 6, 7, 8, 9, 10	1st Adm. Brig.	—	—	10½	630	—	—	—	—	—	—	630			
	1	· · ·	—	—	—	—	—	—	4	160	—	—	160			

Enrolled Strength of the Volunteer Force on the 1st of April 1862—cont.

County	No. of Corps	Organization	Light Horse		Artillery		Engineer		Mounted Rifle		Rifle		No. of Arm in each County	Total 1862	Total 1861	Total 1860
			Troops	Enrolled Members	Batteries	Enrolled Members	Companies	Enrolled Members	Companies	Enrolled Members	Companies	Enrolled Members				
Fife—cont.	1 2 3 4 5 6 7 8 9	1st Adm. Batt.	—	—	—	—	—	—	—	—	11	920	920			
														1,710	1,720	1,455
Flint	1 2 3 4	1st Adm. Batt.	—	—	—	—	—	—	—	—	4	266	266	266	261	226
Forfar	1 2 3 4	1st Adm. Brig.	—	—	6	374	—	—	—	—	—	—	374			
	3 5 7 13	1st Adm. Batt.	—	—	—	—	—	—	—	—	6	621				
	2 8 9 11 12	2nd Adm. Batt.	—	—	—	—	—	—	—	—	6	433		-		
	1		—	—	—	—	—	—	—	—	8	630				
													1,684	2,058	1,940	1,680
Glamorgan	1		1	40	—	—	—	—	—	—	—	—	40			
	3 4	1st Adm. Brig.	—	—	4	355	—	—	—	—	—	—				
	1		—	—	1	89	—	—	—	—	—	—				
	2		—	—	1	55	—	—	—	—	—	—	499			
	1		—	—	—	—	1	70	—	—	—	—	70			
	1 5 5 7 9 11 15 17	1st Adm. Batt.	—	—	—	—	—	—	—	—	13½	1,119				
	16 2 8 10 12 13 14 16 19	2nd Adm. Batt.	—	—	—	—	—	—	—	—	9½	737				
	3		—	—	—	—	—	—	—	—	4	337				
	4		—	—	—	—	—	—	—	—	6	634				
													2,827	3,436	3,226	1,892
Gloucester	1		—	—	5	207	—	—	—	—	—	—				
	2		—	—	1	52	—	—	—	—	—	—				
	3		—	—	7	71	—	—	—	—	—	—				
	4		—	—	3	96	—	—	—	—	—	—	446			
	1		—	—	—	—	1	70	—	—	—	—				
	2		—	—	—	—	2	163	—	—	—	—	233			
	3 5 6 8 9 11 12 15 16	1st Adm. Batt.	—	—	—	—	—	—	—	—	11½	965				
	7 10 13 14	2nd Adm. Batt.	—	—	—	—	—	—	—	—	4	304				
	1		—	—	—	—	—	—	—	—	10	854				
													2,123	2,802	2,823	2,226

Enrolled Strength of the Volunteer Force on the 1st of April 1862—*cont.*

County.	No. of Corps.	Organization.	Light Horse.		Artillery.		Engineer.		Mounted Rifle.		Rifle.		No. of Arm in each County.	Total 1862.	Total 1861.	Total 1860.
			Troops.	Enrolled Members.	Batteries.	Enrolled Members.	Companies.	Enrolled Members.	Companies.	Enrolled Members.	Companies.	Enrolled Members.				
HADDINGTON	1	- - -	—	—	1	69	—	—	—	—	—	—	69			
	2,3,4,5,6	1st Adm. Batt.	—	—	—	—	—	—	—	—	5½	509	509			
														578	473	397
HANTS	1	- - -	1	43									85			
	2	- - -	½	42												
	1,2,3	1st Adm. Brig.	—	—	9	471	—	—	—	—	—	—	471			
	1	- - -	—	—	—	—	1	54	—	—	—	—	54			
	1,11,13,15,16,18	1st Adm. Batt.	—	—	—	—	—	—	—	—	6½	447				
	4,5,6,23	2nd Adm. Batt.	—	—	—	—	—	—	—	—	6½	507				
	7,8,12,17,20,21,22	3rd Adm. Batt.	—	—	—	—	—	—	—	—	7½	504				
	2	- - -	—	—	—	—	—	—	—	—	6	401				
	3	- - -	—	—	—	—	—	—	—	—	1	80				
	10	- - -	—	—	—	—	—	—	—	—	1	66				
	19	- - -	—	—	—	—	—	—	—	—	½	39				
	14	- - -	—	—	—	—	—	—	—	—	1	76				
													2,120	2,730	2,706	2,552
HAVERFORDWEST	1	- - -	—	—	—	—	—	—	—	—	2½	151	151	151	166	
HEREFORD	1,2,3,4,5,6,7,8	1st Adm. Batt.	—	—	—	—	—	—	—	—	8	546	546	546	559	494
HERTFORD	2,3,4,5,7,8	1st Adm. Batt.	—	—	—	—	—	—	—	—	5½	417				
	1,6,9,10,11,12	2nd Adm. Batt.	—	—	—	—	—	—	—	—	7	557				
													974	974	924	639
HUNTINGDON	1	- - -	3	145	—	—	—	—	—	—	—	—	145			
	1	- - -	—	—	—	—	—	—	—	—	2	159	159			
														304	304	228
INVERNESS	1	- - -	—	—	4	234	—	—	—	—	—	—	234			
	1,2,3,4,5,6,7	1st Adm. Batt.	—	—	—	—	—	—	—	—	7	501	501			
														735	758	569
ISLE OF MAN	1	- - -	—	—	2	122	—	—	—	—	—	—	122			
	1,2,3	1st Adm. Batt.	—	—	—	—	—	—	—	—	2½	161	161			
														283	237	

Enrolled Strength of the Volunteer Force on the 1st of April 1862—*cont*

County.	No. of Corps.	Organization.	Light Horse. Troops.	Artillery. Batteries.	Artillery. Enrolled Members.	Engineer. Companies.	Engineer. Enrolled Members.	Mounted Rifle. Companies.	Mounted Rifle. Enrolled Members.	Rifle. Companies.	Rifle. Enrolled Members.	No. of Arm in each County.	Total 1862.	Total 1861.	Total 1860.
Isle of Wight	1, 2, 3, 4, 5	1st. dm. Batt.	—	—	—	—	—	—	—	6½	527	527	527	583	
Kent	7, 8, 1, 2, 4, 5, 9, 11, 12, 13	1st Adm. Brig.	—	—	11 760	—	—	—	—						
	10, 14	" "	—	—	7 402 / 5 280	—	—	—	—			1,442			
	3, 4, 7, 8, 13, 18, 25, 27, 28, 32, 34	1st Adm. Batt.	—	—	—	—	—	—	—	13	1,130				
	11, 14, 17, 23, 33, 35	2nd Adm. Batt.	—	—	—	—	—	—	—	5½	377				
	1, 9, 12, 15, 19, 20, 22, 31, 39, 45	3rd Adm. Batt.	—	—	—	—	—	—	—	11	876				
	5, 6, 16, 24, 29, 36, 37, 38, 40	4th Adm. Batt.	—	—	—	—	—	—	—	6	468				
	41, 42, 43, 44	5th Adm. Batt.	—	—	—	—	—	—	—	6	428				
(Cinque Ports.)	3, 26	" "	—	—	—	—	—	—	—	16	951	4,230	5,672	5,692	5,969 (including C.P.)
Kincardine	1, 2, 3, 4	" "	—	—	2 123 / 25 / 35 / 28	—	—	—	—	—	211				
	1, 2, 3, 4, 5, 6, 7	1st Adm. Batt.	—	—	—	—	—	—	—	6½	495	495	706	723	560
Kinross	1	{ with 1st Fife Adm. Batt. }	—	—	—	—	—	—	—	—	—	—	—	69	
Kircudbright and Wigton	1, 2, 3, 4, 5, 1, 2, 3, 4	1st Adm. Batt.	—	—	—	—	—	—	—	7½	534	534			

Enrolled Strength of the Volunteer Force on the 1st of April 1862—cont.

County.	No. of Corps.	Organization.	Light Horse.		Artillery.		Engineer.		Mounted Rifle.		Rifle.		No. of Arm in each County.	Total 1862.	Total 1861.	Total 1860.
			Troops.	Enrolled Members.	Batteries.	Enrolled Members.	Companies.	Enrolled Members.	Companies.	Enrolled Members.	Companies.	Enrolled Members.				
KIRCUDBRIGHT —cont.	1	. . .	—	—	1	50	—	—	—	—	—	—	50	584	362	317
LANARK .	1 2 3 4 5 6 7 8 9 10 12 13 14 15	1st Adm. Brig.	—	—	15	888										
	11	. . .	—	—	1	52							940			
	1 2	. . . . . .	— —	— —	— —	— —	1 1	105 66			— —	— —	171			
	16 42 44 52 56 57	1st Adm. Batt.	—	—	—	—	—	—	—	—	6	496				
	30 31 38 45 46 47 75 84 86 88 96	2nd Adm. Batt.	—	—	—	—	—	—	—	—	11	813				
	37 55 73 94	3rd Adm. Batt.	—	—	—	—	—	—	—	—	4	313				
	1 3 4 5 19 25 29 32 43 48 49 95 97	. . . .	— — — — — — — — — — — — —	— — — — — — — — — — — — —	— — — — — — — — — — — — —	— — — — — — — — — — — — —	— — — — — — — — — — — — —	— — — — — — — — — — — — —	— — — — — — — — — — — — —	— — — — — — — — — — — — —	16 9 10 12 15 8 1 1 1 1 — 1 4	989 579 616 783 924 531 83 57 55 71 3 63 254	6,630	7,741	7,920	7,455
LANCASTER .	1 2	. . . . . .	1 1½	58 95	—	—	—	—	—	—	—	—	153			
	1 2 6 7 13	1st Adm. Brig.	—	—	10½	650										
	9 12 17	2nd Adm. Brig.	—	—	8	501										
	5 18 22 23	3rd Adm. Brig.	—	—	7	425										
	4 8 10 11 15 19 21	. . . .	— — — — — — —	— — — — — — —	8 8 1 6 2 4 4	535 452 58 367 103 265 260							3,625			
	1 2	. . . . . .	— —	— —	— —	— —	8 1	64 97	— —	— —	— —	— —	161			

Enrolled Strength of the Volunteer Force on the 1st of April 1862—*cont.*

County.	No. of Corps.	Organization.	Light Horse.		Artillery.		Engineer.		Mounted Rifle.		Rifle.		No. of Arm in each County.	Total 1862.	Total 1861.	Total 1860.
			Troops.	Enrolled Members.	Batteries.	Enrolled Members.	Companies.	Enrolled Members.	Companies.	Enrolled Members.	Companies.	Enrolled Members.				
LANCASTER— *cont.*	4, 7, 17, 57, 84, 87	3rd Adm. Batt.	—	—	—	—	—	—	—	—	7	536				
	46, 53, 60, 67, 76, 10	4th Adm. Batt.	—	—	—	—	—	—	—	—	6	439				
	37a, 57b, 37c, 52, 53, 73	5th Adm. Batt.	—	—	—	—	—	—	—	—	8	570				
	11, 44, 59, 61	6th Adm. Batt.	—	—	—	—	—	—	—	—	7	523				
	1	" " "	—	—	—	—	—	—	—	—	10	561				
	2	" " "	—	—	—	—	—	—	—	—	4	405				
	5	" " "	—	—	—	—	—	—	—	—	10½	608				
	6	" " "	—	—	—	—	—	—	—	—	13	885				
	8	" " "	—	—	—	—	—	—	—	—	4	349				
	9	" " "	—	—	—	—	—	—	—	—	4	250				
	13	" " "	—	—	—	—	—	—	—	—	1	69				
	15	" " "	—	—	—	—	—	—	—	—	5	297				
	21	" " "	—	—	—	—	—	—	—	—	2	134				
	22	" " "	—	—	—	—	—	—	—	—	2	85				
	23	" " "	—	—	—	—	—	—	—	—	4½	301				
	24	" " "	—	—	—	—	—	—	—	—	3	253				
	25	" " "	—	—	—	—	—	—	—	—	2	193				
	26	" " "	—	—	—	—	—	—	—	—	2	128				
	27	" " "	—	—	—	—	—	—	—	—	6	450				
	28	" " "	—	—	—	—	—	—	—	—	9	639				
	29	" " "	—	—	—	—	—	—	—	—	1	67				
	31	" " "	—	—	—	—	—	—	—	—	3	221				
	33	" " "	—	—	—	—	—	—	—	—	6	382				
	40	" " "	—	—	—	—	—	—	—	—	10	731				
	41	" " "	—	—	—	—	—	—	—	—	1	83				
	42	" " "	—	—	—	—	—	—	—	—	2	125				
	45	" " "	—	—	—	—	—	—	—	—	2	146				
	47	" " "	—	—	—	—	—	—	—	—	8	530				
	48	" " "	—	—	—	—	—	—	—	—	1	71				
	49	" " "	—	—	—	—	—	—	—	—	1	65				
	51	" " "	—	—	—	—	—	—	—	—	5	532				
	54	" " "	—	—	—	—	—	—	—	—	1	59				
	56	" " "	—	—	—	—	—	—	—	—	4	257				
	62	" " "	—	—	—	—	—	—	—	—	1	90				
	65	" " "	—	—	—	—	—	—	—	—	1	70				
	67	" " "	—	—	—	—	—	—	—	—	1	63				
	70	" " "	—	—	—	—	—	—	—	—	1	74				
	73	" " "	—	—	—	—	—	—	—	—	1	60				
	74	" " "	—	—	—	—	—	—	—	—	3	182				
	76	" " "	—	—	—	—	—	—	—	—	1	64				
	77	" " "	—	—	—	—	—	—	—	—	1	43				
	78	" " "	—	—	—	—	—	—	—	—	6	556				
	80	" " "	—	—	—	—	—	—	—	—	8	646				
	82	" " "	—	—	—	—	—	—	—	—	1	75				
	83	" " "	—	—	—	—	—	—	—	—	1	59				
	64	" " "	—	—	—	—	—	—	—	—	2	157				
	71	" " "	—	—	—	—	—	—	—	—	2	136				
														13,207	17,146	17,961	12,713
LEICESTER	1, 2, 3, 4, 5, 6, 7, 8, 9, 10	1st Adm. Batt.	—	—	—	—	—	—	—	—	10	636	636	636	638	405
LINCOLN	1, 2, 6, 7, 9, 11, 12, 19, 20	1st Adm. Batt.	—	—	—	—	—	—	—	—	11	812				

Enrolled Strength of the Volunteer Force on the 1st of April 1862—*cont.*

County.	No. of Corps.	Organization.	Light Horse. Troops.	Artillery. Batteries.	Artillery. Enrolled Members.	Engineer. Companies.	Engineer. Enrolled Members.	Mounted Rifle. Companies.	Mounted Rifle. Enrolled Members.	Rifle. Companies.	Rifle. Enrolled Members.	No. of Arm in each County.	Total 1862.	Total 1861.	Total 1860.
Lincoln—*cont.*	3, 5, 6, 15, 18	2nd Adm. Batt.	—	—	—	—	—	—	—	6	441				
	4, 13, 16, 17	3rd Adm. Batt.	—	—	—	—	—	—	—	4	253	1,506			
	1, 2, 3	1st Adm. Brig.	—	—	5½	346	—	—	—	—	—	346	1,852	1,863	1,592
Linlithgow	1	. . .	—	—	—	—	—	—	—	1	84				
	2	. . .	—	—	—	—	—	—	—	1	91				
	3	. . .	—	—	—	—	—	—	—	1	91	266	266	230	241
London	1	. . .	—	—	—	1	85	—	—	—	—	85			
	1	. . .	—	—	—	—	—	—	—	16	1,217				
	2	. . .	—	—	—	—	—	—	—	4	278				
	3	. . .	—	—	—	—	—	—	—	12	831				
	4	. . .	—	—	—	—	—	—	—	8	480				
	5	. . .	—	—	—	—	—	—	—	2	160	2,966	3,051	2,419	In Middlesex.
Merioneth	1	. . .	—	—	—	—	—	—	—	1	53				
	2	. . .	—	—	—	—	—	—	—	1	56				
	3	. . .	—	—	—	—	—	—	—	1	123	232	232	243	118
Middlesex	1	. . .	2	101	—	—	—	—	—	—	—	101			
	1	. . .	—	4	233	—	—	—	—	—	—				
	2	. . .	—	2	134	—	—	—	—	—	—				
	3	. . .	—	8	461	—	—	—	—	—	—	828			
	1	. . .	—	—	—	8	698	—	—	—	—	698			
	3, 12, 13, 14, 33, 41	2nd Adm. Batt.	—	—	—	—	—	—	—	11	562				
	26, 42	5th Adm. Batt.	—	—	—	—	—	—	—	6	427				
	16, 24, 30, 43, 44, 45	7th Adm. Batt.	—	—	—	—	—	—	—	8½	614				
	1	. . .	—	—	—	—	—	—	—	8	561				
	2	. . .	—	—	—	—	—	—	—	16	1,337				
	4	. . .	—	—	—	—	—	—	—	8	280				
	9	. . .	—	—	—	—	—	—	—	8	583				
	11	. . .	—	—	—	—	—	—	—	6	440				
	15	. . .	—	—	—	—	—	—	—	10	673				
	18	. . .	—	—	—	—	—	—	—	2	115				
	19	. . .	—	—	—	—	—	—	—	10	702				
	20	. . .	—	—	—	—	—	—	—	14	1,041				
	21	. . .	—	—	—	—	—	—	—	8	520				
	22	. . .	—	—	—	—	—	—	—	19	1,503				
	23	. . .	—	—	—	—	—	—	—	6	772				
	28	. . .	—	—	—	—	—	—	—	10	497				
	29	. . .	—	—	—	—	—	—	—	10	773				
	32	. . .	—	—	—	—	—	—	—	2	112				
	36	. . .	—	—	—	—	—	—	—	4	297				
	37	. . .	—	—	—	—	—	—	—	8	606				
	38	. . .	—	—	—	—	—	—	—	3	235				
	39	. . .	—	—	—	—	—	—	—	8	696				
	40	. . .	—	—	—	—	—	—	—	9	564				
	46	. . .	—	—	—	—	—	—	—	8	576				
	47	. . .	—	—	—	—	—	—	—	1	68				
	48	. . .	—	—	—	—	—	—	—	8	481	14,878	16,505	16,639	12,922
Midlothian	1	. . .	—	8	463	—	—	—	—	—	—				
	2	. . .	—	2	138	—	—	—	—	—	—	601			
	2, 3, 5	1st Adm. Batt.	—	—	—	—	—	—	—	5½	372				
	1	. . .	—	—	—	—	—	—	—	8	449				
	4	. . .	—	—	—	—	—	—	—	4	60	881	1,182	1,646	In Edinburgh.

Enrolled Strength of the Volunteer Force on the 1st of April 1862—cont.

County.	No. of Corps.	Organization.	Light Horse.		Artillery.		Engineer.		Mounted Rifle.		Rifle.		No. of Arm in each County.	Total 1862.	Total 1861.	Total 1860.
			Troops.	Enrolled Members.	Batteries.	Enrolled Members.	Companies.	Enrolled Members.	Companies.	Enrolled Members.	Companies.	Enrolled Members.				
Monmouth	1	-	-	-	2	105	-	-	-	-	-	-	105			
	1,3,4,10	1st Adm. Batt.	-	-	-	-	-	-	-	-	7	486				
	5,6,7,8,9	2nd Adm. Batt.	-	-	-	-	-	-	-	-	9½	452				
	2	-	-	-	-	-	-	-	-	-	6	696	1,634	1,739	1,729	761
Montgomery	1,2,4,5	1st Adm. Batt.	-	-	-	-	-	-	-	-	3½	373				
	3	-	-	-	-	-	-	-	...	-	2½	149	522	522	401	284
Nairn	1	-	-	-	2	125	-	-	-	-	-	-	125			
	1	-	-	-	-	-	-	-	-	-	½	18	18	143	170	104
Newcastle-on-Tyne	1	-	-	-	-	205	-	-	-	-	-	-	205			
	1	-	-	-	-	-	2	131	-	-	-	-	131			
	1	-	-	-	-	-	-	-	-	-	-	705	705	1,041	1,065	In Northumberland.
Norfolk	1	-	-	-	4	229	-	-	-	-	-	-	229			
	1	-	-	-	-	-	-	-	½	42	-	-	42			
	6,10,11,12,13,15,19	1st Adm. Batt.	-	-	-	-	-	-	-	-	6½	369				
	7,8,9,14,18,20,21,22	2nd Adm. Batt.	-	-	-	-	-	-	-	-	6	289				
	1	-	-	-	-	-	-	-	-	-	6	422				
	2	-	-	-	-	-	-	-	-	-	4	412				
	5	-	-	-	-	-	-	-	-	-	1	111				
	16	-	-	-	-	-	-	-	-	-	1	61				
	17	-	-	-	-	-	-	-	-	-	1	71				
	23	-	-	-	-	-	-	-	-	-	½	41	1,776	2,047	2,065	1,488
Northampton	1	-	-	-	-	-	-	-	½	50	-	-	50			
	1,2,4,5,6,7,8	1st Adm. Batt.	-	-	-	-	-	-	-	-	10	906	906	956	944	446
Northumberland	1	-	-	-	6	427	-	-	-	-	-	-				
	2	-	-	-	2	114	-	-	-	-	-	-				
	3	-	-	-	2	57	-	-	-	-	-	-	598			
	2,3,4,5,6,7,10,1 (City of Berwick)	1st Adm. Batt.	-	-	-	-	-	-	-	-	7½	544				
	1,8,9	2nd Adm. Batt.	-	-	-	-	-	-	-	-	6½	486	1,030	1,628	1,474	1,716

Enrolled Strength of the Volunteer Force on the 1st of April 1892—cont.

County	No. of Corps.	Organization.	Light Horse.		Artillery.		Engineer.		Mounted Rifle.		Rifle.		No. of Arm in each County.	Total 1892.	Total 1891.	Total 1890.
			Troops.	Enrolled Members.	Batteries.	Enrolled Members.	Companies.	Enrolled Members.	Companies.	Enrolled Members.	Companies.	Enrolled Members.				
Nottingham	2, 3, 4, 6, 7, 8	1st Adm. Batt.	—	—	—	—	—	—	—	—	7	494				
	1	. . .	—	—	—	—	—	—	—	—	10	908				
	5	. . .	—	—	—	—	—	—	—	—	1	80	1,482	1,482	1,511	1,181
Orkney	1	. . .	—	—	1	72	—	—	—	—	—	—	72			
	1	. . .	—	—	—	—	—	—	—	—	½	57	57	129	133	145
Oxford	2, 3, 4, 5, 6, 7, 8, 9	1st Adm. Batt.	—	—	—	—	—	—	—	—	7½	50.7	*			
	1	. . .	—	—	—	—	—	—	—	—	6	567	1,070	1,070	1,023	924
Peebles	1	. . .	—	—	—	—	—	—	—	—	1	63				
	2	. . .	—	—	—	—	—	—	—	—	1	76				
	3	. . .	—	—	—	—	—	—	—	—	1	45				
	4	. . .	—	—	—	—	—	—	—	—	1	—	184	184	264	178
Pembroke	1	. . .	—	—	1	53	—	—	—	—	—	—	53			
	1, 2, 3, 4	1st Adm. Batt.	—	—	—	—	—	—	—	—	4½	324	324	377	355	201
Perth	1, 5, 6, 7, 8, 9, 11, 13, 14, 15, 16	1st Adm. Batt.	—	—	—	—	—	—	—	—	12½	957				
Argyll	3, 10, 9	2nd Adm. Batt.	—	—	—	—	—	—	—	—	6	446	1,403	1,403	1,331	1,078
Radnor	1	. . .	—	—	—	—	—	—	—	—	1	64				
	2	. . .	—	—	—	—	—	—	—	—	1	60				
	3	. . .	—	—	—	—	—	—	—	—	½	44	168	168	169	140
Renfrew	1, 5, 10, 11, 22	1st Adm. Batt.	—	—	—	—	—	—	—	—	8	602				
	3, 6, 9, 14, 15, 17, 20, 24	2nd Adm. Batt.	—	—	—	—	—	—	—	—	8	651				
	4, 7, 8, 16, 19, 21, 23, 25	3rd Adm. Batt.	—	—	—	—	—	—	—	—	8	581	1,834			
	1	. . .	—	—	1	78	—	—	—	—	—	—				
	2	. . .	—	—	1	56	—	—	—	—	—	—				
	3	. . .	—	—	1	52	—	—	—	—	—	—	186	2,020	2,123	1,907

Enrolled Strength of the Volunteer Force on the 1st of April 1862—cont.

County	No. of Corps	Organization	Light Horse		Artillery		Engineer		Mounted Rifle		Rifle		No. of Arm in each County	Total 1862.	Total 1861.	Total 1860.
			Troops.	Enrolled Members.	Batteries.	Enrolled Members.	Companies.	Enrolled Members.	Companies.	Enrolled Members.	Companies.	Enrolled Members.				
Ross	1	- - -	—	—	1	72	—	—	—	—	—	—	72			
	1 }															
	2 }															
	4 } 1st Adm. Batt.	—	—	—	—	—	—	—	—	4½	330				
	5 }															
	6 }															
	3	- - -	—	—	—	—	—	—	—	—	1	68				
													398	470	471	420
Roxburgh	1 }															
	2 }															
	3 } 1st Adm. Batt.	—	—	—	—	—	—	—	—	7	636	636	636	660	441
	4 }															
	5 }															
Selkirk	1 }															
	2 }															
Salop	1	- - "	—	—	2	152	—	—	—	—	—	—	152			
	1 }															
	4 }															
	5 }															
	6 }															
	10 } 1st Adm. Batt.	—	—	—	—	—	—	—	—	8½	624				
	11 }															
	14 }															
	16 }															
	17 }															
	2 }															
	3 }															
	7 }															
	8 } 2nd Adm. Batt.	—	—	—	—	—	—	—	—	8	574				
	12 }															
	13 }															
	15 }															
	18 }															
													1,198	1,350	1,345	1,030
Somerset	1	- - -	—	—	1	64										
	2	- - -	—	—	2	105	—	—	—	—	—	—	169			
	1 }															
	2 }															
	7 }															
	14 } 1st Adm. Batt.	—	—	—	—	—	—	—	—	6½	545				
	17 }															
	18 }															
	22 }															
	3 }															
	5 }															
	8 }															
	9 }															
	11 } 2nd Adm. Batt.	—	—	—	—	—	—	—	—	11	926				
	12 }															
	16 }															
	20 }															
	21 }															
	26 }															
	4 }															
	6 }															
	10 }															
	13 }															
	15 } 3rd Adm. Batt.	—	—	—	—	—	—	—	—	8½	642				
	19 }															
	23 }															
	24 }															
	25 }															
	27 }															
													2,113	2,282	2,278	1,770
Stafford	—	- - -	—	—	1	104	—	—	—	—	—	—	104			
	2 }															
	3 }															
	6 }															
	9 }															
	10 }															
	13 } 1st Adm. Batt.	—	—	—	—	—	—	—	—	12	1,101				
	16 }															
	28 }															
	36 }															
	37 }															
	38 }															
	40 }															

Enrolled Strength of the Volunteer Force on the 1st of April 1862—cont.

County.	No. of Corps.	Organization.	Light Horse.		Artillery.		Engineer.		Mounted Rifle.		Rifle.		No. of Arm in each County.	Total 1862.	Total 1861.	Total 1860.
			Troops.	Enrolled Members.	Batteries.	Enrolled Members.	Companies.	Enrolled Members.	Companies.	Enrolled Members.	Companies.	Enrolled Members.				
STAFFORD—cont.	7, 8, 19, 21, 24, 25, 30	2nd Adm. Batt.	—	—	—	—	—	—	—	—	7	570				
	1, 15, 17, 18, 20, 27, 31, 33	3rd Adm. Batt.	—	—	—	—	—	—	—	—	8	658				
	5, 11, 12, 23, 26, 29, 30, 32	4th Adm. Batt.	—	—	—	—	—	—	—	—	8	654				
	4, 14, 22, 33, 34	5th Adm. Batt.	—	—	—	—	—	—	—	—	4½	387				
													3,370	3,474	3,433	2,744
STIRLING	1		—	—	—	—	1	61	—	—	—	—				
	2		—	—	—	—	1	70	—	—	—	—				
													131			
SUFFOLK	1, 2, 3, 4, 5, 6, 7, 8, 9, 11, 12	1st Adm. Batt.	—	—	—	—	—	—	—	—	10	996				
	10		—	—	—	—	—	—	—	—	1	76				
													1,072	1,203	920	720
	1		—	—	1	69	—	—	—	—	—	—				
	2		—	—	½	40	—	—	—	—	—	—				
	6, 10, 11, 13, 16, 18, 19, 20	1st Adm. Batt.	—	—	—	—	—	—	—	—	8	613		109		
	1, 2, 3, 5, 8, 12, 21	2nd Adm. Batt.	—	—	—	—	—	—	—	—	6½	551				
	4, 7, 9, 14, 15, 17	3rd Adm. Batt.	—	—	—	—	—	—	—	—	6½	529				
													1,693			
SURREY	1		1½	84	3	177	—	—	—	—	—	—	84	1,802	1,777	1,306
	2		—	—	2	180	—	—	—	—	—	—				
	1		—	—	—	—	2	148	—	—	—	—	357, 148			
	1, 2, 4, 8, 20, 26	1st Adm. Batt.	—	—	—	—	—	—	—	—	7	342				
	6, 9, 11, 13, 16	2nd Adm. Batt.	—	—	—	—	—	—	—	—	6½	403				

Enrolled Strength of the Volunteer Force on the 1st of April 1862—*cont.*

COUNTY.	No. of Corps.	Organization.	Light Horse. Troops.	Light Horse. Enrolled Members.	Artillery. Batteries.	Artillery. Enrolled Members.	Engineer. Companies.	Engineer. Enrolled Members.	Mounted Rifle. Companies.	Mounted Rifle. Enrolled Members.	Rifle. Companies.	Rifle. Enrolled Members.	No. of Arm in each County.	Total 1862.	Total 1861.	Total 1860.
SURREY—*cont.*	5, 13, 14, 17, 16, 22, 25	3rd Adm. Batt.	—	—	...		..		—	—	7	485				
	1	" " "	—	..	—	—	—	..	—	—	8	542				
	7	" " "	—	—	—	—	—	—	—	—	6	475				
	10	" " "	—	—	—	—	—	—	—	—	2	178				
	12	" " "	—	—	—	—	—	—	—	—	4	347				
	19	" " "	—	—	—	—	—	—	—	—	8	376				
	21	" " "	—	—	—	—	—	—	—	—	1	103				
	23	" " "	—	—	—	—	—	—	—	—	1½	144				
	24	" " "	—	—	—	—	—	—	—	—	1	91				
	25	" " "	—	—	—	—	—	—	—	—	1	60				
													3,836	4,425	4,122	3,029
SUTHERLAND	1	" " "	—	—	1	71	—	—	—	—	—	—	71			
	1	" " "	—	—	—	—	—	—	—	—	4	354	354	425	354	310
SUSSEX	1, 2, 3, 4, 9	1st Adm. Brig.	—	—	8½	571	—	—	—	—	—	—	571			
	10, 11, 12, 15	1st Adm. Batt.	—	—	—	—	—	—	—	—	4½	336				
	5, 6, 7, 8, 13, 14, 16	2nd Adm. Batt.	—	—	—	—	—	—	—	—	8	572				
	1, 2, 4	3rd Adm. Batt.	—	—	—	—	—	—	—	—	6	608				
													1,516	2,087	2,260	1,890
TOWER HAMLETS.	1	" " "	—	—	2	116	—	—	—	—	—	—	116			
	1	" " "	—	—	—	—	1½	87	—	—	—	—	87			
	3, 7, 10, 11	1st Adm. Batt.	—	—	—	—	—	—	—	—	9	642				
	2	" " "	—	—	—	—	—	—	—	—	7	648				
	4	" " "	—	—	—	—	—	—	—	—	5	296				
	6	" " "	—	—	—	—	—	—	—	—	6	577				
	8	" " "	—	—	—	—	—	—	—	—	1	100				
	9	" " "	—	—	—	—	—	—	—	—	1	99				
	12	" " "	—	—	—	—	—	—	—	—	2	128				
													2,490	2,693	2,723	In Middlesex.
WARWICK	2, 3, 4, 5, 6, 7, 8, 9, 10, 11	1st Adm. Batt.	—	—	—	—	—	—	—	—	9½	658				
	1	" " "	—	—	—	—	—	—	—	—	12	1,067	1,725	1,725	1,715	1,344
WESTMORELAND	1, 3, 4, 5, 6	1st Adm. Batt.	—	—	—	—	—	—	—	—	6	402	402	402	425	420
WIGTOWN	1	" " "	—	—	1	55	In Kirkcudbright		—	—	—	—				
	2	" " "	—	—	1	47			—	—	—	—	102	102	291	240

Enrolled Strength of the Volunteer Force on the 1st of April 1862—*cont.*

County	No. of Corps.	Organization.	Light Horse.		Artillery.		Engineer.		Mounted Rifle.		Rifle.		No. of Arm in each County	Total 1862.	Total 1861.	Total 1860.
			Troops.	Enrolled Members.	Batteries.	Enrolled Members.	Companies.	Enrolled Members.	Companies.	Enrolled Members.	Companies.	Enrolled Members.				
Wilts	1,2,6,8,9,10,13,14	1st Adm. Batt.	—	—	—	—	—	—	—	—	11½	725				
	3,4,5,7,11,12,15,16,17,18	2nd Adm. Batt.	—	—	—	—	—	—	—	—	12	769				
													1,494	1,494	1,506	1,267
Worcester	1,2,3,4,5,6,7,8,9,16,20	1st Adm. Batt.	—	—	—	—	—	—	—	—	11	938				
	10,11,12,13,14,15,17,18,19,21	2nd Adm. Bat.	—	—	—	—	—	—	—	—	10	742				
													1,680	1,680	1,604	1,351
York, E. R.	3,5,6,8,9,10	1st Adm. Batt.	—	—	—	—	—	—	—	—	5¼	385				
	1		—	—	—	—	—	—	—	—	8	398	783			
N R.	1,2,2,3	1st Adm. Brig.	—	—	7	427	—	—	—	—	—	—				
W. R.	3,4		—	—	9	482	—	—	—	—	—	—	909	1,692	1,508	1,268
York, N. R.	1		—	—	8	441	—	—	—	—	—	—	441			
	2,4,5,7,8,9,11,12,14,15,18,19	1st Adm. Batt.	—	—	—	—	—	—	—	—	11	738				
	1,3,6,10,13,16,17	2nd Adm. Batt.	—	—	—	—	—	—	—	—	7½	366				
													1,101	1,545	1,524	1,522
York, W. R.	1,2,4		—	—	6	464	—	—	—	—	—	—				
			—	—	4	253	—	—	—	—	—	—				
			—	—	3	249	—	—	—	—	—	—	966			
	1,2		—	—	—	—	2	155	—	—	—	—				
			—	—	—	—	6	436	—	—	—	—	591			

Enrolled Strength of the Volunteer Force on the 1st of April 1862—*cont.*

County.	No. of Corps.	Organisation.	Light Horse.		Artillery.		Engineer.		Mounted Rifle.		Rifle.		No. of Arm in each County.	Total 1862.	Total 1861.	Total 1860.
			Troops.	Enrolled Members.	Batteries.	Enrolled Members.	Companies.	Enrolled Members.	Companies.	Enrolled Members.	Companies.	Enrolled Members.				
York, W.R.—*cont.*	1, 16, 17, 27, 31, 33, 12, 15	1st Adm. Batt.	—	—	—	—	—	—	—	—	8½	670				
	23, 25, 26, 5	2nd Adm. Batt.	—	—	—	—	—	—	—	—	5	542				
	28, 29, 30, 38, 18	3rd Adm. Batt.	—	—	—	—	—	—	—	—	7½	445				
	19, 20, 21	4th Adm. Batt.	—	—	—	—	—	—	—	—	4	320				
	2	.	—	—	—	—	—	—	—	—	7	628				
	3	.	—	—	—	—	—	—	—	—	6	430				
	4	.	—	—	—	—	—	—	—	—	9	584				
	6	.	—	—	—	—	—	—	—	—	4	355				
	7	.	—	—	—	—	—	—	—	—	9	665				
	32	.	—	—	—	—	—	—	—	—	1	64				
	34	.	—	—	—	—	—	—	—	—	1	134				
	35	.	—	—	—	—	—	—	—	—	1½	106				
	36	.	—	—	—	—	—	—	—	—	1	78				
	37	.	—	—	—	—	—	—	—	—	1	85				
	39	.	—	—	—	—	—	—	—	—	1	85				
													5,220	6,777	6,053	3,654
		Grand Total	—	11½	362	386	24,363	45	2,904	13	656	1,802	134,096	—	162,681	161,400	119,283

(3.)—COPY OF REPORTS FROM THE ASSISTANT INSPECTORS OF VOLUNTEERS.

(Furnished by the Secretary of State for War.)

Sir,   Edinburgh, 15th January 1862.

IN reply to your letter, V Haddington 55, of the 13th instant, enclosing a printed report of a committee appointed by the county of Haddington, and calling upon me for my opinion of the present state of the rural volunteer corps, with special reference to the points raised in the above report, I have the honour to inform you that the financial statement which the report contains is a fair type, in the aggregate, of most of the rural corps in my division.

There are very few self-supporting corps. The 14th Aberdeenshire at Tarland, which is composed of two or three farmers, and the remainder all labourers, paid for their own clothing and accoutrements. The Prince of Wales gave them 20*l.* to start with, but with the exception of a few pounds from their captain they have received no other pecuniary assistance, and this money has been expended on a drill-serjeant, and other incidental expenses. This is the nearest approach to a self-supporting rural corps in my division.

I am of opinion that one fourth only of the members in the rural districts are self-supporting, about one half pay a portion, and one fourth give nothing whatever towards the expenses of their corps.

The 7th Kincardineshire at Durris, numbering about 75 members, composed of a few farmers, and the remainder labourers, are entirely supported by Captain Mackenzie, who rents the house on the estate on which the men are employed; and should he leave the country the corps would certainly fall to pieces. There are about eight or nine other corps similarly circumstanced.

Many of the corps are supported by the proceeds of bazaars and voluntary contributions in the neighbourhood; but I am of opinion that the mode of raising funds by bazaars is not popular in Scotland, as it interferes with charity; it will, therefore, soon cease to exist.

Many corps are supported by voluntary contributions alone. In neighbourhoods where the movement is popular among the richest part of the inhabitants, ample funds are obtained. In other parts of the country, where the movement is not so popular among the rich, the people are willing to enrol themselves, but are restricted from doing so by want of funds.

The officers commanding the rural corps are principally the gentlemen of the county, several being retired officers of the army; consequently these corps are better disciplined, and are more under control than consolidated corps, which are chiefly officered from the leading tradesmen of the town.

The rural corps do not generally move so smartly as urban corps, but I consider that the material of which they are composed would prove to be far the best, should their services be required.

Several of the first enrolled corps, which are the best drilled, now require new clothing; and from personal communication with the officers commanding these corps during my last inspections I found that some were in debt, and others with their funds so reduced, with little or no prospect of further contributions, that it will be impossible to clothe them all. These corps, I fear, will gradually decrease in numbers, and will eventually be broken up, unless some pecuniary assistance is granted to them, such as that mentioned in the report.

I am of opinion that the mode of raising funds by assessment, as suggested in the report, would be very unpopular in Scotland just now, but I think that each county should guarantee to the Government an annual sum, according to its means, for a term of years, and that the Government should grant a like sum. The fund so raised to defray the expense of clothing, &c. Should this fund not be sufficient for all existing expenses, the force in the county should be reduced to a level with the expenditure. A quota might be given for each county so as to keep the numbers in the kingdom within the limits required. I have very little fear but that each county in my division would soon find sufficient funds for the full quota, and that the movement would be permanent and efficient.

I have, &c.

(Signed)   DOUGLAS JONES, Major,
Ass.t Insp.r of Rifle Volunteers.

Inspector-General of Volunteers,
War Office, Pall Mall.

Sir,   Swansea, 17th January 1862.

WITH reference to the War Office letter dated 13th January 1862, V Haddington 55, confidential, enclosing a report of the committee appointed by the county of Haddington, &c., &c., and calling upon me to give my opinion of the present state of the rural volunteer corps in my division, with reference to the points raised in the report in question, I have the honour to state, for the information of Sir George Cornewall Lewis, that the points raised by the committee, and the opinions expressed by them, are very appropriate to and bear with equal strength on the position of the volunteer corps in general in my district; and I am glad to have the opportunity of expressing confidentially my feelings concerning the movement in Wales and Monmouth, and I beg to state that throughout my district I have, in general, observed a great difficulty in keeping the corps together, in consequence of the falling off of subscriptions from the county families and other parties not immediately connected with the volunteers, who at first were willing to assist in supporting the movement, but when a second and third subscription was called for they either withdrew their support altogether or gave it grudgingly, and as a tax.

In most cases the expenses fall nearly altogether on the officers commanding the corps, the junior officers often not being willing to give more than their time, and the expense entailed by their outfit, &c., &c. Subscriptions from members who, for the most part, are artizans and labourers, are, as a rule, very difficult to get in, and I look forward with some apprehension to my inspections this year, as I observed symptoms of collapse in many corps; more, it appeared to me, from want of funds and means, than from an actual unwillingness on the part of the volunteers to attend drills, &c., &c.

I may add, as a rule, that in my conversations with officers commanding corps, they invariably dwelt much on their increasing expenses, in consequence of diminished subscriptions, and they looked with considerable anxiety to the time when it would be necessary to supply new uniforms to their men, as they were, for the most part, paid for out of the first liberal subscriptions obtained; the men themselves, generally, only paying a small portion of the expense, even of their first outfit.

From what I could discover during my tours of inspection last year, there were not throughout my division half a dozen corps actually with funds in hand, and where the captain was not a man of means I felt very doubtful as to their appearing again in any strength this year.

I have, &c.,
(Signed) R. RONEY, Major,
Assistant Inspector of Volunteers.
Colonel McMurdo, C.B.,
Inspector of Volunteers.

Sir,   York, 16th January 1862.

I HAVE the honour to acknowledge the receipt of your letter of the 13th instant, with its enclosure (herewith returned), and in reply to inform you, for the information of Secretary Sir George Lewis, that I feel great diffidence in giving any opinion as to the present financial position of the county volunteer corps in the district under my supervision, as at my several inspections I have never investigated matters connected with the funds of any corps; however, from general observation, and what I have been informed privately, I am convinced that not more than one-fourth, if as many, of the enrolled volunteers in the northern division are self-supporting; in most of the county corps the clothing has all been furnished from funds raised by donations of private individuals, and in no instance have I heard of any provision being made for the renewal of uniforms.

The artizans and labouring class consider that giving their time and service is sufficient, and that they should not be called upon for any subscriptions.

The corps funds generally are barely sufficient to meet incidental expenses, and with such a state of things I consider permanence cannot be reckoned on, though as yet the county corps keep up their numbers, and have generally more effective members than the town corps in proportion to their enrolled strength, in consequence of the personal relations between officers and men being of a more intimate nature (viz., as landlord and tenant) than is the case in towns.

There are no county volunteer funds in the north of England, but in several instances battalion funds are being raised, the principal object of which is to cover the expenses of battalion assemblies, the continuance of which in sufficient numbers, cannot be ensured unless some such provision is made.

In conclusion I fully concur in resolutions 11, 12, and 13, although I cannot suggest the precise manner in which the difficulties are to be met.

I have, &c.,
(Signed)   G. B. HARMAN,
Colonel McMurdo, C.B.,
Inspector-General of Volunteers,   Major, L.A.I.V.
War Office.

Sir,   Liverpool, 17th January 1862.

COMPLYING with the instructions contained in your letters of the 13th inst., I have the honour to acquaint you, for the information of Secretary the Right Hon. Sir George Lewis, that the present state of the rural volunteer corps in this district is, in a general sense, exemplified by the under-mentioned remarks.

1. The original funds raised for the organization of a volunteer force in this district are, in nearly every instance, exhausted.

2. A very great majority of the companies are not self-supporting.

3. In addition to the money originally subscribed for clothing, &c., supplementary contributions have been had recourse to, for the purpose of meeting incidental expenses, which have generally been found far heavier than anticipated.

4. The average annual incidental expenses of a company may be estimated at about 50l.

5. It is highly improbable the annual subscriptions per company will exceed 50l.

6. No corps, as far as has been ascertained, is in a position to meet any part of the expense attending a renewal of uniforms.

7. A very small proportion of the whole force is clothed at their own expense, and there is no prospect of companies being able to raise the sum required for a renewal of uniforms.

8. The estimated cost of uniforms, exclusive of accoutrements and great coats, is about 3l. per head; but if proper judgment and the experience already gained were brought to bear upon this point, this amount might be reduced, especially if cloth of one description and colour was selected by each county.

9. In a general sense, the volunteer force of this district is in a high state of efficiency, and this applies especially to the consolidated battalions, in which, with the assistance of duly qualified adjutants and drill instructors, a proper system of instruction has been established and carried out in accordance with existing regulations.

10. A great majority of the volunteer force in this division is composed of men of the working classes, which comprise labourers, artizans, operatives, &c., and whose circumstances only admit of a very small annual subscription, and, from the very depressed state of trade in the manufacturing districts, many secessions are taking place from the inability of meeting any pecuniary demand.

11. The volunteers have, upon all occasions, shown a highly creditable spirit of discipline and obedience, and it may be instanced that at the late Newton review in Lancashire, where upwards of 9,000 were assembled, the perfect order and cheerful compliance with existing regulations elicited a high encomium.

12. It is considered in this important section of the country most essential that the volunteer force should be maintained; but is unquestionable that a renewal of uniforms would entail its being broken up. Many corps will shortly require new uniforms.

13. There is no prospect of funds being again realized by donations, that source being, for reasons which it may not be advisable to enter into, exhausted.

14. It is an almost unanimous feeling that an annual subscription, however small, should be paid by every volunteer, and there is an earnest desire for Government aid to ensure the permanency of the movement.

15. The rural corps in Cheshire are, perhaps, financially considered, in a more flourishing state than those in Lancashire, principally in consequence of the former not being so much affected by the fluctuations of trade.

I have also the honour to state that in submitting these remarks I have assumed that it would perhaps be considered as exceeding my instructions, if any suggestions as to the most acceptable manner in which Government aid could be rendered to volunteers emanated from me, and for obvious motives I have abstained from specifying reasons, unconnected with pecuniary embarrassments, which, in my opinion, are causing many secessions from the volunteer force.

Appending an approximate annual abstract of incidental expenses,   I have, &c.,
(Signed)   H. H. MANNERS, Major,
Ass^t Inspector of Volunteers, 6th Div^n
Inspector-General of Volunteers.
War-Office, London.

APPROXIMATE ABSTRACT of annual Incidental Expenses for a Volunteer Corps of Ten Companies.*

	£	s.	d.
Orderly room (rent and taxes)	50	0	0
Office commissionaire	26	0	0
Gas and coals	3	0	0
Printing, advertisements, &c.	15	0	0
Squad books, &c., &c.	3	0	0
Rent of rifle range	40	0	0
Rent of drill ground	30	0	0
Drill sheds	70	0	0
Armouries	100	0	0
Repair of arms	20	0	0
Repair and removal of targets	15	0	0
Signal flags, &c., &c.	5	0	0
Uniform for drill serjeants	9	0	0
Uniform for buglers	10	0	0
Carriage of arms, ammunition, &c	10	0	0
	£406	0	0

The above does not include the railway expenses of corps having ranges at a long distance from head-quarters.

(Signed) H. H. MANNERS, Major, Ass^t Inspector of Volunteers, 6th Divⁿ.
Liverpool, 17th January 1862.

SIR, Birmingham, 17th January 1862.

I HAVE the honour to state, for the information of the Right Hon. the Secretary of State for War, in reply to your letter of the 13th instant relative to the present state of the volunteer force in my district, with especial reference to the points raised in the report of the committee appointed by the county of Haddington, that, although in the Midland district there are no county associations (except for prize shooting, &c.), or funds for the support of corps, each corps being dependent on itself and locality for support, yet the chief points raised in the report are applicable to the volunteer force in the midland counties, especially the paragraph at the top of page 8, with reference to the renewal of clothing. There appears to be a feeling of anxiety as to what will be the state of the force throughout the country at the end of this year when the present clothing is worn out, and as to what provision will be made for the renewal of the same; that as a large majority of the force is composed chiefly of men of the artizan and labouring class they should not be called upon to contribute more than their time and service. It seems also that the general public do not furnish the same amount of support which was freely given at the commencement of the movement.

I have, &c.,
(Signed) J. S. T. F. DICK, Major,
Assistant Inspector of Volunteers.
Colonel McMurdo, C.B., War Office.

SIR, Grove House, Durdham Down, Bristol, January.

I HAVE the honour to acknowledge your letter, dated W. O., 13th January 1862, marked V Haddington 55, and in reply beg to state, for the information of Secretary Sir George Lewis:—

From my observations and inquiries, made during my tour of inspection in the five counties under my supervision, I have remarked that the chief expenses to which volunteer corps are subject are, at present, drill instructors, custody of arms, in many places rent for rifle practice grounds, meeting for battalion drill.

The first of these, viz., drill instructors, will be provided for when sufficient men are found, either by recommendation from the different corps now being drilled, or by properly instructed serjeants, sanctioned by the War Office.

These drill instructors, in most cases, would have charge of the arms and ammunition, so that in future these two causes of expense to volunteers would be obviated.

Rent for rifle practice grounds, I presume, cannot be avoided.

Meetings for battalion drill are a source of great expense in many corps. In the county of Cornwall the rifle association allows every man one penny per mile for two battalion meetings in the year, which I have been given to understand covers their travelling expenses, the loss of a day's work being the sacrifice which the volunteer makes for his country. Refreshments are in many instances taken by each company, the officers often providing the whole. I have recommended haversacks being adopted, to enable men to carry their own refreshments, and have seen my advice followed with good effect at reviews, where sutlers generally charge exorbitantly for provisions. In Devon no allowance has been made by the association for battalion drills. The expense has therefore fallen upon the volunteer, and consequently two administrative battalions in the county have never yet been drilled in battalion.

In many instances the captain bears the whole expense. This cannot last.

In Somerset there is no association, all the expense of meeting in battalion being borne by the corps; and although some of the corps have long distances to the head-quarters of their battalion, still there have been many meetings for battalion drill, and one brigade drill during the past year.

In Wilts the association has not provided any assistance for battalion drills. The 1st battalion has met, the expense being borne by the corps individually. The 2nd battalion has not yet met.

In Dorset the corps have met several times during the past year for battalion drills. The expense being, I believe, partially borne by the association.

Other expenses to volunteer corps, such as targets, signal flags, erection of butts, present clothing, &c., have been borne by the original subscriptions, the expense of keeping up all (except the clothing) after the first outlay being comparatively small.

From occasional inquiries I have ascertained that many of the rural corps are very nearly in a state of bankruptcy.

In the county of Cornwall many corps have recruited their finances by getting up bazaars, the proceeds to be vested in the captain for the benefit of the corps; by this means from 150l. to 250l. has been raised by each corps, which will enable, in many cases, uniforms to be provided. In other counties I fear but little has been thought of on the question of renewal of uniforms.

My general impression is, that the volunteer corps which are raised in towns, and some rural corps who have *enthusiastic* and *wealthy* captains, will stand; but that the generality of rural corps, unless some assistance is given to meet the expenditure attendant upon brigade and battalion drills, and necessary field equipments in case of service, will, I fear, after all their funds are expended, gradually fall off and finally disappear.

This being the third year of the movement, I shall have a good opportunity of testing the permanency of the force at the coming inspections, when I shall pay particular attention to the financial state of the corps.

I have neglected to state that one administrative battalion in Devonshire has proposed to have a battalion association, which would be authorized to form committees for a clothing fund, excursion fund, commissariat fund, and prize shooting fund, so as to make the battalion self-supporting. Should the objects aimed at by this association be carried out, the system might with advantage be imitated by other administrative battalions.

The principle of self-support seems to me to be only applicable to large towns. The class of men who volunteer in country places being, to a great extent, artizans, and many of the labouring classes. These men are now well drilled and disciplined, but cannot afford to pay for attending battalion drills, and new uniforms.

In conclusion, my impression is that the permanency of the volunteer force will be tested when the corps in rural districts require new uniforms. In towns I imagine the difficulties on that point will be slight in comparison. Voluntary contributions are uncertain and not to be relied on.

I have, &c.,
(Signed) GUSTAVUS HUME, Major Unattached,
A. I. Volunteers.
Colonel McMurdo, C.B.,
Inspector-General of Volunteers,
War Office.

SIR, 4, Onslow Square, S.W., 17th January 1862.

IN compliance with the request in your letter of the 13th inst. (No. as per margin), enclosing the report of the committee of Commissioners of Supply of the county of Haddington, dated 25th November 1861, I have the honour to acquaint you, for the information of the Secretary of State for War, that in my opinion the statements embodied in the resolutions in that report with reference to the pecuniary difficulties of the volunteer corps in the county of Haddington will apply with equal force to many of the rural corps in the East Midland division.

Corps are certainly falling off in numbers, from the unwillingness of some members, and the inability of others, to continue the annual subscriptions to meet the expenses of butts, targets, armouries, uniforms, &c.

There are certain corps supplied with ample funds entirely by voluntary subscriptions, but I believe that further assistance will be required from Government to ensure the permanence and efficiency of many corps in the rural districts.

I have, &c.
(Signed) C. P. INNERTSON, Lieut.-Col.,
Assistant Inspector Volunteers,
East Midland Division.
Colonel McMurdo, C.B.,
Inspector-General of Volunteers, War Office.

---

* Applicable only to a consolidated battalion.

Sir, Farnham, 15th January 1862.

I HAVE the honour to acknowledge the receipt of your letter, dated 13th instant (marked as above), enclosing a printed report of a committee of supply of the county of Haddington, as to the expenditure on account of the volunteers of that county, and asking for my opinion on the same subject, as regards the rural volunteer corps in my division.

From my first appointment to the volunteer force I have carefully abstained from inquiry into financial matters. I considered that this would be intruding myself into private affairs with which I was not called on to interfere; I am, therefore, not able to speak with statistical accuracy on the subject, but I have often conversed in a general manner with the volunteers on their prospects, and from what I have gathered I am of opinion that, in the rural districts, expense is the great source of fear to the volunteer cause. I think that volunteers of all degrees find that the expense has proved heavier than they expected. They were willing, and are willing, to give up their time—to many money's worth—and to take the trouble of learning their drill, and to expend a certain amount of money in uniforms; but they have found that this is not all, that volunteer meetings mean, besides drill, travelling, eating and drinking—pleasant, but expensive amusements—and I fear, therefore, that when the suit of uniform now in wear is worn out, and another must be got, many of the volunteers, though with their hearts still thoroughly in the cause, will feel themselves called upon to resign. They will say, "I have learnt " any drill; I am able, if the enemy invade us, to fall in in " the ranks, and I will do so; but meanwhile, in justice to " my family, I cannot afford to spend as much money as " I have been spending in volunteering."

Doubtless much of the expense has arisen from want of judgment, spending money on useless things, such as bands, feathers and shakos, and expensive uniforms, and the corps in which this has been done, will, I think, be the first to give way; but even where it has not, many members will, I fear, retire when their present uniform is worn out.

I am, therefore, of an opinion similar to that at which the Haddingtonshire committee has arrived, viz., that assistance of some sort must be given in order that county volunteers may be maintained. The committee recommend one of three ways of rendering assistance:

1. Direct assistance from Government.
2. Assessment.
3. Combined assessment and Government assistance.

But all these methods appear to refer to *pecuniary* assistance.

In this I venture to disagree with the committee. I think assistance must be given; I think Government should give it, but not in money.

If the county are willing to assess themselves, that is their affair, and it will be for them to see that the money is properly and economically expended; but I venture to think it would be unwise that aid in money should be given by Government. It would entail close examination of all the volunteer accounts; restrictions, irksome to the volunteers, would have to be laid down in order to ensure economy; and the movement would thus lose much of its volunteer character, and the Government would find itself frequently at variance with the feelings of the volunteers.

Additional aid *in kind* is, therefore, the description of assistance which I would venture to recommend on the part of Government.

The nature of assistance which Government might render may be ranged under the following heads:

1. Arms and ammunition.
2. Drill instructors.
3. Making of ranges.
4. Targets, &c. for ball practice.
5. Travelling expenses.
6. Clothing.

1. *Arms and Ammunition* have already been given.

2. *Drill Instructors.*—Much has been given, but there is a class of corps in *rural* districts which requires this nature of aid, and has not received it; viz., corps consisting of a subdivision only; these being weaker and therefore poorer than a company, require assistance more, but are not allowed a drill instructor by existing regulations. I beg to recommend most strongly that a drill instructor be allowed to rural volunteer subdivisions. To save expense he might be only of the rank of corporal; but that such corps should have an instructor of some kind, I think essential.

3. *Making of Ranges.*—Many corps have been put to great expense on this score; some of the poorest have been put to the most expense, such expense arising from purely local causes, and through no extravagance on the part of the corps. To other corps, having Government rifle ranges at hand, or from other local reasons, the expense has been trifling. It appears to me but just that all should be put on an equality, that it is most important that every corps should have a range so that its members may become fair shots, and that this expense may most fairly fall on the public, who are to be protected by the volunteers. To those corps, therefore, that have gone to expense for ranges, I would suggest that an allowance be made by Government after the value of the work done has been assessed by some competent surveyor, appointed by Government; and that for the future, when a range requires to be made, it should be constructed by Government; and as the most economical method I would suggest that a non-commissioned officer of Royal Engineers be sent to superintend the work.

4. *Targets, Flags, &c. for Ball Practice.*—This also appears to me an expense which may fairly fall on the public. Allowance on this head is already made to artillery volunteers, though not to riflemen. I would, therefore, suggest that the value of the number of targets, &c. which are required by a corps, according to the extent of its range, be allowed to those corps which have already supplied themselves, and that in future such stores be issued gratuitously.

5. *Travelling.*—This becomes a very heavy item to some corps, while others being near the head-quarters of the battalion do not feel it at all; and probably the distant are also the poorer corps of the battalion. It seems fair that the men who give up their day's work, and spend many hours on the road besides, should not be called on to pay also for conveyance to battalion drill. I am convinced that this is the cause of the unfrequency of battalion drills in rural districts. Battalion drills are most important in the training of volunteers. I would then suggest that an allowance of a penny a mile (the Government fare by rail) per man be granted in rural districts to all corps upwards of a certain distance, say six miles, from the place of battalion assembly for a certain number of battalion drills per annum, such allowance, of course, only to be granted for the actual number of effective men who attended the battalion drill, exclusive of bands, as proved by the signature of the officer actually in command of the battalion each day.

6. *Clothing.*—In the clothing of the volunteers it has always appeared to me that their distinct difference from the line is a disadvantage which has not been sufficiently considered. It seems to me of very great importance in case of invasion, that the volunteers should not be at once distinguished from the line; that at a distance an enemy ought not to be able to know the one from the other. The great variety of uniforms of volunteers (even of corps belonging to the same battalion) is also a minor disadvantage, and I think that both may be overcome, and really useful aid in kind be given by Government, if a gratuitous issue of a part of the clothing were to be made to volunteers.

Urban corps, who are generally better off, might prefer to wear and be able to afford their present uniforms, but in rural corps I think such an issue would be an acceptable present. There seems to be strong objection on the part of volunteers to be dressed in scarlet. This, I think, is natural. It requires some little time for a soldier to become accustomed to a red coat. People used to wear sombre clothing feel shy at appearing in public in so striking a colour. Scarlet is easily stained, and is conspicuous; therefore, I think, it would be unwise to insist on the volunteers adopting red as their uniform; but perhaps the option might be given them, by battalions, on this point.

To the volunteers, I think, might be issued gratuitously;

1. Cap.
2. Blouse, red or grey.
3. Belts, &c.
4. Leggings.

1. *Cap,* of blue or grey cloth, or a low shako like that lately issued to the rifle brigade, badge or ornament to be added by the corps.

2. *Blouse,* to be made of serge or some such inexpensive stuff; loose, to as to be worn over the man's usual waistcoat, or in cold weather over a coat, and to require no fitting to the individual. Two sizes would probably fit all men.

3. *Belts, pouches, &c.,* of brown leather, requiring no cleaning but soap and water.

4. *Leggings,* black, like those worn with knickerbockers. The volunteer would then only have to provide himself with trousers (on actual service these might be of any sort), boots, and under-clothing.

To insure uniformity with the line, I would beg to suggest that to the regulars should also be issued a grey blouse, instead of the present red fatigue jacket, which is a poor

H h

skimpy garment, cold in winter, and from its tightness very unfit for hard fatigue duty. The blouse would pack away easily in the knapsack, and in case of invasion, by putting it on *over* the red coat, it would be impossible for the enemy to know the regulars from the volunteers. If those regiments lately returned from India and China (the Buffs and 60th Rifles, for instance) be consulted on this point, I feel sure they can tell from experience what a comfortable dress the blouse is, and how glad they would be to wear it again.

If in the above remarks I seem to be interfering with the dress of the regular army—a subject on which I have not been consulted—I beg to state, as my excuse, my anxiety that in the day of trial the regulars and volunteers may appear alike, and with the objection of the volunteers to red, I see no other method of ensuring this desirable end.

To ensure due care being taken of the clothing issued, I think that on its receipt a proportion of its value should be deposited by the volunteer with his captain, and by the captain with the Government, to be forfeited in case of neglect, or if the volunteer should leave the corps under a fixed period, and to be returned to him if at the expiration of the time the clothing is calculated to last the volunteer wishes to retire from the volunteer service.

I hope it may not be considered that I have gone into unnecessary details on the subject on which my opinion was asked. I think that assistance should be rendered by Government, and being firmly of opinion that it should be *in kind* and not in money, I have endeavoured to show plainly how I think it may best be done.

If with such assistance as I have suggested the volunteer movement should die, I fear that die it must; but even if it should, we are in a better position than before its birth, in that those who have learnt their drill can never thoroughly forget it, and will always be more ready for the ranks than if they had never been in them.

I have, &c.
(Signed)   R. G. A. LUARD, Lieut.-Colonel,
                    Assistant Inspector, S.E.D.
Colonel McMurdo, C.B.,
Inspector-General of Volunteers.

SIR,   Head-quarters, Glasgow, 17th January 1862.

IN reply to your letter of the 13th instant, number as per margin, enclosing the report of a committee appointed by the county of Haddington to inquire into the financial position of the county volunteer corps, I have the honour to report, for the information of the Secretary of State for War, that my opinion and firm belief is, that with one or two solitary exceptions, the whole of the rural corps in this division are not entirely self-supporting, but in a great measure dependent on annual subscriptions from honorary members and others, donations, &c., &c. for the requisite funds; and when the present uniforms are worn out there will be much difficulty in having them renewed, and it is to be feared there will be a considerable diminution in numbers in many corps in consequence.

I beg to enclose the "Annual Report of the 7th Dumfriesshire Rifle Volunteers," showing its financial position, and which may be taken as a fair criterion of the state of the other corps in that county, but it should not be inferred from this that all the other rural corps in the several counties of this division, are as equally independent.

I have, &c.
(Signed)   R. YOUNG, Major,
Inspector-General of Volun-   Ass.t Inspr of Volunteers.
teers, War Office.

(4.)—COPY OF A LETTER FROM LIEUT.-COLONEL ACLAND, ON THE PROVISION OF DRILL INSTRUCTORS, &c.

(*Furnished by the Secretary of State for War.*)

Sprydoncote, Exeter,
MY LORD,   March 11, 1862.

I BEG leave to submit to your Lordship, for the consideration of Her Majesty's Secretary of State for War, some remarks on the local working of the Volunteer Regulations 147A to 167A, and also some suggestions having for their object to enable scattered corps to obtain, without further delay, some aid towards the expenses of good drill instruction.

Before making the following representation to your Lordship, I have deemed it advisable to summon a meeting of the officers of corps composing or attached to the 1st administrative battalion, and I may say, that they generally concur with me in thinking some change in the present arrangement desirable; nor is this concurrence confined to the officers of my own battalion.

The majority of the corps under my command, that is, seven out of ten, have up to this time been unable to derive any assistance from the Parliamentary grant. In two of the other three corps the appointments made are so far not satisfactory that the officer of a subdivision contiguous to those two corps feels that it would be a disadvantage to his corps to be drilled by either of the two instructors paid by the Government.

Commanding officers have been informed that the applications for drill instructors are so numerous that there is little probability of the supply being equal to the demand for some time to come.

It is further stated, that really well-qualified drill instructors are unwilling to accept the terms offered to them by the Government for the duty of drilling volunteers, and prefer other situations affording greater advantages.

Some officers are unwilling to deprive their corps of the services of serjeants of militia, who are unquestionably good instructors, and under whom their corps have made rapid progress. They are not unreasonably apprehensive of the risk that serjeants unsuited to the duty of drilling volunteers may be permanently posted to their corps. My own experience has taught me the extreme caution necessary in estimating recommendations of serjeants from the army. And, therefore, although I am fortunate enough to have myself the services of one very good serjeant, I do not think this apprehension unreasonable.

It is an important element in the case of administrative battalions (both as regards discipline and expense,) that the whole time of a highly qualified drill instructor is not required by any one detached corps. In ordinary cases an attendance once a week, in some cases less, would suffice. The services of a good instructor, if paid for according to the market value in this neighbourhood, at the current rate of about 5s. per drill, need not cost more than from 12l. to 25l. per annum.

There are, however, other duties of a military nature, such as the custody and cleaning of arms, assisting at battalion or skeleton drill, and at target practice, which may be usefully performed by an old soldier of good character, although he be incapable of acting alone as a drill instructor. It conduces, no doubt, much to the stability and good order of a volunteer corps that the services of a man accustomed to military discipline should be engaged for such purposes; and local arrangements of this kind can be made in many parts of the country at a moderate cost.

I do not venture to call in question the military or financial reasons which may influence the Government, in desiring to retain permanently the services of a staff of qualified drill instructors by payment at a uniform rate per diem; but (without saying more on the scarcity and consequent high value of such men at present) I think that little reliance is to be placed on the sanctions of military law, and the supervision provided in the volunteer regulations, 159 A, 160 A, 161 A, for ensuring the zealous training of volunteers, in comparison with the motives afforded by the prospect of full employment on liberal terms, or by the fear of losing an engagement in consequence of not giving satisfaction to immediate employers.

I therefore venture to suggest (at least as a temporary expedient) that, in the provision of personal military assistance to volunteer corps, the two kinds of military duty above distinguished be separately dealt with; and that market prices and local circumstances be, more than heretofore, regarded in the aid given towards drill instruction.

I have not sufficient knowledge of official practice to propose regulations in detail, but the following proposals appear to me in substance adapted to the circumstances falling under my own observation:—

1. That commanding officers of detached corps be permitted to apply either for aid towards the payment of an *occasional drill instructor*; or for aid towards the payment of retired soldiers, qualified for the duties above referred to, as not requiring for their discharge a superior drill instructor; or for aid towards both objects.

That the aid for either object should not exceed the allowance for a temporary drill instructor specified in regulation 163 A.

That, if aid be granted for both purposes, the total amount of aid should not exceed the allowance for a serjeant instructor in regulation 152 A.

2. That the greatest possible latitude (within prescribed limits) for settling the terms of the engagement with a drill instructor, or other retired soldier, be left to the commanding officer of each corps, who, as one of them has well said, "can make a pound go much further than the Government "can;" and especially that full powers to terminate an

engagement, which proves unsatisfactory, be given to such officers.

3. That the adjutant and the field officer be held responsible for giving to the Government, through the assistant inspector, their explicit opinion upon each arrangement proposed by the commanding officer of a corps, and on the qualifications of the person or persons proposed to be employed, both when application is made for aid, and also when the renewal of the aid is applied for. I assume that the arrangement I propose, will, if adopted, be treated as provisional and temporary.

4. That, with a view to give full force to the foregoing proposals, and to supply to volunteers generally, and especially to officers, an adequate motive for concentrating their efforts on the attainment of real efficiency, the continuance of aid, whether in the way of ammunition, drill instruction, or otherwise, to any corps be contingent on the fulfilment by its members (or by a proportion to be determined by local circumstances), of certain conditions as to attendance at drill, or as to *certified proficiency*, and as to systematic musketry instruction and target practice. And that adjutants and field officers be responsible for obtaining sufficient records of these facts.

The foregoing proposals would, in my opinion, lead to the following advantages:—

The officers and non-commissioned officers would be from time to time thrown on their own resources, as the occasional instructor could not always be at hand, and must, for his own credit, try to make them able to act without him.

The adjutant also, while collecting and digesting information as to the progress of his battalion, could at the same time supply a motive for emulation, as, for example, in reference to the figure of merit in shooting.

Considerable efforts have been made in this country (and elsewhere) to systematize the action of administrative battalions, and to methodize the arrangements for the drill and shooting of companies, with a view to prevent that waste of time without a definite object, which is more dangerous to the permanence of the volunteer system among the middle classes, than any want of pecuniary aid from the public funds.

I beg leave to express my own strong conviction that if the Government will require the public aid to be *earned by results*, they will do much to support the efforts of officers in the direction referred to; while if a number of vested interests are created by stereotyped appointments, volunteer officers will be left to extract work from old soldiers deprived of adequate motives for exertion. The position of a serjeant instructor of volunteers has little in common with that of a regimental serjeant in the regular service, and is full of temptation to indolence.

I have only to add, in conclusion, that many corps are now earnestly engaged in a course of spring drill.

Should the Government entertain the above proposals, an early indication of their intention to assist in providing the expenses of the only drill instruction at present available would have a very encouraging effect.

I have, &c.
T. D. ACLAND, Junr.,
Lt.-Col., 1st. Adm. Bat.
Devon Rifle Volunteers.

(5.)—COPY OF A LETTER FROM THE HONBLE. E. C. CURZON, ON CADET VOLUNTEER CORPS.

(Furnished by the Secretary of State for War.)

MY LORD, Whitehall, 31st March 1862.

WITH reference to the interview I had with your Lordship on Saturday last, on the subject of the volunteer cadet corps being recognized by the Government, when you desired me to embody the substance of our conversation in writing,

I have to submit for the consideration of the Secretary of State for War—

1. That cadets have been enrolled up to the age of 16, and formed into corps attached to several of the volunteer rifle regiments, wearing the same uniforms, and subject to the rules of these regiments.

2. That drill instructors have been specially provided for them, paid out of the funds subscribed by them.

3. That cadet corps have been raised and formed in the country by the exertions and to a considerable extent at the expense of private individuals which are not attached to any volunteer battalion.

4. That some large schools have, through the exertions of their heads or governors, become remarkably efficient in company and battalion drill, but have not yet been put into uniform or attached to any volunteer battalion.

5. That the cadet corps have been formed mainly for the purpose of filling up the ranks of the adult volunteers.

6. That the proper training of youths while cadets, whereby they must acquire habits of self dependence, submission to authority and command, eminently qualifying them for any position they may hold in after life, either in the army, volunteers, or otherwise, is of the highest importance to the country.

To give encouragement and permanence to this force, I have the honour to submit that—

1. Superior officers (probably as supernumeraries) might be commissioned to have the special charge of the cadets.

2. Subordinate officers might be commissioned, subject to the exigencies of the service, depending on the numbers and localities of the cadet corps.

3. That arms should be provided for them (the Irish constabulary carbine now used is supplied to them at 7s. each by the Government), and a limited number of small rifles for ball practice for the senior youths who have passed through their musketry instruction.

4. That at the annual reviews or inspections an officer might be authorized to attend and report on their progress.

5. That a proper certificate of efficiency should entitle a cadet competing for admission to any Government employment or academy to a certain number of marks.

There are many deputy lieutenants and magistrates who, like myself, have taken an active part in attesting and organizing volunteers, and I venture to suggest that through them, as well as commanding officers of volunteers, the names of gentlemen to whom parents would be willing to entrust the military control of their sons, and who would undertake the seriously responsible duties of commandants of cadets might be easily ascertained.

If some such recognition of the existence of cadet corps were made there can be no doubt that, in consequence of the feelings of self respect to be acquired by the youths from being officially connected with the Government, there would be a considerable increase in their numbers, and with very great national advantage.

I have the honour to be, &c.
E. C. CURZON,
President of the Committee,
2nd (South) Middlesex Volunteers.

The Right Honourable
The Earl de Grey and Ripon.

(6.)—LETTERS ADDRESSED TO THE CHAIRMAN OF THE COMMISSION.

(From the Duke of Manchester.)

Great Stanhope Street, W.,
MY DEAR LORD EVERSLEY, 2nd July 1862.

I GREATLY regret that, having mislaid the communication I received from the Secretary to your Commission, I have inadvertently neglected to comply with the request therein expressed.

But, apart from the seeming discourtesy, of which I am ashamed, my absence cannot have been of much consequence. For, unless there were any questions from you to which I could have furnished you with replies, there were few suggestions of my own which I had to make. I should have stated my entire agreement with what was on one occasion said by the Earl of Ellenborough to the effect that it was desirable that volunteer corps should have opportunities of seeing other corps manœuvre—especially that they should see regular troops at drill. This is even more necessary for scattered provincial corps than for those in large towns. But this can scarcely be carried out to an adequate extent at the expense of the volunteers themselves. If possible, all the cost, or at least a portion of the cost of their military instruction, ought to be borne by the community; either by local rates, or by payments from the national Exchequer; and in this instruction I should include the assembling of volunteers for combined movements, at military stations where that is practicable.

I am further of opinion that any contributions towards volunteer expenses should be made towards the regimental funds for regimental expenses, and not as payments to individuals.

Another way in which it seems to me that volunteers

might, most unobjectionably, be assisted is by supplying them from the Government stores, not only with the materials for clothing, but with the articles of clothing and equipment made up at cost price. For local tradesmen make but little difference between the cost of making up materials and that of supplying the whole.

But then I am of opinion that, if volunteer corps accept more assistance from the State, they should be prepared to give more service, not limiting it to the case of actual or threatened invasion. The more they receive, the more they should resemble the position and liabilities of the yeomanry and militia. I think this liability to service might vary in different corps according to the pecuniary assistance each wishes to receive. For the members of some corps are in such a position as to require but little assistance, and they would probably be put to great inconvenience if they were called out for service on any but the last emergency; while others might be ready to act even in case of local disturbances.

If there are any other points on which you wish to know the results of my experience, I shall esteem it an honour to place it at your service. In the meantime allow me to repeat my regrets at my seeming want of attention, and to assure you that,

I remain, &c.
MANCHESTER.

The Viscount Eversley,
&c. &c.

(*From Captain Darby.*)

MY LORD,   Markly Hurst Green, July 17th 1862.

I AM desirous that there should not be any misapprehension respecting the replies which I gave to Major Harcourt before the Royal Commission. The proper understanding of my answers to his questions depends upon the signification which may be attached to the word "organization;" if the sense in which I believe the word to have been used by him and accepted by me, be adopted, I have no desire to qualify any one of my answers. I did not intend to imply that the authority which was delegated by the Crown under the Volunteer Act should, as regards artillery volunteers, be taken out of the hands of those to whom it was so delegated, and transferred to other authority, but it being admitted that the constitution of both artillery and rifle volunteers must be identical, that the organization of the one, under that constitution, requires to be very different from that of the other. To render an artillery corps efficient each man must acquire a knowledge of the duties belonging to each member of a detachment in the various operations incident to the work which an artilleryman ought to perform with safety to himself and others; these can only be learnt in batteries which are under the command of an officer of Royal Artillery, to whom are intrusted, and who is responsible for, all the stores and appliances essential to proper instruction as well as to the performance of an artilleryman's duties on active service. I think to be in constant communication with those versed in the scientific knowledge applicable to this branch of the service, and in constant practice of the active duties belonging to it, is of incalculable benefit to the artillery volunteers; and as the possibility of their being called into active service is contemplated by the very act of their enrolment, the more the Volunteers act in concert with the Royal Artillery the greater confidence will they feel in each other, and the greater will be the use of the volunteers should they be called out on service. It seems to me, therefore, necessary for the officer of Royal Artillery commanding the district to be well acquainted with the number of artillery volunteers within it, and their state of efficiency in every particular, and that an intimate connexion should exist between him and the officers commanding the artillery volunteer corps in his district, as the Volunteers now constantly and readily assist the Royal Artillery when the latter are short of numbers, and as no one can shut his eyes to the fact that in case of any emergency a large body of Volunteers, at least on the south coast, would be required for service.

It seems to follow that the commanding officer of the district ought to have every means of obtaining such information as will enable him to form his own estimate of the state and value of the artillery corps in his district. It was under these impressions I gave the answers I did when before the Royal Commission, which I know conveyed the feelings of those under my command, given under the conviction that should the connexion between the Royal Artillery and the Volunteers be in the slightest degree interrupted, and which I stated I was willing to have increased, I should see no way of maintaining an efficiency which would justify the expenditure of the time, trouble, and money necessary to keep up a corps.

I have, &c.
Viscount Eversley, &c., &c., Chairman,   G. DARBY.
Royal Commission, Volunteers.

(*From Colonel Cuppage, R.A.*)

MY LORD,   The Castle, Dover, July 17th, 1862.

I HAVE always considered myself so identified with the volunteers of this district, and have from the beginning felt it so important a movement for oneself, that I have ventured to place before your Lordship the substance of a letter I wrote some time back when I thought I might be called before the Commission, among the members of which I anxiously sought, when first formed, for the name of an artillery officer, knowing that, however magnificent for the country at large the general feeling was, it was essentially the artillery that must benefit most by it. I am satisfied no half and half measure can ever make them what they can and ought to be; though constitutionally under the War Office, they should be as much as possible under those who eventually must be their commanding officers, and under whose responsibility they must act; besides, more than ever it is essential that a feeling of confidence and good-will should exist between volunteers and those to whom they are to look in time of need, and those who are to benefit by their exertions, and, therefore, the closer that their connexion can be brought the better:—

"It can be no trouble to a commanding officer in command of a district, on his usual round of inspection, to identify himself with the volunteers about his several forts and batteries. At least I have never found it any, and have always asked for and used them in aid of those inspections. Neither can it be trouble in a well-regulated officer, with clerks accustomed to military routine, to receive and keep those reports and returns which must and ought to be at once at hand, to enable the commanding officer to regulate his demands of stores and ammunition for the several corps in his command.

"It must be manifest to any officer holding the responsibility of such a district as this (extending from the North Foreland to Shoreham, and vulnerable at every point) the value of such intelligent drilled auxiliaries as they are becoming, for it must be perfectly known that the country could not afford an adequate portion of trained artillery to the hundreds of guns which its sea-girthed line would oblige to be more or less in a constant state of preparation. It is this conviction which has ever led me (from the first moment Mr. Henry Catt spoke to me at Brighton, during my inspection of 1859, on the possibility of forming what has since extended all over England) to endeavour to aid their advancement and foster a kindly feeling between them and the artillery. For myself, I would fearlessly rest on their services; but then, to make it effective, they must be amenable to command."

I have, &c.,
(Signed)   BURKE CUPPAGE,
Colonel Commanding the Royal Artillery,
South-Eastern District.

The Right Hon. the Viscount Eversley,
&c.   &c.

LONDON:
Printed by GEORGE E. EYRE and WILLIAM SPOTTISWOODE,
Printers to the Queen's most Excellent Majesty
For Her Majesty's Stationery Office.

www.ingramcontent.com/pod-product-compliance
Lightning Source LLC
Chambersburg PA
CBHW031753230426
43669CB00007B/594